1-2-3® Release 3:
The Complete Reference

Mary Campbell

Osborne **McGraw-Hill**

Berkeley New York St. Louis San Francisco
Auckland Bogotá Hamburg London Madrid
Mexico City Milan Montreal New Delhi Panama City
Paris São Paulo Singapore Sydney
Tokyo Toronto

Osborne **McGraw-Hill**
2600 Tenth Street
Berkeley, California 94710
U.S.A.

For information on translations and book distributors outside of the
U.S.A., please write to Osborne **McGraw-Hill** at the above address.

A complete list of trademarks appears on page 1055.

1-2-3® Release 3: The Complete Reference

1234567890 DOC 89

ISBN 0-07-881318-2

CONTENTS

I would like to thank the following individuals who contributed much to this revision:

Cindy Hudson, vice president, Osborne/McGraw-Hill, who took time from her busy schedule to coordinate all the resources necessary to produce a finished product.

Gabrielle Lawrence, who worked along with me day and night to explore all the new features of 1-2-3.

Scott Tucker, who took time from his busy schedule to review the manuscript. Scott's knowledge of the product and keen sense of how the new features should be presented were an immense help.

Kristy Fordham, who created all the Release 3 screens needed for this book.

Laura Sackerman, who patiently handled numerous queries on the chapters as we made changes to keep the manuscript in sync with the latest release of the software.

Madhu Prasher and Margaret Flynn, who handled all the production tasks for the book. Madhu and Margaret juggled all the right pieces and managed to meet our print date.

To the many, many individuals at Lotus who offered help in different ways. With special thanks to Susan Erabino, Mary Beth Rettger, Danielle Romance, Alexandra Trevelyan, and Scott Tucker.

Mary Campbell

ACKNOWLEDGMENTS

Time Saving DISK AVAILABLE NOW

The *1·2·3® Release 3: The Complete Reference Supplementary Disk* contains all the example code used in this book and can save you hours of time and testing.

➡ You don't need to type in code —
All program code from the book is on disk and ready for immediate use.

➡ You don't need to debug your code —
All disk code is thoroughly tested and bug free.

With this *Supplementary Disk,* you can spend your valuable time perfecting your *1·2·3* techniques instead of your typing skills.

➡ **EASY INSTALLATION INSTRUCTIONS ARE PROVIDED!**

Only Order Today!

$19.95 Plus $2.00 Shipping/Handling for 5 1/4" Disk
$21.95 Plus $2.00 Shipping/Handling for 3 1/2" Disk

Toll Free **800-322-3007** Call

(Monday-Friday Between 8:30 A.M. — 4:30 P.M. Pacific Standard Time)
Pay by check or money order, or use your American Express, VISA or MasterCard.

Or fill out the coupon below, clip out and send to:
Osborne/McGraw-Hill, 2600 Tenth Street, Berkeley, CA, 94710, Attention: Supplementary Disk

- -

➡ Please send me:

☐ Copies of *1·2·3® Release 3: The Complete Reference Supplementary Disk — 5 1/4"*
($19.95 each plus $2.00 per disk for postage and handling.)   0-07-881584-3

☐ Copies of *1·2·3® Release 3: The Complete Reference Supplementary Disk — 3 1/2"*
($21.95 each plus $2.00 per disk for postage and handling.)   0-07-881585-1

Name: _____

Company: _____

Address: _____

City: _____ State: _____ Zip: _____

➡ Indicate method of payment.

☐ Check or Money Order #
(Pls. include shipping charge)

☐ VISA Card #   ☐ MasterCard #   ☐ American Express # _____

Expiration Date _____

➡ Signature _____

Allow 2 weeks for delivery — Prices subject to change without notice

This order subject to acceptance by McGraw-Hill. — Offer good only in the U.S.A.

Although 1-2-3 has been available for many years, it is still one of the best-selling microcomputer software packages. Individuals who are new to computing will gain the same benefits that longtime users have realized from the package. Organizations that have been using 1-2-3 for years will benefit from the new features of Release 3.

The introduction of Release 3 in the summer of 1989 adds many new features to the package. Users who are stretching the limits of Release 2.01 will find many new ways to better utilize both their hardware and software using the features offered by Release 3. Features like file linking, three-dimensional spreadsheets, interfaces with external databases, networking support, automatic formatting, and expanded graphics and print options will allow 1-2-3 to maintain its foremost position on the software charts.

Uses of This Book

1-2-3 Release 3: The Complete Reference is designed to serve the needs of both new and experienced 1-2-3 users. Novice users should start at the beginning of the book and work through the first six chapters. After reading these chapters, they may want to enter some of the examples into their systems for practice. Users already familiar with 1-2-3 basics will want to review the table of contents and focus on topics with which they are less familiar, such as data management features, keyboard alternative macros, and command macros.

Experienced users will also find this volume to be a valuable reference tool, describing all of 1-2-3's many features in detail. Each topic has practical examples in addition to a description of specific features. Boxes in the text summarize important information, and a thorough index will help you find the precise topic you are looking for. Reference sections at the end of many of the chapters provide a quick alphabetical guide to commands.

Organization of This Book

This book is divided into three parts. Part One covers the worksheet and all the commands you need to create efficient worksheet models. Part Two focuses on advanced features like database, graphics, macro, and network commands. Part Three consists of four appendixes that offer supplemental information on installation and the Lotus LMBCS codes. You will also find the inclusion of the command card to be very useful. An outline of the chapters follows:

• Chapter One, "An Introduction to 1-2-3," will get you started with the 1-2-3 package. It provides an overview of all the new Release 3 features.

• Chapter Two, "The Access System, Display, and Keyboard," provides an overview of the package by introducing you to some of its most important features. You will learn all about 1-2-3's display in this chapter.

• Chapter Three, "Entering Data in 1-2-3's Worksheet," gets you started in creating worksheet models. You will learn all about the types of entries that can be made on the worksheet.

• Chapter Four, "Changing the Appearance of the Worksheet Display," introduces you to the flexibility 1-2-3 allows in formatting data. You will learn how to override the default display characteristics to create the exact display you want as well as how to take advantage of Release 3's new formats.

• Chapter Five, "Basic Worksheet Commands," covers all the command options pertaining to the worksheet. You will learn how to determine the worksheet status and change options to suit your needs.

• Chapter Six, "Printing," provides explanations and examples of all 1-2-3 printing features. It shows you how to do everything from printing formulas to adding borders to a printed report. You will learn about all the new Release 3 features that fully utilize the features of your printer.

• Chapter Seven, "1-2-3's Built-in Functions," lists and describes each of 1-2-3's built-in functions. You can read about the ones you are interested in or survey them all to discover new uses for the package.

• Chapter Eight, "Working with Files," covers everything you will need to know to save and retrieve files. You will also learn how to link files and save just a section of your worksheet.

• Chapter Nine, "Data Management," introduces you to the sort and query features of 1-2-3. You will learn how to sequence data in any order and extract particular data for any purpose.

• Chapter Ten, "Using Data Management Features in the Worksheet Environment," introduces you to the power that the data management features can add to worksheet models. You will learn about the tools needed to perform a sensitivity analysis, generate matrices, and sort formula entries.

• Chapter Eleven, "Working with 1-2-3's Graphics Features," provides examples of graphic display for your data. You will learn how easy it is to change numeric data into graphics and charts.

• Chapter Twelve, "Keyboard Macros," shows you how to save keystrokes for menu selections and other activities in worksheet cells. These keystrokes can then be reused at will.

• Chapter Thirteen, "Command Language Macros," covers the powerful new command language available in Release 3. Each macro command is described and illustrated with an example.

• Chapter Fourteen, "Using 1-2-3 on a Network," provides information on the networking commands that are part of Release 3.

• Appendix A, "Installing 1-2-3," explains everything you need to know to install the package successfully.

• Appendix B, "1-2-3 Keyboard Guide," shows the keyboards of two popular microcomputers.

• Appendix C, "A History of 1-2-3," explains 1-2-3's popularity in the context of previous spreadsheet solutions.

• Appendix D, "LMBCS Codes" provides the representation for each of the Lotus LMBCS codes.

Conventions Used in This Book

Several conventions used in this book should make your task of learning about 1-2-3 Release 3 easier:

- Command sequences are shown with initial letters in uppercase (as in /Worksheet Erase).

- User input is indicated in boldface.

- Small Capital letters have been used for the names of function keys (as in ALT-F4).

- @Function keywords are shown in uppercase, although you may use either upper- or lowercase when making entries.

- Filenames are shown in uppercase.

- In the chapters on macros, Chapter 12 and Chapter 13, macro keywords are shown in uppercase and range names are shown in lowercase.

1-2-3 Worksheet Reference

PART ONE

An Introduction to 1-2-3

ONE

A Product Designed to Utilize Your Hardware Effectively
New Worksheet Options
@Functions
Undo
Printing
Data Management
Graphs
Macros
Network Support
Development Support

1-2-3 is one of the most popular products ever introduced for microcomputers. Since its first introduction it has set the standard for spreadsheet product offerings on both mainframes and microcomputers. With the introduction of Release 3, Lotus has added many new features to ensure that 1-2-3 maintains its leadership position in the industry. This chapter is an introduction to 1-2-3 for new users, providing an overview of some of its major features. For the experienced 1-2-3 user it is a quick overview of some of the exciting new options in Release 3.

A Product Designed to Utilize Your Hardware Effectively

If you have invested in 286 and 386 computers, you may feel frustrated by the lack of programs that utilize the power of these machines effectively. 1-2-3 Release 3 offers full support for both expanded and extended memory. It provides its own operating system extenders, so you can even utilize your equipment without upgrading to OS/2.

1

New Worksheet Options

The basic worksheet options that allow the recording of numbers, labels, and formulas in 1-2-3's electronic spreadsheet still exist in Release 3. The package continues to be an ideal tool for tasks like budgeting, forecasting, and sales projections—for large and small companies alike. The wide range of 1-2-3's formats and other features allows it to be used in applications as diverse as manufacturing, architectural planning, hospital management, and education. Now new features extend both the range and size of applications that are possible.

3-D Worksheets

The new 3-D worksheet features allow you to have up to 256 worksheets in one worksheet file. Each sheet has the same 256 columns and 8192 rows as the first sheet presented. This capability finally allows you to create applications that parallel your work environment, including the multiple products, subsidiaries, and regions that are part of your overall picture.

Each sheet can contain different types of information, or match other sheets exactly. The new GROUP mode allows you to insert rows and columns, change column widths, and alter formats for one sheet or all the sheets at once.

Figure 1-1 gives you a look at a three-dimensional worksheet; it is a perspective view that splits the screen to show three different sheets at one time. Each sheet displays a level indicator in the upper left corner that allows you to distinguish it from other worksheets. The three sheets shown are all part of one worksheet file—making it possible to create a consolidation of the data shown, with a simple formula in the same file as the detail.

Multiple Files

You have always been able to create multiple files for different types of worksheet information. The difference with Release 3 is that you can bring more than one file into memory at a time. You can have a total of 256 sheets in memory, depending on the size of the sheets and the

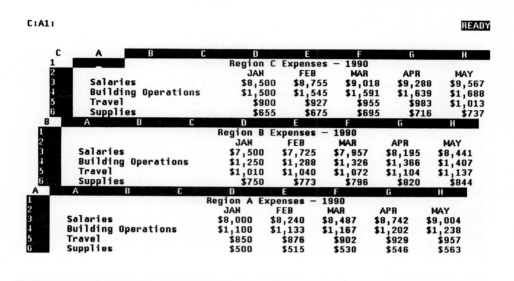

Figure 1-1.   Perspective view of three sheets from a worksheet file

amount of memory in your system. Some of these sheets can be part of a multiple-sheet file, and others can be separate files.

Figure 1-2 shows a perspective window with information from three different files. The first file is active, since it contains the cell pointer. This sheet contains information on current customer purchases. The second file contains a discount table used in computing discounts on all orders based on the amount and the purchase type. The third file contains additional information on the vendors used by the company. The information in this file would be helpful in negotiating a large order, since it may be possible to obtain price concessions or custom features from a vendor if the size of the order is sufficient. Although the screen may look very similar to the multiple-sheet view, you can see that each of the sheets has an A for its level indicator, indicating that it comes from a different file.

File Links

File links are normally used in multiple-file applications. These links can be to other files in memory or on disk. You can use a link to bring

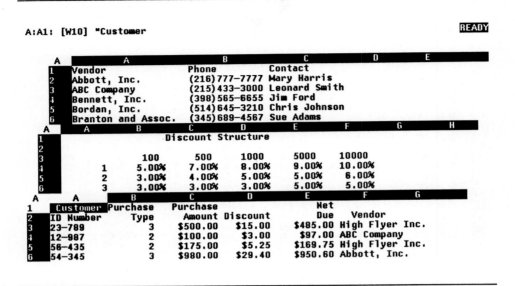

A:A1: [W10] "Customer   READY

	A	B	C	D	E
1	Vendor	Phone	Contact		
2	Abbott, Inc.	(216)777-7777	Mary Harris		
3	ABC Company	(215)433-3000	Leonard Smith		
4	Bennett, Inc.	(398)565-6655	Jim Ford		
5	Bordan, Inc.	(514)645-3210	Chris Johnson		
6	Branton and Assoc.	(345)689-4567	Sue Adams		

	A	B	C	D	E	F	G	H
1			Discount Structure					
2								
3		100	500	1000	5000	10000		
4	1	5.00%	7.00%	8.00%	9.00%	10.00%		
5	2	3.00%	4.00%	5.00%	5.00%	6.00%		
6	3	3.00%	3.00%	3.00%	5.00%	5.00%		

	A	B	C	D	E	F	G
1	Customer	Purchase	Purchase		Net		
2	ID Number	Type	Amount	Discount	Due	Vendor	
3	23-789	3	$500.00	$15.00	$485.00	High Flyer Inc.	
4	12-987	2	$100.00	$3.00	$97.00	ABC Company	
5	56-435	2	$175.00	$5.25	$169.75	High Flyer Inc.	
6	54-345	3	$980.00	$29.40	$950.60	Abbott, Inc.	

Figure 1-2.   Perspective view of sheets from three different files

information from a cell into the current cell, or data in the linked cell or range can be an integral part of a calculation stored in the current cell.

Once linked, you can control when the links are updated. If the files that you are linking are shared files on a network, you will want to refresh the entries as part of a decision-making cycle, and definitely before printing the current entries.

Automatic Format

Automatic format takes the work out of making many entries. Instead of typing a number and selecting the proper format, you can format a range of cells as Automatic. This format is temporary and will be replaced by a more appropriate format once you make an entry. The Automatic format supports Date, Time, Percent, Scientific, Currency, Label, Comma, and Fixed formats.

Figure 1-3 shows a worksheet that was created after selecting an Automatic format for cells in the range A4..E18. The entry 04/03/89 was placed in A4. Since this entry is a valid date entry, 1-2-3 converted the

A:A4: (D4) [W11] 32601   READY

A	A	B	C	D	E	F	G
1		CD Report For The Week Of April 3, 1989					
2							
3	Date	Time	CD Rate	Amount	Quantity		
4	04/03/89	09:00 AM	7.05%	$5,000	10		
5	04/03/89	12:00 PM	7.00%	$5,000	20		
6	04/03/89	04:00 PM	7.10%	$5,000	10		
7	04/04/89	09:00 AM	7.12%	$5,000	15		
8	04/04/89	12:00 PM	7.11%	$5,000	10		
9	04/04/89	04:00 PM	7.12%	$5,000	10		
10	04/05/89	09:00 AM	7.11%	$5,000	15		
11	04/05/89	12:00 PM	7.10%	$5,000	20		
12	04/05/89	04:00 PM	7.10%	$5,000	25		
13	04/06/89	09:00 AM	7.12%	$5,000	15		
14	04/06/89	12:00 PM	7.14%	$5,000	20		
15	04/06/89	04:00 PM	7.13%	$5,000	10		
16	04/07/89	09:00 AM	7.15%	$5,000	10		
17	04/07/89	12:00 PM	7.12%	$5,000	15		
18	04/07/89	04:00 PM	7.15%	$5,000	20		
19							

Figure 1-3.   Worksheet created with Automatic format

cell format to Date 4. The control panel, which shows the current stored contents of the cell, indicates that a date serial number was created for the entry. The entries in the other columns were also made while Automatic was in effect. Column C entries were entered with a % sign. The $ was used with the currency entries in column D. Automatic is a much quicker method than having to apply four different formats to four columns.

Expanded Name Support

1-2-3's range name features offer you the ability to assign names to one or more worksheet cells. You can use these names anywhere a range address is acceptable, and you will find that they make your formulas much easier to understand. New Release 3 features include the ability to assign notes to range names. You can also create tables of range name notes that contain all the information of range name tables, plus the notes attached to them. In Release 3, range names can be used in formulas before they are defined. Although the formula will initially read ERR, the formula can still be finalized.

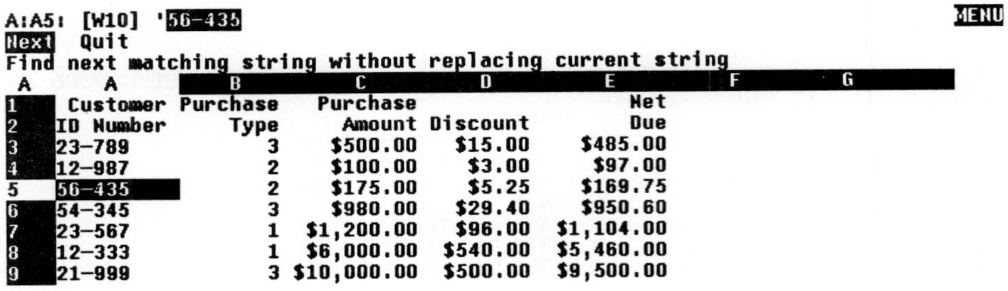

```
A:A5: [W10] '56-435                                                    MENU
Next   Quit
Find next matching string without replacing current string
    A        A        B          C         D         E        F       G
1       Customer  Purchase   Purchase                         Net
2       ID Number   Type       Amount  Discount               Due
3       23-789        3       $500.00    $15.00      $485.00
4       12-987        2       $100.00     $3.00       $97.00
5       56-435        2       $175.00     $5.25      $169.75
6       54-345        3       $980.00    $29.40      $950.60
7       23-567        1     $1,200.00    $96.00    $1,104.00
8       12-333        1     $6,000.00   $540.00    $5,460.00
9       21-999        3    $10,000.00   $500.00    $9,500.00
```

Figure 1-4.   Search looking for a part number entry

Search

Release 3 includes search and replace features that are effective in label and formula entries. You can use them to locate a particular entry like a last name or part number, or to change a phone number or an address.

Figure 1-4 shows several worksheet entries. The /Range Search command was used to locate entries for part number 56-435. 1-2-3 locates the first occurrence of the part number entry and highlights it, as shown in the figure. You have the option of continuing the search to look for additional matching entries or to end the search.

Figure 1-5 shows the same data presented in the previous example, except that the Replace option was used in this example. As you can see from the menu at the top, once the data is located you can choose to replace the matching entry with a string entered previously. Other choices include replacing all occurrences, locating the next occurrence, or quitting the Replace operation.

```
A:A5: [W10] '56-435                                               MENU
Replace  All  Next  Quit
Replace string and proceed to next matching string in range
A       A        B         C         D         E        F       G
1    Customer Purchase  Purchase              Net
2    ID Number   Type    Amount Discount      Due
3    23-789        3     $500.00   $15.00   $485.00
4    12-987        2     $100.00    $3.00    $97.00
5    56-435        2     $175.00    $5.25   $169.75
6    54-345        3     $980.00   $29.40   $950.60
7    23-567        1   $1,200.00   $96.00 $1,104.00
8    12-333        1   $6,000.00  $540.00 $5,460.00
9    21-999        3  $10,000.00  $500.00 $9,500.00
```

Figure 1-5.   Replace options for a part number

Map

You can create a map window for any worksheet. This window lets you look at an overview of the worksheet entries. Different symbols are used to mark labels, numbers, and formulas. You can use this view to identify number entries that should be formulas, or other problems in the work-sheet structure. Figure 1-6 provides a look at a portion of a worksheet that projects expenses for 11 months of the year based on January's actual numbers. When you request a map window, 1-2-3 automatically narrows the columns and displays columns A through AL (from Figure 1-6), as shown in Figure 1-7. The pound symbols (#) represent numbers, quotation marks (") represent labels, and plus signs (+) represent formulas.

@Functions

Release 2 of 1-2-3 included almost 90 @functions that performed tasks like summing a range of entries, computing a payment amount, entering

A:E6: (CO) +D6*(1+0.03)   `READY`

A	A	B	C	D	E	F	G	H
1								
2						Boston Company		
3								
4								
5				JAN		FEB	MAR	APR	MAY
6	Salaries			$8,000		$8,240	$8,487	$8,742	$9,004
7	Building Operations			$1,100		$1,133	$1,167	$1,202	$1,238
8	Travel			$850		$876	$902	$929	$957
9	Supplies			$500		$515	$530	$546	$563
10	Depreciation			$1,200		$1,236	$1,273	$1,311	$1,351
11	Equipment Maintenance			$750		$773	$796	$820	$844
12	Shipping Expense			$400		$412	$424	$437	$450
13	Data Processing Costs			$2,100		$2,163	$2,228	$2,295	$2,364
14	Printing & Duplicating			$640		$659	$679	$699	$720
15	Other			$1,030		$1,061	$1,093	$1,126	$1,159
16	Total Expenses			$16,570		$17,067	$17,579	$18,106	$18,650
17								

Figure 1-6.   Worksheet entries for expense projections

a date and time in a cell, and computing statistical functions within the database environment.

Release 3 provides 16 new @functions, plus expanded capability for some of the existing @functions to support the three-dimensional ranges. You can now sum a range across pages, or reference function arguments on other sheets or even in external files. Figure 1-8 provides a look at the new @INFO function. Depending upon the string argument supplied with the function, you can determine the available memory, the current 1-2-3 mode, the number of active files, the version of the operating system, and the recalculation mode. Although some of the same information is provided in the worksheet status line, you cannot access individual pieces of information with the status line information. With @INFO, you can create macros or formulas that supply results based on the values returned by this function.

Undo

In past releases of 1-2-3, once you invoked a command, a permanent change was effected. There was no way to undo the result of the

A:E6: (C0) [W9] +D6*(1+0.03)   READY

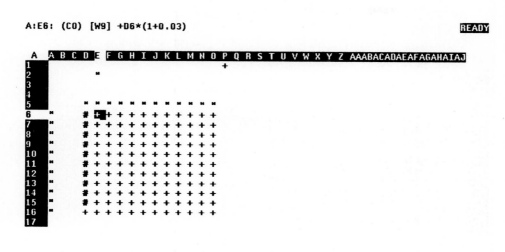

Figure 1-7.   Map window showing cell entry types for an expense projection
worksheet

A:E4: @INFO("memavail")   READY

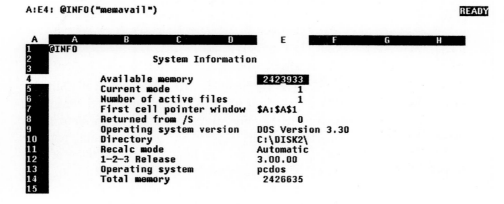

Figure 1-8.   Release 3's new @INFO function

command unless you had the last version of the model stored on disk and available for retrieval. In some cases changing your mind was easy without a disk version, since a change to one format could be altered by the entry of another format command. Other commands that erased data or changed the sequence of the worksheet entries were not as easily undone.

Release 3's Undo feature can be turned on and off through menu selections. When Undo is enabled, any command that does not affect an external device like the disk drive or printer can be undone. The secret is not to execute any intervening commands before attempting to undo the action of a command.

Printing

1-2-3's print features have always been easy to use. They provide basic support for printing spreadsheet data; however, in the past you needed to use the PrintGraph program to print a graph. PrintGraph is no longer required, since graph printing support is available from the Print menu. Print features extend well beyond the basics, with new Release 3 options that support use of most printer features, including different fonts and other customization options for both text and graphs.

New Print Features

A significant addition to 1-2-3's print features is the availability of background printing. You no longer need to sit and wait for a worksheet to print before continuing with your other tasks. You can send many print jobs to the queue, and specify print priorities of default, high, or low. The main Print menu, which used to limit you to a choice of only printer or file, now provides these options:

A:A4: (D4) [W11] 32601   MENU
Printer File Encoded Suspend Resume Cancel Quit
Send print output directly to a printer

The Encoded option allows you to write formatted print output to a file for later printing from the operating system. The file will include all the selected options like colors and fonts. The Suspend option allows you to temporarily stop a print job; Resume allows you to start it again. Cancel eliminates all the print jobs from the queue, including the job currently printing.

The new Options Advanced menu selection allows you to enhance your print output in many ways. You can select options from this menu:

```
A:A4: (D4) [W11] 32601                                              MENU
Device  Layout  Fonts  Color  Image  Priority  AutoLf  Wait  Quit
Select printer name and interface
```

You can now change the print device directly from the print menu, rather than having to modify the default setting. From the Layout selection you can choose Pitch to switch between Standard, Compressed, and Enlarged text, without the need for setup strings. You can change the line spacing from Standard to Compressed. Even the switch between Landscape and Portrait can be made with a Layout menu selection. Fonts can be changed for the header, footer, border, or frame.

With Release 3 you can display a table of graph names on the worksheet, using the Table selection in the Print Options Name menu below:

```
A:A4: (D4) [W11] 32601                                              MENU
Use  Create  Delete  Reset  Table
Use a named group of print settings
```

The graph type, name, and title appear in the table.

Support for Printing Graphs Within 1-2-3

You no longer need to save 1-2-3 graphs for later printing with Print-Graph. With the new Print Printer Image option, 1-2-3 will print the current graph or any named graph.

Image options on the Options Advanced menu allow you to rotate the graph, change the image size, or change the print density of the graph.

Data Management

1-2-3's data management features support the creation of data tables. You can use these features to create a database of client information, or an invoice database. A wide variety of other data management features, in addition to basic query and sort features, include more sophisticated data analysis and the generation of data values.

/Data Query and /Data Sort

1-2-3 supports the creation of databases on the worksheet. The rows of a sheet are the records, and the columns are used for each field. /Data Query features allow you to extract records that match specific criteria, and /Data Sort options allow you to resequence records in any order. Release 3 has expanded the Sort key features beyond the two-key limit of Release 2.01, to allow unlimited sort keys. A new Modify option added to /Data Query in Release 3 allows you to modify records in a database table.

The three-dimensional features of 1-2-3 expand practical applications, allowing you to use the full 8192 rows for the data table. Criteria and an output area can be defined on other sheets as shown in Figure 1-9, where data from sheet A is extracted using the criteria in sheet B and written to the output area in sheet C. Release 3 also has significantly increased the number of database fields from 32 to 256.

/Data Fill

1-2-3's /Data Fill command allows you to generate a series of evenly spaced numbers. You can use it to generate invoice numbers, purchase orders, or day numbers. In Release 3 you will find many new options for this command that allow you to generate date and time serial numbers.

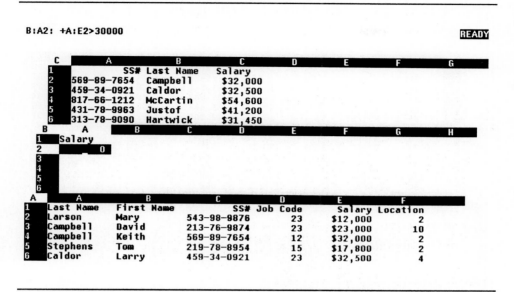

Figure 1-9.   Defining criteria and output areas on other sheets

You can space dates in increments of a week, a month, a quarter, or a year; you can space times in increments of minutes, hours, or seconds.

/Data External

The /Data External commands are new to Release 3. You can use them to exchange information between an external database, like dBASE, and 1-2-3 if you have a DataLens driver file for the database package. The 1-2-3 package provides a sample DataLens driver for dBASE III+. Other database vendors have committed to developing DataLens driver files for their databases.

After establishing a connection with the external file, you can add records to it using your 1-2-3 information. You can also add information to your 1-2-3 file from records in the external database.

Other commands allow you to list tables in an external database or to delete a table. You can also use features that update /Data Query operations or /Data Table commands. Functions and commands that are part of the database program can also be executed, even if you do not

A:B5: @PV(B1,B2,B3)   READY

C	A	B	C	D	E	F	G	H
1	10	9.00%	9.25%	9.50%	9.75%	10.00%	10.25%	10.50%
2	$100	$642	$635	$628	$621	$614	$608	$601
3	$200	$1,284	$1,270	$1,256	$1,242	$1,229	$1,216	$1,203
4	$300	$1,925	$1,904	$1,884	$1,863	$1,843	$1,824	$1,804
5	$400	$2,567	$2,539	$2,512	$2,484	$2,458	$2,432	$2,406
6	$500	$3,209	$3,174	$3,139	$3,106	$3,072	$3,040	$3,007

B	A	B	C	D	E	F	G	H
1	5	9.00%	9.25%	9.50%	9.75%	10.00%	10.25%	10.50%
2	$100	$389	$386	$384	$382	$379	$377	$374
3	$200	$778	$773	$768	$763	$758	$753	$749
4	$300	$1,167	$1,159	$1,152	$1,145	$1,137	$1,130	$1,123
5	$400	$1,556	$1,546	$1,536	$1,526	$1,516	$1,507	$1,497
6	$500	$1,945	$1,932	$1,920	$1,908	$1,895	$1,883	$1,871

A	A	B	C	D	E	F	G
1	Payment						
2	Rate						
3	# of Years						
4							
5	Annuity Value	$0					
6							

Figure 1-10.   Data Table type 3

have a copy of the database program on the computer. Your requests are handled by the DataLens driver for the database program.

Data Tables

1-2-3's /Data Table commands have allowed you to conduct sensitivity analyses or automated "what-if" analyses for your models. With /Data Table 1 you can modify the values for a variable in the model and review the effect of each change on as many formulas as you wish. /Data Table 2 lets you vary two variables within the model, to see which one affects the model the most. With a Data Table type 2 you can only examine the effect on one variable.

Release 3 adds the features of /Data Table 3. You can now systematically vary the values in each of three variables. One set of values is placed down a column, the second set is placed across a row, and the third set is placed across sheets. As with /Data Table 2, only the effect on one formula can be evaluated. Figure 1-10 provides a look at a Data Table type 3.

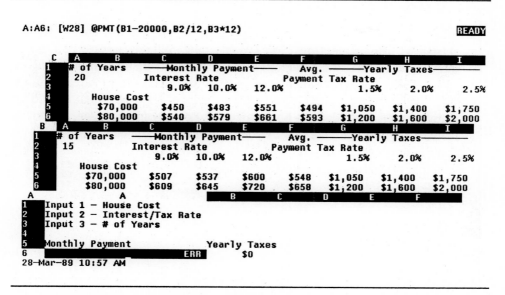

Figure 1-11.   /Data Table Labeled

The /Data Table Labeled command added with Release 3 allows you to create /Data Table 1, 2, or 3 options. /Data Table Labeled offers much more flexibility than the predefined options, allowing you to use more variables or to tailor other entries. You can add blank rows to a table and include formulas within the data table cells. Figure 1-11 shows a table created with the /Data Table Labeled features.

Graphs

Graphs present visual images of the information contained in a worksheet. With the visual appeal of graphs, you can often communicate information that would require considerable time to synthesize from the raw worksheet data. Release 3's many new graph options dramatically improve the quality of graphics output.

A New Graph Window

1-2-3 now allows you to view both a graph and a worksheet on the screen at the same time. The /Worksheet Window Graph command allows you to split the screen in half, with the worksheet data displayed in one half and a graph displayed in the other half. 1-2-3 makes assumptions about how the data in the current area of the worksheet should be graphed and uses default options to create a graph for you automatically. As you make changes to your worksheet data you will be able to see the effect immediately in the graph on the screen. Figure 1-12 is an example of this split screen display.

New Graph Features

Release 3 offers several new graph types and many new graphics options. The new High-Low-Close-Open (HLCO) graphs allow you to track

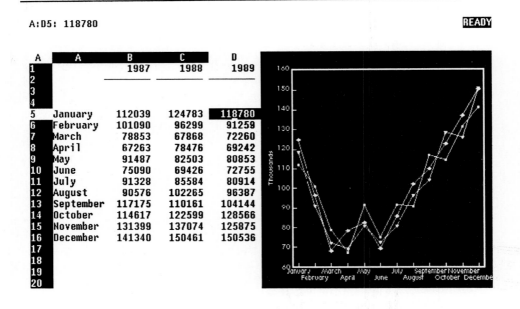

Figure 1-12.   Graph window and worksheet entries

quantities that vary periodically. You might use these graphs to show tides at a particular time of day, along with the high and low tide. Wind speeds, temperature, and barometric pressure can also be shown on these graphs, although stock market prices are normally the data for which HLCO graphs are used (see Figure 1-13).

The new Mixed graph type allows you to combine line and bar graphs. Up to three sets of bars and lines can be shown on each mixed graph. You may choose to show expenses in the bar graph, and use a line graph to show revenues for the same periods.

The options for graphs have increased dramatically. You can now have two different y-axes on a graph, allowing you to show data with two different scales. Other options let you set the colors or hatch mark patterns for the graph. Text can be customized with color and font changes. You can also display each of the data points as a percentage of the total of all the data points — without the need for adding formulas to the worksheet. A 100% option will automatically compute the correct amount for each data point.

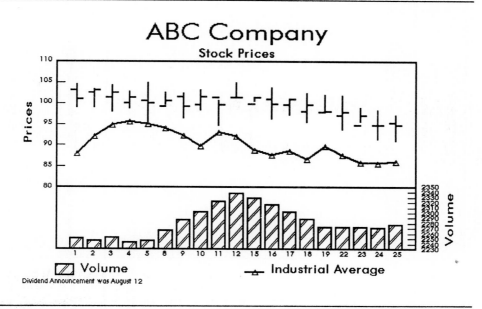

Figure 1-13.   HLCO graph

Macros

1-2-3 macros allow you to automate all types of 1-2-3 tasks. You can use two different types of 1-2-3 macros, the keyboard alternative macro or command language macro. Keyboard alternative macros are nothing more than specially named label cells that contain the letters and symbols representing the keystrokes you would normally type from the keyboard for menu selections and data entry. Command language macros are also labels cells, but they can also contain commands from 1-2-3's command language. This language has commands that allow you to duplicate actions of a programming language, like testing conditions, or executing instructions repeatedly. New command language commands offer important advances, like the ability to create data entry forms. However, the most significant macro enhancement in Release 3 is the addition of an automatic keystroke recorder.

The new keystroke recorder (ALT-F2, RECORD) is always enabled. This means it records everything you type without any special action on your part. The keystroke recorder allows you to access 512 characters of recorded entries. You can copy these entries to a cell and use them as a macro. You can also "play them back" for repetitive tasks that you need temporarily.

Figure 1-14 shows some of the keystrokes captured by the recorder. The Record menu option, Copy, has already been selected in this example; Copy lets you highlight the keystrokes you want to place on a worksheet. Note that the entries enclosed in curly braces, like {U}, indicate cell pointer movement keys such as the UP ARROW key. This abbreviated form used by the recorder maximizes the number of entries that can be stored in 512 characters.

Network Support

Lotus has made a commitment to fully support the use of 1-2-3 within a networking environment. In addition to the single user version of the product, 1-2-3 is also packaged in several popular combinations; you can purchase additional workstation copies, or a LAN package containing

```
A:A4: (D4) [W11] 32601                                                    EDIT
Select keystrokes to copy:
R}{U}/C~{D}.{D 11}~{R}{D}10{D}10{D}15{D}20{D}25{D}15{D}20{D}10{D}{U 7}{L 3}4:00
PM{R}7.12%~{D}{L 2}{ESC}{U}/DF~4/4/89~1~4/5/89~{D}~4/5/89{D}{U}/C~{D}.{D}~{R}9:0
0 AM{R}7.11%{D}{L}12:00 PM{R}7.10%{D}{L}4:00 PM{R}7.10%{D}{L 2}4/6/89~/C~{D}.{D
2}{U}~{R}9:00 AM{D}12:00 PM{D}{ESC}4:00 PM{U 2}{R}7.12%{D}7.14%{D}7.13%{D}{L 2}4
/7/89~/C~{D}.{D}~{R}9:00 AM{D}12:00 PM{D}4:00 PM{U 2}{R}7.15%{D}7.12%{D}7.15%{U
3}{D}{R 2}10{END}10{D}{PGUP 2}{HOME}{D 17}{U}{R 4}15{D}20{D}{L 4}{R 3}/RE~{U 16}
{L 3}{D}/FS{CE}C:\DISK2\FIg1_d~_
```

Figure 1-14.   Keystrokes captured by the keystroke recorder

several copies. The LAN package contains a network administrator's guide, in addition to authorization for the use of 1-2-3 on several machines.

The new 1-2-3 commands in support of a network environment have been added to the File menu structure. Available options allow you to reserve and release files. You can also create a table of file information including the reservation and modification status of files. You can use the new options to refresh the links to files that may have been modified by another user. You can use the File Seal option to seal a file's reservation setting or the entire file.

Development Support

Prior releases of 1-2-3 supported corporate and professional 1-2-3 developers, providing macros and an assembly language-based development tool. Although macros still support applications development at the low end, a new development tool will support more advanced development efforts. This product is packaged and marketed separately and will not be available until several months after Release 3's introduction.

The Pascal-like language, used to create applications with this tool, will appeal to a much larger group than the older assembly language-based tool. You can use it to create custom @functions or complete applications.

The Access System, Display, and Keyboard

The Lotus Access System
The Display
The Keyboard

This chapter will cover the Lotus Access System, your entry into everything 1-2-3 has to offer. It will also take a look at the screen display and the keyboard in some detail. Although this chapter will not require you to type any 1-2-3 commands, you should become comfortable with the keyboard and the information provided by 1-2-3's display as soon as possible. They are designed to assist you in your work with the package.

The Lotus Access System

The Lotus Access System ties together the different programs in the 1-2-3 system. You can use it to enter 1-2-3 and begin working with a worksheet. You can also use the Access System to change your installation selections, or translate another data file into a format that is usable in 1-2-3. The main menu for the Access System is shown in Figure 2-1. You can choose an option from this menu by typing the first character of the desired selection or by highlighting the desired choice and pressing ENTER.

Tip: Highlighting alone does not select a menu option. To avoid a common mistake made by new users, remember to press ENTER after highlighting your desired selection.

```
┌─────────────────────────────────────────────────────────────────┐
│ The Lotus integrated spreadsheet, database, and graphics program  │
│ 1-2-3      Install       Translate       Exit                     │
└─────────────────────────────────────────────────────────────────┘
```

```
┌─────────────────────────────────────────────────────────────────┐
│                                                                   │
│                        Lotus 1-2-3                                │
│                       Access System                               │
│                         Release 3                                 │
│           Copr. 1989 Lotus Development Corporation                │
│                    All Rights Reserved.                           │
│                                                                   │
│ You can run 1-2-3, Install, or Translate from the 1-2-3 Access system. │
│ To select a program to run, highlight the menu item using →, ←, HOME, │
│ or END and press ENTER, or press the first character of the item. │
│                                                                   │
│ To leave the Access system, select Exit from the Access menu.     │
│                                                                   │
│ Press HELP (F1) for more information on the Access system, and press ESC │
│ to leave Help.                                                    │
│                                                                   │
│ If you are running the Access system from a diskette, the Access system │
│ may prompt you to change diskettes.                               │
│                                                                   │
└─────────────────────────────────────────────────────────────────┘
```

Figure 2-1.   Access menu

Just as with any program, you will have to load the operating system before accessing any of the 1-2-3 programs. You will also want to activate the directory containing the 1-2-3 program files. For example, if your 1-2-3 files are stored in the directory 123R3, type **CD\123R3** and press ENTER to make the directory active. You can then access any program directly, or you can key in **Lotus** and press ENTER to load the Access System. From the Access System you can select the options 1-2-3, Translate, Install, or Exit.

If you wish to use a driver configuration file other than 123.CNF, you will need to specify the set name. For example, if you wanted to use a driver configuration file called OFFICE.CNF, you would type **Lotus Office** and then press ENTER.

Tip: You can create a number of driver configuration files. You can use several driver configuration files to establish primary printer or screen displays. Rather than using the menu to change the printer after starting 1-2-3, you can choose the active printer by selecting the .CNF file that is appropriate.

Using the Access System makes it easy to transfer from program to program, since you will be returned to the Access System after working with each program. Because Release 3 requires a hard disk system, you can switch from program to program without having to switch floppy disks, as you may have done with earlier releases.

Tip: Conserve memory requirements by loading only the program you need. If you have limited memory on your system, you will want to load the program you need, rather than using the Access System. To load the Worksheet program, type **123** and press ENTER. To load Translate, type **Trans**; and to load the Installation program, type **Install**.

Now let's review briefly each of the choices on the Access System menu. Most of the attention in this book will focus on the 1-2-3 option, since that is the main part of the package. The Translate program will also receive additional coverage later in the book; you'll see how it can save valuable time when you want to transfer data between 1-2-3 and another program.

1-2-3

1-2-3 is the main option on the Access System menu for all releases of Lotus. You can enter 1-2-3 from the Access System menu, or by typing **123** from the operating system once you have activated the 1-2-3 directory. This latter approach will save a little memory, since the Access System routines will not have to be loaded into memory.

However you elect to load 1-2-3 into memory, you will need to have the operating system active in the system before you begin. To fully utilize the power of the package, you will want to respond to the operating system date and time prompts with the correct information if your system is not set for the proper date and time. Each of the files that you create will then automatically have the current date and time in their directory entries. These entries will be taken from the system clock at the time each file is created. In addition, you can both date- and time-stamp your worksheet with the @NOW and @TODAY functions, described in Chapter 7, "1-2-3's Built-in Functions."

You can use the menu and features of 1-2-3 to build spreadsheet models, construct databases, and display graphs on your screen through a series of nested menus. Most of the work you do with the package will be done through the 1-2-3 program. The other Access System features are designed to handle more specialized needs, such as translating data and customizing installation settings.

Returning to the Access System after working with 1-2-3 is easy. Simply type **/Q** from 1-2-3's main menu to quit; then type a **Y** to confirm that you wish to exit. With Release 3, you have built-in protection from accidentally forgetting to save a file. If the current worksheet contains changes that have not been saved, 1-2-3 will display a second prompt before quitting—letting you choose whether or not you wish to save the worksheet. If you initially entered 1-2-3 from the Access System, you will be returned to the Access System menu after quitting 1-2-3. If you entered 1-2-3 directly from the operating system, the operating system prompt, C>, will appear on your screen.

Translate

The Translate program permits data interchange between 1-2-3 and other programs by translating files from other programs into a form 1-2-3 can handle, or by translating 1-2-3 files into a variety of other data formats. If the Translate program is not on your hard disk, insert the Translate disk (if you are working with 5 1/4-inch disks) or the Utility disk (if you are working with the 3 1/2-inch size). If you want to access Translate directly, type **Trans** and press ENTER.

Once Translate is loaded, you will see a menu. This menu will allow you to translate from one of the Lotus formats to such formats as DIF(Data Interchange Format), Symphony, or dBASE III, or to translate from one of the other formats to a Lotus Release 3 format.

The process has been made very simple with the Release 3 version of Translate. First select the type of source file you plan to use as input for translation from the list of products in the left column. After you make this selection, 1-2-3 lists the target file types available for translation of the source file type that you selected. If you select DIF from the first menu, for example, the only target file type available is a 1-2-3 Release 3 file. On the other hand, if you select a 1-2-3 Release 3 file for the source file, you can choose from any of the target file types shown in the menu in Figure 2-2. This option is useful if you have 1-2-3 data that you want to use with other programs like Multiplan. Translate is discussed further in Chapter 8, "Working with Files."

Install

The Install program is discussed in detail in Appendix A, "Installing 1-2-3." You can enter the program from the Access System menu by selecting Install. If you wish, you can enter Install without the Access System by typing **Install**. If the Install program is not on your hard disk, insert the Install/Setup disk before attempting to access it.

Exit

When you finish with one of the Access System options, you will be returned to the main Access System menu. To return to the operating system, you will use the Exit option. When you choose Exit, you will be

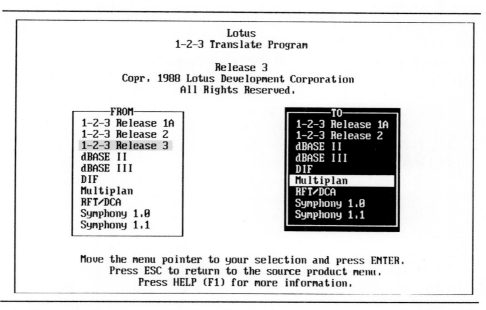

Figure 2-2.   Translate menu

asked to confirm your request by pointing to Yes or No on the screen and pressing ENTER, or by typing **Y** or **N**. This prompt is designed to prevent an exit caused by an accidental selection.

The Display

1-2-3's screen display is divided into three areas: a control panel at the top of the screen, a worksheet area in the middle, and an area at the bottom that displays error messages and descriptions. In Release 3, this bottom area also displays either the current filename or the date and time. A border containing the column names separates the control panel from the worksheet portion of the display. The filename/date area appears at the bottom of the screen below the display of the last row number. Figure 2-3 shows a screen display with all three of the areas labeled.

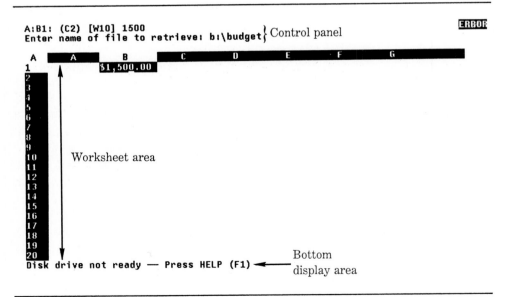

Figure 2-3.   Screen display

The Control Panel

Each of the three lines in the control panel has a specific purpose. The second and third lines will be discussed under "The Menu," later in this chapter. In Chapter 3, "Entering Data in 1-2-3's Worksheet," you will learn that long cell entries will cause the control panel area to expand and display the entire cell entry, up to the maximum of 512 characters. This expanded control panel display will limit the worksheet display to 14 rows.

The top line provides the greatest number of individual pieces of information. At the far left corner you will find the current location of the cell pointer; that is, the highlighted bar visible on the worksheet. In Release 3, this location gives the worksheet level and the specific location of the cell pointer in the current worksheet.

Release 3 supports the use of as many as 256 worksheets within one worksheet file. Release 3 also allows a number of open worksheet files in memory, as long as the total number of worksheets in all files does not exceed 256. For now, let's focus on the first worksheet, which is automatically available and referred to as worksheet A. The A indicates the worksheet level and is followed by a colon and the address of the worksheet cell that contains the cell pointer. In Figure 2-3 the cell pointer is in cell B1 (the intersection of column B and row 1), so the location reads "A:B1".

Immediately to the right of the cell pointer location, in parentheses, you will see any special display attributes assigned to the cell. 1-2-3 allows you to display numbers as currency, percents, and other special formats. Each assigned format has a special code representing the format, such as C for Currency, and this code will appear in the control panel for a cell that has a special format assigned to it. In Figure 2-3, the Currency format with two decimal places has been assigned to the cell, so you see (C2). The C represents Currency, and the 2 shows the number of decimal places. Other commonly used formats are , for Comma, F for Fixed, P for Percent, G for General, and T for Text.

Release 3 also provides information on the protection status of a cell, and the cell width if it is different from the default assigned to the column the cell is in. These features are also represented by special character codes, which will be discussed in Chapter 4, "Changing the Appearance of the Worksheet Display." The codes appear in brackets.

To the right of the format code are the contents of the cell as they were entered. Suppose, for example, that you entered 514.76. If you are displaying the entry as currency with zero decimal places, you will see $515 on the worksheet; but in the control panel you will see your original entry.

On the top line at the far right, in a highlighted area, you will find the mode indicator. This indicator tells you what 1-2-3 is doing, and what it expects from you. It can instruct you to wait, correct an error, point to a worksheet location, or tell 1-2-3 what to do next.

Table 2-1 lists the mode indicators and their meanings. For example, as soon as you begin a cell entry by typing a number, 1-2-3's mode indicator changes from READY to VALUE. If you activate 1-2-3's menu, the mode indicator changes to MENU. Once 1-2-3 is in a certain

Indicator	Meaning
EDIT	Cell entry is being edited. EDIT can be generated by 1-2-3 when your entry contains an error and 1-2-3 wants you to edit it. It can also be generated by pressing the F2 (EDIT) key to change a cell entry.
ERROR	1-2-3 has encountered an error. The problem is noted in the lower left corner of the screen. Press ESC to clear the error message, and then correct the problem specified in the error message.
FILES	1-2-3 wants you to select a filename to proceed. This message also appears when you request a list of files on your disk with /File List.
FIND	The /Data Query Find command is active.
HELP	A Help display is active.
LABEL	1-2-3 has decided that you are making a label entry.
MENU	1-2-3 is waiting for you to make a menu selection.
NAMES	1-2-3 is displaying a menu of range, print, or graph names.
POINT	1-2-3 is waiting for you to point to a cell or range. As soon as you begin to type, POINT mode will change to EDIT mode.
READY	1-2-3 is currently idle and waiting for you to make a new request.
STAT	Worksheet status information is displayed.
VALUE	1-2-3 has decided that you are making a value entry.
WAIT	1-2-3 is processing your last command and cannot begin a new task until the flashing WAIT indicator changes to READY.

Table 2-1.   Mode Indicators

mode, you have to either follow along with its plans or find a way to change the indicator. For example, if the mode indicator reads LABEL, you will not be able to enter a VALUE entry until you find a way to change the indicator. In some cases this means eliminating your previous selections and starting over. Many of a new user's frustrations come from not understanding and watching the mode indicator. In order to maintain a smooth working relationship with 1-2-3, you must stay "in sync" with 1-2-3's mode indicators.

Tip: When 1-2-3 does not respond as you expect, check the mode indicator first. If the indicator contains anything other than READY, you cannot start a new request. You might think you are in the middle of making menu selections; but if you check the indicator and see ERROR, you will remember to press ESC to acknowledge the error condition.

The Worksheet

The worksheet occupies most of your display screen. This area serves as a window that allows you to look at the information stored in memory in an orderly format. In earlier releases, one worksheet mapped the entire contents of memory. With Release 3, you can have one or more worksheet files in memory at the same time. A single worksheet file may consist of up to 256 separate sheets that have the same row and column orientation as the sheet you see when you first start 1-2-3. This worksheet layout serves as your access to all worksheet entries, and allows you to look at any section you choose on any open worksheet.

Think of the memory in your computer as similar to the workspace on the top of your desk. Just as different sized desks may hold different numbers of file folders or other information, the varying amounts of memory within various computers control the amount of worksheet data they store. You can use the top of your desk for one file of information or many files. A file may contain one large sheet of paper or many smaller sheets. It's the same with Release 3: you can now read one or more files into memory, and each of these files can contain entries on one or more worksheets. The total number of worksheets that may be in memory at one time is 256—regardless of whether they are all in one

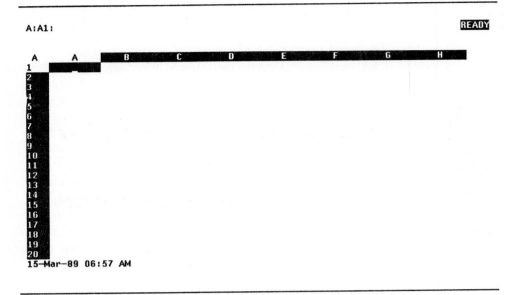

A:A1:   READY

15—Mar—89 06:57 AM

Figure 2-4.   Worksheet display

file or from different files. The size of the worksheets and the amount of memory in your system will determine how close you come to this upper limit.

The worksheet has an orderly arrangement of rows and columns. The row numbers and column letters appear highlighted on the display in Figure 2-4. Since you can have many worksheets within a single 1-2-3 file, the unhighlighted upper left corner of the row and column labels provide the current worksheet level. Later you will learn about an option that allows you to see three worksheet levels at one time, as shown in Figure 2-5.

Every entry you make on the worksheet will be in a specific cell address uniquely identified by the file in which it is stored, its worksheet level, and the row and column location that make up the actual cell address. Cell entries can be numbers, labels, and formulas. You will learn more about the specific worksheet options in Chapter 3, "Entering Data in 1-2-3's Worksheet."

The Bottom Display Area

The area at the bottom of your screen, occupied by a date/time display in earlier releases, can now be used for either a filename or the date and

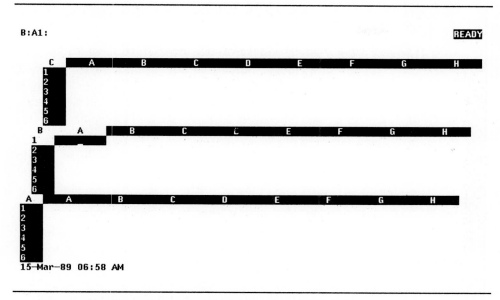

Figure 2-5.   Worksheet perspective of multiple-sheet file

time. The default is to show the filename for worksheets stored on disk. Before a worksheet is saved, this area reflects the date and time display. You may choose an option that changes the default, and displays the date and time in this location at all times. If you elect to display the date and time, it is constantly updated as your screen is refreshed.

Regardless of which display you choose, it will be temporarily suppressed as needed to display error messages such as "Disk Full," "Printer Not Ready," or "Disk Not Ready." Whenever an error message is displayed here, the mode indicator at the top right corner will contain ERROR. To proceed, you must press ESC to eliminate the error message and the ERROR indicator.

Descriptions will also appear in this bottom area to let you know when certain keys have been pressed or when certain other settings for the package are in use. The six key indicators and their meanings are as follows:

CAP   The CAPS LOCK key is depressed. When the CAP indicator is on, the alphabetic keys will produce capital letters.

END   The END key was pressed and 1-2-3 is waiting for you to press an arrow key.

FILE   The FILE key (CTRL-END) was pressed to move to another file in memory. When this key is followed by the HOME key, the first file in memory is active. If the END key is used, the last file in memory is active. CTRL-PGUP and CTRL-PGDN move you to the next and previous files, respectively.

NUM   The NUM LOCK key was pressed. This key allows you to enter a number from the numeric keypad.

OVR   The INS toggle was pressed, allowing keyboard entries in Overstrike mode rather than Insert mode.

SCROLL   The SCROLL LOCK key was pressed; this controls the way information scrolls off your screen. SCROLL LOCK toggles the effect of the arrow keys between moving one row or column in any direction, and shifting the entire screen one row or column in the direction of the arrow. When the SCROLL indicator is on, the entire window will shift when the arrow keys are pressed.

STEP   The STEP mode is in effect for macro execution. This mode is activated by pressing ALT-F2. STEP is discussed further in Chapter 12, "Keyboard Macros."

Eight additional indicators signal more than just one key press. These indicators and their meanings are as follows:

CALC   The worksheet needs to be recalculated. Changes have been made to the data that are not yet recalculated in the screen display. You will see this indicator when recalculation is set to manual, and will need to press F9 to begin recalculation. When set to automatic, the entire worksheet is recalculated as soon as a change is made; however, you will still see this indicator while background recalculation to update the worksheet display is taking place.

CIRC

The worksheet contains a circular reference, that is, a cell that refers back to itself. Release 3 provides special help to locate the defective entry with the /Worksheet Status command.

CMD

Appears during the execution of a macro.

GROUP

The current file is in GROUP mode, causing some commands to affect all the worksheets in the file.

MEM

Less than 4096 bytes of memory remain.

RO

The status of the current file is Read-only. This means that you will not be able to save any of your changes to the file.

SST

This is the macro indicator that appears during single-step execution for a macro. The STEP indicator will change to SST when the execution of a macro begins. SST is discussed further in Chapter 12, "Keyboard Macros."

ZOOM

You pressed ALT-F6 to zoom in for a full-screen view of a perspective view of the worksheet, or a worksheet with multiple windows.

Help Features

You can change your screen to an online reference source at will. All you have to do is press the F1 (HELP) key. 1-2-3 will guess at what your question might be and supply information based on your current task. If you want additional help or help with a different subject, you can use the Help index or ask for one of the other topics listed at the bottom of the Help screen.

Figure 2-6 lists the help that 1-2-3 provides for entering a formula in a cell. This Help screen lists part of the Task index, highlighting the option for "Moving Around the Worksheet." 1-2-3 recognized that a formula entry had been started and selected this option in case additional information on selecting formula references was needed. When ENTER is pressed, additional detail for the highlighted choice, as shown in Figure 2-7, is displayed. If none of the Task index entries meet your needs, you can access the main Help index by highlighting the "Help

```
A:C4:
+C2—
```

```
Task Index (continued)
 Move around the worksheet        — see Moving Around the Worksheet
 Move between worksheets          — see Moving Between Worksheets
 Move between active files        — see Moving Between Active Files
 Password—protect a file          — see /File Save with Password Protection
 Put a page break in a worksheet  — see /Worksheet Page
 Print a worksheet                — see /Print Printer Range
 Print a graph                    — see /Printer Printer Image
 Protect data in a file           — see /File Admin Seal or /WGP
 Save a graph in a file           — see /Graph Save
 Save a graph with a worksheet    — see /Graph Name Create
 Save data in a worksheet file    — see /File Save
 Save data in a text file         — see /Print File
 Save part of a worksheet         — see /File Xtract
 See global default setting       — see /Worksheet Global Default Status
 Sort records in a database       — see /Data Sort
 Start a new worksheet file       — see /File New
 Start over                       — see /Worksheet Erase Yes

Previous                                             Help Index
15—Mar—89 07:00 AM
```

Figure 2-6.   Help screen

Index" entry at the bottom of the screen and pressing ENTER. Figure 2-8 shows the comprehensive list of topics covered by the Help index.

The Menu

Lines 2 and 3 of the control panel can be transformed into a menu of command selections by pressing the slash key (/). Figure 2-9 shows the main menu that this produces. Menus are the backbone of the 1-2-3 program and are your way of accessing all its features. You can make them available at will with the slash key, but they will not clutter the screen when you do not need them.

1-2-3's menus offer an advantage over some earlier spreadsheet programs in that they are self-documenting. The line beneath the individual menu options will reflect a description of the current menu selection. You can point to different menu items (in line 2) with the cell pointer movement keys on the keypad. As you move from item to item, the description line (line 3) will change accordingly. For instance, when you point to the Worksheet option in the menu, the second line will list all the specific Worksheet options: Global, Insert, Delete, Column,

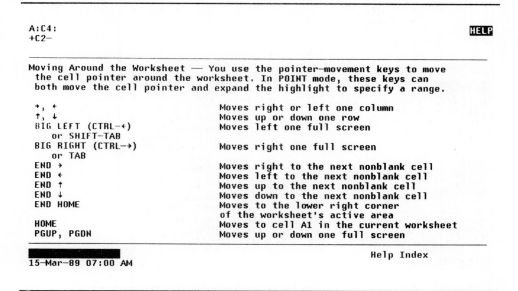

Figure 2-7.   More specific help for a task

Erase, Titles, Window, Status, Page, and Hide. These are not completely descriptive of the functions provided, but they will serve as reminders once you learn the commands.

To select a menu item you can either type the first letter of the menu item (for example, **W** for Worksheet) or point to the item with your cell pointer and press ENTER. Either method will invoke the selected command or present a menu for further selections.

Figure 2-10 presents a map of the menu selections available after pressing **/W** (for Worksheet). Each subsequent menu level is selected in the same manner as the previous selection, with each level refining your choice further. If you choose a menu item in error, you can back out to the previous level by pressing ESC once. Each time you press ESC, you retreat to the next higher menu level until you are eventually back at READY mode.

The Keyboard

You will begin using the keyboard in the next chapter as you make entries in worksheet cells. This section focuses on the keyboard for the

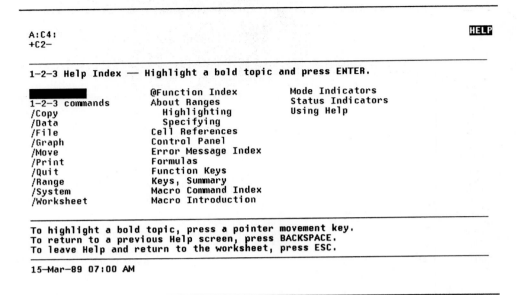

Figure 2-8.   Help index

IBM PS/2. The same keyboard configuration is used for the IBM AT and many IBM-compatible computers. There are some differences between these and keyboards of other popular systems that work with 1-2-3, as Appendix B, "1-2-3 Keyboard Guides" shows. These differences will not require changes in the installation of 1-2-3 or limit your use of the program, but they may affect the keys you use to access 1-2-3's features.

All keys will be covered in this chapter to provide a single reference source for all keyboard functions. Individual features will be pointed out again in later chapters where they will be helpful, so you do not have to worry about absorbing all of this information now.

The IBM PS/2 keyboard has three basic sections, as shown in Figure 2-11. The highlighted keys at the top of the screen are the function keys. These keys are made available to software developers for program-specific use, so there is little consistency between programs in the way function keys are used. Lotus has assigned these keys the special functions shown in Table 2-2. Pressing any of these keys causes 1-2-3 to take the requested action when the system is in READY mode. The only exceptions are F3 (NAME) and F4 (ABS), which function only in

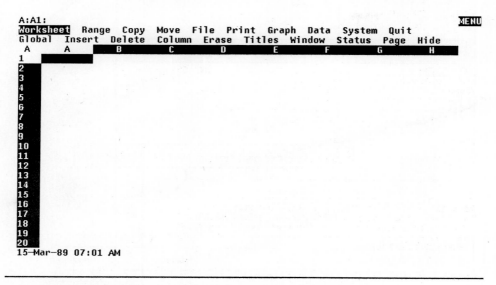

Figure 2-9.   Main 1-2-3 menu

POINT mode. Several of the function keys may be used in combination
with the ALT key to perform additional tasks.

The highlighted keys to the far right serve a dual purpose: they
make up the numeric keypad/cursor movement keys. Table 2-3 explains
where each of these keys will move the cell pointer. You will notice that
these keys also have direction arrows and other writing on them. This
shows their normal function in 1-2-3 when they are used for cell pointer
movement. If you depress the NUM LOCK key, you can also use these keys
for numeric entries. Be careful to press this key only once, though. Like
the CAPS LOCK key, it toggles each time it is pressed. Fortunately, the
newer keyboards like the one on the PS/2 have a second set of cursor
movement keys. This allows you to turn on NUM LOCK and use the numeric
keypad exclusively for the entry of numbers, while the second set of
cursor movement keys is used to change your location on the screen.

Let's look at an example of the use of these keys. A screen display
from 1-2-3 is shown in Figure 2-12. The cell pointer or highlighted area
is found in location C3, as shown by the row and column designators at
the side and top of the display, or at the upper left corner in the control

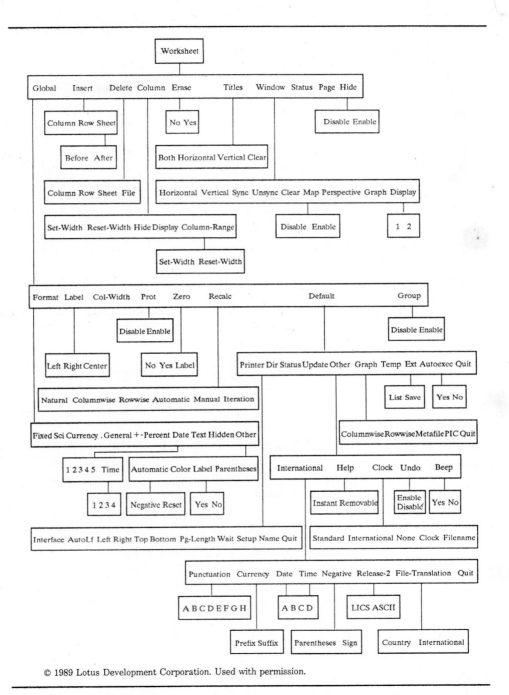

Figure 2-10. Map of 1-2-3 commands

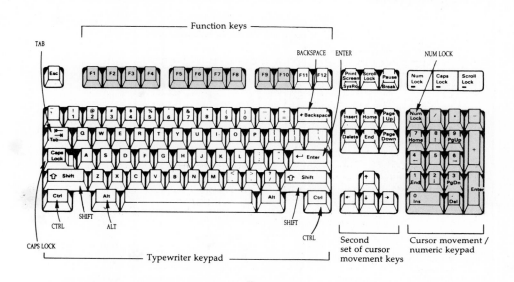

Figure 2-11.   The IBM enhanced keyboard

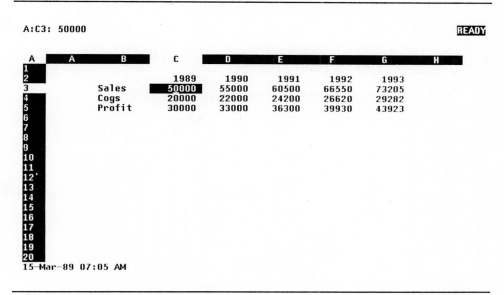

Figure 2-12.   Screen display

panel. Using the keypad keys will move the cell pointer to new locations. The following table shows the new location of the cell pointer if the listed keys are pressed when the cell pointer is in location C3.

Key Sequence	New Cursor Location
LEFT ARROW	B3
RIGHT ARROW	D3
UP ARROW	C2
DOWN ARROW	C4
END followed by DOWN ARROW	C5
END followed by UP ARROW	C2
END followed by RIGHT ARROW	G3
END followed by LEFT ARROW	B3
PGUP	C1 (cell pointer cannot move up 20 rows from its present location)
PGDN	C23
HOME	A1
CTRL-RIGHT ARROW	I3
CTRL-LEFT ARROW	Beeps, since it cannot scroll screen to the left

The function of these keys will become clearer in the next chapter when we put them to work in a worksheet example. There are also keys that allow you to access other levels within the current worksheet, as well as additional files that you might have open in memory.

Tip: Focus first on the basic keys for cell pointer movement. There are many keys that allow you to make your way around a worksheet efficiently, but it can be difficult for a novice to remember all the options. Five basic entries are all you need to get started. Press the HOME key to move to A1, and use the arrow keys to move in other directions. If you hold down the arrow keys, they will repeat and move you around very quickly.

Function Key	Assignment
F1 (HELP)	Provides context-sensitive help.
F2 (EDIT)	Allows you to alter the contents of the current cell without reentering all the information. You can add or delete just a few characters if you wish.
F3 (NAME)	Displays a list of your range names when you are in POINT mode. When pressed a second time, this key provides a full-screen display of the range name information. In Release 3 this key is also used to display a list of function, macro, or file names.
F4 (ABS)	Like F3, F4 functions only when you are in POINT mode. It allows you to toggle from a relative address to an absolute or mixed address.
F5 (GOTO)	Moves your cell pointer to the range or address you enter after pressing the key.
F6 (WINDOW)	Functions as a toggle, moving you into the other window when there are two windows.
F7 (QUERY)	Causes 1-2-3 to repeat the last query operation.
F8 (TABLE)	Repeats the most recent table operation from the Data menu option.
F9 (CALC)	Causes the entire worksheet to be recalculated. Useful when recalculation of the worksheet is set at manual.
F10 (GRAPH)	Redraws the most recent graph.
ALT-F1 (COMPOSE)	Used when creating international characters.
ALT-F2 (STEP)	Causes macros to execute a step at a time, or allows you to use a 512-byte buffer for recording keystrokes.
ALT-F3 (RUN)	Runs a selected macro.
ALT-F4 (UNDO)	Undoes the effect of all actions since the last READY indicator if UNDO is enabled.
ALT-F6 (ZOOM)	Toggles the current window between its current size and full screen size.
ALT-F7 (APP1)	Starts an Add-in application.
ALT-F8 (APP2)	Starts an Add-in application.
ALT-F9 (APP3)	Starts an Add-in application.
ALT-F10 (ADDIN)	Displays a menu that allows you to access Add-in applications.

Table 2-2.   Function Key Assignments with 1-2-3

Keys	Action
HOME	Moves the cell pointer to the home position or upper leftmost corner of the worksheet.
	When in EDIT mode, moves the cell pointer to the beginning of the entry.
UP ARROW	Moves the cell pointer up one cell on the worksheet.
DOWN ARROW	Moves the cell pointer down one cell on the worksheet.
RIGHT ARROW	Moves the cell pointer one cell to the right.
LEFT ARROW	Moves the cell pointer one cell to the left.
PGUP	Moves the cell pointer up 20 rows.
PGDN	Moves the cell pointer down 20 rows.
END followed by one of the arrow keys	Moves the cell pointer to the end of your entries in the direction indicated by the arrow key when the cell pointer is on a cell containing an entry.
	When the cell pointer is on a blank cell, takes the cell pointer to the next cell in the direction that has an entry.
CTRL-RIGHT or CTRL-LEFT ARROW	Moves your window into the worksheet a full screen to the right or left.
CTRL-HOME	Moves the cell pointer to A1 in the current worksheet.
END-CTRL-HOME	Moves the cell pointer to the last nonblank cell in the current file.

Table 2-3.   Numeric Keypad Functions

Multiple worksheets and files offer you a considerable amount of flexibility. There are special keyboard options that allow you to move with ease from sheet to sheet and file to file.

Table 2-4 lists the keys that allow you to move between worksheets when there are multiple worksheets in one file. These additional worksheets must be added to a file when you want to use more sheets than the single default sheet that is provided. You will learn more about the /Worksheet Insert Sheet command in Chapter 5.

Assume that you have four worksheets in the current worksheet file, and worksheet C is active. The cell pointers within each worksheet are in these locations: A:C3, B:B4, C:A1, and D:B3, as shown in Figure 2-13. The following table indicates which worksheet is made active when you use the listed keyboard options while in worksheet C:

CTRL-PGDN	B:B4
CTRL-PGUP	D:B3
END CTRL-PGDN	A:A1
END CTRL-PGUP	D:A1

Since you can work with a number of worksheets in memory at one time with Release 3, you will want to move between them effectively. You can use the keys in Table 2-5 to change the active file. Assume that five files are placed in memory with the /File Open After command in

Keys	Action
CTRL-PGUP (NEXT SHEET)	Moves the cell pointer to the next worksheet
CTRL-PGDN (PREVIOUS SHEET)	Moves the cell pointer to the previous worksheet
END-CTRL-PGUP (END NEXT SHEET)	Functions similar to the END key, except moves across sheets from the current sheet toward the last sheet. The cell pointer remains in the same location as in the present worksheet, except the current worksheet becomes the worksheet with a nonblank entry at an intersection of blank and nonblank cells.
END-CTRL-PGDN (END PREV SHEET)	Functions similar to the END key, except moves across sheets toward the first sheet. The cell pointer remains in the same location as in the present worksheet, except the current worksheet becomes the worksheet with a nonblank entry at an intersection of blank and nonblank cells.

Table 2-4.   Keys for Moving Between Worksheets

the following order: Budget, Expenses, Tax, Vendors, and Employ. TheTax file contains six worksheets. If you could look into memory and see the worksheets, they would look like Figure 2-14. If the first worksheet in the Tax file is currently active, the following table shows the effect of pressing the various keys while in the first Tax worksheet:

Key Sequence	New File Location
CTRL-PGUP	Moves to the second sheet in the Tax file
CTRL-PGDN	Moves to the Expenses file
CTRL-END, HOME	Moves to the Budget file
CTRL-END, END	Moves to the Employ file
CTRL-END CTRL-PGUP	Moves to the Vendors file
CTRL-END CTRL-PGDN	Moves to the Expenses file

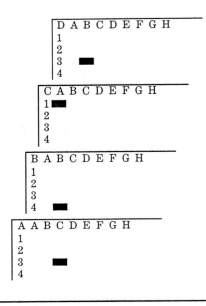

Figure 2-13.   Multiple sheets in one file

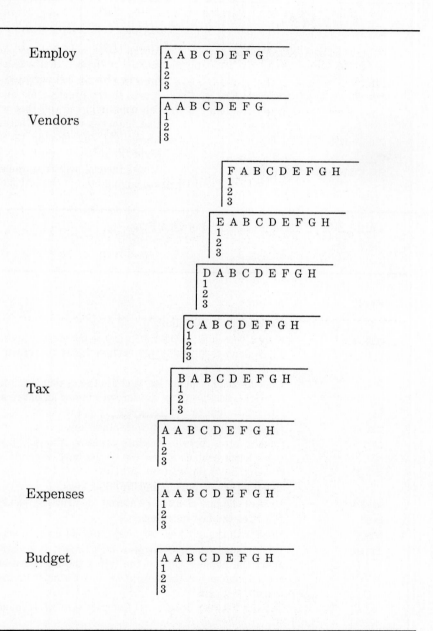

Figure 2-14.   Multiple worksheet files in memory

Keys	Action
CTRL-END CTRL-PGUP (NEXT FILE)	Moves to the next file and places the cell pointer in the cell that was active in that file when it was last accessed.
CTRL-END CTRL-PGDN (PREV FILE)	Moves to the previous file and places the cell pointer in the cell that was active in that file when it was last accessed.
CTRL-END-HOME (FIRST FILE)	Moves the cell pointer to the cell last highlighted in the first file.
CTRL-END-END (LAST FILE)	Moves the cell pointer to the cell that was last highlighted in the last file.

Table 2-5.   Keys for Moving Between Files

Keys	Action
ESC	Cancels the last request.
CTRL-BREAK	Places you in READY mode, canceling one or more selections. Equivalent to pressing ESC enough times to return to READY mode.
TAB	Equivalent to CTRL-RIGHT ARROW; shifts the display an entire screen to the right. SHIFT-TAB shifts the screen window an entire screen to the left; equivalent to CTRL-LEFT ARROW.
CTRL	Used only in combination with other keys.
SHIFT	Causes letter keys to produce capitals. Allows you to access all the special symbols at the top of the keys. Sometimes called the CAPS key, but it differs from CAPS LOCK.
ALT	Used only in combination with other keys.
BACKSPACE	Deletes the last character entered (destructive backspace).
ENTER	Finalizes the last entry made.
PRTSC	Used with the CAPS key (SHIFT key) to print current screen.
CAPS LOCK	Produces all capitals. Toggles each time it is pressed. Does not affect the number keys at the top of the keyboard or any of the special symbols at the tops of keys. (SHIFT must be used to access these.)
INS	Toggles between Insert and Overstrike in EDIT mode.

Table 2-6.   Special Key Combinations

NUM LOCK	Toggles numeric keypad between cell pointer movement and numeric entries.
SCROLL LOCK	Toggles scroll display between scrolling a line of the display every time an arrow key is pressed, and just moving the pointer on a stationary display.

Table 2-6.   Special Key Combinations (*continued*)

Commands for adding and removing files from memory are covered in detail in Chapter 8, "Working with Files."

The keys in the center of your keyboard are in most cases identical to the key assignments on a regular typewriter. Table 2-6 lists some of the special keys and additional uses for the regular typewriter keys.

Entering Data in 1-2-3's Worksheet

**T
H
R
E
E**

Learning how to make entries on 1-2-3's worksheet is one of the most important steps in gaining full use of the package's features. Everything you do with 1-2-3 depends on the entries you make in worksheet cells. These entries will be the basis for financial models and projections. They will also be the basis for files used in the data management environment, since data records are nothing more than a special organization of data entered into worksheet cells. Furthermore, these entries will be the basis for the graphs you create, because graphs are created by referencing entries in your worksheet.

The Worksheet

The discussion in Chapter 2, "The Access System, Display, and Keyboard," of the worksheet display focused on the visible upper left corner of the worksheet. The 8 columns and 20 rows you saw on the screen are a very small part of the whole sheet. In its entirety, the Release 3 worksheet has 256 columns and 8192 rows. The entire worksheet, though not visible all at once, is organized just like the small section you examined.

Release 3 also supports the use of multiple sheets in one worksheet file, with each sheet arranged like the first sheet. The only difference between the first sheet and any others you add is the sheet level indicator at the intersection of the row and column labels. The letters assigned to sheets always start with the initial A level that is present in every worksheet file. Subsequent sheets are assigned letters that are incremented sequentially as you insert sheets. The letters B through Z are assigned first, followed by AA through AZ, BA through BZ, and so on, until the 256th level (IV) is assigned.

Additional sheets are never added to a worksheet automatically. You must use the command /Worksheet Insert Sheet to add worksheets after the A level sheet. It is unlikely that you will need to use all the levels in one worksheet file. Moreover, you may be limited to far fewer than 256 sheets by the memory in your computer.

Tip: In similar applications, use sheets consistently. If you create multiple-sheet worksheets, try to establish a pattern for your entries. Don't use sheet A for the consolidated information one time and sheet D the next time. The same advice is true for the location of macros, data critera entries, and an extract range. It will be easier to find your entries in any application if you follow guidelines that apply to all your models.

Since the worksheet is a replacement for green-bar columnar pads, it may be interesting to make a size comparison. The space for one entry on a green-bar sheet is about 1 1/8 inches by 1/4 inch. If you multiply this area by the number of cells in the 1-2-3 worksheet, you will find that the equivalent of your electronic sheet would require a piece of green-bar paper over 23 feet wide and 170 feet long! Release 3's multiple sheet capability actually provides 256 of these sheets. The electronic version is certainly more practical in the space it requires for storage, and it offers the added advantage of automatic recalculation.

1-2-3's worksheet has not always been this large. Release 1A had only 2048 rows. Release 2.01 provided 8192 rows but was limited to one sheet in each file. Even if you are using an earlier release, however, you still have a generous area for performing calculations or storing data. If you use the Translate utility to convert a Release 3 worksheet into a worksheet that is readable by an earlier release, you will be limited by the restrictions that apply to the earlier release. For example, entries placed below row 2048 will not appear in the Release 1A worksheet. If you want to translate a multiple-sheet Release 3 file into a Release 2.01 file, you will need to have several Release 2.01 worksheets to contain the Release 3 sheets.

Figure 3-1 shows the layout of the electronic worksheet. You can use the screen as a window into any part of a worksheet you wish to see. If you have multiple sheets in a file, you can use the special key combinations in Chapter 2, "The Access System, Display, and Keyboard," to move to any of these sheets. It is as if all the sheets are stacked in memory as shown in Figure 3-2.

If you have multiple files in memory, you can also use special keys to change the worksheet displayed on the screen to a sheet within one of these other files. These sheets are also stacked in memory. Unlike moving from sheet to sheet in one file, however, as you move from sheet to sheet in several files you will see the name of the file change at the bottom of the screen. Since each worksheet file begins with a level A sheet, you will find that the same level indicators may appear more than once.

You can make entries in any of the cells on any sheet, within the memory limitations of your system. Each cell can only contain one entry at a time, however. If you make a second entry in a cell that already contains information, the existing information will be replaced by the new information.

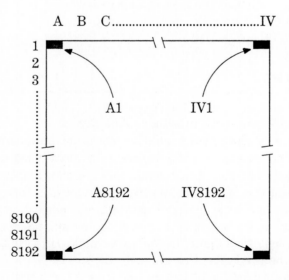

Figure 3-1.   Worksheet layout

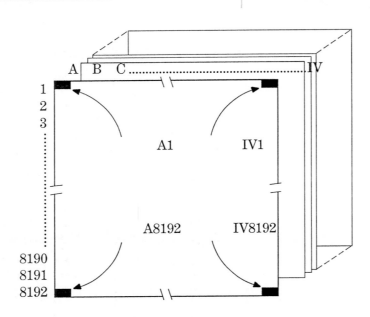

Figure 3-2.   Multiple sheets available in each file

Types of Entries

1-2-3 categorizes entries as either label entries or value entries. These two entry types serve as the building blocks for both simple and sophisticated worksheet models. *Label entries* contain at least one text character. Examples include Accounting, Sales, John Smith, 111 Simmons Lane, and 456T78. Even the last example, which is composed mostly of numbers, has one letter character and therefore is categorized as a label entry. Label entries cannot be used in arithmetic operations. *Value entries,* on the other hand, are either numbers or formulas. Most value entries can be used in arithmetic operations.

1-2-3 determines the type of entry for a particular cell by reading the first character you type in the cell. Once 1-2-3 determines the entry

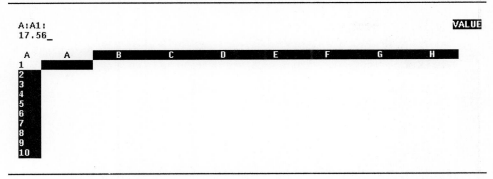

Figure 3-3.   Edit line entry

type, the only way you can change its mind is by either pressing ESC and
starting a new entry in the cell, or editing the cell to remove or add a
label indicator. A *label indicator* is a single character that appears at
the front of each label entry and tells 1-2-3 how to display the entry in
the cell. You can enter a label indicator or have 1-2-3 generate one for
you.

Tip: Learn to check the mode indicator as you perform data entry.
You will save yourself considerable time and frustration as you start
using 1-2-3 if you watch the mode indicator. One quick look will tell you
whether 1-2-3 is treating your entry as a number or a label, and allow
you to make a quick correction if you need to before completing the
entry.

   As you make an entry into a cell, 1-2-3 displays the entry on the
second line of the control panel at the top of your screen. This line is
referred to as the Edit line. A sample entry in the Edit line appears in
Figure 3-3. In Release 3, as soon as your entry fills the first Edit line,
the control panel expands to give you six and one-half lines for the Edit
area. This allows you to make an entry containing as many as 512
characters and to view and edit your complete entry.
   Once you finish your entry and review its contents in the Edit lines,
you can *finalize* it by pressing ENTER or by moving to a new cell with one
of the cell pointer movement keys. This causes the entry to appear in
the worksheet cell, as shown in Figure 3-4.

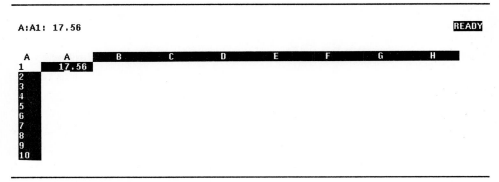

Figure 3-4.   Finalized cell entry

Tip: Use the cell pointer movement keys to finalize your entry. You can save a keystroke on most entries if you finalize by moving the cell pointer rather than pressing ENTER and then moving to a new cell.

When the entry is a formula, the results of the formula's calculation will appear on the worksheet. For example, if cell A1 contains 10 and A2 contains 5, entering the formula +A1/A2 in cell A3 will cause a 2 to appear in A3 on the worksheet. Otherwise, the entry will appear as typed, except that the current format option will be applied. For example, if you enter .4 and the format is Percent, your entry will display as 40% in the cell. In the top line of the control panel, however, the entry will appear exactly as you typed it.

Tip: Use the special keys introduced in Chapter 2, "The Access System, Display, and Keyboard," to position the cell pointer for an entry. Although the arrow keys will move you to any location on the worksheet, there are some shortcuts. You can press the F5 (GOTO) key, type an address like **D3** or **C:F2**, and 1-2-3 will immediately position the cell pointer in the new address. The END-HOME key sequence is another useful combination; it takes you just beyond the last entry on the current worksheet.

Label Entries

You will use label entries whenever you want to enter text or character data into a worksheet cell. Labels can contain descriptive information, as well as character data. There are no restrictions on the characters that can be entered within a label.

1-2-3 supports the full set of LMBCS characters, including numbers and symbols. LMBCS codes are the full set of characters that can be represented by Release 3; they provide access to international symbols and many special characters not directly accessible from the keyboard. They provide access to two different groups of codes as described in Appendix D, "LMBCS Codes."

The code group being accessed and the character desired can be entered with the @CHAR function described in Chapter 7, "1-2-3's Built-in Functions," or through the Compose key sequence. To use Compose, press ALT-F1 twice, type either a **0** or **1** for the code group, and then the key combination representing the desired character. For example, to generate an uppercase *E* with a circumflex, you could use the @CHAR function with the entry 210, as in @**CHAR(210)**; press ALT-F1 twice, type a **0** followed by **210**; or press SHIFT-F1 once and type an **E** and a **caret** (^). In either case, the special E circumflex character would display (Ê).

Some of the key rules concerning label entries are summarized in the box called "Rules for Labels." Labels can be up to 512 characters in length. 1-2-3 will display as much of the label as possible in the cell you use for the entry. If the label is longer than your cell width and the cells to the right are empty, 1-2-3 will borrow space from them to permit the complete display of the label. If the adjacent cell is not empty, 1-2-3 will truncate the display at the number of characters that will fit. The extra characters are not lost; they are stored internally and will be displayed if the cell is widened or the contents of cells to the right are erased.

As descriptive information, a label might be a report heading containing the company name placed in a cell near the top of the worksheet. Labels can also be column headings indicating the months of the year, row headings indicating account names, or descriptors placed anywhere on the worksheet.

1
2
3

Rules for Labels

Labels cannot be longer than 512 characters.

An entry is automatically recognized as a label if the first character is an alphabetic character or any character other than 0 through 9, or any of the following:

. + − $ or (

Any entry that contains alphabet letters or editing characters is considered a label, even if it also contains numbers. When a label begins with a numeric digit or symbol, a label indicator must be typed before the label.

Labels longer than the cell width will borrow display space from the cells to the right if those cells are empty.

Label entries can also record text data anywhere on the worksheet. Part numbers, employee names, sales territories, and warehouse locations are all examples of data containing text characters. A worksheet to project salaries might contain employee names as label entries. Worksheets that deal with suppliers, inventory items, product sales projections, and client accounts are all likely to have some label entries.

When you type a letter as the first entry in a cell, 1-2-3 will generate a default label indicator that establishes the entry as a label and controls the display of the entry within the cell. If a label begins with a number, you must enter a label indicator before you type that first number in the label entry, since 1-2-3 determines the type of an entry by the first character entered in a cell. However it is generated, the label indicator will appear in the top line of the control panel but will not show in the worksheet cell. Only the effects of the indicator appear on the worksheet.

Tip: Spaces and special characters that are not numeric characters are treated as labels. If you start an entry with a space or a nonnumeric character, you can save a keystroke by not entering the label indicator. 1-2-3 will automatically generate it for you.

Label Indicators

1-2-3 provides a default label indicator of ', which will left justify a label. This default can be changed with a menu command (see Chapter 6) or by typing a different indicator at the beginning of the label entry. The label indicators and their effects are as follows:

'	Left justified — the default setting
"	Right justified
^	Center justified
\	Repeat the character that follows until the cell is filled
¦	Sends the code which follows to the printer when the worksheet is printed, although the label does not print. Can also be used to prevent data in a worksheet row from printing. If a printer code is not encountered at the beginning of the entry, there is no effect on printing the worksheet.

You can use label indicators to control placement of an entry in a cell. 1-2-3 provides three placement label indicators for this purpose, as the box called "Label Indicators" shows. The single quotation mark is the default label indicator, that is, the one 1-2-3 generates for you when you enter character data. It causes an entry to be left justified within the cell. You must type the single quotation mark yourself if your entry begins with a number, or begins with a number but contains text — for example, '134 Tenth Street or '213-78-6751. (The hyphens in this latter entry count as text.)

If you do not enter the label indicator, 1-2-3 will not let you finalize the first example (the address) in a cell. The second example (the social security number) can be finalized without a label indicator, but it will not appear as a social security number. 1-2-3 will interpret the hyphens as minus signs and perform two subtractions, resulting in an entry of −6616. If you edit the cell containing this erroneous entry by pressing

F2 (EDIT) and moving to the front of the entry, you can type a label indicator, instructing 1-2-3 to treat the minus signs as hyphens and display the entry as a social security number.

The other two label indicators that can be used for entry placement are the double quotation mark (") and the caret (^). The double quotation mark causes label entries to be right justified, while the caret causes entries to be centered within the cell.

Let's look at a few examples of label entries, to clarify the differences shown in the entries in Figure 3-5.

1. The word **Sales** was entered in B1. As soon as the first character was entered, 1-2-3 changed the READY mode indicator to LABEL. When the entry was completed, the top line of the control panel showed 'Sales, since 1-2-3 generated a single quotation mark. The entry was left justified in the cell and appeared without the quotation mark.

2. ^**Sales** was typed in B2. The caret (^) caused the entry to be centered in the cell.

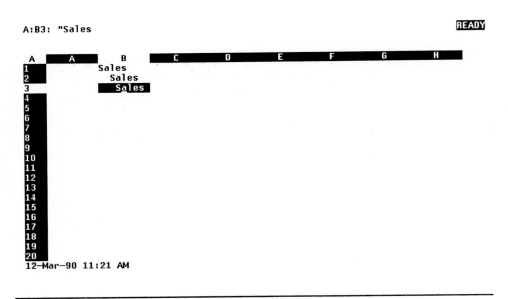

Figure 3-5.   Different orientation possible for label entries

3. "**Sales** was typed in B3. This caused the entry to be right justified.

In Chapter 5, "Basic Worksheet Commands," you will learn how to alter the default label indicator with /Worksheet Global Label. For now, though, if you want something other than left justification, enter the appropriate label indicator before you start typing your entry.

Two additional label indicators perform special functions. The backslash (\) causes the characters that follow it to be repeated until the entire cell is filled with this pattern. For example, entering \— will fill the cell with dashes. Figure 3-6 shows how * has been used to enter asterisks in all the cells in one row of the worksheet to serve as a dividing line between the worksheet assumptions and the calculation section. (You can use any character to create dividing lines.) You can also use the \ to make multiple characters repeat: \+ — would result in a pattern of + and — symbols repeated for the width of the cell.

Labels provide readability to a worksheet and allow you to enter text data. Since a worksheet is primarily involved in projections and calculations, however, you clearly also need a way to deal with numeric entries.

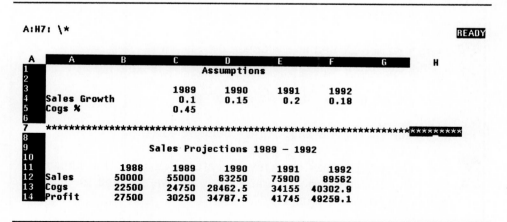

Figure 3-6.   Repeating label entry

Value Entries

Value entries are treated as numeric entries by 1-2-3. They must follow much more rigid rules than label entries. There are two basic types of value entries: *numbers* and *formulas*. Like labels, numbers are constants; they do not change as the result of arithmetic operations. Formulas are not constants, since the results they produce depend on the current values for the variables they reference. We will examine each category separately, because 1-2-3 handles each differently.

Numbers

The rules for entry of numeric constants are summarized in the box called "Rules for Numbers." Numeric entries do not have a special beginning indicator like labels, but they can contain only certain characters.

Rules for Numbers

Numbers cannot exceed 512 characters; however, the limitation for decimal accuracy and significant digits is 18.

If the first key you press is a numeric digit or one of these symbols,

$$+ \; - \; . \; (\; \$$$

the entry will be treated as a number.

Only the following symbols can appear in a number entry:

$$0 \; 1 \; 2 \; 3 \; 4 \; 5 \; 6 \; 7 \; 8 \; 9 \; . \; + \; - \; \$ \; (\;) \; E \; @ \; \char`\^ \; \%$$

The last four of these cannot begin a numeric entry.

Only one decimal can be used.

Spaces and commas can only be entered as part of a numeric entry with automatic formats, and when you have changed the international punctuation settings.

- Any of the numeric digits from 0 through 9 is acceptable.

- Other allowable characters at the beginning of a number are as follows: . + − $ (

- Other characters from the Lotus International Multi-Byte Character Set that represent foreign monetary units such as yen, pounds, and guilders can be substituted for the $. The LMBCS codes for these other currency symbols are found in Appendix D. To use another currency symbol at the beginning of a number you must first change the default currency symbol with the /Worksheet Global Default Other International Currency command.

- A % can be used to indicate a percentage but cannot begin a numeric entry. It must be placed at the end of the entry.

- Spaces, commas, and other characters cannot be added to a numeric entry, except the letter *E* when it is used to denote a Scientific notation entry. Or, when you are using the Automatic format (described in Chapter 4, "Changing the Appearance of the Worksheet Display"), any valid format for the supported value entries is acceptable.

- Alphabetic characters with similar appearance cannot be substituted for numeric digits as they can on a typewriter. Using the lowercase *L* for a numeric 1, or a lowercase *O* for a numeric 0 (zero) will cause an invalid entry for a value.

- For date and time entries, the Automatic format allows additional characters in numeric entries. Any characters in one of 1-2-3's valid date or time entries will be accepted and stored as a date or time number. These are discussed in further detail in Chapter 4.

Size   Numbers can be as large as $10^{\wedge}99$ or as small as $10^{\wedge}-99$, where the caret symbol ($\wedge$) represents exponentiation (that is, 10 raised to the 99th power or 10 raised to the −99th power). Up to 512 characters can be used to represent the numbers, although you must still adhere to the numeric limits of the package.

If you wish, you can use the Scientific notation to enter large numbers. Scientific notation is a method of entering a number along with the power of ten that it will be multiplied by. In this format, the letter *E* (either *E* or *e* may be used) separates the number from the positive or negative power of 10 that will be used. This kind of notation offers the advantage of representing very large or very small numbers in a minimum of space. The following examples should help clarify Scientific notation:

$9.76E+4 = 97,600$
$6.543e+5 = 654,300$
$6.71E-02 = .0671$
$3.86e-5 = .0000386$

The number that follows E must be between -99 and 99 to conform with the entry size that 1-2-3 allows. Although you cannot exceed this limitation for entries, 1-2-3 can store calculated numbers that are much larger and smaller. The storage limitations are numbers between 10^-308 and 10^308 when the number is the result of calculations.

Tip: Entries you think of as numbers may be labels to 1-2-3. It is common to refer to social security numbers, phone numbers, part numbers, and purchase order numbers. Although these entries are called numbers, they may not be considered number values to 1-2-3 due to the presence of alphabetic characters or special symbols. They must be entered as labels in 1-2-3.

Entry   In one sense, entering numbers is easier than entering labels, since all you do is make your entry using the allowable characters and then press either ENTER or an arrow key. You do not need a special character at the beginning of a numeric entry.

As soon as you type any of the allowable characters, the mode indicator will change from READY to VALUE. Once 1-2-3 has determined that you are entering a value, you must continue entering only allowable characters. If you attempt to finalize an entry containing unallowed characters, 1-2-3 will place you in EDIT mode so that you can make necessary corrections. If you realize your error before trying to finalize the original entry, you can use BACKSPACE to remove the incorrect characters, or press ESC to eliminate the entire entry. Later you will learn other error correction methods to save time.

Looking at a few numeric entries may clarify the entry process and the way 1-2-3 displays such entries in a cell, as shown in Figure 3-7.

Figure 3-7.   Numeric entries

1. With the cell pointer on C1, .0925 was entered, and the cell pointer was moved to C2 to finalize the entry.

2. **51279** was entered in C2.

3. **4.35E + 05** was entered in C3.

Notice that 1-2-3 converted the third entry to 435000, since the number was not too large for decimal display. The first two entries were displayed just as entered, except that a zero was added in front of the decimal in C1. There is no consistency in the number of decimal places displayed because the General format is in effect. General format is the default format for all new worksheets. In Chapter 4, "Changing the Appearance of the Worksheet Display," you will learn how to change the format so that entries are displayed as currency, percentages, or with a consistent number of decimal places. In the next section of this chapter you will get a closer look at the display with the General format in effect.

Display   The numbers you enter are shown both in the control panel and in the worksheet. They are also stored internally. The form of the numbers may be slightly different in each case. Internally 1-2-3 can store up to 18 significant digits for an entry. If you enter a number with more than 18 significant digits, the display of the number will be rounded to fit within the 18-digit display limitation. The display on the worksheet will depend on the format for the cell and the length of the number in relation to the cell width.

When 1-2-3 displays a number in a cell, it will display all the digits up to one less than the cell width. Numeric entries which are longer than this limit are not handled by borrowing space from cells to the right, as is done with labels. The entries are either shown in Scientific notation, a rounded form, or as asterisks representing an overflow situation. The cell format and the composition of the number determines the display.

If the General format is in effect, 1-2-3 will display the number as you have entered it if at all possible. If the integer portion of the number is too large, 1-2-3 converts the display to Scientific notation if the General format is in effect. If the integer portion of the number fits but some or all of the decimal digits do not, the cell value will be rounded to fit within the display. In both cases when the General format is not in effect, 1-2-3 displays the number as a series of asterisks (*********). The default cell width is nine positions, so you can see that long numbers will not fit unless you expand the width of the column. You will learn how to do that in Chapter 4, "Changing the Appearance of the Worksheet Display."

The following example shows how 1-2-3 reacts to long numeric entries, as shown in Figure 3-8.

1. .000000000134 was entered in cell C4. The worksheet display changed this to Scientific notation and displayed it as "1.3E − 10."

2. 9578000000 was entered in C5. 1-2-3 performed another conversion and shows the entry as "9.6E + 09" in the cell. The entry appears in its original form in the control panel.

You have no control over format in the control panel or the internal storage of a number. In both cases 1-2-3 will retain as much accuracy as possible (18 decimal digits maximum for the control panel and internal

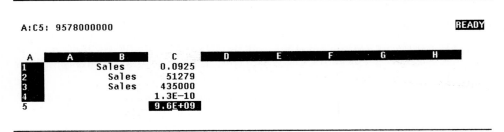

Figure 3-8.   Long numeric entries

storage). You can control the accuracy of the number that appears on the worksheet by selecting a format. You will learn how to do this in Chapter 4, "Changing the Appearance of the Worksheet Display." In Chapter 4 you will also learn how to format date and time numbers.

Formulas

Formulas are the second type of value entry. Unlike number and label entries, they produce variable results depending on the numbers they reference. This ability makes formulas the backbone of worksheet features. They allow you to make what-if projections and to look at the impact of changing variable values. To produce an updated result with a formula, you do not need to change the formula. Simply change one of the values the formula references, and the entire formula can be recalculated for you. Formulas follow the same basic rules as numbers in terms of allowable characters. In addition, formulas also support the use of cell references, range names assigned to a group of cells, and operators that define specific operations to 1-2-3.

Early releases of 1-2-3 provided only two types of formulas, arithmetic formulas and logical formulas. Release 2 added string formulas. These formulas are summarized in the box called "Formula Types."

A few rules pertain to all formulas:

- Formulas cannot contain spaces, except for the spaces in range names or string variables.

- The first character of a formula must be one of the following:

  $+ - (@ \# \$. 0 1 2 3 4 5 6 7 8 9$

- Formulas contain special operators to define the operation you wish performed. Operators are assigned priorities in 1-2-3, as shown in the box called "Operation Priorities."

- Formulas can also contain numeric constants or string constants (such as 77 or "sales total"), cell references (such as F4 or Z3), special built-in functions (such as @MIN), or range names (such as TOTAL).

1
2
3

Formula Types

1-2-3 provides three types of formulas for your use: arithmetic formulas, logical formulas, and string formulas.

Arithmetic formulas involve constants, cell references, and the arithmetic operators (+ - * / ^). Arithmetic formulas calculate the formula entered and return its result. Examples are A2*A3, or Sales-Cogs (where Sales and Cogs are names of cells that contain numerical data).

Logical formulas involve cell references, constants, and comparison operators (<> = <= >= < >). These formulas evaluate the condition listed to determine whether it is true or false. If the condition is false, the formula returns 0; if true, a 1 is returned. An example of a logical formula is +C2<=500.

String formulas permit the joining of two or more character strings. The concatenation character (&) can be used to join string variables or constants—for example, +"Sales for the "&"Midwest "&"Region".

Functions provide predefined formulas for a variety of calculations, including mathematical formulas, financial calculations, logical evaluations, statistical computations, and string manipulation. Functions have a unique appearance: they begin with the @ symbol and contain a list of specific values for arguments within parentheses.

Arithmetic Formulas   Arithmetic formulas calculate numeric values. These formulas are built with *arithmetic operators* and references to values in other cells in the current worksheet file, or to values in other worksheets. The value references are to either the cell address in the current sheet (such as A1 or Z10), cells in other sheets within the current file (such as B:A1 or D:F10), cells in other files on disk, or a name that has been assigned to a cell or cells (such as Cash or Interest). For now, you will concentrate on references to cells in the current file, using both the current worksheet and other sheet references. Linkages to external files are covered in Chapter 8, "Working with Files ." You will learn how to assign range names in Chapter 5, "Basic Worksheet Commands."

Operation Priorities

1-2-3 has a variety of operators for arithmetic, logical, and string formulas. Often more than one operator is used in a formula. In this situation it is important to know which operation 1-2-3 will evaluate first. This table provides the priority order for each operation within 1-2-3, with the highest number being the highest priority. If several operators in a formula have the same priority, they will be evaluated from left to right.

Priority	Operator	Operation Performed
8	(	Parenthesis for grouping
7	^	Exponentiation
6	+ −	Positive and negative indicators
5	/ *	Division and multiplication
4	+ −	Addition and subtraction
3	= <> < >	Logical operators
	< = > =	
2	#NOT#	Complex not indicator
1	#AND# #OR# &	Complex and, complex or, and string operator

The *arithmetic operators* used in 1-2-3 are + for addition, − for subtraction, / for division, * for multiplication, and ^ for exponentiation. An instruction to multiply 3 times 4 would be written as 3*4. These operators are listed in the "Operation Priorities" box.

Tip: Ignoring 1-2-3's operator priorities will result in incorrect formula results. You must use parentheses to group references if you do not want to use the established priorities. A difference in the order of operations can cause a dramatic difference in results.

There are some things to keep in mind when entering cell references. Cell references without sheet letters preceding them are assumed to reference cells on the sheet where the formula is being entered. Since all worksheet files start with only one sheet, and additional sheets must be added with the /Worksheet Insert Sheet command, you cannot reference cells on sheets that you have not added to the current file. For example, the entry **+B:C1+D:F10** cannot be finalized unless the current file has sheets B and D.

In examining the sample formulas, you may have wondered why a plus sign was placed at the beginning of the formula. If you want to multiply the current contents of C1 by the contents of C2, you might think that entering C1*C2 would seem logical. This will not work, however. The problem here is the initial C. As soon as 1-2-3 realizes a C has been entered, it flags the cell as a label entry. It will show the entry as a label on the worksheet, rather than giving the result of the formula calculation.

You need a formula indicator, and the + is the logical choice, since it requires only one additional keystroke and does not alter the formula. (Actually any numeric character that does not affect the formula result is acceptable.) Therefore, place a + at the front of all formulas that begin with a cell address. The formula just discussed can be entered as **+C1*C2**, for example. This formula is entered in cell D1 on the worksheet shown in Figure 3-9. The result of the formula appears on the worksheet, while the formula itself is displayed in the top line of the control panel. Formula results will be displayed on the worksheet automatically unless you change the worksheet format to Text.

Entering a formula similar to the one used in the previous example, but with references to cells on different sheets, requires a minor modification. The sheet letter precedes both of the cell addresses. In Figure

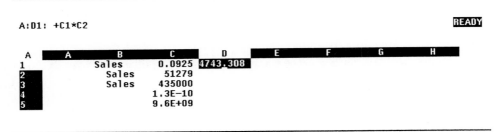

Figure 3-9. Formula in D1

3-10, to compute the total sales of widgets, you need the number of units stored in cell B2 on sheet B, and the cost of a widget stored in B2 on sheet C. So, you would enter the formula in A:B2 as **+B:B2*C:B2**. You could enter similar formulas for the stoves and pipes if the detail data for these were with the widget data on the other sheets.

The results of formulas are not affected by the sheet from which the values are obtained. 1-2-3 always uses its operations priority sequence to determine the order in which operations are completed. Parentheses in arithmetic expressions are the only option for changing the order of operations. For example, 3+4*5 equals 23, but (3+4)*5 equals 35. Otherwise operators in formulas will be evaluated according to the priority list, proceeding from left to right within the expression if there is more than one operator at the same level. In the first expression, multiplication has a higher priority than addition, so it will be carried out first. This produces the expression 3+20, which is equal to 23. In the second expression, the parentheses take priority. Therefore, 3 will be added to 4 first, making the expression 7*5, or 35.

1-2-3 allows many sets of parentheses in one expression, so you can use them liberally to override the natural priority order. With nested parentheses, the priority sequence will apply within each set of parentheses. Here is an example of priority order within nested parentheses:

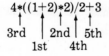

You have learned how to build a formula by typing cell addresses and arithmetic operators. This method will work well if you are

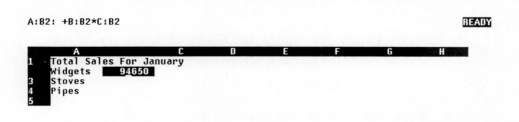

Figure 3-10.   Formula with a reference to other sheets

good at remembering the cell addresses you want to use and do not make mistakes in typing. However, a second method of formula construction can alleviate both these potential problems. This new method lets you point to the cell references you wish to include in the formula and then type only the arithmetic operators. After you type an operator, simply move your cell pointer to the cell whose value you wish included in the formula. Watch the mode indicator change from VALUE to POINT as you move your cell pointer. To finalize the selection of the cell reference, either type the next operator or, if you have reached the end of the formula, press ENTER. If you type another operator, the cell pointer returns to the formula's entry cell, and 1-2-3 then waits for you to move your cell pointer to a new location.

Tip: Blank cells have a zero value. If you reference a blank cell in a formula, the result is the same as referencing a cell that contains a zero.

Thus +A1*A2 equals zero if either A1 or A2 contain a zero.
Here is a sample worksheet that was developed using this method:

To produce this example, .0925 was entered in C1, and **51279** was entered in C2. The cell pointer was then moved to D1, and a + was typed. Then the cell pointer was moved to C1, putting 1-2-3 in POINT mode. An asterisk for multiplication was then typed, causing the cell pointer to return to D1. With 1-2-3 still in POINT mode, the LEFT ARROW and DOWN ARROW keys were used to move to C2. Finally, pressing ENTER caused the formula to appear in cell D1, as shown in the example.

You can use the pointing method when there are multiple sheets in a file and you want to access cell values from more than one sheet. Use the special key combinations introduced in Chapter 2, "The Access System, Display, and Keyboard," to move to another sheet and then move around within the sheet to select the correct cell. When you complete the current selection, 1-2-3 returns the cell pointer to the sheet and cell where the formula is being recorded.

This may seem like a lot of work compared to typing in cell references. However, once your worksheet becomes large or you are using a number of sheets, the pointing method can save considerable time. It speeds up the testing and verification process for your model, because it forces you to visually verify cell references and therefore eliminates many formula errors that could result from incorrect cell or sheet references. When you use the pointing method, 1-2-3 picks up the worksheet letter even if the cell referenced is the same sheet as the formula.

Tip: Make the pointing method mandatory for all your formulas that reference other sheets. Otherwise, you are using guesswork. It is too easy to type in an incorrect reference. The effects of errors in worksheet entries can be devastating if they are not recognized until after decisions have been made.

Logical Formulas   Logical formulas use the *logical operators* to compare two or more values. Such formulas can be used to evaluate a series of complex decisions or to influence results in other areas of the worksheet. As noted in the "Operation Priorities" box, the *logical operators* are = for equal, < > for not equal, < for less than, > for greater than, < = for less than or equal to, and > = for greater than or equal to. The logical operators all have the same priority and will be evaluated from left to right in an expression. All the logical operators are lower in priority than the arithmetic operators.

Logical formulas do not calculate numeric results like arithmetic formulas. They produce a result of either zero or one, depending on whether the condition that was evaluated is true or false. If it is a true condition, 1 will be returned; if the condition is false, 0 will be returned. For example, if C1 contains .0925, the logical expression + C1 > = 500 will return 0, since the condition is false.

1-2-3 also has a few *compound operators*. These operators are used either to negate a logical expression or to join two logical expressions. The negation operator #NOT# has priority over the other two compound operators, #AND# and #OR#. These latter operators can join two expressions, as in C1>=500#AND#C2=50. In this example the expression will return a 1 for true only if both conditions are true.

The function of #NOT# is to negate an expression. For instance, the formula #NOT#(A1=2#AND#D2=1) will return a 1 for true only if the contents of cell A1 are not equal to 2, and those of cell D1 are not equal to 1. (If #OR# replaced #AND# in this formula, the formula would be true if either cell A1 were not equal to 2, or cell D2 were not equal to 1.) For practical purposes, you are more likely to use the not equal logical operator, <>, than the more cumbersome #NOT# operator. The formula A1<>2#AND#D2<>1 is easier to read than is #NOT(A1=2#AND#D2=1), and its meaning is identical.

One application of logical operators in a worksheet might be the calculation of a commission bonus. Figure 3-11 shows a calculation on a worksheet to determine the quarterly commission check for salesperson John Smith. The calculation has two components: the regular commission, and a bonus for meeting sales quotas.

The regular commission is 10% of total sales. The bonus is calculated by product. Each salesperson has a $50,000 quota for each of three products. A bonus of $1,000 is given for each product for which the sales quota is met. A salesperson could thus gain $3,000 by meeting the quota for all three products.

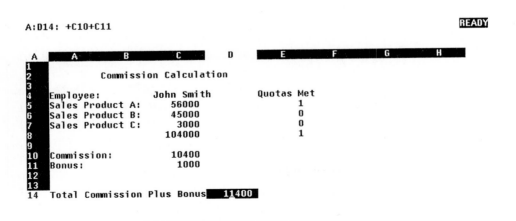

Figure 3-11.   Total pay calculation

Let's look at the steps taken to build the model shown in the figure. First a number of labels are entered in cells B2 through A7. Next, **John Smith** is entered in C4; and **56000**, **45000**, and **3000** are entered in C5 through C7. These numbers are totaled in C8 by entering the formula **+C5+C6+C7** in that cell. The label **Quotas Met** is entered in E4.

The logical formula **+C5>50000** is now entered in E5. When ENTER is pressed, if sales of product A are greater than 50,000, a 1 will be returned, but if they are equal to or less than this number, a 0 will be returned. Similarly, **+C6>50000** is entered in E6, and **+C7>50000** is entered in E7. Pressing ENTER produces the result of the logical formula in both cases. The total formula, **+E5+E6+E7**, is placed in E8 to determine the number of bonus categories.

Additional labels **Commission:** and **Bonus:** are entered in A10 and A11. **+C8*.1** is then entered in C10, and **+E8*1000** is entered in C11. A label for total commission is placed in A14, and the final formula is entered in D14 as **+C10+C11**.

String Formulas   String or text formulas allow you to join or concatenate two or more groups of characters. This allows you to access and manipulate character data to build headings, correct errors, and convert text formats to a satisfactory format for reporting. There is only one operator for string formulas, the ampersand (&). If you want to join the string John with the string Smith, you could enter the string formula **"John"&"Smith"** to produce JohnSmith, or **"John"&" "&"Smith"** to produce John Smith.

String formulas let you alter data previously entered in a worksheet, so you can use them to correct errors or change formats. For example, if names have been entered in a worksheet with the last name first, and you wish to reverse the sequence, you can combine string functions such as @RIGHT, @LEFT, and @MID to produce that result. (String functions are explained in Chapter 7, "1-2-3's Built-in Functions.") String formulas also offer a creative approach to producing new reports by providing an opportunity to join data from two or more locations on your worksheet. For instance, string formulas can be used in combination with cell references to produce flexible report headings.

Figure 3-12 shows a report heading created by combining string constants and string variables. There are three string constants in this formula: "Monthly Statistics for the ", " ", and "Warehouse". The constants were enclosed in quotation marks and entered into the formula.

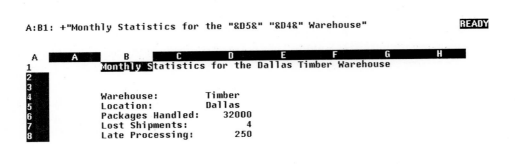

Figure 3-12.   A string formula

The variables are references to cell addresses that contain text data. The two variables here are D5 and D4, which contain Dallas and Timber, respectively.

Tip: String references to blank cells result in ERR. Since blank cells are equivalent to zero, referencing a blank cell in a string formula returns ERR, indicating an error in the formula. If you make an entry in the cell, ERR will disappear. You can enter a label indicator if you want the cell to represent an empty string, often known as the null string. You can also use the @S function described in Chapter 7.

The & operator, along with #AND# and #OR#, have the lowest priority of all the operators. This does not diminish the usefulness of these operators; it just means they are the last operators to be evaluated in an expression.

Functions   1-2-3's built-in *functions* are a special category of formulas. They can be used alone or as part of a formula you create. The entire algorithm or formula for the calculations represented in a function have been worked out, tested, and incorporated into the package features. 1-2-3 will supply all the operators for a function; all you need to supply are the values that the operators work with. There are functions to perform arithmetic operations, string manipulation, logical evaluation, statistical calculations, and date and time arithmetic. They all have the same general format and must abide by the same rules. Regardless of the function type, all are regarded as value entries because they are formulas.

Functions all start with an @ sign. This is followed by a function keyword, which is a character sequence representing the calculation being performed. The keyword is followed by arguments enclosed in parentheses. The arguments define the function's specific use in a given situation. A few of 1-2-3's functions are

@MAX	Calculates the maximum value
@SUM	Calculates a sum or total
@ROUND	Rounds a number to a certain number of decimal places
@NPV	Calculates the net present value

Release 3 of 1-2-3 has over 100 of these built-in functions, spanning calculations in financial, mathematical, logical, statistical, string, and other applications. Functions will be covered thoroughly in Chapter 7, "1-2-3's Built-in Functions."

Figure 3-13 shows an example of the use of the @SUM function to produce a total. After entering appropriate numbers and labels, the sum formula was entered in E6 by typing **@SUM(**. The cell pointer was then moved to C6 (the beginning of the range to be summed), and this reference was locked in place as the beginning of the range by typing a period. The cell pointer was next moved to the value in D6 and another

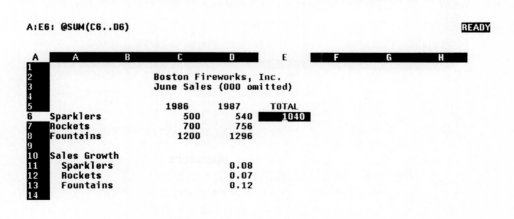

Figure 3-13.   Using @SUM

period was typed. As a last step, the closing parenthesis) was entered, and ENTER was pressed to produce the sum shown in the figure. The remaining two @SUM formulas could be added in the same way.

The @SUM function can also be used across sheets in Release 3. Figure 3-14 shows the data for three of a company's subsidiary operations in sheets B through D. To produce a consolidated travel expenses total in sheet A, the following formula can be entered in sheet A:

@SUM(B:B4..D:M4)

The formula in sheet A can be entered by either typing or pointing. To use the pointing method, place the cell pointer in A:B3 and type @SUM(. Press CTRL-PGUP to move to B4 in sheet B, and type a period to fix the beginning of the range. Next, use END-RIGHT ARROW to move the cell pointer to M4 in sheet B; this key combination will move the cell pointer to the last nonblank cell in the direction specified. The last step is to use CTRL-PGUP twice and move to cell M4 in sheet D. Type the closing parenthesis) and press ENTER. The @SUM formula procedure can be duplicated for other expenses as shown in Figure 3-15.

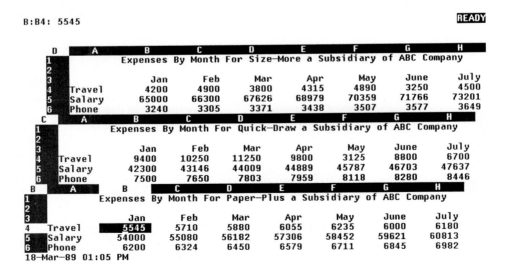

Figure 3-14.   Subsidiary data on three sheets in one file

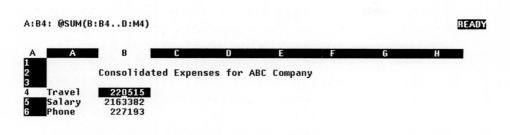

A:B4: @SUM(B:B4..D:M4)   READY

```
A      A          B         C       D       E       F       G       H
1
2                 Consolidated Expenses for ABC Company
3
4    Travel        220515
5    Salary       2163382
6    Phone         227193
```

Figure 3-15.   @SUM reference to all the data for travel expenses

How 1-2-3 Treats Formulas   You need to know some facts about formulas beyond the procedure for their entry. 1-2-3 offers a number of recalculation options that affect the timeliness of recalculation and the order of formula evaluation. You will probably begin your use of the 1-2-3 package with the default settings, but you should be aware that other alternatives can enhance your use of the package when you begin to build models with greater sophistication.

With the default settings in Release 3, minimal intelligent background recalculation is used. This string of adjectives means a much more efficient method of dealing with recalculation than past releases offered. 1-2-3 now has the intelligence to determine which cells require recalculation, and it recalculates only this minimum number of cells rather than the entire worksheet every time you change a variable on a sheet. Even this more efficient recalculation is accomplished in the background, thereby allowing you to continue with additional worksheet entries. Instead of the WAIT mode indicator that you saw during recalculation for past releases, you will see the CALC indicator at the bottom of the screen until the background recalculation is completed. Unless your worksheet is very large, you will hardly notice the amount of time required to perform these calculations. 1-2-3 is one of the fastest spreadsheet packages marketed.

Release 3 offers further processing efficiency for users who have 80287 or 80387 math coprocessor chips installed in their systems, because it can automatically recognize and use these chips. The math coprocessor provides noticeable speed improvements for iterative calculations, including the /Data Table features explained in Chapter 10,

"Using Data Management Features in the Worksheet Environment," and reduces the time involved for recalculation when a worksheet contains numerous trigonometric or mathematical functions.

In addition to fast recalculation, 1-2-3's speed in format changes, cell pointer movement, window switching, and copying functions sets standards for the other spreadsheet packages. This is not to say that you will never become impatient with the package, since most users want no delay at all. At these times you can take comfort in knowing that 1-2-3 is using the features of your computer to the fullest. Furthermore, as you will learn in Chapter 5, "Basic Worksheet Commands," there is a method to temporarily turn off recalculation when you have data entry tasks to perform.

Early spreadsheet packages had a fixed recalculation order. You had a choice of calculating by row or column. If you chose row, every formula in row 1 would be calculated, then every formula in row 2, and so on down the worksheet. Similarly, if you chose column sequence, column 1 was calculated, then column 2, and so on. With fixed recalculation order, great care had to be taken in worksheet design. A formula in column 1 could not refer to a calculated value in column 3 without creating a backward reference (reference to a value that had not yet been calculated). Undetected backward references could result in projection printouts that were not in sync.

Fortunately, this problem can be resolved with 1-2-3's default setting of natural recalculation order. In this setting, 1-2-3 bears the burden of determining the appropriate order for evaluating formulas. Backward references do not occur.

Reference Types   The cell address references in 1-2-3's formulas can be relative, absolute, or mixed. These three reference types will be covered in detail in Chapter 5, "Basic Worksheet Commands," in connection with the /Copy command. They are mentioned here as well, however, because references must be entered in one of the three formats when you type in your original formulas, even though the reference type does not have any effect on the original calculation. The "Reference Types" box provides examples of the three reference type formats.

You will notice that the mixed type addresses have several different options, since mixed is a combination of relative and absolute. Only portions of the address are absolute; the other part of the address may vary depending on the location to which it is copied. It is important to know that the way you enter cell references in your original formula can have long-term and widespread consequences if the formula is copied.

Adding Notes to Formulas

With Release 3 you can annotate formulas with text to describe your entry. This feature allows you to describe the logic behind a formula.

Reference Types

1-2-3 has three different reference types. These types do not affect the original formula, but do affect Copy operation. You can type the $'s where required or add them with the F4 (ABS) key when you are in POINT mode. The mixed reference type actually has a number of forms, depending on which parts of the address are held constant and which are allowed to change. See Chapter 5, "Basic Worksheet Commands."

Relative references: A:A2, A:B10, A:Z43
Absolute references: $A:$A$2, $A:$B$10, $A:$Z$43
Mixed references: $A:A$2, $A:$A2, A:B$10, A:$B10, A:$A$3, $A:A2

Although you can also annotate a number, 1-2-3 will convert the number to a formula if you do. You enter the number or formula followed by a semicolon (;). Then type the text for the note after the semicolon, up to the maximum length of 512 characters for a cell entry. Figure 3-16 shows a note added at the end of a formula. You can see the note in the control panel, but when the entry is finalized only the result of the formula displays in the cell.

You can print the note along with the numbers or formulas entered in the cells if you use the /Print Printer Options Other Cell-Formulas option covered in Chapter 6, "Printing."

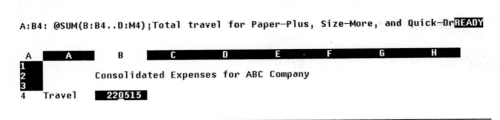

A:B4: @SUM(B:B4..D:M4);Total travel for Paper—Plus, Size—More, and Quick—Dr`READY`

Figure 3-16.   Note added to the end of a formula

Correcting Errors in Entries

1-2-3 offers a variety of error correction techniques. They are summarized in the "Error Correction Methods" box. The method you use will depend mostly on whether the entry to be corrected has been finalized (by pressing ENTER or one of the arrow keys).

When an entry is short and has been finalized, retyping is a good correction method. This will replace the incorrect contents of the cell with your new entry. If the Undo feature is active, you can press ALT-F5 (UNDO). This will eliminate the effect of your last entry. (If Undo is currently disabled, you can use /Worksheet Global Default Other Undo Enable to activate UNDO for subsequent use, although it will not help in eliminating the current entry.)

A quick-fix option for an unfinalized entry is pressing ESC, which will make your entire entry disappear. However, if you have not finalized an entry, the most common error correction technique is to use the BACK-SPACE key. It functions as a destructive backspace, deleting the previous character each time you press it. This approach is ideal when you realize that the last character you typed was incorrect.

Placing yourself in EDIT mode by pressing the F2 (EDIT) key is a good way to correct errors in entries that have been finalized. When this key is pressed, the mode indicator in the upper right corner of the screen changes to EDIT, and a small cursor will appear at the end of the entry in the Edit line of the control panel. This small cursor marks your place in the entry as you move within it and make changes. EDIT mode is also a good solution for long, incomplete entries where the error is near the beginning of the entry.

Error Correction Methods

If data is in the control panel but not yet entered in the cell:

Use the ESC key to erase the entire entry.

Use the BACKSPACE key to delete one character at a time until the erroneous character has been eliminated.

Press F2 (EDIT); then use HOME, END, RIGHT ARROW, and LEFT ARROW to move within the entry. Use BACKSPACE to delete the character in front of the cursor, and DEL to erase the character above the cursor. INS can be used to toggle between INSERT and OVER-STRIKE modes.

If data has already been entered in the cell:

Retype the entry; the new entry will replace the old.

Press F2 (EDIT), then use HOME, END, RIGHT ARROW, and LEFT ARROW to move within the entry. Use BACKSPACE to delete the character in front of the cursor, and DEL to erase the character above the cursor. INS can be used to toggle between INSERT and OVER-STRIKE modes.

If the UNDO feature is enabled, press ALT-F4 (UNDO). This will eliminate the entry only if there have been no intervening actions.

The cell pointer movement keys take on new functions in EDIT mode, as follows:

• HOME moves you to the first character in your entry — not to A1 as it does outside of EDIT.

• END moves you immediately to the last character in your entry. You do not have to press an arrow key to have END take an action, as you do in READY mode.

• The RIGHT ARROW and LEFT ARROW move you one character at a time in your entry.

- BACKSPACE still performs its destructive function.

- DEL also eliminates characters from entries. Rather than deleting the previous character, DEL removes the character above the small Edit cursor.

Tip: Using the POINT mode to modify an existing formula is more difficult than EDIT. Since EDIT changes the operation of many of the special keys, like RIGHT and LEFT ARROW, it is often easier to type a formula change rather than point to it. If you want to use POINT, use either the UP or DOWN ARROW before attempting to move to the left or right. If you want to add additional formula references to the end of a formula, just press F2 (EDIT) twice to move from READY to EDIT and then VALUE mode. Once in VALUE mode you can point in any direction.

If you have left out a character in an entry, move the cursor to the character that follows the desired location, and type the character you wish to add. It will be inserted, as long as you have not changed the default setting of Insert mode. (If you should want to change this setting, so that what you type will overlay an existing character rather than be inserted, you can press INS. To change the setting back again, just press INS again; this key functions as a toggle switch.)

Let's look at a brief example using EDIT mode to make a correction. In this situation, "sales" has been entered in B1 and finalized. To change the first letter of "sales" to a capital, follow these steps:

1. Move the cell pointer back to the cell containing the error, B1.

2. Press F2 (EDIT) to place 1-2-3 in EDIT mode.

3. Use HOME to move to the beginning of the entry, and then RIGHT ARROW to move under the *s* (the extra character at the front of the entry is the label indicator).

4. Press the DEL key to remove the *s*, leaving the cell pointer under the *a*.

5. Type S, then press ENTER to finalize your corrected entry.

You can also use the error correction techniques to change the justification of a label entry by altering the label indicator that appears at the beginning of the entry. Simply press F2 (EDIT), then HOME to move to the front of the entry. Press DEL to remove the label indicator, then type a caret (^). When ENTER is pressed, this entry will be centered. This same approach works with long label entries and complicated formulas.

Errors can be frustrating, but having several options makes the correction process as painless as possible.

Ranges

Most of the formulas discussed in this chapter have operated on individual cells—for example, C1*C2 or B:C2+D:F2, where the value in one cell was multiplied by the value in another cell, or the values in two cells were added. The one exception was the use of a *range* of cells in the @SUM function example (Figure 3-14). When using 1-2-3's built-in functions and other commands, you will often work with more than one cell at a time. This is not difficult as long as the range of cells forms a contiguous rectangle. Figure 3-17 presents examples of valid and invalid ranges. The examples on the left are invalid because the cell groups do not form one contiguous rectangle. Ranges can be large rectangles of cells, or they can be as small as a single cell.

A range specification always includes two cell addresses separated by periods. If you are typing a range address, you only need to type one period; 1-2-3 will supply the second one. If you are specifying a range address by pointing, and if the address already appears in a range format with two addresses separated by a period, you can use the arrow keys to enlarge or contract a range.

The entries B1..B10, F2..F2, and A3..C25 are all examples of range specifications. Any single cell address can be changed to a range reference within a formula by typing a period after the address as you are specifying the range. For example, an entry of B1 will appear as B1..B1 if you type a period after B1 while 1-2-3 is expecting a range specification. With @SUM, type @SUM(, then point to B1 and type a period, then type). The entry will read "@SUM(B1..B1)". To expand the range, move the cell pointer down or to the right before typing the closing parenthesis.

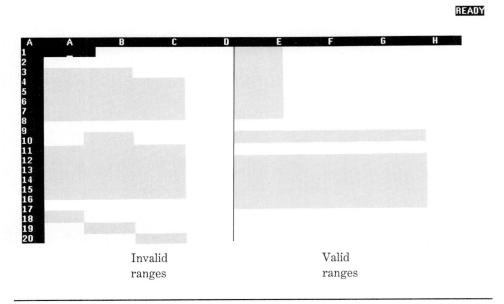

Figure 3-17.   Valid and invalid ranges

Cell ranges can be typed in just like a single address, or highlighted with your cell pointer, or specified with a range name (explained in Chapter 5, "Basic Worksheet Commands,"). To specify the cells of a range, use the cell names of two diagonally opposite corners of the rectangle, separated by one or two periods. For example, the range shown in Figure 3-18 can be specified as B4.C8, B4..C8, B8..C4, B8.C4, C8..B4, C8.B4, C4..B8, or C4.B8. However, the most common way to represent a range is by specifying the left uppermost cell first and the right lowermost cell last. Also, since 1-2-3 will supply the second period, you might as well save a keystroke and just type **B4.C8**.

Tip: Type a decimal point to change the orientation of a range. If you have a range highlighted and need to expand or shrink it from the beginning rather than the end, one option is to press ESC and start over. A better approach is to press the period. This changes the orientation; it makes a different corner of the current range active and allows you to use the arrow keys to push and pull on the range from this corner. For

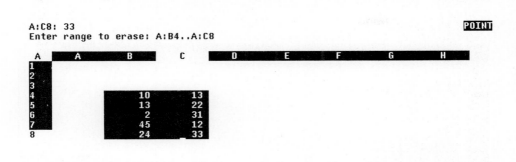

Figure 3-18.   Highlighted range

example, the range A1..D10 initially has D10 as the active corner. The first time you press the period, A10 is active, the second time A1, and the third time D1.

Ranges in Release 3 can also span sheets in a file. You saw one example of this with the @SUM function used to consolidate travel expenses. When specifying ranges across multiple sheets, you must choose diagonally opposite corners for the range on the first and last sheet in the range. Figure 3-19 shows a valid range that spans sheets in a multiple-sheet file. The size of the range in each sheet is always the same. The period option allows you to change the beginning and ending sheets for the range by switching the diagonally opposite corners that specify the range. Each time you type a period, it changes the corners used to indicate the range. The importance of this option is that it allows you to change the anchor point for the range, and expand or contract it from different sides of the range.

When specifying a range encompassing multiple cells on each sheet, you can specify all the cells in the range on the first sheet (as in B:D2..B:E4) and then use CTRL-PGUP to extend the range to other sheets like C, D, and E, with a final range specification of B:D2..E:E4. Another approach to specify this same range is to start with the cell pointer in B2 of sheet B, and extend the range to the remaining sheets so that it reads B:D2..E:D2; then extend the range on the last sheet. Both methods produce the same range.

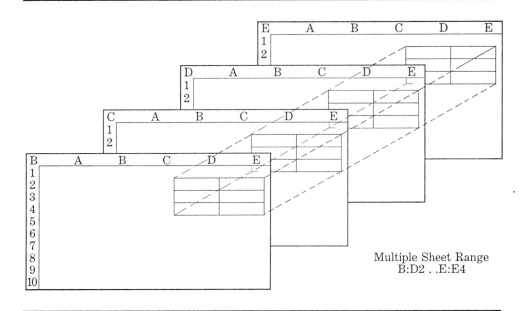

Multiple Sheet Range
B:D2 . .E:E4

Figure 3-19.   A range which spans sheets

Storage Capacity

Improved memory management techniques allow Release 3 to control data storage more effectively than earlier releases. The location of entries on the worksheet is no longer a factor in the amount of memory utilized. Be aware, however, that a worksheet with ten entries on one sheet will require less memory than a worksheet with one entry on each of ten sheets, because additional memory is required as new sheets are added to a worksheet file.

With Release 2, 1-2-3 was restricted to 640K of RAM; this could be extended with as much as 8MB of additional memory through an add-on card that supported the Lotus Intel Microsoft Expanded Memory Specification (LIM-EMS) for expanded memory. The amount of data that could be entered in a worksheet or data file with expanded memory depended on a number of factors, including whether the entries were constants or formulas, whether numbers were decimal numbers or integers, and the range options used (formatting, justification, and so on).

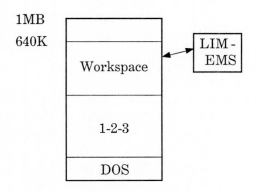

Figure 3-20.   Memory utilization with Release 2.01

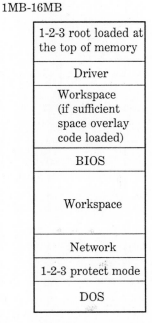

Figure 3-21.   Memory utilization with Release 3.0

Under Release 2 and the LIM-EMS memory standard, only formulas, labels, pointers to integers, and nonintegers were stored in expanded memory. This meant RAM memory would probably be fully utilized, and expanded memory would still be available.

Release 3 runs under either OS/2 or DOS. With OS/2, the operating system itself can manage up to 16MB of memory. Under DOS, the 640K limitation still exists, although Lotus has developed DOS extenders to allow you to access both extended or expanded memory in your machine. This utilization makes effective use of memory without the restrictions present in earlier releases.

Figure 3-20 shows memory utilization under Release 2. Release 3 makes effective use of program overlays when there is not sufficient memory to bring in the entire program and still leave adequate space for models. The diagram in Figure 3-21 shows the utilization of memory under Release 3. In Chapter 6, "Printing," you will learn how to monitor utilization of existing memory.

Changing the Appearance of the Worksheet Display

Global, Range, and GROUP Changes
Worksheet Changes
Format Options
Advanced Features
Conclusion
COMMAND REFERENCE: Worksheet Display

/Range Format
/Range Format Other
/Range Justify
/Worksheet Column
/Worksheet Delete
/Worksheet Global Col-Width
/Worksheet Global Default Other Clock
/Worksheet Global Default Other
International

/Worksheet Global Default Other Undo
/Worksheet Global Default Update
/Worksheet Global Format
/Worksheet Global Format Other
/Worksheet Global Group
/Worksheet Global Zero
/Worksheet Hide
/Worksheet Insert
/Worksheet Window Perspective

Using what you have learned up to now, you can make entries on the worksheet that convey useful information. The format of the numeric portion of this information, however, probably is not as attractive as you would like. It has no dollar signs, commas, or aligned decimal points. 1-2-3 can provide these special edit characters for you. The only time you will enter the edit characters yourself is when you are using Release 3's new Automatic format. In this case, the special edit characters will be the clue that tells 1-2-3 what type of format you want for the cell.

This chapter describes the features 1-2-3 provides for formatting your worksheet. It will demonstrate global and range formatting options, which give you a choice in the design of all or just a portion of your worksheet. It will teach you commands to change the width of your worksheet columns when the formats you have chosen require additional display space. This chapter will introduce you to the power of Release 3's GROUP mode, which allows you to affect all the sheets in the current worksheet file as you make changes to the current sheet. It will also describe some advanced ways to change 1-2-3's default display options. You will learn how to add and delete rows, columns, and sheets. For an overview of the commands covered in this chapter, see the command map at the start of the Worksheet Display Command Reference Section.

Global, Range, and GROUP Changes

1-2-3 has several menu commands for improving the appearance of your worksheet. These commands can work their magic globally, changing the entire worksheet at once, or they can affect only a single range of cells. Moreover, if you turn on the GROUP mode, your entries will affect either the current range on every sheet in the current file, or the entire file—depending upon whether or not your changes are range or global changes. The /Worksheet Global Format command changes the appearance of the entire worksheet from the global setting of General to another display format. If GROUP mode is on, every sheet in the file will have its global format altered. Figures 4-1 and 4-2 show the impact of a global format change with and without GROUP mode on.

The /Range Format command changes the appearance of just the cells within a specified range. Again, the range affected is in the current sheet, or, with GROUP mode on, the same range in all sheets. If the changes in Figures 4-1 and 4-2 had been made with a /Range command rather than with a global format change, the results would have been identical. Without GROUP mode, formatting the range in sheet A would have left sheets B and C unaffected. The same change with GROUP mode on would apply to sheets B and C also.

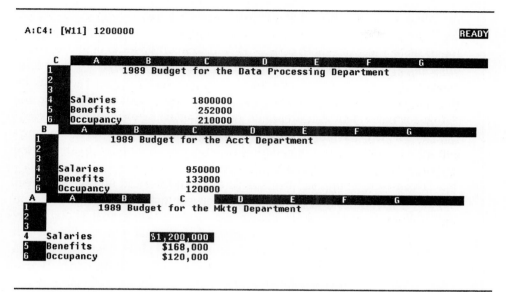

Figure 4-1.   Global format change with GROUP mode off

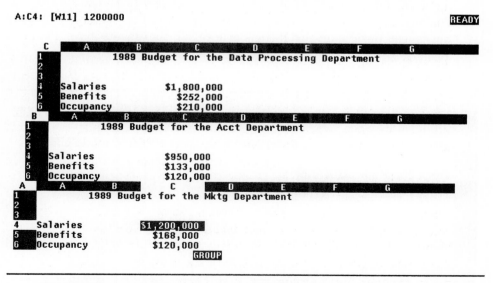

Figure 4-2.   Global format change with GROUP mode on

A Range Format option has priority over a Worksheet Format option. This means you can select a Worksheet option that matches your needs for most of the worksheet cells, and still tailor individual cells to have a different appearance. In Figure 4-3 the /Worksheet Global Format command was used to set the overall format to Currency, and then /Range Format was used to change C3..C5 to Percent format. Changing the global format again would change every numeric worksheet cell except C3..C5. Those cells would not be affected by a worksheet format change because a range format instruction was previously applied to them, and the range format has priority.

If you were using six sheets in one file and wanted all but one sheet to have a global format of Currency, you could turn GROUP mode on (with /Worksheet Global Group Enable), enter /Worksheet Global Format Currency, and press ENTER to accept two decimal places. This action formats all the sheets as Currency, including the sheet that you want to show in a different format. On that sheet, turn GROUP off (with /Worksheet Global Group Disable) and then use /Worksheet Global Format Percent, or another desired format. Similarly, if you want several cells on one worksheet to use a different format from all the other cells, you can use the /Range Format command after GROUP mode is disabled. Be careful: if you accidentally turn GROUP mode back on at a later time, you will find that the active sheet's range and global settings at the time you invoke GROUP mode will be applied to all the sheets. For this reason GROUP mode is best reserved for the beginning of your worksheet design or for models where all the sheets have identical formats.

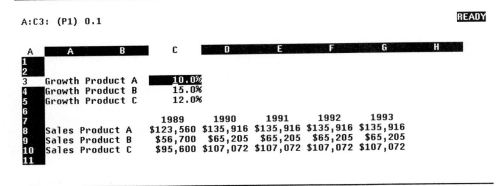

Figure 4-3.   Combining global and range formats

Before making a change to your worksheet, you should always determine the extent of the change you wish to make. You can then select the command that makes just the amount of change you need. This chapter will look separately at global changes and range changes, and take an in-depth look at each format option that 1-2-3 provides, both for global and range applications. Since the GROUP mode option can affect both range and global options, its coverage will be integrated with options in both sections.

You will need to be especially careful with GROUP mode, unless your sheets are identical for different products or subsidiaries. A GROUP mode indicator appears in the bottom status area when GROUP mode is active. Changes will take place as soon as you activate GROUP mode, based on the settings for the current sheet. All sheets in the file will assume the range format, range and worksheet protection status, worksheet column settings, labels, titles, and zero settings from the current worksheet. All worksheets are affected if you use any of these commands with GROUP on:

/Range Format
/Range Label
/Range Prot
/Range Unprot
/Worksheet Column
/Worksheet Global Col-Width
/Worksheet Global Format
/Worksheet Global Label
/Worksheet Global Prot
/Worksheet Global Zero
/Worksheet Insert
/Worksheet Delete
/Worksheet Titles

In addition, GROUP mode moves you from sheet to sheet, keeping the cell pointer on the same column and row. This means if you are in cell A3 on Sheet A when you press CTRL-PGUP, you will still be in cell A3, but on Sheet B. Without GROUP mode, CTRL-PGUP would have placed you in the cell that was active the last time you used Sheet B.

Worksheet Changes

All the /Worksheet commands are accessed through the Worksheet option on the main menu, which looks like this:

```
A:A1:                                                                    MENU
Worksheet  Range  Copy  Move  File  Print  Graph  Data  System  Quit
Global  Insert  Delete  Column  Erase  Titles  Window  Status  Page  Hide
```

Select Worksheet either by pressing ENTER while the command is highlighted, or by typing **W**.

This chapter will discuss the Worksheet menu options that are found under Insert, Delete Column, and Global on the Worksheet submenu. In addition, Worksheet Window options that change the appearance of the display will be introduced.

If you make a series of mistakes and wish to eliminate all the entries on your worksheet, you can use /Worksheet Erase Yes. This command makes the ultimate change in worksheet appearance: it clears the screen. Since it also eliminates all the underlying data, affecting more than the display, it is covered in Chapter 5, "Basic Worksheet Commands." A similar command, /Range Erase, clears a range on one or more worksheets; it is also covered in Chapter 5, since it affects the cell entries rather than the display format.

Undoing Worksheet Changes

Release 3 provides a powerful Undo feature that can return a worksheet to its former status. When Undo is enabled, pressing ALT-F4 (UNDO) and typing a **Y** to confirm that you want to undo your last action will reverse (undo) all the actions taken since the last time 1-2-3 was in READY mode. Pressing ALT-F4 (UNDO) when Undo is disabled has no effect. The Undo option will also have no effect on eliminating a series of actions if another series of actions are executed before you press ALT-F4 (UNDO).

You can use Undo to eliminate format changes, worksheet insertions and deletions, sorting, the effects of macros, and most other changes that affect the worksheet. External activities like printing or saving a file cannot be undone with Undo.

To enable Undo, use /Worksheet Global Default Other Undo Enable. To eliminate Undo's actions, use /Worksheet Global Default Other Undo Disable.

When Undo is enabled, the amount of memory required for 1-2-3 is increased. The exact requirements are determined by the type of command that you are undoing. For example, undoing a cell format requires a minimum of additional memory, whereas undoing a sort of a large database can require extensive storage space.

Insert Commands to Add Rows, Columns, or Sheets

The /Worksheet Insert command adds blank rows or columns to a worksheet. This same command adds blank sheets to a worksheet file, up to 256 sheets in memory or in a file.

The addition of sheets works a little differently from the addition of rows and columns. Adding rows and columns is a little like cutting rows and columns from the end of the sheet and pasting them back at another location, since the full complement of both rows and columns are in a sheet from the beginning. With sheets, only the first sheet is part of a new worksheet file. Subsequent sheets must be added before or after the first sheet.

You can use inserted rows and columns to add a heading for a report, or to include new or unexpected information. Adding blank rows and columns can also improve your worksheet design by making it more readable. Adding sheets offers an opportunity for restructuring your entire worksheet. You might choose to use a sheet for each product line or department. You can also store tables and macros on separate sheets from the main model components.

The /Worksheet Insert command is position-dependent, in that rows and columns can be added at the cell pointer location if you position it before entering the command. New sheets can be added before or after the current sheet.

Inserting Rows and Columns

With rows and columns you need not make a second menu choice to indicate the position of the new row or column. Position your cell pointer in the *column to the right* of where you wish to insert, or in the *row below* where you wish to insert. 1-2-3 always inserts columns to the left of the cell pointer, and rows above the cell pointer. After you enter **/Worksheet Insert**, 1-2-3 will ask whether you want to add rows, columns, or sheets. Make the appropriate selection. 1-2-3 will then ask for the range you wish to insert, if you have chosen row or column. You can expand your cell pointer across columns or down rows, covering the number of rows or columns you wish to insert. If you forget to position your cell pointer prior to entering the command, you can always type in the range, or use ESC to free the beginning of the range so you can move it. If you are inserting sheets, 1-2-3 asks how many sheets you wish to insert, rather than requesting a range for the insertion.

Figure 4-4 presents a worksheet that needs the insertion of additional blank spaces to improve its appearance. To make the insertions, move the cell pointer to A1 to insert blank columns to the left, enter **/Worksheet Insert Column**, and then move the cell pointer to expand the range to B1. When you press ENTER, two new columns will be inserted to the left of column A, causing the worksheet to appear as shown in Figure 4-5. Next, place the cell pointer in A1 to insert blank rows above the cell pointer, and enter **/Worksheet Insert Row**. Move the cell pointer down three rows to A3 and press ENTER to add three rows. The final version of the worksheet, after the insertion of both rows and columns, is shown in Figure 4-6.

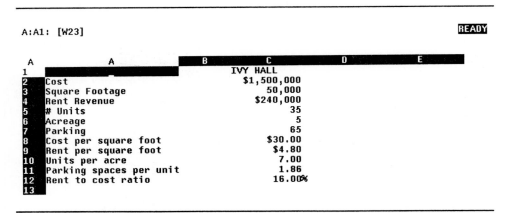

A	A	B	C	D	E
1			IVY HALL		
2	Cost		$1,500,000		
3	Square Footage		50,000		
4	Rent Revenue		$240,000		
5	# Units		35		
6	Acreage		5		
7	Parking		65		
8	Cost per square foot		$30.00		
9	Rent per square foot		$4.80		
10	Units per acre		7.00		
11	Parking spaces per unit		1.86		
12	Rent to cost ratio		16.00%		
13					

Figure 4-4.   Sample worksheet

A:A1:   READY

```
   A     A        B              C              D            E
1                                                         IVY HALL
2                         Cost                          $1,500,000
3                         Square Footage                    50,000
4                         Rent Revenue                   $240,000
5                         # Units                              35
6                         Acreage                               5
7                         Parking                              65
8                         Cost per square foot             $30.00
9                         Rent per square foot              $4.80
10                        Units per acre                     7.00
11                        Parking spaces per unit            1.86
12                        Rent to cost ratio               16.00%
13
```

Figure 4-5.   Worksheet after adding columns

When rows, columns, or sheets are inserted in the middle of a range, the range is automatically expanded to allow for the insertions. This applies to range names that have been assigned, and to ranges used in formulas. For example, Figure 4-7 shows a @SUM formula for departmental expenses. When two additional rows are inserted in the middle of the range, the formula is automatically adjusted to include two extra cells, as shown in Figure 4-8. If entries were made in these rows, a new total would display, as shown in Figure 4-9.

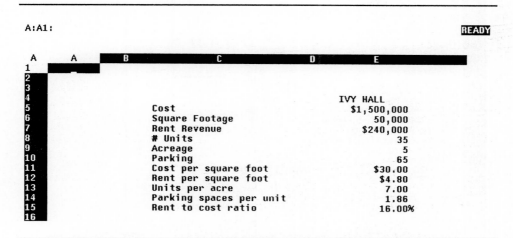

A:A1:   READY

```
   A     A        B              C              D            E
1
2
3
4                                                        IVY HALL
5                         Cost                          $1,500,000
6                         Square Footage                    50,000
7                         Rent Revenue                   $240,000
8                         # Units                              35
9                         Acreage                               5
10                        Parking                              65
11                        Cost per square foot             $30.00
12                        Rent per square foot              $4.80
13                        Units per acre                     7.00
14                        Parking spaces per unit            1.86
15                        Rent to cost ratio               16.00%
16
```

Figure 4-6.   Worksheet after adding rows

A:D16: (CO) [W11] @SUM(D6..D15)   `READY`

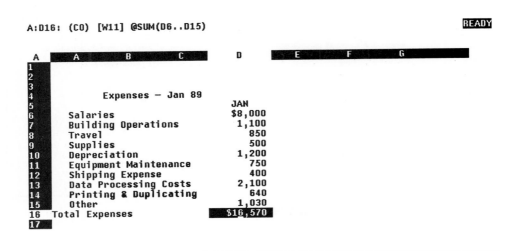

Figure 4-7. Worksheet computing department expense

A:D18: (CO) [W11] @SUM(D6..D17)   `READY`

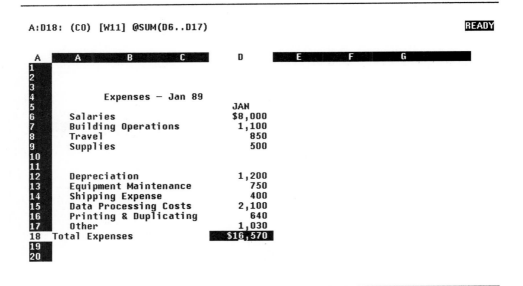

Figure 4-8. Worksheet after adding two rows

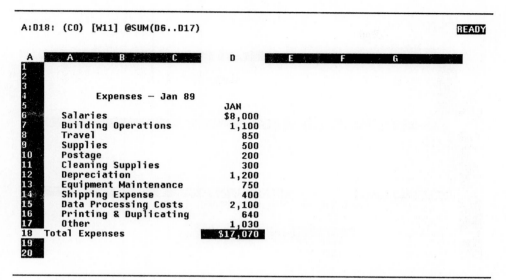

A:D18: (C0) [W11] @SUM(D6..D17)   READY

Figure 4-9.   Worksheet with two rows inserted and filled

When insertions are made before the first entry or after the last entry, no adjustment is made to the range. Whenever you wish to expand a range, therefore, pick a spot somewhere in the middle for your insertion.

Inserting Sheets

Each new worksheet file automatically provides sheet A. If you were to use the /Worksheet Window Perspective command (described later in this chapter), you would see a perspective view of up to three sheets—but only the first would contain a sheet, as shown in Figure 4-10. To expand the file to contain multiple sheets, use /Worksheet Insert Sheet. The next step is deciding whether the new sheets should be inserted before or after the current sheet. 1-2-3 prompts for the number of sheets to insert.

To insert two sheets after sheet A, enter /**Worksheet Insert Sheet After.** Type a **2** in response to the following prompt:

A:C4: [W11] 1200000   EDIT
Enter number of worksheets to insert: 2_

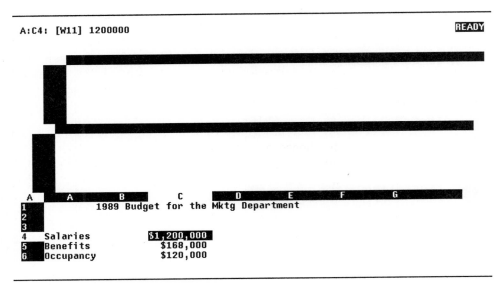

Figure 4-10.   A perspective window for a file with only one sheet

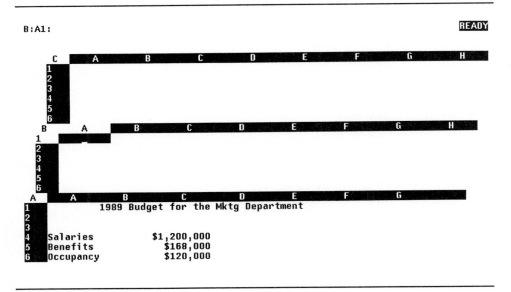

Figure 4-11.   Worksheet after adding two sheets after the current one

The perspective window will change to match Figure 4-11. Notice that the cell pointer is positioned in the first new sheet (level B). If you want to add a new sheet before sheet A, you first need to move to sheet A with CTRL-PGDN. Next, enter /**Worksheet Insert Sheet Before** and type a **1** in response to the prompt for number of sheets. Your display would match Figure 4-12.

Tip: Use a new sheet for different types of data. In the past you had no alternative but to choose different areas of one sheet for an entire model. You can create a much more organized application if you place each table, each new type of data, or your macros on different sheets. It is easy to move from sheet to sheet, since 1-2-3 remembers the correct cell pointer location for each sheet (as long as GROUP mode is not on).

Deleting Rows, Columns, or Sheets

1-2-3 also provides a command that will delete complete rows, columns, or sheets that are no longer required. Just as with the Insert command, it is easiest to use the Delete command when you position your cell pointer prior to execution. If you are deleting rows, place the cell pointer in the uppermost row to be deleted. If you are deleting columns, the cell pointer should be in the leftmost column to be deleted. If you

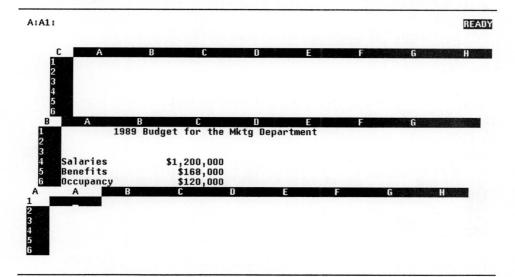

Figure 4-12.   Worksheet after adding a sheet before the current one

are deleting sheets you should have the pointer in the first sheet you wish to delete. Note that protected cells cannot be deleted when worksheet protection is enabled.

The rows, columns, or sheets deleted can be blank, or they can contain worksheet data, including formulas. When deleting rows or columns, be sure that the formulas and data in them are not referenced by other worksheet cells. If such references exist, incorrect data may be referenced after the deletion, or an error condition may occur if the new cells are no longer numeric. Figure 4-13 shows the resulting error message when a critical column is accidentally deleted. Before making large-scale deletions, you will want to save your worksheet to disk or make sure that the Undo command is enabled. (To enable Undo when it is off, enter **/Worksheet Global Default Other Undo Enable.**)

Figure 4-14 presents a worksheet with extraneous blank columns in locations A through C. To delete these columns, move the cell pointer to A1 and enter **/Worksheet Delete Column.** Extend the cell pointer to

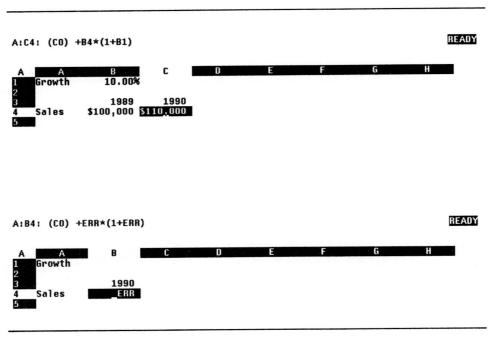

Figure 4-13.   Worksheet before and after deleting critical cells

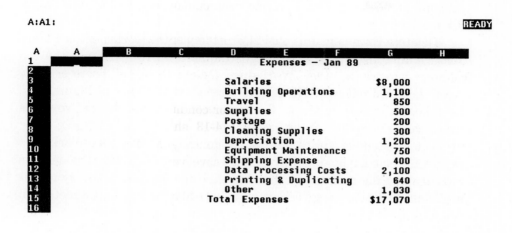

Figure 4-14.   Worksheet with extra columns

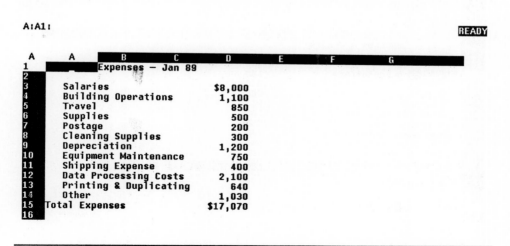

Figure 4-15.   Worksheet after deleting extra columns

column C by pressing RIGHT ARROW twice, then press ENTER. All three columns are deleted with this one command, producing the display in Figure 4-15.

Deleting rows is just as easy. For example, the worksheet in Figure 4-16 contains data that is no longer required, in row 4. Move the cell pointer to that row, enter /**Worksheet Delete Row**, and press ENTER to delete just that one row. The altered worksheet is shown in Figure 4-17. 1-2-3 is able to adjust the @SUM function, since the deleted row was taken from the middle of the range.

You can delete entire sheets full of entries with the /Worksheet Delete Sheet command. Be cautious; 1-2-3 does not verify the deletion first, making file backups or the Undo feature the only recovery means available. After entering the command, specify the range of sheets that you wish to remove.

Tip: Save the file before deleting entire sheets. Deleting the wrong sheets can quickly destroy an afternoon's work if you have not saved your file. You will want to save your work frequently in case you request the /Worksheet Delete Sheet command by accident.

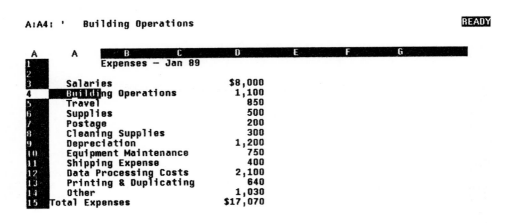

Figure 4-16.   Worksheet with an extra row

Window Perspective Command

1-2-3 provides a number of Window commands that allow you to change your view of the worksheet data. One of these commands is covered here so you can learn how to view more than one sheet on the screen at a time. You will be introduced to additional Window options in Chapter 5, "Basic Worksheet Commands."

To view the worksheet with a perspective view of three sheets, shown in some of the earlier examples in this chapter, use /Worksheet Window Perspective. 1-2-3 uses the current sheet as the first sheet, and shows you the two following sheets if they exist. If there are no additional sheets in the file, 1-2-3 still displays three worksheet areas, but only the first area is used.

If you want a close-up look at the active screen in a perspective view, you can press ALT-F6 (ZOOM). Pressing it a second time returns you to the three-sheet perspective. To eliminate the perspective view and return to a single-sheet view on a permanent basis, use /Worksheet Window Clear.

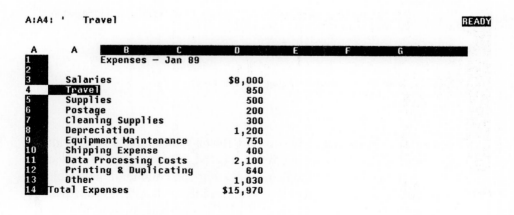

Figure 4-17.   Worksheet after deleting extra row

Column Commands

Every column on a new worksheet is the same width. Unless you change the default width, each column is nine positions wide. This means that labels with nine characters, or numeric entries with eight digits can be entered in the cell. (Numeric entries are always restricted to one digit less than the cell width.)

When you enter labels that are too long for this width, they are truncated for display if the cells to their right are not empty. If the adjacent cells are empty, 1-2-3 borrows space from them to show the complete label entry. Numbers that are too long are either rounded to fit the cell width or displayed as asterisks, depending on the format in effect for the cell. In earlier releases of 1-2-3 the General format truncated numbers without rounding. Release 3 follows these rules governing the General default display of numbers:

- 1-2-3 attempts to display your entry as you enter it.

- If the integer portion of the entry exceeds the cell width, 1-2-3 switches to Scientific notation.

- If the integer portion fits within the cell width but the decimal portion does not, 1-2-3 rounds the value.

Set-Width

The /Worksheet Column menu looks like this:

```
A:A1:                                                          MENU
Set-Width  Reset-Width  Hide  Display  Column-Range
Specify current column width
```

The first two options, Set-Width and Reset-Width, change the width of the column where the cell pointer is located. You will therefore want to position your cell pointer before requesting the command. The Column-Range option also changes the column width, but allows you to affect more than one column at a time. With Column-Range, you also specify whether you want to set or reset width. Instead of assuming the current column is to be changed, 1-2-3 will ask you to specify the affected range.

The following display shows account names that were entered in column A but are too long to display in that column's default width of 9.

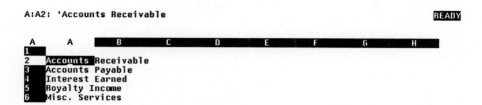

The entries could be allowed to borrow space from adjacent columns, or column A's width could be changed with Set-Width, so that the entries could be shown in that column. This option is especially useful if you already have an entry in column B, and the label in column A therefore is being truncated.

First, make sure your cell pointer is in column A. Then invoke the command by entering /**Worksheet Column Set-Width**. Next, you can either enter the desired number of characters and press ENTER; or you can move with the RIGHT and LEFT ARROW keys until the column is the desired width, and press ENTER. The latter method is best, since guessing wrong about the desired number of characters means you have to start over with /Worksheet Column Set-Width.

In the following example, the width was set at 19.

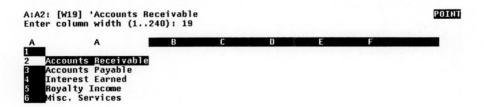

This width could have been set either by typing the entire entry, then /**Worksheet Column Set-Width 19**, and pressing ENTER, or by using the RIGHT ARROW key to widen the column one position at a time. If you wanted to enter similar names in other sheets within the same file, using

/Worksheet Global Group Enable before changing the column width would make the width change affect all the sheets in the file.

The Set-Width option can also be used when numbers are too large to display in the default column width. In Figure 4-18, numeric entries were made for the account balances. These cells are formatted as Currency with two decimal places, meaning that 1-2-3 added a $, and a comma after the thousands position. (To produce this format, type **/Range Format Currency**, press ENTER, type **B2..B6**, and press ENTER again.) The asterisks appear in these cells because the values they contain are too large for the cell width once the dollar sign and comma are added to the existing digits. This column can be widened sufficiently by typing **/Worksheet Column Set-Width** and moving the RIGHT ARROW three times before pressing ENTER. Figure 4-19 shows the display after the cells were changed to a width of 12.

Reset-Width

Once you have used /Worksheet Column Set-Width to change the width of a column, its width will be different from its neighbors'. If that width ceases to be useful, you can return the column to the global column width with the Reset-Width command. In Figure 4-19, placing the cell

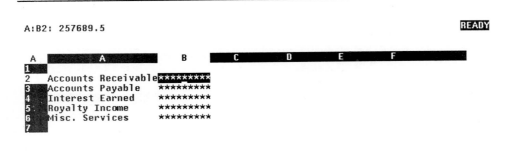

Figure 4-18. Currency format with entries that will not fit in cell

pointer in column C and entering /**Worksheet Column Reset-Width** will return the column to a width of 9, causing the asterisks to reappear.

If you are uncertain of the current global width, you can make a quick check by typing /**Worksheet Status**. A display similar to Figure 4-20 will appear, allowing you to review the status information; you can return to your model by pressing ESC to return to READY mode.

When the width of a column is changed with /Worksheet Column Set-Width, that width is conveniently displayed in the control panel for each cell in that column. In other words, if you place your cell pointer on any cell in a column where a special width has been used, you will see the width in brackets in the command line (the top line) of the control panel. For example, [W8] means width 8, [W4] means width 4, and [W25] means width 25. Widths from 1 to 240 can be assigned to any column.

Hidden Columns

/Worksheet Column Hide allows you to eliminate individual columns from the display. In effect, it cuts a section of the worksheet temporarily. You can use this option to eliminate confidential or proprietary information from the display. Hidden sections can be restored to the

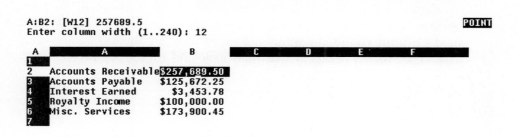

Figure 4-19.   Column widened to 12 to show numbers

```
                                                                    STAT

Available memory: 1463424 of 2417952 Bytes (61%)

Processor: 80386
Math coprocessor: None

Recalculation:
  Method.......... Automatic
  Order........... Natural
  Iterations....... 1

Circular reference: (None)

Cell display:
  Format.......... (G)
  Label prefix..... '
  Column width..... 9
  Zero setting..... No

Global protection: Off

                                                        CALC
```

Figure 4-20.   Results of /Worksheet Status command

display at any time, since the data has not been erased. When you press
ENTER after typing /Worksheet Column Hide, the column where the cell
pointer is located will be hidden. You may also use the RIGHT and LEFT
ARROW keys or specify a range of columns before pressing ENTER.

Figure 4-21 shows a worksheet before Hide is invoked. To hide
columns C and D, place the cell pointer in column C and type /**Worksheet Column Hide** followed by a decimal point (.), the RIGHT ARROW, and
ENTER. The same worksheet will then look like Figure 4-22. Note that

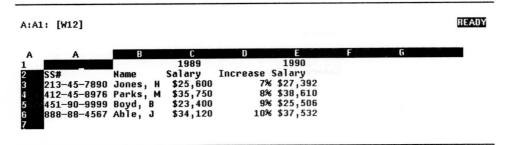

<figure>
A:A1: [W12]   READY

     A   A   B   C   D   E   F   G
 1   1989   1990
 2   SS#   Name   Salary   Increase Salary
 3   213-45-7890 Jones, H $25,600   7% $27,392
 4   412-45-8976 Parks, M $35,750   8% $38,610
 5   451-90-9999 Boyd, B $23,400   9% $25,506
 6   888-88-4567 Able, J $34,120   10% $37,532
 7
</figure>

Figure 4-21.   Worksheet before hiding columns

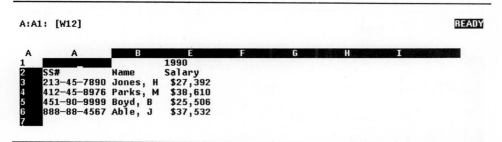

Figure 4-22.   Worksheet after hiding columns C and D

columns C and D have disappeared. The data in the two hidden columns can still be accessed in formulas.

Tip: Use /Range Format Hidden to eliminate any range from display, and thus display a group of cells as blank. This allows you to hide the information in a row or rectangle on the worksheet.

The /Worksheet Column Display command redisplays hidden columns. It displays the column letters of the formerly hidden columns with asterisks next to them, as shown in Figure 4-23. After typing the command, you can move the cell pointer to the column you want to redisplay and press ENTER, or you can select a range if you want to redisplay adjacent columns.

Tip: Column Hide and Delete Column have very different results. When you hide a column it is only eliminated from the display temporarily. When you delete a column, the column and its contents are

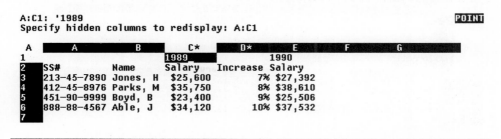

Figure 4-23.   Selecting columns to redisplay

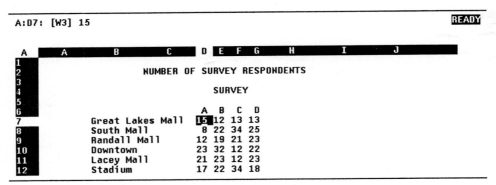

Figure 4-24.   Worksheet with columns D, E, F, and G using a width of 3

permanently removed from the worksheet. Other columns are renamed with the letter from the deleted column—but its entries are lost unless you have a retrievable copy of the model on disk.

Column-Range

If you need to change the width of four or five consecutive columns, Column Set-Width or Reset-Width must be executed once for each column that you wish to change. However, Release 3 offers an addi-

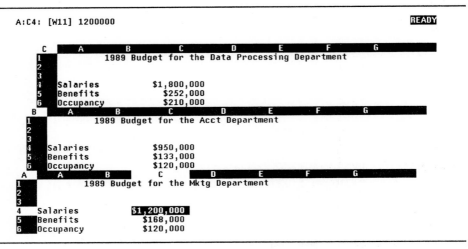

Figure 4-25.   Worksheet file with multiple sheets

tional, far more efficient approach: you can use the /Worksheet Column Column-Range command to change multiple columns at one time. Figure 4-24 shows a model where the width of columns D through G was changed to 3. This was accomplished by entering **/Worksheet Column Column-Range Set-Width**, highlighting the columns to change, pressing ENTER, typing a **3**, and pressing ENTER. Using /Worksheet Column Set-Width would have required four separate command entries.

The Reset-Width option resets the column width for the range of affected columns to the default global column width. You can enter **/Worksheet Status** to check the current setting before making a change if you wish.

Like the other /Worksheet Column commands, the use of GROUP mode with this command will cause the column width changes to affect all the sheets in the current file.

Hiding Sheets

Release 3 offers the /Worksheet Hide command to allow you to remove sheets from display and then redisplay them. You can use this command for one or more consecutive sheets at once. Figure 4-25 shows three of the sheets in the current worksheet file. Many additional sheets exist, representing other departments in the company. To work with sheets A, D, and E, moving between them frequently, you will want to hide sheets B and C. You cannot move the cell pointer to hidden sheets, even with the F5 (GOTO) key.

Figure 4-26 shows a perspective view of the file with sheets B and C still active. Move to sheet B and enter **/Worksheet Hide Enable**. Expand the range to include sheet C by typing a period (.); then press CTRL-PGUP followed by ENTER. Your screen will now display sheets A, D, and E (Figure 4-27).

The /Worksheet Hide command is also a good option when you want to eliminate confidential or proprietary data from view. An alternative measure is to use /Worksheet Global Format Hidden to hide all the data on a worksheet.

Global Commands

Global commands affect the entire worksheet. Every row, every column, and every cell in each row and column are affected by the changes you make with the /Worksheet Global command options, although most of the Global options will affect only numeric cell entries. When you invoke GROUP mode first, the global change affects not only every cell in the current sheet but every sheet in the current file. The options available under the Global menu are shown here:

```
A:A1:                                                          MENU
Format  Label  Col-Width  Prot  Zero  Recalc  Default  Group
Fixed  Sci  Currency  ,  General  +/-  Percent  Date  Text  Hidden  Other
```

In this chapter you will have the opportunity to use Global Col-Width, Format, Zero, and Default. In addition, you have already had several occasions on which to benefit from the GROUP mode setting, which is also a global change. The first three commands will be examined next; the more advanced options offered under Default will be discussed at the end of the chapter. Additional Global options will be described in Chapter 5, "Basic Worksheet Commands."

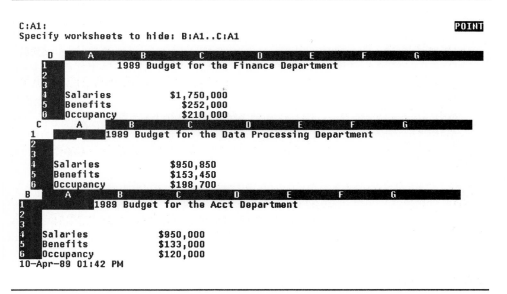

Figure 4-26. Hiding the B and C sheets

Column-Width

Changing the column width for the entire worksheet with the /Worksheet Column option would take much too long. You could use /Worksheet Column Column-Range, but if you want to affect every column, it is more efficient to use a global change. In addition, a global change will be documented on the status screen, so it is easy to see the width that is currently selected. 1-2-3 allows you to change the width of every column on the worksheet with one command: /Worksheet Global Col-Width. With this option you can make all the columns on your worksheet any width from 1 to 240, instead of the default setting of 9 positions.

Since this command will affect the entire worksheet, there is no need to position your cell pointer before invoking it. The example in Figure 4-28 shows columns of numbers, all of which contain fewer than the default setting of 9 positions. Shrinking the size of the columns would allow you to display more information on the sheet. By typing **/Worksheet Global Col-Width 5** and pressing ENTER, you could change the display to match the one shown in Figure 4-29.

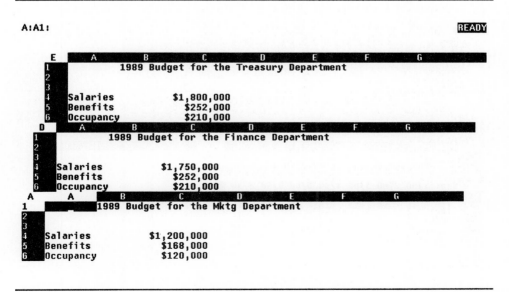

Figure 4-27.   Worksheet file after hiding sheets

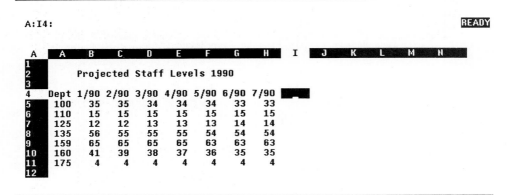

```
A:A1:                                                                      READY

  A        A         B         C         D         E         F         G         H
1
2           Projected Staff Levels 1990
3
4   Dept     1/90      2/90      3/90      4/90      5/90      6/90      7/90
5    100       35        35        34        34        34        33        33
6    110       15        15        15        15        15        15        15
7    125       12        12        13        13        13        14        14
8    135       56        55        55        55        54        54        54
9    159       65        65        65        65        63        63        63
10   160       41        39        38        37        36        35        35
11   175        4         4         4         4         4         4         4
12
```

Figure 4-28.   Worksheet using a default column width of 9

The /Worksheet Column command takes precedence over the Global Col-Width command. You could use both commands if you had a worksheet where all but one column could be narrow. /Worksheet Global Col-Width could set the narrow width for the entire worksheet. You would then move your cell pointer to the column requiring the wider width, type **/Worksheet Col Set-Width,** and specify the wider width needed for that column only.

A look at a more complicated example illustrates how all the options can be combined to efficiently tailor a worksheet to your needs. Let's say sheets A through D in a worksheet file require a column width of 10,

```
A:I4:                                                                      READY

  A     A    B    C    D    E    F    G    H    I    J    K    L    M    N
1
2          Projected Staff Levels 1990
3
4   Dept 1/90 2/90 3/90 4/90 5/90 6/90 7/90
5    100   35   35   34   34   34   33   33
6    110   15   15   15   15   15   15   15
7    125   12   12   13   13   13   14   14
8    135   56   55   55   55   54   54   54
9    159   65   65   65   65   63   63   63
10   160   41   39   38   37   36   35   35
11   175    4    4    4    4    4    4    4
12
```

Figure 4-29.   Worksheet using a default column width of 5

and Sheet E requires a width of 5 for all columns except column B, which needs a width of 12. Follow these steps:

1. Turn on GROUP mode with /**Worksheet Global Group Enable**.

2. Globally change the width for all sheets to 10 with /**Worksheet Global Col-Width 10** followed by ENTER.

3. Move to Sheet E and turn off GROUP mode with /**Worksheet Global Group Disable**.

4. Globally change Sheet E to a width of 5 with /**Worksheet Global Col-Width 5**. Since GROUP is off, only sheet E is affected this time.

5. Move to column B of sheet E and enter /**Worksheet Col Set-Width 12**. Only column B on Sheet E is affected by this change, since GROUP mode is still off. Important: Remember that invoking the GROUP mode again later will cause you to lose the changes made to individual sheets.

As you tailor the column widths for any application, consider what you want the sheets to look like. With each sheet, you must decide whether to alter the width of all the columns of the current sheet or just one or two. You must also decide whether or not to use GROUP mode, so that the current sheet's column width changes are applied to all the sheets that are part of the worksheet file. You must make any GROUP mode changes the first step, before customizing the worksheets. If you do not want all the sheets affected by your changes, you may need to modify each sheet individually.

Format

Format can also be changed on a global basis. The default setting is General format, but if you want all your entries to be in Currency, Percent, Scientific, or any of the other available formats, every worksheet cell can be reformatted with the /Worksheet Global Format command and the format specification of your choice. Figure 4-30 displays a worksheet created with the General format setting. The appearance of this worksheet can be markedly improved by use of a single command,

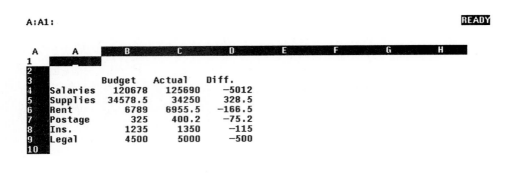

Figure 4-30. Worksheet using the General format

/Worksheet Global Format Currency. After the initial command sequence, type **0** to indicate zero decimal places and press ENTER. The newly formatted worksheet looks like Figure 4-31.

Any one of the options listed in the Format Options box can be used. Some formats require more worksheet space than others, however. If the display turns to asterisks when you change your format, you will have to widen your columns to accommodate the new format. As you

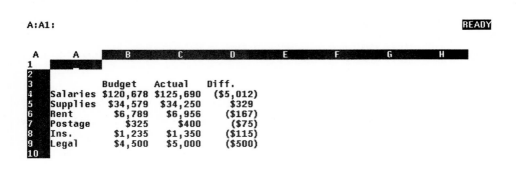

Figure 4-31. Worksheet using the Currency format

will learn later in the chapter, a /Range Format command always takes precedence over a /Worksheet Global Format change.

Using the GROUP mode while making a formatting change causes the change to affect all sheets in the active file. If you choose Currency in the active sheet, all the sheets in the current file will have a format of Currency. Sheets added to the file at a later time will automatically assume the characteristics of the existing sheets. Also when you first invoke Group mode, the format, column width, and zero suppression characteristics of the active sheet affect all the sheets in the file.

Zero Display

You can choose how zero values are displayed on the worksheet. In the past, a zero value always resulted in a cell containing a 0. The zero value options in Release 3 can hide zero values, display zero values, or display a label in every zero location on the worksheet. The zero values remain the same, as they can be referenced for calculations; but any cell with a zero value can appear, be hidden, or appear as a label.

To suppress the display of zeros on the worksheet, use /Worksheet Global Zero Yes. To restore the display, use /Worksheet Global Zero No. To display the zero values as labels, use /Worksheet Global Zero Label and enter a label to display in place of zero values. The label will be right aligned unless you provide a different alignment prefix character.

The one problem with zero suppression is that 1-2-3 will write over a zero-suppressed cell if you type a new entry there, because the cell appears blank. A solution for this problem is discussed under "Protection" in Chapter 5. Figure 4-32 shows a worksheet with the Zero option set to Yes; Figure 4-33 shows the same worksheet with Zero set to Label, and "None" as the label.

Tip: Zeros may still appear in a worksheet, even when Global Zero is suppressing zeros or displaying them as labels. The worksheet will display zeros if it contains cells that appear as zero due to the cell's format. To convert these values to actual zeros, use the @ROUND function covered in Chapter 7, "1-2-3's Built-in Functions."

Format Options

This table provides a quick reference to the formatting features offered by 1-2-3.

Format	Entry	Display
Fixed	5678	5678.00
2 decimal places	−123.45	−123.45
Scientific	5678	5.68E + 03
2 decimal places	−123.45	−1.23E + 02
Currency	5678	$5,678.00
2 decimal places	−123.45	($123.45)
, (Comma)	5678	5,678.00
2 decimal places	−123.45	(123.45)
General	5678	5678
	−123.45	−123.45
+/−	4	+ + + +
	−3	− − −
	0	.
Percent	5	500%
0 decimal places	.1	10%
Date	31679	24-Sep-86
(D1)		
Time	.5	12:00:00 PM
(T1)		
Text	+ A2*A3	+ A2*A3
Other Automatic	$5	$5
	15-Aug-92	15-Aug-92
Other Color Negative	−17	**−17***
Other Parentheses with Currency	−5	(−$5)
Other Label	123r7	'123r7

* The display is in color on a color monitor and in boldface on a monochrome monitor.

```
A:A1:                                                                    READY

   A        A           B           C          D          E        F   .    G            H
 1                              Absences by Month
 2
 3                       Jan         Feb         Mar        Apr       May       June         July
 4     Dept 4           0           2           3          2         0         0            1
 5     Dept 5           1           1           0          0         0         0            2
 6     Dept 7           2           2           2          2         0         0            0
 7    .Dept 8           0           0           0          0         1         1            0
 8     Dept 9           3           3           1          1         0         0            2
 9
```

Figure 4-32.   Hiding zeros

Range Format Commands

Range format changes do just what their name implies: they change the format for a specified range of cells on the worksheet. Any of the valid ranges described in Chapter 2, "The Access System, Display, and Keyboard," can be affected. The range can be as small as one cell, or it can be a row, column, or rectangle of cells on one or many sheets.

Tip: Plan your format layout as you plan your worksheet design. You will not create well-designed models without adequate planning. As you lay out a worksheet design on paper, add color highlighting or some other indication of the formats you want to use. You can make the format changes as a first step in the model creation process.

```
A:B4:  0                                                                 READY

   A        A           B           C          D          E        F        G            H
 1                              Absences by Month
 2
 3                       Jan         Feb         Mar        Apr       May       June         July
 4     Dept 4          None         2           3          2        None      None          1
 5     Dept 5           1           1          None       None      None      None          2
 6     Dept 7           2           2           2          2        None      None         None
 7     Dept 8          None        None        None       None       1         1          None
 8     Dept 9           3           3           1          1        None      None          2
 9
```

Figure 4-33.   Displaying labels instead of zeros

Let's look at an example of the /Range Format command in action. The worksheet shown in Figure 4-34 has three different types of entries. Two of these worksheet entries have already been formatted, and one is in the process of being changed. To change the format of these cells, follow these steps:

1. Move your cell pointer to the upper leftmost cell in the range you wish to format. Placing the cell pointer in this location will allow you to specify the range using only the arrow keys.

2. Type /**Range Format**.

3. Select the Percent format from the menu, either by typing **P** or by pointing and pressing ENTER.

4. If the format requires a certain number of decimal places, either press ENTER to accept the default of two places, or enter the desired number of decimal places and then press ENTER. In our example, 1 was entered to replace the default.

5. 1-2-3 will request the range to format. Specify the range by using the RIGHT and DOWN ARROW keys to move to the lower rightmost cell you wish to format. If you are formatting just one cell, do not move the cell pointer. After all the cells to be formatted are highlighted, press ENTER, and they will be displayed with the new format. The worksheet will then look like Figure 4-35.

Just as with /Worksheet Global Format changes, changes in format for a range of cells do not affect the internal storage accuracy of your

```
A:F4: 0.1                                                              MENU
Fixed  Sci  Currency  ,  General  +/-  Percent  Date  Text  Hidden  Other  Reset
Percent format (x.xx%)
  A        A        B        C        D        E        F        G        H
1                Currency          Fixed            Percent
2                2 decimals        0 decimals       1 decimal
3
4                $54.56            123              0.1
5                $34.10            234              0.234
6                $2.30             55               0.999
7                $17.99            1                0.3211
8
```

Figure 4-34.   Worksheet with numbers in different formats

numbers and calculated results. Suppose you decide to display an entry with no decimal places, but internally six or more places are stored. When that cell is used in a calculation, the full internal accuracy will be applied, because 1-2-3 maintains entries with an accuracy of approximately 18 decimal digits. Later, in Chapter 7, "1-2-3's Built-in Functions," you will learn a way to change the internal accuracy as well.

/Range Format commands always take priority over /Worksheet Global Format commands. You can use this fact to your advantage. Before constructing a new worksheet, plan its design. Determine which format will be used more than any other, and use /Worksheet Global Format to establish this format. Then, where necessary, use /Range Format commands to alter the format of individual cells or ranges.

The /Range Format commands have a feature not found in /Worksheet Global Format commands. Once a cell has been formatted with a /Range command, the top line in the control panel will show the format for the cell. "(F2)" means Fixed with two decimal places, "(C0)" means Currency with zero decimal places, and so on.

You can use the /Range Format commands with multiple sheet files in two ways. First, with the GROUP mode option, you can choose to make a format change on the current sheet and have it apply to every sheet in the file. Second, you can leave GROUP mode turned off and specify a range that spans sheets. In this second case, you might choose to format cells F2..H25 as Currency on sheets B, C, and D, by entering the range **B:F2..D:H25** in response to the prompt.

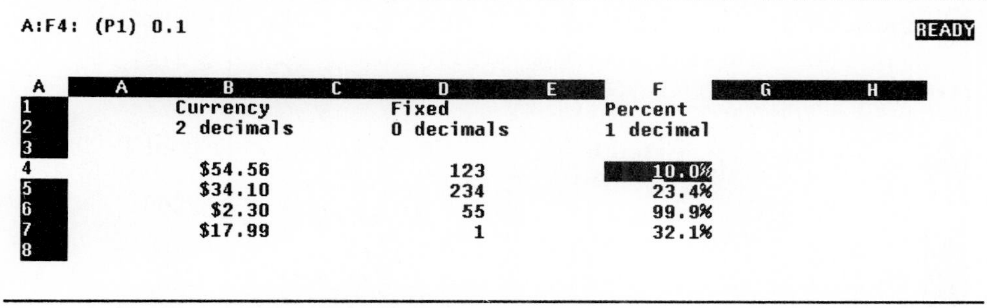

```
A:F4: (P1) 0.1                                                    READY

  A       A         B         C         D         E         F         G         H
  1                 Currency            Fixed               Percent
  2                 2 decimals          0 decimals          1 decimal
  3
  4                   $54.56              123                  10.0%
  5                   $34.10              234                  23.4%
  6                    $2.30               55                  99.9%
  7                   $17.99                1                  32.1%
  8
```

Figure 4-35.   Formatting Percent numbers

Format Options

Each of the format options in this section, with the exception of Reset, can be used with either the /Worksheet Global Format or the /Range Format command. Since Reset is used to reverse a /Range Format command by changing the range back to the global setting, this option is not needed on the /Worksheet Global Format menu. The following format options are summarized for you in the "Format Options" box shown earlier in the chapter.

Fixed Format

The Fixed format lets you choose the number of places to the right of the decimal point that you wish to display. Like General format, it does not display dollar signs or commas.

If you use the Fixed format option and the numbers you enter or calculate with formulas do not contain a sufficient number of decimal places, zeros will be added. For example, if you enter **5.67** in a cell that you formatted as Fixed with four decimal places, your entry will display as 5.6700. The zeros used for padding are always added to the right. With Fixed format you may select from 0 to 15 decimal places. If the column is not wide enough, asterisks will appear. Leading zero integers are always added for decimal fraction numbers.

If, conversely, you enter or calculate numbers with more decimal places than have been specified, they will be rounded to the appropriate number of decimal places. Any number of 5 or above will be rounded upwards by 1-2-3. The following table may help you remember the action 1-2-3 will take in various circumstances.

Entry	Fixed 0	Fixed 2	Fixed 4
7.23	7	7.23	7.2300
8.54	9	8.54	8.5400
3.5674	4	3.57	3.5674
.98	1	.98	.9800

After you apply a Fixed format to a range of cells, the command line of the control panel will display an indicator like (F0), (F2), or (F4). The number following the F (for Fixed) is the number of decimal places that you specified for your display.

The Fixed format option presents an appealing display when cells have many decimal numbers. This format is particularly useful when these decimal numbers are the result of formulas, since it permits numbers to be displayed with the decimals aligned, which General format does not.

Scientific Format

This format displays numbers in exponential notation. This option appears as Sci in the formatting option. You can choose from 0 to 15 decimal places in the first, or multiplier, portion of the expression, which makes the Scientific format option different from the Scientific notation display generated by the General format option. With General, if Scientific notation is required for a very large or very small number, 1-2-3 will determine the number of decimals in the multiplier. With Scientific format, you make the determination when you establish the format.

The following table shows entries as they are made in a worksheet cell, and the display that results when each of several Scientific decimal settings is established for the multiplier.

Entry	Scientific 0	Scientific 2	Scientific 4
100550000	1E + 08	1.01E + 08	1.0055E + 08
7896543	8E + 06	7.90E + 06	7.8965E + 06
.00005678	6E-05	5.68E-05	5.6780E-05

The indicator for Scientific when the /Range Format command is used is an S combined with the number of decimals. It is displayed within parentheses in the command line of the control panel in the same way the Fixed format indicator was. Thus, you will see (S0), (S2), (S4), and so on.

Scientific notation is useful when you need to display very large or very small numbers in a limited cell width. It is used primarily in scientific and engineering applications and would not be acceptable on most business reports.

Currency Format

The Currency format places a dollar sign ($) in front of each entry. It adds a comma separator between thousands and hundreds and between millions and thousands. This format shows negative numbers in parentheses.

From 0 to 15 decimal places can be specified for this format, although the most common settings are 0 for whole dollars, and 2 to show both dollars and cents. The default setting is 2. Thus, when you want to show dollars and cents, you only have to press ENTER after selecting Currency as either the /Worksheet Global Format or /Range Format options. With the /Range command, you also need to specify the size of the range to be formatted.

The /Worksheet Global Default Other International command can change the way the Currency option works. In the "Advanced Features" section near the end of this chapter, you will learn to use symbols for other currencies such as pounds and guilders, and to place the symbol either in front of or behind the currency amount. In addition, the symbols used for the comma separator and the decimal point can be changed to meet your needs in working with international currencies. Further, the parentheses around negative numbers can be changed to a minus sign.

Let's look at the impact on several numeric entries of using different Currency formats.

Entry	Currency 0	Currency 2	Currency 4
34.78	$35	$34.78	$34.7800
−123	($123)	($123.00)	($123.0000)
1234.56	$1,235	$1,234.56	$1,234.5600

To display these entries, the column width must be widened to 10 for the middle column and to 12 for the column on the far right.

The indicator for the Currency format is a C followed by the number of decimal places. Like the other format indicators, this will appear in parentheses in front of the cell entry on the command line in the control panel.

The Currency format is used frequently in business reports because of the many dollar figures shown in such reports. If you want to conserve space when printing your reports, remember that you can use a format of (C0) and an appropriate column width without losing the additional stored decimal accuracy.

Comma Format

The Comma format is just like the Currency format, except that the dollar sign is not used in the Comma format. Just as with the Currency format, negative numbers are shown in parentheses and commas are added as separators.

From 0 to 15 decimal places can be shown with this format. Enter the number of decimal places when prompted with the default. If you wish to accept the default (2), just press ENTER.

Here is a sample of the displays created with the Comma format:

Entry	, 0	, 2	, 4
34.78	35	34.78	34.7800
−123	(123)	(123.00)	(123.0000)
1234.56	1,235	1,234.56	1,234.5600

You will notice that the same entries were used for this table as for the Currency format. This allows you to compare their use.

A comma and the number of decimal places are used as the indicator for this format. Thus (,0), (,2), and (,4) in the command line represent this format with zero, two, and four decimal places, respectively.

The Comma format is frequently combined with the Currency format for financial statements. As in Figure 4-36, the top and bottom line of a financial statement typically have the $ added, whereas the other numbers are shown in Comma format. The best strategy for producing this layout is to use /Worksheet Global Format, followed by /Range Format Currency commands for the top and bottom line of the display.

General Format

Since General is the default format, it is the one you have seen in the entries made on your worksheet until now. This format does not provide

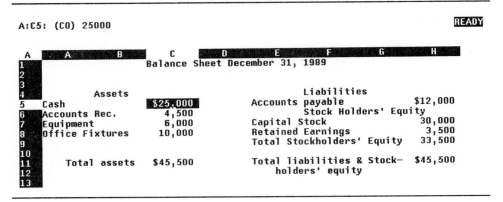

Figure 4-36.   Using Comma format to format numbers

consistent displays as the other formats do, since it depends on the size of the number you enter. As you saw in Chapter 3, "Entering Data in 1-2-3's Worksheet," very large and very small numbers will display in Scientific format when General format is in effect. Some numbers will appear as they are entered, while others will be altered to have a leading zero added, or be rounded to a number of decimal digits that will fit in the cell width you have selected. This format also suppresses trailing zeros after the decimal point, so if you have used them, they will not appear in the display.

General format does not provide a choice of the number of zeros for the display, and it often results in a display that has varying numbers of decimal places in the entries. There is also no way to establish the number of digits for the multiplier when the Scientific format option is used for very small and very large numbers.

Looking at the way various entries appear in General format will help you decide when it is an appropriate format for your needs.

Entry	General Display
10000000000	$1.0E + 10$
2345678	2345678
234.76895432	234.7689

An indicator of (G) is used for General format. A numeric digit is not present, since the command does not expect you to decide the number of decimal digits to be shown.

Although it is the default worksheet setting, General format is seldom selected as the display of choice. For most applications you will want a more consistent display, even if it does require more room on the worksheet. This format would be particularly useful, however, if you were really short of space, since it automatically converts to Scientific notation when the entry becomes too large or small to fit in the cell width.

+/− Format

This is one of the most unusual formats available in 1-2-3. It creates a series of plus (+) or minus (−) signs as a representation of the size of the number in the cell, producing a sort of bar graph. These signs will change to asterisks if the size of the bar exceeds the column width. When the value of the cell is zero, a period (.) will display on the left side of the cell.

The +/− format creates the following horizontal displays from the entries shown:

Entry	+/− Display
0	.
5	+ + + + +
−4	− − − −
−3.85	− − −

The indicator (+) or (−) will appear in the command line when the cell pointer is on any cell that has been formatted with the +/− format using the /Range Format command.

The +/− format can be used to create a series of small bars to show, for example, growth or decline in sales over a period of time. In this situation you may want to divide the sales figure by 100 or some other appropriate number, so that the result can be shown in a reasonable cell width. This approach has been used to create the bar graph shown in Figure 4-37.

This format can also be used to highlight positive and negative values on your worksheet. You could add a column for the + and − displays, and place a formula in each cell within the column that is simply a reference to the corresponding value in the column being monitored. You could then scan this second column quickly to see which values were positive and negative.

Percent

With the Percent format you can display percentages attractively, with the % symbol added to the end of each cell. You can choose any number of decimal places between 0 and 15.

Entries to be formatted as percentages are entered as decimal fractions; for example, ten percent is entered as .1. When the Percent format is applied, the number you have entered is multiplied by 100

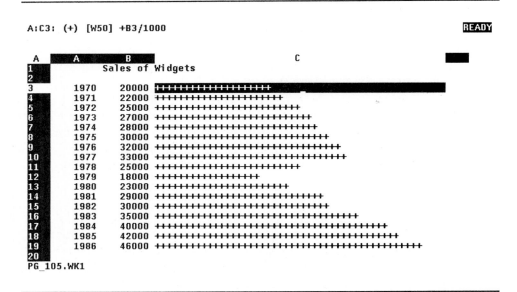

Figure 4-37.   Bar graph created with +/− format

before the % symbol is added. Thus, an entry of .1 becomes 10%, and an entry of 10 becomes 1000%. You can see why it is important to enter the correct decimal fraction for the percent you want.

In the Percent format the following entries will display as shown, depending on how many decimal places you specify:

Entry	0	2	4
5	500%	500.00%	500.0000%
−.089635	−9%	−8.96%	−8.9635%
.45	45%	45.00%	45.0000%
−1	−100%	−100.00%	−100.0000%
.12	12%	12.00%	12.0000%

The Percent format is used in many areas of business reports. Percentage growth rates, interest on loans, and sales increases all can be computed and formatted as percents.

Date/Time Format

This format is used for date and time entries. Release 3 can provide a single serial number that represents both the date and the time. The whole number portion of the entry represents the date, and the fractional portion of the entry represents the time.

Tip: Use the Automatic format if you need to enter a number of date or time serial numbers. Automatic format provides a quick way to enter dates and times without the need for @functions. You can enter the date or time in any of 1-2-3's formats if the cell is formatted as Automatic.

A number of built-in @functions of the package allow you to enter dates and times in worksheet cells. There are also package functions that allow you to access the system date and time. These functions will all be described in Chapter 7, and two will also be considered here. These are the @TODAY function, used in Release 1 and Release 1A to **access the current system date,** and the @NOW function, used in

Release 2 to access both the current system date and time. Release 2 will also accept @TODAY and convert it to @INT(@NOW). Release 3 will accept either @TODAY or @NOW and display both as today's date if the proper format is applied. In Release 3, @TODAY is no longer converted to the integer portion of @NOW, @INT(@NOW), as it was in Release 2.01. Neither @NOW nor @TODAY requires function arguments; they are entered into worksheet cells simply as either @NOW or @TODAY.

Using either of these functions requires that you respond with the proper date and time to the DOS prompts during the booting process. If you do not respond to the date and time prompts and your system does not have a clock card to keep track of date and time for you, the date will appear as "Jan 1 1980." If you respond to the DOS prompt, the value you give will be stored internally in your system for later reference and can be accessed with the @NOW and @TODAY functions.

1-2-3 shows dates as serial numbers representing the number of days from December 31, 1899, to the current day. The serial number for September 24, 1986, is 31679, for example. Without formatting, that is exactly the way the number will appear on your worksheet. Fortunately, Date formats provide a number of other options. You can display the date as 24-Sep-86, 24-Sep, or Sep-86. With Release 3 you also have such options as 09/24/86 and 09/86. Any of these present a much more understandable version of the date than the serial date that displays in a cell under General format.

Assuming that @NOW was entered in each of several cells and generated the serial number shown in the Entry column, here are the displays you would see with different Date formats:

Entry	DD-MMM-YY	DD-MM	MMM-YY	Long Int	Short Int
31679	24-Sep-86	24-Sep	Sep-86	09/24/86	09/24

The indicators for dates vary depending on which Date format you select. The following table lists the Date formats found in Release 3 and the indicators that will appear in the control panel for cells that have these formats added with a /Range command.

Indicator	Format
D1	(DD-MMM-YY)
D2	(DD-MMM)
D3	(MMM-YY)
D4	(MM/DD/YY)
D5	(MM/DD)

For each cell you will have to decide whether to apply a Date or a Time format, since both formats cannot be applied to the same cell. This means that although the @NOW function places both a time and a date in a cell, you will be able to see only one at a time. The one you see depends on the format you choose.

The whole number 1 makes up one day. To represent time, therefore, 1-2-3 uses decimal fractions of the number 1. Twelve hours is .5 and six hours is .25, for example. As you can see, the fractions are based on a 24-hour clock. As with dates, you will probably want to use the special Time formats to make the time easier to read. The Time format options are just as varied as the Date formats. A time of 10:00 PM can be represented as 10:00:00 PM, 10:00 PM, 22:00:00, or 22:00.

Time formats are accessed through the Date format option by selecting Time. There are four Time formats. Two use the AM and PM designation, and the other two are international formats that use a 24-hour day like military time.

The effect of format selection on the display of time in worksheet cells can be seen in the table that follows.

Entry	T1	T2	Long Int	Short Int
.25	06:00:00 AM	06:00 AM	06:00:00	06:00
.5	12:00:00 PM	12:00 PM	12:00:00	12:00
.75	06:00:00 PM	06:00 PM	18:00:00	18:00

Date and time entries are used in a variety of applications, such as to represent shipment receipts or line processing time. They can also be used to represent loan due dates, appointment dates, or order dates.

Text Format

Text format allows you to display actual formulas on the worksheet, rather than displaying the results of formula calculations, as will happen with any of the other formats. Using Text format causes a cell to display exactly what you enter. If your entry was a formula, 1-2-3 also remembers the result of the formula, and the results can be accessed with a reference to the cell.

The following table shows how different entries appear when a cell is formatted as text:

Entry	Text Display
+A1+A2	+A1+A2
+A3*A4/A5	+A3*A4/A5
Sales	Sales
23.56	23.56

When the cell pointer is on a cell formatted as text with a /Range command, the indicator (T) will appear in the upper line of the control panel.

The Text format can be used to create a documentation copy of a worksheet, containing the actual formulas used in worksheet calculations. For example, to create a documentation copy of the worksheet shown in Figure 4-38, follow these steps.

1. Use **/Worksheet Global Format Text** to set the global format to Text. This will not completely change the display, because some of the entries have been formatted with /Range commands, which always override global settings. Only columns R, S, and T are affected.

2. Use **/Range Format Reset P1..X15** and ENTER to reset all the Range formats back to global settings.

3. Move your cell pointer to column T. Use **/Worksheet Column Set-Width,** and press the RIGHT ARROW until column T is 51 characters across. Press ENTER to select 51 as the column width. Now you

have a copy of the worksheet with all the formulas documented. It should look like Figure 4-39.

After you learn about saving files in Chapter 8, "Working with Files," you will want to make sure that you never save a documentation file under the same filename you used for your original file. If you do, you will lose all the formats and column widths that you worked so hard to establish for it. In Chapter 6, "Printing," you will learn how to print a documentation copy of your worksheet so you will have a paper to file away and refer to if your disk copies are ever damaged or destroyed.

Hidden Format

Hidden format causes a cell to display as a blank; that is, 1-2-3 will suppress the display of the cell. The cell's contents have not been lost,

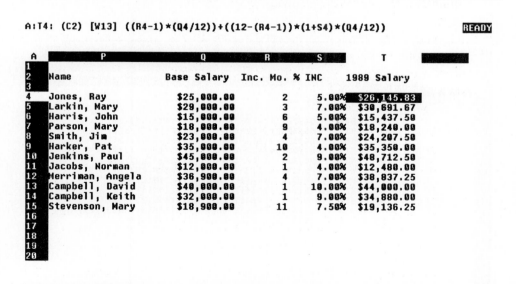

Figure 4-38.   Worksheet displaying results of formulas

even though they do not appear on the worksheet. They are still stored internally and are accessed when you reference the cell in a formula. In fact, the contents of the cell will display in the control panel when you move your cell pointer to the cell. You can hide the contents further by enabling worksheet protection as discussed in Chapter 5, "Basic Worksheet Commands." When a worksheet is protected, 1-2-3 displays "PR" in the control panel when the cell pointer is on a hidden cell.

With the Hidden format, all entries regardless of type will appear as blanks. The control panel indicator for a hidden cell, when the format is applied with a /Range command, is (H). In Figure 4-40, you see the cell pointer in a hidden cell, and the contents displayed in the control panel.

The main use of hidden cells is in macro applications. If the application is kept completely under macro control, the Hidden format could provide a measure of security. For more about macros, see Chapters 12 and 13.

Other Formats

Unlike the rest of the format options, the Other category provides access to a menu of four different format choices that are all new to

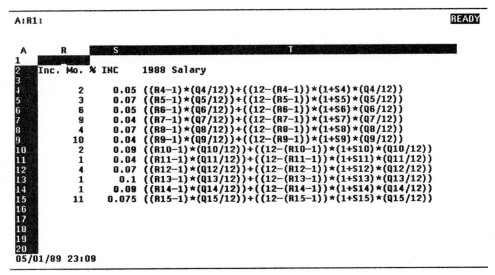

Figure 4-39.   Documentation copy displaying formulas

Release 3. The Other options essentially provide an extension to the options in the main Format menu, although each of the new formats is somewhat unique — providing either a temporary format, a format to be used with the existing formats, or a conversion to a label type entry.

Automatic

The Automatic format is the most powerful of all the formatting choices within 1-2-3. This format is a temporary format that will be converted to one of the other format types as soon as you make an entry in the cell. Automatic can supply the correct format for a variety of different data types. It allows you to make entries as you ultimately wish to see them, and uses the edit characters within your first entry in a cell to determine how the data will display. 1-2-3 then stores the data from your entry in a basic form.

A cell with an Automatic format can successfully handle Currency, Comma, Fixed, Percent, Scientific, Date, and Time formats. Entries in Date/Time format are automatically stored as date and time serial numbers. If you change a cell with an existing entry to Automatic, 1-2-3 will use the General format.

Figure 4-41 shows the effect of Automatic format in column B, assuming the entries in column A were entered exactly as shown.

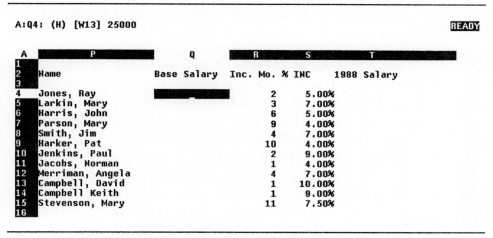

Figure 4-40.   Numbers hidden with the Hidden format

```
A:B19: [W17]                                                         READY

   A        A              B                      C              D
1   Entry Typed Automatic Format           Entry Stored  Format After Entry
2         $5                ($5)                      5            (C0())
3      $5.45             ($5.45)                   5.45           (C2())
4        7%                 (7%)                   0.07           (P0())
5     7.79%              (7.79%)                 0.0779           (P2())
6     5.678              (5.678)                  5.678           (F3())
7  8,125,145         (8,125,145)                8125145           (,0())
8  5.695E+03         (5.695E+03)                   5695           (S3())
9   12:05PM           (12:05 PM)        0.0534722222222           (D7())
10    15:30             (15:30) 0.645833333333333333             (D9())
11   3/15/90           (03/15/90)                 32947           (D4())
12  12-Mar-90         (12-Mar-90)                 32947           (D1())
13
```

Figure 4-41.   Effects of Automatic format

Column C shows how these entries are stored, and Column D shows the actual cell format after completing the entry shown in Column B. After you type your entry and press ENTER, the (A) for Automatic format is replaced by one of 1-2-3's other format entries.

If you want the cell entry formatted as Currency, precede your entry with a dollar sign. The entry $6 in a cell formatted as Automatic will display as $6. The entry 6.52 will display as 6.52, with a format of Fixed with 2 decimal places (F2). An entry of 4.2% will be stored as .042, with a format of Percent with 1 decimal place (P1), so it displays as you entered it. The entry .09987E+04 is stored as 998.7 in the cell, and displays as entered. An entry of 5,192 is stored as 5192 in the cell, with a display format of Comma with 0 decimal places (C0).

Using the Automatic format with date and time entries provides even more dramatic results, since it allows you to supply a date or a time in any of 1-2-3's date and time formats. This means you can generate the proper date and time serial numbers without the use of @functions. The entry 04/15/89 or 15-Apr-89 is stored as 32613, the date serial number for 4/15/89, and formats the cell as dictated by the style of your entry. Thus, if you use 04/15/89, the format for the cell is (D4); if you use 15-Apr-89, the format is (D1). A time entry of 12:30 or 12:30 PM is stored as .5208333333, and formats the cell with either (D9) or (D7), depending on which of the entries you used.

Tip: Automatic format occurs only once for a cell. Once an entry is made into an Automatic format cell, 1-2-3 changes the cell's format to match the format of the entry. New entries made in the cell retain the cell format of the first entry. If you want to change the format, you must use the /Range Format command.

Color

In many business models, negative numbers sound an alarm. Negative profits, cash flows, or sales trends need immediate attention. The Other Color Negative format can highlight these conditions with a different color while retaining the original format of the cell. Thus cells formatted as Currency, Comma, or Percent can have the added feature of a color that will change if they contain a negative number.

If your monitor does not support color display, 1-2-3 uses highlighted entries to signify negative entries. You can quickly scan a worksheet for the variation in the display, and focus on situations requiring urgent attention. The following worksheet displays a row of values in the Other Color Negative format. Note the difference in intensity of the negative numbers in D3 and E3. If you later decide to eliminate the color or highlighting from negative numbers, use the Other Color Reset option.

A:B3: (−) 89000   READY

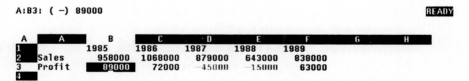

Label

This format adds a label indicator at the front of values entered after the format is applied. Existing value entries are not changed to labels. Cells formatted with the Other Label format have an (L) indicator in the control panel. This type of format is ideal for numbers that you do not want treated as values, such as social security numbers, zip codes, and phone numbers.

The effect of this format only applies to entries that you type. When 1-2-3 generates a series of entries with /Data Fill, the label prefix is not added, and the values display in General format.

The year numbers in the following worksheet are all generated after using the Other Label format on the range of cells where these numbers were to be entered. The current setting for global label prefix is used.

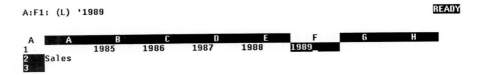

A:F1: (L) '1989

Parentheses

This format causes 1-2-3 to encase all numeric values in parentheses. The unique feature of this format is that it is supplemental to any existing format. A cell formatted as Currency will remain formatted as Currency while it is encased in parentheses, as in ($5). Likewise, cells formatted as Percent, Date, Time, or Scientific all retain their existing format. Even the format indicator in the control panel shows both formats, with Currency and Parentheses represented as "(C0( ))".

Figure 4-42 shows entries that were initially entered as Automatic, reformatted with Other Parentheses Yes. Notice how each of the formats generated by the entry into the Automatic cell were retained. To remove the parentheses from entries, use Other Parentheses No.

Advanced Features

The three options discussed in this section are not features you will need to change every day, like the other formatting options, but you may occasionally want to use them. One is the /Worksheet Global Default Other International option, which changes the way 1-2-3 handles punctuation, currency, date, and time displays, as well as negative numbers.

A:C20: [W21]

A	A	B	C	D
1	Entry Typed	Automatic Format	Entry Stored	Format After Entry
2	$5	$5	5	(C0)
3	$5.45	$5.45	5.45	(C2)
4	7%	7%	0.07	(P0)
5	7.79%	7.79%	0.0779	(P2)
6	5.678	5.678	5.678	(F3)
7	8,125,145	8,125,145	8125145	(,0)
8	5.695E+03	5.695E+03	5695	(S3)
9	12:05PM	12:05 PM	0.0534722222222	(D7)
10	15:30	15:30	0.645833333333333	(D9)
11	3/15/90	03/15/90	32947	(D4)
12	12-Mar-90	12-Mar-90	32947	(D1)
13				
14				

Figure 4-42.   Enclosing entries with parentheses

A related command, /Worksheet Global Other Clock, alters the clock display format on your screen. The third feature, the justification options available under /Range Justify, manipulates a column of text-type entries in your worksheet. Let's look at each of these options in more detail.

Other International Format Options

The /Worksheet Global Default Other International command is the longest command sequence discussed so far. This command allows you to customize the display for numeric punctuation, currency, date, and time.

Punctuation

The numeric punctuation indicators you can control are the point separator (that is, the decimal indicator in a number like 55.98), the thousands separator for numbers, and the argument separator in @functions. The default point separator is a period (.), but you have the option of changing it to a comma (,). The default thousands separator is a comma, and can be changed to a period (.) or a space. The argument separator is initially set as a comma; it can be changed to a period (.) or a semicolon (;). The Punctuation options are not chosen individually, but rather in a threesome, as follows:

Option	Point	Argument	Thousands
A (default)	.	,	,
B	,	.	.
C	.	;	,
D	,	;	.
E	.	,	space
F	,	.	space
G	.	;	space
H	,	;	space

The next table shows how each choice affects the display of numbers, and the arguments for @functions like @SUM.

Punctuation Option	Numeric Entry in Current Format	Function Arguments
A (default)	$1,200.50	@SUM(D2,A8..A10)
B	$1.200,50	@SUM(D2.A8..A10)
C	$1,200.50	@SUM(D2;A8..A10)
D	$1.200,50	@SUM(D2;A8..A10)
E	$1 200.50	@SUM(D2;A8..A10)
F	$1 200,50	@SUM(D2.A8..A10)
G	$1 200.50	@SUM(D2;A8..A10)
H	$1 200,50	@SUM(D2;A8..A10)

International Currency

This option allows you to change the currency symbol from the standard $ to one of the international currency symbols found in the LMBCS codes. In addition, you may choose to place the symbol at the end of your entry rather than at the beginning, as in the default setting. Examples of currency symbols you may wish to use are those for Dutch Guilders, Pounds, Yen, and Pesetas. The Compose sequence for these entries are as follows:

Currency	Compose Sequence	Symbol
Dutch guilders	ff	ƒ 67,893.00
Pounds	L=	£ 67,893.00
Yen	Y=	¥ 67,893.00
Pesetas	PT	₨ 67,893.00

To change from $ to one of these symbols, invoke /Worksheet Global Default Other International Currency, and then use COMPOSE (ALT-F1) with the appropriate character sequence, followed by ENTER. The Compose sequence allows you to enter more than one character in a single position. To access it, hold down the ALT key while you press F1, then type the characters specified in the table. For Pounds you would type an **L** followed by =, for example.

When this International Currency option is combined with the numeric punctuation options, you have an effective way to display international currency amounts. Another option is accessing the full set of LMBCS codes. Pressing ALT-F1 (COMPOSE) twice, type the LMBCS group from Appendix D, and then type a hyphen, followed by the three-digit Key code from the LMBCS appendix for the character you wish to generate. Once you select the currency character, 1-2-3 prompts you to determine whether you want the character to be a suffix or a prefix.

International Date

The international date formats—D4 and D5—can be altered with the Date option from the /Worksheet Global Default Other International command. The initial setting for the international date is MM/DD/YY. This can be changed to three other forms. The choices for this setting are shown on the following page.

A	MM/DD/YY
B	DD/MM/YY
C	DD.MM.YY
D	YY-MM-DD

The application of these formats to D4 and D5 are shown in the following table for the entry of September 24, 1986:

Option	D4	D5
A	09/24/86	09/24
B	24/09/86	24/09
C	24.09.86	24.09
D	86-09-24	09-24

International Time

The appearance of the international time formats can be changed with this option. Format D8 shows hours, minutes, and seconds; format D9 shows only hours and minutes. The initial international time setting is HH:MM:SS. Each of the four options is indicated by a letter, as follows:

A	HH:MM:SS
B	HH.MM.SS
C	HH,MM,SS
D	HHhMMmSSs

Using these settings to display the time for 12:30:25 PM would result in the following:

Option	D8	D9
A	12:30:25	12:30
B	12.30.25	12.30

C	12,30,25	12,30
D	12h30m25s	12h30m

Negative

The Worksheet Global Default International Negative option allows you to customize how negative numbers in the Comma or Currency format will be displayed. The default setting is to enclose these numbers in parentheses, but you can also use a minus sign. Once you select this command you can choose either parentheses or a minus sign to affect all the entries in the spreadsheet.

Update

Any changes made with /Worksheet Global Default Other International commands are in effect only for the current session. Next time you load 1-2-3, the original worksheet global default settings will be in effect. If you wish to make your changes permanent, invoke the /Worksheet Global Default Update command to save your custom settings. This will make your changes the new global default values, and they will be in effect the next time 1-2-3 is loaded into memory.

Clock Display

The clock display on your screen, when the current worksheet is not on disk, changes to the current filename as soon as you save the current file or retrieve a file that is stored on disk. If you would prefer to retain the clock display, you can change the setting for this option and 1-2-3 will display the clock at all times. You have several format options for the clock display. Use /Worksheet Global Default Other Clock, and select Standard, International, None, Clock, or Filename, (see Figure 4-43).

Standard is the default display for the clock. It displays the date in the long format: DD-MMM-YY. The time displays as HH:MM AM/PM. This display will only be used before a file is saved to disk or when the clock is active on the screen.

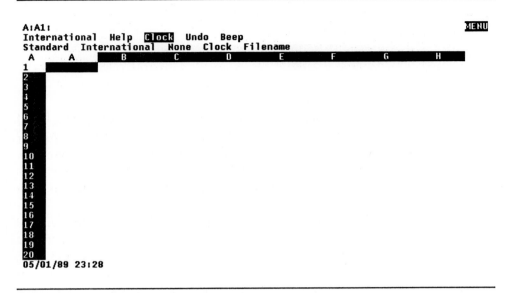

Figure 4-43.   Menu for /Worksheet Global Default Other

Selecting International changes the display of both date and time when they are on the screen. Time becomes the short international format, D9. Date displays in the long international format, D4. The clock display with International chosen looks like Figure 4-43.

Choosing None eliminates the time display from the screen. This is useful for applications where you do not wish to have part of the screen dedicated to a time and date display.

The Clock option ensures that the clock display is always on the screen. It will use either Standard or International display, depending on your earlier selection.

Choosing Filename for the Clock display restores the filename display if you previously changed it to Clock. Filename is the default setting for this feature.

/Range Justify

The /Range Justify command is as close as 1-2-3 comes to providing word processing features. It adjusts the length of a line of text to fit within margin limitations.

With this command, you can enter one or more long labels in a column and then, after the entry is complete, decide how many characters wide the display of this information should be. The width of the display is determined by selecting a justify range. If that range is two cells wide, for example, the long labels will be redistributed so that they take up more rows but display only in two columns.

/Range Justify does not provide full word processing support, but it does allow you to write readable documentation on the screen, or write a short memo that references worksheet data. It frees you from having to concentrate on the length of your entry as you type. When all your data is typed in, 1-2-3 will adjust the line length according to your specifications.

Figure 4-44 contains an example of long labels entered into A1..A6 of the worksheet. The labels all have different lengths. Suppose you decide that the display should be confined to columns A through C. (The labels are entered in column A and will remain in that location; what you are changing is the space they borrow for display purposes.) To make the change, take the following steps:

1. Move your cell pointer to the beginning of the range you will use for display—A1 in the example.

2. Type /**Range Justify**.

A:A1: 'To test the /Range Justify command, we will type a series   `READY`

A	A	B	C	D	E	F	G	H
1	To test the /Range Justify command, we will type a series							
2	of long labels in Column A. Then we will attempt to confine the							
3	display of these long labels to the first three columns.							
4	To do this we will use /Range Justify and specify our justify range							
5	as A1..C1. The labels will be shortened to use only the allotted							
6	spaces and will require additional spreadsheet rows for the display.							
7								

Figure 4-44.   Worksheet containing long labels

3. Highlight the cells in the range A1..C1 with the RIGHT ARROW key.

4. Press ENTER. Your justified data should look like Figure 4-45.

To make the display wider again, move your cell pointer to A1 and start the process over. For example, you might want to specify A1..F1 as the justify range. The first six columns would then be used for the display.

If there is information in column A, in cells after the end of the justify range, the /Range Justify command will displace that information as it expands the long label down the worksheet. Since the label was originally entered in column A, *only* the cell entries in column A will be displaced. Even if the justify range includes columns A..C, and there is information in the cells to the right of column A, it will not be displaced. For instance, a table in cells B10..C14 would be unaffected by the paragraph rearrangement shown in Figure 4-45. Instead, the label display in column A would be truncated in rows 10 through 14, just as it is when an entry to the right of any long label causes the label display to be truncated.

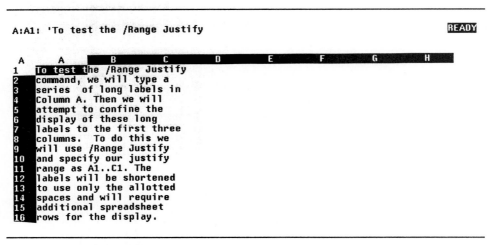

Figure 4-45.   Worksheet with long labels justified

Conclusion

In this chapter you have learned how to make many changes in the appearance of your worksheet. These changes do not alter the internal accuracy of your data, and they can make the difference between an amateur and a professional presentation of the information contained in a worksheet. You should now feel confident in using either /Worksheet or /Range commands to change the worksheet format.

In the next chapter you will learn how to use many additional /Range and /Worksheet commands for model building.

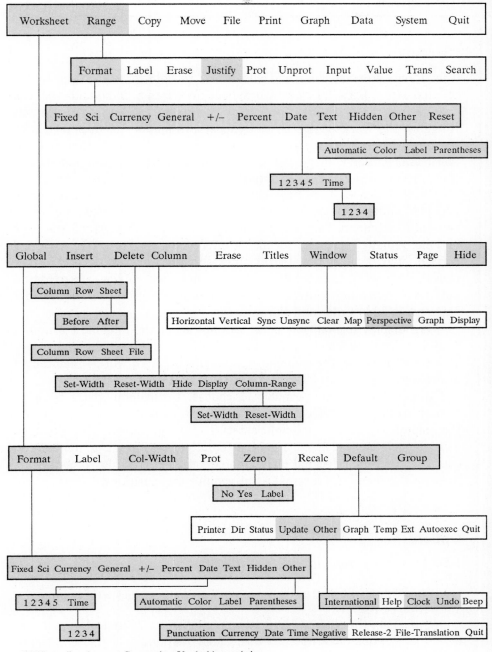

WORKSHEET DISPLAY

/Range Format

Description

The /Range Format command allows you to determine the appearance of numeric entries on your worksheet. With this command you can change the specific display format for one or many cells in a contiguous range on the worksheet. You can choose the number of decimal places displayed (0 to 15) for most formats, and determine whether the numeric information is displayed as currency, a scientific notation, a date, a time, or one of several other options.

With Release 3, a new category of format options have been grouped under /Range Format Other. These are outlined later as a separate command, due to the number and significance of the new options. A new Automatic format is offered to speed up the entry and correct display of a variety of value entries. This Automatic format provides a special time savings for date and time entries, since you do not need @function entries. Additional options in the Other format category include Color and Parentheses.

The display format you select will not affect the internal storage of numbers. You can elect to display a number with seven decimal places as a whole number, for example, but all seven places will be maintained internally.

Regardless of the format you choose, the column must be wide enough to display your selection. For all the formats except General, if the column is not wide enough, asterisks (*) will appear. For example, using a column width of 3 and attempting to format a number as Currency with two decimal places would result in a display of asterisks, because the $ and the decimal point require two positions.

Options

1-2-3 provides a menu of the following /Range Format options:

Fixed Sci Currency , General +/− Percent Date Text Hidden Other Reset

To employ the /Range Format command, enter **/Range Format** and select the option you wish to use. Then respond to 1-2-3's prompts concerning the number of decimal places (or the Date format) you desire. Finally, select the range of cells to be formatted by entering either the cell address, or a range name, or by highlighting the cells with your cell pointer.

Fixed   Fixed format allows you to display all entries with a specific number of decimal places. Two places are the default, but you may select any number between 0 and 15. Examples with three decimal places are .007, 9.000, and 4.156.

Sci   Scientific format displays numbers in exponential form, showing the power of 10 that the number must be multiplied by. This format allows you to concisely represent very large or very small numbers. From 0 to 15 places can be specified for the multiplier. Some examples with two decimal places are 6.78E-20, 4.11E+5, and 0.78E+8.

Currency   Currency format will cause your entry to be preceded by a dollar sign ($). It will also insert a separator such as a comma between the thousands and hundreds positions. You may specify from 0 to 15 decimal places for this format; 2 is the default. Negative amounts will appear in parentheses. Examples with two decimal places are $3.40, $1,400.98, and ($89.95).

, (Comma)   Comma format is identical to the Currency format, except that Comma lacks the dollar sign ($). Comma format uses the thousands separator. You may specify any number of decimal places you want between 0 and 15; 2 is the default. Negative numbers are displayed in parentheses. Examples with two decimal places are 1,200.00, (5,678.00), and 45.00.

General   General is the default format for 1-2-3. With it the leading zero integer will always appear, as in 0.78, but trailing zeros will be suppressed. If the number is very large or very small, it will appear in Scientific notation. Examples of numeric displays with the General format are 15.674, 2.7E+12, and 0.67543.

+/−   +/−format produces a horizontal bar graph showing the relative size of numbers. Each integer is represented by a symbol. For example, −3 would be − − −, and 5 would be + + + + +. A period (.) is used to represent 0.

Percent   Percent format displays your entries as percentages. Each entry will be multiplied by 100, and a % symbol will be added to the end. Because of this multiplication, you must enter percents as their decimal equivalent. For example, enter .05 for 5%. If you enter 5 and format the cell as Percent, it will display as 500%. You may specify from 0 to 15 decimal places; 2 is the default. Examples with two decimal places are 4.00%, 3.15%, and 1200.00%.

Date   The Date option provides a second menu of possibilities. From this second menu you can select specific formats for the date. The formats accessible through the Date option are

D1	(DD-MMM-YY)	08-Sep-86
D2	(DD-MMM)	08-Sep
D3	(MMM-YY)	Sep-86
D4	(MM/DD/YY)	09/08/86*
D5	(MM/DD)	09/08*

*These formats can be changed to a number of other formats with the /Worksheet Global Default Other International command.

Time formats are accessed through the Date format. When you select Time from the Date options, a menu of four Time formats are presented. Two of the formats use the AM and PM designation, the other two are International formats that use a 24-hour day like military time. The formats available for the display of time in your worksheet cells are

(D6) T1	HH:MM:SS AM/PM	06:00:00 AM
(D7) T2	HH:MM	06:00 AM
(D8) T3	Long International	06:00:00*
(D9) T4	Short International	06:00*

*These formats can be changed to a number of other formats with the /Worksheet Global Default Other International command.

Text   Text format displays specified cells exactly as you have entered them. In the case of formulas, the formula rather than the result will be displayed.

Hidden   Hidden format causes the selected cells to appear blank on the screen. If you move your cell pointer to a hidden cell, the control panel will display the cell's contents.

Other   The Other selection offers a number of new Release 3 formatting options. Due to the significance of these options they are covered separately under the command /Range Format Other.

Reset   This option returns the specified range of cells to the default format setting. The only two options for eliminating a /Range format are to use /Range Format Reset, or apply a new /Range format. Erasing a range on the worksheet with /Range Erase does not affect the format of the cells in the range.

/Range Format Other

Description

The /Range Format Other command provides additional formatting options. All of these selections are new to Release 3 and offer the potential for additional model customization. The Automatic formatting option found in this group of commands also offers time savings in data entry.

Like the other /Range Format options, the features available through this command can affect any block of cells on one or more sheets in a multiple-sheet file.

Options

The formatting features available in the Other category provide a diverse range of options. The Automatic feature affects new entries, and should only be used on blank cells. The other /Range Format Other options can be used either before or after you make your entries.

Automatic   Existing values in a range formatted as Automatic will display in the General format, even if they were previously assigned another format. New entries will be formatted according to the style of the entry made. This feature supports Fixed, Scientific, Currency, Comma, Percent, Label, Date and Time formats. Date and time entries must be in one of the acceptable Date or Time formats. New entries assume the format established by the initial cell entry after the Automatic format is applied. This format stores labels that start with numbers and invalid formulas as labels.

Note

The Automatic format option only works for the initial entry of a number. Using it for existing entries will eliminate the existing format, and may not provide the results that you want.

Color   This format option displays negative numbers in a different color or in a brighter intensity, or resets the color option to eliminate special treatment for negative numbers. The original format applied to the cell remains when the Color option is selected. The two Color options are Negative and Reset.

Label   This format adds a label prefix for new entries only. Existing entries are displayed in the General format without a label prefix added.

Note

Entries made with the /Data Fill command are not converted to labels, even if the Other Label format is in effect for the affected cells.

Parentheses   This format either encloses all numeric values in parentheses or removes parentheses added with this command. Like the

Color option, this format retains the original format for the cell. The two options are Yes to add parentheses, and No to remove them.

/Range Justify

Description

The /Range Justify command lets you change the way a label is displayed. Once a label is entered (for instance, a long label entered in cell A1), you can use /Range Justify to redistribute the label so that it is displayed differently. For instance, the long label in cell A1 might be displayed in the range A1..C3. The width of the display is determined by selecting a justify range, which may be one to several cells wide (the maximum is 512 characters) and one to several rows long.

If you use /Range Justify to redistribute a label in cell A1 to the single-row justify range A1..C1, the label is reformatted to display in columns A through C. Sufficient rows are used to display the full label. The label will be contained only in the cells of column A, however.

Information in cells to the right of a justify range is not displaced when you use /Range Justify. Instead, the display of a label in the justify range is truncated—even though the contents of the cells containing the label are not affected.

Options

You have the option of specifying one or more rows for the justify range. If you specify one row, 1-2-3 will include all labels from that row down to either the bottom of the worksheet or the first row that does not contain a label. Cells containing nonlabel entries below the justify range may be shifted up or down, depending on the space requirements for the justified labels.

If you specify more than one row with /Range Justify, you assume the burden of allowing sufficient space for the justification. If there is not enough space in the range you choose, you will see the error message "Justify Range Is Full Or Line Too Long." With a selection of more than one row for the range, only the labels in the range down to the first nonlabel entry will be justified. Also, when you specify more than one row, cells outside the justify range will be unaffected.

Note

Do not use this command for cells that have been assigned range names. Although the contents of the cell may be displaced, the range name will still be assigned to the same cell.

/Worksheet Column

Description

The /Worksheet Column command allows you to change the characteristics of the worksheet columns. You can use the command to change the column width and to hide and display columns.

Note

When the GROUP mode indicator is on, all worksheets in the current file are affected by this command.

Options

After entering /Worksheet Column, you will be presented with the following options:

Set-Width Reset-Width Hide Display Column-Range

Set-Width   After choosing this option, either use the RIGHT and LEFT ARROW keys to change the column width of the current column, or type in the exact width desired for that column. With Release 3, any width between 1 and 240 is acceptable. If you choose a column width narrower than the width of your data, the value data will display as asterisks.

Reset-Width   This option returns the width setting for the current column to the default setting—that is, either the initial default of 9, or the setting established with /Worksheet Global Col-Width if that command has been used.

Hide   This option affects the display and printing of worksheet data. You can hide one or many columns, depending on the range you specify for this command. The hidden columns will not appear on your display. They also will not be printed, even if the print range spans cells on both sides of them. These hidden columns only appear when 1-2-3 is in the POINT mode; an asterisk will appear next to the column letter.

Hide will not affect the data in the cells. At any time you can bring the data back into view with the Display option.

Display   This option allows you to redisplay one or more hidden columns. Each hidden column will have an asterisk next to the column letter. The columns can be redisplayed either by highlighting a cell within each column you wish to redisplay, or by entering a range that includes the hidden columns you wish to redisplay.

Column-Range   This option allows you to change the width in one or more columns on the current worksheet. Column-Range functions the same as the /Worksheet Set-Width and Reset-Width commands, except that it allows you to work with more than one column. Any group of adjacent columns on the current worksheet can be changed. The two selections available for this choice are Set-Width and Reset-Width.

/Worksheet Delete

Description

The /Worksheet Delete command allows you to delete unneeded rows, columns, and sheets. These rows, columns, and sheets may be blank, or they may contain data. You can use this command to delete single or multiple rows and columns. Deletions from the middle of a range cause 1-2-3 to automatically adjust the range to compensate for the deletions.

Options

The /Worksheet Delete command provides four options: Row, Column, Sheet, and File. The last option, File, is covered in Chapter 8, "Working with Files." You also have the option of deleting one or many rows, columns, or sheets with one execution of the command. The best approach is to place your cell pointer on the top row or left column to be deleted (if you are deleting rows or columns). Enter **/Worksheet Delete Row** or **/Worksheet Delete Column**, and then move your cell pointer to include all the rows or columns you wish to have deleted. To delete sheets, place the pointer anywhere on the first sheet you wish to delete.

Notes

A complete row, column, or sheet must be deleted, since 1-2-3 does not provide a feature for deleting part of the selected segment. You may want to make sure that Undo is enabled before deleting, or you can save the file before you begin as a precaution.

When the GROUP mode indicator is on, deleting rows or columns affects all the sheets in the active file.

/Worksheet Global Col-Width

Description

The /Worksheet Global Col-Width command allows you to change the default column width for every column on the worksheet.

Options

After entering /Worksheet Global Col-Width, either use the RIGHT and LEFT ARROW keys to change the column width, or type in the exact width desired. With Release 3, any width between 1 and 240 is acceptable.

Note

With the GROUP mode indicator on, the global column width is changed in all active sheets in the current file. Without the GROUP indicator on, only the current sheet is changed.

/Worksheet Global Default Other Clock

Description

This command lets you display the format for the date and time in the left corner of your screen.

Options

This command provides the following five options:

Standard International None Clock Filename

Standard   This is the default setting used when the clock displays. It displays the date as DD-MMM-YY, and the time as HH:MM AM/PM.

International   This option displays the date in the current long International format (month, day, and year will be shown), and the time in the current short international format (hours and minutes based on a 24-hour clock). The International format options are discussed in more detail under /Worksheet Global Default Other International. This option does not override the default display of the filename.

None   This option suppresses the filename or the date and time display in the lower left corner of the screen.

Clock   This option causes the clock to display at all times, overriding the default display of the filename.

Filename   This is the default setting for the clock. It causes 1-2-3 to display the filename for file on disk. On a new worksheet that has not been saved, the clock continues to display.

/Worksheet Global Default Other International

Description

The /Worksheet Global Default Other International command allows you to customize the display for numeric punctuation, currency, date, and time.

Options

Select from these Other International options:

Punctuation Currency Date Time Negative Release-2 File-Translation Quit

Since the Release-2 and File-Translation options are directly related to files, they are covered in Chapter 8, "Working with Files."

Punctuation   The numeric punctuation indicators you can control are the point separator (the decimal indicator in numbers like 55.98), the thousands separator for numbers, and the argument separator used in @functions. The default point separator is a period (.), but you have the option of changing it to a comma (,). The initial thousands separator is a comma; It can be changed to a period (.) or a space. The argument separator is initially set as a comma; It can be changed to a period (.) or a semicolon (;). The options are not chosen individually, but in a three-some after you select Punctuation. The options available are shown in the following table:

Option	Point	Argument	Thousands
A	.	,	,
B	,	.	.
C	.	;	,
D	,	;	.
E	.	,	space
F	,	.	space

G	.	;	space
H	,	;	space

Currency   This option allows you to change the currency symbol from the standard $ to one of the international currency symbols found in the LMBCS codes. You can also use any of the other LMBCS codes if the currency symbol you want is not in the table. You have the further choice of placing the symbol at the end of your entry rather than at the beginning, as in the initial setting.

To change the currency indicator, invoke /Worksheet Global Default International Currency, and then use COMPOSE with the appropriate two character sequence. Or press COMPOSE twice, type the LMBCS group you want to use, then a hyphen, followed by the Key code for the LMBCS character you want to use. The Compose sequence allows you to enter more than one character in a single position. To access it, hold down the ALT key while you press F1, then type the characters specified. (For example, you would type l followed by = for Pounds.) To access the LMBCS characters using the Key codes, you must press ALT-F1 (COMPOSE) twice.

Date   The International Date formats (D4 and D5) can be altered with the Date option under the /Worksheet Global Default Other International command. The initial setting for the International Date (option A) is MM/DD/YY. This can be changed to three other options, as follows:

B	DD/MM/YY
C	DD.MM.YY
D	YY-MM-DD

Time   The appearance of the International Time formats can be changed with this option. Format D8 shows hours, minutes, and seconds; format D9 shows only hours and minutes. The initial International Time setting (option A) is HH:MM:SS. The three options to which this setting can be changed are

B	HH.MM.SS

C	HH,MM,SS
D	HHhMMmSSs

As an example, using these settings to display the time for 12:30:25 PM would result in the following:

Option	D8	D9
A	12:30:25	12:30
B	12.30.25	12.30
C	12,30,25	12,30
D	12h30m25s	12h30m

Negative   This option allows you to set 1-2-3 to use either minus signs or parentheses for negative numbers in the Comma and Currency formats.

/Worksheet Global Default Other Undo

Description

This command allows you to enable and disable 1-2-3's Undo feature (ALT-F4). When it is enabled, you can reverse (undo) the last command sequence. If Undo is disabled, the ALT-F4 (UNDO) key will have no effect on the worksheet.

Options

The Undo command has two options: Enable and Disable.

/Worksheet Global Default Update

Description

The /Worksheet Global Default Update command allows you to save changes you have made to 1-2-3's default global settings with the /Worksheet Global Default commands, so that the new settings will be available the next time you work with 1-2-3. The settings will be saved in the 123.CNF file on your 1-2-3 disk.

/Worksheet Global Format

Description

The /Worksheet Global Format command allows you to change the default display format for the entire worksheet. All numeric entries on the worksheet will use the format chosen with this command unless they have been formatted with the /Range Format command, which has priority over /Worksheet Global Format.

Options

To define your format selection, select among these menu options:

   Fixed Sci Currency , General +/− Percent Date Text Hidden Other

Fixed   Fixed format allows you to display all entries with a specific number of decimal places. Select any number between 0 and 15; 2 is the default. Examples with three decimal places are .007, 9.000, and 4.156.

Sci   Scientific format displays numbers in exponential form, showing the power of 10 that the number must be multiplied by. This format allows you to concisely represent very large or very small numbers. From 0 to 15 places can be specified for the multiplier. Some examples with two decimal places are 6.78E −20, 4.11E + 5, and 0.78E + 8.

Currency   Currency format will cause your entries to be preceded by a dollar sign ($). It will also insert a separator such as a comma between the thousands and hundreds positions. You may specify from 0 to 15

decimal places for the Currency format; 2 is the default. Negative amounts will appear in parentheses. Examples with two decimal places are $3.40, $1,400.98, and ($89.95).

, (Comma)   Comma format is identical to the Currency format, except that Comma lacks the dollar sign ($). Comma format uses the thousands separator. You may specify the number of decimal places you want between 0 and 15; 2 is the default. Negative numbers are displayed in parentheses. Examples with two decimal places are 1,200.00, (5,678.00), and 45.00.

General   General is the default format for 1-2-3. With it the leading zero integer will always appear, as in 0.78, but trailing zeros will be suppressed. If the number is very large or very small, it will appear in Scientific notation. Examples of numeric displays with the General format are 15.674, 2.7E+12, and 0.67543.

+/−   +/− format produces a horizontal bar graph showing the relative size of numbers. Each integer is represented by a symbol. For example −3 would be − − −, and 5 would be + + + + +. A period (.) is used to represent 0.

Percent   Percent format displays your entries as percentages. Each entry will be multiplied by 100, and a % symbol will be added to the end. Because of this multiplication, you must enter percents as their decimal equivalent. For example, you must enter .05 for 5%. If you enter 5 and format the cell as Percent, it will display as 500%. You may specify from 0 to 15 decimal places; 2 is the default. Examples with two decimal places are 4.00%, 3.15%, and 1200.00%.

Date   The Date option provides a second menu of possibilities. From this second menu you can select specific formats for the date. The formats accessible through the Date option are as follows:

D1	(DD-MMM-YY)	08-Sep-86
D2	(DD-MMM)	08-Sep

D3	(MMM-YY)	Sep-86
D4	(MM/DD/YY)	09/08/86*
D5	(MM/DD)	09/08*

*These formats can be changed to a number of other formats with the /Worksheet Global Default Other International command.

Time formats are accessed through the Date format. When you select Time from the Date format options, a menu of four Time formats will be presented. Two of the formats use the AM and PM designation, and the other two are International formats that use a 24-hour day like military time. The formats available for the display of time in your worksheet cells are

(D6) T1	HH:MM:SS AM/PM	06:00:00 AM
(D7) T2	HH:MM	06:00 AM
(D8) T3	Long International	06:00:00*
(D9) T4	Short International	06:00*

*These formats can be changed to a number of other formats with the /Worksheet Global Default Other International command.

Text   Text format displays specified cells exactly as you have entered them. In the case of formulas, the formula rather than the result will be displayed.

Hidden   Hidden format causes the selected cells to appear blank on the screen. If you move your cell pointer to a hidden cell, the control panel will display the cell's contents.

Other   The Other selection options provide a variety of new options under Release 3. Due to the variety of options possible, the Other formats are covered separately under /Worksheet Global Format Other.

/Worksheet Global Format Other

Description

This command provides access to a variety of new Release 3 format possibilities.

Options

This command has the following options:

Automatic When Automatic formatting is used, new entries will be formatted according to the style of the entry made. This format supports Fixed, Scientific, Currency, Comma, Percent, Date and Time formats. Date and time entries must be in one of the acceptable Date or Time formats. New entries assume the format established by the initial cell entry after the automatic format is applied. Stores labels that start with numbers and invalid formulas as labels.

Note

The Automatic format option only works for the initial entry of a number. Using it for existing entries will eliminate the existing format, and may not provide the results that you want.

Color This format option displays negative numbers in a different color or in a brighter intensity, or resets the color option to eliminate special treatment for negative numbers. This option is used in addition to any other format that may have been applied to the cell. The two Color options are Negative and Reset.

Label This format adds a label prefix for new entries only. Existing entries are displayed in the General format without a label prefix added.

Note

Entries made with the /Data Fill command are not converted to labels even if the Other Label format is in effect for the affected cells.

Parentheses   This format either encloses all numeric values in parentheses or removes parentheses added with this command. The two options are Yes to add parentheses, and No to remove them. Parentheses are in addition to any other format the cell might have.

/Worksheet Global Group

Description

This command allows you to determine whether or not you wish to work only with the current sheet, or with all of the sheets in the file. When GROUP mode is in effect, a status indicator appears at the bottom of the screen. With GROUP on, /Range Format, /Range Protect, /Range Unprotect, /Worksheet Titles, /Worksheet Page, /Worksheet Insert and /Worksheet Delete operate on all the sheets in the current worksheet file. The /Worksheet Global commands Col-Width, Format, Label, Prot, and Zero also affect all worksheets when GROUP is enabled.

GROUP mode also affects the movement of the cell pointer from sheet to sheet. While in GROUP mode, the cell pointer is moved to its same position in any new sheets displayed. Without GROUP mode on, the cell pointer is moved to the position it was in the last time the new sheet was viewed.

As soon as GROUP is activated, the global and format changes for the current worksheet are applied to all sheets in the file. The column widths are affected in the same manner.

Options

The two options for this command are Enable to activate GROUP mode, and Disable. When GROUP is disabled, only the current sheet is affected by commands. The default is for GROUP to be disabled.

/Worksheet Global Zero

Description

This command allows you to select how 1-2-3 displays cells that have a value equal to zero. The options let you display a zero, hide the zero, or display a label.

Options

The /Worksheet Global Zero Command presents three options: Yes, No, and Label. The default is No, which allows zero values to display. Choosing the Yes option will suppress the display of zero values. The Label option, which is new in Release 3, prompts you for a label (other than 0) that 1-2-3 will display for cells that have a zero value. With all of these options, the original value (a zero or a formula) still appears in the control panel when the cell is highlighted.

/Worksheet Hide

Description

This command allows you to hide and redisplay sheets in the active worksheet file. You can indicate a range of one or more adjacent sheets.

Options

This command's two options are Enable to eliminate the sheets from view and access, and Disable to make them available again. Once you select one of these options, you must select one cell from the adjacent worksheets that you want to hide or redisplay.

Note

Changes made during GROUP mode affect hidden sheets. Also, a reference to a range that spans the hidden worksheets includes the appropriate cells in the hidden worksheets.

/Worksheet Insert

Description

The /Worksheet Insert command can be used to add blank rows, columns, and sheets to your worksheet files. These blank areas can be used to improve readability or to allow for the addition of new information to your worksheet.

Inserts made to the middle of a range of cells will automatically expand the reference for a range name applied to those cells. The same is true for formulas that reference this range; they will automatically be expanded to allow for the additional rows, columns, or sheets.

Options

This command provides three options: Row, Column, and Sheet, which are listed on a menu. Columns are always added to the left of the cell pointer location or the range you specify. Rows are always added above the cell pointer or the range you specify. New sheets can be added before or after the current sheet. After you select whether you want the new sheets before or after the current worksheet, 1-2-3 prompts you for the number of worksheets you want to insert. Enter a number between 1 and 255. 1-2-3 limits the total number of worksheets to 256.

/Worksheet Window Perspective

Description

This command allows you to view three consecutive sheets at one time. 1-2-3 automatically sizes the screen for the three sheets. To restore the display, use /Worksheet Window Clear for a permanent change, or ALT-F6 (ZOOM) for a temporary change.

Basic Worksheet Commands

This chapter focuses on menu commands that will extend your productivity in using the worksheet. In the chapter you will learn additional commands on the Worksheet menus.

You will also use /Range commands — to name worksheet cells and create notes regarding their contents. Other /Range commands will help you find and optionally change entries within formulas or labels. /Range commands let you transpose data from a row layout to a column layout, or from a layout across worksheets to a row or column on another worksheet. You can also use /Range commands to establish a restricted input area.

The /Copy command and the /Move command will improve your skill at developing new worksheets. You will also be introduced to a variety of new Worksheet options that allow you to use your Worksheet data more effectively.

By the time you have finished reading this chapter, you will have experience with all the worksheet commands except the ones with a very specialized purpose. A complete list of the commands you will work with in this chapter is shown on the command tree at the beginning of the Basic Worksheet Command Reference Section.

Working with Ranges

In Chapter 4 you learned to use some of the /Range commands to change the appearance of your worksheet. In this chapter you will expand your range options with commands that allow you to access cells through range names rather than cell addresses. You will also learn /Range commands that can change a worksheet column into a worksheet row. With Release 3, you can also change the layout of data that spans multiple sheets, transposing rows into columns, or taking data displayed across sheets and placing it in a single row or column of a single sheet. You will find out how to freeze formulas at their existing values for a large or small range of cells. You will be introduced to additional commands that alter the worksheet format, either erasing all entries for a range or changing the justification for labels stored in the range. Finally, you will learn how to use the new search features that locate matching entries in a formula or label.

Methods of Specifying Cell Ranges

You can communicate with 1-2-3 in a variety of ways about the range you wish to work with. The easiest method is using the arrow keys to point to the desired range. Pointing offers the advantage of letting you visually verify the range you have chosen, since it highlights the range cells as you expand or contract the range with the arrow keys. Pointing works only after a complete range is suggested. If a command references a single cell, type a period to turn the single cell address into a range, thereby locking the beginning of the range in place at this address. You can then expand the range to include additional cells by moving the cell pointer until you reach the end of the range you want.

In Figure 5-1, 1-2-3 suggests a range beginning at a location where you are using the /Range Format command from Chapter 4. If your cell pointer is positioned at the beginning of the range before you invoke the menu with a slash (/), you need only move with the arrow keys to complete the range, as shown in Figure 5-2. Notice that 1-2-3 highlights the range when you use this method.

If you forget to position your cell pointer properly before invoking one of the /Range commands, you will have to unlock the beginning of the range before you can change it. To do this, press ESC and move the cell pointer to the desired location. You must again lock in the beginning of the range by entering a period before you begin to expand the range with the cell pointer movement keys. If the beginning of a range is not locked into place, 1-2-3 displays only the beginning of the range, as shown in Figure 5-3. If you then move to the end of the range without locking the beginning in place, only the last cell in the range is highlighted.

You can use other keys in combination with the arrow keys to save time when pointing out a range. For example, in Figure 5-4 the cell pointer is located in A1. If you invoke a command that suggests a range,

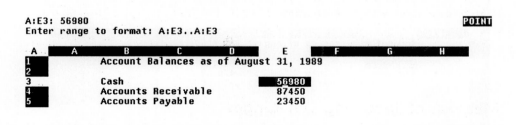

Figure 5-1.   Example of a range being formatted

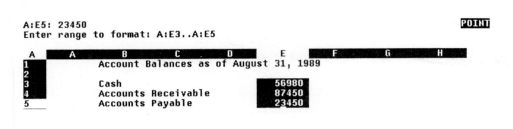

Figure 5-2.   Highlighting the range to be formatted

it will display the range as A:A1..A:A1, indicating a single-cell range that begins and ends in cell A1 on sheet A. To select the complete rectangle of cells shown, in response to the prompt for the range, press END followed by RIGHT ARROW. This moves your cell pointer to the last entry on the right. To move to the bottom of the column, press END and DOWN ARRROW. This will include all the filled cells in the selected range, as shown in Figure 5-5.

The END key can be used in other situations with a little planning. Let's say you want to format all the cells in row 3 but there are not entries in every cell. First move to the beginning of row 3 (cell A3), invoke /**Range Format Fixed,** and press ENTER. END and RIGHT ARROW will not work here because of the breaks in the entries. But if row 1 has entries in every cell and you press HOME to move to A1, and then END and RIGHT ARROW, you can then press the DOWN ARROW twice for the exact selection you wanted, as you can see in Figure 5-6.

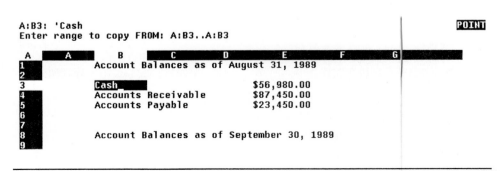

Figure 5-3.   1-2-3 displays only the first cell in the range

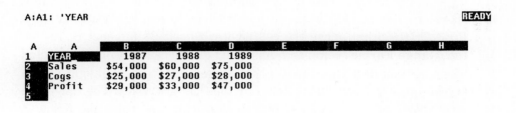

Figure 5-4.   Worksheet with the cell pointer in A1

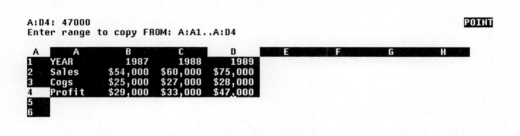

Figure 5-5.   A range highlighted using the END and arrow keys

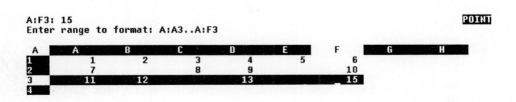

Figure 5-6.   Using other keys with the END and arrow key combinations

Release 3 lets you specify multiple sheet ranges that span two or more worksheets, although it is not possible to create one range that spans worksheet files. Suppose you wish to format the range of cells B:B3..D:D10. First, move the cell pointer to cell B3 in sheet B. Invoke the /**Range Format** command. Assuming all the cells within the selected range contain data, you can use the END key method to highlight all the entries quickly. Press END followed by the RIGHT ARROW key. The range will now read B:B3..B:D3. Press the END key again, but this time follow it with DOWN ARROW. The range now reads B:B3..B:D10. For the last step, press the CTRL-PGUP key twice. The range now reads B:B3..D:D10. Press ENTER to finalize the range.

It is preferable to have 1-2-3 generate the cell addresses in a range whenever possible, but you always have the option of typing a cell reference in response to one of the range prompts. When you use the pointing method, 1-2-3 always adds the level numbers, even if the references are both on the same sheet. If you are typing the range yourself, you only need to type the cell addresses, unless the data is in another sheet or file.

When you type a single period in a reference (D4.D10)—either with the pointing method or when you type the complete entry—1-2-3 will duplicate it so that two periods display (D4..D10). You can enter any two opposite corners of a rectangle of cells to specify a range. Normally, however, the upper left and the lower right corners are used for a single-sheet range (as in A2..F10). For a multiple-sheet range, use the upper left corner on the sheet with the lowest level and the lower right corner on the highest sheet, as in A:A2..G:F10. Remember, if you type a period after pointing to a range address, 1-2-3 will move the active corner (the corner containing the cell pointer) in the range, allowing you to expand or contract the range from a different side.

Tip: Some commands remember the last range they used. Commands like /Print and /Data Fill (described in Chapters 6 and 8, respectively) remember the range last used, and suggest it for the next use of the command. To change these suggested ranges you can use ESC to eliminate the range, or BACKSPACE to replace the cell pointer in its location before the command was invoked.

Naming Cell Ranges

In some respects, all worksheet cells automatically have names, since they have unique cell addresses by which they can be referenced. You are already familiar with column/row addresses such as A2, U7, or AX89 from a single sheet perspective, and D:A2, D:F10, G:A2 from a multiple sheet perspective. It is clear exactly what cell you mean when you use these addresses. If you leave out the sheet level indicator, 1-2-3 assumes you mean the current sheet. Although it is never wrong to add a sheet level, it is only required when the cells referenced are on another sheet. Likewise, a file reference is only required when you are referencing a range in another file.

However, though the location of the cell is evident, it is not clear what is contained in cells named A2, U7, or AX89. Is it the interest rate, the number of employees, or the Los Angeles Dodgers' batting average? It can take time to move the cell pointer every time you need to remember a particular cell's contents.

The /Range Name commands provide a solution for this dilemma. With these commands you can assign names to ranges of any size—that provide meaningful information about the contents of the groups of cells they reference. If cell A10 contains sales for 1989, for example, you might assign it the name SALES_89. If cells B3..B25 contain all the expenses for a certain department, you might assign a range name like TOTAL_EXPENSES.

In Release 3, range names assume added importance. With the ability to access multiple worksheets in one file, it is more convenient to be able to access data in other sheets by using a name like Sales rather than remember that you stored it in D13..D42. This feature also makes it easier to link data across several files. Range names can only be assigned within active worksheet files (that is, files in memory), although you must use sheet or file indicators to assign names to sheets other than the current sheet.

1-2-3 allows you to assign any name to any range of cells, provided that the name does not exceed 15 characters and does not start with a number. Once you assign a range name, you can use it the same way that you use a cell address. For example, you could create a formula for a profit calculation using assigned range names: +SALES_89−TOTAL_EXPENSES. Unlike Release 2, when you include a named range in the formula, 1-2-3 Release 3 keeps the range name in the formula, even when you edit it. The box called "A Few Pointers for Creating Range Names" provides some additional tips on range names.

Release 3 has many new range name options, including the ability to add a note for a range name. Since the named range can span many cells, the semicolon method used to add a note after a value or a formula will not work. Instead, you need to use the /Range Name Note command. Another new Release 3 option is support for undefined range names: you can finalize a formula even if it includes range name references that do not yet exist. If you delete an assigned range name used in a formula, 1-2-3 converts the range name reference to the corresponding range address. In Release 3, when you edit a formula that contains range names, the range names still appear in the formula. In conjunction with this feature, there is a new /Range Name Undefine command that retains an existing range name but disassociates it from any specific range reference.

Assigning Range Names

There are two basic methods for assigning range names. Usually you will invoke the /Range Name Create command to enter your range names. In special cases where the name you want to use will be assigned to a single cell and already appears in an adjacent worksheet cell, you can use the /Range Name Labels command.

Creating New Names   The easiest way to name a range of cells is to move your cell pointer to the upper left corner of the range. If you are planning to create a name for a range that spans multiple sheets, you will also want to be in the first sheet in the range. After positioning the cell pointer, type **/Range Name Create**, type your range name, and press ENTER. If you want to name just one cell, simply press ENTER again. For a range larger than one cell, move your cell pointer to the lower right cell in the range and then press ENTER again.

Alternatively, you can leave your cell pointer on any worksheet cell, type **/Range Name Create**, type the range name, and press ENTER. You then type the cell coordinates corresponding to the range and press ENTER again. For example, consider the commands /Range Name Create SALES D:A1 and /Range Name Create EXPENSES B2..B6. In the first

**1
2
3**

A Few Pointers for Creating Range Names

1-2-3 has few restrictions in range names, but it is helpful to add a few for the sake of clarity.

- 1-2-3 does not prevent you from using spaces in range names, but it is preferable to avoid using them. The name TOTAL SALES could be mistaken for two range names by someone just glancing at a formula, but TOTAL _ SALES is clearly one name.

- You are also allowed to use arithmetic operators in range names, but they, too, can cause problems. TOTAL*SALES could be confusing as a range name; it might be interpreted as a request for an arithmetic operation that would multiply TOTAL by SALES.

- Another permitted type of name to avoid is a name that could be confused with a cell address, such as A3 or D4.

- Remember that numbers cannot be used as range names unless they are used in combination with letters. For example, SALES _ 86 is acceptable, but 56 is not acceptable as a range name.

- Do not name ranges with the same name as @functions, macro commands, or 1-2-3 key names.

- Do not start range names with numbers because they cannot be included in a formula.

example, the range being named can be on another sheet in the active file. In the second example, the range must be in the current sheet of the active file since the sheet level is not supplied.

1-2-3 allows you to assign more than one name to a range. For example, suppose you have data in cells F4..F25 that represent expenses for 1989, and you name this range EXPENSES _ 89. Now suppose you wish to use these expenses to project next year's budget. You might then want to assign this same range of cells the name PRE-

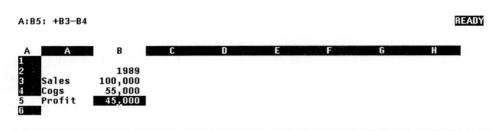

Figure 5-7. A worksheet where range names can be used

VIOUS_YR_EXP for use in your budget calculations. 1-2-3 permits you to assign both names.

The worksheet in Figure 5-7 offers several opportunities to use the /Range Name Create command. Suppose you want to name the cells containing the figures for Sales and Cost of Goods Sold (Cogs). To do this, place the cell pointer in B3 on the amount for sales, and enter **/Range Name Create**. In response to the request for a name, enter SALES_89, like this:

```
A:B5: +B3-B4                                          EDIT
Enter name to create: Sales_89_
```

Then press ENTER. The next prompt wants the address of the range you are naming. Since the name is for just this one cell, simply press ENTER again. You will see

```
A:B3: 100000                                         POINT
Enter name to create: Sales_89        Enter range: A:B3..A:B3
```

Now move the cell pointer to B4 and repeat the process, using the name COGS_89.

You can see from the formula for profit shown in Figure 5-8 that 1-2-3 will use range names in the display of an existing formula once you have assigned them. You can also reference range names when you construct new formulas. Once a name has been assigned to a cell or a range of cells, you may use this name anywhere you would use a cell or range reference. This means you can use range names when formatting,

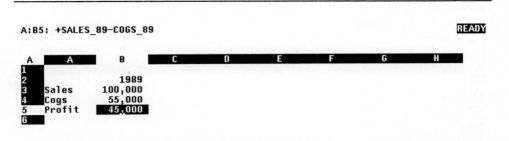

Figure 5-8.   Profit formula with range names displayed

copying, moving, printing, or graphing data, in addition to formula building. When you use a range name that refers to a multiple cell range in a formula in which only single-cell references are allowed, Release 3 returns ERR.

Tip: 1-2-3 only replaces range references in formulas. If you use a cell address, like A1 in a formula, assign a name like SALES to the range A1..A1; 1-2-3 will not make a substitution. Since A1 is a cell address, not a range, 1-2-3 will not equate the two references, and the formula will continue to display A1.

1-2-3 has a special feature for accessing names once they have been assigned: the F3 (NAME) key. When you are using a command that expects a range, you can press F3(NAME) to access the list of names you have assigned. You can then select a name from the list for use with the command you entered.

Using Existing Worksheet Labels to Create Range Names   The /Range Name Labels command can save you data entry time when assigning range names if conditions are right. First, the name you plan to use must already exist on the worksheet as a label entry. It must also be in a cell adjacent to the cell you plan to name. With this command you can assign a range name only to a single cell, so if you are naming more than one cell in a range, you must use the /Range Name Create command. One advantage of /Range Name Labels is that you can use it to assign several range names at once.

The cells in B3..B10 in Figure 5-9 can all have range names assigned with one execution of the /Range Name Labels command. To do

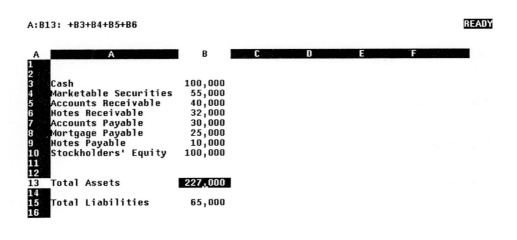

Figure 5-9. A range suitable for /Range Name Labels

this, position the cell pointer in A3 and enter /**Range Name Labels**. Since the range of cells you are naming is on the right of the labels, choose Right next. Finally, move the cell pointer to A10, as shown in Figure 5-10, and press ENTER.

In Figure 5-9, note that cell addresses appear in the formula shown in the control panel. In Figure 5-11, the names of some of the cells just named with the /Range Name Labels command have been substituted in the formula. Notice that some of the labels have been truncated, since 1-2-3 enforces a 15-character limit on range names.

Deleting Range Names

Assigned range names use a small amount of 1-2-3's internal memory. If you are not using some of your old range names, consider deleting them to free up the space they use. It is best to delete a range name as soon as you know it is no longer required, since later on you may forget whether you need it or not.

To delete a range name, enter /**Range Name Delete**. 1-2-3 will then present a list of all the assigned range names at the top of your screen, as shown in the example in Figures 5-12 and 5-13. (Note the NAMES mode indicator.) You have the option of typing the name to delete, or

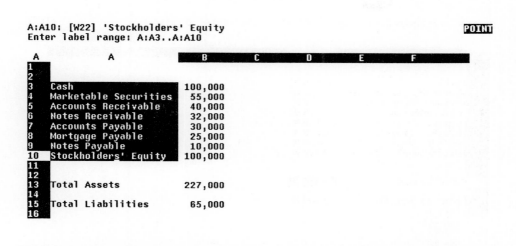

Figure 5-10.   Specifying the label range

using the highlighted bar in the control panel to point to the name to delete. In either case, press ENTER after making your selection. This action causes the selected range name to disappear permanently.

Resetting Range Names

The /Range Name Delete option is ideal when you have only a few names to delete. If you have many names to delete, however, this option is slow. The /Range Name Reset command can speed up the process when you are deleting most or all of your range names. /Range Name Reset deletes all range names, so it is perfect for situations when you want to start fresh and create all new names. When you have a large number of names and want all but a few deleted, it may be quicker to delete them all and then use /Range Name Create to reenter the names you want to keep—rather than delete the names one by one with /Range Name Delete. Figure 5-14 shows the options presented with /Range Name Delete after /Range Name Reset has been used. Since all range names have been deleted by /Range Name Reset, there are no remaining names to delete.

/Range Name Undefine also removes range names from the active list of range names. An important distinction between this command and

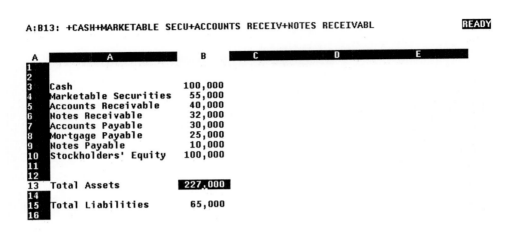

Figure 5-11.   Formula with range names substituted for cell addresses

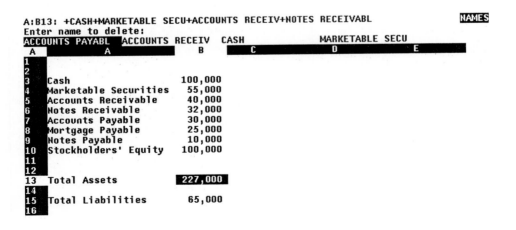

Figure 5-12.   Partial list of names to delete

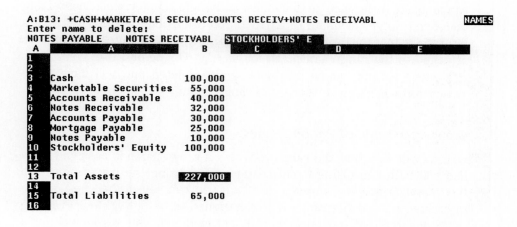

Figure 5-13.   End of alphabetized list to delete

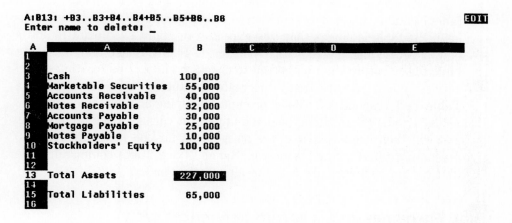

Figure 5-14.   List after /Range Name Reset was used

/Range Name Delete is that the Undefine command does not eliminate notes that may be attached to range names. It also does not remove the range name reference in formulas, although the formulas containing undefined ranges evaluate to ERR. If you use /Range Name Create at a later time to reinstate undefined range names, the notes will still be attached to the range names. If you use the Delete or Reset commands to remove a range name, the note is also deleted and will have to be re-entered when you reinstate the range name.

Creating a Table of Range Names

One way of checking the range to which a range name is assigned is by using the /Range Name Create command to bring the list of names to the screen. Once the names are listed, you can select the one you are interested in, and the range it was assigned to is highlighted. Pressing ENTER ensures that the assignment is not changed. This works well for a single range name; however, it is not a good alternative when there are a number of ranges you need to check, since repeating the sequence for each range takes too much time.

A better solution is to use the /Range Name Table command to build a table of range names and the cell addresses they identify. This table, built in any empty area of the worksheet, can serve as documentation for all the range names used in your worksheet.

Before executing the required command sequence, choose a good table location—one where you won't overwrite data or important formulas if the table is longer than you expect. You might even want to add a new sheet to the model with /Worksheet Insert Sheet and place the table there, rather than bothering to check the impact on existing model entries. When you are ready to create the table, enter **/Range Name Table** and respond to 1-2-3's prompt by typing in the table location. 1-2-3 permits you to supply just the upper left corner of the table range, and will then use as much space as it needs for the table. Figure 5-15 presents a table created with the /Range Name Table command. Note that the range names are listed in alphabetical order.

Using Filenames and Wildcard References with Range Names

Although range names like SALES or B:SALES are the most common form of reference used, you can also use a filename as part of the range

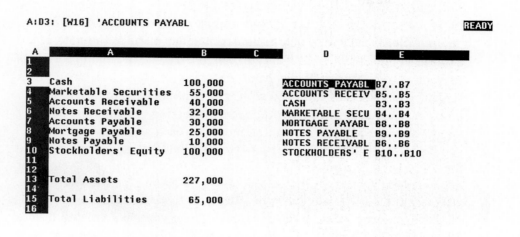

Figure 5-15.   Output of /Range Name Table

name reference when you want to access a range in a file other than the current file. The standard double angle bracket notation < < > > is used around the filename, as in < < C:\123R3\BUDGET.WK3 > > SALES.

You can also use a question mark within the angle brackets as a wildcard, indicating a match regardless of the filename, and 1-2-3 will search all active files. Use the wildcard notation only when the range name is unique among the active files. If you enter this notation in a command or formula, 1-2-3 will display an error message if it does not find a match, or if it finds multiple matches. To look for the range name SALES in this manner, you would enter < <?> > **SALES** in a formula or a command that expects a range.

Tip: 1-2-3 does not convert wildcard references to range addresses when you delete the range name. Normally if you delete a range name, 1-2-3 converts formula entries that reference the deleted name to the appropriate range address. This does not occur when the formula reference is to a wildcard reference.

Creating and Using Range Name Notes

You can attach notes to range names to describe the contents of the range, the individual entering the note, or the date and time it was entered. Since the range may include a number of cells, the note is not entered in a particular cell like the notes entered at the end of formulas or values. The /Range Name Note command displays a submenu that remains on the screen until you select the Quit option. This allows you to make multiple selections from the menu—creating, editing, and deleting notes without having to invoke the menu for each activity.

The /Range Name Note Create command allows you to enter a note for an existing range name. If a range name is undefined, you must define it before adding a note. A note can be as long as 512 characters, although the entire note does not display in the control panel on multiple lines the way a long cell entry does. Once you have created a note for a range name, you can also use the Create option to edit the note entry. Use the cursor control keys to move within the control panel line when you are editing. If you save the worksheet file after entering the note, it will be available for all future sessions.

To eliminate a note from a defined range name, invoke the /Range Name Note Delete command. Type the name of the range for which you want to delete the note, or highlight it in the list of defined range names. When the note is deleted, the range name is unaffected and is still assigned to the range.

If you want to eliminate all notes attached to all range names, use /Range Name Note Reset. This one command deletes all notes in the current file without prompting you to confirm your decision.

Tip: Remember to check the file you are in before using /Range Name Note Reset to delete all range notes. If Undo is not enabled, there is no way to restore notes you have Reset, unless you have a copy of the worksheet on disk that you can retrieve. To safeguard all of your hard work in note creation, check the active file to ensure that you are in the file you want to be in before invoking the Reset option.

You have learned that the /Range Name Table command creates a table of range names. /Range Name Note Table adds a third column to this table, to display any notes attached to the range names. /Range Name Note Table also lists undefined range names that have notes attached to them.

Practical Applications for Range Names

Assigning range names may seem like so much extra work that you may wonder why you should bother using them. For very small models they may not be worthwhile, but for larger ones— especially multiple-sheet models—range names offer a significant payback. They make formulas much more readable, for one thing. They also help prevent incorrect formula references, since you will see a descriptive name rather than a cryptic cell address. As data becomes farther removed from the formula location, the payback becomes greater, because you cannot see the data at the same time as the formula, and verify the accuracy of the cell addresses used.

When range names are used, you will find that rows, columns, and sheets can be inserted in the middle of a range, and the range reference will be adjusted automatically. The references will also be updated if you delete rows, columns, or sheets from the middle of a range. If you want to see the updated references in a table, however, you will need to execute /Range Name Table or /Range Name Note Table again since neither command dynamically updates the worksheet.

Transposing Data

Sometimes you will want to rearrange a range of entries that you have made in a worksheet. You may have changed your mind about the best presentation method, or you may want to use an existing worksheet as the basis for a new worksheet but must reorganize the presentation to make this possible.

1-2-3 provides the /Range Trans (Transpose) command to permit you to change data entered horizontally across a row, to a vertical column presentation or vice versa. You can also reorganize in a number of different ways the information stored in a three-dimensional range. When you use the command on a two-dimensional range, it automatically transposes column data into a row, and row entries into a column, using a special copy process. When you use the command with three-dimensional ranges, a submenu of additional selections appears so you can specify exactly how you want the transposition to occur. The steps for transposing data are summarized in the box called "Steps for Transposing Data."

Since the /Range Trans command will operate on single or multiple rows or columns in single or multiple sheets, there are a wide variety of options to cover. Before using any of these options, you will want to be sure the formulas in any cells that you are transposing have up-to-date values. If CALC is showing at the bottom of your screen, press F9 (CALC) to recalculate the worksheet before beginning. Also, if the cells that you are transposing contain links to other files, you might want to refresh these links before starting (with /File Admin Link-Refresh).

To begin the transpose operation enter /**Range Trans** and press ENTER. Next, select a From range (the original location of your data) in response to 1-2-3's prompt, and press ENTER. For a single-sheet transposition, you can specify either a single row or column of entries, or a rectangular range of data. For a multiple-sheet transposition, the From range can be any range that spans sheets.

Next you are asked to specify a To range (the new location). You can enter a range that has the opposite orientation but the same number of entries as the From range. However, the easiest approach is to enter the beginning cell of the To range and let 1-2-3 figure out the size of the range that it needs.

Caution: In specifying the To range in three-dimensional transpositions, make certain there are a sufficient number of open sheets to accommodate the requirements of the To range. For example, if your From range was A2..B10, your To range might be D2..M3—the same number of cells but with a row rather than a column orientation. Never use overlapping To and From ranges. You can use a To range in another file, but it must be active.

With a single-sheet operation, 1-2-3 completes the transposition after the entry of the To range. However, with a three-dimensional transposition you must select how you want 1-2-3 to handle the process.

Steps for Transposing Data

Transposing data in your worksheet allows you to reorganize an entire application without reentering data. The steps you need to follow are:

1.   Use F9 (CALC) and /File Admin Links-Refresh if you need to update calculations or links to external files.

2.   Move the cell pointer to the first cell in the range you wish to transpose.

3.   Enter /**Range Trans** and use the cursor movement keys to highlight the entire range containing entries that you want to transpose.

4.   Highlight the first cell in the To range, and press ENTER. If both of your ranges are single-sheet ranges, the transposition will occur now. 1-2-3 implicitly performs a /Range Value command with the /Range Trans command, since it copies the values instead of the formulas to the To range.

5.   If either range was a multiple-sheet range, select the type of change you want. The selections are

• Rows/Columns to change the orientation of data within each sheet

• Worksheets/Rows to change rows of data in several worksheets to a row on another worksheet

• Columns/Worksheets to perform the same transition as Worksheets/Rows, except with a column orientation.

Note: If you want to transpose a single-sheet range to a multi-sheet range, you must specify a To range that spans the correct number of worksheets.

The Rows/Columns option performs the same transpose operation as the single-sheet operation. Within each sheet, the data in the From range is reversed from a row to a column orientation in the To range and vice versa. With the Worksheets/Rows selection, the data in the first row of each worksheet's From range is copied to the first worksheet. Data from the second row in each worksheet is copied to the second worksheet, with the process continuing until all the rows in the From range have been transposed. With a Columns/Worksheets transposition the first column in the From range on each worksheet is copied to the first worksheet in the To range, and the data from the second column of each worksheet is copied to the second worksheet until all the columns in the From range have been transposed.

If some of the cells in the To range already contain data, their contents will be replaced as a result of the transposition operation. With Release 3, as formulas in a From range are copied to a To range, the resulting entries in the To range are always the converted value of the formula. Looking at examples for each of the options will help to clarify the operation of this command.

Single-Sheet Transposition

The original worksheet entries for a single-sheet transposition are shown in cells A3..B5 in Figure 5-16. To complete the operation, enter **/Range Trans**, highlight A3..B5, and press ENTER. Highlight D1 as the beginning of the To range and press ENTER to complete the transposition. The results are shown horizontally in D1..F2 in Figure 5-17.

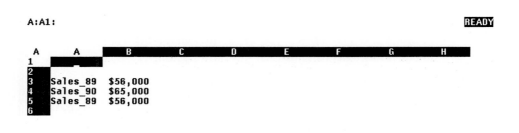

Figure 5-16.   Entries for a transposition operation

Figure 5-17.   Results of the transposition operation shown in D1..F2

Multiple-Sheet Transpose Operations

Multiple-sheet transpose operations can either transpose several sheets as if you had performed several single-sheet transpose operations, or it can slice through a series of sheets and bring the data from a row or column of these sheets into one sheet.

The first sample multiple-sheet transpose operation shows a way to complete several row-to-column transitions without the need for separate requests. The data in Figure 5-18 shows a section from three different worksheets that display discount percentages by customer type and amount purchased for three different regions. To change the orientation of these three individual tables and place Customer Type /Amount data across the top row rather than down the left-hand column, you can use the Rows/Columns option.

First, enter /**Range Trans**. Specify the From range as A:A3..C:E6 and press ENTER. Next, specify the To range as A:A10—the upper left corner of the range on the first sheet—and press ENTER. Although you may want the new orientation to replace the old data, you do not want to use overlapping From and To ranges. So first transpose the data; then you can move it to replace the old entries, to ensure an error-free operation. Select Rows/Columns from the menu and press ENTER. The worksheet now shows both sets of entries. The new entries are shown in Figure 5-19.

In the next example, a series of worksheets showing sales contest winners from three regions is shown in Figure 5-20. If you would like all the first-place winners in one list, second-place in another, and third in another, the Columns/Worksheets option can handle the task. The first step is setting up a form on the file to receive the data. Since sheets D,

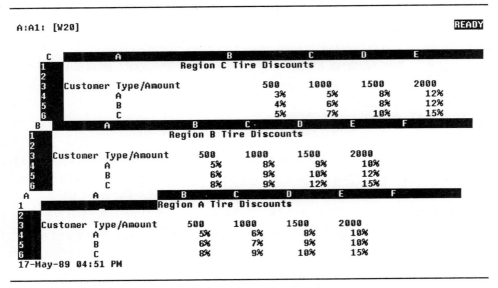

Figure 5-18. Entries from three different range name tables

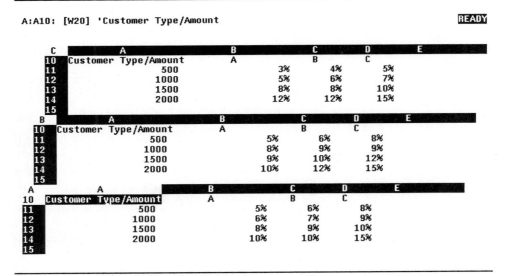

Figure 5-19. Entries from the three sheets in Figure 5-18 transposed in a new location

E, and F contain the data to be transposed, sheets A, B, and C can contain the new entries. These sheets were set up with headings in B2, and the words "Western Region," "Eastern Region," and "Southern Region" in C3..C5 of each sheet. After the preliminary setup, move the cell pointer to D:C3 and enter **/Range Trans**. Next, highlight D:C3..F:C5 and press ENTER. Specify the To range as A:D3, planning for 1-2-3 to transpose the data so it displays on the sheets as shown in Figure 5-21.

The third type of multiple-sheet transposition that you might need is moving data from several worksheets and placing it into the first row on one sheet. In Figure 5-22, there are three sheets that display the total sales information for three regions by year. In a set of consolidated reports by year, you might want to show all the 1989 data for all three regions on one sheet. Enter /**Range Trans**, highlight A:B3..C:D5 as the From range, and press ENTER. Highlight D:B3 as the To range, assuming that you want to use the prepared sheets in Figure 5-23 for the results. Press ENTER to see the transposed data in Figure 5-24.

Converting Formulas to Values

At times during the model creation process, you may want to change some of your projections to fixed values, rather than allowing them to be revised each time the worksheet is recalculated. One example is the budgeting process. As you prepare a budget, you want to look at various possibilities. Once the budget is submitted, however, the projections you made are recorded and will serve as the target for your operation throughout the budget period. You may thus wish to freeze some of the formulas used to make the budget projection. 1-2-3 provides the perfect way to do this via the /Range Value command.

The /Range Value command copies the values produced by formulas to a new location. It copies only the values displayed in worksheet cells, not the formulas used to produce these values. Thus the original worksheet can still change as new values are entered for assumptions, but the copy will not be affected by changes in the assumptions. To use this command to freeze formula values, use the same range for From and To. Thus, the original formula values are replaced with fixed values.

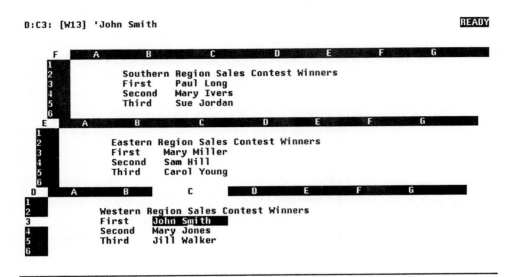

Figure 5-20.   Sales contest winners from three regions

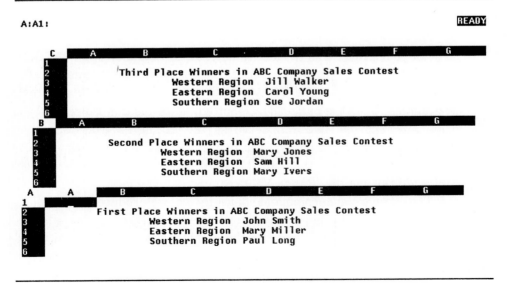

Figure 5-21.   Data from Figure 5-20 after transposition

A:A1:   READY

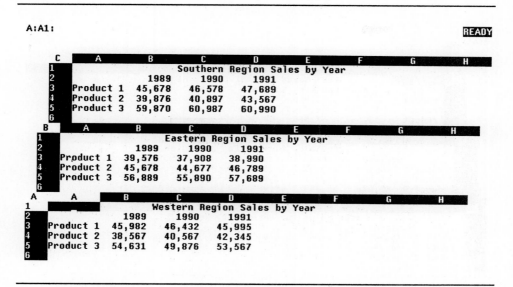

Figure 5-22.   Total sales information

D:B3: (,0)   READY

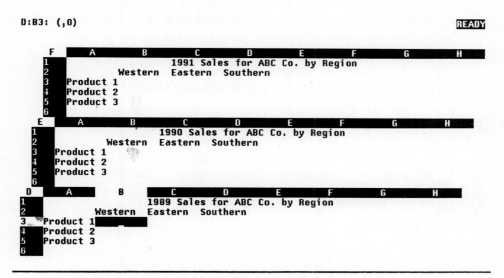

Figure 5-23.   Sheets prepared for the transposed data

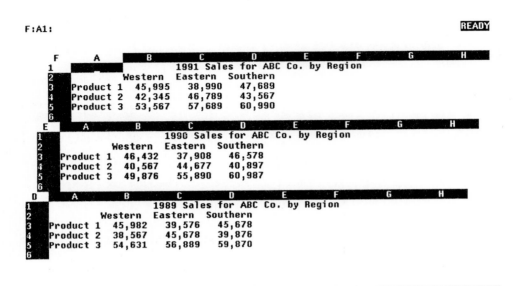

Figure 5-24. Results of the transposition of Figure 5-22

Tip: Be sure all your formula values are up to date before converting formulas to fixed values. If the CALC indicator appears at the bottom of your screen, press F9 (CALC) to update all formulas before proceeding. If you are referencing linked cells in shareable files, use /File Admin Links-Refresh to insure the most recent values.

As an example of fixing values, the entry in B3 in the following worksheet displays in the worksheet cell as a number but as a formula in the control panel:

The same cell after using /Range Value, with B3 as a From and a To range, is now a value in both places:

You will notice that the worksheet display is the same, but the control panel now shows the cell as containing a value, not a formula.

You can also use /Range Value on ranges that span worksheets, if you have a multiple-sheet range that you wish to convert.

Changing the Justification of Labels

As a default, 1-2-3 begins labels at the left side of cells. You have already learned that you can change the alignment of an individual label by preceding it with a caret (^) for center justification or a double quotation mark (") for right justification. Using these options can be very time consuming, however, when you want to change the alignment of a whole range of cells.

The /Range Label command can handle this situation much more efficiently. You simply specify the range for which you want to change the labels and then execute the command. 1-2-3 ensures that existing label entries in the specified cells receive the correct label indicator. Neither entries made after /Range Label are entered nor nonlabel entries in the specified cells will be affected. New label entries will receive the default label prefix.

With this command you can select left, right, or center justification for an existing range of labels. Labels originally entered using the default label prefix of a single quotation mark (') are left justified, as shown in Figure 5-25. If you enter /Range Label and select Right to change the orientation of the labels to the right side of each cell, the results look like Figure 5-26. Entering the command again and choosing Center causes each label to display in the center of the cell as shown in Figure 5-27. The Left option could be used to change either of these results back to the original display format.

Erasing Cell Ranges

The /Range Erase command eliminates the entries in a range of cells. It does not matter whether the entries are numbers, labels, or formulas.

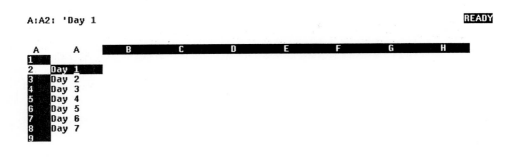

Figure 5-25.   Left aligned labels

Using this command will not affect the numeric format assigned to the cell, its width, or its protection status.

Figure 5-28 shows a worksheet containing miscellaneous entries in E1..G15 that are no longer required. To remove these entries, move the cell pointer to E1 and type /**Range Erase.** Then move the cell pointer to G15 to extend the range, and press ENTER to achieve the results shown in Figure 5-29. Note that if worksheet protection has been enabled, the /Range Erase command will not work. If Undo is enabled, you can restore the entries removed with /Range Erase as long as no actions intervene between /Range Erase and the use of ALT-F4 (UNDO).

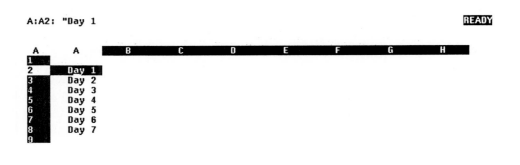

Figure 5-26.   Right aligned labels

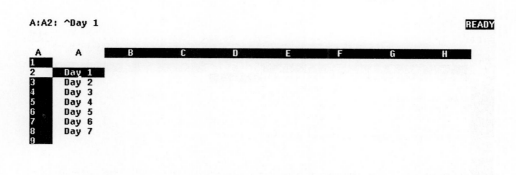

Figure 5-27.   Centered labels

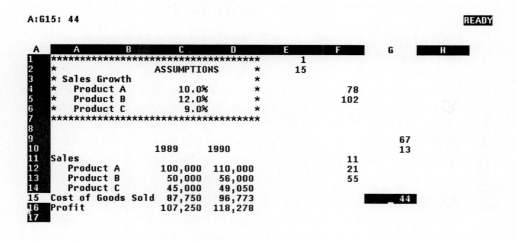

Figure 5-28.   Extraneous worksheet entries

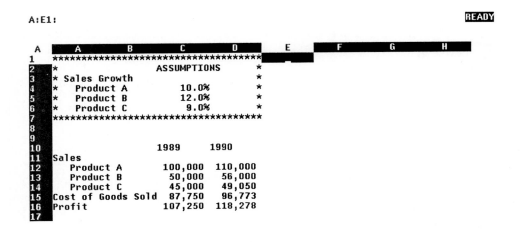

Figure 5-29.   Results of /Range Erase

Protecting Worksheet Cells

A completed worksheet often represents hours or days of work in planning, formula entry, and testing. Once you have created a well-planned and tested worksheet application, you will want to protect it from accidental keystrokes or option selections that could cause you to overwrite formulas or other vital data. 1-2-3 provides features that will prevent this damage to important cells. These features can also make other users more comfortable in using models that you create for them, because they know they cannot destroy the models.

Tip: Watch your screen for information about the current Protection status. Use /Worksheet Status to see the Global Protection Status for the current file. Look in the control panel for "PR" to identify individual entries with a Protected status.

The Protection features of 1-2-3 let you determine which cells will be protected and which ones will accept entries. There is also an easy way to temporarily disable the Protection mechanism without changing a cell's basic definition as a protected or unprotected cell. Finally, 1-2-3 provides a command that is used in conjunction with Protection to restrict the cell pointer to a single input range on the worksheet.

Tip: Group input entries onto one sheet where possible. Rather than spread input entries across many sheets, gather them on an input form on one sheet if possible. This approach will save operator entry time, and also make it easy for you to apply Protection to the cells in all the other sheets and eliminate it from the entry cells on the input sheet.

1-2-3's Protection process requires that you first decide which worksheet cells you wish to have protected. All cells are protected as an initial default. If you wish to allow entries in certain cells, you can unprotect them with /Range Unprot. You can then turn on the Protection features of the package, and these unprotected cells will still permit entries. Protection is turned on with a Global option under the Worksheet menu.

Remember: The effect of GROUP mode applies to /Range Prot and /Range Unprot. Changes made to the Protection status of the current worksheet with GROUP mode on will apply to all the sheets in the file.

Deciding What Cells to Protect

1-2-3 establishes a default status of Protected for every worksheet cell. This might sound strange, since you can make an entry anywhere on a new worksheet. You can do that because the Protection features of the package are initially turned off. If you turn on the Protection features, the Protected status of each cell is energized, and 1-2-3 rejects any additional entries. It is therefore important to decide what cells should accept entries before you turn on Protection.

You might find it useful to think of 1-2-3's Protection feature as a fence placed around every cell. The fences do not protect the contents of cells in a new worksheet, since none of the fence gates are closed. The /Worksheet Global Prot Enable command will close all the gates, thereby protecting the contents of the cells. Cells that you do not wish to have protected should have their fences torn down with /Range Unprot. Then, when the gates are closed with /Worksheet Global Prot Enable, you can still change these cells, because a gate without a fence does not offer effective protection.

The /Range Unprot command is used to strip cell Protection from a range of one or many cells. To unprotect a range, enter /**Range Unprot**, and either point to the limiting cells or enter the range. If you change your mind and decide that a cell should be protected again, you can use the /Range Prot command to restore Protection for the cell. Unprotecting a cell highlights it on a monochrome display, or makes it green on a color display. Removing Protection has no other effect on a cell unless the Global Protection features (discussed in the next section) are turned on. In addition, a "U" appears after the cell address in the top line of the control panel when the cell pointer is on the unprotected cell (see Figure 5-30).

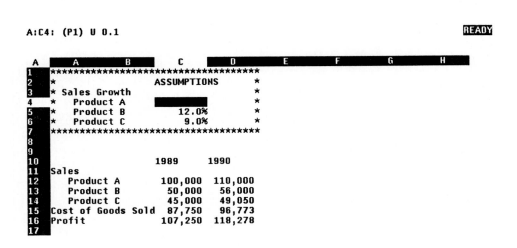

Figure 5-30.   Unprotected cell highlighted

Enabling Worksheet Protection

As noted in the analogy established previously, the /Worksheet Global Prot Enable command "closes the gate" on every protected worksheet cell, ensuring that protected cells cannot be altered. It also places the entry "PR" in the control panel for every protected cell.

Unless you have altered the default cell protection with /Range Unprot, you cannot make entries in any worksheet cell once Protection is enabled with this command. You can enter characters from the keyboard while pointing to one of these cells, but when you attempt to finalize the entry, the error message shown in Figure 5-31 appears, alerting you to the protected status of the cell. If you have used the /Range Unprot command to remove Protection from some of the cells, you will still be able to make entries in these cells.

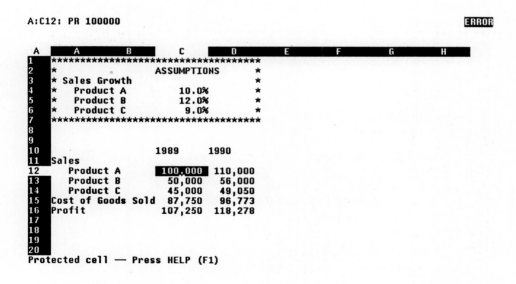

Figure 5-31.   Error message from attempt to write in protected cell

You may need to turn Protection off after enabling it; if so, you can enter **/Worksheet Global Prot Disable**. This command allows you to temporarily suspend Protection so you can make a change to a formula, for example.

Tip: If you need more protection use /File Admin Seal. Anyone who knows how to enable Worksheet Protection also knows how to disable it. Use /File Admin Seal to lock the current worksheet settings; a password is then required to unlock it.

Specifying an Input Range

The /Range Input command is used in conjunction with the Protection features. Once a worksheet is protected, the /Range Input command allows you to restrict cell pointer movement to unprotected cells within the input range. /Range Input is useful for focusing attention on the cells available for entry during data input. The steps for using this command are as follows:

1. Set up the worksheet with all needed labels and formulas. In other words, design your worksheet before restricting the cell pointer.

2. Remove Protection from the cells requiring data entry, using /Range Unprot.

3. Enable the Protection feature, using /Worksheet Global Prot Enable.

4. Enter **/Range Input** and select the range of cells in which you want to allow input.

Your screen will display the input range in the upper left corner. You can edit cells in the specified range or enter new data in them. You can also use ESC, HOME, END, ENTER, F1 (HELP), F2 (EDIT), BACKSPACE, or any of the arrow keys in completing your entries. The cell pointer will always remain within the input range, since that is the only area where entries can be made. While /Range Input is in effect, the END and HOME keys will move you to the end or the beginning of the input range. Pressing either

ESC or ENTER without making an entry cancels the /Range Input command. This command is used in the macro environment to assist with automating applications, and is ideal for use with the new input form capability offered in Release 3 (see Chapter 13, "Command Language Macros").

Cutting and Pasting

Cutting and pasting can extend your productivity with 1-2-3 by allowing you to move or copy existing entries to new locations. You can thus restructure a worksheet to meet new needs without reentering data. You can also use the /Worksheet Insert and /Worksheet Delete commands from Chapter 4, "Changing the Appearance of the Worksheet Display," to add new rows, columns, or sheets and to eliminate rows, columns, and sheets that are no longer required.

Moving Information

Creating a worksheet can sometimes be a trial-and-error process, during which you attempt to obtain the most effective placement of data. 1-2-3 provides a /Move command that permits you to move a range of cells to another location on one of the sheets in the active file. The command requires that you specify both a From and a To range. The From range marks the original location of the data to be moved, and the To range is the new location you have selected. 1-2-3 will prompt you for these ranges when it is time to enter them. You can use any of the normal methods for specifying a range location, including range names, cell addresses, and pointing.

Tip: Use /Move to restructure worksheets created in Release 2.01 to utilize the multiple-sheet features of Release 3. If you have a number of different kinds of data in a Release 2.01 worksheet, you can reorganize it quickly. Use /Worksheet Insert Sheet to add the required number of sheets, and /Move to handle the remainder of the task.

It is easiest to specify the From range for the /Move command if you place your cell pointer on the upper left cell in the range to be moved before invoking the command. That is because 1-2-3 assumes that the current cell is the range you wish to move. To expand this range, simply move the cell pointer in the direction you want; the beginning cell remains anchored in place. You can move a single-sheet range or a multiple-sheet range.

If you want to change the beginning of the range 1-2-3 suggests, press ESC or BACKSPACE to unlock the beginning of the range. Move your cell pointer to the upper left cell in the range you wish to move, type a period, and move to the end of the range. Alternatively, you can just type a new range when presented with 1-2-3's suggestion.

Unless you are typing the range reference, you must move your cell pointer for the To range—even if you position your cell pointer prior to executing the command. This is because 1-2-3 suggests the same range for To as it suggested for From. Since the suggestion for To is a single cell, you will not need to press ESC to unlock the beginning of the range. Just move to whatever beginning cell you wish for the To range, or enter the beginning cell from the keyboard. Only the beginning cell needs to be specified for To, even if many cells are being moved.

The /Move command can be used to move one or many worksheet cells. The example in Figure 5-32 shows a long label that is not in the center of the worksheet. To reenter the label in a more central location would be time consuming; you can move it more quickly with /Move. Place the cell pointer in A3 and enter /**Move**. Since the From range is

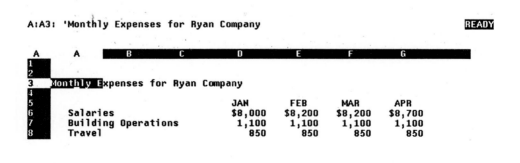

Figure 5-32.   Long label to be moved

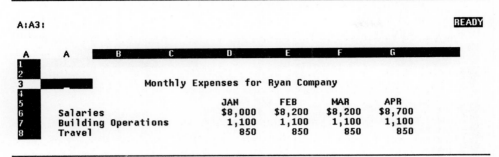

Figure 5-33.   Result of moving label

the cell pointer location, press ENTER to accept the current cell address for the From range. Then move the cell pointer to C3, and press ENTER to accept C3 as the To range. Figure 5-33 presents the worksheet after the move is complete. Although the label displays in multiple cells, you are able to move it by specifying only one cell each for the From and To ranges.

As another example, suppose that in the worksheet shown in Figure 5-34 you want to move the entries in cells A2..C15 to the right. These cells contain numbers, labels, and formulas. (The formulas are shown in

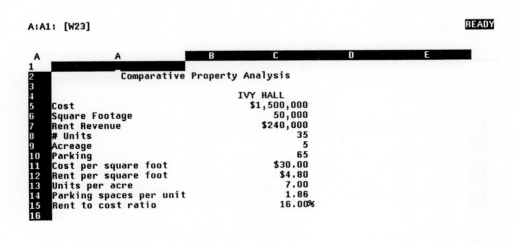

Figure 5-34.   Entries in A2..C15 to be moved

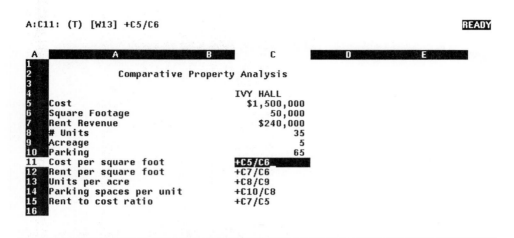

Figure 5-35.   Display of formulas

Figure 5-35.) To move all these entries at once, enter /**Move** and the From range A2..C15. When the To range is requested, enter B2. Only one cell is needed to tell 1-2-3 where to begin the To range; it will automatically use B2..D15 as the complete To range. Figure 5-36 shows

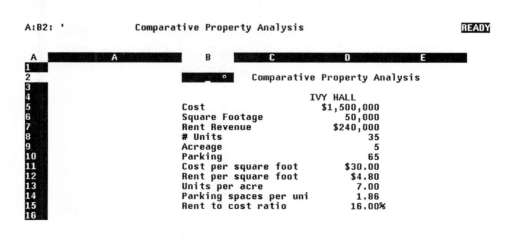

Figure 5-36.   Result of /Move in Figure 5-34

the worksheet after the move, including the way in which the formulas have been adjusted to reflect their new locations. Note also that there is an overlap between the From and To ranges. 1-2-3 is able to handle this.

Duplicating Existing Entries

The copying features of 1-2-3 extend your productivity with the package more than any other single feature. /Copy permits you to enter a label, formula, or number in one cell and copy it to many new locations. This feature is especially valuable for formulas, since 1-2-3 is able to adjust the formulas to conform with their new locations. With the new three-dimensional features, you can set up calculations for one business entity on one sheet and copy it to 5, 10, or 20 additional sheets, letting you enter data for other business entities immediately, without entering any formulas.

Copy Options

The /Copy command will perform its task in a variety of situations. You can /Copy the contents of one cell to another cell, or to a range of many cells. You can speed up the copying process by copying a range of cells to a second range of the same size. Lastly, this command can copy a range of cells to a second range whose size is a multiple of the original range. The data you are copying can be in the current sheet, another sheet in the current file, another active file, or a file on disk. The area to which you copy must be in any active file. Let's look at an example for each of these uses.

Suppose a label entry is placed in cell A1, like this:

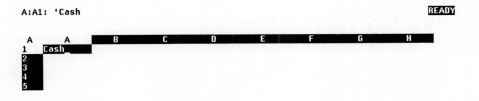

To copy this label to another cell, the easiest approach is to place your cell pointer on A1 before beginning. When you enter /**Copy**, 1-2-3 asks what you want to copy from. Since your cell pointer is already positioned on A1, just press ENTER. (If the cell pointer is not where you want it to be, press ESC before moving it to the correct From location.) After the From location is specified, 1-2-3's next prompt requests the To range. In the preceding illustration, to copy the label entry to B3, move the cell pointer to B3 in response to this prompt and press ENTER. The completed copy operation generates a second label in B3, like this:

The next example will again start with the entry of "Cash" in A1, but this time the entry will be copied to many cells. The beginning of the but this time the entry will be copied to many cells. The beginning of the operation is the same: place the cell pointer on A1 and enter /**Copy**. Press ENTER in response to the From range prompt. The entry is to be copied to D1..D51; therefore, when the prompt for a To range appears, move the cell pointer to D1. Enter a period to lock the beginning of the To range in place. Move the cell pointer down to D51, and then press ENTER. The result is the label copied into every specified cell from D1 down, like this:

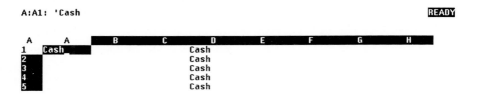

Figure 5-37 shows a worksheet with labels in A3..A15. /Copy can be used to copy these labels to a second range of the same size and shape as the original. The best way to begin is to place the cell pointer in the upper left cell in the range, A3 in this example. Type /**Copy**. Then,

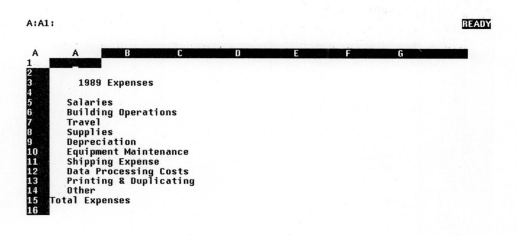

A:A1:   `READY`

```
      A    A        B        C        D        E        F        G
 1
 2
 3          1989 Expenses
 4
 5          Salaries
 6          Building Operations
 7          Travel
 8          Supplies
 9          Depreciation
10          Equipment Maintenance
11          Shipping Expense
12          Data Processing Costs
13          Printing & Duplicating
14          Other
15   Total Expenses
16
```

Figure 5-37.   Label entries to be copied

instead of pressing ENTER, move the cell pointer to the bottom of the From range as shown in Figure 5-38 (the entries are all long labels within column A). Press ENTER, and 1-2-3 requests the To range. At this point, move the cell pointer to the top cell in the To range; in Figure 5-38, this is E3. Since 1-2-3 knows that the To range must match the From range in size and shape, you need specify only the upper left corner of the To range. Then press ENTER, producing the results shown in Figure 5-39. With just a few keystrokes, an entire range of label entries has been duplicated much faster than anyone could enter them.

The next use of /Copy is even more powerful, since it copies one row or column of entries to many rows or columns in one operation. Let's use the labels found in Figure 5-40. To copy them, place the cell pointer in A3 and enter /**Copy**. Move the cell pointer to A15 in response to a request for the From range, and press ENTER. This time the labels are to be copied into B3..B15, C3..C15, D3..D15, and E3..E15. When 1-2-3 requests the To range, therefore, move the cell pointer to the top of the first column where the labels will be copied, B3, and enter a period to lock the beginning of the range in place. Since 1-2-3 knows it is copying a partial column of labels that will extend down to row 15, it needs to be told only how far across the worksheet this partial column should be

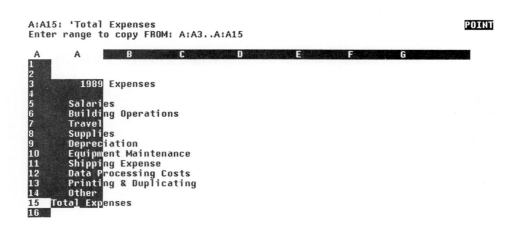

Figure 5-38. From range for labels

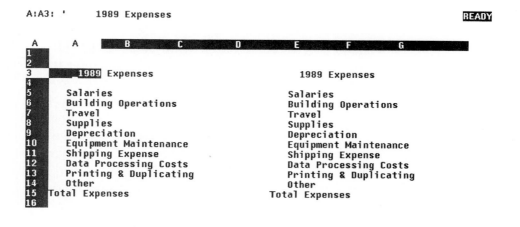

Figure 5-39. Result of copying labels

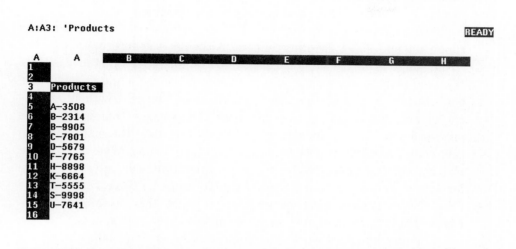

Figure 5-40.   Column of label entries

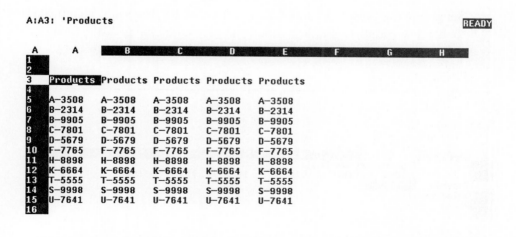

Figure 5-41.   Result of copying to many locations

copied. To do this, move the cell pointer to E3 and press ENTER. The display in Figure 5-41 is produced with this operation.

The last option to be examined is copying entries in a rectangular range on one sheet to other sheets. Although the information in the From range is on the same sheet in this example, it can just as easily be obtained from another sheet. First, highlight the rectangle of cells to be copied. In Figure 5-42, this will be A:A1..A:G3. The cells without entries as yet are in this range; they are part of the range that includes the entries across the top and down the sides. Including the empty cells in this copy operation offers another advantage if you have used range formats on the empty cells: the copy operation will copy the range formats as well as the data. Specify the To range as B:A1..D:A1 — or the first cell in each worksheet where you want this rectangle copied. Figure 5-43 shows part of the data copied to three new sheets.

Copying numbers works the same way as copying labels. Copying formulas can be even more valuable. Although the mechanics of copying formulas are the same from your standpoint, it is important to understand exactly how 1-2-3 treats cell references when copying formulas.

Copying Formulas

Since copying formulas requires adjusting cell references, it is important to have a complete understanding of cell addressing. This topic was

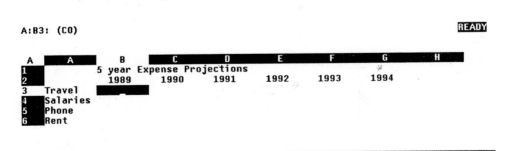

Figure 5-42.   Range to be copied

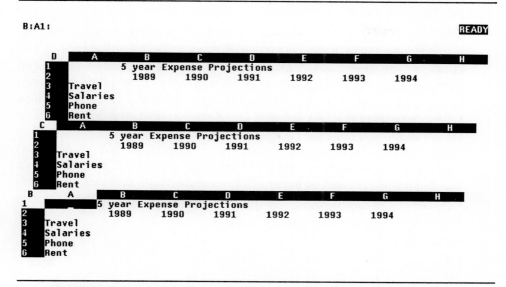

Figure 5-43.   Multiple-sheet range to which the range is copied

introduced in Chapter 4, "Changing the Appearance of the Worksheet Display," but will be expanded in this section to cover the three addressing options completely.

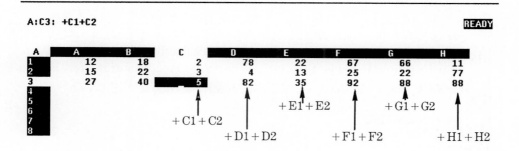

Figure 5-44.   Result of copying formulas across a row

Relative References

Relative references are the addresses generated when you enter regular cell addresses into formulas. A19, D2, and X15 are all relative references, as are D:H5 and A:Z2. This is the normal reference style used with formulas in 1-2-3. When a formula is created with this reference style, 1-2-3 not only records the cell addresses for the formula, but also remembers their relative distance and direction from the cell containing the formula.

For example, when you enter the formula +A1+A2 in A3, 1-2-3 remembers facts that are not shown in the worksheet. Specifically, in the illustration presented here, 1-2-3 remembers the distance and direction that must be traveled to obtain each of the references in the formula.

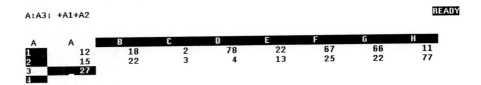

For A1, 1-2-3 knows that this reference is in the same column as the formula result, but is two rows above it. A2 is in the same column, one row above the result. This concept adds great power to the /Copy command. Let's say you want the same type of formula in B3, and you want it to add the values in B1 and B2 together. /Copy can handle this, since it remembers the directions for the formula's relative references.

To make this transfer, place the cell pointer on A3, enter /**Copy**, and press ENTER. Then move the cell pointer to B3 as the To location and press ENTER again. The formula is replicated into B3 and, in addition, adjustments are made that make the formula appropriate for B3, as shown here:

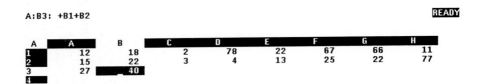

Let's try this again, but this time copy from B3 across the remainder of the row. Enter /**Copy** with the cell pointer on B3, and press ENTER. Move the cell pointer to C3 as the beginning of the To range, enter a period, move the cell pointer to H3, and press ENTER again. Figure 5-44 shows that the appropriate formulas were copied across the row.

Relative references can be used in formulas any time you want the formula adjusted during the copying process. Figure 5-45 shows another worksheet with a column of formulas. To copy the formulas, position the cell pointer on C3 and enter /**Copy**. Then move the cell pointer to C5, which expands the highlighting, and press ENTER. Move the cell pointer to D3, type a period, and move the cell pointer across to F3, before pressing ENTER to finalize the To range. Figure 5-46, which contains the results of the copying process, has been changed to a text format so that you can review 1-2-3's work in copying the formulas.

Figure 5-47 shows some formula entries in an earlier model, where labels were copied across sheets. Now that the formulas have been added you can copy them across sheets as well. The absolute reference (see next section) to Expense Growth on sheet A ensures that the entries for all four regions will use the same growth rate projection. First, move the cell pointer to A:A1 and enter /**Copy**. Expand the range to A:G6 and press ENTER. Next, use CTRL-PGUP to move the highlighting to the same cell as the beginning of the range, but in the next sheet. Type a decimal point, press CTRL-PGUP two more times, and then ENTER to produce the results in Figure 5-48.

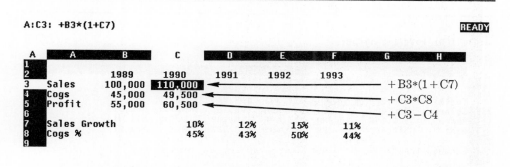

Figure 5-45.   A column of formulas

A:F3: (T) [W11] +E3*(1+F7)   **READY**

A	A	B	C	D	E	F	
1							
2		1989	1990	1991	1992	1993	
3	Sales	100,000	+B3*(1+C7)	+C3*(1+D7)	+D3*(1+E7)	+E3*(1+F7)	
4	Cogs	45,000	+C3*C8	+D3*D8	+E3*E8	+F3*F8	
5	Profit	55,000	+C3−C4	+D3−D4	+E3−E4	+F3−F4	
6							
7	Sales Growth		10%	12%	15%	11%	
8	Cogs %		45%	43%	50%	44%	
9							

Figure 5-46.   Result of copying formulas, displayed as text

Absolute References

Absolute references are references that you want held constant. In other words, you do not want these references to be adjusted when they are copied to a different location. This is the kind of reference you want for, say, a single interest rate, a specific value in an assumption block, or a table that is in a fixed location. Even when you copy this formula to other sheets, the sheet, column, or row portions of an absolute address are not updated.

Entering absolute cell references in formulas requires a little more work, because absolute references must have a $ in front of the column, the row, and the sheet portions of the address. $A:$A$A, $F$87, and $X$1 are all absolute references. 1-2-3 does not remember the relative

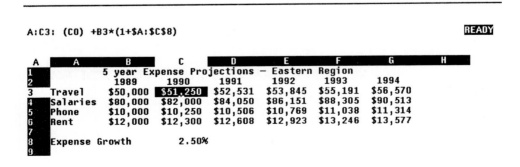

A:C3: (C0) +B3*(1+$A:$C$8)   **READY**

A	A	B	C	D	E	F	G	H
1		5 year Expense Projections − Eastern Region						
2		1989	1990	1991	1992	1993	1994	
3	Travel	$50,000	$51,250	$52,531	$53,845	$55,191	$56,570	
4	Salaries	$80,000	$82,000	$84,050	$86,151	$88,305	$90,513	
5	Phone	$10,000	$10,250	$10,506	$10,769	$11,038	$11,314	
6	Rent	$12,000	$12,300	$12,608	$12,923	$13,246	$13,577	
7								
8	Expense Growth		2.50%					
9								

Figure 5-47.   Data from the multi-sheet model used earlier

Basic Worksheet Commands   **223**

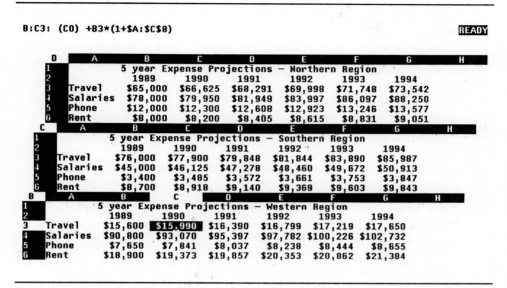

Figure 5-48.   Result of copying formulas across sheets

direction and distance that must be traveled to obtain these values when they are used in a formula. Instead, it remembers the absolute cell address.

There are two ways to enter the $s during formula entry. You can type them wherever they are required, or you can have 1-2-3 enter them for you. To get 1-2-3 to do the work, you must enter your formulas with the pointing method. For example, the worksheet in Figure 5-49 requires formulas that use both relative and absolute references, since

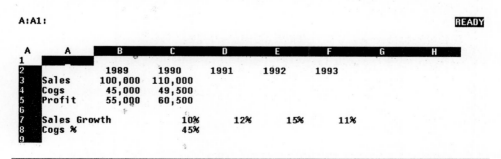

Figure 5-49.   Model requiring relative and absolute references

there are varying Sales Growth rates but one fixed Cogs (cost of goods sold) percentage that applies to all years. The formulas that were already entered for the 1989 sales used only relative references. The formula for cost of goods sold (row 4) requires both a relative reference to sales for the current year, and an absolute reference to the Cogs % (cell C8). An absolute reference is required because the same Cogs % will be used for all years. The formula will be +C3*$C$8 for 1990, +D3*$C$8 for 1991, and so forth.

To enter this formula in cell C4 (it will later be copied to other cells in row 4), place the cell pointer in C4 and enter a +. The first cell reference needed in the formula is the 1990 Sales figure in C3, so use the UP ARROW to point to C3. Since you want to multiply this figure by the Cogs %, enter an *, representing multiplication, next.

Now, move the cell pointer to C8 to reference the Cogs %. If you needed a relative reference, you would press ENTER now, but since you want an absolute reference to this cell, $s are needed first. 1-2-3 will enter them for you from the POINT mode if you press F4 (ABS). The first time you press this key, the reference becomes $A:$C$8. You can continue to press it to cycle through all the possibilities:

Absolute reference	$A:$C$8 — first time
Mixed address	$A:C$8 — second time
Mixed address	$A:$C8 — third time
Mixed address	$A:C8 — fourth time
Mixed address	A:$C$8 — fifth time
Mixed address	A:C$8 — sixth time
Mixed address	A:$C8 — seventh time
Relative reference	C8 — eighth time

The F4 (ABS) key will cycle through the possibilities again if you continue to press it.

Once the cell reference has the dollar signs added in both positions, press ENTER to accept it. If another arithmetic operation were required in the formula, typing the arithmetic operator would also have accepted the $ placement. (For instance, entering + to continue the formula would accept the $A:$C$8 reference.)

```
A:C4: +C3*$A:$C$8                                                  READY
```

```
   A        A          B          C          D          E          F          G          H
   1
   2                 1989       1990       1991       1992       1993
   3    Sales      100,000    110,000    123,200    141,680    157,265
   4    Cogs        45,000     49,500     55,440     63,756     70,769
   5    Profit      55,000     60,500     67,760     77,924     86,496
   6
   7    Sales Growth            10%        12%        15%        11%
   8    Cogs %                  45%
   9
```

Figure 5-50.   Result of copying relative and absolute references

The formula +A:C3*$A:$C$8 is now entered, containing both an absolute and a relative reference. The result of the calculation is the same as if both relative references had been used. Only when the formula is copied to new locations will the difference become apparent.

Before this is demonstrated, let's examine one more formula in Figure 5-49—the one needed to calculate the profit for 1990. This formula is simply +C3-C4, with both references relative. All three years' formulas will be copied at once. To do this, move the cell pointer to the top cell in the range to be copied, C3, and enter /**Copy**. Move the cell pointer down twice to highlight the entire From range. Next move to D3 as the first location in the To range and enter a period. Then move across to F3, and press ENTER. Figure 5-50 shows the results of the copying process.

The formulas in the different cells are shown in Figure 5-51. If an

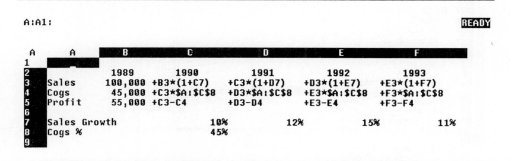

```
A:A1:                                                             READY
```

```
   A        A          B             C              D              E              F
   1
   2                 1989          1990           1991           1992           1993
   3    Sales      100,000    +B3*(1+C7)     +C3*(1+D7)     +D3*(1+E7)     +E3*(1+F7)
   4    Cogs        45,000    +C3*$A:$C$8    +D3*$A:$C$8    +E3*$A:$C$8    +F3*$A:$C$8
   5    Profit      55,000    +C3-C4         +D3-D4         +E3-E4         +F3-F4
   6
   7    Sales Growth           10%            12%            15%            11%
   8    Cogs %                 45%
   9
```

Figure 5-51.   Formulas from Figure 5-50 displayed

absolute reference had not been used for the Cogs %, 1-2-3 would attempt to increment the cell reference for each new formula, and blank cells would be referenced for years beyond 1990.

As you can see from this example, you can combine relative and absolute references to create formulas that meet your exact needs.

Mixed Addresses

1-2-3 has one more reference type that extends the package features still further. This reference type is a *mixed address*, which combines relative and absolute features in one cell reference.

Since a cell address is composed of a sheet, a row, and a column reference, it is possible to make one component absolute while leaving the others relative. This gives you the flexibility, for example, to have the column portion of an address updated when a formula is copied across the sheet, while keeping the row portion of the same address constant when the formula is copied down the worksheet.

Figure 5-52 presents an application where the mixed addressing feature is useful. In this worksheet the 1989 figures are historic numbers, and all of the projections for subsequent years use these figures as base numbers. Sales projections for each product will use the appropriate growth factor from C4..C6. For Product A, for example, the sales

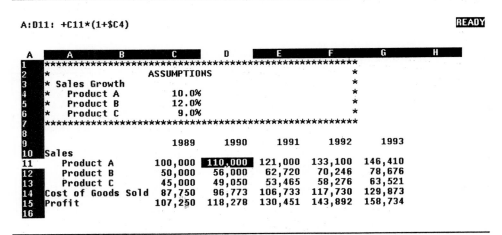

Figure 5-52.   An application of mixed addressing

figure from 1989 will be multiplied by 110%. This formula could be written in cell D11 as +C11*(1+C4). It would work for this one year, but it would cause a problem when copied across to subsequent years, since C4 would be updated to D4, E4, and so on.

Using $C$4 in this formula would present another problem, since the Product A formulas could not be copied down for Product B and Product C. If an absolute reference were used for C4, the copied formulas could not reference C5 and C6. The ideal situation would be to freeze the column portion of the address, but allow the row portion to vary. Mixed addressing provides this capability. If the formula reference is written as $C4, only the column portion of the address will be absolute; the row portion will be allowed to vary during the copy process.

A little thought and planning is required to decide how to construct the address type you need. You might elect to just use a different formula for each of the product types. That is all right, but for twenty-five products rather than three, the mixed addressing feature really saves significant time, since it allows you to devise one formula to work for all situations.

The formula devised for D11 is +C11*(1+$C4). Mixed addressing allows this formula to be used for all the sales projections. First copy it down column C to C12 and C13. Then copy the range C11..C13 across to column D through column G. The formulas automatically created in E11..G13 are as follows:

```
E11: +D11*(1+$C4)
F11: +E11*(1+$C4)
G11: +F11*(1+$C4)
E12: +D12*(1+$C5)
F12: +E12*(1+$C5)
G12: +F12*(1+$C5)
E13: +D13*(1+$C6)
F13: +E13*(1+$C6)
G13: +F13*(1+$C6)
```

Using mixed addressing, you can enter one formula and have 1-2-3 generate the other 11 formulas for you. Although mixed addressing is not useful in all models, its payback under appropriate circumstances is significant enough to make it a desirable part of your model building toolkit.

Using 1-2-3's Search and Replace Features

Through /Range Search, Release 3 offers you the ability to search for character strings within formulas and labels. This feature is especially useful in a large worksheet where you need to locate a particular entry with no knowledge of its cell address. The area that you search can span sheets in a multiple sheet file if you are uncertain which sheet you want to search. With the Find option you can find the first occurrence of your entry, or continue to search through a specified range of the worksheet file. You can use /Range Search to search either formulas, labels, or both.

The /Range Search command offers a Replace option in addition to its Find features. With the Replace option, you supply a replacement string which 1-2-3 uses as a substitute for the character string you find within matching entries. This feature is useful if you need to replace cell references or range names in a large range of formula entries. You can replace the first occurrence or all occurrences. If you prefer, you can proceed through the selected range, finding one occurrence at a time.

Tip: You may want to replace matching entries one at a time until you are certain that the search string you entered is matching correctly. This isn't necessary if you need to change all occurrences of A:$D$9 to D:$A$9, because you will probably only find correct matches. But, if you want to change the A in A:$D$9 to D, searching for A and replacing it with D could be a disaster if you choose All. Entries like AB10 would be changed to DB10, and all A's in range names would be changed to D's. As a rule, be as specific as possible when doing a replace.

Using Search

The /Range Search command lets you locate a string of characters in a range of formulas or labels. If the range you choose spans sheets, 1-2-3 will be able to scan many sheets for you much more quickly than you can visually yourself. You might want to scan a large range of data for a vendor name, or a range name that you are considering deleting. When looking for a range name, you will want to use the Formulas option for this command, to scan only the cells with formula entries. When looking for text stored in a label cell, you can restrict your search to cells that contain labels.

To find the name Campbell in the data in Figure 5-53, enter /**Range Search** and highlight the cells that contain name entries. This range might be the cells that are visible, or it could include a much longer column or additional columns on other sheets. After selecting the appropriate range, press ENTER. Type **campbell;** since upper- and lowercase are equivalent in a search string, you do not need to capitalize your entry. Select Labels, and then Find from the next menu. The first occurrence of the cell containing the first occurrence of the string will be highlighted. Select either Next to look for additional occurrences or Quit to end the Find operation.

A:A1: [W12] 'Last Name   `READY`

A	A	B	C	D	E	F
1	Last Name	First Name	SS#	Job Code	Salary	Location
2	Wilkes	Caitlin	124-67-7432	17	$15,500	2
3	Campbell	David	213-76-9874	23	$23,000	10
4	Parker	Dee	659-11-3452	14	$19,800	4
5	Hartwick	Eileen	313-78-9090	15	$31,450	4
6	Preverson	Gary	670-90-1121	21	$27,600	4
7	Smythe	George	560-90-8645	15	$65,000	4
8	Justof	Jack	431-78-9963	17	$41,200	4
9	McCartin	John	817-66-1212	15	$54,600	2
10	Campbell	Keith	569-89-7654	12	$32,000	2
11	Deaver	Ken	198-98-6750	23	$24,600	10
12	Caldor	Larry	459-34-0921	23	$32,500	4
13	Miller	Lisa	214-89-6756	23	$18,700	2
14	Patterson	Lyle	212-11-9090	12	$21,500	10
15	Hawkins	Mark	215-67-8973	21	$19,500	2
16	Larson	Mary	543-98-9876	23	$12,000	2
17	Samuelson	Paul	219-89-7080	23	$28,900	2
18	Lightnor	Peggy	560-55-4311	14	$23,500	10
19	Kaylor	Sally	312-45-9862	12	$32,900	10
20	Stephens	Tom	219-78-8954	15	$17,800	2

Figure 5-53.   Section of large worksheet

Using Replace

The Replace option not only locates strings but allows you to replace them with other entries. The data in Figure 5-53 can be used again for this example. Let's say you want to change the second occurrence of the last name Campbell to Camper. You could find the entry, quit, and then change it; or you can use Replace. Begin a Replace operation in the same way by entering /**Range Search**, highlighting the range containing the name entries, and pressing ENTER. Next, type **Campbell** and press ENTER. Select **Labels** followed by **Replace**. Type **Camper** and press ENTER. The first occurrence of Campbell is not the one you want to replace, so select Next to move to the next occurrence without changing the current entry. The second occurrence highlighted is the one you want, so select Replace to complete the change. Since there are no additional entries, you are finished. You can press ESC to return to READY mode.

Other menu options for Replace are All to change all the records at once, and Quit to return to READY mode when you do not wish to make further changes. Figure 5-54 shows the altered data.

```
A:A10: [W12] 'Camper                                          ERROR
Replace  All  Next  Quit
Replace string and proceed to next matching string in range
    A       A          B            C      D        E      F
1   Last Name    First Name      SS# Job Code   Salary Location
2   Wilkes       Caitlin    124-67-7432     17   $15,500      2
3   Campbell     David      213-76-9874     23   $23,000     10
4   Parker       Dee        659-11-3452     14   $19,800      4
5   Hartwick     Eileen     313-78-9090     15   $31,450      4
6   Preverson    Gary       670-90-1121     21   $27,600      4
7   Smythe       George     560-90-8645     15   $65,000      4
8   Justof       Jack       431-78-9963     17   $41,200      4
9   McCartin     John       817-66-1212     15   $54,600      2
10  Camper       Keith      569-89-7654     12   $32,000      2
11  Deaver       Ken        198-98-6750     23   $24,600     10
12  Caldor       Larry      459-34-0921     23   $32,500      4
13  Miller       Lisa       214-89-6756     23   $18,700      2
14  Patterson    Lyle       212-11-9090     12   $21,500     10
15  Hawkins      Mark       215-67-8973     21   $19,500      2
16  Larson       Mary       543-98-9876     23   $12,000      2
17  Samuelson    Paul       219-89-7080     23   $28,900      2
18  Lightnor     Peggy      560-55-4311     14   $23,500     10
19  Kaylor       Sally      312-45-9862     12   $32,900     10
20  Stephens     Tom        219-78-8954     15   $17,800      2
No more matching strings — Press HELP (F1)
```

Figure 5-54.   Data altered with the Replace option

Making Other Worksheet Changes

Several additional features bring advanced capabilities to worksheet preparation. In this section you will look at options that allow you to change label justification for the entire worksheet, to erase the complete worksheet with one command and to change the beep that occurs when you make a mistake. 1-2-3 also includes a Help access command for compatibility with previous releases. An additional capability, for embedding page breaks in a worksheet, is discussed in Chapter 6, "Printing."

Changing Default Label Justification for the Worksheet

The default worksheet setting for labels provides left justification for every label entry. This means that a single quotation mark will be generated as the first character of every label entry. As you learned in Chapter 3, "Entering Data in 1-2-3's Worksheet," you always have the option of center justifying a label entry by typing the center justification character yourself. For example, entering ˆ**Sales** would center justify the label Sales in the cell where it was entered. You can also right justify a single entry by beginning your label entry with a double quotation mark (").

1-2-3 offers further flexibility with the /Range Label command, which lets you change the justification of label entries that are already in cells. But if you want all of your labels to default to a new justification, neither the single entry method nor the Range option is exactly right. For such circumstances, 1-2-3 provides the /**Worksheet Global Label** command to change the default label prefix for every new worksheet entry. To make the change, enter /**Worksheet Global Label** and select the justification you want from the menu, as shown in this example.

With the Worksheet option, existing entries are unaffected, but new entries will have the new label prefix. Just the opposite is true with /Range Label. With both options you should remember that numeric and formula entries are unaffected by changes made to the label prefix.

Erasing the Worksheet

1-2-3 provides a command to erase the entire contents of the worksheet currently in memory. This feature is useful when you have made so many mistakes that you want to wipe the slate clean and start over again, or when you have saved all your completed worksheets on disk and want to begin a new application without having to delete each worksheet individually.

When you enter **/Worksheet Erase** to request this feature, 1-2-3 presents the following screen:

You must confirm your selection from this menu or abandon the operation. This confirmation step is provided because of the dramatic effect of Erase.

Caution: Your only hope for restoring the effect of /Worksheet Erase is with ALT-F4 (UNDO), and only then if your Undo feature is enabled at the time of the erase operation and there have been no intervening actions. In other words, once you have erased a worksheet, there is no way to bring the contents of memory back without UNDO, unless you have saved a copy of the worksheets on disk.

You will notice that the cell pointer is initially positioned over the No option on the confirmation screen, so if you accidentally press ENTER without looking, you will not lose your worksheet files. To erase the worksheets you will have to take an action, either typing **Y** or pointing to the Yes option before pressing ENTER.

Tip: /Worksheet Erase has a more dramatic effect in Release 3 than in earlier releases. When you used /Worksheet Erase in prior releases, it did erase all of memory. However, since memory could only contain one worksheet, your risk was minimized somewhat if you accidentally executed the command. With Release 3, you might erase 15 files with one execution of this command.

Controlling the Beep Option

The default setting for 1-2-3 causes your computer to sound a bell when you make an error or execute 1-2-3's {BEEP} macro instruction. This sound is designed to alert you to an error situation, but it can be disabled if you would prefer not to hear it.

To change the setting for Beep in the current session, enter **/Worksheet Global Default Other Beep No**. You can enable it again later with the Yes option of this same command. If you wish to make this change permanent, enter **/Worksheet Global Default Update**; 1-2-3 will alter the file 123.CNF that contains the default parameters for each new session. To check the status of the current Beep or other default settings, enter **/Worksheet Global Default Status**. You cannot change any of the options from this screen.

Help Access Setting for Release 2 Compatibility

When you press the HELP (F1) key, 1-2-3 opens the 123.HLP file to display the Help information. Pressing ESC closes the file. Opening and closing the Help file allows 1-2-3 to run faster. In earlier versions, you could set 1-2-3 to open the Help file when 1-2-3 was loaded and close the file when you quit 1-2-3. Release 3 still has the /Worksheet Global Default Other Help command for compatibility, but the two options, Removable and Instant, have no effect.

Recalculating the Worksheet

1-2-3's recalculation abilities provide the power behind its formula features. A new improved calculation method offers minimal, intelligent, background recalculation. The essence of these adjectives is that 1-2-3 no longer recalculates the entire worksheet every time a new entry is made in a worksheet cell. It only recalculates the formulas affected by the new entry and has the intelligence to determine which cells are affected. Recalculation now takes place as a background activity, so that you can continue with your other worksheet tasks while 1-2-3 is updating the worksheet formula results.

Some tasks—like printing, changing formulas to values with /Range Value, or altering the layout of entries with /Range Trans—should only be done when the recalculation has completed. You can watch for this to occur by waiting for the CALC indicator to disappear from the bottom of the screen. Or press F9 (CALC) to cause 1-2-3 to do the calculations in the foreground. The latter approach is better, since you cannot proceed until 1-2-3 finishes, and all of your machine's resources are dedicated to the recalculation effort. All the recalculation options are accessed through the /Worksheet Global Recalc command.

Default Recalculation Settings

1-2-3's recalculation features have three different setting categories, all selected from the following menu:

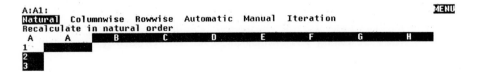

One group determines whether recalculation will be automatic or only upon request. The second group controls the order in which the worksheet formulas will be reevaluated. The last recalculation option specifies how many times each formula will be reevaluated during recalculation.

Timing of Recalculation

The default setting for a new worksheet is Automatic recalculation. This means that any new number, changed number, or new formula will cause 1-2-3 to recalculate all worksheet formulas affected by your change. The time needed for this recalculation depends on the number and complexity of the worksheet formulas and the number of formulas affected by your change. Since 1-2-3 recalculates in the background, you will be able to continue with other tasks, although part of your computer's resources will be dedicated to the recalculation. If you have a whole series of entries to make and are not concerned with the impact of each individual entry, you can use Manual recalculation, so that 1-2-3 does not do any recalculations until you request them.

Order of Recalculation

The default setting for recalculation order is Natural. This means that 1-2-3 will examine each worksheet formula for dependencies on other formulas, and determine which formulas must be calculated first to provide the results needed by the formulas to be reevaluated next. This Natural recalculation order set a new standard for other spreadsheets when it was first introduced. Before then the only options were Rowwise or Columnwise recalculation.

Rowwise recalculation evaluates all the formulas in row 1, then all the formulas in row 2, and so on. The problem with this method is that if a formula in row 1 references a value in a row further down the worksheet, the earlier formula will reference a value from a prior recalculation. The same type of problem occurs with columnwise recalculation, when early columns reference values further to the right that have not yet been recalculated. These deficiencies in existing recalculation methods made 1-2-3's Natural recalculation order a welcome addition.

Iterations of Recalculation

The default setting for the number of iterations for a recalculation is once. This means that each formula requiring recalculation is computed once each time the worksheet is recalculated. If you set this number higher than one, 1-2-3 will perform multiple recalculation when the order of calculation is rowwise or columnwise, or if there is a circular reference with Natural recalculation order.

Changing the Recalculation Settings

If you do not want the default settings, each of the three categories of recalculation options can be changed. The various recalculation options and appropriate circumstances for their use are summarized in the box called "Recalculation Options and Potential Pitfalls."

Timing of Recalculation

To turn off Automatic recalculation, enter /**Worksheet Global Recalc Manual**. When the Manual option is in force, the worksheet will not recalculate unless you turn Automatic back on, or press the F9 (CALC) key. The Manual option can speed up your data entry, since you can enter everything before requesting a recalculation.

Order of Recalculation

If you want recalculation done in Rowwise or Columnwise order, rather than Natural order, you can obtain these options by entering /**Worksheet Global Recalc Rowwise** or /**Worksheet Global Recalc Columnwise**, respectively. You might want to use the other recalculation orders when you import data from another worksheet package. If you bring a model created with a package like VisiCalc into 1-2-3, you might want to retain the recalculation order used with the original model.

Iterations of Recalculation

In calculations that involve a circular calculation pattern, one iteration is not sufficient. This is because each calculation depends on the result of some other calculation, with the final result referring back to one of the earlier calculations. In situations like this, 1-2-3 is not able to identify a clear recalculation sequence for the formulas. Multiple calculations are

Recalculation Options and Potential Pitfalls

The recalculation options control three different features of recalculation. Each of these settings remains in effect until changed, or until a file is loaded into memory with /File Retrieve or /File Open. Here are the specific options, along with a few tips for their use:

Automatic This option, which causes the worksheet to recalculate automatically after every worksheet entry, is the default setting. You can stop the Automatic recalculation by invoking /Worksheet Global Recalc Manual.

Manual This option turns off the Automatic recalculation feature. The worksheet will not recalculate with this option in effect unless you use F9 (CALC). You can restore Automatic recalculation with /Worksheet Global Recalc Automatic.

Natural This option controls the order in which formulas are recalculated. This is the default setting, and makes 1-2-3 responsible for determining which formula to evaluate first. You can change to either Rowwise or Columnwise recalculation.

Rowwise This option disables the Natural recalculation sequence and switches to recalculation by rows. Row 1 is calculated from left to right, then row 2, and so on beginning on sheet A of the worksheet. The potential problem with this approach is early references that refer to values not yet recalculated.

Columnwise This option disables the Natural recalculation sequence and switches to recalculation by columns. Column 1 is calculated from top to bottom, then column 2, and so on from left to right on the worksheet. Again, the potential problem with this approach is early references to values not yet recalculated.

Iterations The normal setting for this option is 1, meaning that each formula is recalculated once during every worksheet recalculation. Circular references and other applications requiring iterative calculations to refine approximations require the iteration count to be set higher. The highest number 1-2-3 will accept is 50.

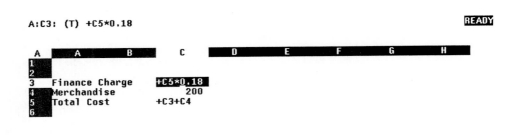

Figure 5-55. Example of a circular reference

required so that each will approximate the correct answer a little more closely.

Increasing 1-2-3's iterative count can solve the problem with circular references. This increase means that 1-2-3 will recalculate more than once each time the worksheet is automatically calculated or the F9 (CALC) key is pressed.

An example of a circular reference requiring iteration for resolution is shown in the formulas in Figure 5-55. When the formulas are first entered, C3 displays as 0 and C5 displays as 200. Since these two formulas are dependent on each other, each recalculation refines the accuracy of the result. The results after several recalculations with the F9 (CALC) key appear in the worksheet as shown in Figure 5-56. Slight changes continue to occur over the next several recalculations, until a final approximation is reached. All of these calculations could have been performed the first time the worksheet was calculated if the iteration count had been set higher.

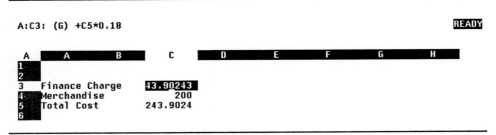

Figure 5-56. Using F9 (CALC) to update the formula results

Modifying the Screen Display

1-2-3 has several screen display options that are especially useful for large worksheets. One option allows you to lock the titles or descriptive labels at the side or top of your screen so that you can look at data in remote parts of the worksheet and still have these labels in view. Another feature lets you split the screen vertically or horizontally and use each section as a window into a different part of the worksheet. The third option allows you to create a map of the worksheet in order to easily identify cells that contain formulas, values, and labels.

Freezing Titles

The /Worksheet Titles command presents the following menu:

```
A:A1:                                                            MENU
Both  Horizontal  Vertical  Clear
Freeze all rows and columns above and to the left of the cell pointer
  A       A         B         C         D         E         F         G         H
1
2
```

With these options you can elect to freeze titles at the top of your screen, the side of your screen, or both. The command is position dependent in that it freezes titles that are above and to the left of the cell pointer location at the time you invoke the command.

Once titles are frozen on the screen, you will not be able to use the arrow keys to move into these cells. If you need to make spelling corrections or other changes in these cells, you can use the F5 (GOTO) key. Pressing this key temporarily brings two copies of the titles to the screen, as shown here:

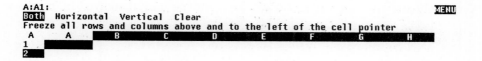

```
A:A1:                                                                  MENU
Horizontal  Vertical  Sync  Unsync  Clear  Map  Perspective  Graph  Display
Split the screen horizontally at the current row
  A       A         B         C         D         E         F         G         H
1                        New Employees By Department
2
3   DEPT.         1975      1976      1977      1978      1979      1980      1981
4          100      23        69        58        24        34        74        31
```

This double title will disappear when you scroll away from the title area.

Tip: GROUP mode will cause title changes to apply to all sheets in the active file. If GROUP mode is on, titles will be frozen at the same time in all active models.

Freezing Horizontal Titles

If you choose /Worksheet Titles Horizontal, the titles above the cell pointer will be frozen. Figure 5-57 presents a section from a worksheet with many entries. If you move your cell pointer toward the bottom of the entries, the top lines will scroll off. Figure 5-58 shows the worksheet with the two top lines, including the identifying labels, scrolled off. The remaining numbers are difficult to interpret without the labels.

To freeze the labels in row 1, move the cell pointer to A2 on the original screen and select /**Worksheet Global Titles Horizontal**. Now, when the cell pointer is moved down the worksheet, the titles remain visible, as shown in Figure 5-59. Notice that the figure starts with row 1, which displays the horizontal titles, but the data displayed is from row 4 to 22.

A:A1: 'Part No.   `READY`

A	A	B	C	D	E	F	G	H
1	Part No.	Cost	Warehouse					
2	1502	$0.25	3					
3	1234	$1.79	4					
4	2134	$1.25	3					
5	5678	$2.35	2					
6	8543	$2.45	1					
7	6752	$5.90	2					
8	3412	$9.99	3					
9	2134	$7.50	3					
10	5432	$6.25	3					
11	8765	$0.59	2					
12	6667	$3.35	4					
13	5567	$2.00	5					
14	5543	$1.00	2					
15	4435	$2.25	2					
16	4432	$3.45	2					
17	7789	$7.80	3					
18	8876	$0.79	1					
19	9931	$2.00	1					
20	4452	$1.50	4					

Figure 5-57.   Worksheet with many entries down the sheet

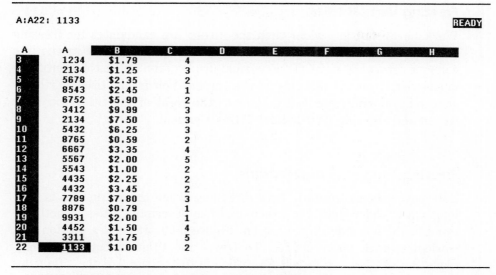

A:A22: 1133   READY

A	A	B	C	D	E	F	G	H
3	1234	$1.79	4					
4	2134	$1.25	3					
5	5678	$2.35	2					
6	8543	$2.45	1					
7	6752	$5.90	2					
8	3412	$9.99	3					
9	2134	$7.50	3					
10	5432	$6.25	3					
11	8765	$0.59	2					
12	6667	$3.35	4					
13	5567	$2.00	5					
14	5543	$1.00	2					
15	4435	$2.25	2					
16	4432	$3.45	2					
17	7789	$7.80	3					
18	8876	$0.79	1					
19	9931	$2.00	1					
20	4452	$1.50	4					
21	3311	$1.75	5					
22	1133	$1.00	2					

Figure 5-58.   Top row title lines scroll off the screen

A:A22: 1133   READY

A	A	B	C	D	E	F	G	H
1	Part No.	Cost	Warehouse					
4	2134	$1.25	3					
5	5678	$2.35	2					
6	8543	$2.45	1					
7	6752	$5.90	2					
8	3412	$9.99	3					
9	2134	$7.50	3					
10	5432	$6.25	3					
11	8765	$0.59	2					
12	6667	$3.35	4					
13	5567	$2.00	5					
14	5543	$1.00	2					
15	4435	$2.25	2					
16	4432	$3.45	2					
17	7789	$7.80	3					
18	8876	$0.79	1					
19	9931	$2.00	1					
20	4452	$1.50	4					
21	3311	$1.75	5					
22	1133	$1.00	2					

Figure 5-59.   Titles remain on the screen after freezing

Freezing Vertical Titles

Worksheets that are wider than the screen are candidates for freezing titles vertically. Doing so will allow you to move across the screen into columns far to the right of the normal display, and still have identifying labels visible on the left side of the screen. You freeze titles vertically simply by moving your cell pointer to the right of the titles you want frozen and entering /**Worksheet Titles Vertical**.

Freezing Titles in Both Directions

You may want to freeze in both directions when the worksheet is both longer and wider than the screen, and has descriptive titles at both the top and the left side of the screen. Figure 5-60 presents a portion of a worksheet with many entries. To freeze the titles in both directions, move the cell pointer to cell B4, which is to the right of the side titles and below the top titles, and then enter /**Worksheet Titles Both**. When the cell pointer is moved to J26, causing information to scroll off the top and left of the screen, both sets of titles are still visible, as you can see in Figure 5-61.

A:A1:   `READY`

A	A	B	C	D	E	F	G	H
1			New Employees By Department					
2								
3	DEPT.	1975	1976	1977	1978	1979	1980	1981
4	100	51	66	83	82	73	53	43
5	120	33	93	31	38	29	12	71
6	130	20	28	95	25	39	78	35
7	140	88	59	0	33	53	73	56
8	145	23	31	32	7	22	39	27
9	150	84	18	72	59	47	76	78
10	160	64	89	62	55	26	21	54
11	175	85	22	27	93	46	37	17
12	180	5	92	17	8	60	73	98
13	190	21	36	41	76	6	9	57
14	195	5	65	14	91	83	5	39
15	200	0	85	41	48	87	13	32
16	210	62	45	11	60	61	19	52
17	220	31	23	39	65	31	20	30
18	225	61	5	38	42	18	74	64
19	228	50	47	85	1	49	49	57
20	230	33	96	73	46	9	77	70

Figure 5-60.   Worksheet with extra width and depth

```
A:J26: @SUM(J4..J23)                                               READY

A     A       D       E       F       G       H       I       J
1             yees By Department
2
3   DEPT.    1977    1978    1979    1980    1981    1982    1983
10     160     62      55      26      21      54      42      92
11     175     27      93      46      37      17      50      45
12     180     17       8      60      73      98      15      87
13     190     41      76       6       9      57      94      16
14     195     14      91      83       5      39      23      87
15     200     41      48      87      13      32      94      16
16     210     11      60      61      19      52      23      87
17     220     39      65      31      20      30      94      44
18     225     38      42      18      74      64      19      28
19     228     85       1      49      49      57     100      23
20     230     73      46       9      77      70       6       9
21     235     70      73      82       4       2      57      62
22     240      9       7      88      34      36      18      43
23     245      5      28       1       9      76      51      28
24
25
26  TOTAL     845     937     910     775     994     820     902
```

Figure 5-61.   Titles frozen in both directions

Clearing Titles

/Worksheet Titles Clear eliminates any titles that you have frozen. This command is not position dependent. It will remove the titles regardless of your cell pointer location.

Adding a Second Window

Having two windows in your screen display—available with /Worksheet Window—allows you to look at information in two completely different areas of the current worksheet file at the same time. When you learn how to open additional worksheet files in Chapter 8 "Working with Files," you can use the second window to display a different worksheet file. You can split the screen into two vertical or horizontal sections and then move your cell pointer within either window to bring whichever cells you choose into view.

There are also several special views of the worksheet available with the Window option, including the /Worksheet Window Map that provides a view of the types of data within the worksheet. The /Worksheet

Window Perspective command described in Chapter 4 allows you to look at three sheets in the same file or three files at once. In Chapter 11, "Working with 1-2-3's Graphics Features," you will learn about another /Worksheet Window command that displays a graph on your screen at the same time as other worksheet entries.

If you decide to divide the screen into horizontal or vertical windows, the size of each window depends on the cell pointer location at the time the split is requested. The split is placed to the left of or above the cell pointer location, based on whether the split is vertical or horizontal.

The command to split the worksheet is /Worksheet Window, which produces the following menu:

```
A:A1:                                                               MENU
Horizontal  Vertical  Sync  Unsync  Clear  Map  Perspective  Graph  Display
Split the screen horizontally at the current row
   A       A        B         C         D         E         F         G         H
   1                        New Employees By Department
   2
   3   DEPT.          1975      1976      1977      1978      1979      1980      1981
   4          100       23        69        58        24        34        74        31
```

You will notice there is no option for splitting the screen in both directions at once. This is due to 1-2-3's two-window limitation.

In addition to the Horizontal and Vertical options, the /Worksheet Window command has options that decide whether movement in one window will cause a corresponding shift of information in the second window. These options are Sync and Unsync.

Splitting the Screen Horizontally

A horizontal screen split is appropriate when you need the entire screen width to show two different sections of a worksheet report. To split the screen horizontally, move the cell pointer to a location within the row immediately below the desired split location. For example, Figure 5-62 shows the cell pointer positioned in A12. When you enter /**Worksheet Window Horizontal**, the screen splits into two different windows, with the size of the two windows being dictated by the cell pointer location at the time of the request. Figure 5-63 shows the result of the split in our

A:A12: 180   `READY`

A	A	B	C	D	E	F	G	H
1			New Employees By Department					
2								
3	DEPT.	1975	1976	1977	1978	1979	1980	1981
4	100	51	66	83	82	73	53	43
5	120	33	93	31	38	29	12	71
6	130	20	28	95	25	39	78	35
7	140	88	59	0	33	53	73	56
8	145	23	31	32	7	22	39	27
9	150	84	18	72	59	47	76	78
10	160	64	89	62	55	26	21	54
11	175	85	22	27	93	46	37	17
12	180	5	92	17	8	60	73	98
13	190	21	36	41	76	6	9	57
14	195	5	65	14	91	83	5	39
15	200	0	85	41	48	87	13	32
16	210	62	45	11	60	61	19	52
17	220	31	23	39	65	31	20	30
18	225	61	5	38	42	18	74	64
19	228	50	47	85	1	49	49	57
20	230	33	96	73	46	9	77	70

Figure 5-62.   Cell pointer positioned for horizontal window split

A:A26: 'TOTAL   `READY`

A	A	B	C	D	E	F	G	H
1			New Employees By Department					
2								
3	DEPT.	1975	1976	1977	1978	1979	1980	1981
4	100	51	66	83	82	73	53	43
5	120	33	93	31	38	29	12	71
6	130	20	28	95	25	39	78	35
7	140	88	59	0	33	53	73	56
8	145	23	31	32	7	22	39	27
9	150	84	18	72	59	47	76	78
10	160	64	89	62	55	26	21	54
11	175	85	22	27	93	46	37	17
19	228	50	47	85	1	49	49	57
20	230	33	96	73	46	9	77	70
21	235	21	99	70	73	82	4	2
22	240	42	66	9	7	88	34	36
23	245	26	55	5	28	1	9	76
24								
25								
26	TOTAL	805	1120	845	937	910	775	994

Figure 5-63.   Horizontally split screen

example. F6 (WINDOW) has been pressed to move the cell pointer into the second window.

Once the screen is split, you can use the arrow keys to move the cell pointer around in either window. In Figure 5-63, the cell pointer is in the TOTAL line. You can also move the second window to a different sheet while the first window remains on the original sheet.

Splitting the Screen Vertically

A vertical screen split is appropriate when you would like the full length of the screen to show sections of the worksheet but do not require the full width. Cell pointer position at the time of the request will again determine the size of the two windows. The split will occur to the left of the column in which the cell pointer is located.

Figure 5-64 presents a worksheet in which the screen will be split vertically at the cell pointer location. To produce this split, position the cell pointer in column E and enter /**Worksheet Window Vertical**. If you then press the F6 (WINDOW) key and move the cell pointer to column I, the display shown in Figure 5-65 will be produced. Notice that, just as with

A:E11: 93   READY

A	A	B	C	D	E	F	G	H
1			New Employees By Department					
2								
3	DEPT.	1975	1976	1977	1978	1979	1980	1981
4	100	51	66	83	82	73	53	43
5	120	33	93	31	38	29	12	71
6	130	20	28	95	25	39	78	35
7	140	88	59	0	33	53	73	56
8	145	23	31	32	7	22	39	27
9	150	84	18	72	59	47	76	78
10	160	64	89	62	55	26	21	54
11	175	85	22	27	93	46	37	17
12	180	5	92	17	8	60	73	98
13	190	21	36	41	76	6	9	57
14	195	5	65	14	91	83	5	39
15	200	0	85	41	48	87	13	32
16	210	62	45	11	60	61	19	52
17	220	31	23	39	65	31	20	30
18	225	61	5	38	42	18	74	64
19	228	50	47	85	1	49	49	57
20	230	33	96	73	46	9	77	70

Figure 5-64.   Worksheet ready for vertical split

```
A:I11: 50                                                            READY
```

A	A	B	C	D	A	F	G	H	I
1			New Employees By D		1				
2					2				
3	DEPT.	1975	1976	1977	3 1979	1980	1981	1982	
4	100	51	66	83	4	73	53	43	5
5	120	33	93	31	5	29	12	71	12
6	130	20	28	95	6	39	78	35	8
7	140	88	59	0	7	53	73	56	7
8	145	23	31	32	8	22	39	27	59
9	150	84	18	72	9	47	76	78	43
10	160	64	89	62	10	26	21	54	42
11	175	85	22	27	11	46	37	17	50
12	180	5	92	17	12	60	73	98	15
13	190	21	36	41	13	6	9	57	94
14	195	5	65	14	14	83	5	39	23
15	200	0	85	41	15	87	13	32	94
16	210	62	45	11	16	61	19	52	23
17	220	31	23	39	17	31	20	30	94
18	225	61	5	38	18	18	74	64	19
19	228	50	47	85	19	49	49	57	100
20	230	33	96	73	20	9	77	70	6

Figure 5-65.   Vertical split screen

the Horizontal option, the cell pointer was moved into the second window with F6 (WINDOW). Each time F6 (WINDOW) is pressed, the cell pointer will move into the opposite window.

Moving in Both Windows at Once

1-2-3's default setting has its two windows synchronized. This means that if you move in one window, the other window automatically scrolls to match it. With horizontal windows, moving the cell pointer from column A to column Z in one window causes the other window to automatically scroll to match. With vertical windows, moving from row 1 to row 120 in one window automatically updates the other window to display row 120, as well.

Moving in One Window at a Time

Sometimes you will want information, such as a table, to remain stationary while you move in the other window. You can make this change from either window using /**Worksheet Window Unsync**. With Unsync, the contents of the two windows are totally independent. If you choose, you can show the same information in both windows. To return to a synchronized mode, invoke /**Worksheet Window Sync**. This causes the two windows to move in tandem again. The Sync and Unsync options also affect window movement when a three-sheet perspective view is used.

Clearing the Second Window

When you decide to return to a single window display, enter /**Worksheet Window Clear**. If the screen was split horizontally, the returning single window obtains its default settings from the top window. If the screen was split vertically, the settings for the left window are used.

Using the Map Option to View Worksheet Information

As a worksheet grows large, it can be difficult to monitor all the entries it contains. Release 3's Map window can help you with this task by allowing you to audit the entries in the worksheet to determine if they contain numbers, labels, or formulas. This can be important. You might think that a model contains an entire column of formulas that add the data in each row. If you accidentally change a formula to a number, changes in the data will no longer update the total in this column.

Because the Map window narrows the display of the columns, many columns can be displayed on the screen at once. Label entries are displayed as double quotation marks ("), numbers are displayed as number signs (#), and formulas are displayed as plus signs (+). To invoke this view, enter /**Worksheet Window Map Enable**; to clear it again, enter /**Worksheet Window Map Disable**.

Figure 5-66 shows a model with 1989 budget entries. These entries extend to column N, and are totaled in column O and at the bottom of each column. If one of the @SUM functions is accidentally entered as a number, the Map window will reveal the error. After pressing /Worksheet Window Map, the display in Figure 5-67 is the result. You can see from this display that column O and row 13 do contain formulas in the required location, based on the "+" entries. If you encountered a "#" in any of these locations, you would need to explore the model further and make the required changes.

A:A1:   **READY**

A	A	B	C	D	E	F
1						1989 Budget f
2						
3			Jan	Feb	Mar	Apr
4	Salaries		$1,200,000	$1,218,000	$1,236,270	$1,254,814
5	Benefits		168,000	170,520	173,078	175,674
6	Occupancy		120,000	121,800	123,627	125,481
7	Phone		259,500	263,393	267,343	271,354
8	Advertising		1,050,000	1,065,750	1,081,736	1,097,962
9	Utilities		19,000	19,285	19,574	19,868
10	Supplies		67,000	68,005	69,025	70,060
11	Postage		3,500	3,553	3,606	3,660
12						
13	Total		$2,887,000	$2,930,305	$2,974,260	$3,018,873
14						

Figure 5-66.   Model with budget entries for an entire year

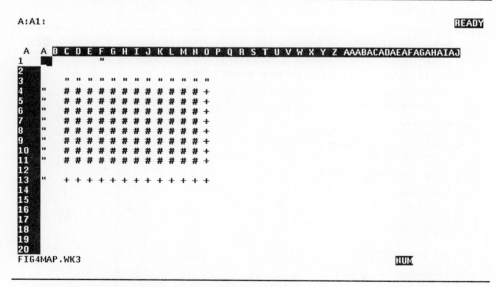

Figure 5-67.   Map view of the worksheet

Displaying Current Status of Worksheet Options

When you go back to a worksheet you used earlier, you may not remember all the options you chose for it. Conveniently, 1-2-3 lets you see the settings for all the worksheet options on one screen.

Enter /**Worksheet Status** to display the status of the options listed in Figure 5-68. With this command you can monitor the available memory, the existence of a math coprocessor to speed numeric calculations, the recalculation options, the default options for cell display, the global Protection status, and any cell causing a circular reference in the worksheet. The box called "A Closer Look at the Status Settings" provides a detailed look at the various status items listed. You cannot make changes to any of the options through the status display.

Tip: You can use both /Worksheet Status and /Worksheet Global Default Status to obtain a complete picture of 1-2-3's current settings, including selections, hardware, and system defaults.

```
                                                              STAT

Available memory: 2411100 of 2416256 Bytes (100%)

Processor: 80386
Math coprocessor: None

Recalculation:
  Method.......... Automatic
  Order........... Natural
  Iterations...... 1

Circular reference: (None)

Cell display:
  Format.......... (G)
  Label prefix..... '
  Column width..... 9
  Zero setting..... No

Global protection: Off

Build Number:    {79T5}
```

Figure 5-68.   Status display

A Closer Look at the Status Settings

There is a variety of information to monitor from the Status screen. Even though these settings are not individually selectable because they relate to different features of the worksheet, you will regard them as options and discuss each separately.

- **Available Memory** This portion of the display reports the amount of available memory you have used. This information helps you plan the remainder of your worksheet entries. When memory is almost full, you can split your worksheet in two.

- **Processor** This section reports the computer's resident processor. 1-2-3 automatically determines this display. Examples include 8088, 80286, and 80386.

- **Math Coprocessor** Release 3 supports the use of a math coprocessor chip. This section reports whether one of the supported chips is installed on your system.

- **Recalculation** This section reports on all the recalculation options. You can observe whether recalculation is set at Automatic or Manual. You can also monitor the current recalculation order to see whether it is set at Natural, Rowwise, or Columnwise. The current number of recalculation iterations set to occur is also displayed. To change any of the recalculation options use /Worksheet Global Recalc.

- **Circular Reference** It shows you the address of the first cell that is causing the CIRC indicator to appear at the bottom of your screen.

- **Cell Display** This section of the Status screen provides four different pieces of default information: the global format settings, the current label prefix, the column width, and whether zero suppression is on or off. These defaults can be changed through the Worksheet Global Menu option.

- **Global Protection** The last area of the Status screen shows whether global Protection is enabled or disabled. Changes to this setting can be made with /Worksheet Global Prot.

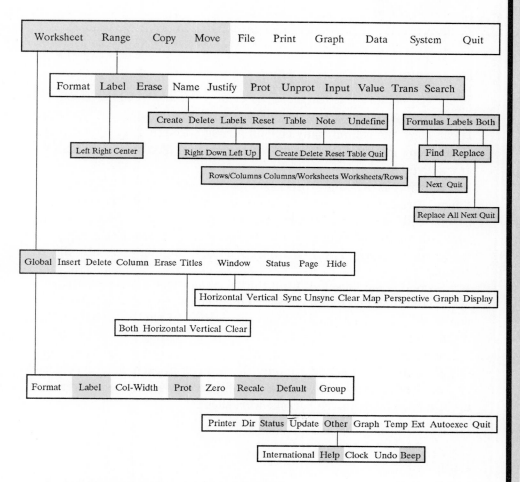

Worksheet   Range   Copy   Move   File   Print   Graph   Data   System   Quit

Format   Label   Erase   Name   Justify   Prot   Unprot   Input   Value   Trans   Search

Create   Delete   Labels   Reset   Table   Note   Undefine   Formulas   Labels   Both

Left Right Center   Right Down Left Up   Create Delete Reset Table Quit   Find   Replace

Rows/Columns Columns/Worksheets Worksheets/Rows   Next Quit

Replace All Next Quit

Global   Insert   Delete   Column   Erase   Titles   Window   Status   Page   Hide

Horizontal Vertical Sync Unsync Clear Map Perspective Graph Display

Both Horizontal Vertical Clear

Format   Label   Col-Width   Prot   Zero   Recalc   Default   Group

Printer Dir Status Update Other Graph Temp Ext Autoexec Quit

International Help Clock Undo Beep

© 1989 Lotus Development Corporation . Used with permission.

/Copy

Description

The /Copy command is the most powerful command 1-2-3 has to offer. It copies numbers, labels, and formulas to new locations on the worksheet. It can copy one cell or many cells in a range, to either a cell or a range. It can copy information from any file, including files stored on disk into any active file.

Copying is a simple process that requires telling 1-2-3 only two things. First, it wants to know where to copy from. The From range can be one cell or many. Multiple cells to be copied can be arranged in a row, column, or rectangle on one or more sheets. The From range can be typed, referenced with a range name, or highlighted with the cell pointer.

Secondly you must tell 1-2-3 the To range. This defines whether you are making one or several copies, and specifies the exact location where you would like them placed. Each duplication of the From information requires only that the top left cell in the To range be entered. For example, if you were copying A1..A15 to B1..E15, you need only enter B1..E1 as the To range, since only the top cell in each copy is required. If you do not specify a sheet level or a file reference, the cells referenced are assumed to be in the current worksheet.

Options

The /Copy command supports four copying procedures:

- One cell to one cell

- One cell to many cells

- A range of cells to a range the same size as the original range

- A range of cells to a range whose size is a multiple of the original range. For example, a column of five cells can be duplicated in several additional columns of five cells

Any of these options can be used with a single-sheet worksheet, a multiple-sheet worksheet, or with two different files. The specification of the From and To range determines what type of copying will take place.

/Move

Description

The /Move command allows you to move a range of worksheet entries to any location on the worksheet. This command will adjust the formulas within the range to correspond to their new location.

Options

This command permits you to move one or many cells to a new location. For example, you can move A2 to B3 by entering /**Move A2**, pressing ENTER, and then **B3** and pressing ENTER. To move a range of cells to a new location, you might enter /**Move A2..B6** and press ENTER, then enter a new destination like D2 and press ENTER. With a multiple sheet range, 1-2-3 will move the entire range, locating the contents of its upper leftmost cell (A2) in the designated To cell. You can use any of the options for specifying ranges, such as pressing F3 (NAME), pointing to the range, or typing the complete range address.

/Range Erase

Description

The /Range Erase command eliminates entries you have made in worksheet cells. Without this command your only options for removing a cell entry would be one of the following: make a new entry in the cell, edit the cell's contents, use the SPACEBAR to replace the entry with blanks, or press ALT-F4 (UNDO) immediately after making the entry. Only the Undo method leaves a label cell completely blank, however; the other approaches place a label indicator at minimum in the cell.

Options

There are no special options for this command. Your only choices are whether to specify a single cell or many cells in the range, and whether to type the range reference or highlight the included cells by pointing.

Note

The /Range Erase command does not affect cell formats. A cell formatted as Currency is still formatted as Currency after /Range Erase is used. (To eliminate a format, use /Range Format and a new format option, or use /Range Format Reset to return the range to the default setting.) The /Range Erase command also does not affect Protection or cell width. Protected cells cannot be erased when Worksheet Protection is enabled. In this situation 1-2-3 will present you with an error message instead of erasing the protected cells.

/Range Input

Description

This command is used to restrict cell pointer movement to unprotected cells. To use the command, first construct a worksheet and make sure the desired input cells are unprotected with /Range Unprot. Then enable Worksheet Protection with /Worksheet Global Prot Enable. Next, enter **/Range Input** and select a range of unprotected cells for the input area. Remember that ranges must be rectangular; this command will not work on input cells scattered across the entire worksheet.

Options

While using the /Range Input command, you can employ many of the cell pointer movement keys to move among the unprotected cells in the selected area. HOME moves to the first unprotected cell, and END moves to the last unprotected cell. The arrow keys will move you within the selected range. ESC can be used to cancel an entry, but if you have not made an entry, it will cancel /Range Input. ENTER can be used to finalize entries, but if no entries have been made, it will cancel /Range Input. Selections cannot be made from the command menus, although some of the function keys are operational. These are F1 (HELP), F2 (EDIT), and F9 (CALC).

Note

/Range Input is especially useful in the macro environment, where you are attempting to automate applications for inexperienced 1-2-3 users. See Chapter 13, "Command Language Macros," for more details.

/Range Label

Description

The /Range Label command is used to change the justification (placement) of existing worksheet labels. Cells within the range that are blank, however, will not save the label indicator you enter with /Range Label and apply it to later entries. These later entries will use the default worksheet setting.

Options

/Range Label has three options: Left, Center, and Right. These selections dictate the label indicator that will be used for existing cell entries. Left changes the label indicator to ' for all entries in the range, and left justifies them in the cells. Center places a ^ at the front of the labels and centers them in the cells. The last option, Right, places " at the beginning of the labels and right justifies them in the cells.

/Range Name Create

Description

The /Range Name Create command allows you to assign names to cell ranges. Using names rather than cell addresses makes formulas easier to understand and helps you develop worksheet models that are self-documenting. Range names can be used anywhere cell addresses can be used.

Options

After entering **/Range Name Create**, you have two options: working with an existing range name or entering a new one. If you choose to work with an existing range name, you can select a name from the list of existing range names in the menu and have 1-2-3 highlight the cells that are currently assigned this name. At this point you can use ESC to undo the existing range name assignment and specify a new range name.

To establish a new range name, after entering **/Range Name Create**, type a new range name of up to 15 characters and press ENTER. Next, respond to 1-2-3's prompt for the range by pointing to or entering the range and then pressing ENTER. The range name you choose should be as meaningful as possible.

1-2-3 does not restrict you to a single name for a given range of cells. If a range is used for more than one purpose, you can assign multiple names to it by using /Range Name Create a second time.

/Range Name Delete

Description

The /Range Name Delete command allows you to delete range names that are no longer needed. Each execution of this command removes a single range name. To delete a range name, enter **/Range Name Delete**, point to the appropriate name in the list 1-2-3 provides, and press ENTER. Alternatively, type the name that you wish to delete after entering the command sequence.

Options

There are no options with this command.

Note

This command also deletes any note associated with the range name.

/Range Name Labels

Description

The /Range Name Labels command allows you to use worksheet label entries for range names in certain situations. With this command, each label can be assigned as a name only to a single cell. Furthermore, the label must be in a cell adjacent to the cell you wish to assign the name to. If you choose a label that exceeds the 15-character limit for range names, the label will be truncated. The /Range Name Labels command is most useful when you have a column or row of labels and wish to assign each one to its adjacent cell as a range name. One execution of this command can assign all of the range names.

Options

The /Range Name Labels command has four options on a submenu. They let you tell 1-2-3 the direction in which to go for the cell needing assignment of the label. The choices are Right, Down, Up, and Left.

/Range Name Note

Description

The /Range Name Note command provides a number of options that allow you to create, modify, and view notes created for range names.

Options

There are five options for this command. Use Create to enter or edit notes for any assigned range name. Each note can be a maximum of 512 characters. The Delete option deletes a note associated with a range name, although the range name itself is not affected. The Reset option deletes all the range name notes in the current file. The Table option creates a table of range names, their addresses, and associated notes. If a range name has either a note or an assigned address, it will appear in this table. Quit eliminates the Range Name Note menu and returns you to READY mode.

/Range Name Reset

Description

The /Range Name Reset command is equivalent to a "delete all" option. Rather than using /Range Name Delete to eliminate range names one by one, use this command to eliminate all range names in a file at once.

Options

There are no options for this command.

Note

/Range Name Reset also deletes any notes associated with range names it deletes.

/Range Name Table

Description

The /Range Name Table command lets you access a list of all the range names in a file, and the range to which each name has been assigned. Decide what area of your worksheet will be used to store the table of range names and assignments before executing the command. After you enter **/Range Name Table**, all you have to do is specify the table location. 1-2-3 will do the rest.

Options

The only options you have with this command are whether to specify the entire area for the table or just the upper left cell in the table range. If you specify the entire range, and if the range is not large enough to contain all the entries, 1-2-3 will not use additional space. If you specify only the upper left corner, 1-2-3 will use as much space as required, and will overwrite worksheet entries if they are present in the cells used for the table.

/Range Name Undefine

Description

The /Range Name Undefine command "disconnects" the range address from a specified range name. The action does not affect any formula that uses the range name, although the formula will evaluate to ERR. The range name and note, if any, remain in the worksheet file. This allows you to redefine the range name, associating it to a new range of data that 1-2-3 immediately uses in any formula referencing that range.

Options

After entering this command, you must select or type the range name to undefine.

/Range Prot

Description

The /Range Prot command is used for reprotecting cells that you have unprotected with the /Range Unprot command. It allows you to change your mind and reestablish the Protection features that are initially provided by 1-2-3 for every worksheet cell. Using the /Range Prot command has no apparent effect on a cell while the Worksheet Protection features are turned off. Once Protection is turned on, cells that are protected will not accept entries of any type.

Since /Range Prot must be used in combination with /Worksheet Global Prot, you will also want to read the entry for that command.

Options

The only options for /Range Prot are ones for entering the range once you have requested the command. You can type the range address, use POINT mode to expand the cell pointer to include the entire range, or type the range name that you wish to use.

/Range Search

Description

The /Range Search command allows you to perform either a Search or Replace operation. The command will search for a character string in either formulas or labels, and can optionally be used to replace the string with a new entry.

Options

After specifying the search range and search string, the first set of Search options lets you choose whether to search formulas, labels, or both. Next you tell 1-2-3 to find the string, or find it and replace it with another entry. If you choose Find, 1-2-3 looks for the first occurrence of your entry and highlights it. You can then continue to look for the next occurrence, or quit. If you choose Replace, 1-2-3 asks for the replacement string and highlights the first occurrence of the search string. You are then given the options to confirm this replacement, replace all occurrences of the search string, skip this replacement and move to the next matching string, or quit the Search and Replace operation.

This command skips hidden columns but includes cells with a Hidden format.

/Range Trans

Description

The /Range Trans command provides additional flexibility in restructuring a worksheet. It will copy data from either a row or column orientation to the opposite orientation; that is, data stored in rows can be copied to columns, and vice versa.

Note

The Release 3 version of /Range Trans works a little differently from earlier releases. First, the Release 3 version of the command copies the value associated with any cell in the From range, rather than the formula. Earlier releases copied the formula, but would not adjust the formula's references—often necessitating the use of /Range Value before /Range Trans. This required that the From range be frozen. Second, /Range Trans now offers new options that allow more flexibility in dealing with transposition in a multiple-sheet environment.

Options

The two /Range Trans options control the selection of a From range with either a row or a column orientation. The choice is not made with a menu selection, but rather by specifying a cell range. With a single-sheet transposition, 1-2-3 interprets this range as having either a row or a column orientation, and produces a To range with the opposite orientation.

In a multiple-sheet transposition, a submenu appears that allows you to select from Rows/Columns, Worksheets/Rows, and Columns/Worksheets. The Rows/Columns option transposes the data on each sheet from a row to a column orientation. The Worksheets/Rows option copies the rows of the worksheets in the From range to the worksheets in the To range. The last option, Columns/Worksheets, converts column entries from the worksheets in the From range to the worksheets in the To range.

/Range Unprot

Description

The /Range Unprot command is used to change the cell protection characteristics of a range of cells. Using this command will allow entries in the selected cells after Worksheet Protection features are enabled.

Unless the /Range Unprot command is used, all worksheet cells have a status of Protected. This means entries cannot be made in the cells once the Worksheet Protection features are enabled. To remove the Protected status from a group of cells, simply enter /**Range Unprot**, and specify the range to unprotect.

Options

The only options for this command are the ones for entering the range once you have requested the command. You can type the range address, use POINT mode to expand the cell pointer to include the entire range, or type the range name that you wish to use.

/Range Value

Description

The /Range Value command is used to copy the values displayed by formula cells without copying the formulas. The cells containing the values can be copied to a different range on the worksheet or to the location containing the original formulas. In both cases the cells that receive the data will not contain formulas, they will contain only the values resulting from the formulas.

Options

This command provides two options. When you enter **/Range Value** and specify the From range, you can specify a different To range in order to retain the original formulas and just make a copy of the values they contain. Or you can specify the same range for To and From, thus eliminating the original formulas and retaining just the values.

/Worksheet Erase

Description

The /Worksheet Erase command can be equivalent to a destroy instruction. It erases all the active files from memory. Unless you have Undo enabled, or have another copy of the worksheets stored on disk, you will not be able to retrieve the worksheets after using the /Worksheet Erase Yes option.

Options

The command presents a submenu with two options. One is Yes, indicating you want to proceed with the erasure of memory. The No selection is the default. The No option abandons the erase operation.

/Worksheet Global Default Other Beep

Description

This command allows you to enable or disable the computer bell that sounds when an error occurs, and when you execute the macro {BEEP} command.

Options

The two options for this command are Yes, which is the default and enables the beep, and No, which disables it.

/Worksheet Global Default Other Help

Description

This command sets the Help access method for 1-2-3. This command is only for compatibility with earlier releases. Release 3 uses Removable Help, which opens the Help file when F1 (HELP) is pressed, and closes the file when ESC is pressed.

Options

Although this command has two options, Removable and Instant, they have no effect.

/Worksheet Global Default Status

Description

The /Worksheet Global Default Status command provides a screen snapshot of the worksheet settings made with /Worksheet Global commands. No changes to any of the settings can be made from this screen.

Options

In one sense there are no options for this command, since /Worksheet Global Default Status has no submenu. A variety of information is presented on the status screen, however. Even though the different items are not individually selectable, they can be regarded as options. All of the data listed are the results of selections made with other /Worksheet Global Default commands. When you press a key, 1-2-3 returns to the /Worksheet Global Default menu.

/Worksheet Global Label

Description

The /Worksheet Global Label command allows you to change the default label prefix, and therefore the default justification (placement in the cell) for all label entries on the worksheet. Entries made prior to the use of this command retain their original label indicators and their existing justification. Entries made in any cell after the command is used have the new label indicator at the front of the entry.

Options

This command has three options: Left, Right, and Center. Left generates a " as the label prefix; Right generates a '; and Center generates a ˆ at the beginning of each label entry.

Note

The Global Label option takes a different approach from that of the /Range Label command, which changes the label prefix and justification for existing entries but does not affect new entries into cells within the range. Entries made after the employment of /Range Label use the default label prefix.

/Worksheet Global Prot

Description

The /Worksheet Global Prot command allows you to enable Worksheet Protection for all worksheet cells that have a Protected status. It is also used to disable Protection for the entire worksheet. The command works with the /Range Prot command to determine which worksheet cells are protected and which are unprotected. If this command is used to enable Protection for a new worksheet, you will not be able to make entries in any worksheet cells, since all the cells have a default status of Protected.

Once Protection has been enabled, you will see "PR" in the control panel when your cell pointer is in cells that are protected. The color and highlighting created with the /Range Unprot command is maintained. With a color monitor, unprotected cells are highlighted in green, providing a "green light" signal that you can proceed with entries for that cell. Other cells remain their normal color. With a monochrome display, the unprotected cells are highlighted to indicate that you can make entries in these cells. Cell contents of Hidden format cells do not appear in the Control Panel while worksheet protection is enabled.

Options

This command has two options. The Enable option turns Protection on for the entire worksheet. Entering **/Worksheet Global Prot Enable** will prevent entries to cells that have a Protected status and allow entries only to those cells that have a status of Unprotected.

The second option is Disable. This option turns off Protection for the entire worksheet and permits entries to all cells. This command can be used to temporarily turn off Worksheet Protection so that you can modify a formula, erase or delete worksheet entries, or unprotect some of the worksheet cells.

Note

It is necessary to use the /Range Unprot command before you enable Worksheet Protection. Otherwise, you will be locked out of all worksheet cells.

/Worksheet Global Recalc

Description

This command provides access to all the recalculation options. With the use of /Worksheet Global Recalc you can affect the number of recalculations for a worksheet, determine whether the recalculation is automatic, and specify the order in which formulas are recalculated.

Options

The options for this command affect three different features of recalculation.

Automatic   This option causes the worksheet to recalculate automatically after every worksheet entry. With the more efficient recalculation methods of Release 3, only the required recalculations are performed.

Manual   This option turns off the Automatic recalculation feature.

Natural   This option gives 1-2-3 the responsibility for determining which formula to evaluate first.

Rowwise   This option disables the Natural recalculation sequence and switches to recalculation by rows.

Columnwise   This option disables the Natural recalculation sequence and switches to recalculation by columns.

Iterations   The normal setting for this option is 1, meaning that every formula is recalculated once during every worksheet recalculation. It can be reset by typing in the number of iterations you want.

/Worksheet Status

Description

This command provides a screen snapshot of your current worksheet environment. It allows you to monitor available memory, as well as many of the default worksheet settings. No changes to any of the settings can be made from this screen.

Options

In one sense there are no options for this command, since /Worksheet Status has no submenu. A variety of information is presented on the status screen, however. Even though the different items are not individually selectable, they can be regarded as options.

Available Memory   This portion of the display reports on the amount of available memory that you have used. This information helps you plan the remainder of your worksheet entries. If memory is almost fully used, you may have to split your worksheet in two.

Processor   This section reports the computer's resident processor. 1-2-3 automatically determines the display. Examples include 8088, 80286, and 80386.

Math Coprocessor   Release 3 supports the use of a math coprocessor chip. This item on the Status screen reports whether one of the supported chips is installed in your system.

Recalculation   This section reports all the recalculation options. You can observe whether recalculation is set at Automatic or Manual; whether the current recalculation order is set at Natural, Rowwise, or Columnwise; and the current number of recalculation iterations. To make changes to any of the recalculation options, you must use /Worksheet Global Recalc.

Circular Reference   Anyone who has struggled to find a circular reference in earlier releases of 1-2-3 will appreciate this display. It shows you the address of the cell causing the CIRC indicator to appear at the bottom of your screen.

Cell Display   This section of the Status screen provides four different pieces of information: the global format settings, the current default label prefix, the current default column width, and whether zero suppression is turned on or off. Changes to format can be made with /Worksheet Global Format. The label prefix is changed with /Worksheet Global Label. Changes to column width are made with /Worksheet Global Col-Width. Changes to zero suppression are made with /Worksheet Global Zero.

Global Protection   The last area of the Status screen shows whether global Protection is enabled or disabled. Changes to the Protection status can be made with /Worksheet Global Prot.

Note

This command is different from the /Worksheet Global Default Status command, which allows you to look at the default settings for each 1-2-3 session.

/Worksheet Titles

Description

The /Worksheet Titles command allows you to freeze label information at the top or left side of the screen. This is useful when you have a worksheet that is either wider or longer than the screen. Without the titles frozen on the screen, you would not see any descriptive information as you scroll and move through the worksheet.

The cell pointer movement keys will not move your cell pointer to the titles area once it is frozen on the screen. If you want to move there, you will have to use the F5 (GOTO) key. This will cause the title area to be shown on the screen twice. When you scroll away from this area, the double view of the titles will disappear from the screen.

Options

The options for this command are Both, Horizontal, Vertical, and Clear.

Both   This option freezes information above and to the left of the cell pointer on your screen.

Horizontal   This option freezes information above the cell pointer on your screen.

Vertical   This option freezes information to the left of the cell pointer on your screen.

Clear   This option frees titles that have been frozen.

/Worksheet Window

Description

The /Worksheet Window command allows you to create two separate windows on your screen. This has advantages for large worksheets where you cannot view the entire worksheet on one screen. Window lets you view two different sections of the worksheet through the two windows created by this command. The windows' size is controlled by the location of your cell pointer at the time you request the screen split. When the screen is split vertically, a dividing line will replace one of the worksheet columns; in a horizontal split, the dividing line will replace one of the rows. You can move easily between windows with the F6 (WINDOW) key. F6 always moves you to the window opposite the one you are in. You can use the windows to look at different files or sheets at once.

This command also allows you to look at three different sheets or files on the screen at once. Another option provides a map of the types of entries in the cells. You can also use this command to switch between two different display monitors, or to display a graph and a worksheet on the screen at the same time.

Options

There are nine options for the Window command: Horizontal, Vertical, Sync, Unsync, Clear, Map, Perspective, Graph, and Display. All options are covered in this chapter except Graph, which is introduced in Chapter 11, "Working with 1-2-3's Graphics Features."

Horizontal   This option splits the screen into two horizontal windows. The dividing line is inserted immediately above the cell pointer.

Vertical   This option splits the screen into two vertical windows. The dividing line is inserted immediately to the left of the cell pointer.

Sync   This option causes scrolling in the two windows to be synchronized. That is, when you scroll in one window, the other window will automatically scroll along with it. This is the default setting when you create a second window. This setting affects a perspective view.

Unsync   This option allows you to scroll in one window while the other window remains stationary. This setting affects a perspective view.

Clear   This option removes the second window from the screen or eliminates a special window option like Map or Perspective. When you clear a two-window screen, the window that remains is the top window when the split was horizontal, and the left window when the split was vertical.

Map   This option displays the worksheet with a Map view. Each column is 2 characters, wide and displays " for cells containing labels, # for cells containing numbers, and + for cells containing formulas or annotated numbers.

Perspective   This option displays three windows sloped to the right. Each sheet uses one third of the screen.

Graph   This option is covered in Chapter 11, "Working with 1-2-3's Graphics Features."

Display   This option selects the Display driver 1-2-3 uses. The selections for this option (1 and 2) are the same as the 1 and 2 for the Display drivers selected in the Install program.

You have learned a great number of worksheet commands in this chapter. You will want to practice with important commands like /Copy and /Move before continuing on to Chapter 6. Although all the commands presented in this chapter are important, /Copy and /Move are the workhorses that will help you most to create professional quality worksheets.

Printing

Print Destination
Print Range
Controlling the Printer from the Keyboard
Exiting the Print Menu
Background Printing
Printing Options
Global Printer Defaults
Other Worksheet Commands for Printing
COMMAND REFERENCE: Printing

/Print Cancel

/Print Encoded

/Print File

/Print Printer

/Print Printer Align

/Print Printer Clear

/Print Printer Go

/Print Printer Hold

/Print Printer Line

/Print Printer Options

/Print Printer Options Advanced

/Print Printer Options Borders

/Print Printer Options Footer

/Print Printer Options Header

/Print Printer Options Margins

/Print Printer Options Name

/Print Printer Options Other

/Print Printer Options Pg-Length

/Print Printer Options Quit

/Print Printer Options Setup

/Print Printer Page

/Print Printer Quit

/Print Printer Range

/Print Printer Sample

/Print Quit

/Print Resume

/Print Suspend

/Worksheet Global Default Printer

/Worksheet Global Default Update

/Worksheet Page

Working with your models on the screen is great if you want to make changes and see their immediate impact. But when you have to go to a meeting and reference these same numbers, the screen in your office is no help. Fortunately, 1-2-3 Release 3 has extensive print features that allow you to create anything from a quick hardcopy of important figures to a professional looking multi-page report.

Preparation for using the print features of 1-2-3 begins before you build your first model. With Release 3, you must install your package before you can print any model. The installation process creates a driver configuration file that can speak the correct language for your particular printer. If you have not yet installed your package, you will want to review Appendix A, "Installing 1-2-3," for detailed directions on completing this vital step.

In this chapter you will have an opportunity to work with all of 1-2-3's commands related to printing, which are shown in the command tree at the beginning of the Command Reference section for this chapter. In addition to Print menu commands, you will explore the Global Default Printer options and other /Worksheet commands that affect printing. With these commands you will be able to set up default parameters, such as margins and page length, that will be used every time you work with 1-2-3. By the time you finish this chapter you should have mastered simple printing tasks, and also be familiar with the more advanced print options that 1-2-3 provides.

Release 3 offers a number of exciting new features that give you additional options for printing worksheet reports. Support for *background printing* allows you to use your time for additional spreadsheet activities while 1-2-3 is printing completed worksheets in the background. You no longer have to sit and wait for print output to end before continuing your work on additional worksheet tasks. Also, 1-2-3 now lets you access printer features like font selection, line spacing, and character spacing through menu selections, instead of the setup strings required by earlier releases.

Print Destination

The first choice you must make when selecting Print from the main menu is the destination of your printed output. You must decide whether you want the information sent directly to your printer or written to a disk file. You will choose between the Printer, File, and Encoded destinations.

When you send the output to a file, you can select whether or not the file contains formatting codes specific to a printer (the Encoded option). Often other factors make this decision for you. If you do not have a printer attached to your system, for example, a disk file will be your only choice. Likewise, if your printer is broken or you want to use a different printer, you will want to choose Encoded. If you want to save the output to a file for use by another program, you will want to choose File, since it omits the printer codes an encoded file contains.

When 1-2-3 writes your print file to disk, it will assign the extension .ENC for encoded files, or .PRN for nonencoded files, to the filename. This distinguishes the print file from the worksheet files on your disk, which have a suffix of .WK3. If you want to review the contents of your print file, you can use DOS commands like TYPE to scroll through the output on your screen. You can also use your word processor to view the print file. If it is an encoded file, the file contains several special characters that alter the worksheet appearance. To print an encoded file, use the DOS COPY command to copy the file to the printer (LPT1).

Once you select Printer, Encoded, or File, you may select any of the Print options that tell 1-2-3 such things as what part of the worksheet you want printed, and what left and right margins you want. All the /Print command options can be used with Encoded, File, and Printer. As you make your selections from 1-2-3's Print menus, be aware that several of the Print menus do not disappear like other menus after you have made your selection. They remain on screen long enough for you to select other options. To eliminate these menus from your screen, select Quit from the Print menu.

Print Range

Whether you are printing to your printer or a disk file, you will have to decide what worksheet cells you want to print. You can print every cell that contains entries, or just a few. In either case you will need to specify the range of cells to 1-2-3. These cells can reside on one sheet, or several sheets in a multi-sheet file. You can even specify several areas in a worksheet file as separate print ranges—all with one Range command.

You specify the cells you wish to print through the Range option in the main Print menu shown in Figure 6-1. To see how this works, assume you want to print the model shown in Figure 6-2. If you have never printed this worksheet before, 1-2-3 will assume that the starting location for printing is the current cell pointer location. Therefore you will probably want to position your cell pointer on A1 before typing /**PP** to tell 1-2-3 to print to the printer.

To tell 1-2-3 what range to print, follow these steps:

1. Type **R** to select the Range option.

2. Lock the beginning of the range in place at A1 by typing a period.

3. Move to the end of the model by pressing the special key sequence of END followed by HOME.

4. Press ENTER to tell 1-2-3 that the range has been selected.

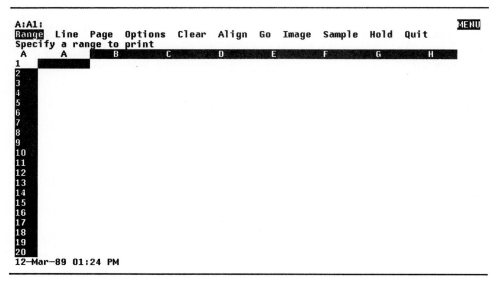

Figure 6-1.   Range option on the main Print menu

5. Assuming that all the default settings are acceptable, check to make sure the printer is turned on and the paper is aligned properly; then select Go from the Print menu. You should get the printout shown in Figure 6-3.

Note: If you have chosen File rather than Printer, selecting Go will start the process for writing your information to the disk.

The default margins and page length used in producing 1-2-3 printouts are illustrated in Figure 6-4. Options to change these and other settings affecting the appearance of your printed output will be covered later in the chapter. Changes in the default settings would be made between steps 4 and 5 in the print procedure previously described.

When the selected range includes long labels that extend beyond their cells, you must include in the range the cells from which the labels borrow space. This keeps the labels from being truncated in the printout. For example, if G4 contains "Date of Report: March 16, 1990" and the cell width is 9, the label will use G4, H4, and I4 for its display. If

A:A1:   `READY`

A	A	B	C	D	E	F	G
1							
2				Boston Company			
3				First Quarter Expenses			
4							
5				JAN	FEB	MAR	
6	Salaries			$8,000	$8,200	$8,200	
7	Building Operations			1,100	1,100	1,100	
8	Travel			850	850	850	
9	Supplies			500	500	500	
10	Depreciation			1,200	1,200	1,200	
11	Equipment Maintenance			750	750	750	
12	Shipping Expense			400	400	400	
13	Data Processing Costs			2,100	2,100	2,100	
14	Printing & Duplicating			640	640	640	
15	Other			1,030	1,030	1,030	
16	Total Expenses			$16,570	$16,770	$16,770	

Figure 6-2.   Worksheet example for specifying print range

```
                         Boston Company
                      First Quarter Expenses

                              JAN        FEB        MAR
        Salaries            $8,000     $8,200     $8,200
        Building Operations  1,100      1,100      1,100
        Travel                 850        850        850
        Supplies               500        500        500
        Depreciation         1,200      1,200      1,200
        Equipment Maintenance  750        750        750
        Shipping Expense       400        400        400
        Data Processing Costs 2,100      2,100      2,100
        Printing & Duplicating 640        640        640
        Other                1,030      1,030      1,030
Total Expenses             $16,570    $16,770    $16,770
```

Figure 6-3.   Printed output from worksheet example

these three cells are not included in the print range, 1-2-3 will not print them. 1-2-3 only prints the portion of the label that appears in the selected range.

Changing the Print Range

There may be one additional step in the printing procedure if you have already printed a worksheet before, and now want to print a new area from it. This is done by reissuing the /Print Printer Range command. 1-2-3 remembers and highlights the last selected range. To select a new range, press ESC or BACKSPACE to change the range address to a single cell address. You can then reposition and anchor again before moving to the opposite corner of the range you want to print.

Tip: When the /Print Printer Range command is executed, 1-2-3 remembers and highlights the last range you printed. To expand and contract the print range, move the cell pointer to different corners of the range. To change the corner of the range that is most active, press the period; 1-2-3 will then move the active corner in a clockwise direction. The *active corner* determines the direction in which expansion and contraction of the range occurs. The first cell address in the control

Name	Base Salary	Inc. Mo.	% INC	1989 Salary	Benefits
Alpen, Pat	$35,000.00	10	4.00%	$35,350.00	$4,949.00
Arbor, Jim	$23,000.00	4	7.00%	$24,207.50	$3,389.05
Bunde, Norman	$12,000.00	1	4.00%	$12,480.00	$1,747.20
Campbell, Keith	$32,000.00	1	9.00%	$34,880.00	$4,883.20
Campbell, David	$40,000.00	1	10.00%	$44,000.00	$6,160.00
Denmore, Mary	$18,900.00	11	7.50%	$19,136.25	$2,679.08
Farper, David	$40,000.00	1	10.00%	$44,000.00	$6,160.00
Fork, Angela	$36,900.00	4	7.00%	$38,837.25	$5,437.22
Guest, Norman	$12,000.00	1	4.00%	$12,480.00	$1,747.20
Guest, Paul	$45,000.00	2	9.00%	$48,712.50	$6,819.75
Guiness, Pat	$35,000.00	10	4.00%	$35,350.00	$4,949.00
Harker, Pat	$35,000.00	10	4.00%	$35,350.00	$4,949.00
Harper, Angela	$36,900.00	4	7.00%	$38,837.25	$5,437.22
Harper, Pat	$40,000.00	1	10.00%	$44,000.00	$6,160.00
Harris, Jim	$23,000.00	4	7.00%	$24,207.50	$3,389.05
Harris, John	$15,000.00	6	5.00%	$15,437.50	$2,161.25
Harvey, Jim	$23,000.00	4	7.00%	$24,207.50	$3,389.05
Hitt, Mary	$18,000.00	9	4.00%	$18,240.00	$2,553.60
Jacobs, Norman	$12,000.00	1	4.00%	$12,480.00	$1,747.20
Jenkins, Paul	$45,000.00	2	9.00%	$48,712.50	$6,819.75
Jones, Ray	$25,000.00	2	5.00%	$26,145.83	$3,660.42
Just, Ray	$25,000.00	2	5.00%	$26,145.83	$3,660.42
Kaylor, Angela	$36,900.00	4	7.00%	$38,837.25	$5,437.22
Kiger, Keith	$32,000.00	1	9.00%	$34,880.00	$4,883.20
Kommer, John	$15,000.00	6	5.00%	$15,437.50	$2,161.25
Korn, Pat	$35,000.00	10	4.00%	$35,350.00	$4,949.00
Larkin, Mary	$29,000.00	3	7.00%	$30,691.67	$4,296.83
Litt, Norman	$12,000.00	1	4.00%	$12,480.00	$1,747.20
Merriman, Angela	$36,900.00	4	7.00%	$38,837.25	$5,437.22
Morn, Pat	$35,000.00	10	4.00%	$35,350.00	$4,949.00
Nest, Paul	$45,000.00	2	9.00%	$48,712.50	$6,819.75
Parden, Mary	$29,000.00	3	7.00%	$30,691.67	$4,296.83
Parker, Mary	$29,000.00	3	7.00%	$30,691.67	$4,296.83
Parson, Mary	$18,000.00	9	4.00%	$18,240.00	$2,553.60
Piltman, Mary	$18,000.00	9	4.00%	$18,240.00	$2,553.60
Polk, Mary	$18,900.00	11	7.50%	$19,136.25	$2,679.08
Rensler, Jane	$12,000.00	1	4.00%	$12,480.00	$1,747.20
Rolf, John	$15,000.00	6	5.00%	$15,437.50	$2,161.25
Rolf, Mary	$18,000.00	9	4.00%	$18,240.00	$2,553.60
Sarper, Angela	$36,900.00	4	7.00%	$38,837.25	$5,437.22
Smith, Jim	$23,000.00	4	7.00%	$24,207.50	$3,389.05
Stanbor, Jim	$23,000.00	4	7.00%	$24,207.50	$3,389.05
Stark, Nancy	$18,900.00	11	7.50%	$19,136.25	$2,679.08
Stedman, David	$40,000.00	1	10.00%	$44,000.00	$6,160.00
Stephens, Paul	$45,000.00	2	9.00%	$48,712.50	$6,819.75
Stevenson, Mary	$18,900.00	11	7.50%	$19,136.25	$2,679.08
Stone, Mary	$29,000.00	3	7.00%	$30,691.67	$4,296.83
Stone, Ray	$25,000.00	2	5.00%	$26,145.83	$3,660.42
Tolf, John	$15,000.00	6	5.00%	$15,437.50	$2,161.25
Tolf, Mary	$18,000.00	9	4.00%	$18,240.00	$2,553.60
Tone, Mary	$29,000.00	3	7.00%	$30,691.67	$4,296.83
Trundle, John	$15,000.00	6	5.00%	$15,437.50	$2,161.25
Umber, Paul	$45,000.00	2	9.00%	$48,712.50	$6,819.75

Figure 6-4.   Default margins and page length

panel is the anchored corner, and the second address is the corner that you can change. Although there are a few times when 1-2-3 might not respond as expected, this method is worth a try.

Printing Multiple Ranges

One of the new features of Release 3 is the ability to print multiple ranges. This feature is ideal when you want to print several different areas on a sheet or when you need to print data from several sheets.

To print more than one range, highlight the first range that you want to print. Then, type a semicolon instead of ENTER. 1-2-3 finalizes the first range and repositions the cell pointer at the current position so you can highlight another range. Once you select all the ranges that you want to print, press ENTER. 1-2-3 prints all of the specified ranges, in the order they are specified. If you use the /Print Printer Range command again, 1-2-3 lists all of the selected ranges and highlights the last one for you to alter, if desired. You can edit the other ranges by pressing F2 (EDIT) to edit the range addresses.

Controlling the Printer from the Keyboard

1-2-3 provides several methods of controlling the paper in your printer from the keyboard. The three Print menu options involved are Line, Page, and Align.

Advancing Printer Paper a Line at a Time

The /Print Printer Line command moves the paper in the printer up by one line. It acts just as if you turned your printer off line and pressed the line feed button, with one important exception. The printer's line feed does not alter the internal line count that 1-2-3 maintains to determine when a new page is needed. The Line command, however, will add one to 1-2-3's internal line count, so it will stay in sync with the paper.

Line assumes that you have positioned your paper at the top of a form before turning your printer on. If you did not, printing will start on the same line on all pages as on your first page, since 1-2-3's line count does not change. The Align command, discussed later in this section, can remedy this problem.

Advancing Printer Paper a Page at a Time

The /Print Printer Page command moves the paper in your printer to the top of the next form. When you select this command, 1-2-3 checks its internal line count to determine how many lines must be spaced to complete a full page and reach the top of the next page. The result is similar to pressing form feed with your printer off line, except that the Page command will print a footer (if you define one) for the bottom of your page; form feed will not. Like Line, Page assumes that you started printing at the top of a form.

Using Align to Reset the Printer Line Count

The /Print Printer Align command is another page adjustment command. Rather than moving the paper in the printer, it resets the line count to zero to represent the top of a page, and resets the page number to 1. Every time you position your paper at the top of a new form with /Print Printer Page or the printer control buttons, you should also use Align to tell 1-2-3 to restart the line count for a new page. If you do not remember to use Align, your new page will not be filled completely, since 1-2-3 will continue to use its existing line count even though it does not match the page currently in the printer.

Exiting the Print Menu

The /Print Printer Quit command is the selection to make when you are finished with the Print menu. All "sticky" menus in 1-2-3 (that is, menus that do not automatically disappear when you select a command) provide the Quit option as a means of exiting. Pressing ESC is another way to exit. Leaving the Print menu finishes the print job and resets 1-2-3's page number to 1. If you are printing to a file, it closes the file. If you are printing to a network or a printer spooler, it directs the network or spooler to begin printing the output.

Background Printing

Before Release 3, you had to wait until 1-2-3 finished printing before you could continue using the other features of 1-2-3. Release 3 introduces *background printing*, which allows you to continue using 1-2-3 while worksheets are printed. 1-2-3 performs background printing by storing the print output in memory and sending portions of it to the printer when 1-2-3 is not performing other tasks and the printer is capable of accepting more information.

1-2-3 stores each printing task as a print job in a queue. Documents are normally printed in the order they are created, but you can change the print order by assigning priority levels. During background printing, you have the option of temporarily or permanently halting the print jobs. If you temporarily suspend a print job, you can restart it.

Assigning Priority Levels

As you create print jobs, you will want some worksheets printed before others. One way to set the order in which 1-2-3 prints your jobs is to request them in the order you want them printed. Another option for controlling the print order is assigning priority levels to the print jobs. 1-2-3 has three priority levels: High, Default, and Low. Within each priority level, 1-2-3 prints the print jobs in the order they are created. To assign a priority to the print job you are creating, use the /Print Printer Options Advanced Priority command. 1-2-3 first prints jobs with a priority of High, then Default, then Low.

As an example, suppose you need to print a labor summary report and the detailed analysis. You might assign a High priority to the summary report and a Low priority to the detailed analysis. After you create both print jobs and are working on other worksheets, and if you add print jobs with a High or Default priority, 1-2-3 will print these jobs before the detailed analysis.

Halting and Restarting Print Jobs

As 1-2-3 prints your document, you may need to stop the printing temporarily or permanently. You may notice that the printer is about to run out of paper, or realize that the print output contains a mistake, or want to stop printing so you can use another computer package. If you suspend printing, you can start printing again when you are ready.

To temporarily stop the printing, use the /Print Suspend command. This command stops 1-2-3 from sending more information to the printer. If the printer has a buffer, the printer will not stop immediately, since the printer usually has information stored that it has not printed yet. The printer will stop when it prints the information that has already been transferred to its buffer.

Once you are ready to restart printing, the /Print Resume command will begin sending information to the printer at the point where 1-2-3 stopped sending information after you used /Print Suspend. /Print Resume is also used if 1-2-3 halts the printer due to a printer error, or if the printer uses a single sheet feeder. When 1-2-3 encounters a printer error or has finished printing a page on a single sheet feeder printer, 1-2-3 displays an error message in the status line. Unlike other error conditions, it does not prevent you from continuing to work with other 1-2-3 features.

There may be situations where you want to abort printing without the need to restart it. To permanently stop printing, use the /Print Cancel command. This command stops 1-2-3 from sending more information to the printer. If the printer has a buffer, the printer will stop when its buffer is empty. Unlike the /Print Resume command, the /Print Cancel command removes all print jobs from the queue. You cannot restart the print jobs. After performing this command, you will want to realign the printer and use the /Print Printer Align command, so that subsequent print jobs are properly aligned.

Printing Options

You have had an opportunity to explore some of the default settings for printing. In this section you will learn how to tailor printing to the task at hand, making changes that affect only the current session or worksheet. Later, you can reset the default according to what you need most of the time, and still make temporary changes by using the /Print Printer Options menu, shown here.

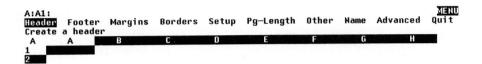

While you are making changes to the print settings, you may want to return to the worksheet. For example, you may want to change some worksheet data before including it in a print range. You may also find that you need to open another worksheet file before specifying another print range. However, if you leave the Print menus, you end the current print job. If you were writing several ranges to a file, leaving the Print menu would close the print file. For situations where you want to return to READY mode without ending the current print job, use the /Print Printer Hold command. This command returns you to the worksheet and holds the print job you are currently creating until you return to the Print menus and finish it.

Tip: To temporarily change the appearance of a range before you print it, open a second window (/Worksheet Window). Modify the format and column widths in the second window. After printing the range from the second window, close it; 1-2-3 will retain the formatting selections from the first window.

Headers and Footers

Headers and *footers* are lines printed at the top and bottom, respectively, of every page of your report. A header or footer may be, for example, a date, company name, report name, department, page number, or a combination of these elements. Except for page numbers, they are usually the same for each page.

Since 1-2-3 allows you to use a header or footer total width equal to the maximum printed report width of 512 characters, and permits you to divide both headers and footers into separate segments for the right, left, and center sections of each line, you can place more than one information element in a header or footer. 1-2-3 requires that all of the information for a header and footer fit on one line, so you will need to consider your line length when planning the contents of a header or footer. Rules for setting up headers and footers are summarized in the box called "Header and Footer Rules."

Headers and footers in 1-2-3 are specified through the /Print Printer Options Header and Footer commands. To separate the information you are entering into each section of the header or footer, use the vertical bar character (|). Any spaces included between the vertical bars will be counted as characters to be included in the heading, and will affect the alignment of the heading sections. For example, to place the company name of Adams & Associates on the left, and the report number 1234 on the right of a heading, enter

Adams & Associates ‖ Rpt. No. 1234

at the prompt, as shown in Figure 6-5. This would display on your report as shown in Figure 6-6. To place a heading only at the right of each page, precede the header information with two vertical bars (‖).

Using Special Characters in a Header or Footer

Two special characters can be used in headers and footers to have 1-2-3 add the page number and date. Use # to represent the location where you want 1-2-3 to add a page number. 1-2-3 will begin with 1 and automatically increment the number for each page. If you want to start with a different number, enter two # signs and the number you want to

1
2
3

Header and Footer Rules

Several characters are essential to creating headers and footers: the vertical bar (¦), the at sign (@), the pound sign (#), and the cell reference (\).

¦   This character is used to divide the three sections of a header or footer (right, left, and center). For example, if you enter the header Accounting Department ¦ Texas Company ¦ Rpt: 8976, the department name will print at the left, the company name in the center, and the report identification at the right. The heading ¦ ¦ Rpt 4356 places the report identifier on the far right; the left and center portions of the header are empty, as indicated by the two vertical bars.

@   This character can be used anywhere in a header or footer to incorporate the current system date. It can be combined with a character string, such as Today's Date:, to provide additional description.

This character can be placed anywhere in a header or footer to incorporate the current page number. It, too, can be combined with character strings for additional description, such as Page-Number:. If you want the page number to start with a specific number, enter two # signs, followed by the page number you want to start with.

\   This character can be placed in a header or footer, followed by a cell address. 1-2-3 will then use the header or footer stored in the cell referenced. For example, if the cell A3 contained Acme Company - Toy Division ¦ Page # ¦ @, the header entry \A3 would place Acme Company - Toy Division on the left side of the header, the page number in the middle section, and the date at the far right. Using a cell reference for different entries would allow you to change header and footer information quickly.

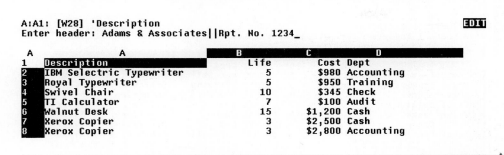

Figure 6-5.   Entering a header

use. If you use page numbers on a report, you will need to align and
reset the printer options (with /Print Printer Align) before printing
again. Otherwise, the second report's paging sequence will begin where
the first report stopped, instead of with 1.

Use @ to represent the location where you would like 1-2-3 to place
the current date. 1-2-3 will use the system date, which is stored in your
computer's memory. The only way to change this date is to access the
DOS DATE command (using /System on the main menu; see Chapter 8),
enter a new date, and then use EXIT to return to 1-2-3.

The # and @ characters can be entered in any header or footer
segment and can be combined with other text, such as **Page No:** or
Today's Date:. Figure 6-7 shows the construction of a header; the
finished product appears at the top of the report in Figure 6-8.

```
Adams & Associates                                        Rpt. No. 1234


Description              Life    Cost Dept        Type        Inv Code
IBM Selectric Typewriter   5    $980 Accounting   Office         54301
Royal Typewriter           5    $950 Training     Office         54455
Swivel Chair              10    $345 Check        Furniture      54789
TI Calculator              7    $100 Audit        Office         54177
Walnut Desk               15  $1,200 Cash         Furniture      54138
Xerox Copier               3  $2,500 Cash         Processing     54392
Xerox Copier               3  $2,800 Accounting   Processing     54999
```

Figure 6-6.   Print output with a header

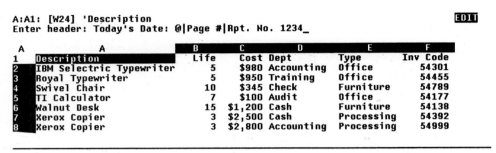

Figure 6-7.   Using date and page number in a header

Tip: To automatically date stamp every page of output you create, use the @ to represent the current date in either a header or footer on every worksheet printed.

Storing Headers and Footers in Worksheet Cells

If you need to use different headers and footers when printing different sections of a worksheet, the easiest approach is to store the complete header or footer in a worksheet cell. Rather than typing the long header or footer entry into the Options menu with each change, you can instead reference the cell address for the appropriate header or footer after selecting the menu option. Use \ and a cell address to represent the referenced cell's contents.

```
Today's Date: 17-Mar-89           Page 1                Rpt. No. 1234

Description                Life      Cost Dept       Type        Inv Code
IBM Selectric Typewriter      5      $980 Accounting  Office        54301
Royal Typewriter              5      $950 Training     Office        54455
Swivel Chair                 10      $345 Check        Furniture     54789
TI Calculator                 7      $100 Audit        Office        54177
Walnut Desk.                 15    $1,200 Cash         Furniture     54138
Xerox Copier                  3    $2,500 Cash         Processing    54392
Xerox Copier                  3    $2,800 Accounting   Processing    54999
```

Figure 6-8.   Printed output with the date and page number

Since 1-2-3 updates the information in the header each time it uses a header, referencing a cell instead of retyping the contents provides the current contents of the cell. An example of the backslash in a footer entry is \A28. In this example, each time 1-2-3 prints the footer, it checks the current value of cell A28 and uses that value in the footer. The referenced cell can include the header and footer special characters.

Margins

The /Print Printer Options Margins command controls the amount of white space at the top, bottom, and sides of your printed document. A graphic representation of the page layout, including margins, can be seen in Figure 6-9. If you are printing a narrow range of cells, for example, you might want to increase the side margin settings to center the output on the paper, as shown in Figure 6-10. On the other hand, if you want to spread a great deal of data across a page, you might want to use very small side margin settings, like those in Figure 6-11.

The four Margins options are Left, Right, Top, and Bottom. These options get their default values from settings specified with /Worksheet Global Default Printer. A fifth option, None, sets the top, bottom, and left margins to 0, and the right margin to 1000. This option is for printing a worksheet to an unencoded file that will later be imported into another computer package.

The default setting for the left margin is 4, but you can change it to any number between 0 and 1000. The default for the right margin is 76. These numbers indicate the number of characters from the left edge of the paper. You can assign any value from 0 to 1000. To use values greater than 80, you will either need to use compressed print when the worksheet is printed (specified through /Print Printer Options Advanced Pitch Compressed), Landscape mode which prints sideways (an Advanced Layout option), or have a wide-carriage printer with paper wider than eight inches across. The top margin default is 2 lines, but it can be revised to any number from 0 to 240. The bottom margin accepts the same settings as the top margin.

To change any margin setting, simply type the new number after specifying the appropriate Margins option. If you prefer, you can also use the RIGHT ARROW and LEFT ARROW keys to expand and contract these

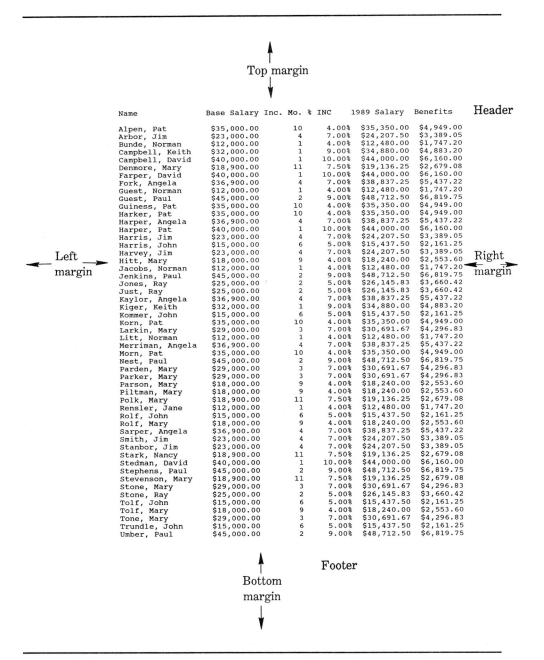

Figure 6-9. Page layout

```
                                      JAN
              Salaries              $8,000
              Building Operations    1,100
              Travel                   850
              Supplies                 500
              Depreciation           1,200
              Equipment Maintenance    750
              Shipping Expense         400
              Data Processing Costs  2,100
              Printing & Duplicating   640
              Other                  1,030
        Total Expenses             $16,570
```

Figure 6-10. Wide margins

settings, just as you can with column width settings. The changes you make to the margin settings are saved with the document when you save it to disk after updating the Print options.

Borders

The /Print Printer Options Borders command allows you to include the identifying information found at the top of columns and at the left side

---

```
                                          Boston Company

                         JAN       FEB       MAR       APR
    Salaries           $8,000    $8,200    $8,200    $8,700
    Building Operations 1,100     1,100     1,100     1,100
    Travel                850       850       850       850
    Supplies              500       500       500       500
    Depreciation        1,200     1,200     1,200     1,200
    Equipment Maintenance 750       750       750       750
    Shipping Expense      400       400       400       400
    Data Processing Costs 2,100    2,100     2,100     2,100
    Printing & Duplicating 640       640       640       640
    Other               1,030     1,030     1,030     1,030
Total Expenses        $16,570   $16,770   $16,770   $17,270
```

Figure 6-11. Narrow margins

of rows in your worksheet, on every printed page of a report. This feature is useful if you have used the months of the year as column heads across the worksheet, for example, and have more data than will fit on one printed page. You can print the worksheet with these column heads at the top of each page, if the row containing the months is specified as a *border*.

Similarly, if your report is wider than it is long, you can print the information found at the far left of your worksheet on every page of your report. This information could be account names or other identifying descriptions.

The range of worksheet cells you specify for printing will then be printed either to the right of or below the border information.

Caution: Do not include the border rows or columns as part of your print range, or you will get duplicate border information on the first page of your output. Rules for borders are summarized in the box called "Border Rules."

Border Rules

The Borders option allows you to print descriptive information on each page of a multi-page report. The descriptive information may be in columns, rows, or both. To include a row or column in a border, you only have to select one cell from a row or column to select the entire row or column. When 1-2-3 prints the range, it prints the rows and columns that apply to the rows and columns for the print range. For example, a worksheet can have a print range of A:B2..M:L24 and use column A and row 1 as the border. When 1-2-3 prints B2..H24 (the portion of the worksheet in worksheet B that can fit across the page) it prints B:A1..B:A24 as the column border and B:A1..B:H1 as the row border.

Release 3 supports the addition of row numbers and column labels as a frame around the range of print data. When a frame is added with the /Print Printer Options Border Frame command, 1-2-3 supplies row numbers above and column letters to the left of the printed range. Figure 6-12 shows a printed worksheet that uses a frame. You can use a frame in combination with row and column borders, or separately. This option can be used to document a worksheet by changing the default format to Text and then printing the worksheet with a frame. To remove a frame, use the /Print Printer Options Borders No-Frame command.

Tip: When you specify a print range for a worksheet, do not include the border rows and columns in the print range, since 1-2-3 will print them twice.

Column Borders

The /Print Printer Options Borders Columns command is used when you have more columns than will fit across one page, and there are labels or other information in a column or columns on the left side of the worksheet that are needed to identify data printed on subsequent pages of your report. Selecting these columns as borders will cause the columns to print on each page of the report.

The expense worksheet containing monthly figures, shown in Figure 6-13, serves as an example. If the print range A1..O16 is used, the descriptive account names will only appear with the first months printed. However, if you specify these account names as a column border, you can print them on each page. To do this, select /Print

A	A	B	C	D	E	F	G
1							
2						Boston Company	
3							
4							
5				JAN	FEB	MAR	APR
6	Salaries			$8,000	$8,200	$8,200	$8,700
7	Building Operations			1,100	1,100	1,100	1,100
8	Travel			850	850	850	850
9	Supplies			500	500	500	500
10	Depreciation			1,200	1,200	1,200	1,200
11	Equipment Maintenance			750	750	750	750
12	Shipping Expense			400	400	400	400
13	Data Processing Costs			2,100	2,100	2,100	2,100
14	Printing & Duplicating			640	640	640	640
15	Other			1,030	1,030	1,030	1,030
16	Total Expenses			$16,570	$16,770	$16,770	$17,270

Figure 6-12.   Printout with a row and column frame

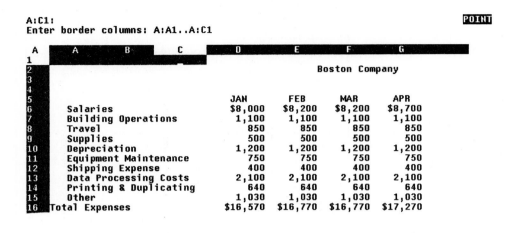

Figure 6-13. Entering the border columns

Printer Options Borders Columns. In response to the prompt for columns, enter the range **A1..C1**. Then, when you print the worksheet, begin your print range with D1. (If you begin it with A1, the account name column information will be printed twice, as shown in Figure 6-14.) The correct multi-page printout should look like Figure 6-15.

		JAN
Salaries	Salaries	$8,000
Building Operations	Building Operations	1,100
Travel	Travel	850
Supplies	Supplies	500
Depreciation	Depreciation	1,200
Equipment Maintenance	Equipment Maintenance	750
Shipping Expense	Shipping Expense	400
Data Processing Costs	Data Processing Costs	2,100
Printing & Duplicating	Printing & Duplicating	640
Other	Other	1,030
Total Expenses	Total Expenses	$16,570

Figure 6-14. Columns printed twice

	JAN	FEB	MAR	APR	MAY
Salaries	$8,000	$8,200	$8,200	$8,700	$8,700
Building Operations	1,100	1,100	1,100	1,100	1,100
Travel	850	850	850	850	850
Supplies	500	500	500	500	500
Depreciation	1,200	1,200	1,200	1,200	1,200
Equipment Maintenance	750	750	750	750	750
Shipping Expense	400	400	400	400	400
Data Processing Costs	2,100	2,100	2,100	2,100	2,100
Printing & Duplicating	640	640	640	640	640
Other	1,030	1,030	1,030	1,030	1,030
Total Expenses	$16,570	$16,770	$16,770	$17,270	$17,270

	JUNE	JULY	AUG	SEPT	OCT
Salaries	$7,500	$7,500	$10,000	$10,000	$10,000
Building Operations	1,100	1,100	1,100	1,300	1,300
Travel	850	850	850	850	850
Supplies	500	500	500	500	500
Depreciation	1,200	1,200	1,200	1,200	1,200
Equipment Maintenance	750	750	750	750	750
Shipping Expense	400	400	400	400	400
Data Processing Costs	2,100	2,100	2,100	2,100	2,100
Printing & Duplicating	640	640	640	640	640
Other	1,030	1,030	1,030	1,030	1,030
Total Expenses	$16,070	$16,070	$18,570	$18,770	$18,770

	NOV	DEC
Salaries	$10,000	$10,000
Building Operations	1,300	1,300
Travel	850	850
Supplies	500	500
Depreciation	1,200	1,200
Equipment Maintenance	750	750
Shipping Expense	400	400
Data Processing Costs	2,100	2,100
Printing & Duplicating	640	640
Other	1,030	1,030
Total Expenses	$18,770	$18,770

Figure 6-15.   Three pages of print using border columns

Row Borders

The /Print Printer Options Borders Rows command is used when the identifying data you want repeated on each page is located in rows at the top of your worksheet. Use this option if there are more rows of data to print than will fit on one page. First enter the command. Highlight a cell at the top of the border range, and anchor it with a period (.); then highlight a cell in the last row you want to use as a row border, and press ENTER. Once you have defined the border, Quit the Options menu and select a print range that does not include the border cells.

The example shown in Figure 6-16 has a set of column headings in row 1, and seven rows of data below it. On a page with a normal layout, this information would fit. However, if you selected very large top and bottom margins, allowing only the heading and the first four lines to fit on page 1, you would also need to have the descriptive information from row 1 placed at the top of page 2. To do this, select this row as a border row. The following steps show you how; this procedure also includes instructions for creating a header and a footer, and setting margins.

1. Before beginning, move your cell pointer to A1.

2. Select /Print Printer Options Borders Rows.

3. You only need to select one cell in the row you want to use as a border; then press ENTER. (If you want to use more than one row in your border, specify a range that includes one cell in each border row.)

A:A1: [W24] 'Description   `READY`

A	A	B	C	D	E	F
1	Description	Life	Cost	Dept	Type	Inv Code
2	IBM Selectric Typewriter	5	$980	Accounting	Office	54301
3	Royal Typewriter	5	$950	Training	Office	54455
4	Swivel Chair	10	$345	Check	Furniture	54789
5	TI Calculator	7	$100	Audit	Office	54177
6	Walnut Desk	15	$1,200	Cash	Furniture	54138
7	Xerox Copier	3	$2,500	Cash	Processing	54392
8	Xerox Copier	3	$2,800	Accounting	Processing	54999

Figure 6-16.   Purchases worksheet for multi-page printout

```
A:A1: [W24] 'Description                                    EDIT
Enter header: @||Rpt No:2657_

A           A              B      C      D          E          F
1  Description            Life   Cost Dept        Type       Inv Code
2  IBM Selectric Typewriter  5   $980 Accounting  Office      54301
3  Royal Typewriter          5   $950 Training    Office      54455
4  Swivel Chair             10   $345 Check       Furniture   54789
5  TI Calculator             7   $100 Audit       Office      54177
6  Walnut Desk              15 $1,200 Cash        Furniture   54138
7  Xerox Copier              3 $2,500 Cash        Processing  54392
8  Xerox Copier              3 $2,800 Accounting  Processing  54999
```

Figure 6-17.   Entering a header

4. If you want a header and footer for the report, select Header next. Enter a header such as @ ‖ **Rpt No:2657**, as shown in Figure 6-17. This entry will place the date at the left of the header, and the report number on the right.

5. Now select Footer. To produce the page number, enter ¦ **Page No: #** as shown in Figure 6-18.

6. The remaining two entries needed are Margins Top and Margins Bottom. In our example, the top margin was set at 5 and the bottom margin at 50—leaving only five print lines on a 60-line page (for Hewlett-Packard LaserJet Series II) once the header, footer, and other blank lines at the top and bottom are included.

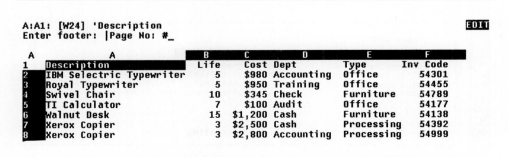

```
A:A1: [W24] 'Description                                    EDIT
Enter footer: |Page No: #_

A           A              B      C      D          E          F
1  Description            Life   Cost Dept        Type       Inv Code
2  IBM Selectric Typewriter  5   $980 Accounting  Office      54301
3  Royal Typewriter          5   $950 Training    Office      54455
4  Swivel Chair             10   $345 Check       Furniture   54789
5  TI Calculator             7   $100 Audit       Office      54177
6  Walnut Desk              15 $1,200 Cash        Furniture   54138
7  Xerox Copier              3 $2,500 Cash        Processing  54392
8  Xerox Copier              3 $2,800 Accounting  Processing  54999
```

Figure 6-18.   Entering a footer

7. Finally, press **Q** to quit the Options menu; then select Range to tell 1-2-3 what range to print. In this case, specify A2 to F8, carefully excluding the border row so it will not print twice. Then select Go from the Print menu.

The product of this process will be the two report pages shown in Figure 6-19. If you had extended the top and bottom margins a little further, you could have produced a report with only one data line per page.

Using Printer Features

Most printers have a variety of special features that you can access if you "speak the language" of the printer. 1-2-3 has the ability to speak the language of most popular printers if you supply it with the correct entries. Some of the requests the printer understands are available in

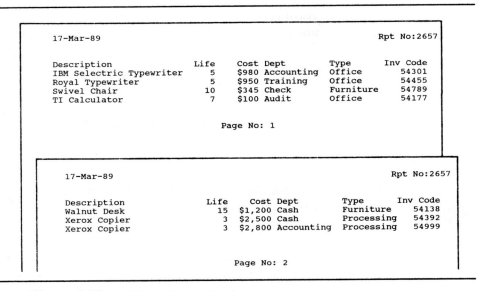

Figure 6-19.   Printout using border rows

1-2-3 through the /Print Printer Options Advanced command; they include boldface, compressed print, orientation, and color. Other printer features are accessed through 1-2-3 using *setup strings*.

Since each printer can offer its own unique set of features, 1-2-3 will print a sample worksheet and graph combination, to show you how it will print the current selections on your particular printer. To print this sample, use the /Print Printer Sample command, and select Go. The sample displays the current print settings; a sample worksheet; how the printer prints fonts 1 through 8, standard, compressed, and expanded pitch; standard and compressed spacing; and two sample graphs showing various 1-2-3 graphic features. If your printer does not support all of these features, the sample will show how 1-2-3 will choose to print them.

Using Menu Commands for Printer Features

Your printer may have features like compressed print, the option of printing six or eight lines to the inch, boldface printing, and enlarged print. These common options are available through the /Print Printer Options Advanced command. These options assume that the printer you direct 1-2-3 to use matches the printer that is attached to your system. Since the Options Advanced option adds printer-specific codes to the print output, you want to avoid sending codes that your printer will not interpret properly. If you do, the worksheet will not look like you expect it to. When an option you selected with /Print Printer Options Advanced is not available, the closest possible substitution will be made. These options have no effect when you are printing to a .PRN file.

The /Print Printer Options Advanced command has three options that access printer features: Layout, Fonts, and Color. The Layout option controls the character width (pitch), number of lines printed per inch (line-spacing), and whether 1-2-3 rotates the printed output by 90 degrees (orientation). The Fonts option selects the font, or character style 1-2-3 uses to print the range, header and footer, border, and frame. When you use this option, 1-2-3 prompts for the area you are printing, and a font selection. Then it lists the numbers 1 through 8, representing different fonts, along with a description of the font in the line below. The Color option controls the color 1-2-3 uses to print the worksheet.

Boston Company

	JAN	FEB	MAR	APR	MAY	JUNE	JULY	AUG	SEPT	OCT	NOV
Salaries	$8,000	$8,200	$8,200	$8,700	$8,700	$7,500	$7,500	$10,000	$10,000	$10,000	$10,000
Building Operations	1,100	1,100	1,100	1,100	1,100	1,100	1,100	1,100	1,300	1,300	1,300
Travel	850	850	850	850	850	850	850	850	850	850	850
Supplies	500	500	500	500	500	500	500	500	500	500	500
Depreciation	1,200	1,200	1,200	1,200	1,200	1,200	1,200	1,200	1,200	1,200	1,200
Equipment Maintenance	750	750	750	750	750	750	750	750	750	750	750
Shipping Expense	400	400	400	400	400	400	400	400	400	400	400
Data Processing Costs	2,100	2,100	2,100	2,100	2,100	2,100	2,100	2,100	2,100	2,100	2,100
Printing & Duplicating	640	640	640	640	640	640	640	640	640	640	640
Other	1,030	1,030	1,030	1,030	1,030	1,030	1,030	1,030	1,030	1,030	1,030
Total Expenses	$16,570	$16,770	$16,770	$17,270	$17,270	$16,070	$16,070	$18,570	$18,770	$18,770	$18,770

Figure 6-20.   Worksheet printed with compressed print

These three options were only available in previous releases of 1-2-3 with the use of setup strings or external utilities. Since these features apply to either the entire worksheet or to a general area, a worksheet can still incorporate setup strings to change the formatting within a range or another area. These features can be combined.

Figure 6-20 shows a worksheet that uses compressed pitch from the Layout option. With this feature, a printer that normally prints a page 80 columns across and 66 rows down, using standard size characters, will print a page of 132 columns and 88 rows of compressed characters.

Using Setup Strings for Printer Features

Unfortunately, not all printer features can be added with menu commands. Also, you may want to change printer features in the middle of a print range. In these cases, you must access printer features with *setup strings*.

Each printer has its own "language," or directions that tell the printer what to do. When you use setup strings, you will have to look in your printer manual for the language required by that printer model. Look for a set of decimal codes assigned to that printer's features. The "Setup String Chart" box provides a handy form for making a reference list of the printer codes you'll need. Add your own entries for additional fonts or features and make your own list.

Setup String Chart

Setup strings allow you to utilize the full capacity of your printer. You must use a setup string customized for your printer to access the features your printer supports — when you want to design a small area of the worksheet, or when you want to use a printer feature that 1-2-3's menus do not support. This fill-in list will serve as a convenient reference for your printer's setup codes once you have looked them up in your printer manual. Add other features to this list as needed, so you can have all your codes in one place.

Begin Boldface   _____

End Boldface   _____

Begin Emphasized   _____

End Emphasized   _____

Begin Italic   _____

End Italic   _____

Begin Auto Underline   _____

End Auto Underline   _____

If you want the printer codes to affect all of your output, enter them through the command /Print Printer Options Setup. (If you want to affect the printing of only a small area of the worksheet, you will need to embed the codes in worksheet cells using a process described later.) To enter the desired printer code or codes as a setup string for the entire print range, enter the command sequence **/Print Printer Options Setup** and press ENTER. If another setup string is already displayed, press ESC before entering a new string. Next enter the printer code or codes you want, preceding each three-digit decimal code with a backslash (\), and each two-digit decimal code with a backslash and a zero. This will produce entries such as \027, \018, and \100. After the complete setup string is entered, press ENTER again. Then select Quit from the Options menu, and Go from the main Print menu to obtain your printout.

Setup strings can include more than one code. For instance, you may want both underlining and a special font. You may include up to 512 characters in a setup string. The feature your setup string creates will remain in effect, in most cases, until you enter another setup string to turn off or change the feature you selected. For example, the setup string for underlining on the Hewlett-Packard LaserJet Series II printer is \027\038\100\068. The underlining will remain in effect until the setup string \027\038\100\064 is transmitted to turn off the underlining feature, or the printer is turned off to erase its print buffer. Figure 6-21 shows the setup string for a different font on the Hewlett-Packard LaserJet Series II, and Figure 6-22 shows a report printed with this feature.

It is also possible to embed setup strings in worksheet cells. The advantage of this approach is that it allows you to change print characteristics more than once while printing a worksheet. Place these entries in blank rows, since the entire row is ignored after the setup string is processed. Setup strings in a worksheet cell must be preceded by two vertical bars (‖). For example, to embed \015 in a cell, enter ‖\015.

Suppose you have a worksheet on which you would like to print only the company name in boldface. You have a Hewlett-Packard LaserJet Series II printer, so you need to use the codes for this printer. Enter the printer code for boldface, ‖\027(s3B, on the line above the company name as shown in Figure 6-23. (Notice that this print code includes

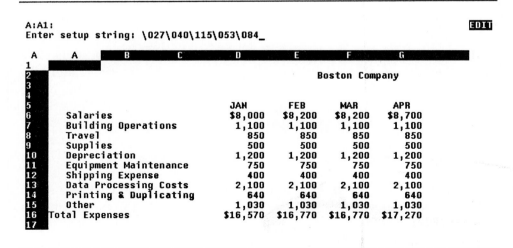

Figure 6-21.   Entering a setup string

```
                                    Boston Company

                          JAN      FEB      MAR      APR
          Salaries       $8,000   $8,200   $8,200   $8,700
          Building Operations
                          1,100    1,100    1,100    1,100
          Travel           850      850      850      850
          Supplies         500      500      500      500
          Depreciation   1,200    1,200    1,200    1,200
          Equipment Maintenance
                           750      750      750      750
          Shipping Expense 400      400      400      400
          Data Processing Costs
                         2,100    2,100    2,100    2,100
          Printing & Duplicating
                           640      640      640      640
          Other          1,030    1,030    1,030    1,030
   Total Expenses       $16,570  $16,770  $16,770  $17,270
```

Figure 6-22.   Printout using a different font

letters and symbols. Many print codes combine decimal codes with
letters and symbols; check your manual for the correct codes for your
printer. Since 1-2-3 converts the characters to their ASCII values, it is
important that the order and case is correct for the code.) On the line
below the company name, enter the code to stop boldface, ‖\027(s0B.
(Note that only one vertical bar displays in the cell .)

A:A1: ||\027(s3B   READY

```
A        A.        B      C      D      E      F      G      H
1   |\027(s3B
2                   The Smith Company
3   |\027(s0B
4
5                   Unit Sales        $ Sales
6
7   Product 1        3,450          $57,600
8   Product 2        5,670          $78,900
9   Product 3        5,312          $76,598
10  Product 4       12,679          $87,953
11  Product 5        2,341         $120,900
12  Product 6       10,900          $45,246
```

Figure 6-23.   Entering setup strings on the worksheet

If you then enter the range A1..E12 and select Go from the Print menu, the report shown in Figure 6-24 will be produced. Of course, the lines containing the print codes do not print on the report.

Tip: There is an alternative to using setup strings in a worksheet to change printer features within a range. Instead, print each area of the worksheet that uses a specific printer feature separately, so you can use the 1-2-3 commands to select printer features. For example, if you want to print the bottom half of the worksheet in compressed pitch, first print the top portion of the worksheet using standard print size. Then, before you print the second half of the worksheet, execute the /Print Printer Options Advanced Layout Pitch Compressed command. The rest of the sheet will print in smaller characters.

Page Length

Page length is the number of lines that could be printed on a sheet of paper, assuming every line was used. With the default options in effect, and 6 lines printed per inch, only 56 lines will be printed for a page length of 66. This is because lines 1, 2, 65, and 66 are reserved for top and bottom margins. Line 3 is left blank for a header, and lines 4 and 5 are blank to make space between header and text. Similarly, line 64 is left blank for a footer and lines 62 and 63 for space. Lines 6 through 61 are used for printing your worksheet data.

If you elect to print at 8 lines per inch by using the /Print Printer Options Advanced Layout Line-Spacing command, you can increase the

---

The Smith Company

	Unit Sales	$ Sales
Product 1	3,450	$57,600
Product 2	5,670	$78,900
Product 3	5,312	$76,598
Product 4	12,679	$87,953
Product 5	2,341	$120,900
Product 6	10,900	$45,246

Figure 6-24.   Heading printed in boldface

page length to 88 on the same 11-inch sheet of paper. You can reset the default page length with the /Print Printer Clear Format command sequence.

Other Options

The /Print Printer Options Other command allows you to decide whether information will be printed with or without formatting that has been added to the text. It also allows you to print formulas rather than the information displayed on your screen. A new option in Release 3 allows you to suppress 1-2-3's automatic use of the top and bottom three lines for headers and footers; you can employ this when you don't intend to have a header and footer.

Printing What You See on the Screen

The default setting, /Print Printer Options Other As-Displayed, will cause your printed report to contain the same information you see on the screen. This means the results of formulas will be printed just as they are displayed on the screen. The formats in effect on your screen display will be used for the printout, as will the column width for the current active window. In short, you will have an exact duplicate of the worksheet portion of the screen display, except that you are not restricted to screen size for your printout. You will be restricted to the limitations of the established page size, however.

Printing Cell Formulas

In Chapter 4, "Changing the Appearance of the Worksheet Display," you learned how to display formulas in cells by using the /Range Format Text command. To print a Text format worksheet like the one described in Chapter 4, you could use the As-Displayed option, since the formulas are already displayed. Alternatively, you could use 1-2-3's built-in formula printing option. With this option you do not have to change the format and width of cells as you did in Chapter 4, because the package does not print the formulas in the shape of the worksheet. Instead, it prints the formulas one per line down the page.

If an entire large worksheet is involved, the documentation produced by this approach can be quite a long list. However, this is an excellent way to print the formulas for a smaller range of cells, because it involves so little work on your part. All you have to do is select your print range and then choose Options Other Cell-Formulas. Quitting the Options menu and selecting Go from the Print menu will then produce a formula listing like the one in Figure 6-25. The formulas print according to the column they are in, with the order being A1, A2, A3, B1, B2, B3, and so on.

Tip: You can also print the notes you have added to cells. When you use the Cell-Formulas option, 1-2-3 includes notes added to both value and formula cells. Printing cell contents with this command bypasses the column width limitation to display lengthy formulas and notes.

Using Format Options for Printing

Like As-Displayed, Formatted is another default setting in the Options Other menu. It uses page breaks, headers, footers, and any other formatting you have done to create a professional report. Formatting is

```
A:A5:  [W18]  'Alpen, Pat
A:A6:  [W18]  'Arbor, Jim
A:B5:  (C2)  [W12]  35000
A:B6:  (C2)  [W12]  23000
A:C5:  10
A:C6:  (F0)  4
A:D5:  (P2)  0.04
A:D6:  (P2)  0.07
A:E5:  (C2)  [W13]  ((C5-1)*(B5/12))+((12-(C5-1))*(1+D5)*(B5/12))
A:E6:  (C2)  [W13]  ((C6-1)*(B6/12))+((12-(C6-1))*(1+D6)*(B6/12))
A:F5:  (C2)  [W11]  +E5*0.14;benefits are 14% of salary
A:F6:  (C2)  [W11]  +E6*0.14
```

Figure 6-25.   Cell-formulas printout

used almost every time a report is printed on a printer. Select this option after using the Unformatted option, when you want 1-2-3 to return to formatting the output.

Eliminating Formatting from Output

When you write files to disk for use with another program, you often do not want formatting characters added. The other program may not recognize them and may try to process them as data. Choosing the Unformatted option alleviates this problem by causing the files to be written without formatting. This means that 1-2-3 will ignore page breaks, headers, footers, and any other formatting you have added to the text.

Use of this option is normally confined to printing to an unencoded disk file. It might also be used when you print a list that barely runs over to the next page. You might prefer to keep such a list together, even if it prints over the page perforation. You could do this by choosing /Print Printer Options Other Unformatted.

Suppressing Blank Headers

When your worksheet does not need a header or footer, you can reclaim the blank lines 1-2-3 reserves for headers and footers, and use them as additional lines for printing worksheet entries. Execute /Print Printer Options Other Blank-Header, and select Suppress. This command tells 1-2-3 to use the six lines on each page that are reserved for the header and footer, and the four blank lines that precede and follow them, for worksheet data. If you later want to again include the blank lines for the header or footer, select the /Print Printer Options Other Blank-Header Print command.

Saving Print Settings

When a worksheet file is saved, the print settings associated with this file are also saved. Saving a worksheet after setting its margins, setup strings, and other options will ensure that you will not have to reenter these settings next time you use the file. Release 3 adds other features that let you assign a name to a group of print settings. These print settings names can also be saved with the file. You can have more than one set of print settings, allowing you to switch between groups of print settings.

To save the current worksheet's print settings, you must first assign a print settings name. Use the /Print Printer Options Name Create command and provide a name up to 15 characters that does not include spaces. To use a named set, execute the /Print Printer Options Name Use command and specify the print settings name to use. This command first removes the current print settings before incorporating the settings you have specified.

To modify the settings associated with a print settings name, use /Print Printer Options Name Use to activate the print settings, modify the settings you want to change (with /Print commands), and save the print settings again using the same name. To remove a single print settings name, use /Print Printer Options Name Delete, and specify the print settings name to remove. To remove all print settings names, use /Print Printer Options Name Reset.

To quickly list the print settings names associated with a worksheet file, use /Print Printer Options Name Table, and select a blank area of a worksheet. 1-2-3 will create a single column table that lists each print settings name in a separate row.

Clearing Print Settings

The Clear options let you eliminate some or all of the special print settings you have used for a report and return to the default settings. The five options presented from the Clear menu are All, Range, Borders, Format, and Image. Since Image is used to print graphs, it is covered in Chapter 11, "Working with 1-2-3's Graphics Features."

Clearing All Settings

The All option restores the default for all of your print settings, including print range, borders, setup strings, and margins. If you want to be more selective, you can use one of the other three options.

Clearing Range Settings

The Range option eliminates only a range print specification made earlier for the worksheet. Other print options are not affected.

Clearing Border Settings

The Borders option cancels the specification of any rows or columns as borders, and removes any frame. Other print options are not affected.

Clearing Format Settings

The Format option returns margins, setup strings, layout, fonts, colors, and page length to their default values, but does not affect a range or borders.

Clearing Device Settings

The Device option returns the device name and interface to the default value. This option is used if a different printer is selected.

Selecting a Printer

There are several reasons why you may want to use a different printer. Perhaps you are printing to an encoded file that you will print later using a different computer. Another reason for selecting a different printer is that you have more than one printer attached to your computer. Since 1-2-3 includes printer codes designed to match the printer, it is important that 1-2-3 knows which printer to use.

Before you can select the appropriate printer for 1-2-3 to use, you must include the printer as one of the selectable options when you install 1-2-3. If the printer you want is not available in 1-2-3's Install menu, refer to Appendix A, "Installing 1-2-3," for instructions on adding a printer to 1-2-3's selection of printers. The printer's default settings are set by the /Worksheet Global Default Printer command.

Selecting a Printer Device

To switch to a different printer, use the options for the /Print Printer Options Advanced command. The Device Name option lets you determine which printer selected from the Install menu 1-2-3 will use. The

Device Interface option allows you to specify the printer interface. The default setting is 1; this is the appropriate setting for a parallel printer adapter. Eight other settings are possible. If you select a serial port, 1-2-3 will prompt you to specify the baud rate.

Automatic Line Feed

The /Print Printer Options Advanced AutoLf command determines whether 1-2-3 needs to generate a line feed after every carriage return. Select No, indicating that your printer does not generate line feeds, or Yes, indicating that it does. If your printed output looks the way you want it to, you do not have to worry about this setting. If extra line feeds are being generated, you will want to set it to Yes. If line feeds are missing, change it to No.

Pausing Between Pages

Use the /Print Printer Options Advanced Wait command to specify whether the printer uses single sheets or continuous feed paper. The No option indicates that the printer uses continuous feed paper and does not need to pause after printing each page. Yes means the printer uses single sheet paper, and 1-2-3 must pause after printing each page until you insert the next page and tell 1-2-3 to continue with the /Print Resume command.

Global Printer Defaults

It takes little effort to get a printed copy of your worksheet, because 1-2-3 does much of the preliminary work for you by setting up default values for many of the print options. These default values are available whenever you load 1-2-3. Sometimes, however, you may wish to change the defaults. You have learned in the previous section how to make changes that apply to just one particular worksheet; this section shows how you can make permanent changes to the defaults.

The command you will need to change the default values is not found in the Print menu. It is /Worksheet Global Default Printer, which presents the following menu:

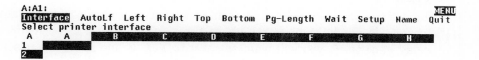

Changing these options to values that meet your particular daily needs will save time; you will not have to change print options every time you load 1-2-3. Notice the Quit option at the end of this menu, which indicates that it is another menu that will remain displayed until you eliminate it with Quit.

Printer Interface

The Default Printer Interface option allows you to specify the default printer interface. The default setting is 1 for a parallel interface; this is the appropriate setting for a parallel printer adapter. Eight other settings are possible. The first three are as follows:

    2 Serial 1 for a serial printer with an RS232 interface
    3 Parallel 2 for a second parallel printer
    4 Serial 2 for a second serial printer

The remaining five options are DOS devices for use when your computer is part of a local area network. Here is a list of them.

    5 LPT1
    6 LPT2
    7 LPT3
    8 COM1
    9 COM2

You will need to specify additional information concerning your network configuration, such as baud rate, when selecting either serial interface.

Automatic Line Feed

The Default Printer AutoLf option determines whether 1-2-3 needs to generate a line feed after every carriage return. The two options are No, indicating that your printer does not generate line feeds, and Yes, indicating that it does. If your printed output looks the way you want it to, you do not have to worry about this setting. If extra line feeds are being generated, you will want to set it to Yes. If line feeds are missing, change it to No.

Left Margin

The Default Printer Left option establishes a default left margin of 4. You can use this option to change the default to any number from 0 to 1000.

Right Margin

The Default Printer Right option establishes a default right margin of 76, four spaces in from the right edge of a form that holds 80 characters across. As with the left margin setting, you can use any setting from 0 to 1000.

Top Margin

The Default Printer Top option is set at 2 for a top margin. You can change this option to allow a default of 0 to 240.

Bottom Margin

The default for the bottom margin is also set at 2. You can change it to any number from 0 to 240, using the Default Printer Bottom option.

Page Length

The default setting for Default Printer Page Length is 66. This is the correct setting for 8 1/2-by-11-inch paper, assuming printing at 6 lines per inch. You can change the default to any number from 1 to 1000.

Paper Feeding

The Default Printer Wait option indicates whether you wish to wait for a paper change at the end of each sheet. The default setting is No, which is appropriate for continuous feed paper. Use the Yes setting when you print on single sheets.

Printer Setup

As you saw earlier in this chapter, setup strings are special codes you can transmit to your printer to access its special features. The default setting is no setup string, but if you use certain features regularly, such as double strike or compressed print, you can add the appropriate setup string to your printer's default settings. Use the /Worksheet Global Default Printer Setup command.

There is no menu under this option because of the wide variations in printer codes from model to model. Your printer manual supplies the decimal codes that represent the available options. In most printer manuals you will find a three-digit decimal code. Precede this code by a backslash (\). If the decimal code has only two digits, also add a zero to transform it into a 1-2-3 setting. For instance, \015 is the 1-2-3 form of the code that tells the Epson printer to use its compressed print feature.

Choosing Your Printer

The Default Printer Name option allows you to specify the name of the printer you wish to use if you have more than one. The menu is customized during installation to include the names of your existing printers.

Exiting the Default Printer Menu

The Quit option is the last /Worksheet Global Default Printer menu choice. Aside from repeatedly pressing ESC, Quit is the only way out of the menu.

Saving Global Default Settings

Changing the Default Printer options does not automatically produce a permanent modification. You must first Quit the Default Printer menu and choose Update from the prior menu. Update stores the default options in your configuration file, called 123.CNF. This file will be on your hard drive if you have one.

Other Worksheet Commands for Printing

Most of the commands that affect printed output are found under the Print option on the main menu. You have seen that most of the default settings are controlled using the /Worksheet Global Default Printer command. There are two additional commands on the Worksheet menu that affect printing. /Worksheet Column Hide affects the worksheet display, and also excludes hidden columns from the printed output. /Worksheet Page inserts a page break anywhere you wish in your document.

Using Hidden Columns to Affect Print Range

If you want to print more than one range from a worksheet, one method is to select the ranges and print them. The second range prints immediately after the first range, as shown in Figure 6-26. You will notice that the columns in the second range do not have descriptive information preceding them.

In many instances it is not possible to fit all the information in your worksheet across one printed page. You can solve this problem by using the /Worksheet Column Hide feature, discussed in Chapter 4, "Changing the Appearance of the Worksheet Display," to choose which columns to print, effectively extending the print features. Figure 6-27 presents part of a worksheet, the result of using /Worksheet Column Hide to eliminate columns D through F. Entering /Print Printer Range A1..I16, and then Go, will create the printed report shown in Figure 6-28.

```
                                Boston Company
                            First Quarter Expenses

                            JAN        FEB        MAR
        Salaries            $8,000     $8,200     $8,200
        Building Operations  1,100      1,100      1,100
        Travel                 850        850        850
        Supplies               500        500        500
        Depreciation         1,200      1,200      1,200
        Equipment Maintenance  750        750        750
        Shipping Expense       400        400        400
        Data Processing Costs 2,100      2,100      2,100
        Printing & Duplicating 640        640        640
        Other                1,030      1,030      1,030
    Total Expenses          $16,570    $16,770    $16,770

            Second Quarter Expenses

        APR        MAY        JUNE
        $8,700     $8,700     $7,500
         1,100      1,100      1,100
           850        850        850
           500        500        500
         1,200      1,200      1,200
           750        750        750
           400        400        400
         2,100      2,100      2,100
           640        640        640
         1,030      1,030      1,030
        $17,270    $17,270    $16,070
```

Figure 6-26.   Two print ranges printed consecutively

Using hidden columns is one way to print a second range with descriptive information. It is also useful when some columns contain data that you do not need in your report.

Inserting a Page Break in the Printed Worksheet

A worksheet with many separate sections could be a printing nightmare in the past. You had two options: you could sit at the printer and

A:I3:   READY

A	A	B	C	G	H	I	J	K
1								
2				Boston Company				
3				Second Quarter Expenses				
4								
5				APR	MAY	JUNE	JULY	AUG
6	Salaries			$8,700	$8,700	$7,500	$7,500	$10,000
7	Building Operations			1,100	1,100	1,100	1,100	1,100
8	Travel			850	850	850	850	850
9	Supplies			500	500	500	500	500
10	Depreciation			1,200	1,200	1,200	1,200	1,200
11	Equipment Maintenance			750	750	750	750	750
12	Shipping Expense			400	400	400	400	400
13	Data Processing Costs			2,100	2,100	2,100	2,100	2,100
14	Printing & Duplicating			640	640	640	640	640
15	Other			1,030	1,030	1,030	1,030	1,030
16	Total Expenses			$17,270	$17,270	$16,070	$16,070	$18,570

Figure 6-27.   Worksheet with hidden columns

request each section separately, trying to remember to Page and Align
during print requests, or you could set up a print macro to do the
remembering for you. Neither way was easy.

	Boston Company		
	Second Quarter Expenses		
	APR	MAY	JUNE
Salaries	$8,700	$8,700	$7,500
Building Operations	1,100	1,100	1,100
Travel	850	850	850
Supplies	500	500	500
Depreciation	1,200	1,200	1,200
Equipment Maintenance	750	750	750
Shipping Expense	400	400	400
Data Processing Costs	2,100	2,100	2,100
Printing & Duplicating	640	640	640
Other	1,030	1,030	1,030
Total Expenses	$17,270	$17,270	$16,070

Figure 6-28.   Printed output with hidden columns

The /Worksheet Page command makes it possible to split the printing of your reports wherever you want. /Worksheet Page causes 1-2-3 to insert a blank line, adding a page indicator (::) at the cell pointer location. A page break can be manually added by placing |:: on a blank row. (The /Range Erase or /Worksheet Delete Row commands can be used to erase an unwanted page break.) 1-2-3 ignores anything in the row after the page break.

Figure 6-29 presents a worksheet with a page break inserted. When A1..G16 is selected as the print range, the output shown on the two pages in Figure 6-30 is produced. The page break indicator causes the page break to occur before the first page is filled.

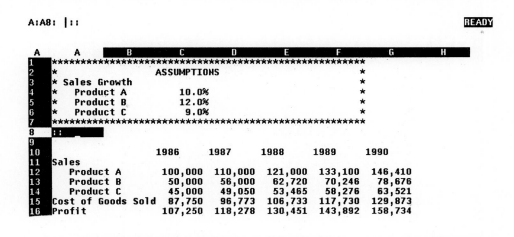

Figure 6-29. Worksheet showing page break

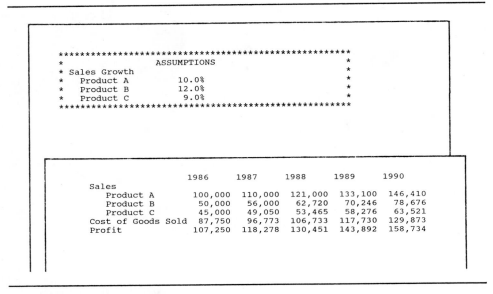

Figure 6-30. Printout using /Worksheet Page

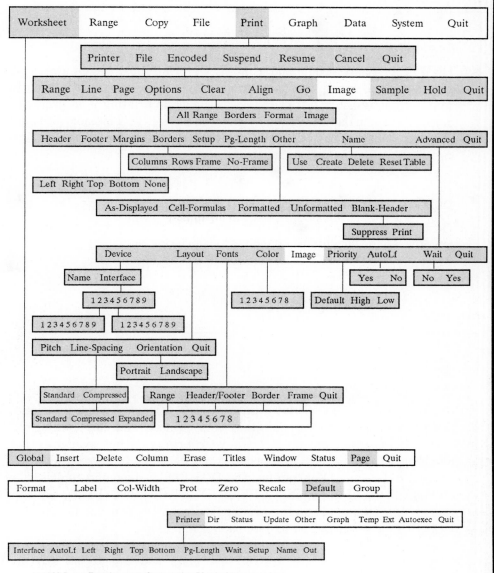

| Worksheet | Range | Copy | File | Print | Graph | Data | System | Quit |

| Printer | File | Encoded | Suspend | Resume | Cancel | Quit |

| Range | Line | Page | Options | Clear | Align | Go | Image | Sample | Hold | Quit |

| All | Range | Borders | Format | Image |

| Header | Footer | Margins | Borders | Setup | Pg-Length | Other | Name | Advanced | Quit |

| Columns | Rows | Frame | No-Frame |

| Use | Create | Delete | Reset | Table |

| Left | Right | Top | Bottom | None |

| As-Displayed | Cell-Formulas | Formatted | Unformatted | Blank-Header |

| Suppress | Print |

| Device | Layout | Fonts | Color | Image | Priority | AutoLf | Wait | Quit |

| Name | Interface |

| Yes | No |

| No | Yes |

| 1 2 3 4 5 6 7 8 9 |

| 1 2 3 4 5 6 7 8 |

| Default | High | Low |

| 1 2 3 4 5 6 7 8 9 |

| 1 2 3 4 5 6 7 8 9 |

| Pitch | Line-Spacing | Orientation | Quit |

| Portrait | Landscape |

| Standard | Compressed |

| Range | Header/Footer | Border | Frame | Quit |

| Standard | Compressed | Expanded |

| 1 2 3 4 5 6 7 8 |

| Global | Insert | Delete | Column | Erase | Titles | Window | Status | Page | Quit |

| Format | Label | Col-Width | Prot | Zero | Recalc | Default | Group |

| Printer | Dir | Status | Update | Other | Graph | Temp | Ext | Autoexec | Quit |

| Interface | AutoLf | Left | Right | Top | Bottom | Pg-Length | Wait | Setup | Name | Out |

/Print Cancel

Description

The /Print Cancel command cancels all print jobs, resets the page alignment, and resets the page number to 1. This command is used to stop print jobs either before they start or while printing is in progress. Since this command removes all print jobs from 1-2-3's memory, it is not for temporarily halting the printing process. To temporarily halt printing, use the /Print Suspend command.

Options

There are no options for this command. Since this command resets the top of the page, realign the paper before printing again.

/Print Encoded

Description

The /Print Encoded command allows you to print a report to a file on the disk. Unlike the /Print File command, /Print Encoded includes printer formatting codes specific to your printer, and can also include graphs. This command is useful if your printer is not available. The resulting file with a .ENC extension is not designed to be read by other computer packages. You can use the DOS COPY command to print the encoded file. For example, COPY BUDGET.ENC TO LPT1 requests that DOS print the file on the printer device LPT1. You can also use the DOS PRINT command to achieve the same results.

Options

All of the /Print Printer options are also available when you choose /Print Encoded. You can select print ranges and apply any of these other options to them.

/Print File

Description

The /Print File command allows you to print a report to a disk file. This command is useful at times when your printer is not available. It can also be used to prepare data for other programs that manipulate 1-2-3's print output. The file created by this command does not include the printer codes that control printing features. This command also cannot accommodate graphs. To print graphs and include printer codes in a file, use the /Print Encoded command.

Options

Most of the /Print Printer options are also available when you choose /Print File. You can select print ranges and apply any of these other options to them.

/Print Printer

Description

This command is used whenever you wish to print information from a worksheet file on your printer. Since 1-2-3 contains default values for most of the Print parameters, printing can be as simple as specifying a print range. When you need greater sophistication or would like to tailor a report to your exact needs, you have a variety of options to work with.

Options

The /Print Printer command has the same options as the /Print Encoded command. You can make simple selections like specifying the range of worksheet cells to print, or you can include more sophisticated information, such as a set of printer control codes to meet your exact print style needs. You can change margins, choose rows or columns that you want to appear on all pages of a report, print the worksheet cells as they display, or print the formulas behind them.

/Print Printer Align

Description

This command will set 1-2-3's internal line count to zero. 1-2-3 then assumes that the printer is aligned at the top of a page. Any entries after this point will begin to add to the new line count.

Options

There are no options for this command. Your only real concern is that the printer carriage be stationed at the top of a form before you enter the command sequence.

/Print Printer Clear

Description

This command can be used to eliminate special print settings, and return the specified print settings to their defaults. For example, if you have added a setup string, header, footer, and borders to a report, and want to print it again without these special features, the Clear option saves you time by eliminating the added settings. Without Clear, you would have to reexecute each of the commands for the special settings and delete the entries you made.

Options

The options for /Print Printer Clear let you decide whether you want to clear all or some print settings.

All   This option eliminates all the special entries made through the Print menus. The current print range is canceled. Borders, headers, and footers are all eliminated. Margins, page length, and setup strings are returned to their default settings.

Range   This option cancels only the current print range.

Borders   This option clears both row and column borders.

Format   This option resets the margin, page length, graph settings, and setup string to the default setting found under /Worksheet Global Default Printer.

Image   This option clears a graph selected to be printed.

Device   This option sets the printer name and interface.

/Print Printer Go

Description

This command tells 1-2-3 to begin transmitting the print range to the printer (if Printer was selected), or to your disk drive (if File or Encoded was selected). If you are printing to a file, the file is not fully saved until you select the Quit option or press ESC to return to the READY mode. If you are printing to a printer in a network or to a spooler, the network or spooler will not start printing the print job until you select the Quit option or press ESC to return to the READY mode.

Options

There are no options for this command. To print multiple ranges for a print job, first select the range and the options for printing the range. Then use this command. After selecting the range, repeat the same steps for the other ranges that you want to print. If you are printing a large file while using large files, 1-2-3 may run out of memory. If this happens, remove some of the worksheets and files from the current session, and then use the /Print Resume command.

/Print Printer Hold

Description

This command returns to the READY mode and remembers all of the /Print command settings for the current print job. This command allows you to temporarily return to a worksheet to make a modification before printing. To complete the print job, return to the Print menus.

1-2-3 permanently halts the current print job if the /Print Cancel or the /Print Printer Options Advanced Device Name command is performed. The print job also ends if a /Print command sends a print job to a different destination. For example, if the /Print Printer command is sending the current print job to the printer and the /Print Printer Hold command temporarily pauses the current print job description, 1-2-3 cancels the current print job if the /Print Encoded command is performed. This command does not affect the job 1-2-3 is printing.

Options

There are no options for this command.

Note

If you are using OS/2, or a print spooler that starts each print job on a new page, use this command to print multiple print jobs on the same page, rather than returning to the READY mode with the Quit option or by pressing ESC.

/Print Printer Line

Description

This command is used to generate a line feed. It allows you to print two ranges with only one line between them, by entering Line after printing the first range, then selecting the second range and printing it. Line adds 1 to 1-2-3's internal line count.

Options

There are no options for this command.

Note

This command offers an advantage over using the printer's line feed button. Since the Line command increments 1-2-3's internal line count by one, it keeps the printing of a page in sync with the page's physical length.

/Print Printer Options

Description

This command provides access to all the bells and whistles 1-2-3 offers for printing. Through the submenu this option presents, you can make many modifications to the appearance of a report.

Options

The Options menu includes choices for Header, Footer, Margins, Borders, Setup, Pg-Length, Other, Name, Advanced, and Quit. These options will be covered individually in the sections that follow.

/Print Printer Options Advanced

Description

This command accesses many of the new print features available with Release 3. The submenu for this command provides access to all the features your printer can offer, including whether 1-2-3 uses line feeds, the colors 1-2-3 uses, which device 1-2-3 prints to, which font 1-2-3 uses to print the worksheet, graphic image options, layout options, priority options, whether 1-2-3 pauses after each page, and returning to the Options print menu. The selections that are available will depend on your printer.

Options

The /Options Advanced command has nine choices: AutoLf, Color, Device, Fonts, Image, Layout, Priority, Quit, and Wait.

Device   This option selects which printer 1-2-3 uses for printing the selected range. After Device is selected, 1-2-3 displays Name and Interface. Name displays a list of numbers with the printers they represent on the third line in the control panel. Each of the printers is defined during installation. Interface displays the of numbers 1 and 2 representing the different output ports. If you select a serial port, 1-2-3 prompts you for the baud rate.

The selections made with this command are saved with the worksheet file, so the next time a range is printed, it uses the same device. To use another printer without saving the settings with the worksheet, change the default printer with the /Worksheet Global Default Printer Name command.

Layout   This option determines the line spacing, the orientation, and the pitch (or width) of each character. It also includes Quit, which returns to the Options Advanced menu.

For Line-Spacing, you must specify Standard or Compressed. On several printers these settings are equivalent to 6 lines per inch and 8 lines per inch, although the actual results depend upon the printer.

For Orientation, 1-2-3 has the two options of Portrait (the default), and Landscape. This option lets you rotate the direction 1-2-3 prints, if this feature is available on your printer.

The Pitch option controls the number of characters per inch 1-2-3 fits on a line. The choices are Standard, Compressed, and Expanded. Changing the pitch automatically changes the number of characters for the left and right margins, to adjust for the changing size.

Fonts   This option lets you select the font for a specific section of the output. After Fonts is selected, you may choose Border, Frame, Header/Footer, or Range as the areas for which you can select a font. Select one of these areas, and 1-2-3 lists the numbers representing the different fonts; font descriptions appear in the third line of the control panel.

The actual fonts available depend upon your printer. If the printer cannot print the selected font, it substitutes its best approximation or uses standard characters. This option does not effect graphs. Changing the font can change the number of characters that will fit across a printed page. Selecting Quit returns to the Options Advanced menu.

Color   This option selects the color of a print range. 1-2-3 can print each range in a separate color, if the printer supports multiple colors. After choosing this option, select the color for the range. The color selected does not affect graphs.

Image   This option is covered in Chapter 11, "Working with 1-2-3's Graphics Features."

Priority   This option assigns a priority level to the current print job: Default, High, or Low. If the current job has a High priority, it is printed after previous jobs with High priority, but before other jobs with Default or Low priority. If the current print job has a Default priority, it is printed after previous jobs except those with a Low priority. If the current print job has a Low priority, it is printed after all previous jobs. Within each priority level, the jobs are printed in the order they are created.

AutoLf   This option determines whether 1-2-3 prints a line feed at the end of each line. This setting only needs to be changed if the selected print device is different from the default printer, and the selected printer uses a different line feed setting. Change this setting to No if the printed output contains unwanted blank lines after each line of output. Change it to Yes if the output is printed on the same line.

Wait   This option determines whether 1-2-3 pauses after printing each page, to wait for single sheet feeding. Continuous feed printers that use a sheet feeder or continuous feed paper will have this set to No. Set it to Yes when the printer must pause after printing each page for a new page to be inserted. After each page, 1-2-3 pauses and displays a message to insert a new sheet, and then prints the next page after you execute the /Print Resume command.

Quit   This option returns to the /Print Printer Options menu.

/Print Printer Options Borders

Description

The Borders option allows you to print a frame, or specified rows or columns as borders on every page. When rows and columns are used as a border, you first select either rows or columns, and then specify the range of cells you wish to have appear as a border on each page. Be careful not to include the border rows or columns in your print job's print range; otherwise, they will be printed twice. Choosing the Frame option adds incremental row numbers and column letters as a frame for the borders.

Options

You have the choice of using either rows or columns as borders, and also of adding a frame containing the worksheet column letters and row numbers.

Rows   Use this option when you have a report that is too long for one page. Select the rows you wish to print as borders on the second and subsequent pages, to provide descriptive information on each page.

Columns   Use this option when your report is too wide for one sheet of paper, and when the left of your worksheet contains identifying information that applies to all pages. You can duplicate the selected column of information at the left side of each page.

Frame   Use this option to include the incremental column letters above the columns of your printed worksheet, and the row numbers to the left of your rows. This option is useful for documenting worksheets. You can display the frame along with the worksheet contents using the Text format so the formulas appear.

No-Frame   Use this option to remove a frame added with the /Print Printer Options Border Frame command.

Note

If you accidentally select the Borders option, the current row or column will become a border, depending on whether you choose Rows or Columns. You can easily undo the damage with the command /Print Printer Clear Borders.

/Print Printer Options Footer

Description

This command allows you to add one line of up to 512 characters at the bottom of each page of a report. The footer text cannot extend for more than one line. Typical footer contents are date, report name or number, company name or department, and page number. 1-2-3 allows you to have three different entries for the footer line.

Options

The three Footer options allow an entry to be placed at the left, center, or right section of the footer. Entries are separated by the vertical bar character. Use a bar to separate each of the sections, even if they are not used (in other words, a single footer entry at the right should be preceded by two bars).

You also have the option of using @, \, and # in your footer. The # represents the current page number; the \ followed by a cell address represents the contents of the referenced cell; and @ represents the current date.

Note

If you include the page number in your footer, you will have to exit the Print menu or use the /Print Align command before printing a second time. Otherwise, 1-2-3 will start the second printing of the report with the next page number, rather than beginning again with page 1. Also, you must use the /Print Printer Page command once 1-2-3 has finished printing the print job to include the footer on the last page.

/Print Printer Options Header

Description

This command allows you to add one line of up to 512 characters at the top of each page of a report. The header text cannot extend for more than one line. Typical header contents are date, report name or number, company name or department, and page number. 1-2-3 allows you to have three different entries for the header line.

Options

Header options allow an entry to be placed at the left, center, or right section of the header. Entries are separated by the vertical bar character. Use a bar to separate each of the sections, even if they are not used (in other words, a single header entry at the right should be preceded by two bars).

You also have the option of using @, \, and # in your header. The # represents the current page number; the \ followed by a cell address represents the contents of the referenced cell; and the @ represents the current date.

Note

If you include the page number in your header, you will have to exit the Print menu or use the /Print Align command before printing a second time. Otherwise, 1-2-3 will start the second printing of the report with the next page number, rather than beginning again with page 1.

/Print Printer Options Margins

Description

This command allows you to control the amount of blank space at the top, bottom, and sides of a printed page. If you do not make an entry for Margins, the default values will be used.

Options

There is a Margins option for each of the four areas where you can control the amount of blank space on a printed page. The None option removes the margin settings made with the other Margin options.

Left   The default setting for the left margin is 4 spaces. You can enter any number from 0 to 1000 to establish a new setting. Make sure the value you enter for the left margin is less than the value entered for the right margin, since it is the difference between these two values that determines how many characters will print in a line of your report.

Right   The default setting for the right margin is 76. You can enter any number between 0 and 1000 to change this margin setting. Make sure the value you enter for the right margin is greater than the value entered for the left margin, since it is the difference between these two values that determines how many characters will print in a line of your report.

Top   The default setting for the top margin is 2. You can change it to any number from 0 to 240.

Bottom   The default setting for the bottom margin is 2. You can change it to any number from 0 to 240.

None   This option sets the top, bottom, and left margin to 0, and the right margin to 1000.

/Print Printer Options Name

Description

This command is for creating named print settings that are saved with the worksheet file. The options are used to create, delete, list, and use print settings. Saved, predefined print settings can be selected and used to create additional groups of print settings. You can access the print settings with a single command, rather than having to redefine them each time you need them.

Options

This command has five options: Create, Delete, Reset, Table, and Use.

Use   This option selects a print settings name, and the print settings stored with the print settings name. It removes the print settings currently defined for the worksheet.

Create   This option assigns a name to the current group of print settings and saves them with the worksheet. You are prompted for a name of up to 15 letters, numbers, and symbols (except < <). If you provide an existing print settings name, the current settings are saved under that name, and the settings previously stored under that name are deleted.

   To change the print settings currently assigned to a name, select Name Use, enter the print settings name, change the settings with /Print commands, and then select Create and specify the same print settings name.

Delete   This option deletes a selected print settings name and the print settings stored with the name.

Reset   This option deletes all of the selected print settings names and the print settings stored with the names.

Table   This option lists the print settings names in the current worksheet file. 1-2-3 will prompt you for a cell location for the table. The table uses a single column, with as many rows as the file has print settings names.

/Print Printer Options Other

Description

This command provides three very different sets of features. First, it lets you decide whether output should be the information as displayed in worksheet cells, or the formulas behind the display. Second, this command lets you determine whether print or file output should be formatted or unformatted. The Unformatted option is especially useful if you are attempting to take 1-2-3 data into another program, since the file will be stripped of headers and other special formats. Third, you can use this command to print three blank lines instead of a header and footer, or to omit these lines altogether.

Options

The Options Other command has five options: As-Displayed, Blank-Header, Cell-Formulas, Formatted, and Unformatted. The As-Displayed and Cell-Formulas pair of options provides opposing actions, as does the Formatted and Unformatted pair.

As-Displayed   This is the default option. It causes your printout to match the screen display in the active window, in terms of cell values, format, and width. If you want to change the as-displayed printout, you can set up a second window (see Chapter 5, "Basic Worksheet Commands"), make width and formatting changes to this window, and print from there. After printing, the second window can be cleared.

Cell-Formulas   This option causes the cell formulas, rather than their results, to be displayed. The formulas are shown one per line down the page.

Formatted   This option prints the output with all of your formatting options, such as headers, footers, and page breaks. This is normally the way you want your output to appear when you send it to a printer.

Unformatted   This option strips all the formatting from your data. In other words, information is written to the output device without page breaks, headers, or footers. This option is useful when you are writing the output to a file for use by another program, or when you want the printer to ignore page breaks.

Blank-Header   This option prints three blank lines instead of a header and footer, or omits these three lines if the header and footer are not provided. This option has two selections. Select Print, the default, when you want 1-2-3 to include three blank lines in place of absent header and footer contents. Select Suppress when you want 1-2-3 to omit these three lines when a header and footer are not specified. When Suppress is selected, 1-2-3 uses the header and footer lines for the worksheet data.

/Print Printer Options Pg-Length

Description

This option determines the number of lines in a page of printed output. The default is 66, but 1-2-3 will accept entries from 1 to 1000. (There are not actually 66 lines of printed output on a default page. Remember that top and bottom margins, headers, footers, and the two blank lines below the header and above the footer must be subtracted from the page length to determine the number of print lines.)

Options

The only option for this command is to enter a page length between 1 and 1000.

/*Print Printer Options Quit*

Description

Use this command to exit from the Options menu. Since this menu stays displayed for you to make your option selections, you need Quit to make an exit when you have finished.

Options

There are no options for this command.

/*Print Printer Options Setup*

Description

This command allows you to transmit a setup string of control codes to your printer, so you can use the special features the printer offers. These special features may include enlarged, compressed, emphasized, or boldface printing, as well as different numbers of lines to be printed per inch. The control codes should be used to activate printer features that are unavailable from 1-2-3 menus. 1-2-3 does not automatically adjust the other printer settings for changes made with control codes. For example, if the control code setup string activates a different font, 1-2-3 does not adjust the margins to accommodate the different size of the characters.

Options

The options available for this command are dictated by the features your printer supports. A few of the options for the Hewlett-Packard LaserJet Series II and their respective setup strings are as follows:

\027(s3B = Start boldface print
\027(s0B = Stop boldface print
\027&dD = Start underline
\027&d@ = Stop underline

The decimal codes you will need for setup strings can be found in your printer manual. When entering them into 1-2-3, precede each code with a backslash, and a zero if necessary, as in the example.

/Print Printer Page

Description

This command advances the paper to the top of the next form. This keyboard command makes it unnecessary to touch the printer. The command prints a footer if one has been specified.

Options

There are no options for this command.

/Print Printer Quit

Description

This command is used to exit the Print menu and place you back in READY mode. Since the Print menu stays displayed while you make selections, you need Quit to leave it. Even after printing, you will not return to READY mode until you have chosen Quit. Pressing the ESC key produces the same result.

This menu option ends the print job. For network environments and spoolers, it will tell the network or the spooler that the print job is completed and that printing can begin. If used after /Print File or /Print Encoded, this command closes the file printed.

Options

There are no options for this command.

/Print Printer Range

Description

This command determines how much of the worksheet will be printed. Any valid range of cells can be specified, from one cell to the entire worksheet. 1-2-3 will decide how much of the range can be placed on one page, based on the margin and page length settings, and will carry the remainder of the range over to additional pages.

Options

The only option for this command is to specify a range. The format used for ranges is cell address..cell address, where the cell addresses specified are at opposite corners of the range of cells to be printed. For example, if you wanted to print cells A1 through D10, you could specify the range as A1..D10, D10..A1, D1..A10, or A10..D1.

This command can print ranges spanning multiple worksheets if the worksheet letter is included before the cell addresses. To print multiple ranges, separate the range addresses and names with the argument separator (a comma or semicolon), such as in SALES;A2..B12. The range should include the cells used by label cells to display their contents. Named graphs included in the range must be preceded with an asterisk (*). Hidden columns included in the range are not printed.

/Print Printer Sample

Description

This command prints a sample worksheet using the current print settings. It lets you determine how your printer will print the worksheet. The sample output contains the current print settings; a sample worksheet; how the printer prints fonts 1 through 8, standard, compressed, and expanded pitch; standard and compressed spacing; and two sample graphs showing various 1-2-3 graphic features. If your printer cannot print some of these features, the printer will print them with its best approximation.

Options

There are no options for this command. 1-2-3 will not start printing the sample until the /Print Printer Go command is performed.

/Print Quit

Description

This command leaves the 1-2-3 Print menus and returns to the READY mode.

Options

There are no options for this command.

/Print Resume

Description

This command restarts printing jobs that were temporarily suspended with the /Print Suspend command, or a printer error, or when 1-2-3 is waiting for the next sheet of paper when /Print Printer Options Advanced Wait or /Worksheet Global Default Printer Wait is set to Yes.

This command also clears a printer error message if a printer error caused the printing suspension.

Options

There are no options for this command.

/Print Suspend

Description

This command temporarily halts the current print job. Use the command when you need to adjust the printer, or to realign computer paper that is jamming. Many printers have a buffer that holds data waiting to be printed, so there may be a delay between executing this command and actual suspension of printing.

Options

There are no options for this command.

/Worksheet Global Default Printer

Description

This command allows you to change the default printer settings. These settings determine the way a document prints if you have not made particular specifications for it through the Print menu. They also determine the default interface between 1-2-3 and your printer. Changes made with this command are not permanent unless you save them with /Worksheet Global Default Update.

Options

This command has eleven options. Each of these options have parallel options in the Print menu.

Interface   This option determines the type of connection between your printer and 1-2-3. There are three basic options with several choices: parallel connection, serial connection, or connection through a local area network. The available options are as follows:

(1) Parallel (default setting)
(2) Serial 1
(3) Parallel 2
(4) Serial 2
(5) DOS device LPT1
(6) DOS device LPT2
(7) DOS device LPT3
(8) DOS device COM1
(9) DOS device COM2

Note

If you select one of the serial interface options, 1-2-3 will also ask you to specify a baud rate (the transmission speed it supports). For 110 baud you will have to set your printer at 2 stop bits, 8 bits, and no parity. For speeds other than 110, 1 stop bit will be sufficient.

AutoLf   This option specifies whether your printer automatically issues line feeds after carriage returns. Installation sets this to correspond with your printer, although the initial setting is No, indicating that the printer does not automatically print line feeds. If you are getting double spacing on everything you print, set AutoLf to Yes. If your paper is not advancing as it should, change this setting to No.

Left   This setting for the left margin has a default value of 4, but you can change it to any number between 0 and 1000.

Right   This setting for the right margin has a default value of 76, but you can change it to any number between 0 and 1000.

Top   This option for the top margin has a default value of 2, but will accept values between 0 and 240.

Bottom   This option for the bottom margin has a default setting of 2, but will accept values between 0 and 240.

Pg-Length   The default page length is 66, but it can be changed to any value between 1 and 1000.

Wait   This option allows you to set the default for continuous feed or single sheet paper. The initial value is No, indicating continuous feed paper. If you change it to Yes for single sheets, 1-2-3 waits after each page is printed.

Setup   This option specifies a setup string of control characters to be sent to your printer before every print request. The default is blank, indicating no print control codes. You may supply any valid control codes up to 512 characters in length. The control codes can be obtained from your printer manual. Precede each code with a backslash (\), and also a zero if necessary to make a three-digit code.

Name   If you installed more than one printer for 1-2-3, this option allows you to specify the printer to use. The default value is the first printer selected during installation.

Quit   This option allows you to exit the Worksheet Global Default Printer menu.

/Worksheet Global Default Update

Description

This command saves entries and changes made with the /Worksheet Global Default Printer command to a file called 123.CNF. This file will be loaded every time you bring up the 1-2-3 package.

Options

This command has no options.

/Worksheet Page

Description

This command inserts an empty row into the current worksheet and puts a page break symbol (::) in the current column of the new row. Before you execute this command, position the cell pointer in the first row that you want on the new page. This command is equivalent to entering a page break symbol on an empty row manually. 1-2-3 ignores worksheet contents on the same row with the page break symbol. To remove the page break symbol, delete the row, erase the cell, or change the cell's contents.

Options

There are no options for this command.

1-2-3's Built-in Functions

Date and Time Functions
Financial Functions
Mathematical Functions
Logical Functions
Special Functions
Statistical Functions
String Functions

1-2-3's built-in functions provide ready-made formulas for a wide variety of specialized calculations. Since the formulas are already designed and tested, you can have instant reliability when you include them in your models. The built-in functions also allow you to perform calculations like square root and cosine, extending your range of formulas beyond those you can create with the formula operators covered in Chapter 3.

The 103 functions in Release 3 are grouped into eight categories. The categories are database, statistical, date and time, financial, mathematical, logical, special, statistical, and string. Each of these groups except the database functions will be covered in this chapter. Since the database functions require a knowledge of 1-2-3's data management features, they will be covered in Chapter 9. The remaining functions will be covered by category. Table 7-1 provides a list of 1-2-3's built-in functions and the category to which each belongs for quick reference.

All the built-in functions follow the same basic format. Each has a special keyword or name that tells 1-2-3 which function you wish to use. Most also require *arguments* that define your exact requirements for

Function	Type	Available Only in Release 3
@@(cell)	Special	
@ABS(number)	Math	
@ACOS(number)	Math	
@ASIN(number)	Math	
@ATAN(number)	Math	
@ATAN2(number)	Math	
@AVG(list)	Statistical	
@CELL(attribute string,range)	Special	
@CELLPOINTER(attribute string)	Special	
@CHAR(code)	String	
@CHOOSE(number,list)	Special	
@CODE(string)	String	
@COLS(range)	Special	
@COS(number)	Math	
@COORD(worksheet,column,row, absolute)	Special	*
@COUNT(list)	Statistical	
@CTERM(interest,future value, present value)	Financial	
@DATE(year,month,day)	Date & Time	
@DATEVALUE(date string)	Date & Time	
@DAVG(input field,criteria)	Database	
@DAY(serial date number)	Date & Time	
@DCOUNT(input field,criteria)	Database	
@DDB(cost,salvage,life,period)	Financial	
@DGET(input field,criteria)	Database	*
@DMAX(input field,criteria)	Database	
@DMIN(input field,criteria)	Database	
@DQUERY(function,list)	Database	*
@DSTD(input field,criteria)	Database	
@DSTDS(input field,criteria)	Database	*
@DSUM(input field,criteria)	Database	*
@DVAR(input field,criteria)	Database	
@DVARS(input field,criteria)	Database	*

Table 7-1.   List of functions

Function	Type	Available Only in Release 3
@D360(start date,end date)	Date & Time	*
@ERR	Special	
@EXACT(string1,string2)	String	
@EXP(number)	Math	
@FALSE	Logical	
@FIND(search string,entire string,starting location)	String	
@FV(payment,interest,term)	Financial	
@HLOOKUP(code to be looked up,table location,offset)	Special	
@HOUR(serial time number)	Date & Time	
@IF(condition to be tested,value if true,value if false)	Logical	
@INDEX(table location,column number,row number[,worksheet number])	Special	
@INT(number)	Math	
@INFO(attribute string)	Special	*
@IRR(guess,range)	Financial	
@ISERR(value)	Logical	
@ISNA(value)	Logical	
@ISNUMBER(value)	Logical	
@ISRANGE(string)	Logical	*
@ISSTRING(value)	Logical	
@LEFT(string,number of characters to be extracted)	String	
@LENGTH(string)	String	
@LN(number)	Math	
@LOG(number)	Math	
@LOWER(string)	String	
@MAX(list)	Statistical	
@MID(string,start number,number of characters to be extracted)	String	
@MIN(list)	Statistical	
@MINUTE(serial time number)	Date & Time	
@MOD(number,divisor)	Math	

Table 7-1.   List of functions (*continued*)

Function	Type	Available Only in Release 3
@MONTH(serial date number)	Date & Time	
@N(range)	String	
@NA	Special	
@NOW	Date & Time	
@NPV(discount rate,range)	Financial	
@PI	Math	
@PMT(principal,interest,term of loan)	Financial	
@PROPER(string)	String	
@PV(payment,periodic interest rate,number of periods)	Financial	
@RAND	Math	
@RATE(future value,present value,number of periods)	Financial	
@REPEAT(string,number of times)	String	
@REPLACE(original string,start location,# characters,new string)	String	
@RIGHT(string,number of characters to be extracted)	String	
@ROUND(number to be rounded,place of rounding)	Math	
@ROWS(range)	Special	
@S(range)	String	
@SECOND(serial time number)	Date & Time	
@SHEETS(range)	Special	*
@SIN(number)	Math	
@SLN(cost,salvage value,life of the asset)	Financial	
@SQRT(number)	Math	
@STD(list)	Statistical	
@STDS(list)	Statistical	*
@STRING(number,number of decimal places)	String	
@SUM(list)	Statistical	
@SUMPRODUCT(list)	Statistical	*
@SYD(cost,salvage value,life,period)	Financial	
@TAN(number)	Math	
@TERM(payment,interest,future value)	Financial	
@TIME(hour,minute,second)	Date & Time	

Table 7-1. List of functions (*continued*)

Function	Type	Available Only in Release 3
@TIMEVALUE(time string)	Date & Time	
@TODAY	Date & Time	*
@TRIM(string)	String	
@TRUE	Logical	
@UPPER(string)	String	
@VALUE(string)	String	
@VAR(list)	Statistical	
@VARS(list)	Statistical	*
@VDB(cost,salvage,life,start-period,end-period,[depreciation-factor],[switch])	Financial	*
@VLOOKUP(code to be looked up,table location,offset)	Special	
@YEAR(serial date number)	Date & Time	

* in the Release 3 column indicates the function is new to Release 3

Table 7-1.   List of functions (*continued*)

the function in a particular situation. The basic format rules for functions are as follows:

- Every function begins with an at sign (@).

- The @ sign is followed by a function name or keyword. When entering this name, you must match 1-2-3's spelling exactly. Either upper- or lowercase can be used, although function names will be shown in uppercase throughout this chapter.

- It is important never to use spaces within a function. You must always write @SUM(A5,A15..A17), not @SUM (A5, A15..A17) or @SUM(A5, A15..A17). If you accidentally include a space, 1-2-3 may remove it, return ERR, or prompt you to edit the function — depending on the space's location.

There are also a few general rules that apply to all function arguments. They are as follows:

• Function arguments must be encased in a set of parentheses.

• Functions that require no arguments do not require parentheses. One example is @RAND, which generates a random number between 0 and 1. The other seven functions that do not require arguments are @PI, @TRUE, @FALSE, @ERR, @NA, @NOW, and @TODAY.

• When a function is used as an argument for another function, you must use a second set of parentheses, because each function must have its arguments enclosed within parentheses. To use the result of @SUM in an @ROUND function, for example, enter the functions like this:

@ROUND(@SUM(A2..A10),2)

• In most cases functions will require arguments to be separated by commas. (The separator character can be changed with /Worksheet Global Default International Punctuation, as described in Chapter 4, "Changing the Appearance of the Worksheet Display.") These arguments can be numeric values, cell addresses, string values, or special codes. The exact requirements for each function will be covered in the expanded description of the function in this chapter.

Different functions require different types of arguments and use them in different ways. Here are some of the format rules that pertain to different function types and uses:

• Some functions, such as @SUM, expect a list of arguments that can be entered in any order. @SUM will add together all the entries in its argument list to produce a sum, for example. If you wanted to sum the values in B1..B10, D4, and D7, you could enter the function as @SUM(B1..B10,D4,D7), @SUM(D7,B1..B10,D4), or any other order of the three entries within the parentheses.

• Arguments that must be provided in a specific order cannot be reordered without causing erroneous results. The @ROUND function is one example. It requires two arguments, the number to be rounded and the position. The latter argument tells 1-2-3 how many places from the decimal to round the number. The function must always be written as @ROUND(number,position), with the numbers or references substituted in the function. If you enter the function as @ROUND(position,number), you will cause an error.

• Arguments that require a specific argument type cannot have another type substituted without causing an error. For example, the @TRIM function removes leading, trailing, and consecutive spaces from a string and requires a string as an argument. An error will result if any argument other than a string is provided.

• For arguments requiring string values, enclose the actual values in double quotation marks—for example, "this is a string". For string arguments you can also enter a cell address (C3), a range name (SALES), or a string formula (+B3&"Company Report"). If you need to review string arithmetic, reread the "String Formulas" section in Chapter 3, "Entering Data in 1-2-3's Worksheet."

• If a function requires a range as an argument, you can specify the range with a range address (A2..A10), a range name (SALES), or a combination (SALES,A2..A10). If the function expects a range and you enter a single cell reference, 1-2-3 may not return the value you expect as it does not convert the single address to a range.

• Functions requiring numeric values will accept them in many formats. You can use actual values (876.54), cell addresses (A2), range names (SINGLE_CELL), formulas (2*A3), functions (@PI), and combinations of the other options (@PI*3+SUM(D2..D4)+NUMBER).

• Some function arguments can use values from other files. To include values from other files as part of the function, enter two less-than (< <) signs (also called opening angle brackets), the filename with file extension, and two greater-than (> >) signs (also called closing angle brackets) before the cell address from the other file. An example is @SUM(< <MONTHTOT.WK3> >SALES), which adds all the values in the SALES range from the MONTHTOT.WK3 worksheet.

• Most functions that support range arguments can use ranges that span multiple worksheets within a file. To select a range that uses multiple worksheets, include the first worksheet letter in the range's beginning address, and the last worksheet letter in the range's ending address. In the following example, the function @SUM(B:G5..M:G15) adds all of the values in the range G5 to G15 for all worksheets from B to M. Some functions require that a referenced range not span worksheets. The @HLOOKUP and @VLOOKUP functions are examples of functions that are limited to one worksheet for the table range. The second example in the description of @VLOOKUP shows how to bypass this restriction.

You will see examples of these various kinds of functions and arguments in use as you proceed through the examples in this chapter. You may want to read through the descriptions of all the function groups, or you may prefer to concentrate on particular categories that meet an immediate need. The descriptive paragraphs at the beginning of the section on each function category provide an overview of the types of formulas offered by the functions in the group. The description of each individual function will cover its format, its arguments if any, and its use. The functions in each category are covered in alphabetical order.

Date and Time Functions

The date and time functions access, create, and manipulate the serial numbers 1-2-3 uses to represent dates and times. For example, you can use date and time arithmetic in your models to determine elapsed time for a production process, to learn whether a loan is overdue, or to age your accounts receivable.

1-2-3 can handle dates between January 1, 1900, and December 31, 2099. A unique serial number is assigned to each of these days, with the number for January 1, 1900, being 1 and December 31, 2099, being 73050. The serial date number represents the number of days since December 31, 1899. Although this may seem a little strange, representing every date in terms of its distance from this date in the past is what provides the date arithmetic features of the package. If all dates have the same comparison point, you can subtract one date from another to determine how many days apart they are. This provides an effective solution for the overdue loan determination, for example, in that the loan due date can be compared to the current date. If the loan due date is less than the current date, the loan is overdue.

Time of day is represented by fractional serial numbers. Midnight is 0.000, 6:00 AM is .25, noon is .5, 6:00 PM is .75, 11:59:59 PM is .99999, and so on. Serial time numbers can be entered in either decimal (.75) or fraction (3/4) format.

Serial date and time numbers will always be used in calculations, but you can use the Format commands to create a more understandable display. Either /Worksheet Global Format or /Range Format can be used to select one of the Date or Time format displays. Since one cell can contain both a whole and a fractional serial number, representing the date and time respectively, you will have to decide which component you would like displayed, since one cell cannot use both a Date format and a Time format. Release 3 provides five Date format options, two of which offer additional options through the /Worksheet Global Default Other International Date command. There are four Time format options. Two are permanent, and two can be altered with the /Worksheet Global Default Other International Time command. As an example, the serial number 32777.75 represents 6:00 PM on September 26, 1989. When the cell containing the entry is formatted with Date format 1, it will display as 26-Sep-89. When it is formatted with D6, or Time format 1, it will display as 06:00:00 PM. Review the Date and Time formats in Chapter 4, "Changing the Appearance of the Worksheet Display," if you are not familiar with these options.

Some of the date and time functions generate serial numbers (@DATE, @NOW), while others expect them as arguments (@DAY, @YEAR). For those functions that expect serial numbers as arguments, entering both an integer and fractional serial number for a function expecting a date will cause 1-2-3 to ignore the fractional part of the entry. The integer number portion would be ignored if a serial time number was expected. If only the integer portion is entered, the value .0, representing midnight, will be used for the time.

@DATE

The @DATE function allows you to create a serial date number when you supply the date components.

Format

@DATE(*year,month,day*)

Arguments

year	a number between 0 and 199. 1900 is represented by 0, 1989 by 89, and 2099 by 199.
month	a number from 1 through 12.
day	a number from 1 through 31. The number must be valid for the month chosen. Since month 9 (September) has only 30 days, for example, 31 is an invalid value for the day when 9 is used for the month.

The arguments must be supplied in the order shown. Selecting an invalid number for any of the arguments will cause 1-2-3 to return ERR.

Use

The @DATE function can be used anywhere you wish to enter a serial date number on a worksheet. Any date used in arithmetic calculations must be in serial form. Figure 7-1 shows an application for the @DATE function. In this example, the charge for each video rental is determined by the number of days a patron has had the video. The date the video was checked out is entered in column C, and the date it was returned is entered in column D. The two serial dates are subtracted, and the result is multiplied by the daily charge of $2.25 to determine the amount the patron should pay—resulting in the formula (D5−C5)*2.25 (see Figure 7-2). The formulas are stored in column E.

A Date format is applied to the range of entries in columns C and D, and Currency format is applied to the range of entries in column E. You can also enter a date in the DD-MMM-YY, DD-MMM, or Long International Date format. 1-2-3 automatically converts entries entered in one of these formats to date serial numbers.

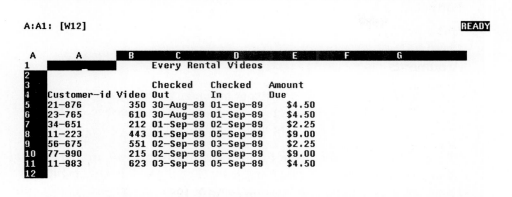

Figure 7-1.   Worksheet using @DATE entries

Note

1-2-3 assigns a serial number to February 29, 1900, even though 1900 was not a leap year. This will cause problems only when you are using dates between January 1, 1900, and March 1, 1900.

@DATEVALUE

The @DATEVALUE function returns a serial date number when you supply a date string in one of the five Date formats.

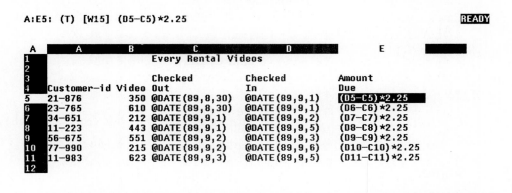

Figure 7-2.   Formulas for @DATE

Format

@DATEVALUE(*date string*)

Arguments

date string	a string argument in quotes, or a cell reference containing a date in one of the five acceptable Date formats.

Three of the acceptable Date formats are fixed, and two are dependent on the format chosen with /Worksheet Global Default Other International Date. Acceptable date string formats for September 29, 1989, are "29-Sep-89", "2-Sep", "Sep-89", and "29.09.89" if D4 (Date format 4) is set at DD.MM.YY; "9/29/89" if D4 is set at MM/DD/YY; "29/09/89" if D4 is set at DD/MM/YY; and "89-09-29" if D4 is set at YY-MM-DD. Acceptable D5 (Date format 5) options are similar except that only the month and day are shown, for example, "09-29".

Use

The @DATEVALUE function is used when you want to perform arithmetic with dates that have been entered in string format. For example, if you were to enter @DATEVALUE("23-Oct-89") in a cell, 32804 would be returned. You could then use this value in a formula. Figure 7-3 provides an example of a model using the @DATEVALUE function. It solves the same problem as the model for video charges in Figure 7-1, except that it uses the @DATEVALUE function and string date formats in the function arguments. The formulas to subtract the two dates are located in column E and follow the format of (@DATEVALUE(D5) − @DATEVALUE(C5))*2.25, as you can see in Figure 7-4.

@DAY

The @DAY function is used to extract the day number from a serial date number.

Format

@DAY(*serial date number*)

A:E5: (C2) (@DATEVALUE(D5)—@DATEVALUE(C5))*2.25   READY

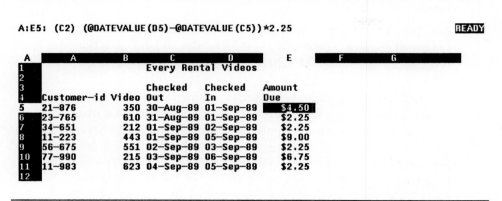

Figure 7-3.   Using @DATEVALUE to work with label (string) dates

Arguments

serial date number   the serial date number of the desired date, which must be between 1 and 73050 to stay within the acceptable range of January 1, 1900, to December 31, 2099. The *serial date number* can be generated by another function such as @NOW, @DATEVALUE, or @DATE.

A:E5: (T) [W40] (@DATEVALUE(D5)—@DATEVALUE(C5))*2.25   READY

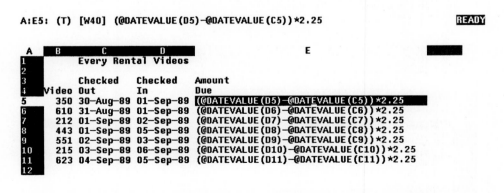

Figure 7-4.   Formulas for @DATEVALUE

Use

This function is used whenever you are interested in only the day portion of a date. Used with @DATE, the @DAY function would be recorded as @DAY(@DATE(89,12,14)) and would return 14. Used with @DATEVALUE, it might be @DAY(@DATEVALUE("24-Dec-89")) and would return a value of 24.

As a sample use for this function, suppose you want to extract the day from a loan origination date so you can use it to generate payment due dates. @DAY can do this. The dates in Figure 7-5 are generated with @DATE, using a day generated with @DAY. The cell must be formatted with one of the Date formats, or the serial date number will display. The advantage of this approach is that the same date formulas could be used for all loans, as only the day numbers will vary. Naturally you would have to make some allowance for February and days 29 through 31. This could be handled with the @IF function, covered later in this chapter.

@D360 (Release 3)

The @D360 function computes the number of days between two dates, based on a 360-day calendar year.

Format

@D360(*beginning date,ending date*)

A:E3: (D1) [W10] @DATE(89,12,@DAY(C3))   `READY`

A	A	B	C	D	E	F	G
1	Loan		Origination		December Payment		
2	Number	Branch	Date		Date		
3	23419	200	14—Jul—85		`14—Dec—89`		
4	45617	908	21—Mar—84		21—Dec—89		
5	23145	540	02—Jun—85		02—Dec—89		
6	22231	200	19—Nov—81		19—Dec—89		
7	87654	313	27—Mar—86		27—Dec—89		

Figure 7-5.   Using @DAY

Arguments

beginning date	the starting date of a period. This is a date serial number which is entered directly or referenced.
ending date	the ending date of a period. This is a date serial number which is entered directly or referenced.

Use

This function is used to determine the number of days between two dates, using a 360-day calendar year. A 360-day calendar year assumes 12 months of 30 days apiece. This function is used primarily for financial applications which use a 360-day calendar in the computations.

A common application is the calculation of interest payments. For example, if you deposit $100,000 in a bank from April 1 to August 16, you may want to know how much interest you will earn if the bank pays 9% interest using a 360-day year. The entry +100000*@D360(@DATE(89,4,1),@DATE(89,8,15))/360*.09 returns 3350, which is the interest your money earns. You need to know the difference in days using a 360-day year rather than a 365-day year because the bank uses a 360-day year in its interest calculations. If you used the formula +100000*(@DATE(89,8,15) − @DATE(89,4,1))/365*.09, the interest amount is $3353.

@HOUR

The @HOUR function extracts the hour from a serial time number, using a military time representation. For example, @HOUR(.75) will equal 6:00 PM.

Format

@HOUR(*serial time number*)

Arguments

serial time number   a decimal fraction between 0.000 and 0.9999. *Serial time number* can be entered as a fraction or a decimal number. It can be generated by @TIME, @TIMEVALUE, or @NOW.

Use

This function is used whenever you wish to work with only the hour portion of a time entry. The function will always return a value between 0 and 23. Used with @TIME, which creates a serial time number when provided with arguments of hour, minute, and second, the function might read @HOUR(@TIME(10,15,25)) and would return 10.

If you were interested in recording the delivery hour for packages received, you might capture the time at receipt and use the @HOUR function to access the specific hour. Figure 7-6 provides an example of using the @HOUR function for this purpose.

@MINUTE

The @MINUTE function extracts the minute from a serial time number.

A:D3: @HOUR(A3)   `READY`

A	A	B	C	D	E	F
1	Time	Package				
2	Received	Number	Recepient	Hour		
3	08:04:06 AM	1761	B. Jones	8		
4	09:11:00 AM	3421	R. Gaff	9		
5	09:30:00 AM	2280	J. Bowyer	9		
6	09:45:00 AM	7891	J. Kiger	9		
7	10:30:00 AM	1975	M. Williams	10		
8	11:05:00 AM	3411	B. Jobes	11		
9	11:15:00 AM	5412	R. Gaff	11		
10	11:55:00 AM	1562	K. Larson	11		

Figure 7-6.   Using @HOUR

Format

@MINUTE(*serial time number*)

Arguments

serial time number	a decimal fraction between 0.000 and 0.9999. *Serial time number* can be entered as a fraction or a decimal number. It can be generated by @TIME, @TIMEVALUE, or @NOW.

Use

This function is used whenever you wish to work with only the minute portion of a time entry. The function will always return a value between 0 and 59. Used with @TIME, which creates a serial time number when provided with arguments of hour, minute, and second, the function might read @MINUTE(@TIME(10,15,25)) and would return 15.

If you were managing a radio station and were interested in recording the exact minutes when you received calls for hourly radio contests, you could use the @MINUTE function to handle the task. Certain types of contests might generate many calls and immediate winners, whereas other types could be announced throughout the hour before a winner called in with the correct answer. You might want to capture the time of receipt of the calls and record whether the caller was the contest winner. Figure 7-7 shows the use of the @MINUTE function for this purpose.

@MONTH

The @MONTH function extracts the month number from a serial date number.

Format

@MONTH(*serial date number*)

A:E3: @MINUTE(C3)   `READY`

A	A	B	C	D	E	F
1	Contest		Time		Minutes	
2	Type	Prize	Of Call	Winner	After Hour	
3	Mystery Guest	$50.00	09:30:00 AM	D. Black	`30`	
4	Golden Oldies	record	10:05:00 AM	P. Silver	5	
5	Wacky DJ Quiz	$125.00	09:08:00 AM	B. Brown	8	
6	Mystery Guest	$75.00	01:05:00 PM	J. Lyson	5	
7	Unknown Music	dinner	02:13:00 AM	F. Pitts	13	
8	Golden Oldies	record	04:20:00 AM	C. Vernier	20	
9	Wacky DJ Quiz	$150.00	02:18:00 AM	D. Gleason	18	
10	Mystery Guest	$300.00	09:45:00 AM	S. Moore	45	
11	Golden Oldies	record	10:02:00 AM	W. Koone	2	
12	Unknown Music	dinner	12:06:00 PM	R. Stork	6	

Figure 7-7.   Using @MINUTE

Arguments

serial date number   the serial date number of the desired date, which must be between 1 and 73050 to stay within the acceptable range of January 1, 1900, and December 31, 2099. The *serial date number* can be generated by another function such as @NOW, @DATEVALUE, or @DATE.

Use

This function is used whenever you are interested in only the month portion of a date. Used with @DATE, the @MONTH function would be written @MONTH(@DATE(89,12,14)) and would return 12. Used with @DATEVALUE, it might be @MONTH(@DATEVALUE("24-Dec-89") and return a value of 12.

One sample use for this function would be to extract employees' vacation months from historic data, so you could monitor vacation schedules to plan for temporary help. You could use this function to extract the month from the vacation start date. The dates in Figure 7-8 are generated with @DATE and used to extract the month number. The advantage of this approach is that the same date formulas can be used for all vacations, as only the month numbers will vary.

A:F4: @MONTH(D4)   READY

A	A	B	C	D	E	F	G
1				1989 Vaction Schedule			
2		YEARS			VACATION	VACATION	VACATION
3	EMPLOYEE	SERVICE	DEPT.	START	STOP	MONTH	
4	G. Brown	5	100	15-Jun-89	29-Jun-89	6	
5	M. Wilson	2	200	03-Jul-89	10-Jul-89	7	
6	N. Staunton	10	100	02-Jun-89	23-Jun-89	6	
7	H. Mailer	3	100	21-Jul-89	28-Jul-89	7	
8	B. Wyler	25	200	03-Aug-89	31-Aug-89	8	
9	K. Wilmer	2	100	22-Jun-89	29-Jun-89	6	
10	D. Jason	5	200	01-Apr-89	15-Apr-89	4	

Figure 7-8.   Using @MONTH

@NOW

The @NOW function is used to stamp a worksheet cell with the current system date and time. The function does not require any arguments and is simply entered as @NOW.

Use

The @NOW function can be used whenever you wish to place the current date or time in a worksheet cell. The integer portion of the serial number generated will be the current date, and the decimal fraction will be the time.

@NOW will appear as a date if formatted with one of the Date format options, and will display as time if formatted with one of the Time formats. @NOW will be recalculated when the worksheet containing it is loaded into memory, and every time the worksheet is recalculated thereafter. This feature can prevent the problem of not being able to tell which one of several printed reports is the most current. If the @NOW function is entered somewhere in every worksheet and always included in your print range, you will always be able to identify the most recent copy of a report.

Figure 7-9 shows a worksheet where two cells, F1 and F2, have @NOW entered in them. One is formatted as a date and the other as a time. Including these cells in the print range when a report is printed

```
A:F2: (D6) [W12] @NOW                                                    READY
```

A	A	B	C	D	E	F	G
1						13–Mar–89	
2						07:31:23 PM	
3				1989 Vaction Schedule			
4		YEARS		VACATION	VACATION	VACATION	
5	EMPLOYEE	SERVICE	DEPT.	START	STOP	MONTH	
6	G. Brown	5	100	15–Jun–89	29–Jun–89	6	
7	M. Wilson	2	200	03–Jul–89	10–Jul–89	7	
8	N. Staunton	10	100	02–Jun–89	23–Jun–89	6	
9	H. Mailer	3	100	21–Jul–89	28–Jul–89	7	
10	B. Wyler	25	200	03–Aug–89	31–Aug–89	8	
11	K. Wilmer	2	100	22–Jun–89	29–Jun–89	6	
12	D. Jason	5	200	01–Apr–89	15–Apr–89	4	

Figure 7-9.   Using @NOW as a date and time stamp

will date and time stamp the report. Since the value of @NOW is calculated only when it is entered and when the worksheet is recalculated, the time display at the bottom of the screen may show a more recent time if the worksheet has not been recalculated recently.

Using F2 (EDIT) followed by F9 (CALC), then pressing ENTER, will freeze the serial date and time number placed in a cell by @NOW, changing it to a fixed value.

Note

This function can be used in conjunction with the @MOD function, covered later in the chapter, to determine the day of the week. @MOD(@NOW,7) will return a value between 0 and 6, since the @MOD function returns the remainder from a division. If the result is 0, the day is Saturday, and if the result is 6, the day is Friday. Each of the other days is represented by one of the other numbers between 0 and 6.

@SECOND

The @SECOND function extracts the second from a serial time number.

Format

@SECOND(*serial time number*)

Arguments

serial time number   a decimal fraction between 0.000 and .9999. *Serial time number* can be entered as a fraction or a decimal number. It can be generated by @TIME, @TIMEVALUE, or @NOW.

Use

This function is used whenever you wish to work with only the second portion of a time entry. The function will always return a value between 0 and 59. If cell A3 contains a serial time number representing 11:08:19, @SECOND(A3) will equal 19. Used with the @TIME function, the @SECOND function might read @SECOND(@TIME(10,15,25)) and would return 25.

@TIME

The @TIME function allows you to create a serial time number when you supply the time components.

Format

@TIME(*hour,minute,second*)

Arguments

hour   must be a number between 0 and 23. Midnight is represented by 0 and 11:00 PM by 23.

minute   must be a number between 0 and 59.

second   must be a number between 0 and 59.

If an invalid number is entered for any of these arguments, a value of ERR is returned by the @TIME function.

Use

This function is used anywhere you want to enter time on a worksheet. When time is entered with this function, you will be able to perform arithmetic operations with the time value, since it will be stored as a serial time number. You can also enter a time by simply typing in the time, because any of 1-2-3's Time formats make times appear, except for the Short International format of HH.MM. 1-2-3 automatically converts the entries entered in one of these formats into time serial numbers.

Figure 7-10 presents a worksheet that uses the @TIME function to record the time vehicles are brought in for repair, and the time the work on each is completed. Entering both sets of numbers makes it easy to perform calculations with the time values, and the /Range Format Date Time command allows you to choose a suitable Time display format. Figure 7-11 shows the worksheet with formulas added in column E to represent the difference between the time each car was brought in for repair and the time it was completed, for example, $+D5-B5$. Using the Short International format under /Range Format Date Time allows you to show just the hours and minutes (represented by the decimal fraction) for the difference between the two time values.

Figure 7-10.   Recording time in a worksheet cell

A:E5: (D9) [W11] +D5-B5   `READY`

```
   A       A        B            C              D         E           F
 1                 QUICK CARE REPAIR - Oct. 1, 1989
 2
 3      Job       Time                          Time     Elapsed
 4      Number    In           Repair           Out      Time
 5            1   08:05 AM  Tire             09:17 AM     01:12
 6            2   08:10 AM  Brakes           10:34 AM     02:24
 7            3   08:30 AM  Steering         01:18 PM     04:48
 8            4   08:32 AM  Lube             09:44 AM     01:12
 9            5   08:40 AM  Transmission     05:04 PM     08:24
10            6   08:45 AM  Brakes           11:09 AM     02:24
11            7   08:47 AM  Muffler          10:35 AM     01:48
12            8   08:59 AM  Tune-Up          12:35 PM     03:36
13            9   09:15 AM  Brakes           11:39 AM     02:24
```

Figure 7-11.   Time arithmetic

@TIMEVALUE

The @TIMEVALUE function returns the serial time number, given the string value of the time.

Format

@TIMEVALUE(*time string*)

Arguments

time string   a single string value conforming to one of
                             the acceptable Time formats and enclosed
                             in double quotation marks.

"HH:MM:SS AM/PM" is acceptable, since it conforms to the D6 (Date Format 6) format, which is the first Time format option; "HH:MM AM/PM" is acceptable, since it conforms to the D7 format, which is the second Time format option. Formats D8 and D9 have more than one option and are changeable through the /Worksheet Global Default International Time command. The acceptable formats for D8 and D9 will depend on which format is in effect. Chapter 4, "Changing the Appearance of the Worksheet Display," provides additional information about Time formats.

Use

This function is used whenever you wish to generate a serial time number from a string value. For example, suppose an entry in your worksheet was originally entered as a string, but you decide you want to use it in a calculation of elapsed time. The @TIMEVALUE function makes this possible. It has the same capability as the @TIME function, but accepts a string for input rather than three separate numeric values for hour, minute, and second. As an example, you might enter @TIMEVALUE("2:14:14 PM"), which gives the value 0.5932175926. This value could then be used in a time formula.

The same worksheet used in Figure 7-10 is reproduced for the @TIMEVALUE example, except that all the times are entered as labels. For example, the entry in D5 is '09:17 AM. This means that the formula in column E will have to be changed, since two label values cannot be used to determine a difference. The formula is changed to use @TIMEVALUE, as shown in cell E5 of Figure 7-12. The entry in this

---

A:E5: (D9) [W11] @TIMEVALUE(D5)-@TIMEVALUE(B5)   READY

A	A	B	C	D	E	F
1		QUICK CARE REPAIR — Oct. 1, 1989				
2						
3	Job	Time		Time	Elapsed	
4	Number	In	Repair	Out	Time	
5		1 08:05 AM	Tire	09:17 AM	01:12	
6		2 08:10 AM	Brakes	10:34 AM	02:24	
7		3 08:30 AM	Steering	01:18 PM	04:48	
8		4 08:32 AM	Lube	09:44 AM	01:12	
9		5 08:40 AM	Transmission	05:04 PM	08:24	
10		6 08:45 AM	Brakes	11:09 AM	02:24	
11		7 08:47 AM	Muffler	10:35 AM	01:48	
12		8 08:59 AM	Tune-Up	12:35 PM	03:36	
13		9 09:15 AM	Brakes	11:39 PM	14:24	

Figure 7-12.   Working with time labels

cell is @TIMEVALUE(D5)−@TIMEVALUE(B5), and the cell is for-matted in the Short International Time format.

@TODAY (Release 3)

The @TODAY function is used to stamp a worksheet cell with the current system date. The function does not require any arguments and is simply entered as @TODAY. It contains the integer portion of the @NOW function.

Use

The @TODAY function can be used whenever you wish to place the current date in a worksheet cell. The advantage of the @TODAY func-tion over the @NOW function is @TODAY's efficiency with regard to minimal recalculation. 1-2-3 only recalculates the @TODAY function when a file containing the function is retrieved, when the date changes, or the cell is edited. The @NOW function is constantly updated since the time serial number portion of the function constantly changes.

@TODAY creates a date serial number that appears as a date if formatted with one of the Date format options. This feature can prevent the problem of not being able to tell which one of several printed reports is the most current. If the @TODAY function is entered somewhere in every worksheet and always included in your print range, you can always identify the most recent copy of a report. As an example, a worksheet can have the following heading:

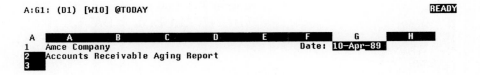

In this worksheet, G1 contains @TODAY, and the result is formatted as a date. Including this cell in the print range when a report is printed will date stamp the report.

Using F2 (EDIT) followed by F9 (CALC), then pressing ENTER, will freeze the serial date number placed in a cell by @TODAY, changing it to a fixed value.

Note

This function can be used in conjunction with the @MOD function, covered later in the chapter, to determine the day of the week. @MOD(@TODAY,7) returns a value between 0 and 6, since the @MOD function returns the remainder from a division. If the result is 0, the day is Saturday, and if the result is 6, the day is Friday. Each of the other days is represented by one of the other numbers between 0 and 6.

@YEAR

The @YEAR function extracts the year number from a serial date number.

Format

@YEAR(*serial date number*)

Arguments

serial date number   the serial date number of the desired date, which must be between 1 and 73050 to stay within the acceptable range of January 1, 1900, to December 31, 2099. The *serial date number* can be generated by another function such as @NOW, @DATEVALUE, or @DATE.

Use

This function is used whenever you are interested in only the year portion of a date. Used with @DATE, the @YEAR function would be recorded as @YEAR(@DATE(89,12,14)) and would return 89. Used with @DATEVALUE, it might be @YEAR(@DATEVALUE("24-Dec-89")) and return a value of 89.

One sample use for this function would be to determine the start year for each of a group of employees. You can reference the date of hire and extract the year number, for an easy reference to the anniversary year, shown in Figure 7-13.

Financial Functions

The primary use of 1-2-3's financial functions is for investment calculations and other calculations concerned with the time value of money. For example, you can use them to monitor loans, annuities, and cash flows over a period of time. Release 3 adds a new variable rate declining balance depreciation function. With this new function and the other depreciation functions, you can quickly compare the effects of different depreciation methods.

Since many of these functions deal with interest rate calculations, you will want to be aware of the two acceptable ways of entering interest rates for these calculations. You can always enter a percent as a decimal fraction, for example, .15 for 15%. Your other option is to enter the percent with the percent sign and have 1-2-3 convert your entry to a decimal fraction for internal storage. For example, 15% would be stored as .15.

Many of the financial functions require a term and a rate as arguments. It is important that the same unit of time be used for both

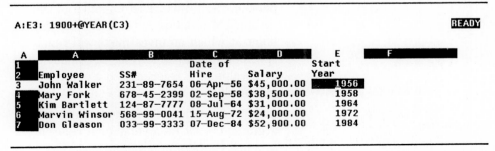

Figure 7-13.   Using @YEAR

arguments. If a term is expressed in years, an annual interest rate should be used. If a term is expressed in months, a monthly interest rate should be used.

@CTERM

Given a present and a future value for an investment, as well as a fixed interest rate, @CTERM will compute the number of time periods it will take to reach the future value.

Format

@CTERM(*interest,future value,present value*)

Arguments

interest	the fixed interest rate per compounding period. It can be expressed as a percent or a decimal fraction within the function, or it can be stored in a cell and referenced with the cell address or a range name. It can also be computed with a formula from within the function.
future value	the value the investment will have at some point in the future. The objective of the @CTERM function is to determine the point at which an investment will reach a specified future value. This argument must be a value or a reference to a cell containing a value.
present value	the current value of the investment. This argument must be a value or a reference to a cell containing a value.

Use

The @CTERM function can provide a quick answer when you want to know how long it will take an investment to grow to a certain value. The formula used by the function is as follows:

$$\frac{\text{natural log(future value/present value)}}{\text{natural log(1 + periodic interest rate)}}$$

As an example, if you have $5000 to invest today and feel you can get an 11% return on your money, you might want to know how long it would take to triple your money at that rate. In Figure 7-14, @CTERM(11%/12,15000,5000) will provide the answer, assuming the compounding occurs monthly. The result is shown in the example worksheet.

@DDB

The @DDB function calculates depreciation expense for a specific period using the *double declining balance method.*

Format

@DDB(*cost, salvage, life, period*)

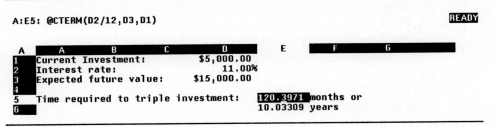

Figure 7-14.   Using @CTERM to compute the time the initial investment needs to earn the future value

Arguments

cost	the amount you paid for the asset. This argument must be a value or a reference to a cell containing a value.
salvage	the value of the asset at the end of its useful life. Like *cost,* this argument must be a value or a reference to a cell containing a value.
life	the expected useful life of the asset; that is, the number of years needed to depreciate the asset from its cost to its salvage value. Normally expressed in years, this argument, too, must be a value or a reference to one.
period	the specific time period for which you are attempting to determine the depreciation expense. Normally the number of the year for which you are calculating depreciation expense, this argument must be a value or a reference to one.

Use

The @DDB function gives you a figure for depreciation expense, using an *accelerated depreciation method* (one that allows you to write off more depreciation expense in the early years of an asset's life). The asset will no longer be depreciated when its book value (that is, cost minus total depreciation to date) equals its salvage value.

The formula used in the calculation of double declining balance depreciation is as follows:

$$\frac{\text{book value for the period} * 2}{\text{life of the asset}}$$

1-2-3 makes adjustments in the calculations to ensure that total depreciation is exactly equal to the asset cost minus the salvage value. Unlike the @VDB function, the @DDB function does not switch to straight-line depreciation when straight-line would be equal or greater.

Figure 7-15 shows the use of this function to determine the proper depreciation expense for each year in an asset's five-year life. The cost of the asset was $11,000, and its salvage value is $1000.

@FV

The @FV function computes the future value of an investment based on the assumption that equal payments will be generated at a specific rate over a period of time.

Format

@FV(*payment,interest,term*)

Arguments

payment	the amount of the equal payments for the investment. This argument must be a value or a reference to a value.
interest	the periodic interest rate earned by the investment. This argument must be a value or a reference to a value.
term	the number of periods for the investment. This argument must be a value or a reference to a value.

Use

This function is designed to perform calculations for an ordinary annuity. It uses the following formula:

$$\text{payment} * \left(\frac{(1 + \text{periodic interest rate}) \text{ raised to the } n \text{ power}}{\text{periodic interest rate}} \right) - 1$$

where n is the number of periods.

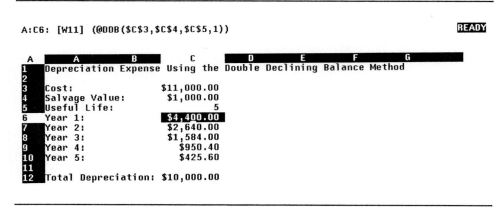

Figure 7-15.   Double declining balance depreciation

Figure 7-16 shows an example of the @FV function used to calculate the value for an ordinary annuity. This worksheet assumes that you plan to deposit $500 a month for each of the next 36 months, and will continue to receive interest on this money at a constant rate of 12% compounded monthly. The formula used is @FV(500,1%,36).

This example is based on the premise that interest is paid at the end of the year and that your next contribution is always made on the last day of the year.

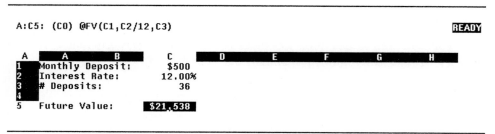

Figure 7-16.   Using @FV to compute the future value of an annuity

Note

The @FV function can be adapted to work with an annuity due, which uses this formula:

@FV(payment,interest,term)*(1 + periodic interest rate)

This is appropriate for a situation where you must make contributions on the first day of the year. Assuming you make annual payments of $5000 at the beginning of each year, and they earn interest at a rate of 10%, the value at the end of ten years would be represented by @FV(5000,10%,10)*(1+10%). This formula would return $87,655.83, the value of your annuity after ten years.

@IRR

The @IRR function calculates the internal rate of return on investments.

Format

@IRR(*guess,range*)

Arguments

guess	an estimate of the internal rate of return. Although any number between 0% and 100% will probably work, you will encounter situations where the correct internal rate of return cannot be closely approximated. If you think the internal rate of return for an investment is between 15% and 25%, 20% is a good guess to start with. A series of cash flows that alternate between positive and negative will result in more than one internal rate of return. The guess you make will affect which of the values is returned. Thirty iterations are the default for this function. If 1-2-3 cannot approximate the result to within 0.0000001 after thirty attempts, ERR will result.

range   the range of cells containing the cash flows
                                 to be analyzed. Negative numbers in this
                                 range are considered outflows, and positive
                                 numbers are inflows. The first number in
                                 the range is expected to be negative, since
                                 it is the cost of the investment opportu-
                                 nity.

Use

The @IRR function is used whenever you wish to find the rate that will
equate the initial investment with the expected future cash flows generated by the investment. Cash flows must be at equal intervals. If the
cash flows are a mixture of positive and negative values, the @IRR
function may find multiple internal rates of return. In this case, 1-2-3
returns the internal rate of return closest to the guess.

Figure 7-17 shows the @IRR function being used to analyze the
stream of Projected Cash Flows shown in A2..A7. As required, the first
number in the range is negative, signifying the cost of the investment
opportunity. A Guess of 12% was placed in D2. The /Range Format
Percent command was used to obtain the percent in D2 and E2. The
formula for the internal rate of return is placed in E2 as
@IRR(D2,A2..A7). In this example, the function returns 19.58%.

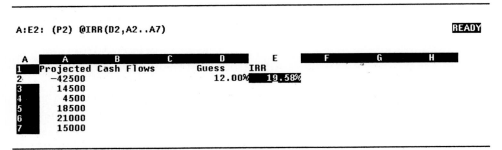

Figure 7-17.   Using @IRR to compute the internal rate of return

@NPV

The @NPV function computes what you should be willing to pay for a projected stream of cash flows, given your desired rate of return.

Format

@NPV(*discount rate,range*)

Arguments

discount rate	a fixed periodic interest rate used to discount expected cash flows, to project their worth in today's dollars.
range	the series of cash flows to be discounted. These cash flows do not have to be equal, but they must be evenly spaced over a period of time (monthly, quarterly, and so forth). They are assumed to occur at the end of a period; the first cash flow will be received at the end of the first period.

Use

This is one of the most frequently used functions in 1-2-3, since it deals with the time value of money.

Figure 7-18 presents a sample use of @NPV. The expected cash flows are shown in B2..G2. You will notice from the column headings that these cash flows are to be received monthly. Yet the interest rate in D4 is expressed as an annual rate. Make note of this discrepancy between the time periods of the interest rate and the payments. The difference can be resolved by changing the interest rate to a monthly figure in the function argument. The formula for the calculation is @NPV(D4/12,B2..G2). It produces a result of $57,396.93, indicating that if the discount rate is 15%, you should be willing to pay $57,396.93 for this investment.

Note

This function is not designed to handle situations where you make an immediate or up-front payment, although you could easily construct a

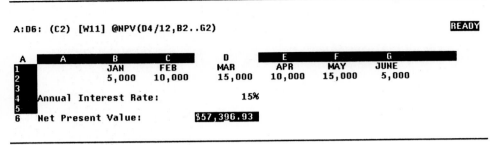

Figure 7-18. Net present value calculations

formula to do this. Since the initial payment is already in today's dollars, there is no need to discount it. Your initial outflow can be added to the result of the @NPV function.

As an example, assume that you must pay $5000 today for an investment that will return $4000, $3000, $2000, and $1500, at the end of each of the next four years, respectively. The formula would be $-5000 + @NPV(.13,B2..B5)$, where .13 is the discount rate and the cash flows are stored in B2..B5.

@PMT

The @PMT function will calculate the appropriate payment amount for a loan when given the principal, interest rate, and term.

Format

@PMT(*principal, interest, term of loan*)

Arguments

principal   a numeric value representing the amount borrowed. It can be provided as a number or as a cell address, formula, range name, or other function.

interest	a numeric value representing the interest rate. It can be provided as a numeric constant in the formula or as a cell reference, formula, or range name. If you elect to enter it in the formula or a cell, you may enter it as a decimal fraction or followed by a %. To specify 9%, for example, you may use .09 or 9%.
term	the number of payments in the loan term. If monthly payments will be made on a loan spanning several years, multiply the years of the term by 12 and use the product for this argument. It can be expressed as a fraction, a formula, a range name, or a cell address.

It is extremely important that the same unit of time be used for both the term and the interest rate. An annual interest rate means a term of a number of years, whereas a monthly interest rate indicates a term consisting of a number of months.

Use

This function can be used wherever you want to calculate the amount of a loan payment. This function makes it easy to calculate your own personal loan tables. Given a specific range of values for the principal and interest rate, you can look at a range of payment amount options and see which are possible given your current monthly income.

Figure 7-19 provides an example of a payment table. Interest rates are entered across row three. The first rate is 9%, in B3. The rates in C3..G3 are generated with a formula entered in C3 to add .005 to B3. This formula is copied across. The entire row is formatted as Percent.

Cells A4..A20 are used for hypothetical principal amounts. The starting point is $100,000, with a $5000 increment. The last number in A20 is $180,000. These principal amounts are formatted as Currency, with no decimal places.

Only one payment formula must be entered; the rest can be copied. @PMT($A4,B$3/12,240) is the formula used. The $s in the arguments are required to keep part of the cell addresses from changing as the

A:B4: (C2) [W10] @PMT($A4,B$3/12,240)   `READY`

A	A	B	C	D	E	F	G
1	LOAN			INTEREST RATE			
2	AMOUNT						
3		9.00%	9.50%	10.00%	10.50%	11.00%	11.50%
4	$100,000	$899.73	$932.13	$965.02	$998.38	$1,032.19	$1,066.43
5	$105,000	$944.71	$978.74	$1,013.27	$1,048.30	$1,083.80	$1,119.75
6	$110,000	$989.70	$1,025.34	$1,061.52	$1,098.22	$1,135.41	$1,173.07
7	$115,000	$1,034.68	$1,071.95	$1,109.77	$1,148.14	$1,187.02	$1,226.39
8	$120,000	$1,079.67	$1,118.56	$1,158.03	$1,198.06	$1,238.63	$1,279.72
9	$125,000	$1,124.66	$1,165.16	$1,206.28	$1,247.97	$1,290.24	$1,333.04
10	$130,000	$1,169.64	$1,211.77	$1,254.53	$1,297.89	$1,341.84	$1,386.36
11	$135,000	$1,214.63	$1,258.38	$1,302.78	$1,347.81	$1,393.45	$1,439.68
12	$140,000	$1,259.62	$1,304.98	$1,351.03	$1,397.73	$1,445.06	$1,493.00
13	$145,000	$1,304.60	$1,351.59	$1,399.28	$1,447.65	$1,496.67	$1,546.32
14	$150,000	$1,349.59	$1,398.20	$1,447.53	$1,497.57	$1,548.28	$1,599.64
15	$155,000	$1,394.58	$1,444.80	$1,495.78	$1,547.49	$1,599.89	$1,652.97
16	$160,000	$1,439.56	$1,491.41	$1,544.03	$1,597.41	$1,651.50	$1,706.29
17	$165,000	$1,484.55	$1,538.02	$1,592.29	$1,647.33	$1,703.11	$1,759.61
18	$170,000	$1,529.53	$1,584.62	$1,640.54	$1,697.25	$1,754.72	$1,812.93
19	$175,000	$1,574.52	$1,631.23	$1,688.79	$1,747.16	$1,806.33	$1,866.25
20	$180,000	$1,619.51	$1,677.84	$1,737.04	$1,797.08	$1,857.94	$1,919.57

Figure 7-19.   Creating a payment table

formula is copied. $A4 indicates that the column for the reference is absolute, although the row can change. The reverse is true of B$3: the row can change, but the column is constant. B$3 is divided by 12 to convert the annual interest into a monthly interest. The term is 20 years, which equates to 240 monthly periods. After this cell is formatted as Currency with two decimal places, the formula can be copied to accommodate the remaining places in the table. You will need to widen some of the columns in order to fit the currency display in the cells.

Note

Financial institutions calculate payment amounts in a number of ways. The formula used by the @PMT function is as follows:

$$\text{principal} * \frac{\text{interest}}{1-(\text{interest}+1)^{-n}}$$

where n is the number of payments.

@PV

The @PV function determines the present value of an investment, assuming a fixed periodic interest rate and a series of equal payments over a period of time.

Format

@PV(*payment,periodic interest rate,number of periods*)

Arguments

payment	the amount of the equal payments, expressed as a value or a reference to a cell containing a value. Only one value may be referenced, since payments are assumed to be equal.
periodic interest rate	the periodic interest rate used to discount the cash flows. This argument must be a value or a reference to a cell containing a value.
number of periods	the term over which the payments will be generated. This argument must be a value or a reference to a cell containing a value.

Use

The @PV function is used whenever you wish to determine today's value of money to be received in the future. You can use the function to assess what you should be willing to pay for an investment today, given that it will return a certain amount of money in future periods. You can also use the function to evaluate a lump sum payment as compared to future periodic payments if you have this option on the sale of a property or the receipt of prize money.

As an example, assume that you have the option of taking a one-time cash payment of $500,000 versus monthly payments of $5000 for the next 20 years. To compare the two options you must look at the present value of the future cash flows. This means you must make an assessment of the rate of return you would receive for investing the $500,000 lump sum payment today. This example assumes that you could get 12% compounded monthly. The present value then becomes @PV(5000,1%,240). The worksheet in Figure 7-20 shows this same formula, except that the numbers are stored in cells to provide easy update capabilities. The result indicates that the best decision, if you are attempting to maximize return, is to choose the lump sum payment.

Note

This comparison of the value of a lump sum payment and periodic payments does not take tax effects into consideration.

@RATE

The @RATE function determines the periodic interest rate that must be earned to increase a specified present value to a future value over a specific term.

Format

@RATE(*future value,present value,number of periods*)

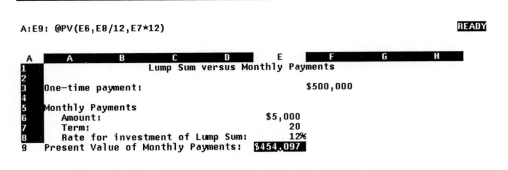

Figure 7-20. Using @PV to compute the present value of an annuity

Arguments

future value	the value of the investment at the end of a specified growth period. This argument must be a value or a reference to a value.
present value	the current value of an investment. This argument can contain a numeric value, a formula, or a reference to one of those two options.
number of periods	the compounding periods over which the investment will grow. This argument must be a value or a reference to a value.

Use

The @RATE function is used to determine the periodic interest rate that is required to realize a desired growth rate. If you give the number of periods in months, you get a monthly rate. You can convert this to an annual rate by multiplying by 12.

Suppose you invested $5000 in a bond maturing in eight years; you could use the @RATE function to calculate the rate of return. This example assumes that the maturity value is $10,000 and that the interest is compounded monthly. The required formula is the @RATE(10000,5000,8*12). This is shown in the worksheet in Figure 7-21 through references to cells that store the arguments. The rate of return is .72%, a monthly rate. To annualize it, multiply by 12 to obtain 8.7%.

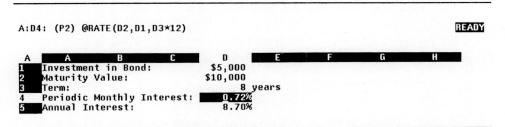

Figure 7-21.   Using @RATE to compute the minimum yield for an investment

@SLN

The @SLN function computes the straight-line depreciation for one period in an asset's life.

Format

@SLN(*cost, salvage value, life of the asset*)

Arguments

cost	the amount paid for the asset. This number can be included in the function or stored in a cell and referenced with an address or range name.
salvage value	the remaining value of the asset at the end of its useful life. This number can be included in the function or stored in a cell and referenced with an address or range name.
life	the number of years of useful life, or the time required to depreciate the asset to its salvage value. This number can be included in the function or stored in a cell and referenced with an address or range name.

Use

The @SLN function can be used whenever you wish to depreciate an asset evenly over its useful life, so that the depreciation expense will be the same for all years. The formula used by the function is as follows:

$$\frac{cost - salvage\ value}{life}$$

As an example, if you purchase a $12,000 machine and estimate its salvage value to be $2000 at the end of its five-year life, you can use

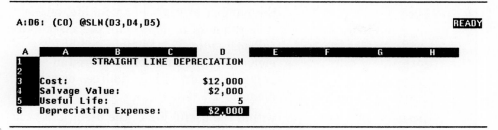

A:D6: (C0) @SLN(D3,D4,D5)   READY

A	A	B	C	D	E	F	G	H
1		STRAIGHT LINE DEPRECIATION						
2								
3	Cost:			$12,000				
4	Salvage Value:			$2,000				
5	Useful Life:			5				
6	Depreciation Expense:			$2,000				

Figure 7-22.   Computing straight-line depreciation with @SLN

@SLN to calculate its depreciation expense. The formula is shown in Figure 7-22.

@SYD

The @SYD function computes depreciation expense for an asset using the sum-of-the-years'-digits depreciation method. This is an accelerated depreciation method that depreciates an asset more in the early years of its life.

Format

@SYD(*cost,salvage value,life,period*)

Arguments

cost   the amount paid for the asset. This num-
                             ber can be included in the function or
                             stored in a cell and referenced with an ad-
                             dress or range name.

salvage value   the remaining value of the asset at the end
                             of its useful life. This number can be in-
                             cluded in the function or stored in a cell
                             and referenced with an address or range
                             name.

life   the number of years of useful life, or the
                                time required to depreciate the asset to its
                                salvage value. This number can be
                                included in the function or stored in a cell
                                and referenced with an address or range
                                name.

period   within the useful life of the asset, the year
                                for which you wish the depreciation ex-
                                pense calculated. This number can be in-
                                cluded in the function or stored in a cell
                                and referenced with an address or range
                                name. It should not be greater than the
                                life of the asset.

Use

The @SYD function lets you calculate the sum-of-the-years'-digits depreciation expense for any period in the life of an asset. The formula
used by the function is

$$\frac{(cost - salvage) * (life - period \ for \ depreciation \ expense + 1)}{(life * (life + 1)/2)}$$

The worksheet in Figure 7-23 shows the sum-of-the-years'-digits
depreciation expense for an asset that was purchased for $12,000 and
has a $2000 salvage value. The cell pointer points to the formula for the
depreciation expense in the first year. This calculation uses the formula

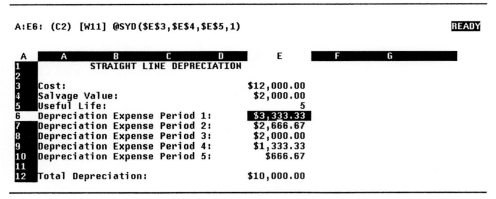

Figure 7-23.   Computing sum-of-the-years'-digits depreciation with
                      @SYD

@SYD(12000,2000,5,1). The worksheet shows the depreciation expense for the other four years, as well. The only difference in the remaining formulas is in the last argument, which indicates the period for which depreciation expense is being calculated.

@TERM

The @TERM function returns the number of payment periods required to accumulate a given future value if the payment amount and interest rate remain fixed.

Format

@TERM(*payment,interest,future value*)

Arguments

payment	a fixed periodic payment, stored as a number in the function, or in a cell that can be referenced by the function.
interest	the fixed interest rate per compounding period. It can be expressed as a percent or decimal fraction within the function, or stored in a cell and referenced with the cell address or a range name. It can also be computed with a formula from within the function.
future value	the value of the investment at some point in the future. The objective of the @TERM function is to determine the point at which the investment will reach its specified future value. This argument must be a value or a reference to a cell containing a value.

Use

The @TERM function is used to calculate the number of periods required for an ordinary annuity to reach a given value. For example, it permits you to determine how long it will take to save for a dream vacation home or luxury yacht, assuming you set aside a fixed amount at the end of each month.

The formula behind 1-2-3's calculations is

$$\frac{\text{natural log } (1 + (\text{future value} * \text{interest/payment}))}{\text{natural log } (1 + \text{interest})}$$

The worksheet in Figure 7-24 shows an example where $350 is set aside at the end of each month for the purpose of accumulating a $25,000 down payment on a vacation home. If the funds are placed in a money market fund paying 10.25%, @TERM will calculate the time that is required to accumulate the down payment. The formula is @TERM(350,.1025,25000).

Note

This function differs from the @CTERM function in that you must provide the payment amount, not the present value. @CTERM focuses on the number of growth periods required for an investment to reach a specific value, while @TERM is concerned with the number of payment periods for an ordinary annuity. To calculate the term of an annuity due, you would need to use the formula @TERM(*payment,interest,future value*)/(1+interest).

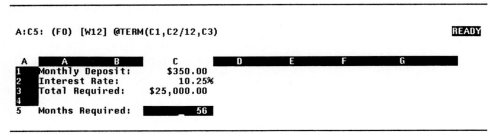

A:C5: (F0) [W12] @TERM(C1,C2/12,C3)   READY

	A	B	C	D	E	F	G
1	Monthly Deposit:		$350.00				
2	Interest Rate:		10.25%				
3	Total Required:		$25,000.00				
4							
5	Months Required:		56				

Figure 7-24.   Using @TERM to compute the number of periods needed for an annuity

@VDB (Release 3)

The @VDB function calculates depreciation expense for a specific period using a variable declining balance method. This function differs from @DDB in that the last function argument contains the percentage, allowing you to control the percentage used in the calculation. With @DDB, the percentage is always 200%. With @VDB, you decide the percentage used in comparison to straight-line depreciation. Also, this function switches to straight-line when straight-line would be equal or greater. Finally, this function can compute depreciation for periods other than a year at a time.

Format

@VDB(*cost,salvage,life,start-period,end-period,*
[*depreciation-factor*],[*switch*])

Arguments

cost	the amount paid for the asset. This argument must be a value or a reference to a cell containing a value.
salvage	the value of the asset at the end of its useful life. Like the *cost*, this argument must be a value or a reference to a cell containing a value.
life	the expected useful life of the asset; that is, the number of years needed to depreciate the asset from its *cost* to its *salvage value*. Normally expressed in years, this argument also must be a value or a reference to one.
start-period	the starting period in the asset's life for which you are attempting to determine the depreciation expense. Normally the beginning of the year for which you are calculating depreciation expense, this argument must be a value or a reference to one, which is between 0 and the value of life. Fractional values represent fractional parts of a year.

end-period	the ending period in the asset's life for which you are attempting to determine the depreciation expense. Normally the number of the year for which you are calculating depreciation expense, this argument must be a value or a reference to one which is between the start-period and life. The difference between start-period and end-period is the time span for which this function computed depreciation.
depreciation-factor	the percentage of straight-line depreciation that the function uses. If this optional argument is not provided, 1-2-3 uses 200%, which calculates the same result as the @DDB function.
switch	a 1 or a 0 that selects whether this function switches to straight-line depreciation when straight-line depreciation is higher. If this function uses a 0 or omits this optional argument, this function switches when straight-line depreciation is greater, which can occur in the later years of the asset's life.

Use

The @VDB function calculates variable declining depreciation expense, using an accelerated depreciation method (one that allows you to write off more depreciation expense in the early years of an asset's life). The asset will no longer be depreciated when its book value (that is, cost minus total depreciation to date) equals its salvage value.

The formula used in the calculation of variable declining balance depreciation is as follows:

$$\frac{\text{book value for the period} * \text{depreciation factor}}{\text{life of the asset}}$$

1-2-3 makes adjustments in the calculations to ensure that total depreciation is exactly equal to the asset's cost minus the salvage value. @VDB automatically switches to straight-line depreciation when that method provides greater depreciation.

```
A:C7: [W11] @VDB($C$4,$C$5,$C$6,0,0.5,$C$2)                          READY
```

```
  A         A          B        C        D                E
  1  Depreciation Expense Using the Double Declining Balance Method
  2  Depreciation Rate:      150.00%
  3
  4  Cost:                $11,000.00
  5  Salvage Value:        $1,000.00
  6  Useful Life:              $5.00    Formulas:
  7  Year 1:               $1,650.00    @VDB($C$4,$C$5,$C$6,0,0.5,$C$2)
  8  Year 2:               $2,805.00    @VDB($C$4,$C$5,$C$6,0.5,1.5,$C$2)
  9  Year 3:               $1,963.50    @VDB($C$4,$C$5,$C$6,1.5,2.5,$C$2)
 10  Year 4:               $1,432.60    @VDB($C$4,$C$5,$C$6,2.5,3.5,$C$2)
 11  Year 5:               $1,432.60    @VDB($C$4,$C$5,$C$6,3.5,4.5,$C$2)
 12  Year 6:                 $716.30    @VDB($C$4,$C$5,$C$6,4.5,5,$C$2)
 13
 14  Total Depreciation: $10,000.00
 15
```

Figure 7-25.   Double declining balance depreciation using 150% straight-line depreciation

Figure 7-25 shows the use of this function to determine the proper depreciation expense for each year in an asset's five-year life. Since the asset was purchased in the middle of the year, it is depreciated over six years with the first and sixth year taking half a year of depreciation. The cost of the asset was $11,000 and its salvage value is $1000. This function uses a 1.5 depreciation factor to calculate depreciation using a 150% declining-balance depreciation rate. Notice how the variable declining balance depreciation method switches to straight-line when straight-line is higher, which occurs in year 3.

Mathematical Functions

1-2-3's mathematical functions perform trigonometric and other numeric calculations. Their primary use is in engineering, manufacturing, and scientific applications.

The angles that some of the functions work with are all expressed in radians, a unit of measure that equates the radius and arc length. If you prefer to work with angles in degrees, multiply radians by 180/@PI to produce the conversion. All angles that you enter for the @SIN, @COS, and @TAN functions should be expressed in radians. If they are in degrees, multiply by the inverse of the conversion factor (that is, @PI/180) to change degrees into radians.

@ABS

The @ABS function returns the positive or absolute value of a number.

Format

@ABS(*number*)

Arguments

number	any value, including references to a cell containing a value. If a string is used for *number*, an error will result.

Use

The @ABS function is used whenever you are interested in the relative size of a number and do not care whether it is positive or negative. A good example might be the need to monitor cash overages and shortages in the registers of a retail establishment. Consistent cash overages and shortages indicate a cash control problem that should be corrected. If you monitored both overages and shortages, adding their + and − signs, they might cancel each other out. Looking at the absolute value of the overages and shortages, however, provides a look at the total amount of the differences.

Figure 7-26 provides a look at a restaurant's cash overages and

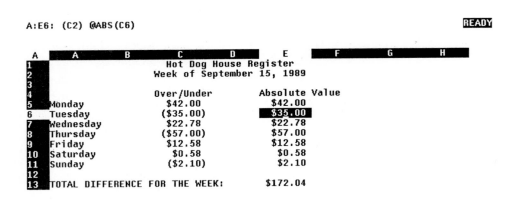

Figure 7-26.   Adding absolute values

shortages by adding absolute values. If @ABS had not been used, the positive and negative numbers would have partially canceled each other, making the cash differences seem less of a problem.

@ACOS

The @ACOS function returns the inverse cosine (arccosine) when you provide the cosine of an angle.

Format

@ACOS(*number*)

Arguments

number	the cosine of an angle, which can be in the range of −1 to 1. This numeric value can be provided within the function or through a reference to a cell or range. If you provide a number outside the allowable limits, ERR will be returned.

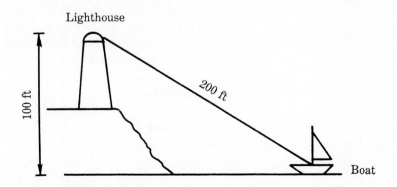

Figure 7-27.   Calculating the angle from the lighthouse to the boat

Use

The @ACOS function is used when you know the cosine of an angle but want to know the angle in radians. If you prefer the angle measurement in degrees, you can multiply the result of this function by 180/@PI.

Suppose you were at the top of a cliff in a lighthouse 100 feet above water and wanted to know the angle needed to make a projectile reach a boat approximately 200 feet away (see Figure 7-27). You could find the cosine of the angle by performing the following calculation:

```
cos of angle  =  100/200
cos of angle  =  .5
@ACOS(.5)*180/@PI  =  60 degrees
```

@ASIN

The @ASIN function is used to determine the arcsine or inverse sine of an angle.

Format

@ASIN(*number*)

Arguments

number	the sine of an angle, which can be in the range of -1 to 1. This numeric value can be provided within the function or through a reference to a cell or range. If you provide a number outside the allowable limits, ERR will be returned.

Use

The @ASIN function returns an arcsine between @PI/2 and $-$@PI/2 and represents an angle in quadrant 1 or 2.

As an example, you can use the @ASIN function to determine the angle of a platform that will be used to roll a barrel into a truck. A diagram of the truck bed and platform is shown in Figure 7-28. The bed

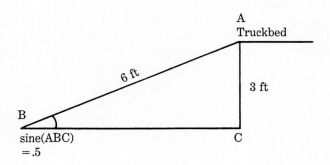

Figure 7-28.   Using a ramp to get merchandise into a truck

of the truck is three feet from the ground, and the platform used to roll
the barrel is six feet long. The sine of the angle between the board and
the ground is equal to 3/6 or .5. @ASIN(.5)*180/@PI equals 30 degrees,
as shown in this worksheet:

@ATAN

The @ATAN function calculates the arctangent or inverse tangent of an
angle for use in trigonometric problems.

Format

@ATAN(*number*)

Arguments

number   the tangent of an angle, which can be in
                            the range of −1 to 1. This numeric value
                            can be provided within the function or
                            through a reference to a cell or range. If
                            you provide a number outside the allow-
                            able limits, ERR will be returned.

Use

The @ATAN function returns an arctangent between @PI/2 and
−@PI/2 and represents an angle in quadrant 1 or 4.

   This function can be used to solve many trigonometric problems.
For example, suppose you are playing a championship game of pool and
need to pass a ball from point A through point B in the diagram shown
in Figure 7-29. The @ATAN function will determine the angle at which
you should hit the ball.

   The location of the ball is three inches from the bumper, and the
location of the pocket in relationship to the bumper is four inches. The
tangent between the pocket and the bumper is equal to 4/3 or 1.333333.
@ATAN(1.333333) is .927295 radians. When this is multiplied by

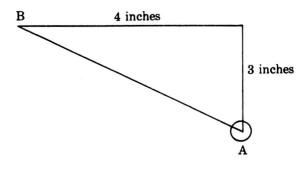

Figure 7-29.   Making the pool shot

180/@PI, it provides the number of degrees, as shown in this worksheet:

@ATAN2

The @ATAN2 function returns the 4 quadrant arctangent, or the angle in radians whose tangent is y/x.

Format

@ATAN2(x,y)

Arguments

x	the x coordinate of the angle, expressed as a number or a reference to a cell containing a number.
y	the y coordinate of the angle, expressed as a number or a reference to a cell containing a number.

Use

The @ATAN2 function is used to solve trigonometric problems where you want to differentiate angles found in the first and third quadrants, from those found in the second and fourth quadrants. Figure 7-30 shows the values of @ATAN2 for the different quadrants. @ATAN2(1,.5) returns .463647 radians.

@COS

The @COS function returns the cosine of an angle.

Format

@COS($number$)

Quadrants

2	1
@PI/2 to @PI	0 to @PI/2
3	4
−@PI to	−@PI/2
−@PI/2	to 0

Values of @ATAN2

Figure 7-30.   Values for @ATAN2 in the different quadrants

Arguments

number   a number representing the radians in an
                                              angle.

Use

The @COS function is used when you have an angle in radians and want
to determine the cosine of that angle. This number can assist you in
making other determinations, such as distances and other angles. Thus,
a surveyor can use the @COS function to determine the length of a side
of a plot of land in the shape of a right triangle (see Figure 7-31).

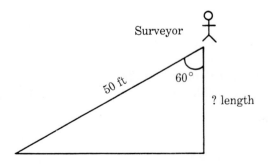

Figure 7-31.   Determining the length of the side of a plot of land

The longest side of the plot of land is 50 feet. There is a 60-degree angle at the point of the lot where the surveyor is standing. He would like to know the length of the side on his left (the adjacent side, in mathematics terminology). He constructs the formula COS (60°) = x/50. The @COS(60*@PI/180) function returns .5, which can be used to solve for x of 250. @PI/180 was needed because the angle was supplied in radians, as shown in this worksheet:

@EXP

The @EXP function raises the base e (2.718282) to a specific power.

Format

@EXP(*number*)

Arguments

number	the power to which you want to raise e. This argument must be a numeric value or a reference to one. *Number* cannot exceed 230 if you wish to display it; it can be as high as 11356 if you just plan to store the number for later calculations.

Use

@EXP is the inverse of @LN and is used whenever you wish to raise e to a specific power. Here are several examples:

@EXP(1) equals 2.718282
@EXP(10) equals 22026.46
@EXP(@LN(5)) equals 5

@INT

The @INT function allows you to truncate the decimal places in a number to produce a whole number.

Format

@INT(*number*)

Arguments

number	any value whose integer portion you wish to use. Any digits to the right of the decimal point in the *number* will be truncated.

Use

This function is used whenever you wish to eliminate the decimal portion of a number. It can determine the number of complete batches finished by a production line, for example. In this situation, partial batches may not be of interest, since they would not be ready for shipment. Similarly, if you needed to calculate the number of items that could be produced from a given amount of raw materials, partial items would be of no interest. In both examples, you would not want the number rounded; you would simply want to truncate the decimal portion of the number to look at the number of units. This can be handled with @INT.

The worksheet in Figure 7-32 shows the use of @INT in calculating the number of wallets that can be created from different sized pieces of cowhide. Partial wallets are not of interest, since one hide will not necessarily match another.

@LN

The @LN function returns the natural log of a number.

Format

@LN(*number*)

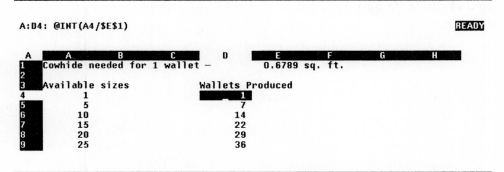

A:D4: @INT(A4/$E$1)   `READY`

Figure 7-32.   Computing the number of finished wallets with @INT

Arguments

number   Any value greater than zero. If *number* is
                            less than zero, ERR will be returned.

Use

Natural logarithms are logarithms to the base *e*, where *e* is approximately 2.718282. @LN is the inverse of @EXP, which means that you can incorporate *e* in any calculation with @EXP(1). @LN(@EXP(4)) equals 4, and @EXP(@LN(8)) equals 8. The primary use of logarithms is to make complex calculations less complex. A few examples follow:

@LN(9) equals 2.197224
@LN(1.5) equals 0.405465

@LOG

The @LOG function computes the base 10 logarithm of a number.

Format

@LOG(*number*)

Arguments

number	Any value greater than zero. If *number* is less than zero, ERR will be returned.

Use

Like natural logs, base 10 logs are primarily used in scientific or other complex calculations where the rules of logarithms can be used to simplify the math involved. The results returned by 1-2-3 from a few examples of @LOG are as follows:

@LOG(10) equals 1
@LOG(100) equals 2
@LOG(190) equals 2.278753

@MOD

The @MOD function returns the modulus or remainder when a number is divided by a divisor number.

Format

@MOD(*number,divisor*)

Arguments

number	any positive or negative number or a reference to one.
divisor	any number other than zero used to divide *number,* as in *number/divisor.*

Use

The @MOD function, which provides the remainder from dividing number by divisor, is useful in a variety of situations, although creativity is often required to see the applications. For example, as the worksheet in Figure 7-33 shows, you can use @MOD to determine how many parts will be left over after building the maximum number of complete items from the parts in an inventory. If you are building windmills that each require 12 blades and you have 750 blades on hand, @MOD(750,12) lets you know that you will have 6 blades left over. To determine how many complete windmills can be built, you can use @INT(750/12).

Note

This function can be used in conjunction with the date functions covered earlier in the chapter to determine the day of the week. @MOD(@NOW,7) will return a value between 0 and 6, since the @MOD function returns the remainder from a division. If the result is 0, the day is Saturday, and if the result is 6, the day is Friday. Each of the other days is represented by one of the other numbers between 0 and 6.

@PI

The @PI function returns an approximation of the constant π, or 3.14159265. The format of the function is simply @PI, since the function does not require any arguments.

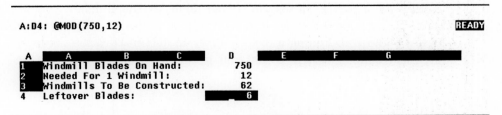

Figure 7-33.   Computing the remaining materials with @MOD

Use

@PI is used frequently in geometric problems involving circumference and area. The circumference of (the distance around) a circle is 2*@PI*radius. Given a circle with a radius of 5 inches, you could find the circumference of 31.4 using the formula shown here:

@RAND

The @RAND function generates random numbers between 0 and 1. The format of the function is simply @RAND; it has no arguments.

Use

This function is useful for generating test data for simulations. Each time the worksheet is recalculated, the @RAND function will take on a new value. You can create rows and columns of a worksheet with this function to generate data for queuing theory problems or other applications. Each @RAND will be a different number, since 1-2-3 uses 15 decimal digits for these numbers.

The worksheet in Figure 7-34 shows numbers generated with the @RAND function. You can control the range of the random number by multiplying the result by a number or adding a number to it. Multiplying @RAND by a factor raises the upper limit to the number you are multiplying by; for example, @RAND*100 provides random numbers between 0 and 100. Adding a fixed number to @RAND raises the lower limit; for example, @RAND*100+50 generates random numbers between 50 and 150.

@ROUND

The @ROUND function is used to round a number in internal storage to a specified number of decimal places.

```
A:G3: @RAND*100+50                                                    READY
```

```
A       A         B         C         D         E         F         G          H
1             @RAND                        @RAND*100                    @RAND*100+50
2
3    0.431114  0.699622            60.62808  54.59137            50.08639  135.5773
4    0.676042  0.012855             9.687157 34.89874            96.96387  72.11447
5    0.163572  0.498771            47.27883  84.85868            91.14005  91.94368
6    0.471293  0.546981            52.74899  1.620516            52.23517  111.9909
7    0.904544  0.193703             60.4402  30.51449            65.64013  63.88647
8    0.494499  0.163512            50.95739  70.24618            123.2612  137.1055
9    0.055141  0.301142            78.22038  96.14122             59.5369  51.18505
10   0.746484  0.315257             6.942702 78.05088            74.96908  94.36844
11   0.792589  0.916827            34.27943   86.2414            149.3278  79.71245
12   0.042985  0.103696            38.23435  94.70303            86.63284  66.27832
13   0.738938  0.925946            96.29573  42.58444            124.7368  118.5138
14   0.714179  0.376207                56.93 32.13369            140.0872  112.5786
15   0.385692  0.397726            80.25431  6.859293            89.28242  75.41769
16   0.836432  0.203177            98.68117  97.86298            109.6018  142.0902
17   0.120962  0.461471            39.83285  30.69028            57.03641  70.48027
18      0.1994 0.250628             8.807727 80.84605            148.7286  141.2814
19   0.687296  0.304674             1.197812 34.57876            103.3868  126.3228
20    0.46161  0.813961            18.35379  83.90102            94.43346    111.14
PG_342.WK1
```

Figure 7-34.   Using @RAND

Format

@ROUND(*number to be rounded,place of rounding*)

Arguments

number to be rounded	any value or reference to a value that you want rounded to a specified number of places.
place of rounding	the number of places to the right or left of the decimal point where rounding should occur. A digit of five or higher after the place where 1-2-3 will round the number will cause the number to the left to be increased by one. Using zero for the place of rounding indicates that you want to round to the nearest whole number. Positive

numbers indicate rounding to the right of the decimal point, with each higher number moving further to the right. Negative numbers indicate rounding to start at the tens position and move further to the left. For example, Figure 7-35 shows the number 12345.678123 rounded to varying numbers of decimal places in column B, using the formulas in column C.

Use

1-2-3 will allow you to display numbers in rounded form, if you specify the number of decimal places you wish to see using the Format options (/Worksheet Global Format or /Range Format). However, the full accuracy of the original number, with all its decimal places, is maintained internally. This can cause displayed column totals to seem inaccurate, because the numbers in the column are displayed as rounded while the internal number has greater decimal accuracy. When all this additional decimal accuracy is summed, it can make the total at the bottom of the column disagree with the display of the detail numbers being summed.

The worksheet in Figure 7-36 shows this discrepancy in column E. The figures in column E are a product of column C and column D, but

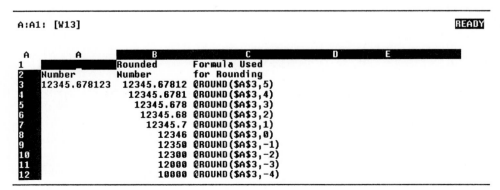

Figure 7-35.   Using @ROUND

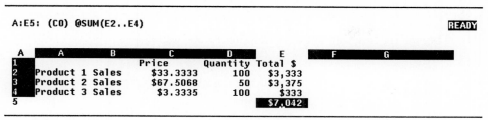

Figure 7-36.   Discrepancy caused by displaying rounded numbers

are displayed as Currency with zero decimal places. The column E figures alone suggest that the total should be $7041, not the $7042 that is shown. The difference of 1 is due to the rounding discrepancy. To solve this problem, more than just a product formula is required. The formula will become an argument for the @ROUND function, which will round the product to the nearest whole number (for example, @ROUND(C2*D2,0)). This makes the internal product agree with the display, and the sum at the bottom of the column will match the displayed numbers, as you can see in Figure 7-37.

Often a complex worksheet model will require that the @ROUND function be used with many of the formulas in the worksheet. To use it, follow the same procedure as shown in the preceding example, making each formula an argument for the @ROUND function.

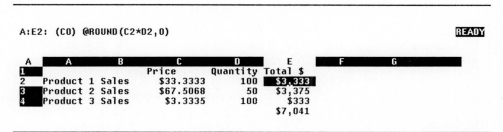

Figure 7-37.   Rounding numbers to prevent discrepancy

@SIN

The @SIN function returns the sine of an angle.

Format

@SIN(*number*)

Arguments

number   a number representing the radians in an
                                angle.

Use

The @SIN function is used when you have the measurement of an angle
in radians and want to determine the sine of the angle. You can use this
information to help you make other determinations regarding physical
aspects of a problem, such as length or other angles. The example that
follows provides one potential application.

The diagram in Figure 7-38 shows terrain containing a large
swampy area that blocks a road crew from traversing the path from
point C to point B. They know that the distance from A to C is 100
meters. If they can determine the distance from B to C, they will be able
to use that number in the Pythagorean theorem to determine the distance from A to B. Their entire distance traveled to avoid the swamp
would be C to A, then A to B. The angle ACB is 30 degrees.

To calculate the distance from C to B, the crew could use the
formula SIN(30) = 100/x. Using the @SIN function to determine the sine
of 30, @SIN(30*@PI/180) would return .5. The @PI/180 converts 30
degrees to the appropriate number of radians. The distance then is
100/.5, or 200 meters. Using the Pythagorean theorem, $a^2 = b^2 + c^2$, they
get $200^2 = 100^2 + s^2$. This means 40,000 equals 10,000, plus the unknown
side squared. The side is thus equal to the square root of 30,000, which
they can find with @SQRT(30,000). This function returns 173.2, so the
distance from C to B is 173.2 meters.

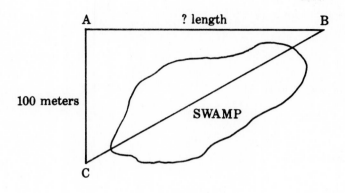

Figure 7-38.   Going around the swamp

@SQRT

The @SQRT function will determine the square root of any positive number.

Format

@SQRT(*number*)

Arguments

number	any positive integer included in the function, or stored in a cell and referenced with a cell address or range name. If *number* is negative, ERR will be returned.

Use

A number of statistical calculations, the Pythagorean theorem, and economic order quantity all require square root calculations. The following are a few examples of the way the square root function operates.

@SQRT(9) equals 3
@SQRT(64) equals 8
@SQRT(100) equals 10

@TAN

The @TAN function returns the tangent of an angle.

Format

@TAN(*number*)

Arguments

number   a number representing the radians in an
                                angle.

Use

The @TAN function returns the tangent, a value useful in solving
trigonometric problems. The diagram in Figure 7-39 requires the

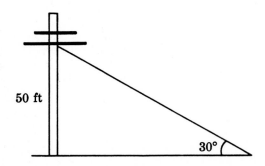

Figure 7-39.   Guide wires for high tension power lines

@TAN function to determine the distance of guide wires for high tension power lines. The electric company has high tension wires at the top of a pole 50 feet high and wants to install guide wires from the top of the pole at a 30-degree angle with the ground. The tangent function can be used to determine the distance away from the high tension wires that the guide wires should be attached. The tangent of 30 must be calculated, and, since the angle was measured in degrees, it must also be converted to radians. The formula thus becomes @TAN(30*@PI/180). The height of 50 feet is divided by the result of .5774 to provide a distance of 87 feet, as you can see here.

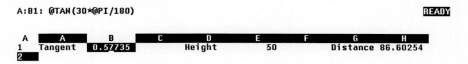

```
A:B1: @TAN(30*@PI/180)                                                    READY
```

```
A     A        B         C        D         E        F       G         H
1   Tangent   0.57735             Height            50             Distance 86.60254
2
```

Logical Functions

1-2-3's logical functions allow you to build conditional features into your models. These functions return logical (true or false) values as the result of condition tests that they perform. A value of 0 means false, and a value of 1 means true.

Some of the logical functions are used when ERR (error) and NA (not available) appear as a result of a formula. Both of these values are regarded as numeric and can be tested. This is a particularly important feature because of the ability of NA and ERR to ripple through all the formulas on a worksheet. As an example, if NA is used to flag a missing grade for a student, that student's average will be shown as NA, and when statistics for all students are combined, the totals will also take on the value NA. The functions @ISERR, @ISNA, @ISNUMBER, and @ISSTRING allow you to check for ERR and NA values and stop their effect on the remainder of the worksheet cells, by replacing ERR and NA with a value of zero.

The logical functions frequently use logical operators. For example, @IF(A2<>5,3,6) uses a simple operator, and the function @IF(A1=1#AND#B3=7,5,2) uses a complex operator. These operators were explained in Chapter 3, "Entering Data in 1-2-3's Worksheet," in detail and are summarized here in the boxes called "The Simple Logical Operators" and "The Complex Logical Operators."

**1
2
3**

The Simple Logical Operators

Simple logical operators are used to compare two or more values. The basic conditions you can check for with these operators are equal to, greater than, and less than. The latter two conditions can also be used in combination with the first condition. The simple logical operators and their meanings are as follows:

=	equal to
>	greater than
<	less than
> =	greater than or equal to
< =	less than or equal to
< >	not equal to

All the simple logical operators have the same evaluation priority. They will be evaluated from left to right in an expression.

@FALSE

The @FALSE function always returns the logical value 0, permitting you to use it to avoid ambiguity in formulas. @FALSE does not use any arguments.

Use

The @FALSE function is a substitute for the number 0 in formulas. It may seem a lot quicker to type 0 than to type @FALSE, but the function is self-documenting and indicates that you want to set up a logical false condition. As an example, consider @IF(A3 = 10,"A3 is equal to 10",@FALSE). If A3 is equal to 10, the string "A3 is equal to 10" will be stored in the cell. If A3 is not equal to 10, a 0 will be stored in the cell.

1
2
3

The Compound Logical Operators

Compound logical operators can be used to join two logical expressions or to negate an expression. The compound logical operators and a sample use for each one are

#AND#	C1 = 2#AND#D1 = 7	Both condition C1 = 2 and condition D1 = 7 must be true for this expression to evaluate as true.
#OR#	C1 = 2#OR#D1 = 7	If either condition is true, the statement evaluates as true.
#NOT#	#NOT#C1 = 3	This statement negates C1 = 3. The #NOT# operator has priority over the other two compound operators.

The worksheet in Figure 7-40 shows @FALSE and its counterpart @TRUE used to determine if the number of items ordered equals the number billed. The formula in D3 checks the numbers ordered and billed for equality, and places @TRUE or @FALSE as the value in the cell accordingly. @FALSE displays as 0 and @TRUE as 1. You can then count these 0s and 1s to determine how many discrepancies were in the orders. Use the @COUNT function to get an item count for the number of entries in C3..C6, which is 4. This function is placed in C7 as @COUNT(C3..C6). @SUM is then used to total the 0s and 1s, returning 3, in D7. Lastly, G9 contains a formula that subtracts D7 from C7 (+C7−D7). The value produced is 1, indicating a discrepancy between number ordered and number billed for one product.

@IF

The @IF function permits you to test a logical condition to determine the appropriate value for a cell.

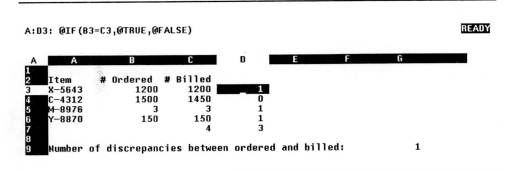

Figure 7-40.   Using @FALSE

Format

@IF(*condition to be tested, value if true, value if false*)

Arguments

condition to be tested   any logical expression that can be evaluated as true or false. Examples are A1 > = 4, D2 = H3, and A2 + D3 < 85. The first expression returns a value of true only if A4 contains a value greater than or equal to 4. When this condition is met, the cell containing the @IF takes on the value for true conditions (1); otherwise, it takes on the value for false (0).

The logical @IF statement can also work with compound conditions joined by #OR# and #AND#. With #AND#, both conditions must be true in order for the true value to be used for the cell. With #OR#, either condition may be true to produce the true value. #NOT# can be used to negate a condition. For example, #NOT#(Sales > 100000) is equivalent to Sales < = 100000. D1 > 8#AND#H3 = 4 means that the numeric value in D1 must be greater than 8, and the numeric value in H3 must be equal to 4 in order for the function to return a value of true.

Conditions can use strings as part of the logical @IF statement. Numbers and blanks in cells involved in the condition test can cause errors. For example, the statement @IF(A1="TEN","TRUE","FALSE") will result in TRUE if A1 contains the label TEN, FALSE if A1 contains any other label entry, and ERR if A1 contains either a blank or a numeric value. The condition @IF(A1=10,"TRUE","FALSE") will result in TRUE if A1 contains the value 10, FALSE if A1 contains any other number or is blank, and ERR if A1 contains a label.

value if true	the value the cell containing the @IF statement will assume if the condition is true. This can be either a value or a label. When labels are included in the @IF statement, they must be enclosed in double quotation marks. If they are stored in a cell, they can be referenced with a cell address or range name. String formulas are also acceptable as labels. Value entries can be numbers, formulas, or references to cells containing numbers or formulas.
value if false	the value the cell containing the @IF statement will assume if the condition is false. All the conditions listed under *value if true* also apply here.

Use

@IF is one of the most powerful built-in functions because it allows you to get around the limitation of having only one entry in a cell. Now you can set up two different values for a cell and determine which one to use, based on other conditions in your worksheet. You can use this function to establish two discount levels, commission structures, payroll deductions, or anything else requiring more than one alternative.

1-2-3 allows you to nest conditions several levels deep, that is, use a second @IF statement for the true and/or false value in the original @IF. As an example, you might want to determine whether a purchase is made by cash or credit and have a code of 1 for cash, assuming that entries without a 1 are credit sales. Once the type of sale is determined, you might want to check the amount of the sale to see if it is over the minimum for a discount. The statement might be coded as

@IF(TYPE = 1,@IF(SALE > 1000,.05,.02),@IF(SALE > 2500,.04,.01))

if TYPE and SALE were named ranges. Regardless of the value for TYPE or SALE, the cell will contain a discount amount, but the amount will depend on the value of both variables. The following chart shows the appropriate discounts.

Type = 1	Discount
Sale > 1000	.05
Sale < = 1000	.02
Type < > 1	
Sale > 2500	.04
Sale < = 2500	.01

Another example is a projection for total salary expenses that uses the logical @IF function to determine allowances for FICA and FUTA taxes. The first part of the model, which does not involve functions, is shown in Figure 7-41. Except for column T, where the salary computation is entered, all the entries in this section of the model are label or value entries. The formula in T4 is as follows:

((R4-1)*(Q4/12)) + ((12-(R4-1))*(1 + S4)*(Q4/12))

The purpose of this rather cumbersome formula is to compute next year's salary expense for the individual, based on the effective month and percentage of increase that has been given. The essence of the formula is to multiply the months at the old salary times the old monthly salary, and add to that the months at the new salary times the new monthly salary.

The @IF function becomes important in the second section of the model, in Figure 7-42. The values for Benefits in column U are calculated by a simple formula that multiplies the projected salary by a flat

A:T4: (C2) [W13] ((R4-1)*(Q4/12))+((12-(R4-1))*(1+S4)*(Q4/12))   `READY`

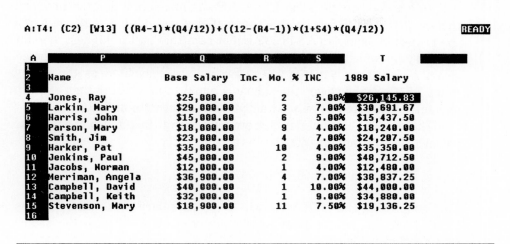

Figure 7-41.   Projecting next year's salaries

A:V4: (C2) [W11] @IF(T4<48000,T4*0.751,48000*0.751)   `READY`

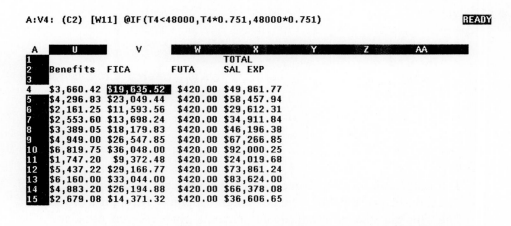

Figure 7-42.   Calculating FICA with the logical @IF

percentage for benefits. The FICA formula in column V is the first one that puts the @IF function to work. It has a condition that compares the projected salary to a $48,000 FICA cap (that is, the highest amount of salary on which an employer would pay FICA tax). If the projected salary is less than $48,000, FICA tax will be calculated as the salary times 7.51%. If, however, the salary is equal to or greater than the cap amount, FICA tax will be paid on $48,000 at the rate of 7.51%.

The FUTA calculation, for unemployment tax, follows a similar pattern. The formula in W4 is

@IF(T4 < 7000,T4*.06,7000*.06)

This states that the FUTA tax will be 6% of salary if the salary is less than $7000, but will be paid on the cap amount of $7000 if the salary exceeds that amount.

@ISERR

The @ISERR function checks for a value of ERR in a cell. It returns 1 if the cell contains an error, and 0 if it does not.

Format

@ISERR(*value*)

Arguments

value	normally this is a reference to a cell value, although it may be a formula or a numeric value.

Use

The @ISERR function is most often used in conjunction with the @IF function, to prevent ERR values from "rippling" through a worksheet. The rippling occurs because any formula that references a cell with ERR will have a result of ERR.

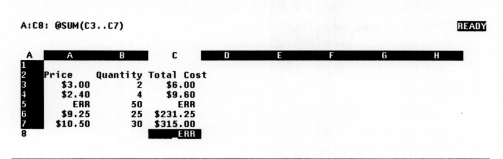

Figure 7-43.   ERR rippling through a worksheet

The worksheet in Figure 7-43 shows ERR for one of the prices in column A. This ERR entry could have been generated by placing @ERR in the cell, or it could be the result of an incorrect formula. When this cell is referenced to supply the unit cost for multiplication, it causes ERR to appear in column C. Again, when the sum is taken in C8, ERR will be the result, since one of the cells in the sum range contains ERR.

If you do not want ERR to ripple through the worksheet like this, use the @ISERR function in conjunction with @IF, as shown in the

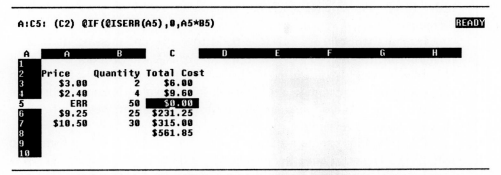

Figure 7-44.   @ISERR preventing ERR from rippling through a worksheet

worksheet in Figure 7-44. This allows you to confine ERR to one location.

@ISNA

The @ISNA function allows you to check for a value of NA in a cell. It returns 1 if the cell contains NA, and 0 if it does not.

Format

@ISNA(*value*)

Arguments

value	normally this is a reference to a cell value, although it may be a formula or a numeric value.

Use

This function is most often used in conjunction with the @IF function in order to prevent NA values from "rippling" through all your worksheet formulas.

In some worksheets @NA is used to represent missing data. Any formula that references a cell with a value of NA will produce a result of NA. If you would like to prevent the NA value from carrying forward in this way, you can use @ISNA to check for the value NA and substitute a zero or some other value, or you can display an error message to show that the value is missing.

Figure 7-45 presents a sample use of the @ISNA function combined with @IF. The @IF function checks the condition @ISNA(D3). If D3 is equal to NA, the condition will be considered true because @ISNA will evaluate as 1. On a true condition, the error message "Missing Unit Price" will display. If D3 is not equal to NA, column E will contain the result of column C times column D.

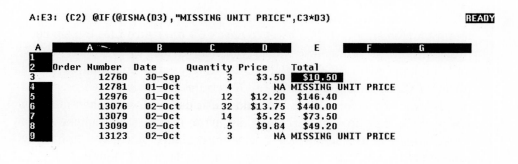

A:E3: (C2) @IF(@ISNA(D3),"MISSING UNIT PRICE",C3*D3)   `READY`

```
A         A ~.        B        C      D       E        F        G
1
2   Order Number  Date     Quantity Price   Total
3         12760   30-Sep       3    $3.50   $10.50
4         12781   01-Oct       4       NA   MISSING UNIT PRICE
5         12976   01-Oct      12   $12.20   $146.40
6         13076   02-Oct      32   $13.75   $440.00
7         13079   02-Oct      14    $5.25   $73.50
8         13099   02-Oct       5    $9.84   $49.20
9         13123   02-Oct       3       NA   MISSING UNIT PRICE
```

Figure 7-45.   Checking for missing data

@ISNUMBER

The @ISNUMBER function allows you to check for a numeric value in a cell. @ISNUMBER returns 1 if the cell contains a number, and 0 if it does not.

Format

@ISNUMBER(*value*)

Arguments

value   normally this is a reference to a cell value, although it may be a formula or a numeric value.

Use

This function is most often used in conjunction with the @IF function to check whether data entries are of the proper type. As an example, an entry of @ISNUMBER(56) in a worksheet cell would return 1, whereas

@ISNUMBER("56") would return 0. Formulas are regarded as numeric entries and will therefore return 1 with this function.

The worksheet in Figure 7-46 shows name and address information entered in column C. If you want to check C7 to ensure that the zip code was entered as a numeric value, you should use the formula in E7, @IF(@ISNUMBER(C6)," ","ERROR - Entry must be numeric"). This formula states that if the entry in C7 is numeric, a blank will be placed in E7, where the formula is located. If the cell contains a non-numeric value, as it does in the worksheet, an error message will appear. This type of error check allows the operator to glance at column E quickly for error flags, rather than having to study entries individually.

@ISRANGE (Release 3)

The @ISRANGE function lets you determine if a defined range name exists. The function returns 1 if the current file contains the specified range name assigned to an address, and 0 if it does not, or if the range name is not assigned an address.

Format

@ISRANGE(*string*)

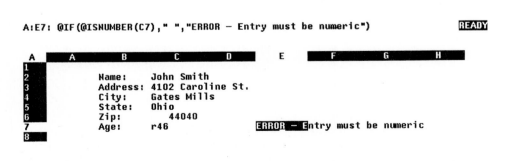

Figure 7-46.   Using @ISNUMBER to validate data

Arguments

string   the name of the range you want to find. It can be entered directly without quotes, or referenced with a cell address that contains a string representing the range name you want to check.

Use

This function is normally combined with @IF, to test for the presence of a range before using it in a calculation or command.

Figure 7-47 shows the first worksheet in a file used to summarize data. If the range the formula will add does not exist, the @IF function displays a message to alert you to the missing range.

@ISSTRING

The @ISSTRING function allows you to check for a string value in a cell. It returns 1 if the cell contains a string, and 0 if it does not.

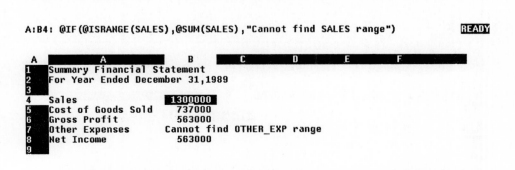

```
A:B4: @IF(@ISRANGE(SALES),@SUM(SALES),"Cannot find SALES range")          READY

A              A              B         C         D         E         F
1  Summary Financial Statement
2  For Year Ended December 31,1989
3
4  Sales                    1300000
5  Cost of Goods Sold        737000
6  Gross Profit              563000
7  Other Expenses           Cannot find OTHER_EXP range
8  Net Income                563000
9
```

Figure 7-47.   Using @ISRANGE to check that a range is defined

Format

@ISSTRING(*value*)

Arguments

value   normally this is a reference to a cell value,
                                 although it may be a formula or a string.

Use

This function is normally used in conjunction with @IF, to test for a
string entry during data entry. @ISSTRING("John") will return 1,
whereas @ISSTRING(56) will return 0. Since ERR and NA are regarded as numeric values, @ISSTRING(ERR) or @ISSTRING(NA)
will return 0.

The worksheet in Figure 7-48 shows name and address information
entered in column C. If you want to check C2..C5 to ensure that the
data was entered as strings, use a formula like the one in E2:

@IF(@ISSTRING(C2)," ","Entry is invalid - it is numeric")

This formula states that if the entry in C2 is a string, a blank will be
placed in E2, where the formula is located. If the cell contains something other than a string value, as shown in the worksheet, an error

Figure 7-48.   Using @ISSTRING to validate data

message will appear. This type of error check can allow the operator to glance at column E quickly for error flags, rather than having to study entries individually.

@TRUE

The @TRUE function always returns the logical value 1, making this function useful in avoiding ambiguity in formulas. The format of the function is @TRUE; it does not use any arguments.

Use

The @TRUE function is a substitute for the number 1 in formulas. It may seem a lot quicker to type a 1 than to type @TRUE, but the function is self-documenting and indicates that you want to set up a logical true condition. Here is an example:

@IF(A3 = 10,@TRUE,"A3 is not equal to 10")

The worksheet in Figure 7-49 shows @TRUE and its counterpart @FALSE used to determine if the number of items ordered equals the number billed. The formula in D3 checks the numbers ordered and

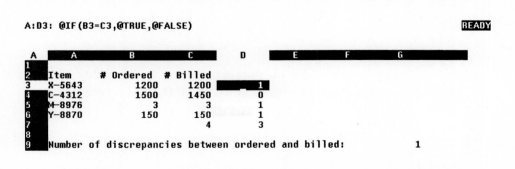

Figure 7-49.   Using @TRUE

billed for equality, and places @TRUE or @FALSE as the value in the cell accordingly. @TRUE displays as 1, @FALSE as 0. You can then count these 0s and 1s to determine how many discrepancies were in the orders. Use the @COUNT function to get an item count for the number of entries in C3..C6, which is 4. Then use @SUM to total the 0s and 1s, returning 3 in D7. Lastly, G9 contains a formula that subtracts D7 from C7 ($+C7-D7$). The value produced is 1, indicating a discrepancy in one of the orders.

Special Functions

1-2-3's special functions perform advanced calculations that do not fit neatly into any of the other categories. Some of them extend the capabilities of the logical features by providing a table lookup feature, and the ability to choose a value from a list of options. Others can be used to trap errors or determine the number of rows or columns in a range of cells. Still others are able to closely examine the contents of worksheet cells, providing information about the cell value or other attributes.

The new functions available in Release 3 can create absolute, mixed, or relative cell addresses, provide information about the current 1-2-3 session, and count the number of worksheets in a range. There is a smorgasbord of sophisticated features that can add power to your models. You will want to examine the functions in this category one by one, gradually adding each of them to your repertoire of 1-2-3 skills.

@@

The @@ function provides an indirect addressing capability that lets you reference the value in a cell pointed to by the cell referenced in the argument of @@.

Format

@@(cell)

Arguments

cell the address of a cell containing a string value that looks like a cell address, such as R10, Z2, or B3; or a range name, such as SALES or PROFIT; or a string formula that will create a string that looks like an address, such as "A"&"A"&"1"&"3", which creates AA13.

Use

The indirect referencing capabilities of the @@ function permit you to set up various values as key variables, and easily change the one you wish to use. The function also provides a way to store file links in .WK1 format.

The worksheet in Figure 7-50 uses @@ to determine which of the key variable values to use. The model shows the annual sales and commissions for a sales staff. Base commission rate for the company is set at 7%, but if it has a profitable year, the company wants the ability

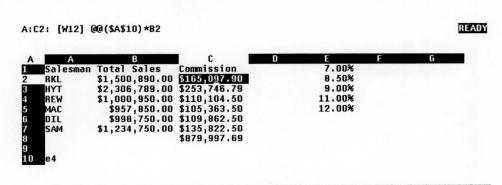

A:C2: [W12] @@($A$10)*B2   READY

A	A	B	C	D	E	F	G
1	Salesman	Total Sales	Commission		7.00%		
2	RKL	$1,500,890.00	$165,097.90		8.50%		
3	HYT	$2,306,789.00	$253,746.79		9.00%		
4	REW	$1,000,950.00	$110,104.50		11.00%		
5	MAC	$957,850.00	$105,363.50		12.00%		
6	DIL	$998,750.00	$109,862.50				
7	SAM	$1,234,750.00	$135,822.50				
8			$879,997.69				
9							
10	e4						

Figure 7-50.   Using @@ function to select commission rate

to increase the commission percentage. The @@ function provides an easy way to do this. You will notice that the formula in C2 is @@($A$10)*B2. A10 in turn contains a reference to one of the commissions in E1..E5. The referenced entry must be a string variable in the form of a cell address. It is currently E4, so the commission is calculated using an 11% rate. Changing the commission to another rate merely requires a change to A10.

You can see in the worksheet in Figure 7-51 that when the entry in A10 is changed to E2, all the commissions are recalculated. Note that a lowercase *e* can be used to reference the cell address.

Tip: The @@ function may require F9 (CALC). 1-2-3 will return a 0 from @@ if you use the function to refer to a location that contains a formula. Pressing F9 (CALC) eliminates the problem by forcing 1-2-3 to recalculate the worksheet.

@CELL

The @CELL function allows you to examine characteristics of any worksheet cell, including the format, content, address, and other detail settings.

A:C2:   [W12] @@($A$10)*B2   **READY**

A	A	B	C	D	E	F	G
1	Salesman	Total Sales	Commission		7.00%		
2	RKL	$1,500,890.00	$127,575.65		8.50%		
3	HYT	$2,306,789.00	$196,077.07		9.00%		
4	REW	$1,000,950.00	$85,080.75		11.00%		
5	MAC	$957,850.00	$81,417.25		12.00%		
6	DIL	$998,750.00	$84,893.75				
7	SAM	$1,234,750.00	$104,953.75				
8			$679,998.22				
9							
10	e2						

Figure 7-51.   Worksheet after changing @@ function's argument

Format

@CELL(*attribute string,range*)

Arguments

attribute string	a character string corresponding to one of the attributes the @CELL function can check, or a reference to a cell containing one. If the characters are included in the function, they must be enclosed in double quotation marks. Acceptable *attribute strings* and the values they return are in the table that follows.
range	a single or multiple cell range, such as A3..A3 or A2..D10. If you enter a single cell address, 1-2-3 converts it to a range address. If the range refers to multiple cells, only the upper left cell will be used.

Attribute String	**Results**
address	the address of the current cell; for example, $K$3
col	a number between 1 and 256, representing the column number
contents	the contents of the cell
coord	the cell address that includes the worksheet letter; for example, $A:$K$3
format	the current format of the cell. Choose from:
	A for Automatic
	C0-C15 for Currency with 0 to 15 decimal places
	D1 for DD-MMM-YY

format	D2 for DD-MMM
	D3 for MMM-YY
	D4 for MM/DD/YY, DD/MM/YY, DD.MM.YY, or YY-MM-DD
	D5 for MM/DD, DD/MM, DD.MM, or MM-DD
	D6 for HH:MM:SS AM/PM
	D7 for HH:MM AM/PM
	D8 for HH:MM:SS, HH.MM.SS, HH,MM,SS, or HHhMMmSSs (all 24-hour)
	D9 for HH:MM, HH.MM, HH,MM, or HHhMMm (all 24-hour)
	F0-F15 for Fixed with 0 to 15 decimal places
	G for General
	H for Hidden
	L for Label format
	P0-P15 for Percent with 0 to 15 decimal places
	T for Text
	S0-S15 for Scientific with 0 to 15 decimal places
	Blank if the cell is empty
	,0-,15 for Comma with 0 to 15 decimal places
	+ for +/− format
	( ) for Parentheses format
	- for no color format
prefix	label prefix for the cell. The label prefix ^ will appear for centered entries, ' for left justified entries, " for right justified en-

prefix	tries, \ for repeating labels, ¦ for non-printing label, and blank for an empty or numeric cell.
protect	Protection status of the cell, with 1 representing Protected and 0 representing Unprotected
row	a number between 1 and 8192 representing the row number
sheet	a number between 1 and 256 representing the worksheet letter
type	the type of data in the cell. The value types are b for blank, v for numeric, and l for label.
width	a number between 1 and 240 representing the current cell width

Use

The @CELL function is primarily used in macros, though you may use it any time you wish to examine the contents of a cell closely. It can be combined with the @IF function to test for certain situations and take appropriate actions.

Figure 7-52 provides a look at all the @CELL options. The main entry for examination is in A1. @CELL functions are stored in column C and are shown again in column E as formulas so you can compare the entry and the results. The formula in C1 reads @CELL("contents",A1..A1) and returns the contents of 123.45, the exact number entered without the addition of formatting characters. The entry in A11 allows you to check the prefix of a label entry. C11 contains the formula @CELL("prefix",A11..A11) and returns a ^, indicating center justification for the entry.

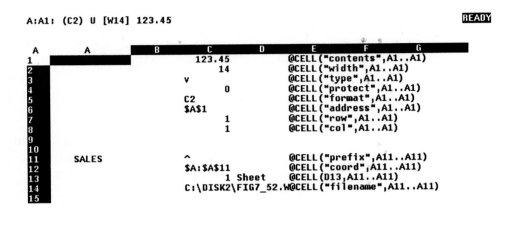

Figure 7-52. Using @CELL for a close-up look at a cell

@CELLPOINTER

The @CELLPOINTER function allows you to examine attributes of the cell where the cell pointer is located. If you move the cell pointer and recalculate, new results will be computed.

Format

@CELLPOINTER(*attribute string*)

Arguments

attribute string a character string corresponding to one of the attributes the @CELLPOINTER can check, or a reference to a cell containing *attribute string*   one. If the characters are included in the function, they must be enclosed in double quotation marks. Acceptable *attribute strings* and the values they return are the same as listed in the tables for @CELL.

Use

The @CELLPOINTER function is primarily used in macros, though you may use it any time you wish to examine the contents of a cell closely. It can be combined with the @IF function to test for certain situations and take appropriate actions.

Figure 7-53 provides a look at most of the @CELLPOINTER options. Since the cell pointer is located in A1, the results of @CELLPOINTER provide information about A1. If you were to move the cell pointer to a new location and recalculate the worksheet with F9 (CALC) or make another entry, you would get updated results. The @CELLPOINTER functions are stored in column C and are shown

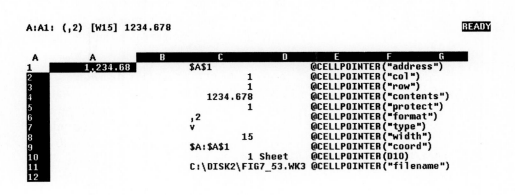

Figure 7-53.   Examining the current cell with @CELLPOINTER

again in column E as formulas, so you can compare the entry and the results. For example, the formula in C1 reads @CELLPOINTER ("address") and returns $A$1, the address of the current cell.

@CHOOSE

The @CHOOSE function allows you to select a suitable value from a list of values.

Format

@CHOOSE(*number,list*)

Arguments

number	the position number in the list of the value that you wish to use. The first value in the list has a position number of 0. This argument can be a number, formula, or a reference to either. *Number* must be smaller than the number of values in the list. If *number* is not a whole number, 1-2-3 uses only the whole number portion for the argument.
list	a group of numeric or string values that are not limited in number, except that the @CHOOSE function must occupy no more than 512 characters. 1-2-3 lets you mix string and numeric values in one *list*.

Use

The @CHOOSE function is ideal when you have a set of codes in your data that are consecutive, and limited in number. Since every number used to find a number in the list must have a value in the list, the number of values in the list must range from 0 to the largest number used to find a value in the list. For example, if you had codes of 1, 20, 300, and 750, @CHOOSE could not be used; you would have to turn to @VLOOKUP or @HLOOKUP. With consecutive and limited codes, however, @CHOOSE can provide a quick solution for supplying varying values.

Here are a few examples of the @CHOOSE function and the values it returns:

@CHOOSE(0,"Bill","Sally","Tom") equals Bill
@CHOOSE(1,"Bill","Sally","Tom") equals Sally
@CHOOSE(2,B10,A3,C2/4,A3*B4) equals the value C2/4
@CHOOSE(INTEREST,.09,.15,.08,.11) equals .15 when INTEREST equals 1.

The worksheet in Figure 7-54 shows the @CHOOSE function being used to determine a shipping cost from a warehouse location. Warehouse 1 adds $5.00 shipping charges, warehouse 2 adds $10.00, warehouse 3 adds $15.00, warehouse 4 adds $3.00, and warehouse 5 adds $20.00.

The Warehouse codes are in column A. The Item numbers are in column B. The Quantity and Unit Prices are in columns C and D respectively. The calculation for shipping cost requires the @CHOOSE formula. A dummy value must be used for warehouse 0, since all

---

A:E2: (C2) @CHOOSE(A2,0,5,10,15,3,20)   READY

A	A	B	C	D	E	F	G
1	Warehouse	Item	Quantity	Unit Price	Shipping	Total Cost	
2	1	2302	3	$50.00	$5.00	$155.00	
3	4	1710	2	$20.00	$3.00	$43.00	
4	5	2350	15	$15.00	$20.00	$245.00	
5	3	3125	13	$3.00	$15.00	$54.00	
6	1	1245	4	$120.00	$5.00	$485.00	
7	4	1111	12	$75.00	$3.00	$903.00	
8	5	2302	4	$50.00	$20.00	$220.00	
9	5	5562	2	$100.00	$20.00	$220.00	

Figure 7-54.   Choosing the correct value

@CHOOSE lists start with 0. A $0 shipping charge will therefore be included in the list. The function is then recorded in E2 as @CHOOSE(A2,0,5,10,15,3,20). The cell is formatted as Currency, and the formula is copied down column E. Total Cost in the model, shown in Column F, is simply the entry in column C times the entry in column D plus the Shipping cost from column E.

@COLS

The @COLS function is used to determine the number of columns within a specified range.

Format

@COLS(*range*)

Arguments

range   a cell range in the format A2..F7 or A:A2..G:F7, or a range name.

Use

This function is used primarily with range names. For example, you may have a range of cells containing employee information across the columns. By knowing how many columns there are in the range, you can tell how many employees are listed. A few more examples may help you understand this function.

@COLS(A2..H3) equals 8
@COLS(EMPLOYEES) equals 26 when EMPLOYEES refers to
the range A3..Z10

Figure 7-55 shows sales figures for a number of months. The range
name SALES_STATS is used to refer to the data for all the months.
You can tell how many months of data are in the range by using
@COLS(SALES_STATS), as shown in D10.

@COORD (Release 3)

This function creates a cell address from the function arguments you
provide.

Format

@COORD(*worksheet, column, row, absolute*)

A:D10: @COLS(SALES_STATS)   READY

A	A	B	C	D	E	F	G	H
1								
2			JAN	FEB	MAR	APR	MAY	
3								
4	Sales — Product A		12,500	13,062	13,650	14,265	14,906	
5	Sales — Product B		5,600	6,328	7,151	8,080	9,131	
6	Sales — Product C		15,750	16,223	16,709	17,210	17,727	
7								
8								
9								
10	Number of months projected			5				

Figure 7-55.   Determining the number of columns

Arguments

worksheet	a number ranging from 1 to 256 representing the worksheet number. The number 1 corresponds to worksheet A, and the number 256 corresponds to worksheet IV.
column	a number ranging from 1 to 256 representing the column number. The number 1 represents column A, and the number 256 corresponds to column IV.
row	a number between 1 and 8192 representing the row number.
absolute	a number between 1 and 8 indicating whether the resulting cell address creates an absolute, mixed, or relative cell reference. The values have the following meanings:

Value	Type of Cell Reference	Example
1	Absolute	$B:$K$3
2	Mixed (worksheet and row absolute)	$B:K$3
3	Mixed (worksheet and column absolute)	$B:$K3
4	Mixed (worksheet absolute)	$B:K3
5	Mixed (column and row absolute)	B:$K$3
6	Mixed (row absolute)	B:K$3
7	Mixed (column absolute)	B:$K3
8	Relative	B:K3

Use

This function is primarily used in macros and as the argument for other functions, although you may use it at any time to create an address. It is often used as the argument for the @@ function.

Figure 7-56 shows detail expense entries for expense codes 1001 and 1002 in sheets B and C. Other sheets contain entries for the company's remaining expense codes. Sheet A allows you to enter the month, year, and expense type for which you want information. In A:B6, the @COORD function uses these values to create a cell address that references the data tables contained in the other worksheets. The @@ function uses this address and returns the value in the cell.

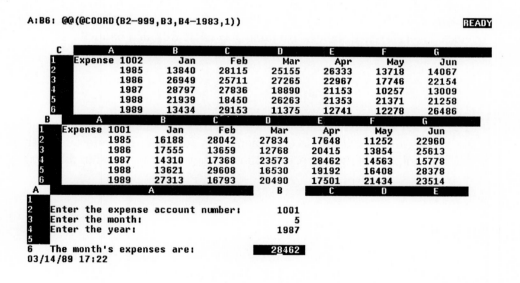

Figure 7-56.   Using @COORD to generate a cell address

@ERR

The @ERR function is used to return the value ERR in a cell and any other cells that reference the cell. The format of the function is @ERR; it has no arguments.

Use

This function is used to flag error conditions. For example, if you combine it with @IF, you can use it to verify that two totals are equal. If the two values are not equal, the cell containing the formula can be flagged with ERR. Such a formula might look like this:

$$@IF(A1 = D2,0,@ERR)$$

Another situation where @ERR is useful is in the verification of data input. An appropriate formula here might be @IF(A6 < 500,0, @ERR). ERR will appear if A6 is greater than or equal to 500. Any cells that reference the cell containing @ERR will also be given a value of ERR.

Note

1-2-3 generates ERR on its own when errors are made in the entry of, or in one of the arithmetic operations in a formula. The effect of both ERR conditions is the same, even though they are generated in different ways.

@HLOOKUP

The @HLOOKUP function allows you to search a table for an appropriate value to use in your worksheet. The distinction between this function and the @VLOOKUP function is that @HLOOKUP stores its table across the worksheet in a horizontal orientation, whereas @VLOOKUP uses a vertical orientation for table values.

Format

@HLOOKUP(*code to be looked up,table location,offset*)

Arguments

code to be looked up	the entry in your worksheet that will be compared against the table entry. When numeric values are used, 1-2-3 looks for the largest value in the table that is not greater than the *code*. When string values are used, the search is for an exact match.
table location	a range containing one or more rows on a worksheet. A table is composed of a set of *codes* and one or more sets of return values in adjacent cells. It can be placed in any area of your worksheet. While the table does not have to be on the current worksheet, the table is limited to a single worksheet. The top row in the range will contain the *codes,* and the subsequent rows will contain return values.
offset	a number that determines which row should be consulted for the return value when a matching code is found. The first row beneath the row of codes has an *offset* of 1, the second an *offset* of 2, and so on. Negative *offset* numbers will cause ERR to be returned, as will *offset* numbers that exceed the range established in the table location. If desired, you may use an *offset* of 0 to return the comparison code.

The following worksheet shows a table in A1..H2. The codes are in A1..H1, and the return values are in A2..H2.

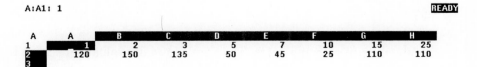

The process 1-2-3 uses for determining the value to be returned is as follows:

- The specified code is compared against the values in the top row of the table.

- The largest value in the top row of the table that is not greater than the code is considered a match. If the code to be looked up in the table is 3.5, the value adjacent to the 3 is returned.

- Offset is used to determine which value in the row that contains the matching table cell will be returned. If offset is 0, the matching code value itself is returned. If offset is 1, the value below the matching value is returned, and so on.

- A code with a value less than the first value in the top row of the table will return ERR.

- A code value greater than the last value in the first row of the table is considered to match the last value.

- If you are using label entries for codes and have label entries in the top row of the table, only exact matches will return table values.

Building a table with numeric codes requires that they be in ascending sequence. They are not required to be consecutive numbers, however; nor do the gaps between numbers have to be of a consistent size. With label entries, the codes do not have to be in any special sequence within the table.

Use

Tables are a powerful feature, useful for everything from tax withholding amounts to shipping rates. They are especially valuable because they allow you to look at potential changes in discount or commission structures, with only a few changes to table values and no alterations in your worksheet formulas.

Figure 7-57 shows a table located in cells C3..F7. The following codes will return the values shown from the table, assuming the offsets listed were provided:

Code	Offset	Return Value
4.5	1	22
11	2	2
15	3	77
0	1	11
99	1	44
4.5	0	4.5
11	1	22
15	2	3
102	1	44
−1	1	ERR

Figure 7-58 provides an example of a purchase discount model for a wholesale store that has a minimum $100 order amount. The model relies on @HLOOKUP to compute the purchase discount. The table is placed in B11..F14, with the comparison codes in B11..F11. The discount rates depend on both the amount of the purchase and the purchase type.

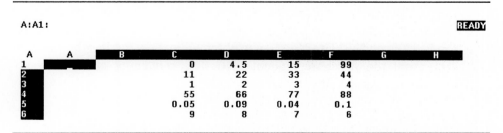

A:A1:   READY

A	A	B	C	D	E	F	G	H
1			0	4.5	15	99		
2			11	22	33	44		
3			1	2	3	4		
4			55	66	77	88		
5			0.05	0.09	0.04	0.1		
6			9	8	7	6		

Figure 7-57.   Sample horizontal table

A:D3: (C2) @HLOOKUP(C3,$B$11..$F$14,B3)*C3   READY

A	A	B	C	D	E	F	G
1	Customer	Purchase	Purchase		Net		
2	ID Number	Type	Amount	Discount	Due		
3	23-789	3	$500.00	$15.00	$485.00		
4	12-987	2	$100.00	$3.00	$97.00		
5	56-435	2	$175.00	$5.25	$169.75		
6	54-345	3	$980.00	$29.40	$950.60		
7	23-567	1	$1,200.00	$96.00	$1,104.00		
8	12-333	1	$6,000.00	$540.00	$5,460.00		
9	21-999	3	$10,000.00	$500.00	$9,500.00		
10							
11		100	500	1000	5000	10000	
12	1	5.00%	7.00%	8.00%	9.00%	10.00%	
13	2	3.00%	4.00%	5.00%	5.00%	6.00%	
14	3	3.00%	3.00%	3.00%	5.00%	5.00%	

Figure 7-58.   Horizontal table lookup

Purchase type 1 corresponds to cash and carry, which requires the lowest overhead and provides the highest discount structure. Purchase type 2 is cash, but requires delivery and uses a lower discount structure. The lowest discount structure of all is for credit sales. The purchase type is used as the offset code to access the proper row of the table. The comparison code in the table is chosen based on the Purchase Amount in column C.

The formula required to find the first discount is @HLOOK-UP(C3,$B$11..$F$14,B3)*C3. This formula looks up the code in C3 in a table located in B11 through F14. The $s indicate absolute addresses for the table range, and thus permit the formula to be copied down the worksheet for calculation of the remaining discounts. The offset for the table is B3, the purchase type. The value returned is multiplied by the purchase amount to compute the discount. For this first entry, this is 3% times $500, or $15. The Net Due is obtained by subtracting the discount (D3) from the purchase amount (C3). The remaining entries are obtained by copying from D3..E3 to D4..D9.

Tip: Compare the code against the 0 column of the table when you need an exact match. Remember that 1-2-3 returns a matching value for numeric codes even if there is not an exact match. So, if you only want to use the value returned by @HLOOKUP or @VLOOKUP when the match is exact, compare it against the values with an offset of 0. Your formula might look like @IF(B7=@HLOOKUP(B7,$TABLE,0), @HLOOKUP(B7,$TABLE,1),"No exact match").

@INDEX

The @INDEX function allows you to retrieve a value from a table of codes by specifying the row, column, and worksheet number of the table you wish to access.

Format

@INDEX(*table location,column number,row number[,worksheet number]*)

Arguments

table location	the location of the table of codes to be accessed by this function. Unlike the lookup functions, @INDEX does not use a comparison value to access the codes. You must specify a row and column address to obtain the code of your choice.
column number	the number of the column in the table from which you want to obtain a code. The leftmost column in the table range is column 0, with the numbers increasing by 1 for each column to the right that you move. The *column number* that you specify must be within the valid range established for the table. If the *number* you supply is not a whole number, the decimal portion will be truncated.

row number   the number of the row in the table from
                             which you wish to obtain a code. The up-
                             per row in the table is row 0. The *row
                             number* specified must be in the relevant
                             range for the table. If it is not a whole
                             number, the decimal portion of the *number*
                             will be truncated. The code returned will
                             be the one at the intersection of the row
                             and column you have specified.

worksheet number   the number of the worksheet in the table
                             from which you want to obtain a code. If
                             the *worksheet number* is not provided, the
                             function uses the first worksheet in the
                             table. The first worksheet in the table
                             range is worksheet 0, with the numbers
                             increasing by 1 for each worksheet the
                             table uses. The worksheet that you specify
                             must be within the valid range established
                             for the table. If the *number* you supply is
                             not a whole number, the decimal portion
                             will be truncated.

Use

The @INDEX function can be used whenever your data values are used
to access the proper row and column of a table. This type of function
works well for quoting insurance rates, shipping charges, and any other
calculation where you can specify the exact code you need from the
table.

Figure 7-59 provides an example of a commission application that
uses Total Sales and Region values to index the proper commission
percentage. The table is located in A1..G3. The row from which the
return value will be selected is the sales region minus 1, since tables
begin with row 0, not row 1. The column from which the return value

```
A:D7:  (C2)  [W11]  @INDEX($A$1..$G$3,(B7/10000)−1,C7−1)*B7                    READY
```

A	A	B	C	D	E	F	G
1	5.00%	6.00%	7.50%	9.00%	12.00%	15.00%	20.00%
2	6.00%	7.00%	8.00%	9.00%	13.00%	18.00%	25.00%
3	8.00%	9.00%	12.00%	15.00%	18.00%	23.00%	30.00%
4							
5							
6	Salesman	Total Sales	Region	Commission			
7	White	$50,000.00	2	$6,500.00			
8	Savage	$30,500.00	3	$3,660.00			
9	Greene	$41,000.00	1	$3,690.00			
10	Parsel	$65,000.00	3	$14,950.00			
11	Murray	$54,500.00	2	$7,085.00			

Figure 7-59.   Finding the appropriate value with @INDEX

will be selected is calculated as (Total Sales amount divided by $10,000) minus 1. The percent obtained from this function is multiplied by the sales figure to determine commissions.

With Release 3, @INDEX can use tables from multiple worksheets. Figure 7-60 shows a formula that uses the @INDEX function to determine the shipping and insurance costs. Each shipping zone has its own table. For each item, the @INDEX function selects the worksheet it needs based on the shipping Zone, the Weight, and the Unit Cost. Since the Unit Cost is divided by 100, the function truncates the noninteger portion. The function returns the number at the intersection of these three values.

@INFO (Release 3)

The @INFO function returns information about 1-2-3 and the operating system. Many of the options return information that is also listed by the /Worksheet Status command.

Format

@INFO(*attribute string*)

`A:F2: (F2) [W14] @INDEX($SHIP_COST,E2/100,C2,D2)` READY

C	A	B	C	D	E	F	G	H
1	Zone = 1	0.00	100.00	200.00	300.00	400.00	500.00	600.00
37	35	14.00	14.30	14.60	14.90	15.20	15.50	15.80
38	36	14.40	14.70	15.00	15.30	15.60	15.90	16.20
39	37	14.80	15.10	15.40	15.70	16.00	16.30	16.60
40	38	15.20	15.50	15.80	16.10	16.40	16.70	17.00
41	39	15.60	15.90	16.20	16.50	16.80	17.10	17.40

B	A	B	C	D	E	F	G	H
1	Zone = 0	0.00	100.00	200.00	300.00	400.00	500.00	600.00
11	9	2.70	2.90	3.10	3.30	3.50	3.70	3.90
12	10	3.00	3.20	3.40	3.60	3.80	4.00	4.20
13	11	3.30	3.50	3.70	3.90	4.10	4.30	4.50
14	12	3.60	3.80	4.00	4.20	4.40	4.60	4.80
15	13	3.90	4.10	4.30	4.50	4.70	4.90	5.10

A	A	B	C	D	E	F	G
1	Item #	Description	Weight	Zone	Unit Cost	Ship & Insur	Total Cost
2	9385	Bookcase	35	1	150.00	14.30	164.30
3	4011	Toss Rug	5	1	65.00	2.00	67.00
4	4637	Desk Lamp	9	0	15.00	2.70	17.70
5	7812	Floor Lamp	15	1	45.00	6.00	51.00
6	4469	Coffee Table	39	0	100.00	11.90	111.90

Figure 7-60. @INDEX using a multiple worksheet table

Arguments

attribute string a character string corresponding to one of the attributes the @INFO function can check, or a reference to a cell containing one of these strings. If the characters are included in the function, they must be enclosed in double quotation marks. Acceptable *attribute strings* and the values they return are as follows:

Attribute String	Results
directory	current directory
memavail	computer memory available

mode	current mode. The mode indicators are

0	WAIT
1	READY
2	LABEL
3	MENU
4	VALUE
5	POINT
6	EDIT
7	ERROR
8	FIND
9	FILES
10	HELP
11	STAT
13	NAMES
99	Any mode not listed above

numfile	current number of active files
origin	cell address of the cell in the upper left corner in the worksheet containing the cell pointer
osreturncode	value returned by the most recent /System command or {SYSTEM} macro command
osversion	current operating system version
recalc	current method of recalculation (automatic or manual)
release	current release of 1-2-3
system	current operating system name
totmem	computer memory, including the memory used by 1-2-3 and the worksheets, and the remaining memory available

Use

This function is primarily used in macros, although you may use it any time you wish to learn about the system. It can be combined with the @IF function or {IF} macro command to test a situation, such as insufficient memory before performing a task. You can respond to the condition test with an appropriate action. 1-2-3 updates this function each time you press F9 (CALC) or make another entry.

Figure 7-61 provides a look at the @INFO options. Column A contains the @INFO command using different attribute strings. The formulas are repeated to the right, and formatted as text.

@NA

This function causes NA, meaning "not available," to appear in the cell where this function is entered, as well as in all cells that reference it. The format for the function is @NA; it has no arguments.

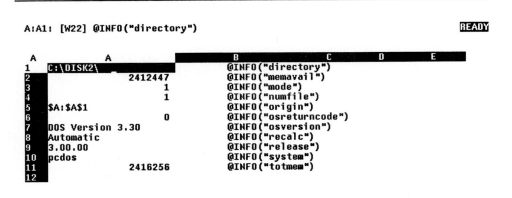

Figure 7-61. @INFO providing information about the current 1-2-3 session

Use

The @NA function is used when data is not available for entry in a cell. It serves as a flag for data that must be entered before correct model results can be computed. NA in one worksheet cell can ripple through a worksheet, since every cell that references a cell containing NA will also contain NA.

The @NA function would be useful for an instructor recording student grades. All students who missed an exam would have NA, rather than a score, recorded. Figure 7-62 shows the effect on the grade point average for students with missing grades. At the end of the semester, the instructor can change all grades that are still NA to 0.

Note

The label NA entered in a cell is not equivalent to entering @NA, which produces a numeric rather than a label entry.

@ROWS

The @ROWS function is used to determine the number of rows within a specified range.

A:F4: (F1) @AVG(B4..E4)   `READY`

A	A	B	C	D	E	F	G
1			Fall Semester − 1989				
2							
3	Student	Exam 1	Exam 2	Exam 3	Final	Average	
4	B. Black	75	NA	82	88	NA	
5	S. Conners	67	78	72	81	74.5	
6	F. Dalton	78	90	89	92	87.3	
7	G. Limmer	88	81	93	87	87.3	
8	S. Melton	67	55	40	60	55.5	
9	P. Stock	67	89	NA	78	NA	
10	J. Zimmer	91	82	75	89	84.3	

Figure 7-62.   The impact of NA on formulas

Format

@ROWS(*range*)

Arguments

    range   a cell range in the format A2..F7, or a range name

Use

This function is used primarily with range names. For example, you may have a range of cells containing order information with the orders listed down the worksheet. If all the order information were included in one range named ORDERS, you could obtain the number of orders with the function @ROWS(ORDERS). A few other examples may help to show how this function works.

    @ROWS(A2..H3) equals 2
    @ROWS(EMPLOYEES) equals 8 when EMPLOYEES refers to the range A3..Z10

The worksheet in Figure 7-63 shows the use of the @ROWS function to determine the number of orders. The range name ORDERS is assigned to A3..C6. Since the number of orders will be the same as the number of rows in the range, @ROWS(ORDERS) will provide the correct answer, as shown in B9.

@SHEETS (Release 3)

The @SHEETS function is used to determine the number of worksheets within a specified range.

Format

@SHEETS(*range*)

Arguments

    range   a cell range in the format A:A2..G:F7, or a range name.

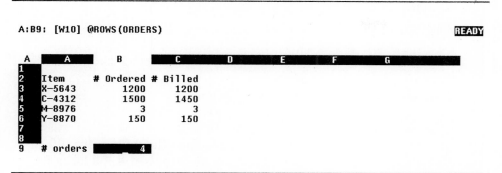

Figure 7-63.   Using @ROWS to determine the number of orders

Use

This function is used primarily with range names. For example, you may have a file containing a named range spanning a number of worksheets, with each worksheet containing the financial information for a division. After checking the number of worksheets in the named range, you know if you have the worksheets for all of the divisions. As you add worksheets between the beginning and end of a range, 1-2-3 automatically expands and contracts the range size. These examples may help you understand this function:

@SHEETS(A:A1..L:K72) equals 12
@SHEETS(DIVISION) equals 20 when the range called DIVISION uses 20 worksheets.

@VLOOKUP

The @VLOOKUP function allows you to search a table for an appropriate value to use in your worksheet. The distinction between this function and the @HLOOKUP function is that @VLOOKUP stores its table down the worksheet in a vertical orientation, whereas @HLOOKUP uses a horizontal orientation for table values.

Format

@VLOOKUP(*code to be looked up,table location,offset*)

Arguments

code to be looked up	the entry in your worksheet that will be compared against the table entry. When numeric values are used, 1-2-3 looks for the largest value in the table that is not greater than the *code*. When string values are used, the search is for an exact match.
table location	a range containing at least two partial columns on the worksheet. A table is composed of a set of *codes* and one or more sets of return values in adjacent cells. It can be placed in any area of your worksheet. While the table does not have to be on the current worksheet, the table is limited to a single worksheet. The left column in the range will contain the *codes,* and the subsequent columns will contain return values.
offset	a number that determines which column should be used for the return value when a matching code is found. The first column to the left of the column of *codes* has an *offset* of 1, the second an *offset* of 2, and so on. Negative *offset* numbers will cause ERR to be returned, as will *offset* numbers that exceed the range established in the table location. If desired, you may use an *offset* of 0 to return the comparison code from the first column of the table.

Figure 7-64 shows a table in A2..D8. The codes are in A2..A8, and the return values are in B2..D8. The process 1-2-3 uses for determining the value to be returned is as follows:

• The specified code is compared against the values in the left column of the table.

• The largest value in the left column of the table that is not greater than the code is considered a match. If the code to be looked up in the table is 3.5, the value adjacent to the 3 is returned.

• Offset is used to determine which value in the column that contains the matching table cell will be returned. If offset is 0, the matching code value itself is returned. If offset is 1, the value to the right of the matching value is returned, and so on.

• A code with a value less than the first value in the left column of the table will return ERR.

• A code value greater than the last value in the first column of the table will be considered to match the last value.

• If you are using label entries for codes and have label entries in the left column of the table, only exact matches will return table values.

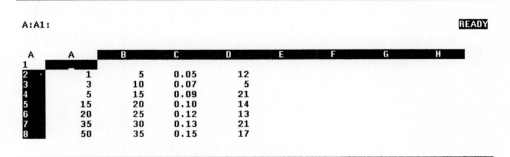

Figure 7-64.   Sample vertical table

Building a table with numeric codes requires that they be in ascending sequence. They are not required to be consecutive numbers, however; nor do the gaps between numbers have to be of a consistent size. With label entries, the codes do not have to be in any special sequence within the table.

Use

Tables are a powerful feature, useful for everything from tax withholding amounts to shipping rates. They are especially valuable because they allow you to look at potential changes in discount or commission structures, with only a few changes to table values and no alterations in your worksheet formulas.

Figure 7-65 provides a portion of a model to project travel costs. The tables for this model are located in J7..L9 and J12..K15 (see Figure 7-66). The first table offers a list of codes that provide an estimate of one night's meal and lodging costs for a travel location on the worksheet, as well as miscellaneous costs such as taxis, phone calls, and so on. The second table lets you assign a second code to a worksheet location, providing an estimate of the airfare costs for reaching that destination.

A:E6: (C2) [W11] @VLOOKUP(B6,$J$7..$L$9,1)*D6   READY

	LOCATION	LODGING CLASS	TRAVEL COST	# TRIPS	LODGING/ MEALS	AIRFARE	MISC.	TOTAL COST
6	Dallas	1	2	12	$1,500.00	$3,600.00	$420.00	$5,520.00
7	Akron	2	2	2	$300.00	$600.00	$90.00	$990.00
8	Chicago	3	1	3	$525.00	$750.00	$150.00	$1,425.00
9	Denver	2	2	12	$1,800.00	$3,600.00	$540.00	$5,940.00
10	Phoenix	2	3	5	$750.00	$1,750.00	$225.00	$2,725.00
11	Atlanta	2	2	4	$600.00	$1,200.00	$180.00	$1,980.00
12	New York	3	2	6	$1,050.00	$1,800.00	$300.00	$3,150.00
13	Portland	2	4	3	$450.00	$1,500.00	$135.00	$2,085.00

Figure 7-65. An application for a vertical table

Two tables are needed because the lodging and meal estimates and the travel cost estimates are based on different criteria.

The model in Figure 7-65 contains city names in column A. Column B contains a numeric code for Lodging Class that categorizes cities according to their relative living costs. Column C contains the numeric code for Travel Cost, assigned on the basis of distance from the origination point. Column D contains the number of trips to the location. This model assumes that all trips are for one night, but you could easily insert another column here to show variable numbers of nights.

The next column contains the first lookup formula. From the three arguments in the function you can see that it looks up B6 in the table with the absolute address of $J$7..$L$9. It uses an offset of 1, referring to the value in the column right next to the code. As a final step, this formula multiplies the returned value by the number of trips, to obtain a total lodging cost for this location.

The next formula, in F6, looks up the travel cost code. This formula is @VLOOKUP(C6,$J$12..$K$15,1). Again the table reference address is absolute, so you can copy the formula down the column for the other cities.

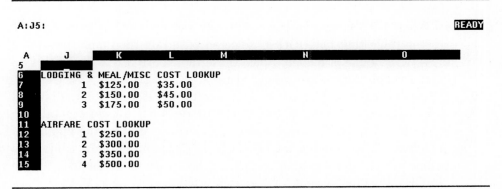

Figure 7-66.   Vertical tables for the travel cost model

The last lookup formula is in column G. The formulas in this column follow the pattern of the formula in G6, which is @VLOOKUP(C6,$J$7..$L$9,2). The difference between this formula and the first @VLOOKUP formula is that here the offset is 2, indicating that the value two columns away from the code should be returned. Total travel costs for a location are obtained with @SUM(E6..G6).

All the formulas described for this model are valid for the other city entries. They will be adjusted automatically if /Copy is used to place them in the other locations.

Note

The @VLOOKUP and @HLOOKUP functions cannot access multiple worksheets for the lookup tables. However, you can bypass this obstacle by combining the @CHOOSE command with the @VLOOKUP and @HLOOKUP command.

Figure 7-67 shows three worksheets. The first one contains employee payroll information, including basic tax information. Column F contains a formula which uses @VLOOKUP to find the Gross Pay in a table, and @CHOOSE to select which sheet in the table to use.

The table is a three-dimensional table that is stored in the file TAXES.WK3. Each worksheet contains a table for a different filing status, and each column in each worksheet contains the federal tax for a different number of dependents. Each row in each worksheet starts with a pay level that the @VLOOKUP function uses to select a row in the table.

When 1-2-3 computes the results for the @VLOOKUP function, it uses the table that @CHOOSE selected based on the employee's filing status. Each table is named. Since these tables are in the TAXES.WK3 file, the range names are preceded by < <TAXES.WK3> >. Once the @VLOOKUP function knows which table to use, it looks for the highest value in the first column of the table that does not exceed the value in column F. Then the function moves to the row chosen by the number of dependents. The intersection of the table, column, and row contains a number which the function returns. This process is similar to the @INDEX function, except 1-2-3 searches for the gross pay in the table's first vertical column.

```
A:G3: @VLOOKUP(F3,@CHOOSE(D3-1,<<TAXES.WK3>>$SINGLE,<<TAXES.WK3>>$MARRIED),  EDIT
@VLOOKUP(F3,@CHOOSE(D3-1,<<TAXES.WK3>>$SINGLE,<<TAXES.WK3>>$MARRIED),E3+1)_
```

B	A	B	C	D	E	F	G	H
1	Married	0	1	2	3	4	5	6
47	290	$35.00	$29.00	$23.00	$18.00	$12.00	$7.00	$1.00
48	300	$36.00	$31.00	$25.00	$19.00	$14.00	$8.00	$2.00
49	310	$38.00	$32.00	$26.00	$21.00	$15.00	$10.00	$4.00
50	320	$39.00	$34.00	$28.00	$22.00	$17.00	$11.00	$5.00
51	330	$41.00	$35.00	$29.00	$24.00	$18.00	$13.00	$7.00

A	A	B	C	D	E	F	G	H
1	Single	0	1	2	3	4	5	6
34	180	$24.00	$18.00	$13.00	$7.00	$2.00	$0.00	$0.00
35	185	$25.00	$19.00	$14.00	$8.00	$2.00	$0.00	$0.00
36	190	$26.00	$20.00	$14.00	$9.00	$3.00	$0.00	$0.00
37	195	$26.00	$21.00	$15.00	$9.00	$4.00	$0.00	$0.00
38	200	$27.00	$21.00	$16.00	$10.00	$5.00	$0.00	$0.00

A	A	B	C	D	E	F	G
1	Social	First	Last	Filing	# of	Gross	Federal
2	Security #	Name	Name	Status	Depend.	Pay	Tax
3	231-89-7654	Mary	Jones	1	1	190	20
4	132-65-4321	John	Cooper	2	3	320	22
5	345-78-4254	Sally	Smith	1	2	225	19
6	657-73-5674	Chris	Winsor	1	1	200	21

Figure 7-67.   @VLOOKUP using @CHOOSE to select the worksheet containing the right table

Statistical Functions

1-2-3's statistical functions perform their magic on lists of values. Frequently these lists are a contiguous range of cells on the worksheet. They can also be a series of individual values or a combination of range and individual values. Blank ranges can be included within the list, but all the values in the blank range will count as 0s. When a range has multiple cells, 1-2-3 will ignore cells containing blanks. If a single blank cell is used in the list, 1-2-3 will assign a 0 to the cell.

The majority of the statistical functions work only with numeric values. @COUNT is the exception, since it counts the number of nonblank cells in a list and will also accept string values.

@AVG

The @AVG function finds the average of a list of values.

Format

@AVG(*list*)

Arguments

list   any set of numeric values. They can be
                                          individual cell references, individual values,
                                          or a range of cells. You can also combine
                                          the options in one *list*. Examples are
                                          @AVG(A2..A9,D4,L2) and
                                          @AVG(D4..D15). Note that the compo-
                                          nents in the *list* are separated by commas.

Use

The worksheet in Figure 7-68 uses @AVG to calculate the average bid
amount received from vendors. The vendor bids are shown in B4..B11,
and the formula is entered in B13 as @AVG(B4..B11).

@COUNT

The @COUNT function determines the number of nonblank entries in a
list. A cell that contains a label prefix will still count as a nonblank, even
though the cell displays as a blank.

Format

@COUNT(*list*)

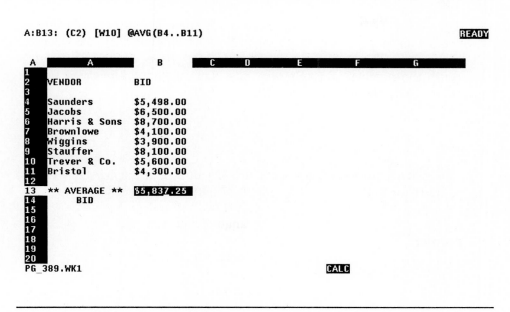

A:B13: (C2) [W10] @AVG(B4..B11)   READY

A	A	B	C	D	E	F	G
1							
2	VENDOR	BID					
3							
4	Saunders	$5,498.00					
5	Jacobs	$6,500.00					
6	Harris & Sons	$8,700.00					
7	Brownlowe	$4,100.00					
8	Wiggins	$3,900.00					
9	Stauffer	$8,100.00					
10	Trever & Co.	$5,600.00					
11	Bristol	$4,300.00					
12							
13	** AVERAGE **	$5,837.25					
14	BID						
15							
16							
17							
18							
19							
20							

PG_389.WK1   CALC

Figure 7-68.   Using @AVG to average vendor bids

Arguments

list

any set of numeric values. They can be individual cell references or a range of cells, although individual cell references may distort your results and should be avoided. A single cell reference increases the count by one, even if the cell is blank. You can also combine the two options in one *list*. Examples are @COUNT(A2..A9,D4,L2) and @COUNT(D4..D15). Note that the components in the *list* are separated by commas.

Use

The @COUNT function does not require numeric data. It will count all the nonblank entries in a list, regardless of whether they are values or characters. The worksheet in Figure 7-69 shows @COUNT used to count the number of employees. The Name field is referenced for the count, using the formula @COUNT(A4..A15).

@MAX

The @MAX function searches a list of values and displays the largest value in the list.

Format

@MAX(*list*)

A:B17: [W12] @COUNT(A4..A15)   `READY`

A	A	B	C	D	E	F
1						
2	Name	Base Salary	Inc. Mo.	% INC	1989 Salary	
3						
4	Jones, Ray	$25,000.00	2	5.00%	$26,145.83	
5	Larkin, Mary	$29,000.00	3	7.00%	$30,691.67	
6	Harris, John	$15,000.00	6	5.00%	$15,437.50	
7	Parson, Mary	$18,000.00	9	4.00%	$18,240.00	
8	Smith, Jim	$23,000.00	4	7.00%	$24,207.50	
9	Harker, Pat	$35,000.00	10	4.00%	$35,350.00	
10	Jenkins, Paul	$45,000.00	2	9.00%	$48,712.50	
11	Jacobs, Norman	$12,000.00	1	4.00%	$12,480.00	
12	Merriman, Angela	$36,900.00	4	7.00%	$38,837.25	
13	Campbell, David	$40,000.00	1	10.00%	$44,000.00	
14	Campbell, Keith	$32,000.00	1	9.00%	$34,880.00	
15	Stevenson, Mary	$18,900.00	11	7.50%	$19,136.25	
16						
17	NUMBER OF EMPLOYEES:	12				
18						
19						
20						

Figure 7-69. Using @COUNT to count the number of employees

Arguments

list

any set of numeric values. They can be individual cell references, individual values, or a range of cells. You can also combine the options in one *list.* Examples are @MAX(A2..A9,D4,L2) and @MAX(D4..D15). Note that the components in the *list* are separated by commas.

Use

The worksheet in Figure 7-70 shows the @MAX function used to obtain the highest bid in a group of vendor bids. The bids are entered in

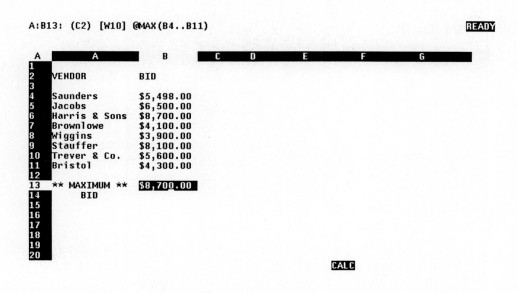

Figure 7-70.   Using @MAX to determine the highest vendor bid

B4..B11, with the corresponding vendor names in column A. The @MAX function is placed in B13 as @MAX(B4..B11); it returns a maximum bid of $8,700.00.

If you entered additional vendor bids, they would be included in the calculation automatically, as long as you inserted them somewhere in the middle of the range. If you added your entries at the beginning or end of the range, 1-2-3 would not automatically expand the range to include them.

@MIN

The @MIN function searches a list of values and displays the smallest value in the list.

Format

@MIN(*list*)

Arguments

list   any set of numeric values. They can be individual cell references, individual values, or a range of cells. You can also combine the options in one list. Examples are @MIN(A2..A9,D4,L2) and @MIN(D4..D15). Note that the components in the list are separated by commas.

Use

The worksheet in Figure 7-71 shows the @MIN function used to find the lowest bid in a group of vendor bids. The bids are located in B4..B11, and the minimum is found with the function @MIN(B4..B11). If you entered additional vendor bids, they would be included in the calculation automatically, as long as you inserted them somewhere in the middle of the range. If you added your entries at the beginning or end of the range, 1-2-3 would not automatically expand the range to include them.

@STD

The @STD function is used to determine the population standard deviation of a set of values, or how much variation there is from the average of the values. It is the square root of the variance.

Format

@STD(*list*)

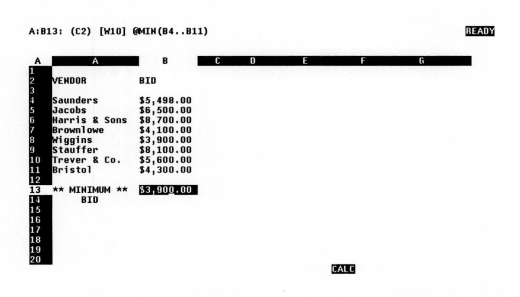

Figure 7-71. Using @MIN to determine the lowest vendor bid

Arguments

list   any set of numeric values. They can be
                               individual cell references or a range of
                               cells. You can also combine the two in one
                               list. Examples are @STD(A2..A9,15,L2)
                               and @STD(D4..D15). Note that the compo-
                               nents in the list are separated by commas.
                               Blank cells within the list will be ignored,
                               but label entries will be assigned a value of
                               0. Including both label entries and single
                               cell references in this list can cause a
                               problem, because @STD uses a count of
                               the entries as part of its calculation.

Use

The @STD function determines the standard deviation when you have
access to the values for the entire population—that is, all the values for
the entire group you are studying. If you are measuring the deviation in
the weight of packages filled in a plant, for example, population would
refer to all packages filled, not just a sample. If you are working with
only a sample of the population, use the @STDS function.

The purpose of the standard deviation calculation is to determine
the amount of variation between individual values and the mean. Suppose, for example, that you determine the average age of your employees to be 40. This could mean that half of your employees are 39 and the
other half 41, or it could mean that you have employees whose ages
range from 18 to 65. The latter case shows a greater standard deviation
because of the greater variance from the mean.

The @STD function is biased, since it uses a count as part of its
calculations. Specifically, it uses the following formula:

$$\sqrt{\frac{\sum (x_i - AVG)^2}{n}}$$

where x_i is the ith item in the list and n is the number of items in the list.

As an example, suppose that the Commemorative Bronze Company has made 50 replicas of antique bronze cash registers and wants to determine the standard deviation in the weight of these products. The worksheet in Figure 7-72 shows the list of weights and the formula for the standard deviation.

@STDS (Release 3)

The @STDS function determines the sample standard deviation of a set of values, for a sample of a population. If the entire population is included in the values, the @STD function is used.

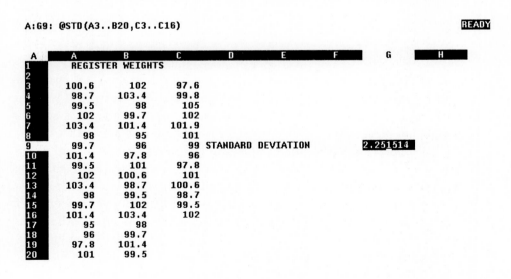

Figure 7-72.   Using @STD to measure the fluctuations in register weights

Format

@STDS(*list*)

Arguments

list	any set of numeric values. They can be individual cell references or a range of cells. You can also combine the two in one list. Examples are @STDS(A2..A9,15,L2) and @STDS(D4..D15). Note that the components in the list are separated by commas. Blank cells within the list will be ignored, but label entries will be assigned a value of 0. Including both label entries and single cell references in this list can cause a problem, because @STDS uses a count of the entries as part of the calculation.

Use

The @STDS function determines the standard deviation when you have access to the values for a sample of a population. For example, if you are measuring the customer responses to a survey, you are using a sample population unless all of your customers respond to the survey.

The purpose of the standard deviation calculation is to determine the amount of variation between individual values and the mean. For example, suppose the companies in a product survey have average sales of $500,000. If the standard deviation is $50,000, you know that most of your customers have approximately the same sales volume. If the standard deviation is $400,000, you know that your customer base includes companies with a wide range of sales volumes. You can use this information to target your advertising to the appropriate companies.

The @STDS function uses the $n-1$, or unbiased, method. The function performs this formula:

$$\sqrt{\frac{\sum (x_i - \text{AVG})^2}{(n-1)}}$$

where x_i is the ith item in the list and n is the number of items in the list.

The difference between the results of the @STD and @STDS function increases as the number of measurements decreases — making it critical to select the proper function. As an example, suppose a worksheet like Figure 7-73 contains product survey information. Each of the questions have an answer between 1 and 5. For each of the questions, the worksheet shows the median and the standard deviation. For

A:B4: @STDS(B6..B64)   READY

A	A	B	C	D	E	F	G	H
1	Survey Response							
2	Question	1	2	3	4	5	6	7
3	Average	3.271186	2.932203	3.118644	2.915254	3.033898	3.016949	3.033898
4	Std. Dev.	0.867627	1.827608	1.340159	1.417722	1.425943	1.547986	1.461767
5	Responses							
6	1	3	3	4	2	5	5	4
7	2	4	5	5	2	5	5	4
8	3	4	1	4	5	1	4	1
9	4	2	4	3	3	4	5	5
10	5	5	1	3	1	5	2	5
11	6	1	2	3	1	1	1	5
12	7	2	3	3	1	2	5	3
13	8	5	1	2	4	3	2	1
14	9	3	2	1	1	1	1	2
15	10	4	5	2	2	2	2	1
16	11	3	2	5	2	2	5	4
17	12	4	1	2	1	4	1	5
18	13	3	2	3	1	3	3	2
19	14	4	3	2	1	1	2	3
20	15	3	2	5	2	4	2	4

Figure 7-73. Using @STDS to measure the fluctuations in survey responses

the first question, the standard deviation is small, which means that most of the responses vary by approximately .87 around the median of 3.27. For the second question, the standard deviation is high; most of the responses vary by approximately 1.83 around the median.

The size of a standard deviation varies depending on the size of the values measured. For example, the standard deviation for the @STD function in Figure 7-72 is 2.25. This standard deviation is a small percentage of each cash register's weight. The deviation of 1.83 for Figure 7-73's survey responses is a larger percentage of the potential survey responses. Since the survey answers vary between 1 and 5, this standard deviation is a larger percentage of the response values than the standard deviation in the cash register weights.

@SUM

The @SUM function totals a list of numeric values.

Format

@SUM(*list*)

Arguments

list   any set of numeric values. They can be individual cell references, individual values, or a range of cells. You can also combine the options in one list. Examples are @SUM(A2..A9,D4,L2) and @SUM(D4..D15). Note that the components in the list are separated by commas.

Use

The @SUM function is used to obtain a total wherever you have more than two values to add together. It is much more efficient than using addition on each individual component. The other advantage offered by @SUM is that when you insert a row or column into the middle of the @SUM range, the range will automatically be adjusted for the extra entry without changing the formula.

The worksheet in Figure 7-74 shows a list of accounts and their current balances. The @SUM function was used to obtain the Total, rather than a formula like +B4+B5+B6+B7, and so on. @SUM-(B4..B11) was entered in B13.

One of the new features Release 3 provides is combining multiple worksheets into one file. The statistical functions—particularly the @SUM function—will frequently use this new feature, because worksheets can now combine figures from multiple worksheets and files. Figure 7-75 shows a worksheet that sums the yearly total from each of the monthly worksheets. To create a yearly report, another worksheet is added before January's worksheet, and the formula @SUM(B5..M5) is

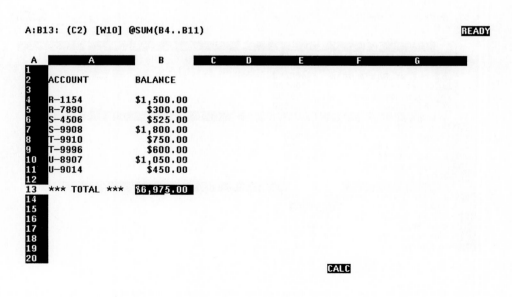

Figure 7-74.   Using @SUM to add account balances

copied from B5 to all of the cells in worksheet A that contain numeric values. If you want to combine worksheets from files instead, include the filename before the field names in the summation formula.

Tip: Make it easy to expand your @SUM range reference. Include a cell with a label entry like ' — — — — — — — — — — at the top and bottom of a column of label entries, and reference these cells as the first and last range entries. This allows you to insert a row at the top or bottom of the range without affecting the accuracy of the computation.

@SUMPRODUCT (Release 3)

The @SUMPRODUCT function multiplies the values in corresponding cells and returns their total.

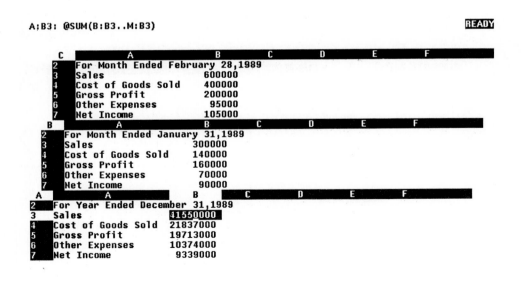

Figure 7-75.   Using @SUM to add across worksheets

Format

@SUMPRODUCT(*list*)

Arguments

list   any set of numeric values contained in
                                specified ranges or range names. Each
                                range in the list must contain the same
                                number of cells. An example is
                                @SUMPRODUCT(C3..C8,E3..E8). Note
                                that the components are separated by
                                commas. The range must have the same
                                orientation. For example, you cannot use
                                A1..C1 with A2..A4 in this function.

Use

@SUMPRODUCT is used to compute a cross product of numbers. An
example of computing a cross product is shown in Figure 7-76, in which
the products on an order form are listed. The total for the entire order
is computed after the last item. @SUMPRODUCT multiplies each item
quantity by its price and adds it to the shipping cost. The shipping cost

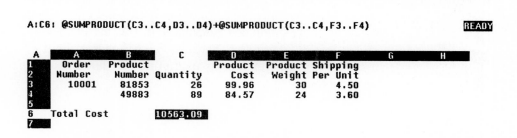

Figure 7-76.   Using @SUMPRODUCT to compute order totals

is the quantity times the weight times the shipping cost per pound. Once the cost for each item is computed, @SUMPRODUCT adds the totals for all of the items for the order. Using the @SUMPRODUCT function reduces the number of formulas the worksheet requires in order to compute the total cost. This function is also used to double-check worksheets that perform the same computations using multiplication and the @SUM function.

@VAR

The @VAR function computes the population variance of values in a population, or the amount the individual population values vary from the average. The variance is equal to the standard deviation squared.

Format

@VAR(*list*)

Arguments

list   any set of numeric values. They can be individual cell references or a range of cells. You can also combine the two in one list. Examples are @VAR(A2..A9,15,L2) and @VAR(D4..D15). Note that the components in the list are separated by commas. Blank cells within the list will be ignored, but label entries will be assigned a value of 0. Including both label entries and single cell references in this list can cause a problem, because @VAR uses a count of the entries as part of its calculation.

Use

The @VAR function determines the variance when you have access to the values for the entire population—that is, all the values for the entire group you are studying. If you are measuring the deviation in the weight of packages filled in a plant, for example, population would refer to all packages filled, not just a sample. If you are working with only a sample of the population, use the @VARS function.

The purpose of the variance calculation is to determine the amount of variation between individual values and the mean. Suppose, for example, that you determine the average age of your employees to be 40. This could mean that half of your employees are 39 and the other half 41, or it could mean that the ages range from 18 to 65. The latter case shows a greater variance because of the greater dispersion from the mean.

The @VAR function is biased, since it uses a count as part of its calculation. Specifically, it uses the following formula:

$$\frac{\sum (x_i - \text{AVG})^2}{n}$$

where x_i is the ith item in the list and n is the number of items in the list. The number of items is critical in determining whether to use @VAR or @VARS. When n is equal to the total population, use @VAR; when n represents a sample of the population, use @VARS.

As an example, suppose that the Commemorative Bronze Company has made 50 replicas of antique bronze cash registers and wants to determine the variance in the weight of these products. The worksheet in Figure 7-77 shows the list of weights and the formula for the variance.

@VARS (Release 3)

The @VARS function determines the sample variance of a set of values, for a sample of a population. If the values include the entire population, use the @VAR function.

Format

@VARS(*list*)

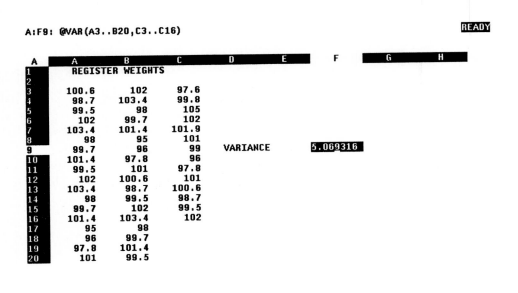

Figure 7-77.   Using @VAR to measure the variance in register weights

Arguments

list

any set of numeric values. They can be individual cell references or a range of cells. You can also combine the two in one list. Examples are @VARS(A2..A9,15,L2) and @VARS(D4..D15). Note that the components in the list are separated by commas. Blank cells within the list will be ignored, but label entries will be assigned a value of 0. Including both label entries and single cell references in this list can cause a problem, because @VARS uses a count of the entries as part of the calculation.

Use

The @VARS function determines the variance when you have access to the values for a sample of a population. For example, if you are measuring the customer responses to a survey, you are using a sample population unless all of your customers respond to the survey.

The purpose of the variance calculation is to determine the amount of variation between individual values and the mean. For example, suppose the companies in a product survey have average sales of $500,000. A variance of 2.5 billion indicates that more of your customers have approximately the same sales volume than if the variance is 160 billion. The variance values accentuate the variances among a set of values. You can use this information to target your advertising to the appropriate companies.

The @VARS function uses the $n-1$, or unbiased, method. The function performs this formula:

$$\frac{\sum (x_i - \text{AVG})^2}{(n-1)}$$

where x_i is the ith item in the list and n is the number of items in the list.

Like the @STD and @STDS functions, the difference between the results of the @VAR and @VARS functions increases as the number of measurements decreases. As an example, suppose a worksheet like Figure 7-78 contains product survey information. Each of the questions have an answer between 1 and 5. For each of the questions, the worksheet shows the median and the variance. For the first question, the variance is small, which means that most of the responses are close to the median of 3.27. For the second question, the variance is high; the responses fluctuate more around the median than the first question responses.

String Functions

String functions provide a variety of character manipulation formulas that give you flexibility in rearranging text entries. You can work with an entire entry and change its order, or you can use just a piece of a cell entry.

1-2-3's string functions often work with the individual characters in a text string. The numbering system that 1-2-3 uses for the characters in a string may not be what you expect. The character at the far left of a string is regarded as character 0, not character 1. The numbering proceeds with 1, 2, and so on, moving to the right in the character string. Understanding these positions within a string is very important, since you will want to be sure you are working with the right characters. String position numbers can range from 0 through 511, since a 512-character string is the largest that 1-2-3 can work with.

A:B5: @VARS(B7..B65)   READY

A	A	B	C	D	E	F	G	H
1	Survey Response							
2	Question	1	2	3	4	5	6	7
3	Average	3.271186	2.932203	3.118644	2.915254	3.033898	3.016949	3.033898
4	Std. Dev.	0.867627	1.827608	1.340159	1.417722	1.425943	1.547986	1.461767
5	Variance	0.752776	3.340152	1.796026	2.009936	2.033314	2.396259	2.136762
6	Responses							
7	1	3	3	4	2	5	5	4
8	2	4	5	5	2	5	5	4
9	3	4	1	4	5	1	4	1
10	4	2	4	3	3	4	5	5
11	5	5	1	3	1	5	2	5
12	6	1	2	3	1	1	1	5
13	7	2	3	3	1	2	5	3
14	8	5	1	2	4	3	2	1
15	9	3	2	1	1	1	1	2
16	10	4	5	2	2	2	2	1
17	11	3	2	5	2	2	5	4
18	12	4	1	2	1	4	1	5
19	13	3	2	3	1	3	3	2
20	14	4	3	2	1	1	2	3

Figure 7-78.   Using @VARS to measure the variance in survey responses

String position numbers must always be expressed as positive integers. A negative integer causes 1-2-3 to return ERR. Using a number with a decimal causes 1-2-3 to drop the decimal and use only the whole number portion of the value. No rounding occurs; for example, 1-2-3 truncates a value of 5.6 to 5 when it is used as a position number in a string. The following shows the positions for entries within a label.

```
T h i s   i s   a   s t r i n g
0 1 2 3 4 5 6 7 8 9 | | | | | |
                    0 1 2 3 4 5
```

It is also important to note that the label indicator that begins a string is not assigned a position number. An empty or null string has a length of 0 positions. A cell with a null string contains no entry except a label indicator. It is not the same as a blank cell without a label indicator.

When you use string values as arguments in a string function, you must enclose them in double quotation marks. These same entries referenced by a cell address will not require quotation marks, however. For example, if you want to use the character string "This is a string" in the @RIGHT string function to remove the last 6 characters on the right, and the entry is stored in D10, you could use @RIGHT(D10,6); but if you put the string itself in the function, it would have to be written as @RIGHT("This is a string", 6).

Some string functions will produce numeric results equating to a position in a string, while others will produce a string value. You will want to become familiar with the workings of string functions before you indiscriminately combine the results of two string functions. Many of the examples in this section will combine several string functions, however, since this is the way string functions are most commonly used.

@CHAR

The @CHAR function is used to return a character that corresponds to a Lotus Multi-Byte Character Set (LMBCS).

Format

@CHAR(*code*)

Arguments

code	any numeric value from 1 to 6143. Decimal fractions will be truncated; only the whole number portion of the entry will be used. Numbers less than 1 or greater than 6143 will return ERR.

Use

The @CHAR function converts an LMBCS code to a displayable and printable character. LMBCS codes above 127 produce foreign currency symbols, accent marks, and other special characters. If the character represented by the code number you specify cannot be displayed on your monitor, a blank or a character resembling the desired character will be substituted. Codes below 32 are returned as the characters for LMBCS codes 257 through 287. Codes above 511 cannot be printed or displayed; 1-2-3 displays these characters as a shaded rectangle. Here are a few examples:

@CHAR(40) equals (
@CHAR(49) equals 1

The primary use for this function is to compose characters from within a macro or a string formula.

@CODE

The @CODE function returns the Lotus Multi-Byte Character Set (LMBCS) code number of the first character in the function argument.

Format

@CODE(*string*)

Arguments

string	any character sequence up to 512 characters. If the characters are included in the function, they must be enclosed in double quotation marks. They can also be stored in a cell and referenced with a cell address or range name. Numeric characters can be used as long as they are preceded by a label prefix. This function uses only the first character in the string.

Use

This function finds its primary application in macros working with composed characters. The purpose of the function is to convert characters to their LMBCS code. A few examples of @CODE are as follows:

@CODE("$") equals 36
@CODE("V") equals 86
@CODE("@") equals 64

Note

Uppercase and lowercase characters have different codes. For example, an uppercase *A* is code 65, but a lowercase *a* is code 97.

@EXACT

The @EXACT function allows you to determine whether two string values are exactly equal.

Format

@EXACT(*string1,string2*)

Arguments

string1	any character sequence that does not exceed 512 characters. If the string is included in the function, the total length of the formula cannot exceed 512 characters, so the string will be restricted to a size that fits within this limitation. If used, the string must also be enclosed in double quotation marks.
string2	any character sequence that does not exceed 512 characters. If the string is placed in the function, the total length of the formula cannot exceed 512 characters, so the string will be restricted to a size that fits within this limitation. If used, the string must also be enclosed in double quotation marks.

Use

The @EXACT function returns 1 when the two strings match exactly, and 0 when they do not. Everything about the two strings must be the same, including blank spaces and capitalization, or 0 will be returned. Although this function can be used by itself, it is normally used with condition tests (that is, with @IF).

Several examples of @EXACT are

@EXACT("Mary Brown","MARY BROWN") equals 0
@EXACT("2144","2144") equals 1
@EXACT(2144,"2144") equals ERR, since string1 is a numeric value
@EXACT(A10,"MARY BROWN") equals 1 if A10 contains MARY BROWN

Note

Use @IF and the equal operator (=) if you do not want to consider case difference. For example, @IF("Tom Jones"="tom jones","True", "False") will return True, since the case difference is not considered.

@FIND

The @FIND function permits you to search a character string to find out if a substring (search string) appears within it. If the search string is found, the function returns the starting location of this string.

Format

@FIND(*search string,entire string,starting location*)

Arguments

search string	a character sequence or a reference to a cell containing one. When the characters are included in the function, they must be enclosed in quotation marks. The maximum length of the search string must be less than or equal to the entire string to be searched. Since @FIND is case sensitive, the search string must exactly match a portion of the entire string.
entire string	a character sequence or a reference to a cell containing one. When the characters are included in the function, they must be enclosed in quotation marks. The maximum length of this string is 512 characters.
starting location	the position in the entire string where you wish to begin your search. Remember that the leftmost character in the string is character 0. The maximum starting location can be one less than the number of characters in the entire string.

Use

The @FIND function is used whenever you wish to locate a string within a string. It can be used to identify the location of the blank space between a first and last name, for example. This information, when combined with other string functions, lets you reverse the name entry so that the last name appears first in the cell. ERR is returned when your starting location number is negative or greater than the last position of the entire string, or when the search string is not found.

Several examples of @FIND are as follows:

@FIND(" –","ABF –6785",0) equals 3
@FIND(" –","213 –46 –2389",4) equals 6
@FIND(" –""ABF –6785",8) equals ERR

The worksheet in Figure 7-79 provides an example of @FIND used to locate the space between first and last names. The formula in C2 is the pattern for the other formulas in column C:@FIND(" ",A2,0). Because of the 0 starting location for strings, the location of the space is equivalent to the number of characters in the first name.

Note

@MID can be used with @FIND to extract the search string. For the formula example, to extract Smith from John Smith, you could use@MID(A10,@FIND(A1,A10,0),@LENGTH(A1)), where A1 contains Smith and A10 contains John Smith.

@LEFT

The @LEFT function allows you to extract a specified number of characters from the left side of a string.

Format

@LEFT(*string,number of characters to extract*)

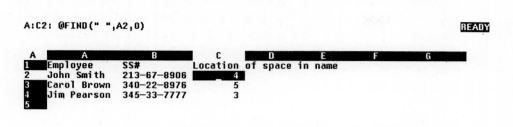

Figure 7-79.   Using @FIND to locate the space between names

Arguments

string	a sequence of characters included in the function, either by enclosing them in double quotation marks or by a reference to a cell address or range name containing the characters.
number of characters to extract	a number representing the characters to be extracted from the string. If you want to extract the first three characters, for example, this number would be 3. ERR will result if this number is greater than the number of characters in the string.

Use

The @LEFT function lets you extract one or many characters from a string. It can be used alone or in combination with other string functions. Some examples are

@LEFT("Lotus 1-2-3",5) equals Lotus
@LEFT("12:30:59",4) equals 12:3
@LEFT("ABC COMPANY",7) equals ABC preceded by four leading spaces

The worksheet in Figure 7-80 shows the @LEFT function coupled with @FIND to extract the first name from worksheet entries. C2 contains the pattern for column C formulas: @LEFT(A2,@FIND (" ",A2,0)). This formula finds the location of the blank space between first and last name and uses it as the number of characters to extract from the string.

@LENGTH

The @LENGTH function returns the number of characters in a string.

Format

@LENGTH(*string*)

Arguments

string   a group of characters that can be included in the function (if they are enclosed in double quotation marks), or placed in a cell and referenced. You can also use a string formula as the string. Numeric entries are not allowed and will return ERR.

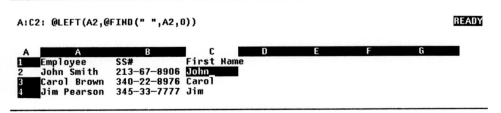

A:C2: @LEFT(A2,@FIND(" ",A2,0)) READY

	A	B	C	D	E	F	G
1	Employee	SS#	First Name				
2	John Smith	213-67-8906	John				
3	Carol Brown	340-22-8976	Carol				
4	Jim Pearson	345-33-7777	Jim				

Figure 7-80. Using @LEFT to extract first name

Use

This function can be used to determine the length of an entry you wish to manipulate, to verify input data, or to determine the length of a line. The following examples should clarify the results produced by @LENGTH:

Function	Length
@LENGTH("sales")	5
@LENGTH("profit "&"and loss")	15
@LENGTH(A2) where A2 contains abc	3

The worksheet in Figure 7-81 shows an example of the @LENGTH function used to determine the number of characters in names. The formula @LENGTH(A2) is copied down column C to return the length of all the entries in column A.

Note

This function is frequently used in combination with other string functions such as @MID, @RIGHT, @LEFT, and @FIND when restructuring label entries.

@LOWER

The @LOWER function converts strings to lowercase.

Format

@LOWER(*string*)

A:C2: @LENGTH(A2)   READY

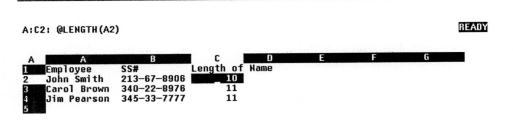

Figure 7-81.   Using @LENGTH to determine the length of an entry

Arguments

string   a group of characters that can be in any
                                  case, such as upper-, lower-, or mixed
                                  upper- and lowercase. The characters can
                                  be included in the function if they are
                                  enclosed in double quotation marks, or
                                  they can be placed in a cell and
                                  referenced. You can also use a string
                                  formula as the *string*. Numeric entries are
                                  not allowed and will return ERR.

Use

This function is valuable when data from several sources must be combined and data entry was not done in a consistent manner. @LOWER is
one of the functions that permit you to change the appearance of data
without reentering it. You can use it to place all data in lowercase
format.

As an example, entering @LOWER("THESE ARE CAPITALS")
returns "these are capitals". The worksheet in Figure 7-82 shows that
changing proper case is just as easy: @LOWER("This Is Proper Case")
returns "this is proper case".

Note

To use this function to change text data entered with incorrect capitalization, first enter the function in an empty area of the worksheet,

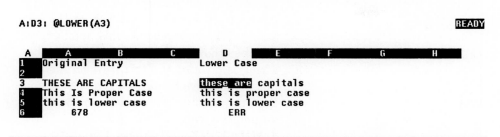

A:D3: @LOWER(A3)   `READY`

A	A	B	C	D	E	F	G	H
1	Original Entry			Lower Case				
2								
3	THESE ARE CAPITALS			these are capitals				
4	This Is Proper Case			this is proper case				
5	this is lower case			this is lower case				
6	678			ERR				

Figure 7-82.   Converting characters to lowercase with @LEFT

referencing the data to be corrected. You will need to restructure the data in a different location before copying it back, and you want to be sure you do not overlay important data in the process of doing so. After the formulas are entered, you can freeze the values in the cells with F2 (EDIT) followed by F9 (CALC). Then transfer them with /Move. Alternatively, you can use /Range Value to freeze the formulas as values and copy them all in one step. After verifying the accuracy of the data, you can erase the work area that originally contained the formula.

@MID

The @MID function extracts characters from the middle of a string when you specify the number of characters to extract and the starting location.

Format

@MID(*string,start number,number of characters*)

Arguments

string   a group of characters that can be included in the function (if they are enclosed in double quotation marks) or placed in a cell and referenced. You can also use a string formula as the string. Numeric entries are not allowed and will return ERR.

start number	a number representing the first character position you wish to extract from the string. When you choose this number, remember that the leftmost position in the string is position 0. *Start number* should not be negative. If *start number* is greater than the number of positions in the string, an empty string will be returned. @MID("ABC",0,1) returns 1 character from the 0 position in the string: "A".
number of characters	a number representing the number of characters you wish to extract from the string. This number can be stored in a cell and referenced by the function through a cell address or range name. When this argument is 0, an empty string is the result. You can set this number at 512 if you do not know how many characters are in the string and you want to extract all of them.

Use

The @MID function can be used whenever you wish to extract a portion of a string. The function offers complete flexibility: you can start anywhere in the string and extract as few or as many characters as you wish. Examples are

@MID("abcdefghi",3,3) equals def
@MID("123"&"456",1,512) equals 23456

The worksheet in Figure 7-83 shows @MID used with @LENGTH and @FIND to reverse a name entry. The formula uses the location of the "," plus 2 to identify the beginning of the first name. The number of characters in the first name is the length of the entire entry less the location of the ",". This is concatenated with a space and the last name. The last name consists of the characters on the left up to the ",". Creating the correct formula may require a little trial and error if you

```
A:C2: @MID(A2,@FIND(",",A2,0)+2,@LENGTH(A2)-@FIND(",",A2,0))&" "&@LEFT(A2,@▓READY
```

```
  A     A         B        C        D        E        F        G        H
1   Name                 Reversed Name
2   Smith, John          John Smith
3   Taylor, Paul         Paul Taylor
4   Zimmer, Mary         Mary Zimmer
5
6
7   Formula in C2
8
9   @MID(A2,@FIND(",",A2,0)+2,@LENGTH(A2)-@FIND(",",A2,0))&" "&
10  @LEFT(A2,@FIND(",",A2,0))
```

Figure 7-83.   Reversing name entries with @MID and other string
functions

are not familiar with string functions, but once you have worked it out,
you can copy it down the column to reverse all the name entries.

Note

The @RIGHT and @LEFT functions are actually special versions of
@MID that extract from the right or left edge of a string, respectiv-
ely.When 0 is used for the start number, @MID is functionally equivalent to @LEFT, since it begins extracting with the leftmost character in
the string.

@MID can be used with @FIND to extract a search string. For
example, to extract Smith from John Smith you could use the formula
@MID(A10,@FIND(A1,A10,0),@LENGTH(A1))   where   A1   contains
Smith and A10 contains John Smith.

@N

The @N function returns the numeric value of a single cell.

Format

@N(*range*)

Arguments

range   a reference to a range, using either the
                                 cell addresses (for example, R2..U20) or a
                                 range name. Even though this function
                                 uses only the upper left cell of the range,
                                 the argument must still be in range for-
                                 mat, that is, A2..A2.

Use

The @N function returns the value of the upper left cell in a range. If
the cell contains a label, a 0 will be returned. The @N function is useful
in macro applications to examine data in a cell. It is also a quick way of
excluding label data from your calculations.

The following worksheet shows an example of @N. In this particular example, the range is a single cell.

@PROPER

The @PROPER function converts strings to proper case (a format
where the first letter of each word is capitalized).

Format

@PROPER(*string*)

Arguments

string   a group of characters that can be in upper-,
                                 lower-, or mixed upper- and lowercase.
                                 The characters can be included in the
                                 function (if they are enclosed in double
                                 quotation marks), or they can be placed in
                                 a cell and referenced. You can also use a
                                 string formula as the *string*.

Use

This function is valuable when data from several sources must be combined and data entry was not done in a consistent manner. @PROPER is one of the functions that permit you to change the appearance of data without reentering it. @PROPER(A2&" "&B3), where A2 contains JOBBARD MILLING COMPANY and B3 contains east dallas division, will return Jobbard Milling Company East Dallas Division. Every word in each string was converted to proper case (lowercase with initial capital). The worksheet in Figure 7-84 shows several additional conversions. Entries are made in column A, and @PROPER formulas are used to obtain the remainder of the display.

@REPEAT

The @REPEAT function is used to duplicate a character string a specified number of times.

Format

@REPEAT(*string,number of times*)

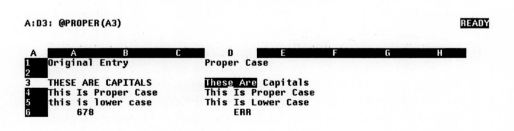

Figure 7-84.   Converting characters to proper case with @PROPER

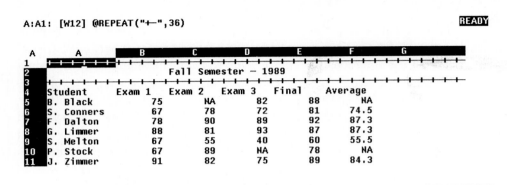

Figure 7-85.   Using @REPEAT to duplicate a label

Arguments

string	a series of characters enclosed in quotation marks or a reference to a cell containing a string. The string can be one character or many.
number of times	a numeric value indicating the number of times to repeat the string.

Use

The primary use for the @REPEAT function is to improve the appearance of a worksheet. @REPEAT can create dividing lines between a report's assumptions and the final result, for example, or between assumptions and the finished model. @REPEAT is in one sense similar to the backslash (\) character, since it repeats characters. It differs because \ is restricted to filling a single cell, whereas @REPEAT can extend across many worksheet cells.

Figure 7-85 provides an example of the @REPEAT function. In this example it is used to create dividing lines on a cumulative grade report.

The formula is placed in A1 as @REPEAT(" + − ",36). This means that + − will be repeated across the screen, since the screen will display 72 characters.

Note

The string returned from this function should not exceed 512 characters. The maximum number of times you can repeat an eight-character string is 64, for example.

@REPLACE

The @REPLACE function replaces characters in a string with other characters.

Format

@REPLACE(*original string,start location,# characters,new string*)

Arguments

original string	a series of characters enclosed in quotation marks or a reference to a cell containing a string. The string can be one character or many. It must specify the complete string entry you wish to work with.
start location	the position number in the original string where you want the replacement to begin. Remember that the first character in the original string is position 0. If *start location* is greater than the length of the *original string,* the new string is added at the end.
# characters	the number of characters to remove from the original string. When *# characters* equals 0, the *new string* is inserted without removal of any part of the *original string.* When *# characters* is the same as the number of characters in the *original string,* the entire string is replaced.

new string   a series of characters enclosed in quotation marks or a reference to a cell containing a string. The string can be one character or many. When *new string* is an empty string, that is, *""*, @REPLACE simply deletes characters from the *original string*.

Use

The @REPLACE function enables you to make changes to a string without retyping the original string. For instance, you can use this function to manipulate a part number into a warehouse location, or an account code into a department number. Sample uses include:

@REPLACE("Department 100",11,3,"200") equals Department 200
@REPLACE("Commissions for: ",17,0,"Mary Brown") equals
Commissions for: Mary Brown
@REPLACE("AX/1265",2,1," −") equals AX −1265
@REPLACE("AX/1265",0,7," −") equals −

The worksheet in Figure 7-86 shows a whole list of part numbers that were changed with the @REPLACE function.

Note

To use this function to change text data entered incorrectly, first enter the function in an empty area of the worksheet, referencing the data to be corrected. You will need to restructure the data in a different location before copying it back, and you will want to be sure you do not overlay important data in the process of doing so. After the formulas are

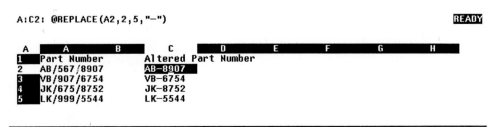

Figure 7-86. Using @REPLACE to revise a list

entered, you can freeze the values in the cells with F2 (EDIT) followed by F9 (CALC). You can then transfer them with /Move. Alternatively, you can use /Range Value to freeze the formulas as values and copy them all in one step. After verifying the accuracy of the data, you can erase the work area that originally contained the formula.

@RIGHT

The @RIGHT function allows you to extract a specified number of characters from the right side of a string.

Format

@RIGHT(*string,number of characters to extract*)

Arguments

string	a sequence of characters included in the function by enclosing them in double quotation marks, or by referencing a cell address or range name containing the characters.
number of characters to extract	a number representing the characters to be extracted from the string. If this number is greater than the number of characters in the *string,* the entire string will be extracted.

Use

The @RIGHT function lets you extract one or many characters from the right side of a string. It can be used alone or in combination with other string functions. Some examples of the function are

@RIGHT("Lotus 1-2-3",5) equals 1-2-3
@RIGHT("1:30:59",5) equals 30:59
@RIGHT("ABC COMPANY   ",8) equals Y with seven trailing spaces

The worksheet in Figure 7-87 shows the @RIGHT function coupled with @FIND and @LENGTH to extract the last name from the worksheet entries. C2 contains the pattern for column C formulas: @RIGHT(A2,@LENGTH(A2)−@FIND(" ",A2,0)−1). This formula finds the location of the blank space between first and last name and subtracts that number plus 1 from the length of the string. The result of this calculation is the number of characters to be extracted from the right side of the string.

@S

The @S function returns a value as a string.

Format

@S(*range*)

Arguments

range   a reference to a range using either cell addresses (such as R2..U20) or a range name. Even though this function uses only the upper left cell of the range, the argument must still be in range format (A2..A2).

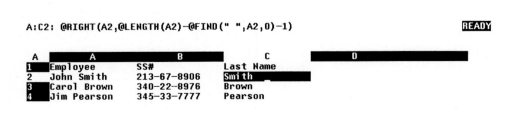

A:C2: @RIGHT(A2,@LENGTH(A2)−@FIND(" ",A2,0)−1)   READY

A	A	B	C	D
1	Employee	SS#	Last Name	
2	John Smith	213−67−8906	Smith	
3	Carol Brown	340−22−8976	Brown	
4	Jim Pearson	345−33−7777	Pearson	

Figure 7-87. The @RIGHT function working with @LENGTH and @FIND

Use

The @S function is used to return the value of the upper left cell in a range. If the cell contains a number, a blank cell is returned. This action can prevent the error condition that occurs if strings and numbers are mixed in one formula. If you have any doubt about the contents of a cell you are combining with a string, you can use @S, which will convert the contents of the cell to an empty string entry if it contains a number.

In the worksheet in Figure 7-88, @S(A3) equals SALES, @S(A4) equals COGS, and @S(B3) equals a blank. To correct potential errors, use @LENGTH(@S(B2)); this returns a 0, whereas @LENGTH(B2) returns ERR.

@STRING

The @STRING function converts numeric values to strings and allows you to specify the number of decimal places to be used for a string.

Format

@STRING(*number,number of decimal places*)

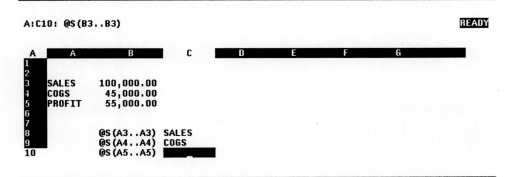

Figure 7-88.   Using @S to look for unwanted numerical entries

Arguments

number	a numeric value or reference to a numeric value
number of decimal places	the number of decimal places to be used when the string is created from the *number*. If the *number* is longer than the specified *number of places,* rounding will occur. If the *number* is shorter, zeros will be used for padding.

Use

The primary use of this function is to permit the combination of numeric values with strings in a string formula. If @STRING is not used to convert numbers first, ERR is returned by any such string formula. The @STRING function uses the Fixed format with the number of places you specify to create the resulting string. The @STRING function ignores formatting characters such as commas and dollar signs. Several examples of @STRING are

@STRING(1.6,0) equals the string 2
@STRING(12,4) equals the string 12.0000
@STRING(2.3E + 04,2) equals the string 23000.00

The worksheet in Figure 7-89 shows the @STRING function used in a string formula to obtain some numeric information and include it in the formula. Without the @STRING function, this numeric information could not have been combined with the string data. Although it may

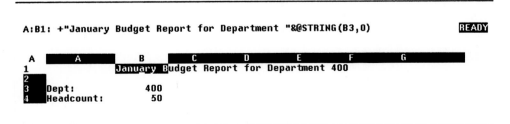

Figure 7-89.   Combining numbers and text with @STRING

appear easier to simply type the 400 in the heading, the string formula approach demonstrated in this worksheet allows a manager to set up templates for use by all departments in an organization, and minimizes the entries each department user has to make. It also eliminates the possibility that someone will forget to update the heading.

@TRIM

The @TRIM function allows you to strip away extraneous blanks from a string entry.

Format

@TRIM(*string*)

Arguments

string	a sequence of characters included in the function by enclosing them in double quotation marks or by referencing a cell address or range name containing the characters.

Use

This function is used to remove trailing, preceding, and multiple internal blanks from a string. It lets you clean up existing entries on a worksheet and establish a consistent format for data storage. @TRIM can be used with string formulas as well as strings. The examples that follow include both types of entries.

@TRIM(" Sales") equals Sales
@TRIM("January "&" Fuel Allowance") equals January Fuel Allowance.
Note that @TRIM retains one space between strings separated by an ampersand (&).

Note

This command can be used in conjunction with some of the long labels transferred from ASCII files. See Chapter 8, "Working with Files," for more information.

@UPPER

The @UPPER function will convert lowercase, propercase, and mixed upper- and lowercase character strings to all uppercase.

Format

@UPPER(*string*)

Arguments

string	a group of characters that can be in proper, lower-, or mixed upper- and lowercase. The characters can be included in the function (if they are enclosed in double quotation marks), or placed in a cell and referenced. You can also use a string formula as the *string*.

Use

This function is valuable when data from several sources must be combined and data entry was not done in a consistent manner. @UPPER is one of the functions that permit you to change the appearance of data without reentering it. @UPPER(A2&" "&B3), where A2 contains Jobbard Milling Company and B3 contains east dallas division, returns JOBBARD MILLING COMPANY EAST DALLAS DIVISION. All of every word in each string is converted to uppercase. The worksheet in Figure 7-90 shows several additional conversions. Entries are made in column A, and @UPPER formulas are used to obtain the remainder of the display.

@VALUE

The @VALUE function is designed to convert a string that looks like a number into an actual numeric value.

Format

@VALUE(*string*)

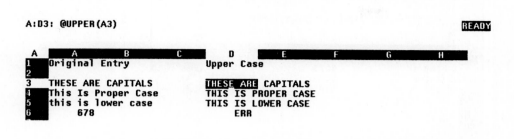

Figure 7-90.   Converting characters to uppercase with @UPPER

Arguments

string a sequence of characters included in the function by enclosing them in double quotation marks, or by referencing a cell address or range name containing the characters. The sequence of characters must look like a number. Acceptable examples are 345.674, 345.1E8, 7, and 7/8 (a fraction). If *string* references an empty string, 0 will be returned.

Use

This function converts strings that look like numbers into actual numeric values so they can be used in calculations. The function removes any leading or trailing blanks from the string. Here are a few examples:

@VALUE("   23.98") returns the number 23.98
@VALUE(Z10) returns 0 if Z10 is blank, and ERR if Z10 contains a label such as abc.

The worksheet in Figure 7-91 shows part numbers in column A that have the weight of the product as the last character in the part number. This last character can be extracted with a formula like @RIGHT(A2,1), but it cannot be used to calculate shipping costs, since a numeric value is

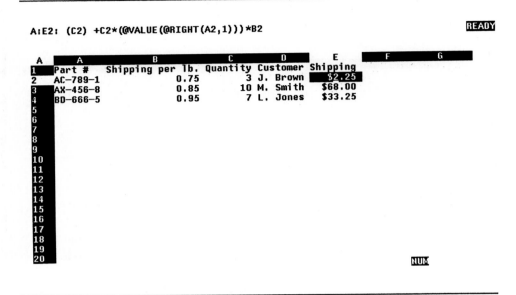

Figure 7-91. Converting characters to numbers with @VALUE

required. The use of @VALUE solves this problem, as shown in the formulas in column E. The formula for E2 is +C2*(@VALUE (@RIGHT(A2,1)))*B2, since the shipping cost for each unit ordered is stored in column B and is multiplied by the weight of the item.

Working with Files

The worksheets discussed so far have all been stored in part of your computer's random access memory (RAM). RAM offers the advantage of instant availability for information stored in it. Changes, additions, and deletions to information stored in RAM can be accomplished very quickly. The disadvantage of RAM storage is that it is very volatile. Losing the power to your computer for even a brief instant causes everything stored in RAM to be permanently lost.

A more permanent means of storage is clearly required and this normally is done with disk files. The 1-2-3 program itself is a file. That is why it is permanently available on your disk. If the program is lost from memory, you can restore it by reloading it from your disk.

This chapter will focus on the data files that contain information on the applications you have created on 1-2-3. You will learn how to save, retrieve, and delete files. You will also learn to combine files, and to perform other file management operations.

Naming and Using Files

1-2-3 uses disk files for the permanent storage of all information. These files can be maintained on either hard or floppy diskettes. They can be transferred from one disk to another by saving the worksheets to several disks with the /File Save command or by using operating system commands. Because 1-2-3 runs under DOS or OS/2, the conventions established by DOS and OS/2 for the naming of files must be followed. A comprehensive discussion of rules for filenames and file storage can be found in your DOS or OS/2 manual.

Filenames and File Types

The 1-2-3 program creates three types of data files: worksheet files, graph files, and print files. 1-2-3 automatically appends a suffix to each filename that allows you to distinguish one file type from another. In addition, 1-2-3 has many files of its own that are part of the program and its various features.

DOS imposes an eight-character limit on filenames, and a three-character limit on filename extensions. A period (.) is used to separate the filename from the extension.

A filename and extension can contain letters, numbers, and many symbols. 1-2-3 automatically changes lowercase characters in your filename entries to uppercase. Symbols are permitted only if the specific release of your operating system allows them. Release 3 of 1-2-3 accepts any LMBCS character as long as your operating system supports the use of the character. Although 1-2-3 allows spaces in the filename if the operating system allows it, many operating systems such as DOS prohibit spaces in filenames. An underscore (_) is a better way to separate filenames into words. Some examples of valid filenames are SALES, REGION _ 1, EMPLOYEE, and SALES _ 85.

If your operating system only accepts a maximum of eight characters for a filename, and you enter a filename longer than that, 1-2-3 truncates the filename after the eighth character. Thus, SALES _ REGION _ 1 becomes SALES _ RE, which would be indistinguishable from truncated versions of SALES _ REGION _ 2, SALES _ REGION _ 3, and other filenames with the same characters in the first eight positions.

1-2-3 distinguishes file types by the extension added to the file. The box called "1-2-3 File Types" lists all the extensions for data files and special file types used by 1-2-3. The three most common types of files and their extensions are as follows:

File Type	Extension
Worksheet	.WK3 (Release 3)
	.WK1 (Release 2)
	.WKS (Release 1A)
Print	.PRN (unencoded)
	.ENC (encoded)
Graph	.CGM
	.PIC

You also have the option of supplying your own extension for any file type. If you supply this extension when you create a file, you must supply it every time you access that file. If you use 1-2-3's default extensions, the package will supply them for you at all times. The only exception to this rule is the use of external file links in 1-2-3. In this situation you will also need to supply the filename extension and the special < < > > symbols that enclose the filename.

1-2-3 File Types

File Type	Extension
Worksheet	.WK3 (Release 3) .WK1 (Release 2) .WKS (Release 1A) .WR1 (Symphony 1.1, 1.2, or 2.0) .WRK (Symphony)
Print	.PRN
Encoded	.ENC
Graph	.PIC,.CGM
Backup	.BAK
Fonts for Graphics	.LRF
Temporary	.TMP
Configuration	.CNF
Programs	.EXE (Release 3)
Program Messages	.RI
Help	.HLP
Drivers	.FBD (graphic image files) .LBD (communications port) .PBD (printers) .VBD (video monitors) .DDF (driver description files) .DLD (Dynamic Link Drivers—the main drivers) .LCF (Lotus configuration file containing a list of the drivers installed)
DOS	.BAT
Driver configuration file	.DCF
Miscellaneous files	.DLL (Dynamic link libraries for OS/2) .XTB (Part of Translate utility) .SCR (Part of Install program) .BCF (Identities database drivers)

Subdirectories

On a hard disk system, you can create subdirectories for the storage of files. Subdirectories create logical rather than physical divisions for the hard disk, and manage the files within a particular directory so it is easy to find related files. The concept of subdirectories is similar to the filing system you may have developed to manage the large number of memos and other paper information you probably receive. Just as you would not throw all this paper in one desk drawer and expect to find something in it with ease, you do not want to randomly place all your files on the hard disk without the organization structure that subdirectories provide.

Using subdirectories lessens the time required for file retrieval because 1-2-3 does not have to search the directory for the entire hard disk to determine the file's location. Since Release 3 of 1-2-3 requires a hard disk, you are probably already using subdirectories for your other applications.

The first directory on your hard disk is automatic and is called the Root directory. You can store files in the Root directory, or you can create subdirectories immediately beneath it. The latter approach is better since it places all your files within the control of a subdirectory. Your operating system provides a command like MD or MKDIR to create new directories at any level within the directory structure.

Within a directory, each filename and extension combination must be unique. You may have two files named BUDGET on the disk, as long as they have different filename extensions. You can use the same filename on a hard disk more than once as long as the files are in different subdirectories. For example, you can have the filename BUDGET.WK3 in the subdirectory ACCT and the subdirectory FIN. The contents of these files may be the same or different. Even if the files originally contain the same data, they are two separate physical files, and an update to one does not affect the other file.

If you are using subdirectories, 1-2-3 must know the drive and the pathname in order to find a file. The drive designation is the drive letter followed by a colon; for example, A:, B:, or C:. The pathname tells 1-2-3 what directory the file is in. Higher level directories are always listed first. \SALES indicates that the file is in the first-level directory SALES, whereas \SALES\REGION\ONE indicates that the file is several levels down from the top directory in a subdirectory called ONE. If you are not familiar with the ins and outs of subdirectories, review your DOS manual for more information on this subject.

The File Menu Options

File is one of the options on 1-2-3's main menu. Most of the commands that manipulate files are options on the File submenu, which is shown in the following illustration. Let's look at each of these menu options in detail.

```
A:A1:                                                               MENU
Retrieve  Save  Combine  Xtract  Erase  List  Import  Dir  New  Open  Admin
Replace the current file with a file from disk
```

Saving a File to Disk

Any worksheet model in RAM must be saved to a disk file if it is to be available in later 1-2-3 sessions. Use the /File Save option to place a copy of the current worksheet on your disk. You will use this command to save a new worksheet, and to save an updated, existing worksheet.

If the current worksheet file has not been saved before, when you invoke /File Save, 1-2-3 will display a default filename. The default filename is FILE0001 or the next highest available default file number. You can accept this filename, or enter a new name in response to 1-2-3's prompt, and press ENTER.

If the file has already been saved in the current session, or if it is a file that you retrieved from disk, 1-2-3 will suggest that it be saved again under the same name. If you agree, press ENTER. When prompted to confirm this decision, select Replace if you want the current worksheet to replace the existing file. If you want to create a backup copy of the worksheet, select Backup to create a backup with a .BAK extension. If you decide not to save the file, select Cancel to return to READY mode.

Tip: Create a Backup version to retain the original and revised versions of a worksheet. When you use /File Save Backup, 1-2-3 saves the original file with the extension .BAK, and saves the current version with the extension .WK3—providing access to both versions of the worksheet.

1-2-3 automatically appends .WK3 to the filename. This assumes that the extension set by the /Worksheet Global Default Ext Save command is .WK3. You can choose any file suffix you wish, but you must then be prepared to reenter this suffix every time you access the file. For example, you can add a .WK1 extension if you want the file translated to a Release 2 format.

Whether you are saving a new or updated file, you may choose to name it with an existing filename. At the /File Save name prompt, press ESC. 1-2-3 will then provide a file list like the following:

```
A:A1:
Enter name of file to save: C:\123R3\*.WK3                          FILES
BASS.WK3              BUDGET.WK3        B.WK3            C.WK3
```

Point to the name you want, and press ENTER.

Once you select a name, 1-2-3 displays the following prompt:

```
A:A1:
Cancel  Replace  Backup                                            MENU
Cancel command; leave existing file on disk intact
```

This prompt asks if you wish to cancel the request, replace the file on the disk with the current contents of memory, or back up the original worksheet first before replacing the file on the disk with the current contents of memory. This is the same prompt that appears when you are saving an updated file using the same filename. This prompt is needed because each disk or subdirectory can have only one file with a particular name. When you reuse a name, only the last data you saved will be in the file when you attempt to retrieve it.

In Release 3 you can save a file to a different drive or directory by specifying the drive and directory designation along with the filename, for example, C:\SALES\REGION\FILE1. If you need to add or delete characters in the current filename and path specification, use the LEFT and RIGHT ARROW to move around.

1-2-3 makes it so easy to save files that you will want to save frequently. If your system goes down, you can then retrieve the most recently saved version of the file; it is easier to reconstruct what was lost if it has not been too long since the last save.

Retrieving a File from Disk

The /File Retrieve command permits you to retrieve a file from your disk. When 1-2-3 loads a worksheet file into RAM memory, it first erases the information currently in RAM memory. If you have not saved that information on disk, there is no way to bring it back.

When you enter this command, 1-2-3 searches the current disk or subdirectory and lists all the files with a .WK3 (Release 3), .WK1 (Release 2) or .WKS (Release 1A) suffix. As shown here, 1-2-3 displays up to four names across the third line of the control panel.

```
A:A1:                                                              FILES
Enter name of file to retrieve: C:\123R3\*.WK*
A.WK1               A.WK3          BASS.WK3          BUDGET.WK3
```

You can use the RIGHT ARROW key to move across the display, scrolling across to additional filenames until you finally cycle through all of them and move back to the beginning of the subdirectory. Using the LEFT ARROW key moves you back toward the beginning of the list.

Other options available with the pointer control keys are as follows:

HOME	Moves the pointer or highlight to the beginning of the file list
END	Moves the pointer or highlight to the end of the file list
DOWN	Presents the next four options in the file list
UP	Presents the previous four options from the file list

If you wish to see all the file names at once, press F3 (NAME). You will see a list like the one in Figure 8-1. Moving your pointer to a particular filename causes the control panel to display the date and time that file

```
A:A1:                                                                    FILES
Enter name of file to retrieve: C:\DISK2\*.WK*
                FIG10_10.WK1    01-Jan-80      02:26 AM        3054
FG12_2&3.WK1        FG12_8&9.WK1        FIG10_10.WK1        FIG10_13.WK1
FIG10_14.WK1        FIG10_15.WK1        FIG10_16.WK1        FIG10_17.WK1
FIG10_18.WK1        FIG10_19.WK1        FIG10_1.WK1         FIG10_2.WK1
FIG10_3.WK1         FIG10_4.WK1         FIG10_5.WK1         FIG10_6.WK1
FIG10_7.WK1         FIG10_8.WK1         FIG10_9.WK1         FIG11_10.WK1
FIG11_12.WK1        FIG11_14.WK1        FIG11_15.WK1        FIG11_16.WK1
FIG11_2.WK1         FIG11_3.WK1         FIG11_5.WK1         FIG11_8.WK1
FIG12_10.WK1        FIG12_11.WK1        FIG12_13.WK1        FIG12_4.WK1
FIG12_6.WK1         FIG12_7.WK1         FIG13_8.WK1         FIG7_13.WK3
FIG7_14.WK3         FIG7_15.WK3         FIG7_16.WK3         FIG7_17.WK3
FIG7_18.WK3         FIG7_19.WK3         FIG7_1.WK3          FIG7_25.WK3
FIG7_30.WK1         FIG7_31.WK1         FIG7_32.WK1         FIG7_33.WK1
FIG7_34.WK1         FIG7_35.WK1         FIG7_36.WK1         FIG7_38.WK1
FIG7_39.WK1         FIG7_3.WK1          FIG7_41.WK3         FIG7_42.WK3
FIG7_43.WK3         FIG7_44.WK3         FIG7_45.WK3         FIG7_46.WK3
FIG7_47.WK3         FIG7_48.WK3         FIG7_49.WK3         FIG7_4.WK1
FIG7_50.WK3         FIG7_51.WK3         FIG7_52.WK3         FIG7_53.WK3
FIG7_54.WK3         FIG7_55.WK3         FIG7_56.WK3         FIG7_57.WK3
FIG7_58.WK3         FIG7_59.WK3         FIG7_5.WK1          FIG7_60.WK3
FIG7_61.WK3         FIG7_62.WK3         FIG7_63.WK3         FIG7_64.WK3
FIG7_65.WK3         FIG7_66.WK3         FIG7_67.WK3         FIG7_68.WK3
FILE0001.WK3
```

Figure 8-1.   Complete filename display generated with F3 (NAME)

was saved, and its size. You can choose a file by pressing ENTER, or cancel the full display by pressing F3 (NAME) a second time.

To retrieve a file in another directory, type the complete pathname for the file. Pressing ESC twice removes the displayed pathname specification. You can also retrieve a file with an extension other than .WK3 by specifying the extension along with the filename.

Using Passwords with Files

Passwords are a form of protection for your files. They were added in Release 2 to offer a measure of protection for the worksheet. When they are in effect, an operator cannot retrieve a file without first supplying the correct password.

Passwords are added to a file when it is saved. If you want to specify a password, after entering the filename press SPACEBAR and type a **p** before pressing ENTER.

```
A:A1:                                                                    EDIT
Enter name of file to save: C:\123R3\newfile p_
```

1-2-3 then prompts for the password, which can be up to 15 characters. When you type in the password, it is not displayed; each character is instead represented by an asterisk in the control panel, like this:

```
A:A1:                                                          EDIT
Enter password: ***************_
```

Your use of upper- and lowercase is recorded, and must be correctly duplicated when you access the file later. When you press ENTER, you will be prompted to enter the password again for verification. If the passwords entered on both occasions are not an exact match, 1-2-3 provides an error message to that effect, as shown here:

```
Passwords don't match — Press HELP (F1)
```

The second prompt for the password also offers a way to stop the addition of the password: simply press ESC. Once you have pressed ENTER for the final time, the password is added to the disk, and you will need to use it when you retrieve the file.

To access a file with a password, enter the command you wish to use in working with the file, such as /**File Retrieve**. 1-2-3 then generates a prompt for the password and waits for you to enter it. If you cannot reproduce the password exactly as it was originally entered, including the correct use of upper- and lowercase, 1-2-3 will not retrieve the file and will display an error message.

To change the password of a password protected file, save the file again. When 1-2-3 displays the filename followed by "[PASSWORD PROTECTED]", press the BACKSPACE key, then the SPACEBAR, and type a **p**. 1-2-3 will prompt you twice, for a new password, just as if you were adding a new password to a new file.

To remove the password of a password protected file, save the file again. When 1-2-3 displays the filename followed by "[PASSWORD PROTECTED]", press the BACKSPACE key and then ENTER.

Combining Information from Two Files

The /File Combine options allow you to bring information from other worksheet files into your current worksheet. With this capability you can produce budget consolidations, or build a new worksheet using components of several existing worksheet files. Unlike /File Retrieve, the Combine options do not erase what is in memory.

The three Combine options are Copy, Add, and Subtract. All three depend on the location of the cell pointer in the current worksheet for the actions they take. The Combine Copy option was essential in earlier releases because they did not support multiple-sheet files, or sheets referenced with external links. Although you can still use the /File Combine Copy command for many applications in Release 3, you will want to consider the potential of links and multiple-sheet files as you work with applications that use several types of data. For example, the /File Combine Add and Subtract options automatically perform arithmetic operations between the contents of the current file and the external file—reference without the need for entering formulas.

Copying Information from a File to a Worksheet

The /File Combine Copy command allows you to replace the contents of current worksheet cells with the contents of cells in a disk file. The replacement begins at the cell pointer location in the current worksheet, and the extent of the replacement will depend on how many cells are being copied from the disk. Values, labels, and formulas can all be copied from the file on disk.

You have two options for determining the extent of the replacement. First, you can bring in an entire file. This operation takes each cell in the file that contains a value, label, or formula, and replaces an appropriate number of cells in the current worksheet to accommodate the imported data. The location of the cell(s) replaced is determined by the location of the cell pointer at the time of the Combine Copy request, and by the contents of the file to be incorporated. Displacement of cells in the current file will match the dimensions of the replacement data, with the base point being the cell pointer location.

Tip: When using /File Combine in Release 3, make sure you have sufficient sheets in the current file for a three-dimensional range to be incorporated. Release 3 will support combining three-dimensional ranges, but the current worksheet must contain a sufficient number of sheets to support the Combine operation.

Suppose you have a file named HEADING that is stored on disk and looks like this:

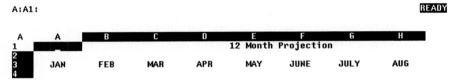

Your current worksheet file looks like Figure 8-2. Position your cell pointer in B1 and enter **/File Combine Copy**. Specify the HEADING filename and choose the Enter-File option. The results should look like Figure 8-3. The /File Combine Copy command will overwrite the existing contents of cells starting at B1.

Tip: If you only need to copy data once, and do not need to update the copy from the external file, use /File Combine, or /Copy with external file references. If you want to refresh the copied data, use a formula that contains external references. You can then update the links at any time with /File Admin Link-Refresh.

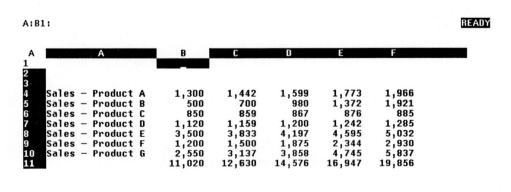

Figure 8-2.   Worksheet without heading entries at the top

A:B1:   READY

A	A	B	C	D	E	F
1						12 Month Projecti
2						
3		JAN	FEB	MAR	APR	MAY
4	Sales — Product A	1,300	1,442	1,599	1,773	1,966
5	Sales — Product B	500	700	980	1,372	1,921
6	Sales — Product C	850	859	867	876	885
7	Sales — Product D	1,120	1,159	1,200	1,242	1,285
8	Sales — Product E	3,500	3,833	4,197	4,595	5,032
9	Sales — Product F	1,200	1,500	1,875	2,344	2,930
10	Sales — Product G	2,550	3,137	3,858	4,745	5,837
11		11,020	12,630	14,576	16,947	19,856

Figure 8-3.   Heading entries added with /File Combine Copy

If you do not need to copy an entire file, and if the disk file has
named ranges, you can use /File Combine Copy's second option, Named-
Range. This option will copy only the range of values that you specify.
For example, suppose the highlighted range of cells named 88_TOT, as
shown in Figure 8-4 is saved in a worksheet file called 88_BUD. You
want to copy 88_TOT to the column headed 88 Sales on the worksheet
shown in Figure 8-5. Place the cell pointer in B4 of 88_BUD and invoke
/File Combine Copy. Then select Named-Range and enter 88_**TOT**,
followed by the file name, 88_**BUD.** The results should look like Figure
8-6.

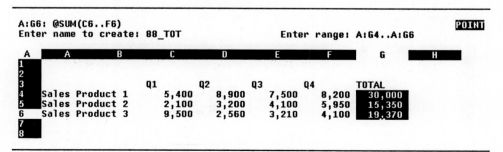

A:G6: @SUM(C6..F6)   POINT
Enter name to create: 88_TOT   Enter range: A:G4..A:G6

A	A	B	C	D	E	F	G	H
1								
2								
3			Q1	Q2	Q3	Q4	TOTAL	
4	Sales Product 1		5,400	8,900	7,500	8,200	30,000	
5	Sales Product 2		2,100	3,200	4,100	5,950	15,350	
6	Sales Product 3		9,500	2,560	3,210	4,100	19,370	
7								
8								

Figure 8-4.   A range named 88_TOT

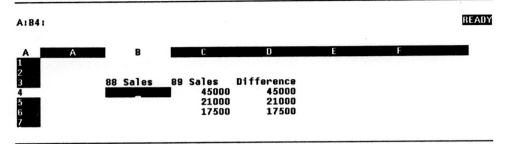

Figure 8-5.   Worksheet where the totals in the named range are needed

Tip: Use range names with the /File Combine command, and name the ranges in the file you are combining. Range names are easier to remember. Also, if you give the same name to all the range names that you are combining, you only have to specify the filename each time you perform the /File Combine command.

Adding Information from a File to a Worksheet

The /File Combine Add command lets you add the values of cells in a disk file to corresponding cells in the current worksheet. The addition begins at the cell pointer location in the current worksheet and the extent of the addition depends on the arrangement of cells added from the disk. Only numeric values are involved in the addition process. Labels and formulas are ignored, and the label and formula entries in

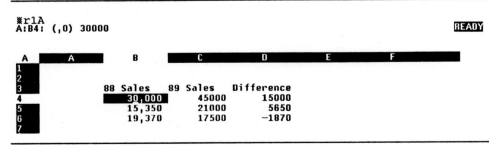

Figure 8-6.   Adding the named range to the existing worksheet with /File Combine Copy

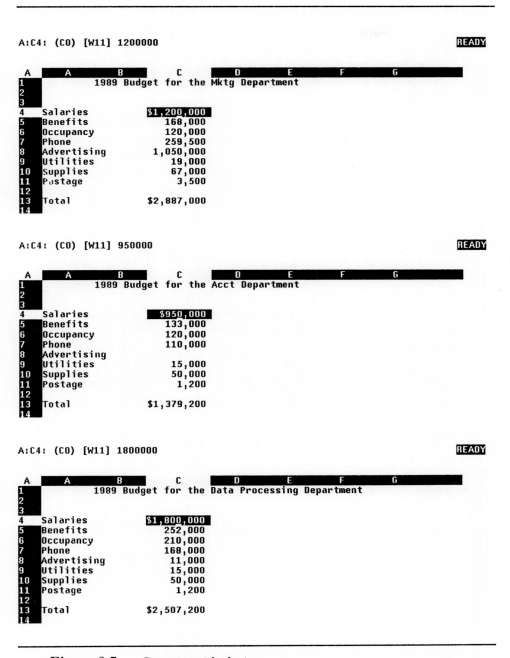

A:C4: (CO) [W11] 1200000   READY

```
A        A         B          C           D        E        F        G
1                    1989 Budget for the Mktg Department
2
3
4     Salaries           $1,200,000
5     Benefits              168,000
6     Occupancy             120,000
7     Phone                 259,500
8     Advertising         1,050,000
9     Utilities              19,000
10    Supplies               67,000
11    Postage                 3,500
12
13    Total              $2,887,000
14
```

A:C4: (CO) [W11] 950000   READY

```
A        A         B          C           D        E        F        G
1                    1989 Budget for the Acct Department
2
3
4     Salaries             $950,000
5     Benefits              133,000
6     Occupancy             120,000
7     Phone                 110,000
8     Advertising
9     Utilities              15,000
10    Supplies               50,000
11    Postage                 1,200
12
13    Total              $1,379,200
14
```

A:C4: (CO) [W11] 1800000   READY

```
A        A         B          C           D        E        F        G
1                    1989 Budget for the Data Processing Department
2
3
4     Salaries           $1,800,000
5     Benefits              252,000
6     Occupancy             210,000
7     Phone                 168,000
8     Advertising            11,000
9     Utilities              15,000
10    Supplies               50,000
11    Postage                 1,200
12
13    Total              $2,507,200
14
```

Figure 8-7.   Department budgets

the current worksheet are retained for those cells. Unlike the Copy option, neither /File Combine Add nor /File Combine Subtract overlays the contents of existing worksheet cells.

You have two options for determining the extent of the addition. First, you can choose Entire-File. This operation will add each cell in the disk file that contains a value, to the appropriate cell in the current worksheet. The location of the cells to which the disk file values are added is determined by the location of the cell pointer at the time of the Combine Add request, and by the amount of the displacement (that is, the location of the cell in relation to the beginning of the file) of the particular cell within the file. The same displacement is used to determine the cells that receive the added data, with the base point being the cell pointer location.

The second option is to choose Named/Specified-Range. In this case, only the cells in the named range will be added. This will begin at the location of the cell pointer in the worksheet.

/File Combine Add provides one solution for budget consolidations. If you have files containing individual department or subsidiary budgets, the /File Combine Add command permits you to add all the figures into one consolidated budget. Figure 8-7 shows a portion of the budgets for each department in a company. Notice that the format for all three is identical: this is required if you want to Combine Add entire files. Add the three files one by one to the Total Budget worksheet (Figure 8-8).

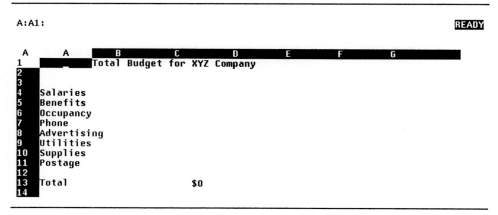

Figure 8-8. Total budget worksheet

Since the entire file is being added in each case, place your cell pointer in A1 before invoking the /File Combine Add command. The final results are shown in Figure 8-9.

Subtracting Information in a File from a Worksheet

The /File Combine Subtract command allows you to subtract the values of cells in a disk file from corresponding cells in the current worksheet. The subtraction begins at the cell pointer location in the current worksheet, and the extent of the subtraction depends on the arrangement of cells from the disk that are being subtracted from the worksheet cells. Only numeric values are involved in the subtraction process. Labels and formulas are ignored, and the label and formula entries in the current worksheet are retained for those cells. /File Combine Subtract does not overlay the contents of existing cells.

You have two options for determining the extent of the subtraction. First, you can choose Entire-File. This operation will subtract each cell in the disk file that contains a value from the appropriate cell in the current worksheet. The location of the cells from which the disk file values are subtracted is determined by the location of the cell pointer at the time of the Combine Subtract request, and by the amount of the displacement of the particular cell within the file. The same displacement will be used to determine the cells that receive the subtracted data

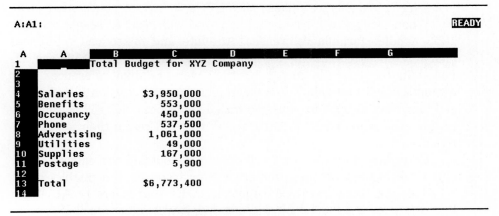

Figure 8-9.   Result of /File Combine Add

with the base point being the cell pointer location. If you choose Named-/Specified-Range, only the cells in the named range will be subtracted. This will begin at the location of the cell pointer in the worksheet.

The subtraction feature is useful after you have completed file consolidation with the /File Combine Add command. /File Combine Subtract allows you to see the effect of taking the budget figures for one department or subsidiary away from the total, thereby simulating the effect of closing it.

Saving Part of a Worksheet

The /File Xtract command permits you to save part of a worksheet. The specified section of the worksheet is saved as a .WK3 or .WK1 file, depending on the extension you provide. This feature is used for saving part of a worksheet file as a 1-2-3 Release 2.01 or 3.0 worksheet. It also lets you save sections of a worksheet for use in constructing new models, or when you have a file that is too large to save on one disk and you need to split it into more than one file. Settings established for the current worksheet are saved in the new file.

Worksheet sections are saved as either Formulas or Values. If you choose Value, 1-2-3 saves the current values of the selected cells. If you choose Formulas, 1-2-3 saves formulas as they were entered, but not the value(s) referenced by the formulas unless they are in the range selected. When labels are extracted, the result will be the same whether you select Formulas or Values, since labels do not reference other cells.

When using the Formulas option, you will need to remember how 1-2-3 handles formula references. Absolute and mixed cell references (cell references containing $s, such as A$2, $A2, or $A:$A$2) are adjusted in the new file just as if they were relative references. For example, a cell that refers to a value four rows away will still refer to a cell four rows away. Absolute and mixed references will still contain the $s after the adjustment. Relative references will retain their same relative directions.

Extracting formulas that reference cells outside the extract range offers the biggest potential for error. For instance, you might extract E1..H12, and there might be a formula in E2 that refers to A1. When this reference is adjusted for the new file, it will refer to cell IS1, since the reference will be computed from A1 of the new worksheet. This cell will therefore not contain what you expected. Similar problems can result from combining extracted formulas with an existing worksheet by using the /Copy command: some of the formulas may reference inappropriate cells in the new worksheet and thereby cause errors.

When using the Values option, only calculated results and labels will be retained in the new file. All formulas will be replaced by the results of the formula calculations.

The procedure for using either option is to enter /**File Xtract** and choose either Formulas or Values. You will be prompted for the filename to use for storage; either type a name or choose one from the list of worksheet files on the disk. If you provide a .WK1 extension, 1-2-3 will save the file in a Release 2 format. You can also make the extracted file password protected by pressing the SPACEBAR after you name the file and typing a **p**. Then you must provide a password, as instructed for password protection with the /File Save command. Next 1-2-3 prompts you to supply the range of cells to extract, by highlighting or typing the address, or supplying a defined range name.

If you choose an existing file name for the extracted file, you must confirm your choice with Replace or Backup. The Replace option erases the original file, and the Backup option renames the original file before storing the extracted data under the specified filename. The other option, Cancel, returns you to READY mode without saving the extract file.

Figure 8-10 shows a worksheet that contains formulas in column E. Suppose you extract the entries in column E and save them as Values. You then place this extract in another worksheet with /File Combine Copy. The result is shown in Figure 8-11, where the formula entries from the previous worksheet appear as calculated values. If you did this

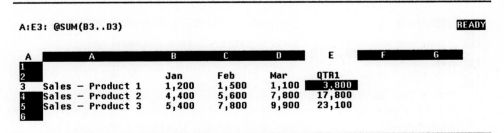

Figure 8-10.   Worksheet containing formulas

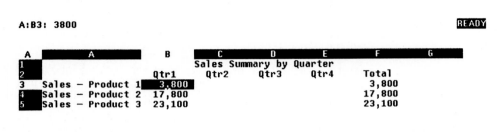

Figure 8-11.   Result of /File Combine Copy with values produced by /File Xtract

again with /Xtract Formulas, you would obtain the results shown in Figure 8-12, since extracted formulas are copied into a new location without the references they used in the original worksheet. Although the results look the same, this is a dangerous situation. Note that the formula in B3 now reads @SUM(IU3..A3); the formula was adjusted, but retains the relative references of the old worksheet.

Erasing Files from the Disk

From time to time you will have files that you no longer require. You can remove them from your disk with the DEL command under DOS, or you can eliminate them from within 1-2-3 with /File Erase. The advantage of /File Erase is that you are still in 1-2-3, so you can retrieve a file and look at it to make sure that you want to delete it.

Figure 8-12.   Result of /File Combine Copy with formulas produced by /File Xtract

The /File Erase command requires first that you specify the type of file you wish to erase. Choose from Worksheet, Print, Graph, or Other, and 1-2-3 then lists all the files of that type on the disk or in the current directory. 1-2-3 also lists the subdirectory names (if any) for the current directory. You can then change directories if you wish.

If you choose Worksheet, all .WK3, .WKS, and .WK1 filenames will be displayed. Select Print to see all files with a .PRN suffix. Graph will display files with the appropriate extension set by the /Worksheet Global Default Graph command. Other will cause 1-2-3 to display all the file-names on the current disk or in the current directory. To change the extension, press F2 (EDIT) and enter the extension of the files you want to see. With F3 (NAME), you can switch between listing the filenames in a single line or using the whole screen.

After selecting the type of file, pick a filename from the display or enter a name yourself. Once the name is entered, 1-2-3 asks you to confirm your choice by responding with Yes. If you elect not to proceed, select No at the confirmation prompt.

The /File Erase command offers wildcard features, just as DOS does. A ? can replace any single character in the filename, and an asterisk (*) specifies that any characters will be accepted from that point to the end of the filename. For instance, J?N would match with JAN, JUN, JON, JEN, and so on. J* would match with all of these options, as well as names like JUNE, JANUARY, JOLLY, and JOINT.

Determining What Files Are on Your Disk

As your list of worksheet models and other 1-2-3 files grows longer, you may have trouble remembering all the files you have on a disk. You can always use the DOS DIR command to see a list of them, but you also have the option of using /File List from the 1-2-3 menu. Release 3 has a new feature which places the file list on a worksheet.

Temporarily Listing Files

1-2-3's /File List command lists files on the screen and displays additional information about the highlighted filename. When you enter /File List, you are first presented with a menu of file type options. Choose from Worksheet, Print, Graph, Other, Active, or Linked, and 1-2-3 lists all the files of that type on the disk or in the current directory. 1-2-3 also lists the subdirectory names (if any) for the current directory. You can then use the cell pointer to change directories if you wish.

If you choose Worksheet, all .WK3, .WKS, and .WK1 filenames will be displayed, as shown in Figure 8-13. Select Print for all .PRN files. Graph displays files with the appropriate extension set by the /Worksheet Global Default Graph command. Choose Other to see all the filenames on the current disk or in the current directory. To change the extension, press F2 (EDIT) and enter the extension of the files you want to see.

Release 3 has a new option—Active—which lists all the worksheet files currently open. Another option new to Release 3 is Linked, which lists the files for which there are formula references in the current worksheet. Regardless of the file type selected, pointing to a filename in the list will display its size and the date and time it was last saved to disk. In addition, the Active option displays the number of worksheets in the file; the flag MOD or UNMOD indicating whether the file has been

```
A:A1:                                                                    FILES
Enter names of files to list: C:\123FILES\*.WK*
            1ST_QTR.WK3      10-May-89        06:03 PM       909
1ST_QTR.WK3          1ST_QTR.WKS     7_11.WK3            7_11.WKS
7_12.WK3             7_9.WK3         BUDGET.WK3          COMM.WK1
DEPREC.WK1           EMPLOYEE.WK1    EMPLOY.WK3          FC029A.WK3
FC5_1.WK3            FC6_18.WK3      FC6_4B.WK3          FC7XXX.WK3
FIG10_7.WK3          FIG10_E.WK3     FIG11_1.WK3         FIG11_2.WK1
FIG11_2.WK3          FIG11_3.WK3     FIG11_4.WK3         FIG11_5.WK1
FIG12_1.WK1          FIG12_1.WK3     FIG12_2.WK1         FIG12_2.WK3
FIG12_7.WK3          FIG12_8.WK3     FIG13_14.WK3        FIG13_2.WK3
FIG13_3.WK3          FIG13_4.WK3     FIG1_10.WK3         FIG1_11.WK3
FIG1_20.WK3          FIG1_8.WK3      FIG2_1.WK3          FIG2_2.WK3
FIG2_3.WK3           FIG2_4.WK3      FIG2_5.WK3          FIG2_6.WK3
FIG2_7.WK3           FIG2_8.WK3      FIG2_9.WK3          FIG2_X.WK3
FIG3_10.WK3          FIG3_11.WK3     FIG3_13.WK3         FIG3_2.WK3
FIG3_4.WK3           FIG3_5.WK3      FIG3_6.WK3          FIG3_8.WK3
FIG5_18.WK3          FIG9_4.WK1      FNC11_1.WK3         FNC11_2.WK3
FNC11_3.WK3          HOUR.WK1        IFKEY.WK3           ILL10.WK3
ILL10_10.WK3         ILL10_5.WK3     ILL10_6.WK3         ILL10_7.WK3
ILL10_8.WK3          ILL10_9.WK3     ILL11_1.WK3         ILL11_2.WK3
ILL11_3.WK3          ILL12_1.WK3     ILL12_2.WK3         ILL12_3.WK1
ILL12_3.WK3          ILL12_4.WK1     ILL12_4.WK3         ILL2_1.WK3
ILL2_2.WK3           ILL2_3.WK3      ILL2_4.WK3          ILL2_5.WK3
16-May-89 02:34 PM
```

Figure 8-13.   List of all the worksheet files on a disk

modified or not; and the flag RO if the file is a read-only file in a network environment. The Linked option also includes the pathname of the linked files.

Listing Files on a Worksheet

1-2-3's /File Admin Table command creates a table in the worksheet containing a list of files and related information. When you enter /**File Admin Table,** you are presented with a menu of file type options. Choose from Worksheet, Print, Graph, Other, Active, or Linked. Then 1-2-3 displays the following prompt:

```
A:A1:                                                          EDIT
Enter current directory: C:\123R3\*.WK?_
```

By editing the pathname, directory, and filename indicator in this prompt, you can determine which files 1-2-3 will include in the table. The selected directory can include the ? and * wildcard characters. For example, if you want all worksheet files that begin with a P, change the prompt to **C:\123R3\P*.WK*.**

If you choose Worksheet, the table includes all .WK3, .WKS, and .WK1 filenames. With Print, the table includes .PRN files. Graph includes files with the extension set by the /Worksheet Global Default Graph command. Other will include all the filenames on the current disk or in the current directory.

Once you select the type of files you want to list, 1-2-3 prompts for the location of the table. Either highlight the cell, or type the cell address or range where you want to place the upper left corner of the table. The table will contain as many rows as are needed by the files to be listed, and four to seven columns depending upon the file type selected. The table will write over the worksheet's current contents, so be sure to select an area where the table has plenty of room.

Regardless of the file type selected, the table lists the filenames, sizes, and the date and time last saved to disk. The Active option's table has three additional columns. These contain the number of worksheets in the file, a 1 or 0 indicating whether the file has changed since it became active, and a 1 if the user can modify the worksheet. The table for the Linked option includes the pathname of files linked with the filenames listed. Figure 8-14 shows a table created with the /File Admin Table Active command.

Adding Text Files to the Worksheet

The /File Import command allows you to transfer to your worksheet the data from a word processing program or other package that generates standard ASCII text input. You must be sure that the word processor does not include special characters in the file. (Most word processors have an option to eliminate special characters from the text file.) A standard ASCII text file is created by 1-2-3 every time you use the /Print File command.

The 1-2-3 program looks for filenames that have the extension .PRN. If the file you want to import does not, you can rename the file so it has a .PRN extension, using the DOS RENAME command. Use the /System command to temporarily exit to DOS. The format of the command is RENAME OLDNAME NEWNAME. Finally, press ESC and type the new filename and its extension when 1-2-3 prompts you for it.

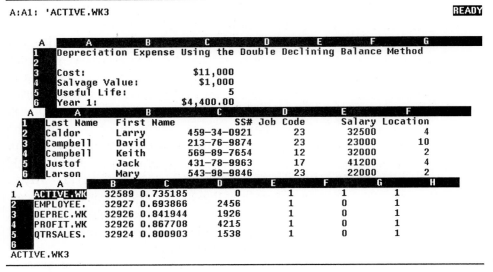

Figure 8-14. Table created with /File Admin Table Active command

There are two basic options for importing text data into a 1-2-3 worksheet: Text and Numbers. These options determine how the data will be placed in the worksheet. Use the Text option when you want to import the entire file. The Numbers option is useful when you want to strip away everything but numeric values, or when you are importing data that is in a delimited format (each piece of data separated by commas).

When you import data as Text, each line of the word processor document will become one long, left justified label. You will thus end up with a column of long labels. Once the data is imported, you can use /Data Parse to split the labels into individual pieces. You can also use /Range Label if you wish to change the alignment of the long labels on the worksheet.

The Numbers option is for importing delimited data files. If you use the Numbers option, characters enclosed in double quotation marks, as well as all numbers, will be imported. Blanks and characters not in quotation marks will be eliminated in the import process. Each number in a line of the text file will generate a numeric cell entry, and each quote-enclosed label will create a left justified label cell. Entries from the same line of a text file will produce entries in the same row of the worksheet, proceeding from left to right of the row with each new entry. Commas separate each piece of data in each line in the imported file.

1-2-3 imposes a size limit on the imported file of 8192 lines. The maximum number of characters in a line is 512 when you are using the Text option. With the Numbers option you can have 512 characters for each entry. This means every comma delimited entry that is enclosed in quotes can contain 512 characters, since 1-2-3 will place each number in a separate field. In contrast, when text is imported the entire entry is placed in one field.

Figure 8-15 shows text entered into a WordStar file named NDOC. PRN. You have two choices for importing the information into 1-2-3. If you place your cell pointer in A1 and use /File Import Text, the results in Figure 8-16 are produced. You will notice in the display of A1 that each of the entries is a long label with the entire WordStar line in the one label. If you chose the Numbers options, the output in Figure 8-17 would result. In this instance only the numbers from the Quantity column are transferred, since the label entries were not enclosed in quotes.

```
  C:NDOC.PRN      L5      C1        Insert
========================= N O N D O C U M E N T   E D I T   M E N U ========
    CURSOR       SCROLL       DELETE     OTHER              MENUS
 ^E up         ^W up        ^G char    ^J help         ^O onscreen format
 ^X down       ^Z down      ^T word    ^I tab          ^K block & save
 ^S left       ^R screen up ^Y line    ^V turn insert off ^P print controls
 ^D right      ^C screen    Del char   ^N split the line  ^Q quick functions
 ^A word left     down      ^U undo    ^L find/replace Esc shorthand
 ^F word right              ^B top bit    again
```

```
Defective Products        Vendor         Quantity            <
Beds                      Quiet Sleeper  10                  <
Openers                   Easy Can       25                  <
Lamps                     Bright Light   15                  <
                                                             ^
```

Figure 8-15.   WordStar text

When 1-2-3 imports text, it uses the setting of the /Worksheet Global Default Other International File-Translation command. This command's default uses the ASCII code page that the computer is set for. If the computer is configured to use code page 850, you need to set the International File Translation option so that 1-2-3 properly translates the characters in the text file to LMBCS characters (see Appendix D, "LMBCS codes").

Changing the Current Directory

The /File Dir command permits you to change the disk drive or directory for your current 1-2-3 session. When you enter **/File Dir**, 1-2-3

```
A:A1: 'Defective Products        Vendor          Quantity         READY

  A     A        B        C       D      E        F       G       H
1   Defective Products        Vendor              Quantity
2   Beds                      Quiet Sleeper       10
3   Openers                   Easy Can            25
4   Lamps                     Bright Light        15
5
```

Figure 8-16.   /File Import with Text

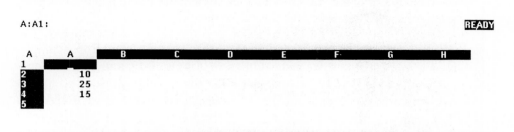

Figure 8-17.   /File Import with Numbers

displays the existing directory. You can press ENTER to accept it, or type a new directory or pathname. If you just want to reach a lower level directory, you can type the new level into the existing directory listing. (First, press F2 (EDIT) to place 1-2-3 in EDIT mode.)

Working with Multiple Files

A new Release 3 feature lets you open multiple files in memory at the same time. Chapter 4, "Changing the Appearance of the Worksheet Display," described how you can have a single worksheet file that contains multiple worksheets. When you have multiple files open in memory, you can move between them just as you can with multiple sheets in the same file. You can copy between files to transfer information from one file to another, but you cannot specify ranges that span files.

You can add new files to 1-2-3's memory, delete files from 1-2-3's memory, and use commands that use data from other commands. 1-2-3 allows you to open as many files simultaneously as you like — as long as the total number of worksheets in all active files does not exceed 256. With multiple files, an *active* file or worksheet is a file or worksheet that 1-2-3 has in its memory. The *current* file or worksheet is the one that contains the cell pointer.

Opening and Closing Multiple Files

When you use one file at a time, you open a file with the /File Retrieve command, and remove it with another /File Retrieve command or the /Worksheet Erase command. To use multiple files, you need to open a file without removing the current files. Release 3's /File Open command opens a file without affecting the other files in memory.

When you use /File Open, 1-2-3 prompts you to determine if you want to open the file before or after the current one. For example, assume you have the worksheet files in Figure 8-18 and you are currently in the YEARLY worksheet file (the second worksheet in the perspective view). If you add the BUDGET file before the YEARLY file, 1-2-3 changes the order of the files to SUMMARY, BUDGET, and YEARLY. If you add the BUDGET file after the YEARLY file, 1-2-3 changes the order of the files to SUMMARY, YEARLY, and BUDGET. When you select Before or After, 1-2-3 inserts the new file before or after the current file rather than the current worksheet. For example, let's say the SUMMARY.WK3 file has three worksheets, and the B worksheet is current. Adding a file before the current file places the opened file before worksheet A of SUMMARY; adding a file after the current file places the opened file after worksheet C of SUMMARY.

Another option for opening a file while keeping other files in memory is to open a new file. The /File New command also has Before and After options that determine whether the new file is placed before or after the current file. Once this choice is made, 1-2-3 prompts for a

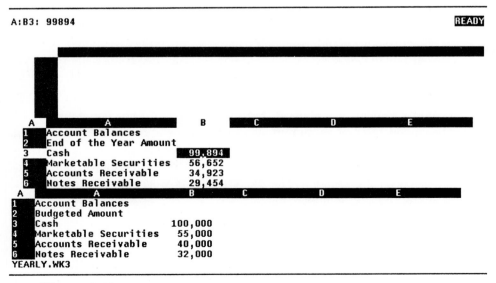

Figure 8-18.   Opening a new file

filename. Like the /File Save command, /File New displays a default filename (FILE0001.WK3 or a higher number). You can enter a new filename or accept the default, and press ENTER. This filename appears in the lower left corner when the file is active. The disk file for the new file is empty until the /File Save command saves its contents.

Once another worksheet file is opened, you can continue to use any of 1-2-3's worksheet features that you can use in single worksheets. To move between files without continually pressing CTRL-PGUP and CTRL-PGDN, try the keys in Table 8-1.

When you have multiple files open, 1-2-3 functions a little differently when some commands are executed. The worksheet settings remain with the worksheet file that originated them. After you open multiple worksheet files, changes that you make with Worksheet commands are saved with the worksheet that is current when the command is invoked. The /File Save command displays [ALL MODIFIED FILES] as the filename to save. Accepting this option saves all files that you have changed since the last /File Save command. If you press F2 (EDIT) with this prompt on the screen, 1-2-3 changes the filename prompt to the current file. Each file allows a range name to be used once, but you can use a single range name in all of the files if you choose.

When you are finished with and have saved a worksheet, you may want to remove it from 1-2-3's memory so you can load other files. To remove an active worksheet file, use the /Worksheet Delete File command. This command removes the current worksheet from 1-2-3's memory. Remember: the contents of this worksheet file are not saved unless you save it with the /File Save command. The /Worksheet Delete File

---

CTRL-END-HOME	Moves to the cell last highlighted in the first active file.
CTRL-END-END	Moves to the cell last highlighted in the last active file.
CTRL-END-CTRL-PGUP	Moves to the cell last highlighted in the next active file.
CTRL-END-CTRL-PGDN	Moves to the cell last highlighted in the previous active file.

Table 8-1.   Keys for Moving the Cell Pointer Between Files

command does not affect any files on the disk. To replace the current file use the /File Retrieve command. 1-2-3 will leave the other active files intact.

Using Multiple Files in Commands

Most 1-2-3 commands can use ranges from different files. For most commands, the file the command uses must be active.

In some cases, the file can be active or be on the default directory—specifically, when you are naming the From ranges for the /Copy, /Range Trans, and /Range Value commands. As an example, assume you want to copy the values in the TOTAL range in a YEARLY worksheet file, to the current worksheet. Use the /Range Value command to copy the values. When 1-2-3 prompts for the From range, enter <<C:\123R3\YEARLY.WK1>>TOTAL. When you press ENTER to select the current cell as the To range, 1-2-3 copies the values from the TOTAL range in the YEARLY.WK3 file starting at the current cell.

Tip: Use range names, rather than cell addresses as From ranges. Since 1-2-3 does not adjust cell references if you move them, you will want to use range names, which are automatically adjusted for their new location in the external file.

External File Links

Release 3 allows you to establish links between the current worksheet and data stored in cells or ranges on disk. You can use this feature to reference data in another file, and 1-2-3 will update the copy of the data that you reference. In previous releases of 1-2-3, if you wanted to use the data from another worksheet, you could use /File Xtract to extract it from the other worksheet, and /File Combine to combine it with the current worksheet. Another option was directly copying the data with /File Combine, using a named range in the other file. In both scenarios, you needed to continue using /File Combine to refresh the imported data when the data in the other file changed. In Release 3, you can create links to external files, and 1-2-3 updates their values every time you load a file or use the /File Admin Link-Refresh command.

To refer to a value in another worksheet file, the cell address, range address, or range name is preceded by the filename surrounded by the file delimiter. (1-2-3 uses double angle brackets (< < > >).) If the file is active, only the filename and extension are necessary. If the file is inactive, the pathname is also needed. 1-2-3 assumes the file is in the current directory unless a path is provided. If you want to include values from a file that you have not saved yet, you should include an empty file reference. Make sure you fill in this empty reference later, as 1-2-3 will not complete it for you.

1-2-3 also supports a wildcard feature that allows you to access a specified range name in any open file. If you use ? as the file reference for a range name's source, 1-2-3 uses the range name in all active files. You cannot include the wildcard ? filename specification with a cell address; if you do, 1-2-3 returns ERR.

Tip: If a file is linked to other files, include the pathname. By including the pathname, the worksheet can find the values it needs even when another directory is current. If 1-2-3 cannot find the file in the current directory, the formula containing the link to an external file returns ERR.

Figure 8-19 shows a formula that computes the yearly total for a company with multiple divisions. Each division has its own worksheet file. The first worksheet of each file contains the summary information

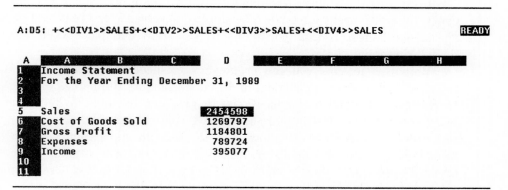

Figure 8-19.   Formula referencing data from another file

for the entire year. The summary worksheet for the entire company adds the different ranges for each of the division's summary worksheets. The formula uses range names rather than cell addresses so that 1-2-3 can adjust the range names if they are moved.

When you have links between files (especially inactive ones), you will want to check that the numbers are still the most current values. This is a recommended step before you print the worksheet, or before you extract values from it to use in another worksheet file. To recalculate values from other files, use the /File Admin Link-Refresh command. With this command, 1-2-3 rechecks all formulas in your current worksheet that refer to values in other files. 1-2-3 only checks values from other files when the formulas is entered, when the /File Admin Link-Refresh command is performed, or when the cell containing a reference to an external file is edited.

Other Ways to Work with Files

1-2-3 provides several commands and features, in addition to those on the File menu, that are useful in working with files.

Creating a Worksheet File That Loads Automatically

1-2-3 provides the ability to automatically load a specific worksheet file every time you bring up 1-2-3. The only requirement for creating this special worksheet is that you name it AUTO123 and place it in the default directory.

With this feature you can create a worksheet that contains help information for your application, and that documents the names of files to retrieve for different applications, to give one example. When you learn about macros in Chapters 12 and 13, you will see further applications for this capability. It allows you to start an application with no intervention from the operator, which eliminates any possibility for error. As soon as 1-2-3 is brought up, the application is started. Creating an automatically executing macro requires a setting of Yes for the /Worksheet Global Default Autoexec command.

Changing the Default Directory Permanently

The /File Dir command is used to change the disk drive or directory for the current 1-2-3 session. To change the default directory permanently, use /Worksheet Global Default Dir followed by /Worksheet Global Default Update to save your changes in the file 123.CNF.

The /Worksheet Global Default Dir command allows you to change the default disk drive or directory that 1-2-3 uses when saving or retrieving data files. If you do not change the default directory, it remains specified as the directory where you installed 1-2-3 Release 3. To change the default directory, enter **/Worksheet Global Default Dir** and then the directory you want to use. After you press ENTER, this directory will be in effect for the remainder of your 1-2-3 session.

To make the change to the default directory permanent, enter **/Worksheet Global Default Update.** This saves any changes made through the Default options, and ensures they will be available for your next 1-2-3 session. The changes are saved in 1-2-3's configuration file, called 123.CNF.

Changing the Default Directory for Temporary Files

1-2-3 sometimes creates temporary files. These files are stored in memory if there is room, and written to disk with the extension .TMP if there is no room in memory. Temporary files are created when you are printing a copy of a worksheet in memory. The default location for these files is in your main 1-2-3 directory, which will be the file server when you are running 1-2-3 on the network. You can improve performance by having temporary files written to your own system rather than the file server. To do this use the /Worksheet Global Default Temp command to change the directory where the temporary files reside.

Tip: When working on a network, do not attempt to write the temporary files to a read-only directory. Choose a location on your own system. If you must choose another location on the file server, at least be certain not to select a read-only directory.

Deleting a File from Memory

If you want to delete a file without erasing all of memory, use the /Worksheet Delete File command. When you execute this command, 1-2-3 displays all the files that are currently in memory. You can highlight the file that you want to delete, and press ENTER. Other files in memory are unaffected by your action, and the copy of the file on disk is not affected. An unnamed file displays as "no name" in this list.

Using Operating System Commands

Release 3 allows you to access DOS commands from within 1-2-3, through the /System command. It allows you to use DOS commands while still retaining your worksheet in memory. The only requirement for using /System is that COMMAND.COM be in the 1-2-3 directory or a directory 1-2-3 can access through DOS's PATH command.

Let's say, for example, that you plan to import a file to the worksheet but forgot to assign it a suffix of .PRN. You can use /System to leave 1-2-3 temporarily and use the DOS RENAME command. Likewise, if you attempt to save a file and the disk is full, you can use /System to access DOS and format a floppy disk, while keeping your current worksheet in memory.

To access DOS commands, enter /**System**. At the DOS prompt, enter the DOS command of your choice. Caution: keep in mind that commands like PRINT, which cause DOS to overlay memory, will erase your worksheet data. Any memory-resident DOS command, such as DIR or COPY, can be used with no problem. However, DOS commands such as GRAPHICS and MODE that require a program to be permanently loaded in memory can cause problems. FORMAT is an externally stored program, but it does not remain permanently resident and thus can be used without problems.

Since 1-2-3 Release 3 adds DOS extenders that allow you to access all of your memory, you may even be able to run some of your other software from this temporary exit. Just be certain that you save your worksheet files before trying this, until you are certain that a specific package will execute smoothly and then let you return to 1-2-3 without having damaged the program or the worksheet in memory. Under OS/2 you may find that fewer restrictions apply, since the OS/2 environment is different from DOS.

The /System command displays the DOS header shown in Figure 8-20. You can enter your DOS commands as usual. When you are finished with DOS, enter **EXIT**; you will return to your 1-2-3 worksheet exactly where you left off.

Translating Files from Other Programs

1-2-3 has several options for translating data from one format to another. 1-2-3 includes a separate program, called Translate, to translate file formats that 1-2-3 commands cannot handle. 1-2-3 also has individual translation programs that you can use instead of the menu-driven Translate Program. Some of the 1-2-3 commands can also translate data.

1-2-3's Translate Program

The 1-2-3 Translate Program is part of the Lotus Access System. It provides the ability to translate 1-2-3 files to other file formats, and files from other programs to the 1-2-3 format. Translate can be accessed directly from DOS or through the Lotus Access System. To use it you must first quit 1-2-3 with /Quit Yes.

Select Translate from the Lotus Access System, or type **trans** at the DOS prompt. When working with Translate, you first have to select the format to translate from. A list of Release 3's From format options is shown in Figure 8-21. After making this selection, you are prompted

```
(Type EXIT and press [RETURN] to return to 1-2-3)


The IBM Personal Computer DOS
Version 3.30 (C)Copyright International Business Machines Corp 1981, 1987
            (C)Copyright Microsoft Corp 1981, 1986

C>
```

Figure 8-20.   DOS header

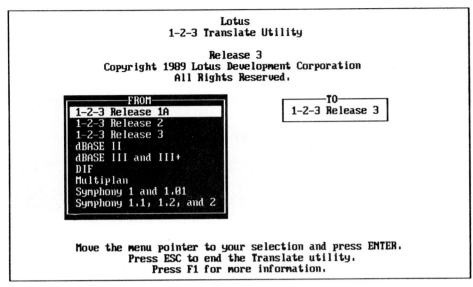

Figure 8-21. From options for Translate

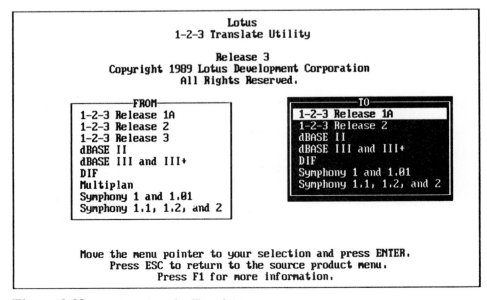

Figure 8-22. To options for Translate

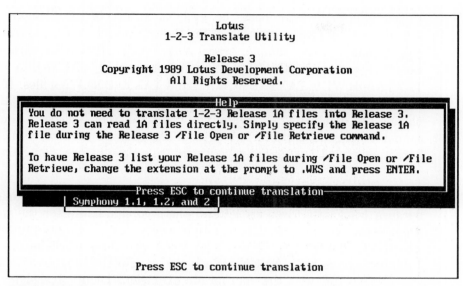

Figure 8-23.   Message that translation is not required

to choose from the list of To formats shown in Figure 8-22. Translate displays a message if the formats you choose do not need translation. As shown in Figure 8-23, you do not need to translate Release 1A files in order to use them with Release 3. Nor do you need to translate Symphony files for use with Release 3 of 1-2-3, or Release 2 files for use with Release 3. However, converting to an earlier version of 1-2-3 eliminates new features from the files translated for earlier releases.

Once you select the To and From data formats, 1-2-3 prompts for the filename in the current directory that you want to translate. You can enter the filename directly, or select it from the list provided. Translate assumes that the translated file (the To file) will have the same filename, with an appropriate extension for the new data format. You can use asterisks and question marks to translate multiple files, such as BUDGET*.WK3 or *.DBF. When you translate multiple files, Translate uses some settings, such as orientation (DIF format), for all of the files. If the file already exists, Translate asks you if you want to write over the existing file. Select Yes to write over the file, or No to abort the translation and return to the file selection list.

If you are translating from 1-2-3 Release 3 to another format, Translate asks you if you want to translate all the sheets in worksheet.

If you select All, 1-2-3 uses the first six letters of the filename you provided and adds two characters for the worksheet letter, to form the new filename. For example, translating TAXTABLE.WK3 with four worksheets to TAXTABLE.WK1 creates the TAXTAB0A.WK1, TAXTAB0B.WK1, TAXTAB0C.WK1, and TAXTAB0D.WK1 files. If you select One, Translate prompts you for the worksheet letter while displaying the default of "A." When you translate from Release 3, the file cannot be password protected. Also, if the file was created with /File Xtract, you must load it and save it with /File Save before translating it.

Tip: The first six letters of a file to be translated should be unique, because 1-2-3 uses these six letters, plus two characters for the worksheet letter, when it translates multiple worksheets. Let's say you translate INVENT.WK3 and INVENTRY.WK3 with three worksheets each. 1-2-3 translates the INVENT.WK3 file as INVENT0A, INVENT0B, and INVENT0C with the appropriate extension. Then it translates the INVENTRY.WK3 file also as INVENT0A, INVENT0B, and INVENT0C with the same extension, and writes over the first set (INVENT.WK3) of worksheets. To prevent this, you can use a different name for one of the output files, such as INV.WK3. Translate will then translate the worksheets to the INV0A, INV0B, INV0C, INVENT0A, INVENT0B, and INVENT0C files.

If you are translating to DIF format, Translate prompts for a row or column orientation. If you are translating to a dBASE II, dBASE III, or dBASE III+ format, Translate asks if you want to translate a named range or the entire file. If you select named range, you must enter a range name when Translate prompts for one.

Finally, Translate prompts if you want to continue. Select Yes to translate the file, or No to return to the initial Translate menu. Once you instruct Translate to continue, Translate converts the file and returns a message telling you that it did or did not successfully translate the file. To exit the Translate Program, press ESC until Translate asks if you want to leave, and select Yes.

When Translate translates a file, it only converts the features that are common to both data format types. For example, when Release 3 converts to Release 1A, it truncates Release 3 labels larger than 512 characters to 240-character labels in Release 1A.

Translation Programs

The individual translation programs are included with the 1-2-3 files. Using these files directly, instead of through the Translate Program, reduces steps and allows you to incorporate the translation programs into a batch file. 1-2-3 has translation programs for each of the data formats handled by the Translate Program. Each translation program translates 1-2-3 files to another format, and files from another program to the 1-2-3 format. The translation programs can be accessed directly from DOS. To use them, you must quit 1-2-3 with /Quit Yes.

At the DOS prompt, enter the name of the translation program you want, the input data file, the output data file, and any flags the translation program uses. The box called "Translation Programs" names the translation programs and tells when you use each one. The individual translation programs use file extensions to determine the data formats of the input and output files. If the default extensions do not match your file names and extensions, you must rename your files before translating them. You can use asterisks and question marks to translate multiple files, such as BUDGET*.WK3 or *.DBF.

The flags used by each translation program consist of the responses to the prompts you see when you use Translate Program to translate files. Flags consist of a hyphen, followed by one or more letters. The -c flag (used by the TRANDIF translation program) transposes the row/column orientation that the DIF files use. The -l# flag (used by all translation programs except TRANSYLK) selects the worksheet letter of the Release 3 input file being translated. The -o flag (used by any translation program) overwrites any existing file with the same name. The -p flag (used by TRANDB2 and TRANDB3 translation programs) names the range of the input worksheet file that the program translates.

Translating with an individual translation program has the same limitations as translating through the Translate Program. For example, if you are translating from 1-2-3 Release 3 to another format, the file cannot be password protected. If the Release 3 file was created with /File Xtract, you must load it and save it with /File Save before translating it. If you are translating multiple worksheets from a Release 3 file, the translation Program follows the same filename conventions of the Translate program—that is, using the first six letters of the name and adding two letters for the worksheet letter.

When a translation program translates a file, it only converts the data that the output file format accepts. For example, when Release 3

1 2 3

Translation Programs

File	Use
TRANDB2	Translates 1-2-3 Release 3 to dBASE II, and vice versa.
TRANDB3	Translates 1-2-3 Release 3 to dBASE III or dBASE III+, and dBASEIII or dBASEIII+ to 1-2-3 Release 3.
TRANDIF	Translates 1-2-3 Release 3 to DIF format files, and vice versa.
TRANSYLK	Translates Multiplan Release 1 and 2 to 1-2-3 Release 3.
TRANWKS	Translates 1-2-3 Release 3 to 1-2-3 Release 1A, 2, and 2.01, and Symphony.

converts to dBASE III+, the TRANDB3 program converts Release 3 formulas to the formula results, and puts the results in the output file.

Translating with 1-2-3 Commands

Some data formats do not need to be translated with the Translate Program because 1-2-3 can translate the data with the /File commands. The /File Retrieve command can retrieve 1-2-3 Release 1A, 2, and 3 files, as well as Symphony (any release). When Release 3 retrieves a Release 1A or Symphony file, it loads the data into memory and creates a file with the same name and a .WK3 file extension. Since this .WK3 file is empty, 1-2-3 will delete it if you do not save the file. Release 3 cannot save files in a Release 1A or Symphony format. The /File Save command can save files in a Release 2 or Release 3 format by using the file extension to tell 1-2-3 which format to use to save the data. If the worksheet does not contain any Release 3 specific features, 1-2-3 saves a file with a .WK1 extension in Release 2 format. If most of the files you are using and saving are Release 2 format, use the /Worksheet Global Default Ext Save and /Worksheet Global Default Update commands to set the default extension to .WK1.

When 1-2-3 retrieves a Release 2 file, it follows the setting of the /Worksheet Global Default Other International Release 2 command. This command has two options. The LICS option enables the LICS character set that Release 2 uses for Compose key characters, to create special characters such as foreign letters. The ASCII option is for Release 2 files created with the ASCII NO-LICS driver available with Release 2.01. You will need to change this setting to ASCII if you load a Release 2 file and special characters in the file do not appear correctly.

When 1-2-3 saves a .WK1 file that has Release 3 features, 1-2-3 makes several conversions. 1-2-3 truncates long labels after 240 characters. Formulas with more that 240 characters are stored intact up to 2000 characters; however, if you edit the formula, 1-2-3 Release 2 will truncate the formula after 240 characters. Release 3 @functions become add-in @functions and evaluate as NA. 1-2-3 deletes range name notes and formula annotations. New command settings that Release 3 saves with the file disappear in the Release 2 worksheet file. Once 1-2-3 makes these conversions, 1-2-3 displays an error message telling you that some information is lost. The /File Save command cannot convert a Release 3 to Release 2 file if it contains multiple worksheets. The /File Xtract command can translate a worksheet by selecting the used portion of a worksheet for the extract range, as long as it is not a range that spans sheets in a three-dimensional file.

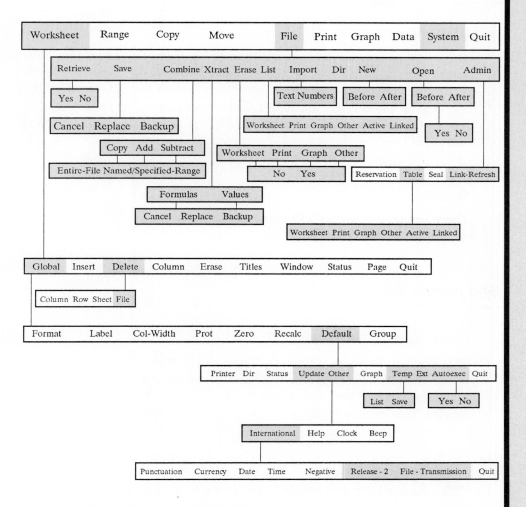

© 1989 Lotus Development Corporation. Used with permission.

/File Admin Link-Refresh

Description

This command recalculates formulas in the current worksheet that have active links to other files. This command is primarily used in network environments where several operators can change the data used by the formulas in the current worksheet. This command is also used when the link to the external file does not include the pathname, and the referenced file is not in the current directory.

Options

There are no options for this command.

/File Admin Table

Description

This command creates a table that lists all the files of the specified type in the current directory. The table is four columns wide (seven columns for listing active files) and as many rows long as the directory has file entries. This command can select which files it retrieves.

Options

This command has six options to select the type of files in the table. The table includes the filenames and extensions, the date serial number when the file was saved last, the time serial number when the file was saved last, and the size. The Active option also includes three other columns. The Worksheet, Print, Graph, and Other options can further limit which files 1-2-3 lists by modifying the filename skeleton. Once you select the type of files 1-2-3 will list in the table, you must specify where you want 1-2-3 to put the information. This area must be unprotected and blank so that the table does not overwrite worksheet information.

Worksheet   This option lists the worksheet files with the file extension set by the /Worksheet Global Default Ext List command.

Print   This option lists the .PRN files. To list the encoded files, type *.ENC when 1-2-3 displays the file skeleton.

Graph   This option lists the graphic image files with the file extension set by the /Worksheet Global Default Graph command.

Other   This option lists all files.

Active   This option lists the active files. The table created with this option contains three additional columns. The first extra column contains the number of worksheets in each file. The second extra column contains a 1 if the file has changed since it became active, or a 0 otherwise. The third extra column contains a 1 if you have the reservation in a network environment or a single user environment, or a 0 otherwise. A 1 in this column allows you to update this file.

Linked   This option lists the files to which the current file is linked by formula references. The first column of the table created with this option contains the pathname with the filename.

/File Combine Add

Description

The /File Combine Add command permits you to add some or all of the values from a worksheet file to current worksheet values. The addition process uses the cell pointer location as the upper leftmost cell to be combined with the first cell in the worksheet or range you are adding. Only cells that are blank or contain values are affected by this process. Cells that contain formulas or labels are unaffected.

The Add option is useful when you are performing a budget consolidation. You can begin with a total budget worksheet that contains nothing more than labels and a few total formulas. As long as all departmental budgets are in exactly the same format as the total work-sheet, you can use /File Combine Add once for each worksheet file to produce a budget consolidation. This command can incorporate data from Release 1A, 2, and 3 files.

Options

Like the other /File Combine options, Add permits you to combine an entire file or a named range. In either case, it begins the combination at the cell pointer location. The cells in the combined range must have the format of the incoming data.

Entire-File   With this option, every value cell in the worksheet file is added to a cell in the current worksheet. Cell A1 in the file is added to the cell where the cell pointer rests in the current worksheet. Remaining values will be added to the cell with the proper displacement from the current cell pointer location.

When you select Entire-File, the names of the worksheet files on the current disk (in the current directory if you are using a hard disk) are displayed. You can either point to one of the filenames or enter another filename you wish to use. 1-2-3 assumes that the file has a .WK3 file extension, unless you provide another one or select a filename from the list that has a different extension. Likewise, you can access files on a different drive or in a different directory if you supply the complete pathname.

Named-Range   With this option, 1-2-3 asks you to specify a range name, and then the file that contains this range name. The range name you specify must be valid for the filename specified. The rules for entering the filename are the same as for Entire-File.

/File Combine Copy

Description

The /File Combine Copy command permits you to replace some or all of the values from the current worksheet with values (including formulas and labels) from a worksheet file. The copying process uses the cell pointer location in the current worksheet as the upper leftmost cell to be replaced with the first cell in the worksheet or range you are copying. Unlike /File Combine Add, current worksheet cells containing formulas and labels are affected by /File Combine Copy. They will be overwritten by the copied information.

The Copy feature is useful when you would like to copy headings and values from an existing worksheet to one you are currently creating. Although formulas can also be copied, you must be sure that the values they require are also copied, or an error could result.

Options

Like the other /File Combine options, Copy permits you to combine an entire file or a named range. In either case, it begins the replacement at the cell pointer location.

Entire-File   With this option, every value cell in the worksheet file is copied to a cell in the current worksheet. Cell A1 in the file is copied to the cell where the cell pointer rests in the current worksheet. Remaining values will be copied to the cell with the proper displacement from the current cell pointer location.

When you select Entire-File, the names of the worksheet files on the current disk (in the current directory if you are using a hard disk) are displayed. You can either point to one of the filenames or enter another filename you wish to use. 1-2-3 assumes that the file has a .WK3 file extension, unless you provide another one or select a filename from the list that has a different extension. Likewise, you can access files on a different drive or different directory if you supply the complete pathname.

Named-Range   With this option, 1-2-3 asks you to specify a range name, and then the file that contains this range name. The range name you specify must be valid for the filename specified. The rules for entering the filename are the same as for Entire-File.

/File Combine Subtract

Description

The /File Combine Subtract command permits you to subtract some or all of the values from a worksheet file from the current worksheet values. The subtraction process uses the cell pointer location as the upper leftmost cell to be combined with the first cell in the worksheet or range you are subtracting. Only cells that are blank or contain values are affected by this process. Cells that contain formulas or labels are unaffected.

The Subtract option is useful when you are performing a budget consolidation. You can begin with a total budget worksheet. Then, to see the effect of closing one of a company's departments or subsidiaries, you can subtract the file containing its budget projections from the total. All subsidiary budgets must be in exactly the same format as the total worksheet, however.

Options

Like the other /File Combine options, Subtract permits you to combine an entire file or a named range. In either case, it begins the combination at the cell pointer location. The cells in the combined range must have the format of the incoming data.

Entire-File   With this option, every value cell in the worksheet file is subtracted from a cell in the current worksheet. Cell A1 in the file is subtracted from the cell where the cell pointer rests in the current worksheet. Remaining values will be subtracted from the cell with the proper displacement from the current cell pointer location.

When you select Entire-File, the names of the worksheet files on the current disk (in the current directory if you are using a hard disk) are displayed. You can either point to one of the filenames or enter another filename you wish to use. 1-2-3 assumes that the file has a .WK3 file extension, unless you provide another one or select a filename from the list that has a different extension. Likewise, you can access files on a different drive or different directory if you supply the complete pathname.

Named-Range   With this option, 1-2-3 asks you to specify a range name, and then the file that contains this range name. The range name you specify must be valid for the filename specified. The rules for entering the filename are the same as for Entire-File.

/File Dir

Description

The /File Dir command allows you to check or change the current Root directory that 1-2-3 is using for file storage and retrieval. With Release 3, the default directory is the subdirectory containing the 1-2-3 files, unless another directory has been set as the default. The /File Dir command lets you make a change only for the current session. If you wish to change the default directory permanently, use /Worksheet Global Default Dir followed by /Worksheet Global Default Update to save your change. This information is stored in the 123.CNF file, which 1-2-3 reads every time it is loaded.

Options

With this command, you can simply review the current directory setting or change it. To review the setting, simply press ENTER after you have seen the /File Dir display.

To change the directory for the session, first decide if you want to change the complete directory that is designated, or to stay in the same directory and just change the subdirectory. You can change the drive, the directory, and the subdirectory with this command.

Drive   To change the drive, type the drive designator followed by a backslash, for example, **B:**. To change the path as well, type the pathname at the same time, for example, **B:\123\SALES**.

Current Directory   If the current directory is ACCT and you want to change it to MKTG, enter **\MKTG**.

A Lower Level in the Current Directory   This allows you to maintain the current directory setting but use a specific subdirectory within it. If your current directory is C:123\SALES and you wish to be in the subdirectory MICHIGAN within SALES, press F2 (EDIT) enter **\MICHIGAN** or **C:123\SALES\MICHIGAN**.

A Higher Level in the Current Directory   To change the directory
to one level higher, enter two periods (..); this is the DOS symbol for a
directory one level higher. If your current directory level is
C:123\SALES\MICHIGAN and you want to be in SALES, you can enter
either **C:123\SALES** or .. (the latter is clearly much quicker).

/File Erase

Description

The /File Erase command is used to remove one or more files from the
disk.

Options

First choose the type of file or files you wish to remove from the disk.
With Release 3, your options are the following:

Worksheet	Worksheet files with the file extension set by the /Worksheet Global Default Ext command
Print	Print files with the .PRN file extension
Graph	Graph files with the file extension set by the /Worksheet Global Default Graph command
Other	Files with any file extension

Once you specify the file type you wish to delete, 1-2-3 lists all the
files of that type that are on the current drive or directory. You can
point to the file you wish to delete, or type in the filename. If the file you
wish to delete is on a different drive or in a different directory, press F2
(EDIT) and change the drive designator and pathname to the path containing the file. After you select the file you want to delete, 1-2-3
prompts for a confirmation. Select Yes to delete the file, or No to cancel
the command.

You can use wildcard characters when specifying the file names you wish to delete. The special characters used in creating wildcard file-names are as follows:

?   Matches any single character in the filename. For example, ?CCT matches ACCT, TCCT, and LCCT.

*   Matches all remaining characters in the filename. For example, S* matches SALES, SALES1, and SALARY.

/File Import

Description

The /File Import command permits you to load information from a Print file into the current worksheet at the cell pointer location. Standard ASCII files that do not exceed 8192 characters in length can be imported.

Options

/File Import offers two options, allowing you to bring either a column of long labels (Text option) or a combination of numbers and labels (Numbers option) into the worksheet. Once you have selected Text or Numbers, 1-2-3 lists the .PRN files in the current directory. To list files with a different extension, type *. followed by the extension you want, and press ENTER. After a filename is selected, 1-2-3 imports the file and places the data starting at the cell pointer's location.

Text   This option brings each line of the imported text file into the worksheet as a single long label. /Data Parse can then split files imported as text into separate entries, rather than one long label (see Chapter 10 for more information). This option imports up to 512 characters from each line into the worksheet.

Numbers   This option searches the imported file for numbers and for text entries enclosed in quotes. Each number is placed in a worksheet cell as a value, and each text entry in quotes is placed in a cell as a left justified label. If more than one number or enclosed text entry is found in a line of the text file, more than one column of the worksheet will be used. When the next line of the imported file is processed, entries will begin again in the same column as the cell pointer.

Note

Special characters added by some word processors can cause problems. Most word processors have an option that excludes these special characters to produce a standard ASCII file.

/File List

Description

The /File List command lists all the files of the specified type in the current directory. This command creates a temporary listing, rather than the permanent listing the /File Admin Table command creates.

Options

With Release 3, you have six /File List choices:

Worksheet	Worksheet files with the file extension set by the /Worksheet Global Default Ext command
Print	Print files with the .PRN file extension
Graph	Graph files with the file extension set by the /Worksheet Global Default Graph command
Other	Files with any file extension
Active	All the active files. The table created with this option contains three additional columns. The first column contains the number of worksheets in each file. The second column contains a 1 if

the file has changed since it became active, or a
0 otherwise. The third column contains a 1 if
you have the reservation in a network environment or a single user environment, or a 0 otherwise.

Linked   Files to which the current file is linked by formula references. The first column of the table
created with this option contains the pathname.

Once you have specified the file type, 1-2-3 displays the filenames of
all files of the selected type. For each filename you highlight, 1-2-3
displays the date serial number when the file was last saved, the time
serial number when the file was last saved, and the file size, at the top of
the list. In addition, the Active option also displays the number of
worksheets in the file; the flag "MOD" or "UNMOD" to indicate if the
file has been modified or remains unchanged; and "RO" if the file is read
only in a network environment. The Linked option list includes the
pathname of the linked files.

/File New

Description

This command creates a blank worksheet and inserts it into the current
worksheets. Use /File New to insert a blank worksheet file that is
separate from the other worksheet files in memory. After executing the
command, the cell pointer is at A1 of the new file. The new file has the
name you provide when you perform this command and the default file
extension specified by the /Worksheet Global Default Ext Save command.

Options

This command has two options, Before and After, which identify the new
worksheet file's location relative to the current file. You cannot insert a
new worksheet file between the worksheets in another file. When 1-2-3
prompts for a filename and displays the default filename (FILE followed
by the next highest number), enter a filename but only provide an
extension if you want to override the default extension.

/File Open

Description

The /File Open command loads a file from disk into the memory of your computer. This command is used to open additional multiple files in memory. The other files in 1-2-3's memory remain in place. You can open a file from the current disk or directory, or from a different one if you specify the pathname. If you want a file from the current directory, you can select it from the list 1-2-3 displays. A file extension only needs to be provided if the file does not have the default file extension specified by the /Worksheet Global Default Ext Save command. 1-2-3 can retrieve files with a .WKS (1-2-3 Release 1A), .WRK (Symphony), WR1 (Symphony), .WK1 (1-2-3 Release 2) and .WK3 (Release 3) extensions.

You can open password-protected files by supplying the correct password when 1-2-3 prompts you. The opened file uses the recalculation and window settings in effect when the file is opened but 1-2-3 remembers the file's original settings when it saves the file.

Options

This command has two options, Before and After, which determine the opened worksheet file's location relative to the current file. You cannot insert a worksheet file between the worksheets in another file. If the file you want to open is used in a network environment and 1-2-3 cannot get the file reservation for you, 1-2-3 displays a Yes or No selection. Select Yes if you want read-only access to the file, or No to cancel the command.

/File Retrieve

Description

The /File Retrieve command loads a file from disk into the memory of your computer. The current worksheet file is erased by the loading of the new file.

Options

You can retrieve a file from the current disk or directory, or from a different one if you specify the pathname. You can retrieve password-protected files by supplying the password when 1-2-3 prompts you. 1-2-3 can retrieve files with extensions of .WKS (1-2-3 Release 1A), .WRK (Symphony), .WR1 (Symphony), .WK1 (1-2-3 Release 2) and .WK3 (Release 3). If the file you are retrieving is used in a network environment and 1-2-3 cannot get the file reservation for you, 1-2-3 displays a Yes or No selection. Select Yes if you want read-only access to the file, or No to cancel the command.

/File Save

Description

The /File Save command allows you to save the current worksheet and any settings you have created for it to a worksheet file. If 1-2-3 has multiple worksheet files in memory, it offers you the option of saving all modified files.

Options

The first time the file is saved, 1-2-3 displays a default filename of FILE*nnnn*.WK3, where *nnnn* is a number beginning at 0001 and incrementing by one as each filename is used. You can save the worksheet file to the current disk by accepting the default name, or entering another filename and pressing ENTER. If you wish to use a disk or directory different from the current one, you must specify the complete pathname.

If the file is already saved on the disk, 1-2-3 will prompt you with the existing filename. Press ENTER to accept it. The next prompt is a choice between Cancel, Replace, or Backup. Cancel stops the /File Save command and returns you to READY mode. Replace places the current contents of memory on the disk under the existing filename, erasing what was stored in the file previously. Backup copies the previous version of the file to a separate file with the same filename and a .BAK file extension, before saving the current version.

If 1-2-3 has multiple files in memory when you enter /File Save, it displays "[ALL MODIFIED FILES]" as the filename. Press ENTER to save all files modified since the last /File Save command. If you only want to save one of the files, press F2 (EDIT) to convert "[ALL MODIFIED FILES]" to the current filename. From this point, you can modify or accept the current filename and press ENTER. If you want to save a file other than the current file, switch to the worksheet in the file you want to save.

This command also allows you to add a password to a file when it is saved. Once a file is saved with a password, you cannot retrieve the file unless you supply the password. After typing the name of the file to be saved, press the SPACEBAR and type **p**. 1-2-3 will prompt you for a password up to 15 characters long. After you enter it, a prompt will ask you to verify it by entering it again. Passwords are case sensitive, so be sure you enter the password in the upper- or lowercase letters that you want for this password. If you wish to abort the password procedure, instead of verifying the password you can press ESC several times to return to READY mode, without saving the file or adding a password.

To change the password, press BACKSPACE to remove "[PASSWORD PROTECTED]" when 1-2-3 displays the filename. Then press the SPACEBAR and type a **p**. 1-2-3 will prompt you for the new password just as if you were adding the password for the first time. To remove password protection from a file, press the BACKSPACE to remove "[PASSWORD PROTECTED]" from the display, and then press ENTER.

This command can save the file in a Release 2 format if you name it with a .WK1 file extension, or set the default extension to .WK1 with the /Worksheet Global Default Ext Save command. For a worksheet to be saved in the Release 2 format, it cannot contain any Release 3 specific features, since the Release 3 features are lost when 1-2-3 translates the file to the Release 2 format. Some of the lost features include function arguments that are new to Release 3, formula notes, and undefined range names. Also, if labels are longer than 240 characters, they will be truncated.

Note

A file with the name AUTO123 will be retrieved every time you load 1-2-3, as long as it is in the default directory as determined by the /Worksheet Global Default Dir command.

/File Xtract

Description

The /File Xtract command allows you to save a portion of the current worksheet in another worksheet file. Settings established for the current worksheet, such as graph and print settings and range names, are saved in the new file.

Options

The /File Xtract command allows you to save either values or formulas from the range specified.

Formulas   This option saves current worksheet formulas, as well as labels and values, in the worksheet file.

Values   This option saves numbers and labels in the worksheet files. Formulas are evaluated to determine the numbers for saving, but the formulas are not saved. When you copy the values, check to see if the values need to be recalculated, or that links to external files need to be refreshed.

After entering /File Xtract and choosing Formulas or Values, select the filename from the menu or enter a new name. Next, enter a range of cell addresses or a range name. If the filename is new, press ENTER to complete the process.

If you are using an existing filename, 1-2-3 asks if you wish to cancel the request; back up the existing file to a .BAK file before replacing the existing file with the contents of the range selected; or replace the existing file with the contents of the range selected. If you supply a .WK1 file extension, 1-2-3 saves the extracted file in Release 2 format, assuming the selected range encompasses only one worksheet. After you have selected the file to hold the extract, specify the range to be extracted, by entering either a range name or range address.

This command also allows you to add a password to an extracted file. For more information on this feature, see /File Save in the Command Reference section in this chapter.

Note

You can use /File Combine to add this extracted information to a worksheet file in memory.

/System

Description

The /System command allows you to use the operating system commands without quitting 1-2-3. This means you can access some of the operating system commands while your 1-2-3 worksheet remains in memory.

Options

Any operating system command that does not overlay memory can be used with /System. Afterwards, EXIT returns you to your worksheet.

Note

It is wise to save your worksheet files before using this temporary exit to the operating system.

/Worksheet Delete File

Description

The /Worksheet Delete File command removes an active file from 1-2-3's memory. This command allows you to remove one file from the active files without affecting the other files. This command does not affect any files saved to disk.

Options

There are no options for this command.

/Worksheet Global Default Autoexec

Description

This command causes 1-2-3 to automatically run autoexecute macros (named \0) when a file containing these macros is retrieved or opened.

Options

This command has two options. If the Yes option is selected, 1-2-3 automatically runs the autoexecute macros when it reads a file that contains one. If the No option is selected, 1-2-3 does not automatically run any macros.

/Worksheet Global Default Dir

Description

Use this command to specify the directory that you want 1-2-3 to automatically look in for your files. Unless you change it, the default is the directory containing the 1-2-3 files.

Options

Normally, when you enter /Worksheet Global Default Dir, you will specify a new default directory. A second option is to clear the existing entry without entering a new one. In this case 1-2-3 will use the directory that was current when 1-2-3 was loaded, as the default for file storage and retrieval.

Note

To make this directory change permanent, use /Worksheet Global Default Update to save the new default to the 123.CNF file.

/Worksheet Global Default Ext

Description

Use this command to set the default worksheet file extension that 1-2-3 assigns for various /File commands.

Options

This command has two options: List and Save. Each option sets the default extension for different file commands.

List   This option sets the default file extension for /File Combine, /File Erase, /File List, /File Open, and /File Retrieve. The default is .WK*, which includes .WKS, .WK1, and .WK3.

Save   This option sets the default file extension for the files created by /File New, /File Save, and /File Xtract.

/Worksheet Global Default Other International File-Translation

Description

This command determines how Release 3 converts characters that the /File Import command imports into Release 3 worksheets.

Options

This command has two options. The Country option uses the IBM character set selected by the Country configuration . The Country configuration is set in the CONFIG.SYS file, which determines which ASCII code page the keyboard uses. Selecting a keyboard page lets you modify the keyboard to match a language's characters. For a U.S.

keyboard, this option uses code page 437. The International option uses code page 850, and is only selected when a text file is created on a computer that uses code page 850.

/Worksheet Global Default Other International Release-2

Description

This command determines how Release 3 converts characters from Release 2, which has the option of using LICS or ASCII.

Options

This command has two options. The LICS option uses the LICS character set that is the Release 2 default. The LICS characters include Compose key sequences to create special characters such as foreign letters. The ASCII option is for Release 2.01 files created with the ASCII NO-LICS driver.

/Worksheet Global Default Temp

Description

This command determines the default directory that 1-2-3 uses for temporary files in such tasks as printing. Temporary files have a .TMP extension and are deleted when you exit 1-2-3.

Options

There are no options for this command.

/Worksheet Global Default Update

Description

This command allows you to save any changes that you have made to the Worksheet Global Default settings, to the 123.CNF file.

Options

There are no options for this command.

Translate Program

Description

The Translate Program allows you to exchange data files between 1-2-3 and other popular programs. It is available from the Lotus Access System menu. You must quit 1-2-3 with /Quit Yes to use Translate. If you entered **123** to open 1-2-3, you will need to enter **trans** to start the Translate Program.

Options

You have two types of options for the Translate Program. You can select from a list of source file formats (From options), and a list of target file formats (To options).

The From options are as follows:

1-2-3 Release 1A
1-2-3 Release 2
1-2-3 Release 3
dBASE II
dBASE III and III+

DIF (VisiCalc and others)
Multiplan
Symphony Release 1.0 and 1.01
Symphony Release 1.1, 1.2, and 2

The To options are as follows:

1-2-3 Release 1A
1-2-3 Release 2
1-2-3 Release 3
dBASE II
dBASE III and III+
DIF (VisiCalc and others)
Symphony Release 1.0 and 1.01
Symphony Release 1.1, 1.2, and 2

Note

You will not need to translate Symphony files and earlier releases of
1-2-3 for use with Release 3 of 1-2-3. this is because the /File Retrieve
command automatically translates these files when it retrieves them.

When you translate one format to another, the Translate Program
only translates the features common to both the source and target file
types. If you are translating a 1-2-3 Release 3 file to another format, you
can select which worksheet you are translating. If you translate all of
them, the Translate Program translates each worksheet to a different
file by replacing or adding the last two filename characters, to indicate
the worksheet letter. If you are translating a file to a DIF format, you
must specify the orientation as row or column. If you are translating a
file to dBASE II, III, or III+, you can select between a named range or
the entire file. If you select range, you must provide the range name
when Translate prompts for that information.

1-2-3's Advanced Features

Data Management

N I N E

In one sense, all the work you have done with 1-2-3 up to this point can be considered data management, because it has all involved the management of information recorded on the worksheet. But data management, as defined by 1-2-3, is a special term that refers to the formalized process of design, entry, and retrieval of information from a database.

The world of data management has its own terminology. A *database*, for example, is a collection of all the information you have about a set of things. These things can be customers, orders, parts in inventory, employees, or anything else. If you created a database of employee information, for example, you would want it to contain information about each of your employees. All the information about one employee would be one *record* in the database. A record is composed of all the pieces of information you have about one thing in the set, such as one employee. These individual pieces of information in a record are referred to as *fields*. Fields you might want to have in each record in an employee database could include name, address, job classification, date of hire, social security number, department, benefits, and salary. When you design a new database, you need to decide what fields will be included in each record.

This chapter describes the /Data commands that permit organization and retrieval of information from 1-2-3's worksheets. You will also read about Lotus' exciting new DataLens capability that lets you access external databases created with popular packages like dBASE, just as easily as if they were part of another worksheet file.

The next chapter will examine the /Data commands that add power to the calculations you do on the worksheet. Some of the commands covered in Chapter 10 serve a dual purpose. They work when information management is your only requirement, but they can also lend assistance when your objective is the more traditional use of the worksheet for calculations. In the next chapter you will find some hints on using these data management techniques with traditional worksheet applications.

The 1-2-3 Database

A 1-2-3 database is a range of cells on a worksheet. It can be in any area of the worksheet, but the field names, that is, the names you use to

A:A1: [W12] 'Last Name   READY

	Last Name	First Name	SS#	Job Code	Salary	Location
1	Last Name	First Name	SS#	Job Code	Salary	Location
2	Larson	Mary	543-98-9876	23	$12,000	2
3	Campbell	David	213-76-9874	23	$23,000	10
4	Campbell	Keith	569-89-7654	12	$32,000	2
5	Stephens	Tom	219-78-8954	15	$17,800	2
6	Caldor	Larry	459-34-0921	23	$32,500	4
7	Lightnor	Peggy	560-55-4311	14	$23,500	10
8	McCartin	John	817-66-1212	15	$54,600	2
9	Justof	Jack	431-78-9963	17	$41,200	4
10	Patterson	Lyle	212-11-9090	12	$21,500	10
11	Miller	Lisa	214-89-6756	23	$18,700	2
12	Hawkins	Mark	215-67-8973	21	$19,500	2
13	Hartwick	Eileen	313-78-9090	15	$31,450	4
14	Smythe	George	560-90-8645	15	$65,000	4
15	Wilkes	Caitlin	124-67-7432	17	$15,500	2
16	Deaver	Ken	198-98-6750	23	$24,600	10
17	Kaylor	Sally	312-45-9862	12	$32,900	10
18	Parker	Dee	659-11-3452	14	$19,800	4
19	Preverson	Gary	670-90-1121	21	$27,600	4
20	Samuelson	Paul	219-89-7080	23	$28,900	2

Figure 9-1.   Portion of an employee database

categorize data, must run across the top row of the range. The records in the database that contain data for each field are placed in the rows immediately following the row of field names. Figure 9-1 presents a section of an employee database in A1..F20. The field names are located in A1..F1, and the first database record is located in A2..F2.

As a database manager, 1-2-3 has both strengths and weaknesses compared to other packages. You may find it helpful to look at some ways in which 1-2-3's features differ from those of its competitors.

- The data in your 1-2-3 database is all stored in memory while you are working with the database. Unlike other packages that must read data from the disk when you need it, 1-2-3 provides unprecedented quick response to requests for resequencing records and finding those that match specific criteria. This feature does require that you have sufficient memory to hold your entire database at once, however. You will need a large memory capacity, a fairly small database, or both.

- 1-2-3's data management commands are similar to its Worksheet commands, which makes them easy for you to learn. By contrast, other packages may require a significant time investment to master their command structure.

• Most data management packages create formatted screens to enter or review one record at a time. With Release 3 macros, you now have the capability to easily design a formatted screen for use with your database.

• Release 3 permits the entry of up to 8191 records in one database table in a worksheet. You can create multiple database tables in a file by putting them on different worksheets. You can combine these database tables in 1-2-3 functions and database commands. The practical limit to a database size is the amount of memory available, since the entire database resides in memory. These limits are sufficient for many applications, but some other database products allow an unlimited number of records.

• 1-2-3 can accommodate up to 256 fields in one database. Some packages allow more and others less.

• 1-2-3 permits each field to have up to 512 characters. Some packages allow more and others less.

Setting Up a Database

The first step in designing a 1-2-3 database is to create a list of fields you want your database to contain. Once you have all the field names recorded, estimate the number of characters that each field will require for storage and the number of records in your database. Add the number of characters for each field plus four additional characters per field to get a record total, and then multiply by the number of records. If the potential number of records exceeds 1-2-3's limits, you will have to find another alternative, such as splitting your file into two sections. Similarly, if the number of records times the length of one record exceeds the available memory in your system, you will not want to proceed with the design process unless you can use multiple subfiles in your application.

Choosing a Location for the Database

The next step is to select an area of the worksheet for storing the database. Here are some considerations to keep in mind as you select a location.

- To allow your database to expand with additional records, choose an area below calculations and other fixed information in your worksheet.

- If you plan to put more than one database in the worksheet, place them side by side so each can expand downward.

- If you have sufficient memory and have two databases in one worksheet, you might want to start one database in A1, and the other one to the right of and beneath the last record in the first database. This allows you to use the /Worksheet Delete and /Worksheet Insert commands to delete and insert records in either database without affecting the other.

- If you want to include other information in the worksheet file with the database entries, place the other information on a separate worksheet in the file. By keeping the database table separate from other information, you can prevent changes made to the database table—like row insertions and deletions—from affecting other data in the file.

Entering Field Names

Record your selected field names across the top row of the database area. Following these rules for field names will help you create a workable database.

- Make sure you record field names in the same order in which they appear in the form you plan to use for data entry. This will minimize the time required for entry.

- Each field name is placed in one cell, and must be unique.

• The names you choose for your fields will be used with some of the other database features. Therefore, choose meaningful names, but not names so long that reentry in other places will lead to misspellings.

• Do not enter spaces at the end of field names. It will not be apparent that you included them, and the names will not match with later entries for other data management features that do not include trailing spaces.

A layout of field names for an employee database might look like this:

Entering Information

The first database record should begin immediately beneath the row of field names. Do not leave blank lines or use special symbols as divider lines.

All entries in corresponding fields of like records should be of the same type. For example, if a field contains numeric data, the value for that field should be numeric in every like record in the database. Mixing numeric values and labels in a single field causes the two types of data to be separated when records are sorted and when you attempt to select a subset of the records. It is acceptable to leave a field blank within a particular record if you lack data. Figure 9-2 presents an employee database after the first ten records have been entered.

As your database grows longer, the field names at the top of your screen will scroll off the screen. You can prevent this by using the /Worksheet Titles Horizontal command to lock the field names in place on your screen. If you have forgotten how this command works, go back to Chapter 5, "Basic Worksheet Commands," for a quick review.

A:F11: 2   READY

A	A	B	C	D	E	F	
1	Last Name	First Name	SS#	Job Code	Salary	Location	
2	Larson	Mary	543-98-9876	23	$12,000	2	
3	Campbell	David	213-76-9874	23	$23,000	10	
4	Campbell	Keith	569-89-7654	12	$32,000	2	
5	Stephens	Tom	219-78-8954	15	$17,800	2	
6	Caldor	Larry	459-34-0921	23	$32,500	4	
7	Lightnor	Peggy	560-55-4311	14	$23,500	10	
8	McCartin	John	817-66-1212	15	$54,600	2	
9	Justof	Jack	431-78-9963	17	$41,200	4	
10	Patterson	Lyle	212-11-9090	12	$21,500	10	
11	Miller	Lisa	214-89-6756	23	$18,700	2	
12							

Figure 9-2.   Employee database with first ten records completed

Tip: To ensure that the data in each field is of the same type, use the /Worksheet Window Map Enable command. 1-2-3 shows the data type of each of the cells. To return the display to normal, use the /Worksheet Window Map Disable command. If you have forgotten how this command works, review it in Chapter 5.

If a database becomes too large to fit on a single worksheet, an alternative is to split the records into multiple database tables in different worksheets. For example, if a customer database is too large for one worksheet, the customers with last names beginning with A through L may be in the first worksheet's data table, and customer names beginning with M through Z may be in the second worksheet's data table.

Making Changes

Entries in a database can be changed with any of the techniques you have used on regular worksheets. An entry can be retyped to replace its current value. The F2 (EDIT) key will insert, delete, and replace characters within an entry.

You can use /Worksheet Insert to add a blank row for a new record or add a blank column for another field. The /Worksheet Delete command can be used to remove records or fields. Bear in mind, though, that the entire worksheet is affected by both of these commands; it is important to assess potential damage to areas outside the database. One good strategy is to save the file before using insertion or deletion commands. Then, if you have a problem, you can restore the file from disk. A better strategy is placing the database table on a worksheet by itself so the changes that you make to the database do not affect other data. Also, the /Copy command can be used to copy field values from other database records.

Sorting Your Data

1-2-3 provides extremely fast sort features because of the storage of the database in RAM. Any change in sequence can take place at the speed of transfer within RAM, which is considerably faster than sorting records from disk.

All the options you will need to specify the records to be sorted, specify the sort sequence, and tell 1-2-3 to begin the sort are located under the /Data Sort command. The submenu for this command looks like this:

```
A:A1: [W12] 'Last Name                                          MENU
Data-Range  Primary-Key  Secondary-Key  Extra-Key  Reset  Go  Quit
```

The steps for resequencing your data using the various Sort options are summarized in the box called "Steps for Sorting Your Data."

Determining What Data to Sort

You can sort all the records in your database or just some of them, depending on the range you specify. Always be sure to include all the fields in the sort, because excluding some fields causes those fields to remain stationary while the remainder of a record is resequenced. If you ever plan to return your records to their original entry sequence after a sort, you will need to include a field for record number

Steps for Sorting Your Data

Sorting is a quick and easy process, but it requires a sequence of commands from the /Data Sort menu. The steps and commands to use are as follows:

1. Enter **/Data Sort** and choose Data-Range.

2. Highlight (specify) all records and fields to be sorted, but do not include the field names within the range.

3. Select Primary-Key from the Sort menu.

4. Highlight any data value within the column you wish to use to control the sort sequence.

5. If you expect duplicate primary keys within your database, choose Secondary-Key from the Sort menu.

6. Highlight any data value within the column that you wish to use as the tie breaker if there are duplicate primary keys.

7. If you expect duplicate primary and secondary keys within your database, choose Extra-Key from the Sort menu.

8. Enter the number of the extra key or accept 1-2-3's default value and press ENTER.

9. Highlight any data value within the column that you wish to use as the tie breaker if there are duplicate primary and secondary keys.

10. Repeat Steps 7 through 9 for each extra key that you want.

11. Select Go from the Sort menu to have 1-2-3 resequence your data.

in the record. A sequential number can be placed in this field at the time of entry.

To set the range for the sort, enter /**Data Sort Data-Range**. Then specify the range for the database as shown in Figure 9-3. Be sure you *do not* include the row of field names. If you do, they will be sorted along with the record values. In Figure 9-3, notice that the range selected includes all of the records and all of the fields, but omits the field names in the first row.

With Release 3, you can sort multiple worksheets. When you select multiple worksheets with a multiple-sheet range, 1-2-3 sorts each worksheet separately. Sorting does not move records between worksheets.

Specifying the Sort Sequence

1-2-3 permits you to specify multiple sort keys. In all cases the primary key will control the sequence of the records. The secondary key will be ignored, even when you specify one, except where duplicate examples of the primary key occur. In this situation, the secondary key will be used to break the tie. When records contain the same data for the primary and secondary keys, 1-2-3 then uses the extra keys to break the tie. These extra keys are a new feature in Release 3; you can specify up to 253 of them. For all sort keys, you may select whether the values are sorted in ascending or descending order.

```
A:F6: 4                                                              POINT
Enter data range: A:A2..A:F6

A        A            B            C          D          E         F
1    Last Name    First Name      SS# Job Code      Salary Location
2    Larson       Mary        543-98-9876       23   $12,000        2
3    Campbell     David       213-76-9874       23   $23,000       10
4    Campbell     Keith       569-89-7654       15   $17,700        2
5    Stephens     Tom         219-78-8954       15   $17,800        2
6    Caldor       Larry       459-34-0921       23   $32,500        4
7
8
```

Figure 9-3.   Sort range selected

Another setting also affects the sort order. This is the collating sequence, which is selected in the Install program. As discussed in Appendix A, "Installing 1-2-3," there are three options for a collating sequence: Numbers First, Numbers Last, and ASCII. The "Effect of Collating Sequence on Sorting" box describes these options in further detail. To make a change, you must reenter Install and select a different collating sequence.

Effect of Collating Sequence on Sorting

The order of your data after a sort is partly dependent on the collating sequence. This sequence is specified during the Install program. Sort order in the three possibilities for ascending sequence is as follows:

- **Numbers last:** Blank cells; label entries beginning with letters in alphabetical order; label entries beginning with numbers in numeric sequence; labels beginning with special characters; values.

- **Numbers first:** Blank cells; labels beginning with numbers in numeric sequence; labels beginning with letters in alphabetical order; labels beginning with special characters; values.

- **ASCII:** Blank cells; labels; values in ASCII order. Capitalization will affect the sort order with this choice.

Sorting in descending order reverses the order.

Choosing a Primary Sort Key

To specify a primary key, enter **/Data Sort Primary-Key** and point to a cell containing data for a particular field within the database. This field (column) becomes your primary sort key. If you prefer, you can type the cell address instead of pointing. In either case you will next be prompted to choose the sort order (A for ascending order and D for descending order). When you choose A, the collating sequence you selected with Install will be used. When you choose D, the sequence will be reversed. Enter the letter for the choice you want, like this:

```
A:A1: [W12] 'Last Name                                            EDIT
Primary sort key: A:D2              Sort order (A or D): A
```

Note that a default sort order may already be present on your screen. This is the order you chose for your previous sort. To keep this default, press ENTER in response to the prompt.

Setting the sort sequence does not automatically resequence your data. You also have to specify the data range and then select Go from the Sort menu.

Choosing a Secondary Sort Key

The secondary sort key serves as a tie breaker. For example, in the case of an employee file where last name has been specified as the primary sort key, you may wish to use first name as the secondary key, to handle instances where more than one employee has the same last name. Within the group of duplicate last names, records are then sorted by first name.

Set the secondary key by entering /**Data Sort Secondary-Key**, and either pointing to a cell containing a data value for the field you want to sort, or by typing the cell address. Then specify A for ascending or D for descending sort order, as you did with the primary key:

```
A:A1: [W12] 'Last Name                                            EDIT
Secondary sort key: A:E2            Sort order (A or D): A
```

Again, the default sequence will be the last order you selected. (Thus, if you selected A last time, the default will be A.) If you wish to keep the current setting, press ENTER in response to this prompt.

Choosing Extra Sort Keys

The extra sort keys in Release 3 serve as additional tie breakers when records contain identical data in their primary and secondary sort key fields. Since 1-2-3 permits up to 253 extra keys, you can select up to 255 different sort keys.

In a large employee database, you may have more than one employee with the same first and last name. You may want to add the social security number as an extra key. In another example, suppose you need to sort expense data that is coded by division, region, branch, and expense code. The data for this example is shown in Figure 9-4. The division can be the primary key, the region can be the secondary key, the branch can be the first extra key, and the expense code can be the second extra key. Once you sort the records, they will look like Figure 9-5.

Specify an extra key by entering /**Data Sort Extra-Key**. 1-2-3 prompts for the extra sort key number by displaying the lowest unselected extra sort key number. You can either accept this number or enter your own. Next, 1-2-3 prompts for the field (column) containing

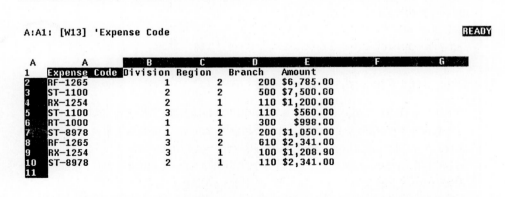

Figure 9-4.   Expense data

```
A:A1: [W13] 'Expense Code                                              READY
```

A	A	B	C	D	E	F	G
1	Expense Code	Division	Region	Branch	Amount		
2	RT-1000	1	1	300	$998.00		
3	RF-1265	1	2	200	$6,785.00		
4	ST-8978	1	2	200	$1,050.00		
5	RX-1254	2	1	110	$1,200.00		
6	ST-8978	2	1	110	$2,341.00		
7	ST-1100	2	2	500	$7,500.00		
8	RX-1254	3	1	100	$1,208.90		
9	ST-1100	3	1	110	$560.00		
10	RF-1265	3	2	610	$2,341.00		
11							

Figure 9-5.   Sorted expense records

the extra sort key. Either point to a cell containing a data value for the
field by which you want to sort, or type the cell address. Here is an
example of the /Data Sort Extra-Key prompt:

```
A:A1: [W13] 'Expense Code                                           EDIT
Extra key: 1     Extra sort key: A:D2          Sort order (A or D): A
```

Specify A for ascending or D for descending sort order, as you did with
the primary and secondary keys. The default sequence will be the last
order you selected. If you wish to keep the current setting, press ENTER
in response to this prompt.

Starting and Stopping the Sort

With the data range and (at a minimum) a primary key selected, you are
ready to resequence your data. Simply select Go from the Sort menu
after completing these other steps, and your data will be sorted in the
specified order. 1-2-3 is very quick. With a small database, the sort will
be complete as soon as you lift your finger after selecting Go.

Figure 9-6 presents an employee database with the records in
random sequence. Suppose the data range is selected as A2..H20, using

A:A1: [W12] 'Last Name   READY

A	A	B	C	D	E	F
1	Last Name	First Name	SS#	Job Code	Salary	Location
2	Larson	Mary	543-98-9876	23	$12,000	2
3	Campbell	David	213-76-9874	23	$23,000	10
4	Campbell	Keith	569-89-7654	12	$32,000	2
5	Stephens	Tom	219-78-8954	15	$17,800	2
6	Caldor	Larry	459-34-0921	23	$32,500	4
7	Lightnor	Peggy	560-55-4311	14	$23,500	10
8	McCartin	John	817-66-1212	15	$54,600	2
9	Justof	Jack	431-78-9963	17	$41,200	4
10	Patterson	Lyle	212-11-9090	12	$21,500	10
11	Miller	Lisa	214-89-6756	23	$18,700	2
12	Hawkins	Mark	215-67-8973	21	$19,500	2
13	Hartwick	Eileen	313-78-9090	15	$31,450	4
14	Smythe	George	560-90-8645	15	$65,000	4
15	Wilkes	Caitlin	124-67-7432	17	$15,500	2
16	Deaver	Ken	198-98-6750	23	$24,600	10
17	Kaylor	Sally	312-45-9862	12	$32,900	10
18	Parker	Dee	659-11-3452	14	$19,800	4
19	Preverson	Gary	670-90-1121	21	$27,600	4
20	Samuelson	Paul	219-89-7080	23	$28,900	2

Figure 9-6.   Employee records in random sequence

/Data Sort Data-Range. Next the Last Name field (A2) is selected as the primary key, with A for ascending sort order. A secondary key of First Name (B2) is then chosen, with A for ascending sort order. Once Go is selected from the /Data Sort menu, the records will be placed in the new sequence shown in Figure 9-7. Notice that the two records with a last name of Campbell are sequenced by first name.

   If you decide to leave the Sort menu without completing the sort operation, you will need to use /Data Sort Quit to get rid of the "sticky" Sort menu. You do not need this command after a normally completed sort, since /Data Sort Go automatically returns you to READY mode after sorting the data.

Starting Over

Once you have made choices for a sort, 1-2-3 will use these settings as a default. Making a new selection for the data range or either of the sort keys will replace the default. If you want to first eliminate your settings

A:A3: [W12] 'Campbell

	A	B	C	D	E	F
1	Last Name	First Name	SS#	Job Code	Salary	Location
2	Caldor	Larry	459-34-0921	23	$32,500	4
3	Campbell	David	213-76-9874	23	$23,000	10
4	Campbell	Keith	569-89-7654	12	$32,000	2
5	Deaver	Ken	198-98-6750	23	$24,600	10
6	Hartwick	Eileen	313-78-9090	15	$31,450	4
7	Hawkins	Mark	215-67-8973	21	$19,500	2
8	Justof	Jack	431-78-9963	17	$41,200	4
9	Kaylor	Sally	312-45-9862	12	$32,900	10
10	Larson	Mary	543-98-9876	23	$12,000	2
11	Lightnor	Peggy	560-55-4311	14	$23,500	10
12	McCartin	John	817-66-1212	15	$54,600	2
13	Miller	Lisa	214-89-6756	23	$18,700	2
14	Parker	Dee	659-11-3452	14	$19,800	4
15	Patterson	Lyle	212-11-9090	12	$21,500	10
16	Preverson	Gary	670-90-1121	21	$27,600	4
17	Samuelson	Paul	219-89-7080	23	$28,900	2
18	Smythe	George	560-90-8645	15	$65,000	4
19	Stephens	Tom	219-78-8954	15	$17,800	2
20	Wilkes	Caitlin	124-67-7432	17	$15,500	2

Figure 9-7. Resequenced employee records

to make sure that you have to reset the data range and primary key before sorting again, you can use /Data Sort Reset. This option eliminates default settings for data range, primary sort key, secondary sort key, and extra sort keys.

Generating a Series of Values

The /Data Fill command can save you considerable time when you are preparing a worksheet model. Use it to generate a series of dates, invoice numbers, purchase order numbers, new account numbers, or identification numbers for new employees, for example. You can combine this feature with sorting records to create record numbers for a database. Whenever you need to enter a series of data with evenly spaced values in either ascending or descending sequence, /Data Fill can handle the task. The /Data Fill command is often used in conjunction with some of the other Data commands covered in this and the next chapter. For example, the next chapter introduces /Data Distribution and /Data Table, which often use the /Data Fill command to generate a numeric series with regular intervals.

To use /Data Fill, place your cell pointer in the upper left cell of the row or column in which you want the series generated, and select /**Data Fill**. Next, enter the range you wish to use for the series. 1-2-3 will then prompt you for the first number in the series (the start value) and suggest the default value of 0. You can press ENTER to accept this value or enter another number. The prompt for the increment is next. To accept the default of 1, press ENTER again; alternatively, enter any positive or negative number for the increment before pressing ENTER. 1-2-3's last prompt is for a stop value. As long as the default stop value of 8191 is greater than or equal to your planned stop value, you can just press ENTER and allow 1-2-3 to determine a stop value, based on the size of the range and other values you have supplied. If 8191 is not large enough, enter a new stop value before pressing ENTER.

For example, suppose you need to enter the data for a group of consecutively numbered invoices. Rather than entering the invoice numbers, you can use the /Data Fill command to create them for you. To enter invoice numbers in cells A2..A20 of a worksheet, place your cell pointer in A2 to begin and enter /**Data Fill**. When 1-2-3 prompts for a range, select A2..A20. For the start value, enter **1004**, representing the first invoice number that you want to enter. For the increment, enter **1**.

Remember that there are two situations that stop generation of entries in a fill series. You must ensure that the range is large enough, and the stop value is high enough. 1-2-3 stops generating values as soon as either condition is exceeded. Consider what happens if you accept the default stop value of 8191. This number exceeds the start value, and it also far exceeds the range, so the range is what stops the generation of fill values. The results are shown in Figure 9-8. If you entered 1009 as the stop value, your results would be quite different, since the stop value would have been reached before the end of the range. In this case, the /Data Fill command would only fill A2..A7.

Tip: If you want /Data Fill to fill every cell in the range, make the stop value sufficiently larger than what you expect the last value in the fill range to be.

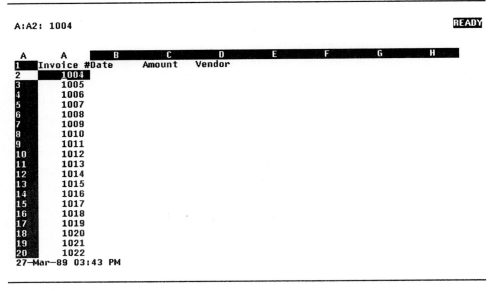

A:A2: 1004   READY

A	A	B	C	D	E	F	G	H
1	Invoice #Date		Amount	Vendor				
2	1004							
3	1005							
4	1006							
5	1007							
6	1008							
7	1009							
8	1010							
9	1011							
10	1012							
11	1013							
12	1014							
13	1015							
14	1016							
15	1017							
16	1018							
17	1019							
18	1020							
19	1021							
20	1022							

27-Mar-89 03:43 PM

Figure 9-8.   Result of /Data Fill

Adding Record Numbers for Sorting Records

1-2-3 does not have an "unsort" feature. Once you have changed the sequence of your records, there is no command that will automatically restore them to their original sequence unless you can use Undo. There is a solution to this dilemma, however, if you plan ahead. You can add a record number field to each record, containing a sequential number based on when the records are added to the database. To return sorted records to their original entry order, you could then simply re-sort based on record number.

You can get 1-2-3 to do the work of sequential record number assignment by using /Data Fill. You have already learned how this command will generate any series of numbers that have even increments, if you specify the start, stop, and increment values you wish to use.

A look at the command in action with the employee database from previous examples will clarify the steps required for this use. Suppose a blank column has been inserted at the left of the employee database for record sequence numbers, and the field name, Sequence, was entered in A1. Record numbers can be used in this field to keep track of the original entry order for the employee records. To make /Data Fill supply the numbers, follow these steps:

1. Move the cell pointer to A2, the upper leftmost cell in the range where the numbers will be generated.

2. Enter **/Data Fill** and specify the fill range as A2..A20, either by pointing or by typing the range reference.

3. At the prompt, enter **1** for the start value, as shown:

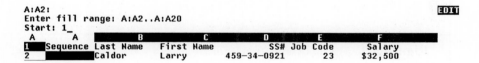

4. The next prompt is for the step or increment value (that is, the amount to add to each value to generate the next number). Enter another **1**.

5. The last prompt is for the stop value—the highest number that can be in the series. You could enter a 19, since this will be the last value in the range. However, as long as the default stop value is not less than the stop value you want, you can let 1-2-3 generate the exact stop value, based on the range and increment you have supplied. To do this, accept the default of 8191 by pressing ENTER, as shown. You can always use this method when 8191 is greater than the last value in your series. 1-2-3 will stop when it fills the range.

```
A:A2:                                                          EDIT
Enter fill range: A:A2..A:A20
Start: 1              Step: 1                    Stop: 8191
```

The result of the /Data Fill operation is shown in Figure 9-9.

A:A2: 1   `READY`

Sequence	Last Name	First Name	SS#	Job Code	Salary
1	Larson	Mary	543-98-9876	23	$12,000
2	Campbell	David	213-76-9874	23	$23,000
3	Campbell	Keith	569-89-7654	12	$32,000
4	Stephens	Tom	219-78-8954	15	$17,800
5	Caldor	Larry	459-34-0921	23	$32,500
6	Lightnor	Peggy	560-55-4311	14	$23,500
7	McCartin	John	817-66-1212	15	$54,600
8	Justof	Jack	431-78-9963	17	$41,200
9	Patterson	Lyle	212-11-9090	12	$21,500
10	Miller	Lisa	214-89-6756	23	$18,700
11	Hawkins	Mark	215-67-8973	21	$19,500
12	Hartwick	Eileen	313-78-9090	15	$31,450
13	Smythe	George	560-90-8645	15	$65,000
14	Wilkes	Caitlin	124-67-7432	17	$15,500
15	Deaver	Ken	198-98-6750	23	$24,600
16	Kaylor	Sally	312-45-9862	12	$32,900
17	Parker	Dee	659-11-3452	14	$19,800
18	Preverson	Gary	670-90-1121	21	$27,600
19	Samuelson	Paul	219-89-7080	23	$28,900

Figure 9-9.   Output from /Data Fill

Using /Data Fill with Dates and Times

Release 3 introduces new features that make the /Data Fill command easier to use with dates and times. One of these features is 1-2-3's recognition of dates and times if they are entered in one of 1-2-3's date and time formats (except Short International format for dates). This lets you enter dates and times as start and stop values making it much easier to generate the required date and time serial numbers than by computing them or using @functions.

The other new Release 3 feature for /Data Fill is the addition of step value options; these are used for the generation of date and time entries. For dates, if the step value contains:

• An integer or an integer followed by a D, 1-2-3 increases the date value in daily increments

- An integer followed by an M, 1-2-3 increases the step value in monthly increments

- An integer followed by a W, 1-2-3 increases the step value in weekly increments

- An integer followed by a Q, 1-2-3 increases the step value in quarterly increments

- An integer followed by a Y, 1-2-3 increases the step value in yearly increments

For example, a step value of 2M increments the date serial numbers in two-month increments.

For times, if the step value contains:

- An integer followed by an S, 1-2-3 increases the time value in second increments

- An integer followed by MIN, 1-2-3 increases the step value in minute increments

- An integer followed by an H, 1-2-3 increases the step value in hour increments

For example, a step value of 30S increments the time serial numbers in thirty-second increments.

A third feature new to Release 3 is the way 1-2-3 formats values generated by /Data Fill. If the range selected for /Data Fill uses the Automatic format, 1-2-3 will automatically format the cells as dates and times using the format of the start, step, and stop values. If the range selected for /Data Fill does not use a date or time format, 1-2-3 displays the time or date serial number using the format established for the range.

For example, suppose you need to enter a series of dates that are each seven days apart. If the first date you need is January 3, 1990, you can enter **@DATE(90,1,3)** and get a serial date number of 32876. Assuming you want to enter the dates in cells A2..A20 of the current worksheet, place your cell pointer in A2 to begin, and enter **/Data Fill**. Next, select A2..A20 as the data range to fill. For the start value, enter **03-Jan-90**. Enter **1w** for the increment and **45000** for the stop value. Since you check the date serial number for the beginning entry you can

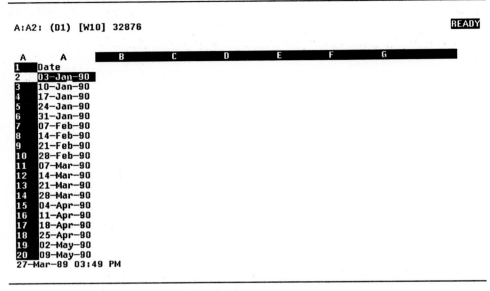

Figure 9-10.   Result of /Data Fill using dates

be certain that 45000 is larger than the last number required to fill the range. The results are shown in Figure 9-10 which has a column width of 10 and an Automatic format. If you entered 33000 as the stop value, your results would have been quite different, since the stop value would have been reached before the end of the range.

Searching the Database

As your database grows large, it becomes increasingly important to selectively review the information it contains. 1-2-3's /Data Query commands provide the ability to work selectively with information in your database and thus offer an exception reporting capability; that is, information can be brought to your attention if it is considered to be outside an established norm. You can also use the selective review feature to clean up your database, or to create reports in response to unexpected requests.

All the commands required to review information selectively are found in the /Data Query menu shown here:

```
A:A1:                                                                    MENU
Input  Criteria  Output  Find  Extract  Unique  Del  Modify  Reset  Quit
Specify ranges or external tables that contain records to manipulate
```

You will need to use at least three of the /Data Query commands to make a selection. Your database must be specified with /Data Query Input, and your selection criteria identified with /Data Query Criteria before you can select a specific action for the Query command to perform. In addition, database records and selection criteria must be entered on the worksheet before you enter a Query command that uses them. The steps required for using /Data Query commands are summarized in the "Steps for Using Query Commands" box. Let's examine each of the Query options in detail.

Telling 1-2-3 Where Your Data Is Located

When you use the Query options, 1-2-3 must know where your field names and data records are located. Contrary to the case with /Data Sort, you *must* include the field names when you specify the range. These field names will be matched against the field names in the selection criteria area to ensure that selections are correct.

The command by which you specify the location of the database is /Data Query Input. After you enter this command, you can point to your data range or type the required cell references. In both cases, be sure to include the field names, as shown in the selection in Figure 9-11. Release 3 lets you select input ranges that are in active files, inactive files, and external tables (which are discussed later in the chapter). If you are planning to insert or replace records with the /Data Query commands, you must use an active file for the input range.

Specifying the Desired Records

To determine what records from the database will be used to fill your query request, 1-2-3 checks the criteria you specify against each record in the selected database range. Records that do not meet the criteria are not used.

1 2 3

Steps for Using /Data Query Commands

The /Data Query commands allow you to access selected records in your database. Obtaining the results you desire involves some preliminary work, as well as a number of /Data Query options. The required steps are as follows:

1. Enter the Query criteria on your worksheet.

2. If you plan to use the Extract, Unique, or Modify options, enter the field names you will be copying in the output area of your worksheet.

3. Enter **/Data Query Input** from the Query menu and specify the range for your database, including field names.

4. Enter **/Data Query Criteria** from the Query menu and specify the location of your criteria.

5. If you plan to use Extract, Unique, or Modify, enter **/Data Query Output** and specify the location of your output area.

6. Select the /Data Query option you wish to use: Find, Del, Extract, Unique, or Modify.

7. If you choose Find, press ESC after you have finished browsing in your file, and then Quit to exit the Query menu.

When entering criteria on the worksheet, keep in mind two things. First, criteria must be positioned on the worksheet in an out-of-the-way location that will not interfere with the expansion of the database. This action must be taken in READY mode, not from within /Data Query, because once you select /Data Query, you cannot make entries on the worksheet. Second, 1-2-3 needs to be told where the criteria are stored, by means of the /Data Query Criteria command.

```
A:F20: [W12] 2                                                    POINT
Enter input range: A:A1..A:F20_
```

A	A	B	C	D	E	F
1	Last Name	First Name	SS#	Job Code	Salary	Location
2	Larson	Mary	543-98-9876	23	$12,000	2
3	Campbell	David	213-76-9874	23	$23,000	10
4	Campbell	Keith	569-89-7654	12	$32,000	2
5	Stephens	Tom	219-78-8954	15	$17,800	2
6	Caldor	Larry	459-34-0921	23	$32,500	4
7	Lightnor	Peggy	560-55-4311	14	$23,500	10
8	McCartin	John	817-66-1212	15	$54,600	2
9	Justof	Jack	431-78-9963	17	$41,200	4
10	Patterson	Lyle	212-11-9090	12	$21,500	10
11	Miller	Lisa	214-89-6756	23	$18,700	2
12	Hawkins	Mark	215-67-8973	21	$19,500	2
13	Hartwick	Eileen	313-78-9090	15	$31,450	4
14	Smythe	George	560-90-8645	15	$65,000	4
15	Wilkes	Caitlin	124-67-7432	17	$15,500	2
16	Deaver	Ken	198-98-6750	23	$24,600	10
17	Kaylor	Sally	312-45-9862	12	$32,900	10
18	Parker	Dee	659-11-3452	14	$19,800	4
19	Preverson	Gary	670-90-1121	21	$27,600	4
20	Samuelson	Paul	219-89-7080	23	$28,900	2

Figure 9-11.   Selecting an input range

Location of Criteria

When you use one of the /Data Query commands that requires the use of search criteria, you must use the /Data Query Criteria command to tell 1-2-3 the location of the criteria. (Remember that the criteria themselves must be entered before you select /Data Query.) Unlike Release 2, Release 3 allows you to leave blank areas in the criteria range without producing wildcard matches with every record in the database table. Entering criteria and telling 1-2-3 where they are located with /Data Query Criteria will not show you the matching records, however. A number of other commands can display the matching records, copy them to a new area, or delete them from your database; these commands are explained later in the chapter.

You can choose any location you desire for your search criteria. A popular location is to the right of the database; this allows the criteria area to be expanded to the right, and does not interfere with the expansion of your database. If your database occupies columns A through M, for example, you may wish to begin your criteria in column R. This allows for the expansion of the database by four new fields before the criteria would have to be moved.

With Release 3, you have the option of putting your criteria on a separate worksheet or a separate file. With this approach, you don't have to plan for expansion or modifications. 1-2-3 does not support search criteria that span sheets and will not allow a multiple-sheet range for the criteria.

Types of Criteria

You can use a variety of different ways to specify which records in the database you wish to query. You can use values that match your database entries exactly; you can use 1-2-3's wildcard characters to specify only a portion of the entry you are looking for; or you can specify formulas. For matches other than formulas, the name of the field in the database you are searching must appear above the specific entry you are searching for. For formula matches you can use any field name, although for documentation purposes it is best to use the name of the field referenced in the formula.

For example, if you want to search the last name field in an employee database to find all records with a last name of Smith, your criteria area might look like this:

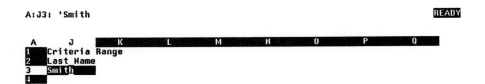

Note that the criteria area is J2..J3. The entry in J1 is documentation. The search value is placed immediately underneath the field name in the criteria area. The field name in the criteria area must be an exact match with the field name in your database. A space at the end of one or the other, or a misspelling, can cause a problem. The safest approach is to copy the field name from its location above the data to the criteria area where you wish to use it.

Note: 1-2-3 is case sensitive to field names when the collating sequence used in sorting is set to ASCII.

In Release 3, you can now leave blank criteria areas without jeopardizing Query operation results. You can include columns with field names but no criteria beneath them; 1-2-3 will still find the records that you want rather than the wildcard matching that occurred in previous releases.

Tip: Copy database field names from the database table to the criteria range, so the spacing and the upper- and lowercase arrangement of the field names in the criteria match the database table.

Values   To search for numeric values in your records, record the desired field name in the criteria area. Underneath this field name enter the value for which you are searching. The criteria value need not have the same format as the values you are looking for. In a search based on the following criteria area, only records for Job Code 23 would match.

Labels   If you want to match label entries, you can enter them in the criteria exactly as they appear in your database, under the name of the field you wish to search. For example, entering **Last Name** in the criteria area and placing **Jones** beneath causes 1-2-3 to select records that contain Jones in the last name field.

1-2-3 has two special characters that are useful when specifying label criteria. These characters are the asterisk (*) and the question mark (?).

The * at the end of a criteria entry indicates that if the first part of the criteria entry matches a database record, any characters from the location of the * to the end of the database entry should be accepted in the match. The following criteria would search the Last Name field for all records beginning with Sm.

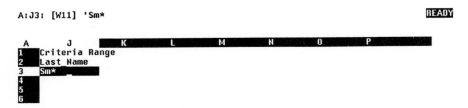

Smith would match, as would Smithfield, Smothers, and Smeltman. The ? replaces any one character in an entry. The question mark says that you do not care what character comes at that location in the data entry, as long as all the other characters match exactly. The following criteria tells 1-2-3 that you do not care what character is located in the second position of the Last Name field, as long as *B* is the first character, and *tman* the third through the sixth characters of the database entry.

Bitman, Butman, Batman, Botman, and Betman would be among the matching entries if records containing these names were in the database. All entries longer than six characters, such as Bitmanson, would be rejected.

Formulas   The ability to create formulas to serve as search criteria offers additional Query power. You can use formula comparisons to check for records that contain values with a specific range, and you can even use string formulas in your criteria. When you enter a formula as criteria, the formula will display as 0 or 1, depending on whether it evaluates to true or false for the first database record. You may want to format the cell of the criteria area as Text, so it will display as the formula you entered.

When you create formulas as search criteria, it is not important that the field name used in the criteria area match with the field referenced in the formula, although for clarity it is always best to use the proper field name. As you construct your formulas to compare values in the database against a specific value, always reference the first value for the field in the database, or the field name.

In the example in Figure 9-11, to find all values in a Salary field located in column E that are greater than $25,000, you might use this criteria formula.

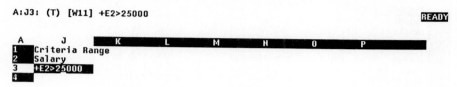

The cell referenced is E2, since that contains the first value in the salary field. Always use a relative reference when referring to database fields. When you format criteria cells as Text, the formulas will display as you enter them. You could also enter the previous formula as **+SALARY>25000**, since 1-2-3 will substitute the field values for the field name. Another shortcut approach is an entry like >25000.

If you need a criteria formula that compares a database field against a value located elsewhere in the worksheet, use an absolute reference as the reference outside the database. Let's say you want to compare the salaries in Figure 9-12 against the average salary amount stored in J10. The criteria in Figure 9-13 will identify all records where the salary exceeded the average by $3,000.

Tip: You may need to start a criteria with a less than (<) symbol. Be aware that when you type a less than symbol in the READY mode, 1-2-3 activates the menus. This feature accommodates foreign language keyboards, where the slash (/) is in an awkward position. So, to start a formula for a criteria range with a less than symbol, type a label prefix before typing the <.

The complex operators #AND#, #OR#, and #NOT# can also be used in formula criteria. Suppose you wish to determine if a salary is less than or equal to $25,000 or greater than or equal to $50,000, for example. The proper criteria formula to use is shown here:

A:A1: [W12] 'Last Name   `READY`

A	A	B	C	D	E	F
1	Last Name	First Name	SS#	Job Code	Salary	Location
2	Larson	Mary	543-98-9876	23	$12,000	2
3	Campbell	David	213-76-9874	23	$23,000	10
4	Campbell	Keith	569-89-7654	12	$32,000	2
5	Stephens	Tom	219-78-8954	15	$17,800	2
6	Caldor	Larry	459-34-0921	23	$32,500	4
7	Lightnor	Peggy	560-55-4311	14	$23,500	10
8	McCartin	John	817-66-1212	15	$54,600	2
9	Justof	Jack	431-78-9963	17	$41,200	4
10	Patterson	Lyle	212-11-9090	12	$21,500	10
11	Miller	Lisa	214-89-6756	23	$18,700	2
12	Hawkins	Mark	215-67-8973	21	$19,500	2
13	Hartwick	Eileen	313-78-9090	15	$31,450	4
14	Smythe	George	560-90-8645	15	$65,000	4
15	Wilkes	Caitlin	124-67-7432	17	$15,500	2
16	Deaver	Ken	198-98-6750	23	$24,600	10
17	Kaylor	Sally	312-45-9862	12	$32,900	10
18	Parker	Dee	659-11-3452	14	$19,800	4
19	Preverson	Gary	670-90-1121	21	$27,600	4
20	Samuelson	Paul	219-89-7080	23	$28,900	2

Figure 9-12.   Salary data

If you use the #AND# operator, the conditions on both sides of the operator must be true for the record to be selected. If you use #OR#, either condition may be true for the record to be selected. #NOT# negates the condition that follows it. When you use a complex operator,

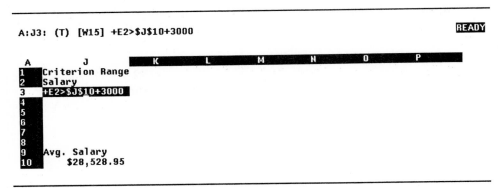

A:J3: (T) [W15] +E2>$J$10+3000   `READY`

A	J	K	L	M	N	O	P
1	Criterion Range						
2	Salary						
3	+E2>$J$10+3000						
4							
5							
6							
7							
8							
9	Avg. Salary						
10	$28,528.95						

Figure 9-13.   Criteria using formulas

you must include the field names or the cell address for the first record. In the previous example, you could not use the criteria $< =25000\#OR\#> =50000$. A criteria like this would look for the string $< =25000\#OR\#> =50000$ in the salary column.

Compound Criteria   Whenever you use more than one field in the criteria area, you are using compound criteria. 1-2-3 allows up to 256 fields to be used for search criteria at one time. These criteria must be joined by implied "and's" and "or's."

If two criteria values are placed on the same line beneath their separate field names, they are joined by an implied "and." The following criteria, for example, will select records where the job code is equal to 23 *and* the salary is less than $16,000.

Notice that the field names in the criteria area are placed in adjacent cells. Note also that the criteria types do not have to be the same; one criterion is a formula, and the other a value. A database record must meet both criteria to be selected.

If one criteria value is placed one row below the other, the two criteria are joined by an implied "or." Perhaps you want records with a job code of 23 or a salary of less than $16,000. The criteria shown here will select records meeting *either* of these conditions:

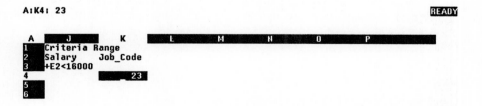

Highlighting Selected Records

Once you have defined your search area and criteria, 1-2-3's /Data Query Find command will highlight records that match the criteria you have defined. The records are highlighted one at a time, beginning at the top of the database. Table 9-1 lists the keys you can use to move through the selected records.

Finding records requires a few preliminary steps. You must have defined your database, including the field names, with /Data Query Input. You must also have entered your search criteria on the worksheet or in a separate area before requesting the Query commands, and then defined the criteria with /Data Query Criteria. Figure 9-14 shows a database that has been defined with /Data Query Input as A1..E10. The following criteria are established in J1...J3 to locate records for the Accounting Department:

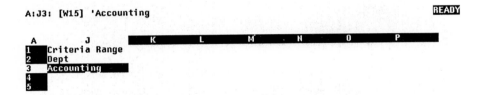

Figure 9-15 shows the first record matching the criteria highlighted on the screen.

The /Data Query Find option is a good one if you need a quick answer to a question concerning data you have stored in your database. The drawback to using it is that all the matching records are not listed at once and cannot be printed out. If you need to do either of these things, you will want to use the /Data Query Extract and /Data Query Unique commands.

Writing Selected Records on the Worksheet

1-2-3 provides three commands that make a copy of selected records and fields from your database to another area of the worksheet. You can add headings to these new areas to create an instant report that can be shared with others. Before you can have 1-2-3 copy database information, however, you must prepare an output location.

Defining an Output Area

First decide on a location and prepare it to receive data. The bottom of the existing database is a commonly selected location. Just make sure you leave some blank rows at the bottom of the database to allow for expansion, or you may find yourself moving the output area around to

Key	Action
DOWN ARROW	Moves to the next record in the input range that meets the criteria. If the cell pointer is on the last record that meets the criteria, 1-2-3 beeps.
UP ARROW	Moves to the previous record in the input range that meets the criteria. If the cell pointer is on the first record that meets the criteria, 1-2-3 beeps.
LEFT ARROW	Moves one field to the left in the selected record. If the cell pointer is on the first field, 1-2-3 beeps.
RIGHT ARROW	Moves one field to the right in the selected record. If the cell pointer is on the last field, 1-2-3 beeps.
HOME	Moves to the first record in the input range that meets the criteria.
END	Moves to the last record in the input range that meets the criteria.
ESC	Ends the /Data Query Find operation and returns to the /Data Query menu.
ENTER	Ends the /Data Query Find operation and returns to the /Data Query menu.
F2 (EDIT)	Switches to EDIT mode for the current field in the selected record. Pressing F2(EDIT) again or ENTER saves your edits and returns to the /Data Query Find operation. Pressing ESC cancels the edits and returns to the /Data Query Find operation.
F7 (QUERY)	Re-executes the most recent query operations or ends the /Data Query Find operation and returns to the READY mode.

Table 9-1.   Cell Pointer Movement Keys for Use with /Data Query Find in Database Records

```
A:A1: [W25] 'Description                                              READY

     A             A           B         C        D           E
 1  Description              Life      Cost Dept          Type
 2  FTY Computer               5       $980 Accounting    Office
 3  Dover Typewriter           5       $950 Training      Office
 4  Swivel Chair              10       $345 Check         Furniture
 5  KL Calculator              7       $100 Audit         Office
 6  Walnut Desk               15     $1,200 Cash          Furniture
 7  Lanver Copier              3     $2,500 Cash          Processing
 8  Lanver Copier              3     $2,800 Accounting    Processing
 9  Computer Table             5       $300 Training      Furniture
10  File Cabinet              10       $450 Audit         Furniture
11
```

Figure 9-14. Asset records

acquire more space. With Release 3, you have the option of placing your output on a separate worksheet or a separate file. This allows both the input and output areas to be as large as 8192 records if you have sufficient memory, and lets you place your output in a location where a growing database will not interfere.

With the location selected, enter the names of the fields you wish to copy from matching records. They need not be in the same sequence as the fields in your database, and you do not have to include every field.

Tip: Use the /Copy command to copy field names from the database table directly to the output range, so the spacing and letter case of the

```
A:A2: [W25] 'FTY Computer                                            FIND

     A             A           B         C        D           E
 1  Description              Life      Cost Dept          Type
 2  FTY Computer               5       $980 Accounting    Office
 3  Dover Typewriter           5       $950 Training      Office
 4  Swivel Chair              10       $345 Check         Furniture
 5  KL Calculator              7       $100 Audit         Office
 6  Walnut Desk               15     $1,200 Cash          Furniture
 7  Lanver Copier              3     $2,500 Cash          Processing
 8  Lanver Copier              3     $2,800 Accounting    Processing
 9  Computer Table             5       $300 Training      Furniture
10  File Cabinet              10       $450 Audit         Furniture
11
```

Figure 9-15. Finding records for a specific department

field names in the criteria match the database table exactly. Once you have all the field names, you can delete field names of the fields you do not want in the output range.

Once the field names are placed in the output area, you are ready to define its location to 1-2-3. This is done with /Data Query Output. If you define the output area as consisting of only the row containing the headings, 1-2-3 will use columns of cells from the heading area to the bottom of the worksheet for writing records that match. If the output area is in a worksheet that contains other data, it is important to be aware of the maximum number of records that can be copied to this area, so that data located in these cells will not be overwritten.

You can also specify the range for the output area to include the number of blank rows beneath the row of field names. If you use this approach, 1-2-3 will stop copying matching database records when the specified output area becomes full. For example, if you select B:A1..B:F10 as the output range, 1-2-3 will only copy the first nine records it finds (it uses the first line for the field names). If 1-2-3 cannot fit the selected records into the output range, it displays an error message in the status line.

Extracting All Matches

To extract matching records, enter **/Data Query Extract** once you have set up the criteria and output areas on your worksheet, and defined the database, criteria, and output to 1-2-3. Every time you select the Extract option, 1-2-3 erases the output area before writing the newly selected records to it. Since so many preliminary steps are required before using this command, let's review them in order, using the database in Figure 9-16 as an example.

1. Add selection criteria to the worksheet, as shown here:

A:J1: [W12] 'Criteria Range   READY

A	J	K	L	M	N	O	P
1	Criteria Range						
2	Dept	Cost					
3	Training	+C2>500					
4							

2. Set up the output area on the worksheet to look like this:

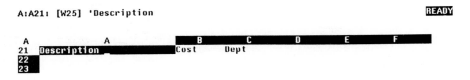

3. Enter the /**Data Query Input** command to define the database as located in A1..E10.

4. Since the Data Query menu remains displayed, all you have to enter is **Criteria** in order to define the criteria location as J2..K3.

5. Define the output area next by entering **Output**, and specifying its location of A21..C21 at the prompt.

6. Enter **Extract**, and the following output will be produced.

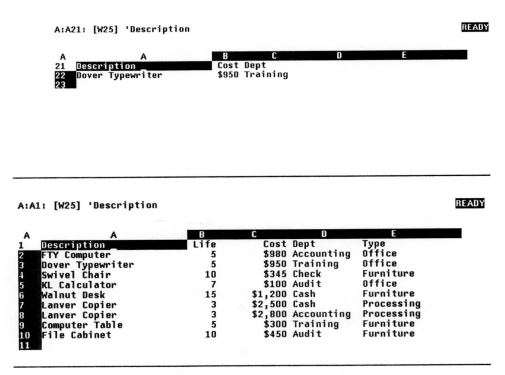

Figure 9-16.   Database used for record extraction process

If you want to turn extracted records into a report, you need only add a report title at the top of the extract area and then print the worksheet range containing the heading and the extract.

Extracting and Replacing Records

Release 3 also has a /Data Query Modify Extract command that you can use to extract records. /Data Query Modify Extract differs from /Data Query Extract in that Modify Extract remembers the extracted records' position in the original database. You can use Modify Extract when you want to edit an extracted group of records, and then use the /Data Replace command to replace the records in the input range with the modified records from the output area.

To extract the matching records, enter /**Data Query Modify Extract** once you set up the criteria and output areas on your worksheet, and define the database, criteria, and output to 1-2-3. Every time you select Modify Extract, 1-2-3 erases the output area before writing the newly selected records to it. 1-2-3 only copies the fields for each record that are in the first row of the outut range. Since several steps are required to extract and replace records, let's again use the data in Figure 9-16 to review them in order.

1. Add selection criteria to the worksheet, as shown here:

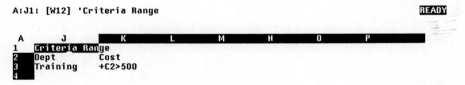

2. Set up the output area on the worksheet to look like this:

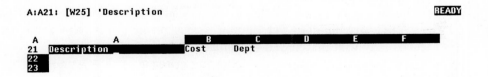

3. Enter the /**Data Query Input** command to define the database as located in A1..E10.

4. Since the Data Query menu remains displayed, all you have to enter is **Criteria** in order to define the criteria location as J2..K3.

5. Define the output area next by entering **Output**, and specifying its location of A21..C21 at the prompt.

6. Enter **Modify Extract**, and the following output will be produced. 1-2-3 then returns to the /Data Query menu.

```
A:A21: [W25] 'Description                                           READY

     A              A                  B        C        D     E
21  Description                       Cost Dept
22  Dover Typewriter                  $950 Training
23
```

7. Select Quit to return to READY mode.

8. Edit the data in the extract; change the Cost of the Typewriter to $850.

9. Enter /**Data Query Modify Replace**. The final output looks like Figure 9-17. Select Quit to return to READY mode.

If you decide not to replace the records, use the /Data Query Modify Cancel command. This command instructs 1-2-3 to forget the original record positions the extracted records had in the database.

Writing Only Unique Records

The Unique option is very similar to Extract in that it writes records to the output area. However, it writes only unique records to this area, so if two selected entries are an exact match, only one will be written. Uniqueness of records is determined by the fields written to the output area.

Be aware that the number of records written to the output area can be affected by the number of fields you plan to write there. If two records are alike in five of the six fields you plan to write to the output area, they are unique; yet, if you select fewer fields, the same two records may well match and therefore not be unique.

For instance, consider the following criteria:

```
A:I3: (T) +F4>60                                                    READY

     A      I          J        K        L       M       N       O       P
1           Criteria Range
2           Rate
3           +F4>60
4
```

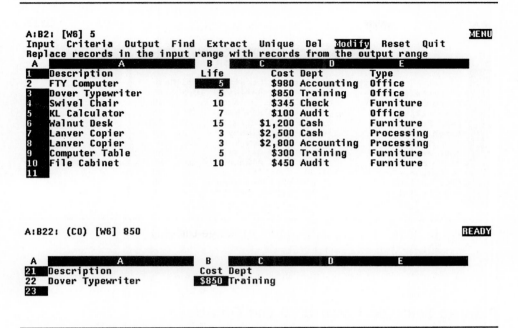

Figure 9-17.   Database after Modify Replace process

and the database records shown in Figure 9-18. 1-2-3 produced the output shown below when Unique was selected from the /Data Query menu. Note that the Tower College record appears only once, even though several qualifying records for it exist in the database.

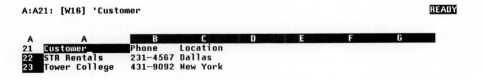

Every time you use the Unique option, the output area is erased so that the newly selected records can be written to it.

```
A:A1:  [W16]                                                          READY

  A            A              B        C         D        E     F      G
1                           CLIENT BILLINGS — SEPTEMBER 1989
2
3   Customer         Type         Phone    Location Hours Rate
4   STR Rentals           5 231—4567 Dallas     10.5   75
5   XCV Company           3 341—4545 Chicago       5   60
6   Tower College         5 431—9092 New York     15   85
7   Lower Rentals         3 498—2123 Dallas       20   60
8   Nelson Products       4 213—9845 Albany        3   60
9   Tower College         5 431—9092 New York     30   85
10  Lower Rentals         3 498—2123 Dallas        2   60
11  Nelson Products       4 213—9845 Albany       14   60
12  XCV Company           3 341—4545 Chicago      15   60
13  Tower College         5 431—9092 New York     22   85
14  Lower Rentals         3 498—2123 Dallas        7   60
15
```

Figure 9-18.   Database used with /Data Query Unique

Adding Selected Records to the Database

The /Data Query Modify Insert command copies records from one database to another. When you use this command, be careful not to have the output range too close below the input range, since as the records are added, they can overwrite the output area. Also, Modify Insert requires that the output range contain both the field names and the records to add. This command adds all records in the selected output area to the bottom of the input area. Blank rows are excluded in this copy operation. If you do not want all the records added, you must remove unwanted records from the selected output area.

As an example, suppose you have the database tables in Figure 9-19. You can add the records in the second database table to the first one with the /Data Query Modify Insert command. Define the input range as A:A1..A:E3, and the output range as B:A1..B:E6. When you perform the /Data Query Modify Insert command, 1-2-3 copies all of the output range to the database (the input range). Figure 9-20 shows the first 3 records added to the input range. Only the data in the fields common to both the input and output range are copied.

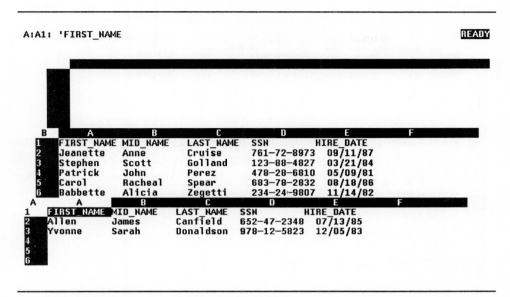

Figure 9-19.   Using Modify Insert to add records

Deleting Selected Records from the Database

/Data Query Del is a powerful yet dangerous command. In one easy process it can purge outdated records from your database—but if you make a mistake in entering your search criteria, it can also purge records you still need. You would be wise to test your criteria with Find or Extract before selecting the Del option.

If you specified the criteria

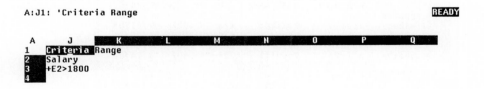

and the database in Figure 9-21, and then chose the Del option, only the following records would remain in the database:

```
A:A1: [W12] 'Last Name                                               MENU
Input  Criteria  Output  Find  Extract  Unique  Del  Modify  Reset  Quit
Delete all records that match criteria
  A      A          B          C          D          E          F
1   Last Name  First Name       SS# Job Code      Salary Location
2   Larson     Mary       543-98-9876       23    $12,000        2
3   Stephens   Tom        219-78-8954       15    $17,800        2
4   Wilkes     Caitlin    124-67-7432       17    $15,500        2
5
```

Tip: Look at database records before you delete them. Use /Data Query Find or /Data Query Extract to view records the /Data Query Del command is going to delete. This step prevents you from deleting records that you want to keep.

Resetting Selection Options

All of the Query specifications can be eliminated with the /Data Query Reset command. This includes the Input specification, the Criteria specification, and the Output specification if you made one.

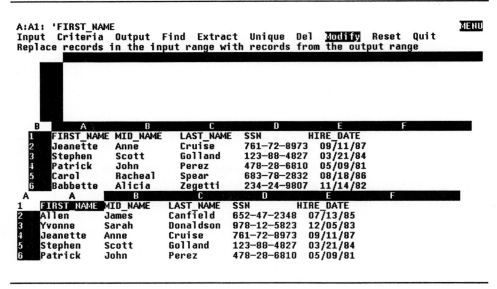

```
A:A1: 'FIRST_NAME                                                    MENU
Input  Criteria  Output  Find  Extract  Unique  Del  Modify  Reset  Quit
Replace records in the input range with records from the output range




  B      A          B          C          D          E          F
1   FIRST_NAME MID_NAME   LAST_NAME  SSN        HIRE_DATE
2   Jeanette   Anne       Cruise     761-72-8973  09/11/87
3   Stephen    Scott      Golland    123-88-4827  03/21/84
4   Patrick    John       Perez      478-28-6810  05/09/81
5   Carol      Racheal    Spear      683-78-2832  08/18/86
6   Babbette   Alicia     Zegetti    234-24-9807  11/14/82
  A      A          B          C          D          E          F
1   FIRST_NAME MID_NAME   LAST_NAME  SSN        HIRE_DATE
2   Allen      James      Canfield   652-47-2348  07/13/85
3   Yvonne     Sarah      Donaldson  978-12-5823  12/05/83
4   Jeanette   Anne       Cruise     761-72-8973  09/11/87
5   Stephen    Scott      Golland    123-88-4827  03/21/84
6   Patrick    John       Perez      478-28-6810  05/09/81
```

Figure 9-20. Database after record insertion

A:A1: [W12] 'Last Name   READY

	A	B	C	D	E	F
1	Last Name	First Name	SS#	Job Code	Salary	Location
2	Larson	Mary	543-98-9876	23	$12,000	2
3	Campbell	David	213-76-9874	23	$23,000	10
4	Campbell	Keith	569-89-7654	12	$32,000	2
5	Stephens	Tom	219-78-8954	15	$17,800	2
6	Caldor	Larry	459-34-0921	23	$32,500	4
7	Lightnor	Peggy	560-55-4311	14	$23,500	10
8	McCartin	John	817-66-1212	15	$54,600	2
9	Justof	Jack	431-78-9963	17	$41,200	4
10	Patterson	Lyle	212-11-9090	12	$21,500	10
11	Miller	Lisa	214-89-6756	23	$18,700	2
12	Hawkins	Mark	215-67-8973	21	$19,500	2
13	Hartwick	Eileen	313-78-9090	15	$31,450	4
14	Smythe	George	560-90-8645	15	$65,000	4
15	Wilkes	Caitlin	124-67-7432	17	$15,500	2
16	Deaver	Ken	198-98-6750	23	$24,600	10
17	Kaylor	Sally	312-45-9862	12	$32,900	10
18	Parker	Dee	659-11-3452	14	$19,800	4
19	Preverson	Gary	670-90-1121	21	$27,600	4
20	Samuelson	Paul	219-89-7080	23	$28,900	2

Figure 9-21.   Database before record deletion process

Quitting the Query Menu

When you want to leave the /Data Query operation, choose Quit from
the Query menu to return to READY mode. This allows you to make
new entries for criteria and perform other tasks. To return to /Data
Query after making changes, you can reenter through the menu. Alternatively, if you want to use the same choices for Input and Criteria and
would like to perform the same query operation as the last one you
performed (Find, Unique, Del, or Extract), you have an easier option.
Simply press F7 (QUERY), and another query will be executed.

Adding a Second Database

With Release 3, you can include more than one database table in the
input range. Using multiple ranges can change the way you use some of
the /Data commands, allowing you to design applications or worksheets

containing multiple database tables. Multiple input ranges are not allowed for the /Data Query Modify Insert and /Data Query Modify Replace commands.

Selecting the Input Range

To select multiple input ranges, you must separate the range names with the default argument separator. This is a comma unless you select another one with the /Worksheet Global Default Other International Punctuation command. Since a semicolon is always a valid argument separator you may prefer to use that character.

External Databases

With Release 3, you can link to databases from other packages while you continue using 1-2-3. Lotus has developed a special facility known as DataLens that allows you to link with these external databases.

You can use this feature to access data from another database that you do not want to enter into 1-2-3. It will access databases that are much too large to bring into a worksheet file. When this is the case, 1-2-3's /Data External commands let you manipulate the external file like a database table in an active 1-2-3 file.

To use an external database, 1-2-3 must have a DataLens driver for the external package. 1-2-3 includes a DataLens driver file for dBASE III+. Other drivers will become available through Lotus or the database program manufacturers. The steps you need to take to access the database are summarized in the box called "Steps for Using an External Database."

Opening an External Database

The first step in using an external database is opening the file from 1-2-3. To open the file, enter the /Data External Use command. 1-2-3 prompts you for the driver name. This is normally the name of the other database management program. 1-2-3 lists the selections it uses. 1-2-3 then prompts you for the database name. (For dBASE III+, you must provide the path to the dBASE file and the database name.) 1-2-3 displays the default directory for the database name. You can either accept this, select another listed one, or press ESC and type one. 1-2-3 prompts you for the table name. You can select a listed table or database filename, or press ESC and type a table or database filename. Finally, 1-2-3 prompts you for the range name for referring to the external database table. 1-2-3 displays a prompt of the table name, unless the name starts with a $ or !, contains a period, or could be interpreted as a cell address. You can accept the default or enter a new range name before pressing ENTER. If the external program requires a password or user name for access to it, 1-2-3 will prompt you for a password or user name before establishing the connection.

You do not need a copy of the other database management program on your system to access its files, if you have 1-2-3 and the proper DataLens driver on your system. This means you can use databases that have been created on other machines. If you are primarily using an external database with 1-2-3, consider placing the external database file in the 1-2-3 default directory.

As an example, suppose you want to use the data in the dBASE III+ file shown in Figure 9-22, which displays the Browse screen. Assume that this file is called INVOICES.DBF and it is in the dBASE directory on drive C. First, enter /**Data External Use**. Then select dBASE as the driver. Next, press ESC and enter **C:\DBASE** before pressing ENTER. When 1-2-3 lists the dBASE files in the C:\DBASE directory, select INVOICES. The prompt at this point looks like this:

```
A:A1:                                                          EDIT
Enter name of table to use: dBASE c:\dbase invoices_
```

When you press ENTER to select the INVOICES database file, 1-2-3 prompts for a range name to assign to the table, and displays IN-VOICES as the default range name. Press ENTER to accept the range name.

Once you establish a connection between a table in an external database and 1-2-3, you can use the external data table in 1-2-3 /Data Query commands, formulas and database functions. When you use the

Steps for Using an External Database

The /Data External commands let you access records in external database tables. Before you can use an external database table, you must create a link between 1-2-3 and the external database table. The required steps are as follows:

1. Enter **/Data External Use.**

2. Enter or highlight the driver name and press ENTER. This is normally the name of the database management program.

3. Enter or highlight the database name and press ENTER. (For dBASE III+, this is the path to the dBASE files.)

4. Enter or highlight the table name and press ENTER. (For dBASE III+, this is the database filename.)

5. Enter a range name, or accept the default range name that 1-2-3 uses to refer to the external database table. The default is the name from Step 4 unless the table name starts with a $ or !, contains a period, or could be interpreted as a cell address. Press ENTER.

6. Select this database table as the input range for /Data Query operations by pressing ESC to return to the Data menu and selecting /Data Query Input. When 1-2-3 prompts for an input range, press F3 (NAME) and select the range name entered in Step 5. Press ENTER to finalize the input range.

external database in 1-2-3, you will refer to it using the range name assigned by the /Data External Use command. The number of links you can create to external databases is limited by your computer's memory.

Records	Fields	Go To	Exit			4:48:47 pm

INVOICE	VENDOR	ITEM_DESCR	QUANTITY	AMOUNT	PAID
K1037	National Hardware	Paint Brushes	400	438.57	T
Q9259	Machine Tool & Die	3/8 HP Drill	100	4944.89	T
L6572	Dutch Hardware	Whitney Punch	50	750.58	
Y7858	National Hardware	Metal Files	150	78.74	T
R4362	Baker Hand Tools	Sanding Disks	500	159.98	
H2963	Cedar Woods, Inc.	Clear Polyurethane	100	549.37	T
P9248	Baker Hand Tools	Wood Round Rasps	175	139.42	T
N2934	Machine Tool & Die	1/4 HP Table Saw	75	200.00	
U8252	Dutch Hardware	C Clamps	200	221.58	

Figure 9-22.   INVOICES.DBF file from dBASE III +

If you establish links with database files on a different directory, and you want to select the directory from a list instead of pressing ESC and entering a new path, you can add the directory containing the database files to your directory list. To do this, edit the LOTUS.BCF file in a text editor such as Metro's Editor, DOS's EDLIN, or MicroPro's WordStar, and add a line at the end of the file:

DB = "database files path" DN = "Driver name that uses this path"

For example, to add the dBASE directory, enter **DB = "C:\DBASE"** **DN = "dBASE"**. You can also add a description to appear above the directory list, by adding **DD = "message"** at the end of the line. The message appears when you highlight the pathname for the database and press NAME (F3) for a full screen list.

If the external database contains characters that are not displaying correctly, such as A appearing as a graphics character, 1-2-3 is not using the correct translation character set. To change the translation character set, use the /Data External Other Translation command. 1-2-3 will display the available character sets. If the external program only has one character set, 1-2-3 automatically sets this option for you; it will appear as if 1-2-3 is doing nothing. Most of the time, 1-2-3 selects the appropriate character set for you.

Listing Information About External Databases

Once you have created links to an external database, you can obtain information from it. Use the /Data External List Tables and /Data External List Fields commands.

The /Data External List Tables command lists the tables that have links established to 1-2-3. It lists the table names in one column; a second column lists the table descriptions if they have one, or NA if they do not. When you execute this command, 1-2-3 first prompts for a range in which to write the list. Figure 9-23 shows a list of external tables created with this command.

/Data External List Fields lists a table definition of an external database. You can use this feature if you plan to create a database similar to one you have already created. This command lists, in columns, the field names, widths, lengths, column labels, and descriptions. If a field lacks any of this information, 1-2-3 displays NA. When you execute /Data External List Fields, 1-2-3 prompts for the first cell to use for

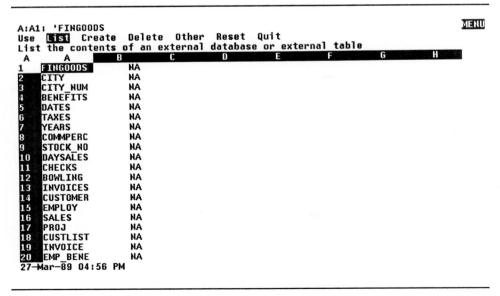

Figure 9-23.   List of external database tables

recording the fields list. The list uses as many rows as the external database has fields. Figure 9-24 shows a list of fields in the INVOICE database, created with this command.

Once you are finished with the /Data External menus, you can return to the READY mode by selecting Quit to leave the /Data External menus.

Tip: Use the /Data External List Fields command to list the field names in the external database table that you want to use with /Data Query commands. Once you have the table definition, you can use the /Copy or the /Range Transpose command to copy the field names to the criteria range. Then you can erase the table definition. This ensures that the field names in the search criteria are correct.

Using External Databases

Once you have created a link to an external database, you can start using its data in 1-2-3 commands. In /Data Query commands, you can specify an external database as an input range by entering its name as assigned by the /Data External Use command. To look at the database's records, use the /Data Query Extract, /Data Query Modify Extract, and /Data Query Unique commands to copy the records to a worksheet. To copy records from an external database table, specify it as the input range name. To copy records to the external database table, specify it as the output range name.

Release 3 can also perform commands in the other database management program if you are familiar with the required command syntax

```
A:A1: 'INVOICE                                                    MENU
Use List Create Delete Other Reset Quit
List the contents of an external database or external table
  A       A         B         C         D         E      F      G      H
1   INVOICE   Character      5         NA        NA
2   VENDOR    Character     20         NA        NA
3   ITEM_DESCCharacter      20         NA        NA
4   QUANTITY  Numeric   4,0            NA        NA
5   AMOUNT    Numeric   7,2            NA        NA
6   PAID      Logical        1         NA        NA
7
```

Figure 9-24.   Table definition for INVOICES.DBF

for the program. To do this, use /Data External Other Command. 1-2-3 will prompt for the database driver, the external database directory, and the database management command.

When you include the external database values in @functions and formulas, 1-2-3 updates their values according to the /Worksheet Global Recalc command and the /Data External Other Refresh command. When both these commands are set to automatic, 1-2-3 reexecutes the last issued /Data Query and /Data Table commands, updates worksheet formulas, and updates database @functions at the interval selected with /Data External Other Refresh Interval. This command also sets the number of seconds between 1-2-3 external database updates. When /Worksheet Global Recalc is set to automatic and /Data External Other Refresh is set to manual, /Data Query and /Data Table commands are only updated each time the commands are executed. The functions and formulas are updated according to the setting in /Worksheet Global Recalc.

Closing an External Database

After you have finished using an external database, you will want to close it. This breaks the connection between 1-2-3 and the database. To close an external database, use the /Data External Reset command. 1-2-3 will prompt you for the driver name, and list the database drivers in memory. Then it prompts for the name of the database, and lists the ones in memory for the driver you named. (For dBASE III +, the listing is the path to the database files.) After you select the database, 1-2-3 prompts you for the range name assigned by /Data External Use to the external database table. Select the range name for the table that you want to close. If the table you select is the only one in the database file, 1-2-3 closes the file. If the closed database file is the only one using a particular driver, 1-2-3 removes the driver from memory.

As an example, suppose you want to close the database table in INVOICES.DBF that you have established with the /Data External Use command. First, enter /**Data External Reset**. Then select dBASE as the driver. Next, enter **C:\DBASE** for the external database name, which is the directory for dBASE III + files. When 1-2-3 lists the open dBASE files, select the range name INVOICES. Once you press ENTER to select the INVOICES range name, 1-2-3 breaks the connection to the INVOICES.DBF file. If this is the only dBASE III+ database open, 1-2-3 removes the dBASE driver from memory.

Creating an External Database

You can create an external database rather than storing all your database information within 1-2-3. This feature is frequently used for transferring information between external databases, or for transferring information from 1-2-3 database tables to external databases. 1-2-3 can serve as the conduit for moving information from one database to another, if there is no built-in link between the two database packages and if 1-2-3 supports interface with both of them. You can also use this feature to transfer 1-2-3 data to another database package, to take advantage of its unique reporting or query features.

To create an external database, you must create an input table definition, create the structure in the external table, and copy information to the external table. The following examples for creating an external database table use the data in the 1-2-3 worksheet shown in Figure 9-25.

CiA1i 'FIRST_NAME   READY

C	A	B	C	D	E	F
1	FIRST_NAME	MID_NAME	LAST_NAME	SSN	HIRE_DATE	
2	Allen	James	Canfield	652-47-2348	07/13/85	
3	Jeanette	Anne	Cruise	761-72-8973	09/11/87	
4	Yvonne	Sarah	Donaldson	978-12-5823	12/05/83	
5	Stephen	Scott	Golland	123-88-4827	03/21/84	
6	Patrick	John	Perez	478-28-6810	05/09/81	
7	Carol	Racheal	Spear	683-78-2832	08/18/86	
8	Babbette	Alicia	Zegetti	234-24-9807	11/14/82	
9	Marlene	Stewart	Galloway	465-27-7937	02/18/89	
10	Andrew	Brandon	Jeck	358-95-2594	11/27/83	
11	Mark	Paul	Jones	324-87-1369	02/28/89	
12	Karen	Allen	Smith	484-62-1669	04/01/88	
13						

Figure 9-25.   Employee database

Selecting Records for the New External Database Table

Before copying records to an external database, select the records that you want to put into the new database table. These records determine the structure of the new database table. Use the /Data Query Input command to select the records. The input range can be a database table in an active worksheet file or in an external database. For the data in Figure 9-25, the input range is A1..E12.

Creating a Table Definition

The first step in creating an external table is assigning a range name to the new table and creating a table definition. This defines the database structure that the new table uses. The format of the table is identical to the fields listing created by the /Data External List Fields command. The steps performed to create a table definition vary depending on which external database product you are using. Refer to the DataLens documentation for your particular database. If you return to the READY mode without creating the new table, you must execute the /Data External Create Name command again.

Creating a Table Definition in a 1-2-3 Worksheet   If the external database that you want to create is unlike other external database structures or 1-2-3 database tables, perform these steps:

1. Move to an empty area in a worksheet that has at least six columns and as many rows as the new database table will have fields.

2. Put the field name in the first column, the field type in the second column, the field width in the third column, the field label in the fourth column, the field description in the fifth column, and the field creation string (if any) in the sixth column. The format of the data must match what the database driver expects.

3. Repeat Step 2 for each field that you want in the created external table, using a new row for each field. An example of a table definition is shown in Figure 9-26.

A:A1: [W11] 'FIRST_NAME   READY

A	A	B	C	D	E	F	G
1	FIRST_NAME	Character	10	NA	NA		
2	MID_NAME	Character	10	NA	NA		
3	LAST_NAME	Character	15	NA	NA		
4	SSN	Character	11	NA	NA		
5	HIRE_DATE	Date	8	NA	NA		
6							

Figure 9-26.   Employee database table definition

Tip: Use the /Data External List Fields command to create a sample table definition that you can refer to as you create another table definition. Referring to a sample prevents errors due to lack of information or an inappropriate format.

4. Enter the **/Data External Create Name** command, and specify the database driver and external database you want to create. Then type the new table name and press ENTER. If the database driver requires an owner name for the database, enter the owner's name before the table name. When 1-2-3 prompts for the range name for the new table, press ENTER to accept the suggested table name or type a new table name before pressing ENTER.

5. Enter **/Data External Create Definition Use-Definition** and select the table definition that you created. For the table in Figure 9-26, the range is A1..E5.

6. Select Go to create the new table. This creates the external database but does not add any records to it. Because selecting Go establishes a link to the new database, you can use the /Data Query commands to copy data into it.

Creating a Table Definition from a 1-2-3 or External Database

Table   The /Data External Create-Definition command can create a table definition from a 1-2-3 database table or an external database table. First name the new table with /Data External Create Name. When you execute this command, you must select a database driver and the external database. Then type a table name and press ENTER. If the database driver requires an owner name for the database, enter the owner's name before the table name.

Next, 1-2-3 prompts for the range name for the new table. To create the table definition, enter /**Data External Create-Definition**; and select the 1-2-3 database table or enter the range name of the external database. Select a range for 1-2-3 to place the table definition. This area must have at least six columns, and as many rows as the 1-2-3 database table or external database table has fields.

When you create a table this way using a 1-2-3 database table, 1-2-3 uses the field names in the top row as the table definition field names, the data types in the second row of the data table as the table definition field types, and the column widths as the field widths. When you create a table this way using an external database table, 1-2-3 uses the field names, field types, and field widths from the external database table. With both types of database tables, 1-2-3 may not assign field widths to fields containing values, depending upon the database driver selected by the /Data External Create Name command. Figure 9-26 shows a table created with this command.

Once you create a table definition, you can create an external database by selecting Go to return to the READY mode. This creates the external database but does not add any records to the new database. Since selecting Go establishes a link to the new database, you can use the /Data Query commands to copy data to the new database. If you need to return to the READY mode before creating the table, select Quit. When you are ready to create the table, you must enter the /Data External Create Name and Use-Definition commands again. You can make changes to the table definition from READY mode.

Copying Records to the New Database Table

Once you have created the external database table, you can copy records to it. Define the new table range name as the output range with the /Data Query Output command, and you can copy in all desired records using /**Data Query Extract**. To limit which records 1-2-3 copies, use criteria specified with the /Data Query Criteria command. The criteria selected must follow all of the criteria rules discussed earlier in the chapter. Figure 9-27 shows the database (sheet C) and the criteria (sheet B) that the /Data Query Criteria and /Data Query Extract will use to copy records to the EMPLOYEE external database table. The

```
C:A1:  'FIRST_NAME                                                      READY

   C        A          B            C            D            E              F
   1    FIRST_NAME  MID_NAME    LAST_NAME    SSN          HIRE_DATE
   2    Allen       James       Canfield     652-47-2348  07/13/85
   3    Jeanette    Anne        Cruise       761-72-8973  09/11/87
   4    Yvonne      Sarah       Donaldson    978-12-5823  12/05/83
   5    Stephen     Scott       Golland      123-88-4827  03/21/84
   6    Patrick     John        Perez        478-28-6810  05/09/81
   B        A          B            C            D            E              F
   1    FIRST_NAME  MID_NAME    LAST_NAME    SSN          HIRE_DATE
   2                                                      >=31048
   3
   4
   5
   6
   A        A          B            C            D            E        F        G
   1    FIRST_NAME  Character    10           NA           NA
   2    MID_NAME    Character    10           NA           NA
   3    LAST_NAME   Character    15           NA           NA
   4    SSN         Character    11           NA           NA
   5    HIRE_DATE   Date         8            NA           NA
   6
   27-Mar-89 05:20 PM                                               NUM
```

Figure 9-27.   Worksheet containing information to be extracted to external
database table

criteria range (sheet B) is A1..E2 which selects records with a
HIRE_DATE on or after January 1, 1985. The /Data Query Extract
command will copy the first two records.

Deleting External Database Tables

Just as you can use 1-2-3 to create external database tables, you can
also delete them with 1-2-3. This permanently removes the table from
the disk.

To delete an external database table, use /Data External Delete.
This command does not require a connection between 1-2-3 and the
external database table. When you execute this command, 1-2-3 prompts
for the driver name and lists the database drivers in memory. Select a
database driver, and 1-2-3 will prompt for the external database, displaying a list of the external databases in memory for a particular

driver. (For dBASE III+, the external database listing is the path to the database files.) After you select one, 1-2-3 prompts you for the external database table name. (For dBASE III+ files, this is the database filename.) Select the table name that you want to delete.

Caution: 1-2-3 deletes the table without confirmation. Once you have deleted the table, you cannot retrieve it from 1-2-3 or the database program that it is designed for. (For deleting dBASE III+ files, this command is equivalent to the /File Erase Other command when you select the database filename to delete.)

As an example, suppose you want to delete the INVOICES.DBF database table. First, enter **/Data External Delete**. Then select dBASE as the driver. Next, select **C:\DBASE** for the external database name (which is the directory for dBASE III+ files). When 1-2-3 lists the dBASE files, select the database name INVOICES. Once you press ENTER to select the INVOICES file, 1-2-3 deletes the file from the disk.

The Database Statistical Functions

1-2-3's database statistical functions are a special category of functions designed to coordinate with the other data management features. Using criteria you enter on your worksheet, they can perform a statistical analysis on selected records in your database. The criteria used is identical to the criteria for the /Data Query commands, except that you may have many active criteria areas. In fact, it is possible to set up a criteria area for each database statistical function that you use.

Each of the database statistical functions has a D immediately following the @ in the function name to show that it is a database function. The characters following the D indicate the exact task the function performs, and also correspond to the name of one of the statistical functions covered in Chapter 7, "1-2-3's Built-in Functions."

@DAVG

The @DAVG function allows you to obtain an average of a selected group of database records.

Format

@DAVG(*input, field, criteria*)

Arguments

input   the location of your database, including field names and all the database records and fields. This argument can be supplied as a range (A1..F67), as a range name assigned to the database (RECORDS), or an external table. This argument can also refer to just a section of the database, as long as the field names for the included fields are within the specified range. To include multiple databases, separate each database table range with an argument separator (a comma or semicolon).

field   the position number of the field in the database you wish to use in the average calculation. This field should contain a field name, or a numeric value representing the number of columns away from the first column you want to use. The first column is 0 and the second column is 1. As you move successively to each field to the right of the first, add 1 to the offset. This argument can be a number or a reference to a cell containing a number or field name. If the input includes multiple database tables, this argument must be a field name enclosed in quotation marks.

criteria   the location of the criteria to be used in selecting records, specified as a range or a range name. Include the field names that appear at the top of the criteria area.

Use

Use the @DAVG function whenever you wish to obtain an average of the values in a field, in a selected group of records in the database. The database and criteria in Figure 9-28 are used with the @DAVG function to calculate an average salary for employees in job code 23 of $21,550. Note that the database is defined as being located in A1..F12. The field the function uses is the Salary field, and the criteria used in the selection are located in A15..A16.

A:F16: (C0) @DAVG(A1..F12,4,A15..A16)   `READY`

A	A	B	C	D	E	F
1	Last Name	First Name	SS#	Job Code	Salary	Location
2	Larson	Mary	543-98-9876	23	$12,000	2
3	Campbell	David	213-76-9874	23	$23,000	10
4	Campbell	Keith	569-89-7654	12	$32,000	2
5	Stephens	Tom	219-78-8954	15	$17,800	2
6	Caldor	Larry	459-34-0921	23	$32,500	4
7	Lightnor	Peggy	560-55-4311	14	$23,500	10
8	McCartin	John	817-66-1212	15	$54,600	2
9	Justof	Jack	431-78-9963	17	$41,200	4
10	Patterson	Lyle	212-11-9090	12	$21,500	10
11	Miller	Lisa	214-89-6756	23	$18,700	2
12	Hawkins	Mark	215-67-8973	21	$19,500	2
13						
14	Criteria Range					
15	Job Code					
16	23		Average Salary for Job Code 23:		`$21,550`	
17						

Figure 9-28.   Using @DAVG

@DCOUNT

The @DCOUNT function allows you to count a selected group of database records.

Format

@DCOUNT(*input, field, criteria*)

Arguments

input	the location of your database, including field names and all the database records and fields. This argument can be supplied as a range (A1..F67), as a range name assigned to the database (RECORDS), or an external table. This argument can also refer to just a section of the database, as long as the field names for the included fields are within the specified range. To include multiple databases, separate each database table range with an argument separator (a comma or semicolon).
field	the position number of the field in the database you wish to use in the count. This field should contain a field name or a numeric value representing the number of columns away from the first column you want to use. The first column is 0 and the second column is 1. As you move successively to each field to the right of the first, add 1 to the offset. This argument can be a number or a reference to a cell containing a number or field name. If the input includes multiple database tables, this argument must be a field name enclosed in quotation marks.
criteria	the location of the criteria to be used in selecting records, specified as a range or a range name. Include the field names that appear at the top of the criteria area.

Use

Use @DCOUNT function whenever you wish to obtain a count of the records in the database that match your selection criteria. The database and criteria in Figure 9-29 are used with the @DCOUNT function to count the salary entries for records with a job code of 23. Note that the database is defined as being located in A1..F12. The offset to refer to the Salary field is 4, and the criteria used in the selection are located in A15..A16. Since @DCOUNT counts only records with a nonblank entry in the specified field, choose carefully the field that you count. For example, some records need not have a location assignment, but all records should have a salary.

Another use of @DCOUNT is to determine the size of the output range. For example, assume you want to determine how many rows you need in an output range for a /Data Query Extract command that you are using on an external database with the range name INVOICES. In a cell enter **@DCOUNT(INVOICES, "invoice",G1..G2)** as in the following worksheet:

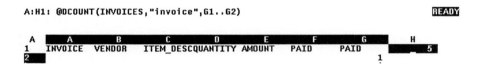

The formula in H1 returns 5 as the number of rows the output range needs. This function uses the criteria range G1..G2. The field names in the criteria range match the field names in the external database table.

Tip: You can use the @DCOUNT function to determine the number of rows the output range requires. To do this, write the @DCOUNT function using the same input range and criteria that the /Data Query commands use. Using this function prevents you from overwriting needed data.

```
A:F16: (F0) @DCOUNT(A1..F12,4,A15..A16)                          READY
```

A	A	B	C	D	E	F
1	Last Name	First Name	SS#	Job Code	Salary	Location
2	Larson	Mary	543-98-9876	23	$12,000	2
3	Campbell	David	213-76-9874	23	$23,000	10
4	Campbell	Keith	569-89-7654	12	$32,000	2
5	Stephens	Tom	219-78-8954	15	$17,800	2
6	Caldor	Larry	459-34-0921	23	$32,500	4
7	Lightnor	Peggy	560-55-4311	14	$23,500	10
8	McCartin	John	817-66-1212	15	$54,600	2
9	Justof	Jack	431-78-9963	17	$41,200	4
10	Patterson	Lyle	212-11-9090	12	$21,500	10
11	Miller	Lisa	214-89-6756	23	$18,700	2
12	Hawkins	Mark	215-67-8973	21	$19,500	2
13						
14	Criteria Range					
15	Job Code					
16	23		Number of Employees in Job Code 2		4	
17						

Figure 9-29.   Using @DCOUNT

@DGET

The @DGET function returns a value for a record that meets a set of criteria. If more than one record fits the criteria, this function returns ERR.

Format

@DGET(*input,field,criteria*)

Arguments

input   the location of your database, including field names and all the database records and fields. This argument can be supplied as a range (A1..F67), as a range name assigned to the database (RECORDS), or an external table. This argument can also refer to just a section of the database, as long as the field names for the included fields are within the specified range. To include multiple databases, separate each database table range with an argument separator (a comma or semicolon).

field

the position number of the field in the database you wish to use in the search. This field should contain a field name or a numeric value representing the number of columns away from the first column you want to use. The first column is 0 and the second column is 1. As you move successively to each field to the right of the first, add 1 to the offset. This argument can be a number or a reference to a cell containing a number or field name. If the input includes multiple database tables, this argument must be a field name enclosed in quotation marks.

criteria

the location of the criteria to be used in selecting records, specified as a range or a range name. Include the field names that appear at the top of the criteria area.

Use

Use the @DGET function whenever you wish to obtain a value from a particular record that matches your selection criteria. The database (sheet C) and criteria (B: C1..B:C2) in Figure 9-30 are used with the @DGET function to return the social security number of the employee with the last name of Canfield. Note that the database is defined as being located in C:A1..C:E12, the SSN field of the record that the function finds is returned, and the criteria used in the selection are located in C1..C2.

@DMAX

The @DMAX function allows you to obtain the maximum value in a field within a selected group of database records.

Format

@DMAX(*input,field,criteria*)

Arguments

input	the location of your database, including field names and all the database records and fields. This argument can be supplied as a range (A1..F67), as a range name assigned to the database (RECORDS), or an external table. This argument can also refer to just a section of the database, as long as the field names for the included fields are within the specified range. To include multiple databases, separate each database table range with an argument separator (a comma or semicolon).
field	the position number of the field in the database you wish to use in the maximum value determination. This field should contain a field name or a numeric value representing the number of columns away from the first column you want to use. The first column is 0 and the second column is 1. As you move successively to each field to the right of the first, add 1 to the offset. This argument can be a number or a reference to a cell containing a number or field name. If the input includes multiple database tables, this argument must be a field name enclosed in quotation marks.
criteria	the location of the criteria to be used in selecting records, specified as a range or a range name. Include the field names that appear at the top of the criteria area.

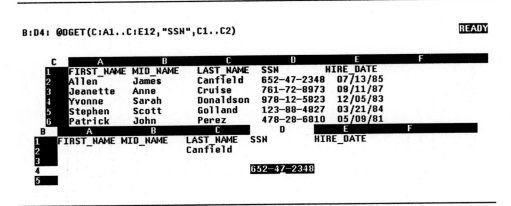

Figure 9-30.   Using @DGET

Use

Use the @DMAX function whenever you wish to obtain the maximum (highest) value in a field for records in the database that match your selection criteria. The database and criteria in Figure 9-31 are used with the @DMAX function to determine the maximum salary for employees

```
A:F16: (C0) @DMAX(A1..F12,4,A15..A16)                           READY
```

	A	B	C	D	E	F
1	Last Name	First Name	SS#	Job Code	Salary	Location
2	Larson	Mary	543-98-9876	23	$12,000	2
3	Campbell	David	213-76-9874	23	$23,000	10
4	Campbell	Keith	569-89-7654	12	$32,000	2
5	Stephens	Tom	219-78-8954	15	$17,800	2
6	Caldor	Larry	459-34-0921	23	$32,500	4
7	Lightnor	Peggy	560-55-4311	14	$23,500	10
8	McCartin	John	817-66-1212	15	$54,600	2
9	Justof	Jack	431-78-9963	17	$41,200	4
10	Patterson	Lyle	212-11-9090	12	$21,500	10
11	Miller	Lisa	214-89-6756	23	$18,700	2
12	Hawkins	Mark	215-67-8973	21	$19,500	2
13						
14	Criteria Range					
15	Job Code					
16	23		Maximum Salary in Job Code 23:		$32,500	
17						

Figure 9-31.   Using @DMAX

with a job code of 23. Note that the database is defined as being located in A1..F12. The field used is the Salary field, and the criteria used in the selection are located in A15..A16.

@DMIN

The @DMIN function allows you to obtain the minimum value in a field within a selected group of database records.

Format

@DMIN(*input, field, criteria*)

Arguments

input the location of your database, including field names and all the database records and fields. This argument can be supplied as a range (A1..F67), as a range name assigned to the database (RECORDS), or an external table. This argument can also refer to just a section of the database, as long as the field names for the included fields are within the specified range. To include multiple databases, separate each database table range with an argument separator (a comma or semicolon).

field the position number of the field in the database you wish to use in the minimum value determination. This field should contain a field name or a numeric value representing the number of columns away from the first column you want to use. The first column is 0 and the second column is 1. As you move successively to each field to the right of the first, add 1 to the offset. This argument can be a number or a reference to a cell containing a number or field name. If the input includes multiple database tables, this argument must be a field name enclosed in quotation marks.

criteria   the location of the criteria to be used in selecting records, specified as a range or a range name. Include the field names that appear at the top of the criteria area.

Use

Use the @DMIN function whenever you wish to obtain the minimum (lowest) value in a field for records in the database that match your selection criteria. The database and criteria in Figure 9-32 are used with the @DMIN function to determine the minimum salary for employees with a job code of 23. Note that the database is defined as being located in A1..F12, the Salary field is used, and the criteria used in the selection are located in A15..A16.

@DQUERY

The @DQUERY function sends a command to an external database management program. This function performs a command in another program without leaving 1-2-3.

A:F16: (CO) @DMIN(A1..F12,4,A15..A16)   `READY`

A	A	B	C	D	E	F
1	Last Name	First Name	SS#	Job Code	Salary	Location
2	Larson	Mary	543-98-9876	23	$12,000	2
3	Campbell	David	213-76-9874	23	$23,000	10
4	Campbell	Keith	569-89-7654	12	$32,000	2
5	Stephens	Tom	219-78-8954	15	$17,800	2
6	Caldor	Larry	459-34-0921	23	$32,500	4
7	Lightnor	Peggy	560-55-4311	14	$23,500	10
8	McCartin	John	817-66-1212	15	$54,600	2
9	Justof	Jack	431-78-9963	17	$41,200	4
10	Patterson	Lyle	212-11-9090	12	$21,500	10
11	Miller	Lisa	214-89-6756	23	$18,700	2
12	Hawkins	Mark	215-67-8973	21	$19,500	2
13						
14	Criteria Range					
15	Job Code					
16	23		Minimum Salary in Job Code 23:		`$12,000`	
17						

Figure 9-32.   Using @DMIN

Format

@DQUERY(*function,ext-arguments*)

Arguments

function	a command in another database management program. This argument is a string, cell reference, or formula that evaluates to a string.
ext-arguments	the arguments the external command uses.

Use

Use the @DQUERY function to execute a command in an external database management program. This function is usually combined with criteria for 1-2-3 database features. 1-2-3 calculates @DQUERY when the /Data Query Delete, /Data Query Extract, /Data Query Modify Extract, or /Data Query Unique commands are executed. The database and criteria in Figure 9-33 are used with the @DQUERY function to locate the employees in the EMP_BENE external database that participate in the company's medical, dental, and long-term disability

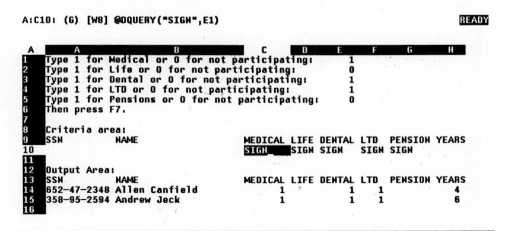

Figure 9-33.   Using @DQUERY

plans. The /Data Query commands use EMP_BENE as the input range, A9..H10 as the criteria, and A13..H13 as the output range. "SIGN" is a dBASE function that returns a 1 if the field contains a positive number, a −1 if the field contains a negative number, or a 0 if the field contains a 0.

@DSTD

The @DSTD function is used to determine the standard deviation of a set of values, or how much variation there is from the average of the values. The values used in this calculation will be from selected records in the database. The standard deviation is the square root of the variance.

Format

@DSTD(*input,field,criteria*)

Arguments

input   the location of your database, including field names and all the database records and fields. This argument can be supplied as a range (A1..F67), as a range name assigned to the database (RECORDS), or an external table. This argument can also refer to just a section of the database, as long as the field names for the included fields are within the specified range. To include multiple databases, separate each database table range with an argument separator (a comma or semicolon).

field   the position number of the field in the database you wish to use in the calculation. This field should contain a field name or a numeric value representing the number of columns away from the first column you want to use. The first column is 0 and the second column is 1. As you move successively to each field to the right of the first, add 1 to the offset. This argument can be a number or a reference to a cell containing a number or field name. If the input includes multiple database tables, this argument must be a field name enclosed in quotation marks.

criteria   the location of the criteria to be used in selecting records, specified as a range or a range name. Include the field names that appear at the top of the criteria area.

Use

Use the @DSTD function to determine the standard deviation when the selected records comprise the entire population you are measuring. If you are working with only a sample of the population, use the @DSTDS function.

The purpose of the standard deviation is to determine the amount of variation between individual values and the mean. If you determine that the average age of your employees is 40, this could mean that half of your employees are 39 and the other half 41, or it could mean that you have employees whose ages range from 18 to 65. The latter case shows a greater standard deviation, due to the greater variance from the mean.

The @DSTD function is biased, since it uses a count as part of the standard deviation calculation. The following formula is used:

$$\sqrt{\frac{\sum (X_i - AVG)^2}{n}}$$

where X_i is the ith item in the list, and n is the number of items in the list.

The database in Figure 9-34 shows the @DSTD function being used to determine the standard deviation of salaries for employees in job code 15. The criteria are located in A15..A16.

```
A:F16: (G) @DSTD(A1..F12,4,A15..A16)                           READY
```

A	A	B	C	D	E	F
1	Last Name	First Name	SS#	Job Code	Salary	Location
2	Larson	Mary	543-98-9876	23	$12,000	2
3	Campbell	David	213-76-9874	23	$23,000	10
4	Campbell	Keith	569-89-7654	15	$17,700	2
5	Stephens	Tom	219-78-8954	15	$17,800	2
6	Caldor	Larry	459-34-0921	23	$32,500	4
7	Lightnor	Peggy	560-55-4311	14	$23,500	10
8	McCartin	John	817-66-1212	15	$17,750	2
9	Justof	Jack	431-78-9963	17	$41,200	4
10	Patterson	Lyle	212-11-9090	12	$21,500	10
11	Miller	Lisa	214-89-6756	23	$18,700	2
12	Hawkins	Mark	215-67-8973	21	$19,500	2
13						
14	Criteria Range					
15	Job Code					
16	15		Standard Deviation for Salaries		40.82483	
17			in Job Code 15:			
18						
19						
20						

Figure 9-34. Using @DSTD

@DSTDS

The @DSTDS function is used to determine the standard deviation of a set of values, or how much variation there is from the average of the values for a sample of the population. The values used in this calculation will be from selected records in the database. The standard deviation is the square root of the variance.

Format

@DSTDS(*input,field,criteria*)

Arguments

input   the location of your database, including field names and all the database records and fields. This argument can be supplied as a range (A1..F67), as a range name assigned to the database (RECORDS), or an external table. This argument can also refer to just a section of the database, as long as the field names for the included fields are within the specified range. To include multiple databases, separate each database table range with an argument separator (a comma or semicolon).

field the position number of the field in the database you wish to use in the calculation. This field should contain a field name or a numeric value representing the number of columns away from the first column you want to use. The first column is 0 and the second column is 1. As you move successively to each field to the right of the first, add 1 to the offset. This argument can be a number or a reference to a cell containing a number or field name. If the input includes multiple database tables, this argument must be a field name enclosed in quotation marks.

criteria the location of the criteria to be used in selecting records, specified as a range or a range name. Include the field names that appear at the top of the criteria area.

Use

Use @DSTDS function to determine the standard deviation when the selected records comprise a sample of the population you are measuring. If you are working with the entire population, use the @DSTD function.

The purpose of the standard deviation is to determine the amount of variation between individual values and the mean. If you determine that the average age of your employees is 40, this could mean that half of your employees are 39 and the other half 41, or it could mean that you have employees whose ages range from 18 to 65. The latter case shows a greater standard deviation, due to the greater variance from the mean.

The @DSTDS function is unbiased. The following formula is used:

$$\sqrt{\frac{\Sigma(X_i - AVG)^2}{n-1}}$$

where X_i is the ith item in the list, and n is the number of items in the list.

The database in Figure 9-35 shows the @DSTDS function being used to determine the standard deviation of salaries for employees in job code 15 when this group is treated as a sample of the population. The criteria are located in A15..A16.

@DSUM

The @DSUM function allows you to obtain the total of values in a field within a selected group of database records.

Format

@DSUM(*input,field,criteria*)

A:F16: (G) @DSTDS(A1..F12,4,A15..A16)   READY

A	A	B	C	D	E	F
1	Last Name	First Name	SS#	Job Code	Salary	Location
2	Larson	Mary	543-98-9876	23	$12,000	2
3	Campbell	David	213-76-9874	23	$23,000	10
4	Campbell	Keith	569-89-7654	15	$17,700	2
5	Stephens	Tom	219-78-8954	15	$17,800	2
6	Caldor	Larry	459-34-0921	23	$32,500	4
7	Lightnor	Peggy	560-55-4311	14	$23,500	10
8	McCartin	John	817-66-1212	15	$17,750	2
9	Justof	Jack	431-78-9963	17	$41,200	4
10	Patterson	Lyle	212-11-9090	12	$21,500	10
11	Miller	Lisa	214-89-6756	23	$18,700	2
12	Hawkins	Mark	215-67-8973	21	$19,500	2
13						
14	Criteria Range					
15	Job Code					
16	15		Standard Deviation for Salaries		50	
17			in Job Code 15:			
18						

Figure 9-35.   Using @DSTDS

Arguments

input   the location of your database, including field names and all the database records and fields. This argument can be supplied as a range (A1..F67), as a range name assigned to the database (RECORDS), or an external table. This argument can also refer to just a section of the database, as long as the field names for the included fields are within the specified range. To include multiple databases, separate each database table range with an argument separator (a comma or semicolon).

field   the position number of the field in the database you wish to use in calculation of the total. This field should contain a field name or a numeric value representing the number of columns away from the first column you want to use. The first column is 0 and the second column is 1. As you move successively to each field to the right of the first, add 1 to the offset. This argument can be a number or a reference to a cell containing a number or field name. If the input includes multiple database tables, this argument must be a field name enclosed in quotation marks.

criteria   the location of the criteria to be used in selecting records, specified as a range or a range name. Include the field names that appear at the top of the criteria area.

Use

Use the @DSUM function whenever you wish to total up the values in a field for records in the database that match your selection criteria. The database and criteria in Figure 9-36 are used with the @DSUM function to determine the total of salaries for employees with a job code of 23. Note that the database is defined as being located in A1..F12, the Salary field is selected to total, and the criteria used in the selection are located in A15..A16.

```
A:F16:  (CO)  @DSUM(A1..F12,4,A15..A16)                                    READY
```

A	A	B	C	D	E	F
1	Last Name	First Name	SS#	Job Code	Salary	Location
2	Larson	Mary	543-98-9876	23	$12,000	2
3	Campbell	David	213-76-9874	23	$23,000	10
4	Campbell	Keith	569-89-7654	15	$32,000	2
5	Stephens	Tom	219-78-8954	15	$17,800	2
6	Caldor	Larry	459-34-0921	23	$32,500	4
7	Lightnor	Peggy	560-55-4311	14	$23,500	10
8	McCartin	John	817-66-1212	15	$54,600	2
9	Justof	Jack	431-78-9963	17	$41,200	4
10	Patterson	Lyle	212-11-9090	12	$21,500	10
11	Miller	Lisa	214-89-6756	23	$18,700	2
12	Hawkins	Mark	215-67-8973	21	$19,500	2
13						
14	Criteria Range					
15	Job Code					
16	23		Total Salaries for Job Code 23:		$86,200	
17						

Figure 9-36.   Using @DSUM

@DVAR

The @DVAR function computes the variance of values in a population,
or the amount that the individual population values vary from the
average. The records used in the computation are selected from the
database with your criteria.

Format

@DVAR(*input,field,criteria*)

Arguments

input   the location of your database, including field names
                 and all the database records and fields. This argu-
                 ment can be supplied as a range (A1..F67), as a
                 range name assigned to the database (RECORDS),
                 or an external table. This argument can also refer

to just a section of the database, as long as the field names for the included fields are within the specified range. To include multiple databases, separate each database table range with an argument separator (a comma or semicolon).

field   the position number of the field in the database you wish to use in the variance calculation. This field should contain a field name or a numeric value representing the number of columns away from the first column you want to use. The first column is 0 and the second column is 1. As you move successively to each field to the right of the first, add 1 to the offset. This argument can be a number or a reference to a cell containing a number or field name. If the input includes multiple database tables, this argument must be a field name enclosed in quotation marks.

criteria   the location of the criteria to be used in selecting records, specified as a range or a range name. Include the field names that appear at the top of the criteria area.

Use

Use the @DVAR function to determine the variance when the selected records comprise the entire population you are measuring. If you are working with only a sample of the population, use @DVARS function.

The purpose of the variance is to determine the amount of variation between individual values and the mean. If you determine that the average age of your employees is 40, this could mean that half of your employees are 39 and the other half 41, or it could mean that you have employees whose ages range from 18 to 65. The latter case shows a greater variance, due to the greater dispersion from the mean.

The @DVAR function is biased, since it uses a count as part of the variance calculation. The following formula is used:

$$\frac{\sum (X_i - AVG)^2}{n}$$

where X_i is the ith item in the list, and n is the number of items in the list.

The worksheet in Figure 9-37 shows the @DVAR function used with criteria located in A15..A16 to determine the variance for salaries of employees with a job code of 15.

@DVARS

The @DVARS function computes the variance of values in a population, or the amount that the individual sample values vary from the average. The records used in the computation are selected from the database with your criteria.

Format

@DVARS(*input, field, criteria*)

A:F16: (G) @DVAR(A1..F12,4,A15..A16)   READY

A	A	B	C	D	E	F
1	Last Name	First Name	SS#	Job Code	Salary	Location
2	Larson	Mary	543-98-9876	23	$12,000	2
3	Campbell	David	213-76-9874	23	$23,000	10
4	Campbell	Keith	569-89-7654	15	$17,700	2
5	Stephens	Tom	219-78-8954	15	$17,800	2
6	Caldor	Larry	459-34-0921	23	$32,500	4
7	Lightnor	Peggy	560-55-4311	14	$23,500	10
8	McCartin	John	817-66-1212	15	$17,750	2
9	Justof	Jack	431-78-9963	17	$41,200	4
10	Patterson	Lyle	212-11-9090	12	$21,500	10
11	Miller	Lisa	214-89-6756	23	$18,700	2
12	Hawkins	Mark	215-67-8973	21	$19,500	2
13						
14	Criteria Range					
15	Job Code					
16	15		Salary Variance for Job Code 15:	1666.667		
17						

Figure 9-37.   Using @DVAR

Arguments

input   the location of your database, including field names and all the database records and fields. This argument can be supplied as a range (A1..F67), as a range name assigned to the database (RECORDS), or an external table. This argument can also refer to just a section of the database, as long as the field names for the included fields are within the specified range. To include multiple databases, separate each database table range with an argument separator (a comma or semicolon).

field   the position number of the field in the database you wish to use in the variance calculation. This field should contain a field name or a numeric value representing the number of columns away from the first column you want to use. The first column is 0 and the second column is 1. As you move successively to each field to the right of the first, add 1 to the offset. This argument can be a number or a reference to a cell containing a number or field name. If the input includes multiple database tables, this argument must be a field name enclosed in quotation marks.

criteria   the location of the criteria to be used in selecting records, specified as a range or a range name. Include the field names that appear at the top of the criteria area.

Use

Use the @DVARS function to determine the variance when the selected records represent a sample of the entire population you are measuring. If you are working with the entire population, use @DVAR function.

The purpose of the variance is to determine the amount of variation between individual values and the mean. If you determine that the

average age of your employees is 40, this could mean that half of your
employees are 39 and the other half 41, or it could mean that you have
employees whose ages range from 18 to 65. The latter case shows a
greater variance, due to the greater dispersion from the mean.

The @DVARS function uses the unbiased method. The following
formula is used:

$$\frac{\sum (X_i - AVG)^2}{n - 1}$$

where X_i is the ith item in the list, and n is the number of items in the
list.

The worksheet in Figure 9-38 shows the @DVARS function used
with criteria located in A15..A16 to determine the variance for salaries
of employees with a job code of 15.

A:F16: (G) @DVARS(A1..F12,4,A15..A16)   READY

	A	B	C	D	E	F
1	Last Name	First Name	SS#	Job Code	Salary	Location
2	Larson	Mary	543-98-9876	23	$12,000	2
3	Campbell	David	213-76-9874	23	$23,000	10
4	Campbell	Keith	569-89-7654	15	$17,700	2
5	Stephens	Tom	219-78-8954	15	$17,800	2
6	Caldor	Larry	459-34-0921	23	$32,500	4
7	Lightnor	Peggy	560-55-4311	14	$23,500	10
8	McCartin	John	817-66-1212	15	$17,750	2
9	Justof	Jack	431-78-9963	17	$41,200	4
10	Patterson	Lyle	212-11-9090	12	$21,500	10
11	Miller	Lisa	214-89-6756	23	$18,700	2
12	Hawkins	Mark	215-67-8973	21	$19,500	2
13						
14	Criteria Range					
15	Job Code					
16	15		Salary Variance for Job Code 15:		2500	
17						

Figure 9-38.   Using @DVARS

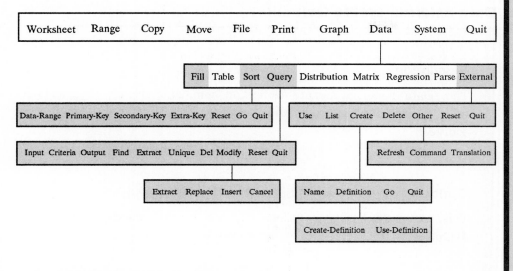

© 1989 Lotus Development Corporation. Used with permission.

/Data External Create Definition

Description

The /Data External Create Definition command creates or selects a table definition. The command options select the table definition's source.

Options

This command has two options that select the source of the table definition.

Create-Definition   This option creates a table definition from a 1-2-3 database table or an external database table. When you select this option, you are prompted for the 1-2-3 database table address, or a range name for a 1-2-3 database table or external database table. A 1-2-3 database table address or range name must include the field names and at least one database table record.

Then this command prompts for the first cell of the range in which to place the table definition. This table uses six columns, and as many rows as are needed by the database table fields. If the input table is a 1-2-3 database table, this command creates a table with the names appearing in the first row of the table as the field names, the data types of the second row determining the field types, and the column widths set the field widths. To modify the table after creating it, select Quit from the /Data External Create menu to return to the READY mode.

Use-Definition   This option selects a worksheet range that contains a table definition. When you use this option, 1-2-3 prompts for the range that contains the table definition. You can point to the range, or type the range address or name directly.

/Data External Create Go

Description

This command creates a new external database table named with the /Data External Create Name command, using the table definition defined with the /Data External Create Definition command. This command only creates the database structure; it does not copy any records to the table. /Data External Create Name and /Data External Create Definition must be executed before this command.

Options

There are no options for this command.

/Data External Create Name

Description

This command names the external database that the /Data External Create Go command creates and defines the 1-2-3 range name that will refer to the table.

Options

When you execute this command, 1-2-3 prompts for you to select the database driver, the database name, and the table name. In some cases you may have to provide a user name and password. Next 1-2-3 prompts for the 1-2-3 range name that other 1-2-3 commands and functions will use. Finally, 1-2-3 prompts for a table creation string. If the database driver that you are using requires one, enter it; otherwise, press ENTER. This command must be performed before the other /Data External Create commands.

/Data External Create Quit

Description

This command leaves the /Data External Create menus and returns to the READY mode. 1-2-3 forgets the settings made with the /Data External Create Name and /Data External Create Definition commands. You must reexecute these to create an external database.

Options

There are no options for this command.

/Data External Delete

Description

The /Data External Delete command removes a table from an external database. This command can be executed without establishing a connection with the /Data External Use command. The /Data External Delete command's actions may be limited by the database administrator restricting your access to the database, or if the database driver does not permit you to delete an external table. The /Data External Delete command may prompt you for a user name and password if the database management program requires this information. When you execute this command, 1-2-3 prompts you to select the driver, the database name, and the table name.

Options

There are no options for this command.

/Data External List

Description

The /Data External List command lists the fields in a table, or tables in a database; the list is displayed in a worksheet range. This command cannot be executed until a connection to an external database is established with the /Data External Use command.

Options

This command has two options for the listed information: Fields and Tables. Select one of these options, and 1-2-3 prompts you to select the driver and the database name from a displayed list. If you select Fields, 1-2-3 lists the table names and prompts you to select one. In both cases, you can either select or type in your entry. Once 1-2-3 has the list specifications, it prompts you for a worksheet location for the list.

The command's output has five columns if the Fields option is selected, and two columns if the Tables option is selected. Both options use as many rows as are necessary to list all the fields or tables. It writes this information over any worksheet contents in the selected output area.

Fields   This option lists in a worksheet the field names, data type, width, column label, and description. NA's appear for the column labels and descriptions when the database management program does not support column labels and descriptions.

Tables   This option lists in a worksheet the table names and table descriptions in a selected external database. NA's appear for the table descriptions if the database management program does not support table descriptions. These table names are not the 1-2-3 range names the /Data External Use command assigns.

/Data External Other Command

Description

/Data External Other Command can execute a command within the database management program that the /Data External Use command has loaded.

Options

When you select this command, 1-2-3 lists the driver and name of the external databases to which the /Data External Use command has connected. Select the one you want or enter a different one. Then, enter the command from the external program that you want to execute, or a cell address containing a label with a command. The command must match the database management program's syntax rules. The features this command can perform are detailed in the specific DataLens driver documentation.

/Data External Other Refresh

Description

The /Data External Other Refresh command determines when 1-2-3 reexecutes the most recent /Data Query and /Data Table commands, and updates worksheet formulas and database @functions.

Options

This command has three options.

Automatic   This option causes 1-2-3 to reexecute the last issued /Data Query and /Data Table commands, and update worksheet formulas and database @functions, at the interval selected with the Interval option. 1-2-3 recalculates the most recent /Data Query and /Data Table commands only when this option is set, and the /Worksheet Global Recalc option is set to Manual.

Interval   This option sets the interval for 1-2-3's reexecution of the most recent /Data Query and /Data Table commands, and update of worksheet formulas and database @functions. The default is 1 second, but the setting can range between 0 and 3600 seconds. If the time needed to perform these recalculations and updates is greater than the interval, the worksheet will continually be recalculated and updated. This interval remains set until the end of the 1-2-3 session or another interval is selected.

Manual   This option causes 1-2-3 to reexecute the last issued /Data Query and /Data Table commands, and update worksheet formulas and database @functions, on a manual basis. The /Data Query and /Data Table commands update their most recent results. The formulas and functions are recalculated as set according to the /Worksheet Global Recalc command.

/Data External Other Translation

Description

The /Data External Other Translation command selects the character set 1-2-3 uses when it transfers data to and from a table in the external database. This command is only used when the information copied from the external table contains inappropriate characters. Most of the time, 1-2-3 selects the appropriate character set for you. When you use this command, 1-2-3 displays the available character sets. If the database management program only has one character set, 1-2-3 automatically sets this command for you. In this case, it appears as if 1-2-3 is doing nothing.

Options

There are no options for this command.

/Data External Quit

Description

The /Data External Quit command permits you to exit the sticky Data External menu.

Options

This command has no options.

/Data External Reset

Description

This command breaks a connection between a table in an external database and 1-2-3. Any further references to the external file may result in errors.

Options

When you execute this command, 1-2-3 prompts you for the range name of the external table from which you are disconnecting. If the range name selected is the only table connected to 1-2-3, this command closes the external database file. If the range name selected is the only external table connection established for a particular driver, this command removes the driver from 1-2-3's memory.

/Data External Use

Description

This command establishes a connection between 1-2-3 and a table in an external database. A 1-2-3 range name is assigned to the external database for other commands and functions to use. You can connect multiple external database tables by using this command for each table. Once a connection is established between 1-2-3 and the external table, you can refer to the table in most of 1-2-3's database functions and commands. To look at the records in the external database, you must copy them to a worksheet with /Data Query commands.

When 1-2-3 connects to an external table, it loads a driver that connects with the database management program. This driver also lets you execute the commands and functions of the database management program from within 1-2-3.

Options

When you execute /Data External Use, 1-2-3 prompts you to select the driver, the database name, and the table name. You can either select a highlighted one or type in your own entry. Then 1-2-3 prompts for a range name; the table name is suggested as the default, unless it starts with a $ or !, contains a period, or looks like a cell address. You can accept the default or enter a new range name before pressing ENTER. Like all range names, it must be unique within the 1-2-3 file. If the database management program requires a user name and password, you must also enter this information.

/Data Fill

Description

The /Data Fill command allows you to produce an ascending or descending list of numbers separated by the same interval. The following series can all be generated with /Data Fill:

```
1  2   3   4   5   6   7   8   9    10  11   12   13   14   15   16
5001  5006   5011   5016   5021   5026   5031   5036
90  88  86  84  82  80  78  76  74  72  70  68  66
03-Jan-90   10-Jan-90   17-Jan-90   24-Jan-90   31-Jan-90
```

When you use /Data Fill, you must specify the range of cells to hold the numeric series. After this you will be prompted for the three variables that provide flexibility in series generation. 1-2-3 continues to fill each cell in the range, from left to right for each row, until it fills the last cell in the range, or until the next value it would use exceeds the stop value.

Options

The /Data Fill options include a start value, a stop value, and an increment or step value. The start value is the beginning number in your sequence and has a default of 0 or the value most recently entered. The stop value is the last value in your sequence: its default is 8191 or the last number that will fit within the range selected. The increment (step) value is the distance between each pair of numbers in the series; its default is 1 or the value most recently entered. Any of these values can be either positive or negative.

The values can also include functions, such as @DATE(89,12,13); formulas, such as + @YEAR(@TODAY) + 1900; or a cell address, range address or range name that evaluates to a value, such as A1, which may contain the number 30. If you provide a range name or range address, 1-2-3 uses the cell value in the upper left corner of the range.

When /Data Fill is used for dates, 1-2-3 offers additional features for the start, step, and stop values. To include a date as a start or stop value, you can enter it in any one of 1-2-3's date formats, except Short International. If the step value contains:

- An integer or an integer followed by a D, 1-2-3 increases the date value in daily increments

- An integer followed by a W, 1-2-3 increases the step value in weekly increments

- An integer followed by an M, 1-2-3 increases the step value in monthly increments

- An integer followed by a Q, 1-2-3 increases the step value in quarterly increments

- An integer followed by a Y, 1-2-3 increases the step value in yearly increments

For example, a step value of 2M increments the date serial numbers in two-month increments.

When the /Data Fill function is used for times, 1-2-3 offers some new features for the start, step, and stop values. To include a time as a start or stop value, you can enter it in any one of 1-2-3's time formats. If the step value contains:

- An integer followed by an S, 1-2-3 increases the time value in second increments

- An integer followed by MIN, 1-2-3 increases the step value in minute increments

- An integer followed by an H, 1-2-3 increases the step value in hour increments

For example, a step value of 30S increments the date serial numbers in thirty-second increments.

Note

If the range selected for the /Data Fill command uses the Automatic format, 1-2-3 will automatically format the cells as dates and times using the format of the start, step, and stop values you specify.

/Data Query Criteria

Description

The /Data Query Criteria command lets you specify the location of the criteria you have entered on the worksheet for database record selection. Criteria must already be entered on the worksheet when you issue this command.

Options

The only option you have with this command is the method you use to specify the criteria range. Pointing, typing the cell addresses, and using a range name are all acceptable methods of specifying the two-dimensional range.

/Data Query Del

Description

The /Data Query Del command searches database records for specified criteria and deletes all the records in the input area that match the criteria. The database records must first be specified with /Data Query Input, and the criteria must already be entered on the worksheet and specified with /Data Query Criteria. This command only works on one data table at a time. 1-2-3 will prompt for confirmation to delete the database records. Select Cancel to leave the command without deleting the record, or Delete to delete the selected records.

Options

There are no options for this command.

Note

Since the /Data Query Del deletion process is permanent, be sure to save your file to disk before using the command. This way you can always retrieve the file if you make a mistake in specifying your criteria and delete too many records. Another protective strategy is to use your criteria to extract records (with Data Query Extract) before using the same criteria for a deletion.

/Data Query Extract

Description

The /Data Query Extract command searches database records for specified criteria, and writes all records from the input area that match your criteria to an output area on the worksheet. Preliminary steps that must be completed before using this command are

   • The database records to be searched must first be specified with /Data Query Input.

   • The criteria for extraction must be entered on the worksheet and specified with /Data Query Criteria.

• An output area must be specified with /Data Query Output. This area must be large enough to hold all the extracted records, and must be out of the way of your other data.

Options

There are no options for this command.

/Data Query Find

Description

The /Data Query Find command searches database records for specified criteria, and highlights one at a time all records from the input area that match those criteria. Before using this command you must specify the database records to be searched, with /Data Query Input. You must also enter the search criteria on the worksheet, and identify them with /Data Query Criteria. This command only works on one data table at a time. It cannot work with external tables.

Options

There are no options for this command.

/Data Query Input

Description

The /Data Query Input command is used to specify the location of the database. Database records should already be entered on a worksheet when you issue this command.

Options

The only option you have with this command is the method you use to specify the input range. Pointing, typing the cell addresses, and entering a range name are all acceptable methods. The input range can include multiple input ranges or external tables. To include multiple tables, type the argument separator (default is a comma) after highlighting an input range; then specify the next input range. If you specify an external table, use the name assigned with the /Data External Use command. The /Data Query Extract command can use an input range from an active file, a file on disk, or an external table. The /Data Query Modify Insert and /Data Query Modify Replace commands can use an input range from an active file or an external table.

Note

The input range should always include the field names at the top of your database.

/Data Query Modify Cancel

Description

The /Data Query Modify Cancel command cancels the actions taken by other /Data Query Modify commands and returns you to the READY mode. Once this command is executed, the /Data Query Modify Replace command has no effect.

Options

There are no options for this command.

/Data Query Modify Extract

Description

The /Data Query Modify Extract command copies records from the input range (set by /Data Query Input) that meet the criteria set by /Data Query Criteria, to the output area set by /Data Query Output.

This command only copies the fields for each record that are in the first row of the output range. Unlike /Data Query Extract, /Data Query Modify Extract remembers the copied records' location in the input range.

Options

There are no options for this command.

/Data Query Modify Insert

Description

The /Data Query Modify Insert command copies records from the output range set by /Data Query Output, to the input area set by /Data Query Input. This command only copies the fields for each record that are in the first row of the output range.

Options

There are no options for this command.

/Data Query Modify Replace

Description

The /Data Query Modify Replace command replaces records in the input range set by /Data Query Input, using records in the output area set by /Data Query Output. This command is used to replace records extracted with the /Data Query Modify Extract command after the extracted records in the output range are edited. This command only copies the fields for each record that are in the first row of the output range.

This command replaces formulas in the input range with their value from the output range. You can prevent this from occurring by changing the name of the field in the output range to a temporary name.

Options

There are no options for this command.

/Data Query Output

Description

The /Data Query Output command permits you to specify the location of the area you plan to use to store information extracted from a database. The field names for the data you extract must already be entered on the worksheet when you issue this command. The other task this command performs is specifying the location of the records to be added to the input range with /Data Query Modify Insert.

Options

You have two options with this command: specifying the entire output area or just the top row. You also have a number of options for specifying the range for the output area.

If you specify a one-row output range that includes only the field names, 1-2-3 will use as many rows as it needs for writing data in the columns selected for the output range. If you specify a multiple-row output range, 1-2-3 will stop extracting records when your output range is full. Options for specifying the range are pointing, typing the cell addresses, and entering a range name. The output range can be in the current file, an active file, or an external table.

/Data Query Quit

Description

This command permits you to exit the sticky Data Query menu.

Options

This command has no options.

/Data Query Reset

Description

This command will clear the range specifications for Input, Criteria, and Output made with the /Data Query commands or /Data External commands.

Options

There are no options for this command.

/Data Query Unique

Description

The /Data Query Unique command copies records from the input range that match the criteria. Unlike the /Data Query Extract command, this command only includes the first record when several identical records exist. The output is sorted according to the field values in the output area. Preliminary steps that must be completed before using this command are as follows.

• The database records to be searched must first be specified with /Data Query Input.

• The criteria for search must be entered on the worksheet and specified with /Data Query Criteria.

• An output area must be specified with /Data Query Output. This area must be large enough to hold all the selected records and must be out of the way of your other data.

Options

There are no options for this command.

/Data Sort Data-Range

Description

The /Data Sort Data-Range command permits you to specify the location of the records you plan to sort. Database records should already be entered on the worksheet when you issue this command.

Options

The only option you have with this command is the method you use to specify the input range. Pointing, typing the cell addresses, and entering a range name are all acceptable methods of specifying the range.

Note

The sort range should not include the field names at the top of the database. If you accidentally include the field names, they will be sorted.

/Data Sort Extra-Key

Description

The /Data Sort Extra-Key command permits you to select additional fields within the database to serve as tie breakers whenever there is more than one primary and secondary key with the same value. When this situation occurs, the sort operation uses the extra keys to provide a sequence for the records containing the duplicate entries. As an example, you may have an employee file with the location field selected as the primary key and job code selected as the secondary key. When you encounter more than one employee with the same job code and location, and have selected last name as the first extra key, the employees with the same location and job code will appear in a sequence determined by their last names.

When this command is executed, 1-2-3 prompts you for an extra key number, and displays the lowest unused extra key number as a default. You can enter another number or press ENTER to accept the default. Extra keys start numbering with 1. An extra key is selected in the same manner as a primary key. Any nonblank cell within a field can be specified as the secondary key.

Options

You can specify either ascending or descending sort order.

/Data Sort Go

Description

The /Data Sort Go command tells 1-2-3 to sort the records. Before this command is executed, the database must be defined with the /Data Sort Data-Range command. The primary key and any additional sort keys must also be specified.

Options

There are no options for this command.

/Data Sort Primary-Key

Description

The /Data Sort Primary-Key command permits you to sort your database records into a new sequence, by selecting a field to control the resequencing. Enter the address of a nonblank cell within the field that you wish to use for controlling the sort sequence.

Options

You can specify either ascending or descending sort order.

/Data Sort Quit

Description

This command lets you exit the sticky /Data Sort menu.

Options

There are no options for this command.

/Data Sort Reset

Description

The /Data Sort Reset command cancels the current settings for the primary, secondary, and extra keys, and the data range.

Options

There are no options for this command.

/Data Sort Secondary-Key

Description

The /Data Sort Secondary-Key command permits you to select a field within the database to serve as a tie breaker whenever there is more than one primary key with the same value. When this situation occurs, the sort operation uses the secondary key to provide a sequence for the records containing the duplicate entries. As an example, you may have an employee file with the last name field selected as the primary key. When you encounter three employees with the last name of Smith, and have selected first name as the secondary key, the three Smiths will appear in a sequence determined by their first names.

A secondary key is selected in the same manner as a primary key. Any nonblank cell within a field can be specified as the secondary key.

Options

You can specify either ascending or descending sort order.

Using Data Management Features in the Worksheet Environment

In Chapter 9, "Data Management," you learned how to use the data management features of 1-2-3 to build your own database of information. In this chapter you will discover ways that data management commands can assist you with calculations and other worksheet tasks. You will see some of the same commands used in Chapter 9, such as /Data Sort, but they will be presented in a new light. You will also explore more sophisticated features that allow you to handle tasks like regression and sensitivity analysis. These features will introduce new commands, such as /Data Table and /Data Regression, including all of the new Release 3 Data Table features.

Performing Statistical Analyses with /Data Commands

The statistical options that are part of the /Data commands allow you to perform sophisticated analyses of your data. You can perform a regression analysis, create a frequency distribution, or prepare a sensitivity analysis.

673

Sensitivity Analysis

The /Data Table options allow you to quickly substitute a range of values in one or more cells referenced by formulas and to record the results of worksheet calculations at the same time. In other words, /Data Table automates the "what-if" analysis you may have been doing with the package as you plugged in new individual variable values and tried to remember the results from previous iterations. The advantage of this automated approach is that 1-2-3 will do all the work, plug in the values, and remember the results for you. The results will be recorded in a table, as you might guess from the command's name.

The /Data Table command provides five options: a one-way table, a two-way table, a three-way table, a labeled table, and a reset option that eliminates settings you have made through any of the other choices.

One-Way Data Tables

A one-way data table allows you to choose a set of values for one variable and record them in a worksheet column. Above and to the right of this column of values you place formulas to be evaluated for each value of the variable. The results are recorded below the formulas to form a complete table.

Let's look at two examples of a one-way table. The first will be used with the worksheet data shown in Figure 10-1. This worksheet computes commissions using the quarterly sales figure for each salesman times the commission percentage in D1. If you were considering changing the commission percentage, you might be interested in what you would have paid out if that commission structure existed in prior periods. You could plug individual values one by one into D1 and monitor the effect on the total commission calculation in C20, but it is faster to have 1-2-3 do the work for you.

The first step is to set up the framework for the table. This step must be completed before you enter /Data Table. Record the values you want to substitute for D1 in a column. The example in Figure 10-2 uses I4..I19, but any empty location can be selected. If you are using values in even increments, you can have /Data Fill generate these values for you. The next step in the setup process is to record the formula or formulas you wish to evaluate, placed one column to the right of the

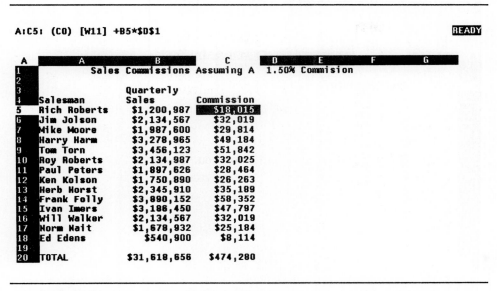

A:C5: (CO) [W11] +B5*$D$1   READY

	A	B	C	D	E	F	G
1	Sales Commissions Assuming A 1.50% Commission						
2							
3		Quarterly					
4	Salesman	Sales	Commission				
5	Rich Roberts	$1,200,987	$18,015				
6	Jim Jolson	$2,134,567	$32,019				
7	Mike Moore	$1,987,600	$29,814				
8	Harry Harm	$3,278,965	$49,184				
9	Tom Torn	$3,456,123	$51,842				
10	Roy Roberts	$2,134,987	$32,025				
11	Paul Peters	$1,897,626	$28,464				
12	Ken Kolson	$1,750,890	$26,263				
13	Herb Horst	$2,345,910	$35,189				
14	Frank Folly	$3,890,152	$58,352				
15	Ivan Imers	$3,186,450	$47,797				
16	Will Walker	$2,134,567	$32,019				
17	Norm Nait	$1,678,932	$25,184				
18	Ed Edens	$540,900	$8,114				
19							
20	TOTAL	$31,618,656	$474,280				

Figure 10-1.   Commission schedule

values and one row above them. In this example, to evaluate total commission, a reference to C20 will suffice. This entry is made in J3. After entering +C20, you can format the cell as Text to display the formula. The table at this time looks like the display in Figure 10-2. After completing these two preliminary steps, you are ready to use the /Data Table command.

Move your cell pointer to I3, the blank cell to the left of the formulas and immediately above the values. Enter /**Data Table** and select 1 for a one-way table. Select the range I3..J19 for the table location. You can use cell addresses, pointing, or a range name for this task.

1-2-3's next prompt is for the input cell. This is the cell into which you want to plug the values from the commission percentage column, one by one. For our example this will be D1. When you press ENTER, 1-2-3 takes the first value in the input column and plugs it into D1 in the model. After the first calculation is completed, 1-2-3 records the result in the table and repeats the process for each of the remaining values. Figure 10-3 shows the level of total commissions at a variety of percent-

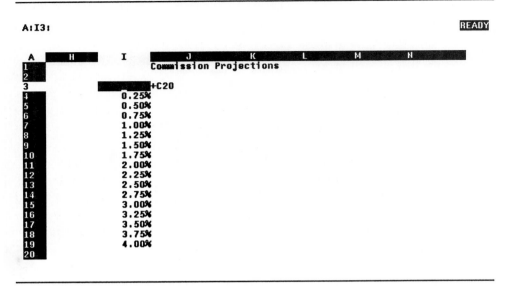

Figure 10-2.   Outline of one-way table

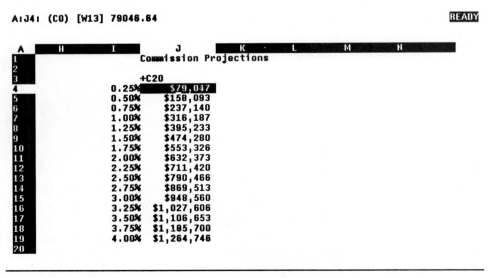

Figure 10-3.   Commission table output

ages. Be aware that if you change the formulas in your model, the table is not updated to reflect these changes. To update the table values, issue the /Data Table command again or press F8 (TABLE).

Now let's look at a second example of a one-way table, this time using more than one formula. Figure 10-4 shows the model and the completed table. The model projects sales, cost of goods sold, and profit through 1991, using a 9% fixed growth rate for sales, and 45% as the cost of goods sold percentage. Suppose you want to look at the impact on sales, costs, and profits of variations in the sales growth factor. Place the variable values in A11..A20. References to the cells containing the formulas you wish to evaluate are placed in B10..D10, as +G4, +G2, and +G3. Using /Data Table 1, define the table as being in A10..D20 and the input cell as C7. This range must include the formulas in the top row and the input values in the leftmost column. The results are shown in cells B11..D20 of the figure.

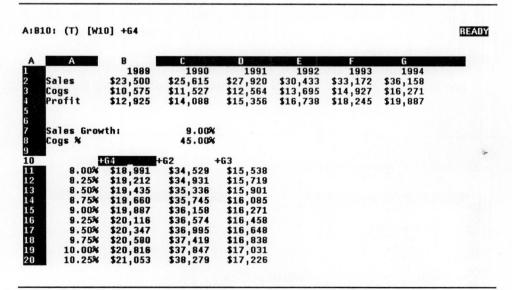

Figure 10-4.   One-way table with multiple formulas

Tip: Use F8 (TABLE) to recalculate tables instead of executing the /Data Table command each time you want to update the values of the formulas. Pressing this key reexecutes the last /Data Table command.

Two-Way Data Tables

The /Data Table 2 command allows you to build a table in which you supply input values for two variables, instructing 1-2-3 to apply these values when recalculating the worksheet and recording the result of one of the worksheet formulas in the table. This kind of table is referred to as a two-way table. It differs from a one-way table in its use of two sets of variable values and its ability to record the results of only one formula. This command allows you to see to which variable the formula being evaluated is most sensitive.

Like the one-way table, the two-way table requires a significant amount of preliminary work. The example uses a two-way table with the model in Figure 10-5 for payment calculations. The payment calculation is dependent on the amount borrowed, the interest rate, and the term of the loan. The amount borrowed may vary, since it will be equal to the cost of the new home minus the equity from the sale of the existing home. While holding the loan term constant, you can use /Data Table 2 to vary both the equity received from the sale of an existing home, and the interest rate.

Values for the first input variable (the interest rate) are stored in one column of the worksheet. If the values are spaced at equal intervals,

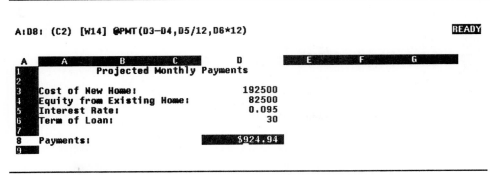

Figure 10-5.   Model used in two-way table

/Data Fill can be used to generate the column of values. Values for the second input value (equity) are placed one row above the top value for input variable 1 and one cell to the right. The values for the second input variable are placed across the row. A formula or a reference to one is then placed in the cell at the top of the column used for input variable 1 and in the same row as the input variable 2.

In the payment example in Figure 10-6, column H is used for the values for input variable 1. Values are in H2..H17, beginning with 9%, adding increments of .25%, and ending with 12.75%. The equity figures start in I1 with 75000 and proceed at increments of 2500, ending with 90000 in O1. Cell H1 contains the formula reference, +D8, representing the payment calculated. If you want this cell to display as a formula, format the cell as Text with /Range Format Text.

With all these preliminaries accomplished, you enter /**Data Table** and choose 2 from the submenu. The first prompt asks for the location of the table, which is H1..O17. The next prompt asks for the cell to use for the first input value, which is D5. Then answer the next prompt with D4, the second input cell. All these locations can be entered as a range, as a range name, or by pointing. After you respond to this last prompt, 1-2-3 provides the results shown in Figure 10-6.

A:H1: (T) +D8   `READY`

A	H	I	J	K	L	M	N	O
1	+D8	75000	77500	80000	82500	85000	87500	90000
2	9.00%	$945	$925	$905	$885	$865	$845	$825
3	9.25%	$967	$946	$926	$905	$884	$864	$843
4	9.50%	$988	$967	$946	$925	$904	$883	$862
5	9.75%	$1,010	$988	$967	$945	$924	$902	$881
6	10.00%	$1,031	$1,009	$987	$965	$943	$921	$900
7	10.25%	$1,053	$1,031	$1,008	$986	$963	$941	$919
8	10.50%	$1,075	$1,052	$1,029	$1,006	$983	$960	$938
9	10.75%	$1,097	$1,074	$1,050	$1,027	$1,003	$980	$957
10	11.00%	$1,119	$1,095	$1,071	$1,048	$1,024	$1,000	$976
11	11.25%	$1,141	$1,117	$1,093	$1,068	$1,044	$1,020	$996
12	11.50%	$1,164	$1,139	$1,114	$1,089	$1,065	$1,040	$1,015
13	11.75%	$1,186	$1,161	$1,136	$1,110	$1,085	$1,060	$1,035
14	12.00%	$1,209	$1,183	$1,157	$1,131	$1,106	$1,080	$1,054
15	12.25%	$1,231	$1,205	$1,179	$1,153	$1,126	$1,100	$1,074
16	12.50%	$1,254	$1,227	$1,201	$1,174	$1,147	$1,121	$1,094
17	12.75%	$1,277	$1,250	$1,223	$1,195	$1,168	$1,141	$1,114
18								

Figure 10-6.   Two-way table for payment calculation

You can use this table of results to determine the monthly payment as long as the interest rate and the amount of money borrowed are in the ranges established for the table. Locate in column 1 the interest rate you feel you can obtain for a loan; then use that row to determine your payments at different levels of borrowing. Similarly, you can use the column for any given borrowing level and determine your payments, based on one of the interest rates in column 1.

Three-Way Data Tables

The /Data Table 3 command allows you to build a three-dimensional table in which you supply input values for three variables; 1-2-3 then applies these values when recalculating the worksheets and recording the result of one of the worksheet formulas in the table. This kind of table, which is new in Release 3, is referred to as a three-way table. It differs from a two-way table in its use of three sets of variable values and its ability to record the results of only one formula. Also, a three-way table uses a separate worksheet for each value of the third input variable. This command allows you to see to which variable the formula being evaluated is most sensitive.

Like the other tables, the three-way table requires a significant amount of preliminary work. The example uses a three-way table with the model in Figure 10-7 for the present value of an annuity calculations. The present value of an annuity is dependent on the amount paid each period, the interest rate, and the number of periods. By adding the loan term as a third variable, you can use /Data Table 3 to vary the periodic payment, the interest rate, and the number of periods.

Values for the first input variable are stored in one column of the data table. If the values are spaced at equal intervals, /Data Fill can be used to generate the column of values. Values for the second input value are placed one row above the top value for input 1 and one cell to the right. The values for the second input variable are placed across the row. Again, evenly spaced values make /Data Fill the ideal choice for making the entries.

Once the first and second input variables are stored in the usual way in the first worksheet of the data table, you can add worksheets to the file for each value of the third variable. Each of the worksheets must use the same rows and columns for the data table. The /Worksheet

A:B5: @PV(B1,B2,B3)   READY

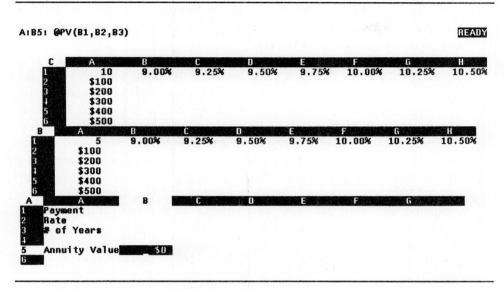

Figure 10-7.   Preliminary work for a three-way table

Insert Sheet command can add all of the worksheets in a single command. Then the values for the first and second variables can be copied in with the /Copy command. Finally, each of the third variables must be entered in the upper corner of the data table in separate worksheets, at the intersection of the column and row of data values already entered for the first two variables.

A worksheet formula or a reference to one must be placed in a cell outside the data table. This formula is used to supply the table entries as the values of the variables change. Other formulas can exist on the worksheet, but one formula is singled out, and its results provide the entries within the table. This formula does not refer to the table cells, but to other formulas or input cells where the variable values in the table will be substituted.

An input cell must be defined for each dimension of the table. The values in the table are plugged into these input cells one by one, and the results of each iteration are captured and stored in the table cells. Systematically, each input cell is assigned new values from the table shell, with the /Data Table command returning the formula results for each of the values of the three variables. This input cell is formatted with /Range Format Text to display as a formula. Unlike /Data Table 1 and /Data Table 2, with /Data Table 3 the formula the command evaluates is outside of the data table.

Let's pull this all together using the annuity example in Figures 10-7 and 10-8. Use the first worksheet for the input variables and the formula for the data table. The formula is stored in B5 of sheet A.

The data table is located in B:A1..F:K6. In the data table, A2..A6 in each worksheet contains the input values for variable 1 (the periodic payment) beginning with $100, adding increments of $100, and ending with $500. B1..K1 in each worksheet is for the input values for variable 2 (the interest rate) beginning with 9%, adding increments of .25%, ending with 11.25%. Once these values are created in worksheet B, the /Copy command can copy the row and column values from B:A1..B:K6 to C:A1..F:A1. A1 in each worksheet is for the input values for variable 3 (the number of periods) beginning with 5, adding increments of 5, and ending with 25. Variable 3 is the only value that changes in each worksheet.

With all these preliminaries accomplished, enter /**Data Table** and choose 3 from the submenu. The first prompt asks for the location of the table; highlight B:A1..F:K6 and press ENTER. (Or enter a range or a range name.) The next prompt asks for the cell containing the formula to be evaluated for each set of values in the data table. In the annuity example, highlight A:B5 and press ENTER. Next, 1-2-3 prompts for the input cell to use for the first input value. In this example the input cell is A:B1, which you can point to or enter as a range name or address. The same procedure works for A:B2, the second input cell, and A:B3, the third input cell. After you respond to this last prompt, 1-2-3 provides the results shown in Figure 10-8.

You can use this table of results to determine the present value of annuities for various payment amounts, interest rates, and payment periods. Move to the worksheet containing the desired number of payment periods in the upper left corner, and look down the column of the table that has the interest rate you want for an annuity, to determine what the annuity is worth. Similarly, you can look across the row for a particular payment amount and determine the present value at various interest rates.

Tip: When you are selecting variables for a three-way table, use the variable with the fewest values as the third input variable. Since each

A:B5: @PV(B1,B2,B3)   `READY`

	A	B	C	D	E	F	G	H
1	10	9.00%	9.25%	9.50%	9.75%	10.00%	10.25%	10.50%
2	$100	$642	$635	$628	$621	$614	$608	$601
3	$200	$1,284	$1,270	$1,256	$1,242	$1,229	$1,216	$1,203
4	$300	$1,925	$1,904	$1,884	$1,863	$1,843	$1,824	$1,804
5	$400	$2,567	$2,539	$2,512	$2,484	$2,458	$2,432	$2,406
6	$500	$3,209	$3,174	$3,139	$3,106	$3,072	$3,040	$3,007

	A	B	C	D	E	F	G	H
1	5	9.00%	9.25%	9.50%	9.75%	10.00%	10.25%	10.50%
2	$100	$389	$386	$384	$382	$379	$377	$374
3	$200	$778	$773	$768	$763	$758	$753	$749
4	$300	$1,167	$1,159	$1,152	$1,145	$1,137	$1,130	$1,123
5	$400	$1,556	$1,546	$1,536	$1,526	$1,516	$1,507	$1,497
6	$500	$1,945	$1,932	$1,920	$1,908	$1,895	$1,883	$1,871

	A		C	D	E	F	G
1	Payment						
2	Rate						
3	# of Years						
4							
5	Annuity Value		$0				
6							

Figure 10-8.   Three-way table

third input cell value creates a table on a different worksheet, using a third variable with many values can fill the computer's memory quickly.

Using Labeled Data Tables in Sensitivity Analysis

Release 3 adds labeled tables to the features you can access with the /Data Table command. The /Data Table Labeled command surpasses the limits of the other /Data Table commands. For example, /Data Table 1 requires that the input values be stored in the first column of the data table. With /Data Table Labeled, you can create one-way tables with the input values in a column, a row, or on multiple worksheets. Also, the /Data Table Labeled command allows you to:

• Include blank rows, columns, and worksheets between the input values and the results, and among the results

• Include more labels than in the other data tables in order to document the table so it is easier to understand

- Evaluate multiple formulas

- Include formulas within the data table that operate on the data table results. This feature can be used to add some of the numbers generated by the table

- Include more than three variables by having multiple variables for a column, row, or worksheet that are assigned different input values

This command can create one, two, and three-way tables.

The /Data Table Labeled command requires the most preliminary work of all the /Data Table commands. Since creating a labeled table requires several steps, reviewing the steps will help you understand this command. The following paragraphs show you how to create a simple one-way labeled table, and a more complicated three-way table. The steps for creating a labeled table are summarized in the box labeled "Creating a Labeled Table."

Creating a Simple Labeled Table

One feature of the /Data Table Labeled command is the ability to create one- and two-way tables that have a different orientation from /Data Table 1 and /Data Table 2 tables. Another advantage of the /Data Table Labeled command is how it can create tables that manipulate more values than the other tables can. The preliminary work of a labeled table that uses these features is shown in Figure 10-9. This table computes the net profit and the after-tax profit using assumptions about the sales growth rate, the cost of goods sold (COGS) percentage, and operating expenses. The formulas (A16..B18) and the income statement (A10..B14) appear using the Text format; the data in rows 3 and 4 are formatted using the Percent format; and row 5 is formatted as Currency.

Figure 10-9 is a one-way table that substitutes three values for each cell in the data table it calculates. For each Guess column, the table substitutes the sales growth rate, the COGS percentage, and the operating expenses in the input cells, and computes net profit and after-tax profit. Since only column variable values are used, this is still a one-way table.

Creating a Labeled Table

A number of steps are required to create a labeled table. They are as follows:

1. Select the input cells you want to use for the formulas and enter labels next to them.

2. Enter the formulas that you want evaluated in the table. List the formula name on one row and the formula itself in the cell below.

3. Select an area in the worksheet file that you want to use for the data table.

4. Enter the values that you want plugged in as column variable values; place them above or below where you want 1-2-3 to fill in the values. If you have multiple column variable values, they must be in adjacent rows.

5. Enter the values that you want plugged in as row variable values; place them to the right or to the left of where you want 1-2-3 to fill in the values. If you have multiple row variable values, they must be in adjacent columns.

6. Enter the values that you want plugged in as sheet variable values; place them outside of the area reserved for the data table. If you have multiple sheet variable values, they must be in the same cell in each sheet.

7. Enter the formula label above or below the data table, or to the left or right of the data table. If the formula label is above or below the data table, it must stretch across all columns the formula will use for input values. It can be stretched by adding the label-fill character (a hyphen) to the beginning and end of the formula label.

8. Enter /**Data Table Labeled Formulas**. Select the formula range created in Step 2; then select the formula label range selected in Step 7.

9. Select the Across option if you have entered column variable values. Specify the cells entered in Step 4. For each row in the column variable values, 1-2-3 prompts for confirmation and the input cell.

10. Select the Down option if you have entered row variable values. Specify the cells entered in Step 5. For each column in the column variable values, 1-2-3 prompts for confirmation and the input cell.

11. Select the Sheets option if you have entered worksheet variable values. Specify the cells entered in Step 6. For each cell in the worksheets, 1-2-3 prompts for confirmation and the input cell.

12. Choose Go to create the table.

To use this table with the /Data Table Labeled command, it must have several additional features shown in the figure. First, the input cells must be selected, in this case, E17..E19. Each of these input cells are labeled.

Next the formulas must be created and labeled. This table has two formulas, Net Profit and After Tax Profit. You must enter the formula's name in the cell above it; this is the *formula range*. The formula name, or label, tells 1-2-3 when to use each formula in the data table. In Figure 10-9, the table uses the Net Profit formula to compute row 7, and the After Tax Profit formula to compute row 8. The names of these formulas in rows 7 and 8 are called the *formula label range*. The formula label range appears above or below the table to indicate which formulas the columns use, or to the left or right of the table to indicate which formulas the rows use. The formulas can reference any cell outside of the data table. As the figure shows, you can add blank rows to a labeled table.

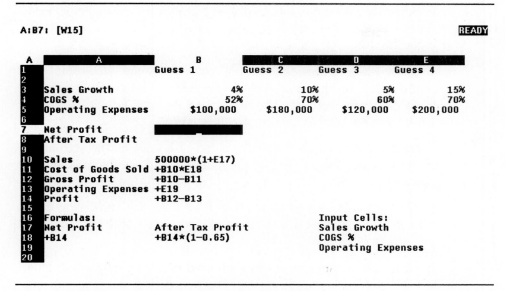

Figure 10-9.   Preliminary work for a labeled table

With the preliminary work finished, you are ready to create the table with the /Data Table Labeled command. 1-2-3 presents a new menu like this:

A:A1:   MENU
Formulas Down Across Sheets Input—Cells Label—Fill Go
Specify the range containing the labeled formulas

You can select the worksheet cells 1-2-3 uses for the labeled data table by following these steps:

1. Select Formulas. 1-2-3 prompts for the formula range, which is A17..B18; this includes the formula name in the first row and the formula in the second.

2. Then 1-2-3 prompts for the formula label range, which is A7..A8; this is the formula name that tells 1-2-3 which formula to use for each row.

3. Since this table has input variables stored across columns, select Across next. When 1-2-3 prompts for the column variable range, enter **B3..E5.**

4. Once 1-2-3 knows the column variable range, it prompts for confirmation of the first row in the column range, and wants to know the input cell for this row. For the Sales Growth variables, 1-2-3 displays B3..E3; the input cell is E17.

5. Next 1-2-3 prompts for confirmation of B4..E4 as the second row in the column range (COGS percentage) and wants to know the input cell, which is E18.

6. Then 1-2-3 asks you to confirm B5..E5 as the third row in the column range (Operating Expenses) and wants to know the input cell, which is E19.

7. Since this finishes your selections, select Go to have 1-2-3 generate the table.

The results are shown in Figure 10-10. You do not need to define a data

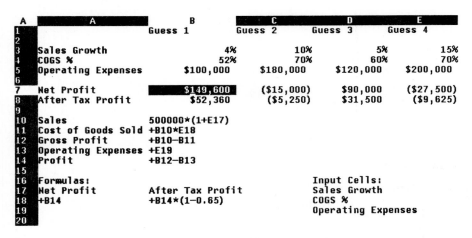

Figure 10-10.   Table after /Data Table Labeled command

table range, since this command uses all cells where formulas and variable ranges intersect.

Tip: Use /Copy or /Range Transpose to copy the formula names into formula label ranges. Since the /Data Table Labeled command does not calculate formulas properly if the formula name is misspelled, use /Copy or /Range Transpose to copy the exact formula names from the formula range to the data table.

Creating a Three-Way Labeled Table

Like the prior example, you can create more advanced tables with the /Data Table Labeled command. The steps you perform to create a three-way table, using the example in Figure 10-11 will show more of the features of this command. Figure 10-11 computes the monthly payment and yearly taxes on a number of houses. An extra computation in the middle of the table computes the average house payment.

Setting Up the Input Cells and Formulas   First, you must label the input cells the table uses. The first input is in B1, the second is in B2,

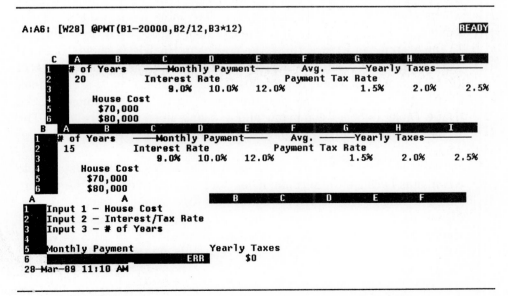

Figure 10-11.   Preliminary work for a three-way labeled table

and the third is in B3. Each of these input cells is labeled for documentation purposes. Notice that the second input cell can contain either the interest rate or the tax rate. You can use an input cell for multiple types of data when the table uses multiple formulas. In this example, all of this information is contained in the first worksheet to keep it separate from the data table. Also, by having multiple worksheets in perspective, you can see the results of two of the worksheets in the data table, as well as the formula and input cells.

Once the input cells are decided and labeled, the formula range can be added. For each formula range, you must enter the formula name and below it the formula. The formula must reference the cell values outside the data range. The first formula, Monthly Payment, assumes that a $20,000 down payment is made on the house so the amount borrowed is $20,000 less than the house cost. The second formula, Yearly Taxes, multiplies the house cost by the tax rate.

Setting Up the Data Table   After you have the input cells and the formulas, you can create the labeled data table. For the example in Figure 10-11, the table uses worksheets B through E. Cell A2 in each worksheet contains the number of years the monthly payment calculation uses. Unlike /Data Table 3 tables, values for input cells that span worksheets can be placed outside the data table if the value is in the same cell in each worksheet; notice the house costs listed in column B. In the example in Figure 10-11, the entries in B5..B10 in sheets B and C were supplied by /Data Fill, with a start value of 70000, a step value of 10000 and a stop value of 120000. While the house cost entries look identical to column entries for the other /Data Table commands, the /Data Table Labeled command allows blank lines in the column. The House Cost label in B4 is ignored, since it is above the first row input value.

The columns in Figure 10-11 look different from other /Data Table commands because the formula label range is combined with the column variable values. The columns determine the formulas that 1-2-3 performs based on formula name range, as well as providing another set of values for an input cell. For the columns headed with Monthly Payment, 1-2-3 evaluates the Monthly Payment formula for each of the possible values listed in row 3.

The formula names in C1 are stretched across all of the columns that use the formula, by using the label-fill character specified with the

/Data Table Labeled Label-Fill command. The default is a hyphen. By filling in the formula label range with this character, you can stretch the label to cover all the columns that you want to use the formula. The Yearly Taxes label in G1 also uses the label-fill character to stretch the formula name across columns G through I.

When the formula label range contains other types of data, such as blanks, other labels, or values, 1-2-3 skips that column in the data table. For example, in Figure 10-11, 1-2-3 skips column F because it contains a label that is not a formula name. When 1-2-3 skips a row, column, or worksheet in a data table, you can fill that row, column, or worksheet with another type of data. For example, cell F5 contains the formula @AVG(C5..E5), which is copied to the other cells in column F. The /Data Table Labeled command does not write over the @AVG functions, and 1-2-3 recalculates the averages based on the values in the data table. The Interest Rate and Tax Rate column headings below the formula names are also ignored, because they are above the column input values. You can use this area to add documentation to the tables.

Once the row and column input variables and labels are entered, you can add worksheets to the worksheet file for the other # of Years values, and copy the first data table to the other worksheet areas. One option is to enable the GROUP mode so all of the formatting and column widths of the first data table are automatically applied to the other worksheet. In the example in Figure 10-11, the /Worksheet Insert Sheet After 4 command inserted four worksheets after the first one, although the last 2 do not appear in the Figure. The formulas and input cells are determined and labeled. Next, the GROUP mode is enabled. As the data values and labels for the first worksheet in the data table are created, the formatting and column widths are automatically applied to the other sheets in the file. Once the table is created in worksheet B, it is copied to worksheets C through E. Then the values of A2 on the various sheets are updated with the /Data Fill command to establish # of Years values, starting with 15 and ascending by increments of 5. Finally, GROUP mode is disabled, and the width of column A in worksheet A is enlarged.

Using the /Data Table Labeled Command

You have really worked hard to accomplish all the preliminary steps, but the payoff is at hand! 1-2-3 will now supply all the calculations for the tables.

1. Enter /**Data Table** and choose Labeled from the submenu.

2. Select Formulas. 1-2-3 prompts for the formula range, which is A:A5..A:B6. This includes the formula name in the first row and the formula in the second. Then 1-2-3 prompts for the formula label range which is B:C1..B:I1. This range displays the formula names used across all the columns in the data table, including the columns the data table skips. 1-2-3 only needs to know the formula label range for the first data table.

3. Since this table uses input values stored in a column, select Down. When 1-2-3 prompts for the row variable range, enter **B:B5..B:B10**. Once 1-2-3 knows the row variable range, 1-2-3 wants to know the input cell for the row variable range. In this example, it is B1.

4. Since this table has input values stored in a row, select Across. When 1-2-3 prompts for the column variable range, enter **B:C3..B:I3**. 1-2-3 knows that the /Data Table Labeled command omits column F because it does not have a formula name in the formula label range. Next 1-2-3 wants to know the input cell for the column variable range; in this example, it is B2.

5. Since this table has input variable values that span worksheets, select Sheets. When 1-2-3 prompts for the worksheet variable range, enter **B:A2..E:A2**. Then, for the worksheet variable range, enter **B3**.

6. Since selecting the row variable range, column variable range and worksheet variable range is all you need to tell 1-2-3 about the data table, select Go, and 1-2-3 generates the table. The results are shown in Figure 10-12.

After you create a labeled table, you may want to perform the table calculations again if you change a variable value. For example, you may want to change the first interest rate to 8%. To make this change, enter .08 in B:C3 and copy it from B:C3 to C:C3..E:C3. To recompute the table, use the /Data Table Labeled Go command, or press F8 (TABLE).

If you want to change one of the table values, use the /Data Table Label Input-Cells command. When you execute this command, 1-2-3 prompts for the row variable range and its input cell; the column

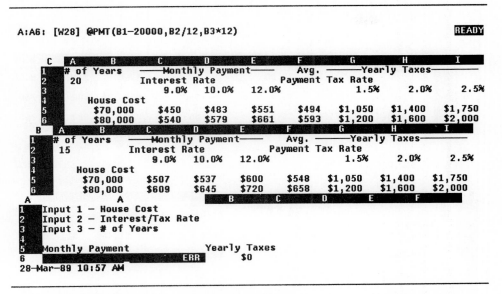

Figure 10-12.   Three-way labeled table

variable range and its input cell; and the worksheet variable range and its input cell. For each of these prompts, 1-2-3 displays the current selection. You can accept it or make a new selection.

Adding Blank Columns, Rows, and Worksheets to the Data Table

One of the advantages of the /Data Table Labeled command is its capacity to insert blank columns, rows, and worksheets into the data table to improve readability. To insert a blank row in a data table, skip the row when you are entering the row variable range. The same applies for skipping columns and worksheets.

Figure 10-13 shows the previous data table after a few modifications. The column containing Avg. Payment is deleted, and a column is added between the 10% and 12% figures. Since column E does not have a value in the column value range, the table leaves column E blank. Also, the column headings in row 2 are deleted to show more of the data table; and a row is inserted between the $70,000 and $80,000 house costs. Since this row does not have a value in the row variable range, the table leaves this row blank. Finally, the 20 in C:A2 is erased. Since this

`D:B1:`   `READY`

	A	B	C	D	E	F	G	H	I
1	# of	Years	────────	Monthly Payment─	─────	────────	──Yearly Taxes─	────	
2	25		9.0%	10.0%		12.0%	1.5%	2.0%	2.5%
3		House Cost							
4		$70,000	$420	$454		$527	$1,050	$1,400	$1,750
5									
6		$80,000	$504	$545		$632	$1,200	$1,600	$2,000

	A	B	C	D	E	F	G	H	I
1	# of Years		────────	Monthly Payment─	─────	────────	──Yearly Taxes─	────	
2			9.0%	10.0%		12.0%	1.5%	2.0%	2.5%
3		House Cost							
4		$70,000							
5									
6		$80,000							

	A	B	C	D	E	F	G	H	I
1	# of Years		────────	Monthly Payment─	─────	────────	──Yearly Taxes─	────	
2	15		9.0%	10.0%		12.0%	1.5%	2.0%	2.5%
3		House Cost							
4		$70,000	$507	$537		$600	$1,050	$1,400	$1,750
5									
6		$80,000	$609	$645		$720	$1,200	$1,600	$2,000

Figure 10-13.   Blank columns, rows, and worksheets in a labeled table

worksheet does not have a variable for the worksheet variable range, the table skips worksheet C in the data table, although it uses worksheets D and E.

Using /Data Table with Database Statistical Functions

The /Data Table command can also be used effectively with the database statistical functions covered in Chapter 9. For example, you can use the command's variable values to supply different criteria values to be used with the database functions. These values may be numeric or label entries, depending on the search criteria you are using.

The database this example will use is shown in Figure 10-14. It contains employee records for a variety of locations and job codes. Let's use the /Data Table 2 command to systematically vary the values for these two variables and obtain an employee count for each job code at each location.

The table is created in B22..E28, as shown in Figure 10-15. In B23..B28, job code values 12, 14, 15, 17, 21, and 23 are listed. Location codes are in C22..E22 as 2, 4, and 10. The formula in B22 is

A:A1: [W12] 'Last Name   `READY`

A	A	B	C	D	E	F
1	Last Name	First Name	SS#	Job Code	Salary	Location
2	Larson	Mary	543-98-9876	23	$12,000	2
3	Campbell	David	213-76-9874	23	$23,000	10
4	Campbell	Keith	569-89-7654	12	$32,000	2
5	Stephens	Tom	219-78-8954	15	$17,800	2
6	Caldor	Larry	459-34-0921	23	$32,500	4
7	Lightnor	Peggy	560-55-4311	14	$23,500	10
8	McCartin	John	817-66-1212	15	$54,600	2
9	Justof	Jack	431-78-9963	17	$41,200	4
10	Patterson	Lyle	212-11-9090	12	$21,500	10
11	Miller	Lisa	214-89-6756	23	$18,700	2
12	Hawkins	Mark	215-67-8973	21	$19,500	2
13	Hartwick	Eileen	313-78-9090	15	$31,450	4
14	Smythe	George	560-90-8645	15	$65,000	4
15	Wilkes	Caitlin	124-67-7432	17	$15,500	2
16	Deaver	Ken	198-98-6750	23	$24,600	10
17	Kaylor	Sally	312-45-9862	12	$32,900	10
18	Parker	Dee	659-11-3452	14	$19,800	4
19	Preverson	Gary	670-90-1121	21	$27,600	4
20	Samuelson	Paul	219-89-7080	23	$28,900	2

Figure 10-14.   Employee database

@DCOUNT(A1..F20,0,J2..K3). The first argument references the database. The second references the first column of the database, which contains last name. That field is a good choice because it is unlikely to be missing from any record. The third argument references a criteria area that you must set up by entering Job Code and Location in J2 and K2 respectively. Then specify the two cells immediately below these, J3 and K3, as input cells. Initially these input cells will be blank, but as the

A:E28: [W12] 2   `POINT`
Enter table range: A:B22..A:E28

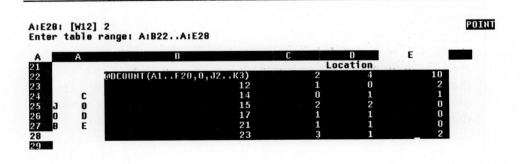

A	A	B	C	D	E
21				Location	
22		@DCOUNT(A1..F20,0,J2..K3)	2	4	10
23			12	1	0	2
24	C		14	0	1	1
25	J 0		15	2	2	0
26	0 D		17	1	1	0
27	B E		21	1	1	0
28			23	3	1	2
29					

Figure 10-15.   Table range selected

```
A:B22:  (T)  [W26]  @DCOUNT(A1..F20,0,J2..K3)                          READY
```

A	A	B	C	D	E
21				Location	
22		@DCOUNT(A1..F20,0,J2..K3)	2	4	10
23		12	1	0	2
24	C	14	0	1	1
25	J 0	15	2	2	0
26	0 D	17	1	1	0
27	B E	21	1	1	0
28		23	3	1	2

Figure 10-16.   Table created using database table

/Data Table 2 command executes, it will supply values for criteria to compute the selective counts of database records.

With all the preliminary work accomplished, enter /**Data Table 2** and specify the table location as B22..E28, the first input cell as J3, and the second input cell as K3. 1-2-3 will then produce the output in Figure 10-16. From this table you can tell how many employees in each job code work at each location.

Regression Analysis

The /Data Regression command is used to perform a simple regression with one independent variable, or a multiple regression with as many as 75 independent variables. You can have up to 8192 observations (that is, values) for each of your variables. All variables must have the same number of observations, however; you cannot have 8192 values for one independent variable, and 50 values for the dependent variable or another independent variable.

The purpose of this statistical technique is to determine whether changes in the independent variables can be used to predict changes in the dependent variable. This potential interrelationship is described quantitatively with *regression analysis*. Details of the theory behind regression analysis can be found in any business statistics book.

The first step in using regression analysis is recording the values for the dependent and independent variables in columns on your worksheet. Figure 10-17 shows the dependent variable—the sales of Product

A:A1: [W11] 'Sales   READY

A	A	B	C	D	E	F	G
1	Sales	Disposable	Advertising				
2	Product A	Income	Expense				
3	110,000	25,000,000	9,000				
4	135,000	31,000,000	9,500				
5	205,000	53,000,000	12,500				
6	215,000	58,000,000	13,000				
7	125,000	42,000,000	9,000				
8	175,000	43,000,000	11,000				
9	210,000	63,000,000	11,000				
10	250,000	67,000,000	12,000				
11							

Figure 10-17.   Regression variables

A—in column A. You can use regression analysis to see whether the
independent variables for which you have historic data for the same
period had an impact on the sales figures for the period. If these
variables do seem to have a relationship to the values for sales, you may
be able to predict sales for future periods—if you know the values for
the other independent variables during the future periods.

Suppose the two independent variables selected are Disposable Income and Advertising Expense. Disposable Income is in column B, and
Advertising Expense is in column C.

You are now ready to enter /**Data Regression**. When you do, the
following menu will be displayed.

A:A1:   MENU
X-Range Y-Range Output-Range Intercept Reset Go Quit
Specify independent variables (X range)

You will need to make a number of selections from this menu. These are
summarized for you in the box called "Creating a Regression Analysis."
Your first step is to select the independent variables with the X-Range
option. You can specify up to 16 columns of values, with as many as 8192

total entries in the columns. This example will use B3..C10. You can use a range name, cell addresses, or the pointing method to inform 1-2-3 of your choice.

---

1 2 3 Creating a Regression Analysis

A number of steps are required to create a regression analysis. They are as follows:

1.   Enter values for the dependent and independent variables in worksheet columns.

2.   Enter /**Data Regression**.

3.   Choose the X-Range option to select the range containing the independent variables.

4.   Choose the Y-Range option to select the column containing the dependent variable.

5.   Choose an output range of nine rows and at least four columns. The number of columns should be equal to the number of independent variables plus two.

6.   Select the Intercept option and choose Zero for a zero intercept, or Compute if you wish 1-2-3 to compute the intercept. If you have not previously done a regression with a 0 intercept during the current session, you can omit this entry if you wish the intercept to be computed, since Compute is the default.

7.   Choose Go to create the regression output.

Your next selection is Y-Range. This selection, used to specify the dependent variable, would be A3..A10 in our example. This can be specified as a range name or cell addresses, or by pointing.

Output-Range is your third selection. You can specify the upper left cell in the range or the complete range. If you choose to explicitly specify the range, keep in mind that it must be at least nine rows from top to bottom, and two columns wider than the number of independent variables, with a minimum width of four columns. If you choose to specify only the left corner, be sure that the space under and to the right of that cell is free, or 1-2-3 will overwrite existing data with your regression results. A21 was chosen for our example.

The fourth menu choice is Intercept. If you wish to have 1-2-3 compute the Y intercept, you can leave this choice blank, since Compute is the default. If you want the intercept set to zero, select Zero rather than Compute.

Once the preliminary setup is finished, enter Go to have 1-2-3 tabulate the regression statistics. The result of the regression for our two variables when 1-2-3 computes the intercept is shown in Figure 10-18. After your analysis is finished, you can use the Reset option to remove previous settings for the command. The Quit option allows you to exit the /Data Regression menu.

In general, the higher the R value, the greater the correlation, although you will want to be aware of the number of observations and the degrees of freedom when determining the reliability of your results. All this is explained in more detail in a book on statistics. The results shown in our example include a computed intercept of −60493.6; a standard error of the estimated Y values; R squared (if you want to know what R is, use @SQRT with R squared as the argument); the

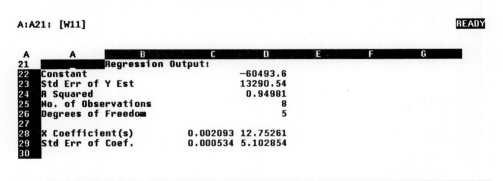

Figure 10-18.   Multiple regression analysis

number of observations for your variables; the coefficients or slopes for the independent variables; and the standard error for the X coefficients.

You can use the same variable values to do two simple regressions. The variable with the highest R squared value will have the closest relationship to the dependent variable. Figure 10-19 presents two regression. output areas. The upper regression output is for disposable income, and the lower regression output is for advertising dollars. The R squared value for disposable income is higher, which indicates that disposable income is a better predictor of sales than advertising dollars. Since the R squared value in Figure 10-18 is higher than either output in Figure 10-19, you can assume that both variables together are stronger predictors than either one individually.

You can also use the regression output to help you determine estimated Y values and the best fitting regression line. The formula you would use to estimate the Y values is as follows:

$$\text{Constant} + \text{Coefficient of X1} * \text{X1} + \text{Coefficient of X2} * \text{X2}$$

You can use this formula to project sales values, assuming that historic relationships are being maintained.

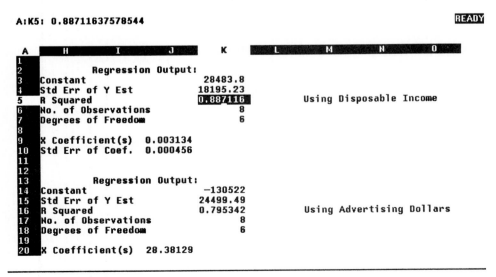

Figure 10-19.   Two simple regression analyses

Frequency Distribution

A *frequency distribution* allows you to count the number of values that fall within specific categories. With the /Data Distribution command features that 1-2-3 provides, you can set up whatever intervals (bins) for categorizing your data that you want. 1-2-3 will then count the number of entries that fall within each of these intervals.

The frequency distribution table is set up prior to using the command by placing the value categories in a location where the column to the right of the categories, and the table cells below the last interval, are blank. Or you can use a separate worksheet to store the bins. The two cells at the bottom of the table location must be blank to record frequencies greater than the largest specified frequency. All category entries must be numeric and in ascending sequence.

When you enter **/Data Distribution** and tell 1-2-3 the locations of the data to be categorized and of the frequency table, 1-2-3 will place each data entry within the range you selected into the smallest category that is equal to or greater than the value in your data. In other words, it will add 1 to the frequency count for that bin. With bin values of 3, 7, and 10, a value of 4 would be counted in bin 7. Each time a value is counted for a category, it increments that category's counter by 1. 1-2-3 ignores cells containing @ERR, @NA, and labels, and cells that are empty.

Figure 10-20 presents a worksheet that contains commission data in C3..C20. The categories for the frequency count are located in E3..E12. These are arbitrary settings and could have been any set of ascending numbers. The area to the right of these categories is blank, as are cells E13 and F13 immediately below the category area. The /Data Distribution command has already been entered, and cells C3..C20 are highlighted in response to 1-2-3's prompt for the range of values requiring categorization. When you press ENTER, 1-2-3 prompts you for the location of the frequency table or bin range. This is shown in Figure 10-21. You may enter just the column bin values, or the entire table area as your range. Press ENTER, and the completed table in Figure 10-22 appears. You can interpret the first entry in the table as meaning that there was one entry less than or equal to 10,000. The last "1," in F13, says that there was one entry greater than the largest bin of 60,000.

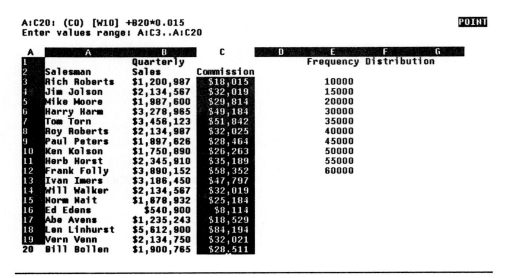

Figure 10-20.   Commission data

/Data Distribution provides a quick way to condense data. It is ideal when you want an overall picture of the data within a category. You can also show the result of a frequency distribution in a bar chart or line graph very effectively.

Frequency distribution can be performed for a category of numeric values, or on the results of a formula calculation like the one found in our example. The frequency count is not updated as changes occur in the data that was categorized, however. If the data is changed, /Data Distribution must be executed again to update the frequency table.

Tip: If the bins are the same interval apart, use /Data Fill to quickly create the bins the /Data Distribution command uses.

Matrix Arithmetic

Matrices can be used to solve problems of econometric modeling, market share, and population study. 1-2-3 offers both matrix multiplication and

POINT

```
A:F12:                                                                    POINT
Enter values range: A:C3..A:C20        Enter bin range: A:E3..A:F12
```

A	A	B	C	D	E	F	G
1		Quarterly			Frequency Distribution		
2	Salesman	Sales	Commission				
3	Rich Roberts	$1,200,987	$18,015		10000		
4	Jim Jolson	$2,134,567	$32,019		15000		
5	Mike Moore	$1,987,600	$29,814		20000		
6	Harry Harm	$3,278,965	$49,184		30000		
7	Tom Torn	$3,456,123	$51,842		35000		
8	Roy Roberts	$2,134,987	$32,025		40000		
9	Paul Peters	$1,897,626	$28,464		45000		
10	Ken Kolson	$1,750,890	$26,263		50000		
11	Herb Horst	$2,345,910	$35,189		55000		
12	Frank Folly	$3,890,152	$58,352		60000		
13	Ivan Imers	$3,186,450	$47,797				
14	Will Walker	$2,134,567	$32,019				
15	Norm Nait	$1,678,932	$25,184				
16	Ed Edens	$540,900	$8,114				
17	Abe Avens	$1,235,243	$18,529				
18	Len Linhurst	$5,612,900	$84,194				
19	Vern Venn	$2,134,750	$32,021				
20	Bill Bollen	$1,900,765	$28,511				

Figure 10-21.   Bin range

matrix inversion options. The word *matrix* indicates a tabular arrangement of data—something that is quite easy to arrange on a worksheet. Both matrix options allow you to perform sophisticated calculations on the data in these tabular arrangements, without the need for complicated formulas. Although many of the mathematical applications are beyond the scope of this book, two different examples are presented. Thus if matrix algebra is a requirement of your application, you will want to know how to invoke these capabilities from 1-2-3.

Matrix Multiplication

One of the applications of matrix multiplication is to streamline formulas where you must multiply a set of variables by another set of variables and add the result of each multiplication together. To illustrate this type of application, consider four different products for which you are trying a number of advertising spots. Each advertising option has a price, and varying numbers of ads are placed for each of the products, in various time slots.

A	A	B	C	D	E	F	G
1		Quarterly			Frequency	Distribution	
2	Salesman	Sales	Commission				
3	Rich Roberts	$1,200,987	$18,015		10000	1	
4	Jim Jolson	$2,134,567	$32,019		15000	0	
5	Mike Moore	$1,987,600	$29,814		20000	2	
6	Harry Harm	$3,278,965	$49,184		30000	5	
7	Tom Torn	$3,456,123	$51,842		35000	4	
8	Roy Roberts	$2,134,987	$32,025		40000	1	
9	Paul Peters	$1,897,626	$28,464		45000	0	
10	Ken Kolson	$1,750,890	$26,263		50000	2	
11	Herb Horst	$2,345,910	$35,189		55000	1	
12	Frank Folly	$3,890,152	$58,352		60000	1	
13	Ivan Imers	$3,186,450	$47,797			1	
14	Will Walker	$2,134,567	$32,019				
15	Norm Nait	$1,678,932	$25,184				
16	Ed Edens	$540,900	$8,114				
17	Abe Avens	$1,235,243	$18,529				
18	Len Linhurst	$5,612,900	$84,194				
19	Vern Venn	$2,134,750	$32,021				
20	Bill Bollen	$1,900,765	$28,511				

Figure 10-22.   Frequency output

Using conventional formulas, determining the total advertising costs for one product would involve multiplying the cost of advertising in time slot 1 times the number of these slots that you purchased. This process must be repeated for each of the advertising slots, each time multiplying the number of slots for the product times the cost of advertising once in that slot. When the cost for each advertising slot has been determined, the values are added together to determine a total advertising cost for the first product. This must be repeated for each of the products. This is a cumbersome process, even when the number of products and potential advertising slots are small.

Matrix multiplication can provide a solution if you can construct your problem according to the rules that matrix operations must follow. After reviewing the rules, you will have an opportunity to see them applied to the advertising problem just discussed.

Matrix Multiplication Rules

There are a few rules of matrix multiplication that you must follow. The restrictions are a combination of matrix algebra rules and the limitations of matrix used in 1-2-3. Each of these rules must be met.

• Matrix multiplication involves multiplying the values in one matrix by the values in a second matrix. The order in which the multiplication is expressed is critical. Multiplying matrix A by matrix B is not equivalent to multiplying matrix B by matrix A.

• Matrix order is determined by the number of rows and columns in the tabular arrangement of the matrix entries. A matrix with x rows and y columns is an x-by-y matrix. When matrices are multiplied, the number of columns (the y) for the first matrix must be equal to the number of rows in the second matrix (the x). The easiest way to test this rule is to write the order of the matrices next to each other, as in 5-by-4 and 4-by-6. When the two inner numbers are the same, as in this example, the matrices are compatible and can be multiplied. Rewriting this as 4-by-6 and 5-by-4 produces a set of matrices that are not compatible, which demonstrates that the order in which the two matrices are multiplied is critical.

• The maximum size matrix that 1-2-3 can multiply is 256-by-256.

• Matrices cannot have blank cells and must have a zero inserted in any cell that is blank before you invoke the matrix command.

Entering the Advertising Matrix

In the advertising problem there are four different products and five different advertising spots. The number of advertising spots for each product is arranged in a 4-by-5 matrix in B11..F14 of the worksheet shown in Figure 10-23. The costs of the spots are arranged in a 5-by-1 matrix in A2..A6. In order for the two matrices to be compatible, the data must be arranged in a 5-by-1 table rather than a 1-by-5 table. It is expected that results will be stored in B17..B20, and appropriate labels are entered around the worksheet to label all the entries.

The /Data Matrix Multiply command is invoked and the first matrix is highlighted, as shown in Figure 10-23. The next prompt is for the second matrix in A2..A6, and this is highlighted as shown in Figure 10-24. The results are placed in B17..B20, as shown in Figure 10-25. The $21,500 represents the total advertising done for the Vectra product. It is obtained as the matrix operation multiplies B11*A2, C11*A3, D11*A4, E11*A5, and F11*A6, and then adds each of these products together. A

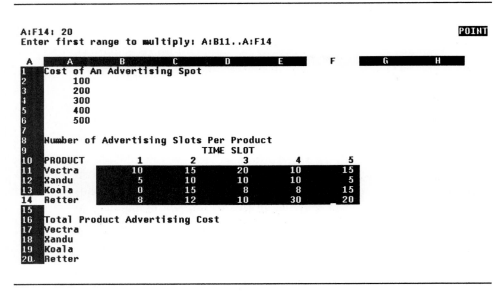

A:F14: 20   POINT
Enter first range to multiply: A:B11..A:F14

	A	B	C	D	E	F	G	H
1	Cost of An Advertising Spot							
2	100							
3	200							
4	300							
5	400							
6	500							
7								
8	Number of Advertising Slots Per Product							
9			TIME SLOT					
10	PRODUCT	1	2	3	4	5		
11	Vectra	10	15	20	10	15		
12	Xandu	5	10	10	10	5		
13	Koala	0	15	8	8	15		
14	Retter	8	12	10	30	20		
15								
16	Total Product Advertising Cost							
17	Vectra							
18	Xandu							
19	Koala							
20	Retter							

Figure 10-23.   Highlighting matrix 1

similar process occurs for Xandu, Koala, and Retter. All this is accomplished without the need for writing a formula.

Matrix multiplication is quite an operation and can be a real time-saver if it fits your application. One drawback is that the results are not automatically updated when a value in either matrix is changed. To do this updating, you would have to execute /Data Matrix Multiply again. A second potential drawback is that matrices are more difficult to document than formulas, and understood less than formulas by most business users. Despite the drawbacks, matrices are a great tool to have for many applications.

Matrix Inversion

Matrix inversion is more difficult, but its potential is even greater. The mathematical concepts behind it are difficult to explain, but in essence they involve the creation of a matrix which, when multiplied by your original matrix, will result in an identity matrix.

An *identity matrix* is one where all of the elements are zero, except one element in each row, which is a 1. The 1 is in a different location in

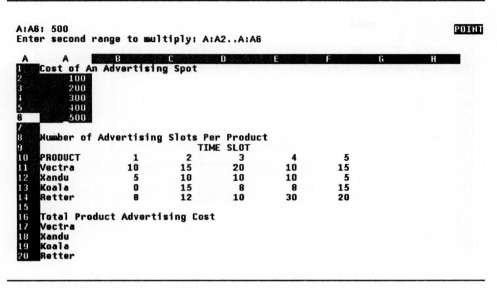

```
A:A6: 500                                                              POINT
Enter second range to multiply: A:A2..A6

A        A          B          C          D          E          F          G          H
1   Cost of An Advertising Spot
2          100
3          200
4          300
5          400
6          500
7
8   Number of Advertising Slots Per Product
9                              TIME SLOT
10  PRODUCT         1          2          3          4          5
11  Vectra         10         15         20         10         15
12  Xandu           5         10         10         10          5
13  Koala           0         15          8          8         15
14  Retter          8         12         10         30         20
15
16  Total Product Advertising Cost
17  Vectra
18  Xandu
19  Koala
20  Retter
```

Figure 10-24.   Highlighting matrix 2

each row. It is easy to remember the location of the 1 for each row, since it is a location identified by the row number. That is, in row 1 the 1 will be in element one; in row 2 the 1 will be in the second element; and so on. You can only convert square matrices (matrices with the same number of columns and rows). 1-2-3 will let you invert matrices up to 80 columns by 80 rows.

If all this seems confusing, you do not really have to understand it all to use the concept, so don't be too concerned. A traditional application for matrix multiplication also uses matrix inversion. It is the same product-mix problem that you solved so often in college algebra. Seeing the solution probably makes you wish you had a copy of 1-2-3 during your college algebra days, when you were trying to solve these with simultaneous equations.

Product-mix problems come in all flavors. Normally there is a limited amount of certain resources, and you have to decide how much of each product to produce. In the sample problem (Figure 10-26), you must determine how much Green Slime and Red Goo should be produced. Green Slime requires two units of resource A, and six units of resource B. Red Goo takes eight units of resource A, and five units of

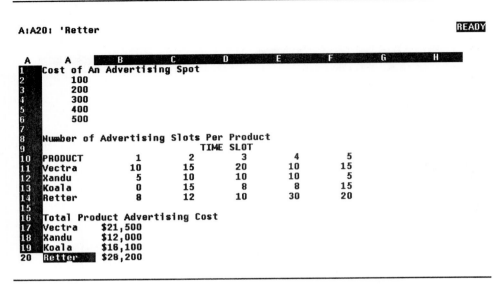

Figure 10-25.   Result of /Data Matrix Multiply in B17..B20

resource B. There are 50 units of A available, and 100 units of B. The matrix operations allow you to optimize your use of these two raw materials.

First, the data of Green Slime and Red Goo are entered in a 2-by-2 matrix. This matrix is inverted to create another 2-by-2 matrix, which will be used in solution. The original matrix is stored in C3..D4, the /Data Matrix Invert command is invoked, and this area is highlighted. A7..B8 is used for the output.

The resulting (2-by-2) inverted matrix is multiplied by a 2-by-1 matrix, which contains the available units of each resource. The result is a new matrix, which is stored in A11..A12 and contains the Optimal Production for each of the products. Since the profit from Green Slime is $10 a unit and the profit from Red Goo is $20 a unit, the whole units produced for each product are multiplied by respective unit profit figures. The @INT function is used to access the whole units for the final formula, which is placed in A15. All of the arbitrary locations used in this example are shown in Figure 10-26, which includes the results.

If you are interested in learning more about applications of matrix inversion, you will want to look for a reference on linear programming.

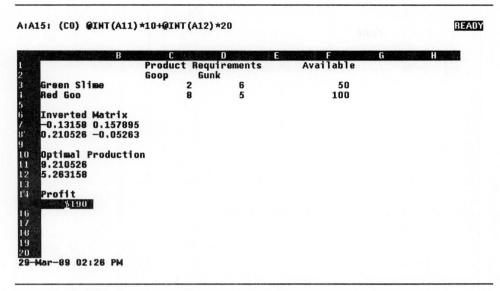

Figure 10-26. Matrix inversion solving simultaneous equations

If you are currently using linear programming, you will be delighted to have these handy techniques incorporated into 1-2-3's features. If you do not need this type of problem-solving tool, keep it in mind in case such a need arises at a later time.

Splitting Long Labels into Individual Cell Entries

The /File Import command can be used to bring information from an ASCII text file into your 1-2-3 worksheet, as described in Chapter 8, "Working with Files." However, it imports this information as a column of long labels, which may not be what you want. Fortunately, the /Data Parse command allows you to split these long labels into various components. These individual pieces can be labels, numbers, or serial time or date numbers.

Using /Data Parse is a multistep process. The steps are summarized for you in the box called "Splitting Text Entries into Cell Values." The options in the /Data Parse submenu are as follows:

```
AiA1i                                                                  MENU
Format-Line  Input-Column  Output-Range  Reset  Go  Quit
Create or edit a format line at the current cell
```

Splitting Text Entries into Cell Values

After importing text into your worksheet, you may need to use /Data Parse to split long labels into individual entries. Follow these steps after using /File Import:

1.   Move your cell pointer to the top of the column containing the labels to be parsed, and enter **/Data Parse**.

2.   Choose the Format-Line option, and then Create to have 1-2-3 generate a suggested format line.

3.   If the generated formatted line requires changes, choose Format-Line Edit and make your changes.

4.   Select the Input-Range option and choose the column of labels to be altered; include the format line in the range.

5.   Select the Output-Range option, and choose the top left cell in a blank area large enough to hold the output, or else specify a range large enough to hold each of the parsed entries. The width of this area is determined by the number of individual fields in the output. The length is the same as the number of labels being parsed.

6.   Select Go.

To use /Data Parse, place your cell pointer on the first cell in the column that needs to be parsed and enter **/Data Parse**. When the command options are presented, select Format-Line and choose Create from its submenu. 1-2-3 will then insert a blank row above your cell pointer and create a format line that shows how it will split the label into component pieces.

The characters used in the format line generated by 1-2-3 are as follows:

D	marks the first character of a date block
L	marks the first character of a label block
S	marks the first character of a block to be skipped during the parse operation. This character is never generated by 1-2-3, but you can enter it manually through the Edit option
T	marks the first character of a time block
V	marks the first character of a value block
>	indicates that the block started by the letter that precedes this character is continued. The entry that began with the letter will continue to be placed in one worksheet cell until a skip or another letter is encountered
*	represents a blank space immediately below the character. This position can become part of the block that precedes it

The pattern established in the format line will be followed in the parsing operation to determine where to split the labels and what type of data is needed for each block. Although you can generate a format line in multiple locations within your column of labels, you will need some consistency in the format of the column in order for this command to be useful.

If you are not pleased with the format line generated by 1-2-3, you can edit it with /Data Parse Format-Line Edit. You can add, replace, or delete any part of the format line after entering the Edit option.

Once the format has been established, the remaining steps for using /Data Parse are quite easy. Choose Input-Column, and then either highlight the cells to be parsed or type in the address of this column of label entries. Be sure to include the format line in the range. Then select Output-Range and enter either the upper left cell or the complete range of cells required. If you choose to supply only the upper left cell, 1-2-3 will determine the space requirements, overwriting data if necessary. If you enter a complete range but do not supply one that is large enough, 1-2-3 will produce an error message rather than overwriting data beyond the range. With the first three menu options set, choose Go to have 1-2-3 restructure the long labels into individual cell entries according to the pattern established by the format line.

The other two options in the Parse menu are Reset and Quit. Reset eliminates any settings you have established for the parsing operation. Quit removes the sticky Parse menu and returns you to READY mode. (Pressing ESC does the same thing.)

A few examples will help clarify the workings of /Data Parse. In this illustration, the entries in A1..A3 are long labels.

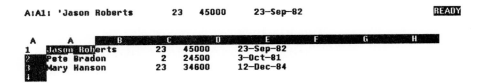

Although at first glance the components of each line may appear to be in separate cells, the control panel shows that each line is in fact a single label entry. The steps to parse these labels are as follows:

1. Move the cell pointer to A1 and enter /**Data Parse Format-Line Create**. 1-2-3 will generate a format line like the one in Figure 10-27. Notice that first names and last names have been treated as separate entries because of the space between them.

2. Choose Input-Column and select A1..A4.

3. To duplicate our example, choose A9 as Output-Range.

4. Select Go, and the output shown in Figure 10-28 is produced.

If you do not want the two name components treated as separate entries, choose Format-Line Edit. Then change the format line to agree with the one in Figure 10-29, and issue Go. You will notice that the

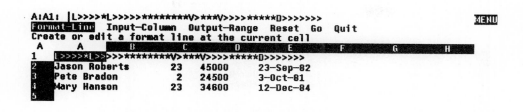

Figure 10-27.   Format line for parsing data

entry "Jason Roberts" is now placed in A9. The display is initially truncated due to the column width, but you can change this easily with /Worksheet Column Set-Width.

Sequencing Worksheet Data

Although the /Data Sort commands were designed primarily for use in the data management environment, they can sometimes be used suc-

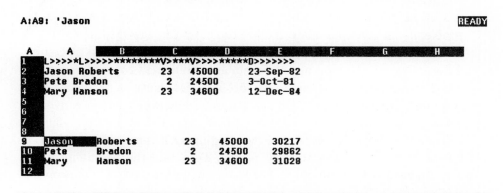

Figure 10-28.   Output from /Data Parse

A:A9: [W9] 'Jason Roberts   READY

```
A     A        B        C        D        E        F     G     H
L>>>>>>>>>>>>>>>★★★★★★★★★V>★★★V>>>>★★★★★D>>>>>>>
1
2  Jason Roberts      23    45000      23-Sep-82
3  Pete Bradon         2    24500       3-Oct-81
4  Mary Hanson        23    34600      12-Dec-84
5
6
7
8
9  Jason Rob          23    45000    30217    30217
10 Pete Brad           2    24500    29862    29862
11 Mary Hans          23    34600    31028    31028
12
```

Figure 10-29.   Output after editing format line

cessfully when your worksheet contains data used solely for calculations. Let's look at an example of a successful and an unsuccessful sort for a worksheet application. If you are not familiar with the /Data Sort command, review its features described in Chapter 9, "Data Management," before using it with your worksheet data.

Before using /Data Sort, you will need to assess whether your worksheet is organized so that sorting the data will not cause problems with your formulas. It would be advisable to save a copy of your worksheet file to disk prior to the sort, just in case you make a mistake and sort formulas that cannot be shuffled without causing an error. Naturally, if you notice the problem right away, ALT-F4 (UNDO) will be the easiest solution. If you enter a command or two before you notice the problem, you will appreciate the backup copy you saved to disk.

As a worksheet is sorted, the rows of your model will be placed in a different order. As long as the formulas within each row reference only other variables in that row, the sort will not cause a problem. When formula references point outside the row, however, errors can occur. Look at the inventory calculations for six months in Figure 7-30; you will see that for each month the new beginning inventory is equal to the inventory at the end of the last period. To obtain the beginning inventory figures, the formula in each month references the appropriate

A:B3: +E2   READY

A	A	B	C	D	E	F	G
1		Beg. Inv.	Purch.	Sales	End Inv.		
2	Jan	1,200	200	300	1,100		
3	Feb	1,100	250	400	950		
4	Mar	950	500	200	1,250		
5	Apr	1,250	350	150	1,450		
6	May	1,450	200	400	1,250		
7	June	1,250	300	300	1,250		
8							

Figure 10-30.   Inventory database

address in the previous month (that is, the prior line of the model). These formulas are shown in Figure 10-31. If you wanted to sequence the data by the Sales figure rather than by month, you might decide to try the /Data Sort command. You would use /Data Sort Data-Range and then specify the range as A2..E7. You would select a primary key of D2 (Sales) and then choose Go. The results shown in Figure 10-32 indicate a problem with the references to previous lines. The reason the errors are confined to the top rows is that the original 1200 entry for January is a numeric constant rather than a reference to a previous line.

A:B3: +E2   READY

A	A	B	C	D	E	F	G
1		Beg. Inv.	Purch.	Sales	End Inv.		
2	Jan	1200	200	300	+B2+C2-D2		
3	Feb	+E2	250	400	+B3+C3-D3		
4	Mar	+E3	500	200	+B4+C4-D4		
5	Apr	+E4	350	150	+B5+C5-D5		
6	May	+E5	200	400	+B6+C6-D6		
7	June	+E6	300	300	+B7+C7-D7		
8							

Figure 10-31.   Inventory database shown with a text format

A:B2: +E1   READY

A	A	B	C	D	E	F	G
1		Beg. Inv.	Purch.	Sales	End Inv.		
2	Jan	End Inv.	250	400	−150		
3	Feb	−150	200	400	−350		
4	Mar	1200	200	300	1100		
5	Apr	1100	300	300	1100		
6	May	1100	500	200	1400		
7	June	1400	350	150	1600		
8							

Figure 10-32.   Sorted inventory database

To avoid this problem, you have two options for sorting the original inventory data. First, you can use /Range Value to freeze the values in column B before sorting. Your other option is to use /File Extract Values to save the portion you want to sort as another file that can be retrieved and sorted separately.

Figure 10-33 shows another worksheet that, at first glance, may appear to have the same kind of problem with the formula in F6. The formula references a table located outside the row of the worksheet. You

A:F6: (C2) [W11] @VLOOKUP(C6,$K$7..$M$9,1)*E6   READY

A	B	C	D	E	F	G	H	I
1								
2								
3		LODGING	TRAVEL	#	LODGING/			TOTAL
4	LOCATION	CLASS	COST	TRIPS	MEALS	AIRFARE	MISC.	COST
5								
6	Akron	2	2	2	$300.00	$600.00	$90.00	$990.00
7	Atlanta	2	2	4	$600.00	$1,200.00	$180.00	$1,980.00
8	Chicago	3	1	3	$525.00	$750.00	$150.00	$1,425.00
9	Dallas	1	2	12	$1,500.00	$3,600.00	$420.00	$5,520.00
10	Denver	2	2	12	$1,800.00	$3,600.00	$540.00	$5,940.00
11	New York	3	2	6	$1,050.00	$1,800.00	$300.00	$3,150.00
12	Phoenix	2	3	5	$750.00	$1,750.00	$225.00	$2,725.00
13	Portland	2	4	3	$450.00	$1,500.00	$135.00	$2,085.00
14								

Figure 10-33.   Travel worksheet

A:F6: (C2) [W11] @VLOOKUP(C6,$K$7..$M$9,1)*E6   `READY`

LOCATION	LODGING CLASS	TRAVEL COST	# TRIPS	LODGING/ MEALS	AIRFARE	MISC.	TOTAL COST
Dallas	1	2	12	$1,500.00	$3,600.00	$420.00	$5,520.00
Akron	2	2	2	$300.00	$600.00	$90.00	$990.00
Chicago	3	1	3	$525.00	$750.00	$150.00	$1,425.00
Denver	2	2	12	$1,800.00	$3,600.00	$540.00	$5,940.00
Phoenix	2	3	5	$750.00	$1,750.00	$225.00	$2,725.00
Atlanta	2	2	4	$600.00	$1,200.00	$180.00	$1,980.00
New York	3	2	6	$1,050.00	$1,800.00	$300.00	$3,150.00
Portland	2	4	3	$450.00	$1,500.00	$135.00	$2,085.00

Figure 10-34.   Sorted travel worksheet

will notice, however, that the formula references the table with absolute addresses. References that are absolute will not change when the sort is performed, so these rows can be sorted without being changed. When /Data Sort is entered and a data range of A6..I13 is specified, with a primary key of A6 for location, the results in Figure 10-34 are produced.

Another situation to watch for is data placed at the side of the data range, like a new field for the database. This data will not be moved, since /Data Sort will move only the specified data range.

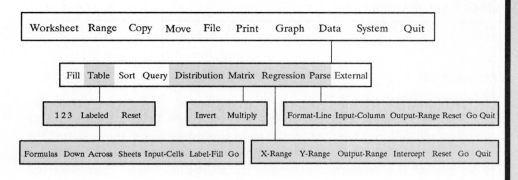

©1989 Lotus Development Corporation. Used with permission.

/Data Distribution

Description

The /Data Distribution command permits you to create a frequency distribution table from the values in a range on your worksheet. This table will tell you how many values in the range fall within each of the intervals you establish. An area of an active worksheet must be set aside to record the frequency intervals (bins) against which your data are analyzed. The frequency for each bin is placed in an adjacent column.

Using the /Data Distribution command requires some preliminary work. First, you must select a location on your worksheet for the bins. 1-2-3 will use the column to the right of the bins for the frequency numbers for each interval, and the row immediately below the last bin for a count of all the values that exceed the last bin value. Second, the values you place in the bins must be in ascending sequence from the top to the bottom of the column you are using.

Here is an example of the way 1-2-3 assigns values to the bins. If you create bin values of 5, 10, and 20, the first bin will contain a count of the values in your list that are less than or equal to 5; the second bin will contain a count of values greater than 5 and less than or equal to 10; and the third bin will hold values greater than 10 and less than or equal to 20. 1-2-3 creates a fourth bin for a count of all values greater than 20. This command ignores blank cells or cells containing labels, @ERR and @NA.

Once /Data Distribution has classified the values in the specified range, a change in one of the values will not cause a reclassification. To reclassify data after a change, you must use /Data Distribution again. This time you only have to press ENTER in response to 1-2-3's prompts, since 1-2-3 will suggest the same ranges used previously.

Options

The only options you have with this command are the size of the intervals you enter in the bin range, and the number of values in the values range.

/Data Matrix

Description

The /Data Matrix command allows you to multiply and invert matrices. Matrices are tabular arrangements of data with a number in each cell. They are specified by their size. The number of rows is specified before the number of columns. Thus, a matrix with 5 rows and 6 columns is a 5-by-6 matrix. A square matrix has the same number of rows as it has columns.

With 1-2-3's matrix multiplication and inversion options you can solve problems relating to market share, projecting receivable aging, inventory control, and other modeling problems for the natural and social sciences. The specifics of the theory behind matrix operations are not examined in this volume.

Options

The /Data Matrix command provides options for two algebraic matrix operations: multiplication and inversion.

Multiply

This option multiplies the individual components of two matrices according to the rules for matrix arithmetic. It assumes that only two matrices will be multiplied and that the number of columns in one matrix is equal to the number of rows in a second matrix. 1-2-3 can multiply matrices up to 256 rows by 256 columns.

When the Multiply option is chosen, 1-2-3 prompts you for the location of the two matrix ranges. You can type the cell addresses, reference the matrices with range names, or use the pointing method for specifying the ranges. When prompted for the output range, you can choose to enter the complete range or a reference to it, or just enter the upper left cell.

Invert

This option inverts any square matrix according to the rules for matrix algebra. 1-2-3 prompts you for the range of the matrix to invert and the output range. When prompted for the output range, you can enter the complete range or a reference to it, or just the upper left cell. 1-2-3 can invert matrices up to 80 rows by 80 columns.

Note

Addition and subtraction on matrices can be handled with the /File Combine Add and /File Combine Subtract options, which are covered in Chapter 8, "Working with Files."

/Data Parse

Description

The /Data Parse command creates shorter, individual field values from the long labels stored in worksheet cells. You will need to use this command after you use /File Import to bring long labels from text files created by your word processor or other program into a column of cells. This column of long labels is limited to descriptive use or a string formula unless /Data Parse is used to split the long labels into individual fields. Then you can also use the results in numeric formulas and graphs.

Assuming some consistency in the format of the labels, /Data Parse can divide each label into a row of individual values, including label, value, date, and time entries. 1-2-3 makes a suggestion for splitting the label into its individual components, but you have the option of changing this recommendation.

Options

When you enter /**Data Parse**, 1-2-3 presents a submenu of six choices.

Format-Line

This is the most important option in the /Data Parse command, since it determines how 1-2-3 will split the long labels into individual cell entries. You can use it to create a new format line or edit an existing one.

Creating a Format Line   The Create option under Parse Format-Line creates a format line above the cell pointer location at the time you make the selection. Position your cell pointer one cell above the first long label in your column to be parsed before entering /Data Parse Format-Line Create, to ensure that the format line is positioned correctly.

1-2-3 places letters and special symbols in the format line to present its interpretation of the way the long label should be split. The letters and symbols used are as follows:

D   marks the first character of a date block

L   marks the first character of a label block

S   marks the first character of a block that is to be skipped during the parse operation. This character is never generated by 1-2-3, but you can enter it manually through the Edit option

T   marks the first character of a time block

V   marks the first character of a value block

>   indicates that the block started by the letter that precedes this character is continued. The entry that began with the letter will continue to be placed in one worksheet cell until a skip or another letter is encountered

*   represents a blank space immediately below the character. This position can become part of the previous block

Editing a Format Line   After 1-2-3 creates a format line, you can use the Edit option to make changes in it if you wish. 1-2-3 only lets you enter valid format line characters.

Input-Column

This is the location for the column of long labels imported from an ASCII text file. The range you specify should include the format line.

Output-Range

This is the location you wish to use for the individual entries generated from the long label. You can enter the upper left cell in an area of the worksheet large enough for the output, or the complete range for the area. Each approach offers a different advantage. If you specify the complete range and it is not large enough, 1-2-3 will provide an error message rather than expand the output area. This prevents data stored near the output range from being destroyed if additional space is needed. If you specify only the upper left cell of the output range, 1-2-3 will determine how much space is required and will write over cells containing worksheet data if it needs the space.

Reset

This option eliminates the settings for input or output area, so you can start over.

Go

The Go option tells 1-2-3 that you have created and verified the accuracy of the format line and have defined the location of the input and output areas. It causes the long labels to be parsed according to the specifications given, and returns to the READY mode.

Quit

This option tells 1-2-3 that you want to leave the /Data Parse menu without parsing the data.

/Data Regression

Description

The /Data Regression command allows you to perform a statistical analysis to see whether two or more variables are interrelated. This command allows you to use from 1 to 75 independent variables for your regression analysis. It will estimate the accuracy with which these independent variables can predict the values of a specified dependent variable.

As an example, your dependent variable may be the sales of hot chocolate at a football concession stand. You may wish to look at outdoor temperature and pregame ticket sales as possible predictors of the number of cups of hot chocolate that will be sold at a game. These two factors would be your independent variables. By applying regression analysis to historic data for the three variables, you can determine how effective the independent variables are as predictors of the dependent variable. When the regression analysis has been completed, 1-2-3 will display the number of observations, the Y intercept or constant, the standard error of estimated Y values and X coefficients, R squared, the X coefficients, and the degrees of freedom.

As with many of the other data commands, using /Data Regression involves a few preliminary steps. First, your dependent and independent variable values must be placed in columns on the worksheet. Each column must have the same number of entries, and all of them must contain numeric values. You can have a maximum of 8192 values; this is one value for each row of the worksheet. Second, choose a blank area of any active worksheet for 1-2-3 to use for output. This area must be at least nine rows in length and four columns wide. The width will need to exceed the number of independent variables by two. After these preliminary steps are completed, use the /Data Regression options to complete your analysis.

Options

The /Data Regression submenu has the following options.

X-Range

This is the column or columns (75 maximum) that contain the values for your independent variables. Enter cell addresses or a range name, or point with your cell pointer to highlight the selected area.

Y-Range

This is the column containing the values for your dependent variable. Enter a range name or cell addresses, or point to the selected column.

Output-Range

This is the area that will contain the results of the analysis. It must be at least nine rows deep and four columns wide, and it must be at least two columns wider than the number of independent variables you are using. You have the option of specifying the entire range or just the upper left corner. If you use the latter approach, 1-2-3 will decide the size of the area to use for the output of the regression analysis. Any existing data in the cells of the output range will be overwritten.

Intercept

This is the Y intercept. You have the option of having 1-2-3 compute this value or setting it to zero. Compute is the default setting.

Reset

This option eliminates all the settings you have established for /Data Regression.

Go

This option completes the regression analysis after you have chosen X-Range, Y-Range, Output-Range, and Intercept.

Quit

This option exits the /Data Regression menu and returns you to READY mode.

/Data Sort

Description

This command allows you to sequence information in worksheet cells. The command is covered fully in Chapter 9, since its primary application is for data management. It is mentioned again here because there are selected instances where it can be used in the worksheet environment. These are described in the chapter.

Options

The options for /Data Sort are covered in Chapter 9.

/Data Table 1

Description

The /Data Table 1 command allows you to use different values of a variable in formulas. This command provides a structured "what-if" feature that substitutes various values in your formulas and records the result of each value.

The /Data Table 1 command builds what is called a one-way table. The table will have one set of input values running down its left side. It can evaluate many formulas.

/Data Table 1 requires that you set up a table area in your worksheet. The purpose of the table is to structure the values that you want to plug into an input cell one by one, while recording the impact of these values on the formulas that are also part of the table. To set up the table, place the input values you wish to use in a column in a blank area of your worksheet. The row of formulas you wish to have evaluated must begin one row above the first input value and one column to the right. You may place new formulas in these cells, or you may reference other cells in the worksheet that contain the desired formulas. For example, to have a formula in A3 evaluated, place +A3 in one of the cells in this formula row. You may also wish to format the formula cells as text for documentation purposes.

The two sets of entries just discussed create the framework for the table. The column of value cells forms the left edge of the table, with the last entry determining the bottom edge of the table. The row of formulas forms the top of the table, with the last entry in the row marking the right edge.

After the initial setup, you are ready to respond to 1-2-3's prompts to define the location of your table and the cell you wish to reference for input.

Options

After your table is defined, tell 1-2-3 the location you have selected for the table. The best way to do this is to position your cell pointer at the upper left edge of the table before you enter the /Data Table 1 command. The table should be a rectangular area that includes all the formulas and all the values you are concerned with. You can use cell addresses, a range name, or the pointing method to communicate the table location.

Next, 1-2-3 asks you what worksheet cell you want to use as an input cell. This is the cell into which 1-2-3 will place the input values from the table column, one by one. Using a given value for the input cell, 1-2-3 evaluates each of the table formulas and places the formula result in the column beneath the formula, on the row for the input value being used.

When 1-2-3 has used each of your values, the table will be complete with formula results. Depending on the size of your table, this takes up to several minutes. When 1-2-3 has completed the table, the input cell still has its original value; 1-2-3 makes its substitutions behind the scenes without affecting the cell entry. A change to a value in the input table does not cause the table to recalculate. To get recalculation, you must reuse /**Data Table**, or press F8 (TABLE). If you wish to reset the table location and input cell before using the command again, use /Data Table Reset to eliminate your previous settings.

/Data Table 2

Description

The /Data Table 2 command allows you to pick any two cells on the worksheet that contain numeric variable values and set up substitution values for these cells, so that the impact of the changes can be measured in the result of a particular worksheet formula. This feature provides a structured approach to "what-if" analysis, in which 1-2-3 does most of the work.

The /Data Table 2 command produces a table that is similar to a one-way table, except that you can substitute values for two variables at once and evaluate only one formula. It allows you to see whether the formula result is more sensitive to changes in variable one or variable two, which provides an easy-to-use sensitivity analysis feature.

/Data Table 2 requires that you set up a table area in your worksheet. The purpose of the table is to structure the values that you want to plug into the two input cells one by one, while recording the impact of these values on the result of a formula that is also part of the table. To set up the table, place the input values for the first variable you wish to use in a column in a blank area of your worksheet. The values for the second variable you wish to use must begin one row above the first input value and one column to the right; place these values across the row. You can use the /Data Fill command to supply them if the increment between values is evenly spaced.

The formula you wish to have evaluated for each value of the input variable is placed in the blank cell at the intersection of the row and column of variable values. You may enter either an actual formula or a reference to a worksheet cell containing a formula. For example, to have a formula in A3 evaluated, place +A3 in the formula cell. You may also wish to format the formula cell as text for documentation purposes.

The two sets of entries just discussed create the framework for the table. The column of value cells forms the left edge of the table, with the last entry determining the bottom edge of the table. The row of value entries forms the top of the table, with the last entry in the row marking the right edge. To have 1-2-3 complete the table entries for you, enter **/Data Table 2** and respond to 1-2-3's requests for specifications.

Options

After your table is defined, tell 1-2-3 the location you have selected for the table. To facilitate this process, position your cell pointer at the upper left edge of the table before entering the /Data Table 2 command. The table should be a rectangular area that includes the formula and all the values with which you are concerned. You can use cell addresses, a range name, or the pointing method to communicate the table location.

Next, 1-2-3 asks you what worksheet cell you want to use as an input cell for the column of values you entered. This is the cell into which 1-2-3 will place the input values from the table column, one by one. 1-2-3 then asks what input cell will be used for the row of values. 1-2-3 then evaluates the formula shown at the upper left corner of the table, using each of the possible value combinations for input cell 1 and input cell 2.

When 1-2-3 has used each of your values, the table will be complete with formula results. Depending on the size of your table, this takes up to several minutes. When 1-2-3 has completed the table, the input cell still has its original value; 1-2-3 alters the values of the input cell only internally. A change to a value in the input table does not cause the table to recalculate. To get recalculation, you must reuse /Data Table, or press F8 (TABLE). If you wish to reset the table location and input cells before using the command again, use /Data Table Reset to eliminate your previous settings.

/Data Table 3

Description

The /Data Table 3 command allows you to pick any three cells on the worksheet file that contain numeric variable values and set up substitution values for these cells, so that the impact of the changes can be measured in the result of a particular worksheet formula. This feature provides a structured approach to "what-if" analysis, in which 1-2-3 does most of the work. This command creates data tables that use multiple worksheets.

The /Data Table 3 command produces a table that is similar to a two-way table, except that you can substitute values for three variables at once and evaluate only one formula. It allows you to see whether the formula result is more sensitive to changes in variable one, variable two, or variable three which provides an easy-to-use sensitivity analysis feature.

/Data Table 3 requires that you set up a table area in your worksheet. The purpose of the table is to structure the values that you want to plug into the three input cells one by one, while recording the impact of these values on the result of a formula that is outside of the table. To set up the table, place the input values for the first variable you wish to use in a column in a blank area of your worksheet. The values for the second variable you wish to use must begin one row above the first input value and one column to the right; place these values across the row. The value for the third variable should be in the upper leftmost cell (usually A1) in each worksheet that is part of the data table. You can use the /Data Fill command to supply these values if the increment between values is evenly spaced.

The formula you wish to have evaluated for each value of the input variables is placed outside of the data table. You may enter either an actual formula or a reference to a worksheet cell containing a formula. For example, to have a formula in A3 evaluated, place +A3 in the formula cell. You may also wish to format the formula cell as text for documentation purposes.

The three sets of values just discussed create the framework for the table. The column of value cells forms the left edge of the table, with the last entry determining the bottom edge of the table. The row of value entries forms the top of the table, with the last entry in the row marking the right edge. The first worksheet with a value in the upper left corner of the data table is the front of the table; the last worksheet containing a third input value determines the back of the table. To have 1-2-3 complete the table entries for you, enter /**Data Table** 3 and respond to 1-2-3's requests for specifications.

Options

After your table is defined, tell 1-2-3 the location you have selected for the table. To facilitate this process, position your cell pointer at the first value for the third input variable, which is the upper left edge of the table in the first worksheet, before entering the /Data Table 3 command. The table should be a rectangular area that includes all the values with which you are concerned. You can use cell addresses, a range name, or the pointing method to communicate the table location.

Next, 1-2-3 asks you for the address of the cell containing the formula. Once 1-2-3 knows where the formula is, it asks for the worksheet cell you want to use as an input cell for the column of values you entered. This is the cell into which 1-2-3 will place the input values from the table column, one by one. 1-2-3 then asks what input cell will be used for the row of values. Finally, 1-2-3 prompts for the input cell for the third input value that is in the upper left cell in each worksheet's table. 1-2-3 will evaluate the formula, using each of the possible value combinations for input cell 1 and input cell 2.

When 1-2-3 has used each of your values, the table will be complete with formula results. Depending on the size of your table, this takes up to several minutes. When 1-2-3 has completed the table, the input cell still has its original value; 1-2-3 alters the values of the input cell only internally. A change to a value in the input table does not cause the table to recalculate. To get recalculation, you must reuse /Data Table, or press the F8 (TABLE) key. If you wish to reset the table location and input cells before using the command again, you can use /Data Table Reset to eliminate your previous settings.

/Data Table Labeled

Description

The /Data Table Labeled command allows you to create "what-if" tables that can contain multiple variables and evaluate multiple formulas. This command has the fewest limitations of the /Data Table commands. /Data Table Labeled can create one- and two-way data tables with a different orientation from those of /Data Table 1 and /Data Table 2. Labeled data tables can have blank columns, rows, and worksheets. You can leave these areas blank or fill them with labels, values, or formulas that use the data in the data tables. This command can create one-, two-, and three-way tables. The /Data Table Labeled command substitutes variables entered in rows, columns, or worksheets and returns the value of one or more formulas to the data table. You can have multiple input values for each set of column, row, or worksheet variables.

/Data Table Labeled requires that you set up an input cell area, a formula range, and a data table area in your worksheet file. The input cell is the cell that the command will substitute for the values in the data table. The formula range contains the formula name in one row, and the formula underneath.

The table contains input values stored in a column, row, and one or more worksheets. Where the specified values meet, 1-2-3 computes a value and treats the intersecting cell as part of the data table. If a cell does not intersect with the selected column, row, and worksheet, 1-2-3 does not include it in the data table. This cell is skipped when the table values are calculated; it can contain any data, and the /Data Table Labeled command will not interfere with it. To set up the table, enter values for an input cell in a column, a row, or the same cell in multiple worksheets. The values for the column variable range and the row variable range cannot be in the same row or column. You can use one, two, or all three of these variable ranges. This command does not order the variable ranges.

To make the data table and input area easier to read, document the values in the table using cells that the command will not use. To supply the data values for column, row, and worksheet variables, you can use the /Data Fill command if the increment between values is evenly spaced.

Select the formula that the /Data Table Labeled command uses by entering the formula name above the row variable values in the column. To select the formula for column variable values, enter the formula to the left of the data table. The formula name above or to the right of the data table is referred to as the formula label range. The formula name can be stretched to cover multiple cells by adding the label-fill character (a hyphen by default).

To have 1-2-3 complete the table entries for you, enter **/Data Table Labeled** and respond to 1-2-3's requests for specifications.

Options

This command has the following seven options:

Formulas

This option selects the formula range and formula label range. The formula range contains both the row with the formula names, and the row with the formulas. The formula label range is the formula name that appears next to or above the data table indicating which formulas 1-2-3 evaluates for the data table. You can use cell addresses, a range name, or the pointing method to communicate the formula range and the formula label range locations.

Across

This option selects the column variable values and the input cell the /Data Table Labeled command uses to evaluate the formulas. You can use cell addresses, a range name, or the pointing method to communicate the column variable values. Then press ENTER to confirm each row in the column variable values and select an input cell for each row. 1-2-3 repeats this step for each row in the column variable values.

Down

This option selects the row variable values and the input cell the /Data Table Labeled command uses to evaluate the formulas. You can use cell addresses, a range name, or the pointing method to communicate the row variable values. Then press ENTER to confirm each column in the row variable values and select an input cell for each column. 1-2-3 repeats this step for each column in the row variable values.

Sheets

This option selects the sheet variable values and the input cell the /Data Table Labeled command uses to evaluate the formulas. You can use cell addresses, a range name, or the pointing method to communicate the sheet variable values. Then press ENTER to confirm each cell for the worksheets in the sheet variable values and select an input cell for each cell. 1-2-3 repeats this step for each cell in the sheet variable values.

Input Cells

This option prompts for the variable values and input cells for the row, column, and worksheet variables. For each of these prompts, 1-2-3 displays the current selection. You can accept or change the selection.

Label-Fill

This option selects a label-fill character for the formula label range and column variable range.

Go

This option generates the table and returns 1-2-3 to the READY mode. For each cell at an intersection of a selected worksheet, row, and column variable, 1-2-3 substitutes the column, row, and worksheet variable values in the input cells and puts the result in the cell. Depending on the size of your table, this takes up to several minutes. When 1-2-3 completes the table, the input cell still has its original value, since 1-2-3 only alters the values of the input cell internally. A change to a value in the input table does not cause the table to recalculate. To recalculate table entries, use /Data Table or the F8 (TABLE) key. If you wish to reset the column, row, and worksheet variable ranges, or the formula range and formula label ranges before using the command again, you can use /Data Table Reset to eliminate your previous settings.

/Data Table Reset

Description

The /Data Table Reset command eliminates the settings you have established for the table location and input cell. Since 1-2-3 will suggest the previous setting the next time you use the command, Reset is convenient when the next table location or input cell setting is far removed from the last use. If you select /Data Table before cancelling your previous settings, you must then press ESC and move your cell pointer to the new location in order to establish new settings. Once Reset is used, your cell pointer will remain in its current location.

Options

The /Data Table Reset command has no options.

Working with 1-2-3's Graphics Features

Creating an Automatic Graph
Viewing Graphs and Worksheets Simultaneously
Creating Graphs
Enhancing the Basic Graph Type
Enhancing the Basic Display
Redrawing Graphs
Storing and Using Graphs
Quitting the Graph Menu
Printing Graphs
Moving Beyond 1-2-3's Graph Features
COMMAND REFERENCE: Graphics

/Graph A B C D E F

/Graph Group

/Graph Name Create

/Graph Name Delete

/Graph Name Reset

/Graph Name Table

/Graph Name Use

/Graph Options Advanced Colors

/Graph Options Advanced Hatches

/Graph Options Advanced Quit

/Graph Options Advanced Text

/Graph Options B&W

/Graph Options Color

/Graph Options Data-Labels

/Graph Options Format

/Graph Options Grid

/Graph Options Legend

/Graph Options Quit

/Graph Options Scale Skip

/Graph Options Scale X-Scale

/Graph Options Scale Y-Scale

/Graph Options Scale 2Y-Scale

/Graph Options Titles

/Graph Quit

/Graph Reset

/Graph Save

/Graph Type

/Graph View

/Graph X

/Print Printer Image

/Print Printer Options Advanced Image
Density

/Print Printer Options Advanced Image
Image-Sz

/Print Printer Options Advanced Image
Quit

/Print Printer Options Advanced Image
Rotate

/Worksheet Global Default Graph

/Worksheet Window Graph

The graphics features of 1-2-3 allow you to display your worksheet information in a format that is easy to interpret. Rather than presenting all the specific numbers, graphs summarize the essence of your data, so that you can focus on general patterns and trends. When you notice something that warrants further analysis, you can return to the supporting worksheet numbers and look at them more closely.

1-2-3's graphics features are popular because they do not require that data be reentered. Indeed, you can use data already entered for your worksheet—without any changes at all. Nor do you need to transfer data to another program or learn a new system in order to print a graph. 1-2-3's graphics menus are just like the other 1-2-3 menus, so you need only learn a few new 1-2-3 commands in order to use the graphics features. They are an integral part of 1-2-3, available from the main menu. After creating your worksheet model, you simply make a few more menu selections to project the data onto a chart.

If you have a color monitor or a graphics card, you will be able to view your graph or chart on the screen. If you have only a monochrome monitor without a graphics card, you will not be able to view your graph, but you can create graphs and print them.

This chapter explores the various options available through the /Graph command, including all of the Release 3 features that significantly expand 1-2-3's graphics ability. The chapter also covers other 1-2-3 commands that affect graphs, such as printing and displaying a worksheet and a graph at the same time.

Creating an Automatic Graph

A quick method for creating a graph is to create an automatic graph, which you can do if your worksheet data is in the proper format. 1-2-3 attempts to create an automatic graph when the /Graph View command is executed, or the F10 (GRAPH) key is pressed, and you have not selected worksheet data to graph.

1-2-3 can create two types of automatic graphs: a rowwise and a columnwise automatic graph. Columnwise and rowwise refer to how 1-2-3 divides the data into data ranges to graph. When you create an automatic graph, 1-2-3 uses the first column or row of the data as the X range, which appears at the bottom of the graph in the X axis. The subsequent columns or rows become the data ranges graphed against the X range. 1-2-3 stops using the worksheet data for the graph when it selects the seventh data range (X and A through F), or when it encounters two blank rows or columns that mark the end of the worksheet data to graph. Once you create an automatic graph, 1-2-3 keeps the data ranges from the automatic graph in its graphics settings. This feature permits you to add enhancements to the automatic graph.

A *columnwise automatic graph* is the default automatic graph. To create a columnwise automatic graph, the data to be graphed must look like the data in Figure 11-1. The worksheet data that 1-2-3 will graph must have two blank rows and columns on all sides to isolate the data to graph from the remaining worksheet data. The edges of the worksheet can serve as one or two of these borders. The automatic graph will use the labels in A5..A16 as the X axis labels. Each column to the right of

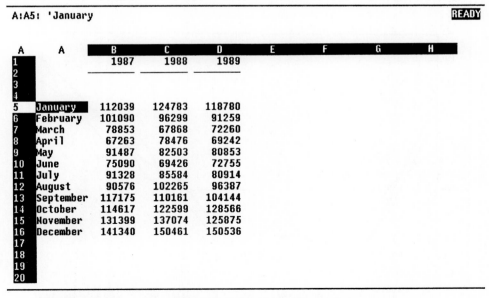

Figure 11-1.   Data for columnwise automatic graph

the labels will become an additional data range. To display this data as an automatic graph, move the cell pointer to the first label (A5), and press F10 (GRAPH). Figure 11-2 shows the automatic line graph for the worksheet in Figure 11-1. 1-2-3 creates a line graph with this data because a graph type is not selected.

The other type of automatic graph is a *rowwise automatic graph.* This option tells 1-2-3 to divide the worksheet data into data ranges for a graph by rows instead of columns. You can choose this option by invoking the /Worksheet Global Default Graph Rowwise command. After executing this command and returning to READY mode, move the cell pointer to the first cell you want to include in the graph. For the data in Figure 11-3, it is D2. A rowwise automatic graph uses the first row for the values along the X axis, and the subsequent rows as the other data ranges. The worksheet has two blank columns, B and C, so 1-2-3 does not include the salespeople's names in the graph. To display this data as an automatic graph, view the graph using the /Graph View command, which is equivalent to the F10 (GRAPH) key. Figure 11-4 shows the automatic graph for the worksheet in Figure 11-3. If you want to

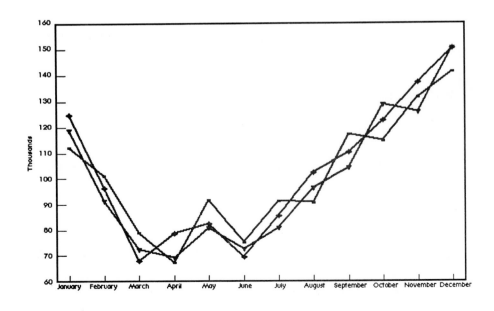

Figure 11-2.   Automatic columnwise graph

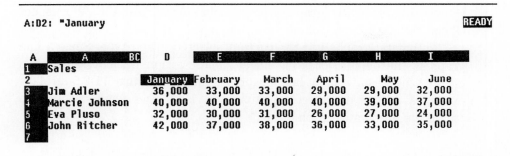

Figure 11-3.   Data for rowwise automatic graph

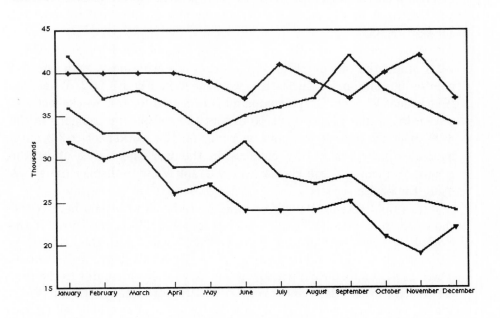

Figure 11-4.   Automatic rowwise graph

return the automatic graph type to columnwise, use the /Worksheet Global Default Graph Columnwise command.

Automatic graphs use the current selected graph type. Since a line graph is the default, creating an automatic graph without selecting a graph type results in a line graph, as in the Figure 11-2 and 11-4 examples. If you do select a graph type, 1-2-3 uses your selection to create the automatic graph data.

Viewing Graphs and Worksheets Simultaneously

As mentioned for automatic graphs, you can view a graph by simply pressing F10 (GRAPH), or by using the /Graph View command. Release 3 has a new feature that allows you to see the worksheet and the current graph at the same time. This is the /Worksheet Window Graph command, which splits the screen at the cell pointer's position and uses the left half to show the current worksheet and the right half to show the current graph.

When you execute this command, the cell pointer determines where 1-2-3 splits the screen. Figure 11-5 shows a worksheet with the cell pointer in column E; this is the worksheet in Figure 11-2. When the /Worksheet Window Graph command is executed for this worksheet, the screen looks like Figure 11-6. Note that the cell pointer remains in the worksheet so you can continue working on the worksheet. 1-2-3 automatically incorporates any changes in the worksheet that affect the graph. You can still use F10 (GRAPH) or /Graph View to display the graph using the entire screen.

In a split-screen, the graph window remains until another /Worksheet Window command is executed or another file is retrieved. If the worksheet does not have a defined graph when a Graph window is created, the Graph window appears blank. 1-2-3 will create an automatic graph in the blank Graph window if you move the cell pointer to the first cell in the graph data and press F10 (GRAPH) or execute /Graph View. When you return to the READY mode, the automatic graph will appear in the Graph window.

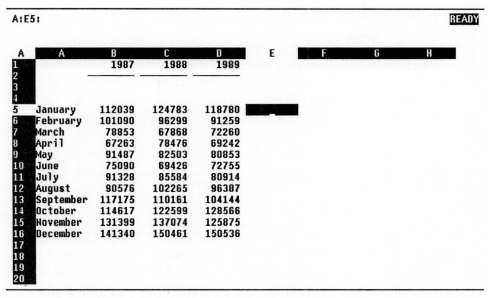

Figure 11-5.   Worksheet before Graph window

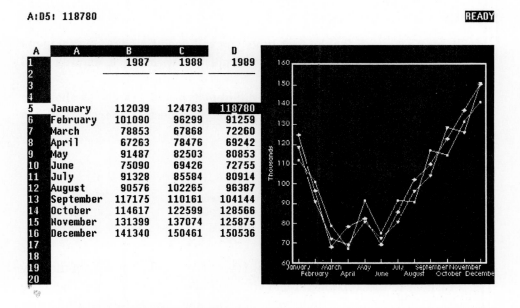

Figure 11-6.   Worksheet with Graph window

Creating Graphs

Most of the options you need to create, modify, display, and save graphs are located under the /Graph command, available from 1-2-3's main menu. When you select /Graph, you will be presented with a menu that looks like this:

```
A:A1: 1                                                               MENU
Type  X  A  B  C  D  E  F  Reset  View  Save  Options  Name  Group  Quit
Line  Bar  XY  Stack-Bar  Pie  HLCO  Mixed  Features
```

Under Type, this menu presents the options for selecting the type of graph you wish to generate. The specific data to be shown in your graph is accessed through options X, A through F, and Group. You can use the Options selections to enhance your graph. Various other selections permit you to view, save, and name your graph.

Selecting a Graph Type

To create a graph for the first time, you will need to make several menu selections. These specify the type of graph you wish to see, and tell 1-2-3 which data to show in the graph.

1-2-3 offers a choice of seven different types of graphs, as shown in the following menu, which appears when you select Type from the main Graph menu.

```
A:A1: 1                                                               MENU
Line  Bar  XY  Stack-Bar  Pie  HLCO  Mixed  Features
Line graph
```

You can easily change from one type of presentation to another by returning to the Type menu and choosing another graph type. The Type options include basic graph types like line and bar, as well as additional

Graph Types for Every Need

The variety of graph types allows you to find a type suitable for presenting almost any kind of data. Here is a description of each type and some suggested uses.

Bar   A bar graph represents the data points in your series with bars of different heights. Although any data can be plotted on a bar graph, it is especially appropriate for comparing the values in several series.

Line   A line graph shows the points of your data ranges plotted against the Y axis. The points in a range may be connected with a line, shown as symbols, or both. The line graph is an excellent choice for plotting trend data over time, such as sales, profit, or expenses.

Stacked Bar   A stacked bar graph places the values in each series on top of each other for each point on the X axis. The total height of a bar thus represents the total values in all the series plotted for any given point. A stacked bar graph is effective for displaying total levels, as well as component levels. Contribution to total company profit of the various subsidiaries could be shown effectively on a stacked bar graph, for example.

Pie   A pie chart shows one range of values. The size of the pie wedge represents each value's percentage of the total. A pie chart is effective for showing the relative size of different components. Pie charts are effective for analyzing different kinds of expenses, or the contribution to profit from different product lines, for example.

XY   An XY graph plots the values in one series against those in another. An XY graph could be used to plot age against salary, machine repairs by age, or time against temperature, for example.

HLCO   An HLCO chart shows the high, low, close, and open values. For each set of data values for each X axis value (such as each day you are recording stock prices), the HLCO graph has a line from the high to the low value. A projection to the left indicates the open value and a projection to the right indicates the close value. Additional ranges appear as a bar graph below this graph, or as a line graph shown with the high, low, close, and open values. This graph type is for graphing financial commodities or statistical results.

Mixed   A mixed graph shows up to three data ranges as a bar graph and up to three data ranges as a line graph. The bar graph and line graph are on top of each other. Mixed graphs can be used to graph profit from different divisions against sales from different divisions.

options available through the Features selection. This flexibility allows you to look at your data in a number of presentation formats, and select the one that seems to show the data most effectively.

Figure 11-7 presents an example of each of the different graph formats. A description of each graph type, along with some suggested uses, is found in the box called "Graph Types for Every Need." By combining the basic graph types with Release 3's Features options, you can create an entire graphics presentation with a different type of graph on each of your slides. The Features options let you rotate the X and Y axes, stack the data ranges, and assign data ranges to a second Y axis.

To select any of the graph types from the menu, simply point to the graph type you want and press ENTER. Alternatively, you can type the first letter of the selection. If you do not select a graph type, 1-2-3 uses a line graph.

Labeling the X Axis

After selecting the graph type, you must define the data to be shown on your graph. The X option in the main Graph menu is used to specify a range of cells containing labels to be placed along the points on the X axis, for all graphs except XY and pie charts. These labels may mark the points of the graph for years, months, or other data values. For the example in Figure 11-8, the cells containing the words "JAN" through "JUNE" were selected as the range after choosing /Graph X. The words in the X range are placed along the X axis, as shown in Figure 11-9.

For pie charts, the X range is used to label the sections of the pie. It might list regions, expense categories, or something similar. X range data for a pie chart must be in the same sequence as the data you provide for the A range, which gives the values for the chart.

For XY charts, the X range data is plotted against corresponding Y values provided by the ranges A through F. Again, use /Graph X to specify the range of cells that contains the entries you wish to use for the X axis. For this type of chart, the entries should be values rather than labels. If an XY type is selected for an automatic graph, 1-2-3 uses the worksheet data differently. The XY graphs skip rows or columns containing labels and use the first numeric row or column as the first data range (the X axis).

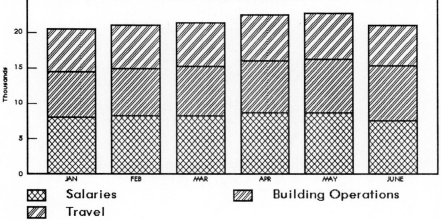

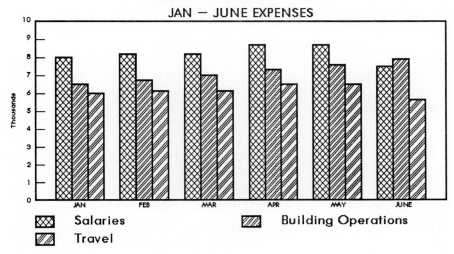

Figure 11-7.   The seven graph types

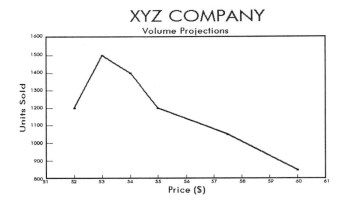

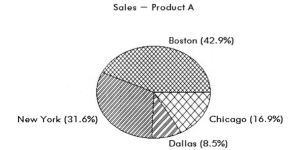

Figure 11-7.   The seven graph types (*continued*)

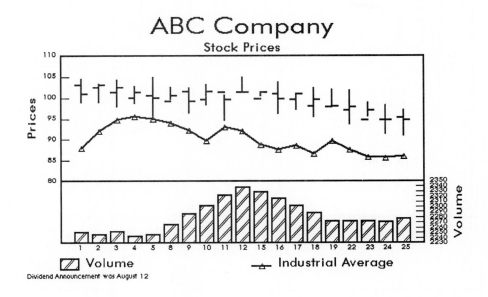

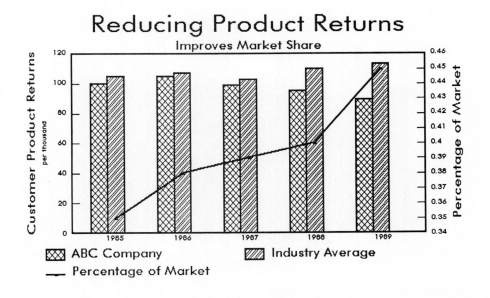

Figure 11-7.   The seven graph types (*continued*)

	A	B	C	D	E	F	G	H	I
1						ABC Company			
2									
3									
4				JAN	FEB	MAR	APR	MAY	JUNE
5	Salaries			$8,000	$8,200	$8,200	$8,700	$8,700	$7,500
6	Building Operations			6,500	6,760	7,030	7,312	7,604	7,908
7	Travel			6,000	6,150	6150	6,525	6,525	5,625
8	Supplies			500	500	500	500	500	500
9	Depreciation			1,200	1,200	1,200	1,200	1,200	1,200
10	Equipment Maintenance			750	750	750	750	750	750
11	Shipping Expense			400	400	400	400	400	400
12	Data Processing Costs			2,100	2,100	2,100	2,100	2,100	2,100
13	Printing & Duplicating			640	640	640	640	640	640
14	Other			1,030	1,030	1,030	1,030	1,030	1,030
15	Total Expenses			$27,120	$27,730	$28,000	$29,157	$29,449	$27,653

Figure 11-8.   ABC Company expenses

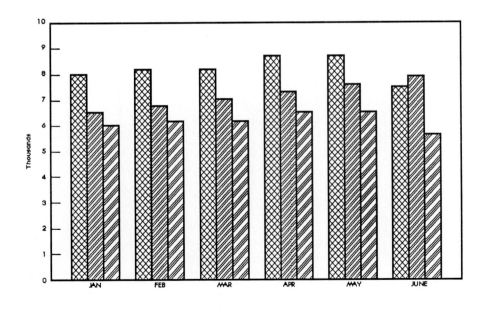

Figure 11-9.   Bar chart showing X range data

If the range you select for X contains too many characters, 1-2-3 will use two rows, with half of the labels on one row and half on the next row, creating a display like the one shown in Figure 11-10. If the X values are too long for two rows, 1-2-3 truncates them if they are labels, or displays them as asterisks if they are values. The X axis can be made easier to read by using fewer or shorter names. Or you can use /Graph Options Scale Skip and enter a skip factor that will cause 1-2-3 to skip some of the labels in the range. A skip factor of 3 will cause every third label in the X range to be used for labeling, for example.

The Y Axis

In contrast to the X axis, the Y axis is labeled automatically once you have selected the data you wish to show on your graph. If 1-2-3 needs to represent your data values in thousands or millions to place them on the graph effectively, it will make the conversion and label the Y axis appropriately.

Selecting Data for a Graph

1-2-3 permits you to show up to six sets of data values on all graph types except the pie chart. A set of data values might represent the sales of a product for a period of months or years, or the number of rejects on a production line for each of the last 16 weeks, to give two examples. Any series of values can be used, as long as they all pertain to the same subject, and are organized according to the points labeled on the X axis. The six different sets of data values are specified for the chart in ranges A through F. To expand our two examples, they might represent sales figures for six different products, or production line rejects from six different factories.

Pie charts are special in that they show what percentage each value is of the total. They therefore would not be appropriate for multiple sets of data. With a pie chart, you use only the A range for your data values. As mentioned earlier, you use the X range to label the sections of the pie. 1-2-3 can use the B and C range to change the appearance of the pie "slices" — as discussed later in the chapter.

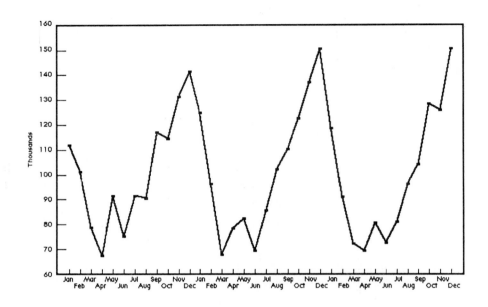

Figure 11-10.   Overlapping X data values

The High-Low-Close-Open (HLCO) graph is another special type of graph because it automatically decides how different ranges are treated. An HLCO graph expects a high-to-low range for each value of X. It is designed for financial applications, such as following the price of a stock. The A range is the high value for each X value; the B range is the low value for each X value. The C range is the closing value, and the D range is the opening value for the X values. The E range is graphed as a second graph below the first one. The F range is a line graph combined with the A through D ranges.

Using the example of tracking a bond price, the X range contains the dates for which you are tracking the bond price. The A range contains the highest sell values for the bond during each day; the B range contains the lowest sell values. The C range contains the closing value of the bond, and the D range contains the opening value of the bond. The E range contains the numbers of shares traded, and the F range contains the average stock price for the industry.

The A through F options on the main Graph menu represent the six possible ranges of data values to be shown on a graph. If you plan to show only one set of data values, choose A and specify the range of cells containing the numeric values you wish to have plotted on the graph. With Release 3, you have the option of including cells from other worksheets and other worksheet files. If you wish to show other sets of data in the graph, select as many of the other range letters as are appropriate, and specify the range of data you wish assigned to each. Remember that you do not have to show all your worksheet data on a graph; you can select just those data ranges that are most important. For example, you may have Sales, Cost of Goods Sold, and Profit data on your worksheet, but you may elect to graph just the Profit data.

Figure 11-11 shows the unit sales of four products for the Boston, New York, Dallas, and Chicago regions of a company. To create a graph from this data, enter /**Graph** to invoke the Graph menu, and then select Type. If you want to see the data for Product 1 as a pie chart, choose Pie. Next, select A for the first data range and specify B5..B8 as the range containing the data. You can specify this range by entering a range name, or pointing after moving to the beginning of the range and locking it in place with a period, or typing the range reference. Select X next, and specify A5..A8 as the X axis range.

Multiple Data Ranges in a Graph

A new feature of Release 3 is the ability to define the data groups for multiple data ranges at once. This reduces the number of steps required to create a graph. The Group option in the /Graph menu selects all the data ranges at once.

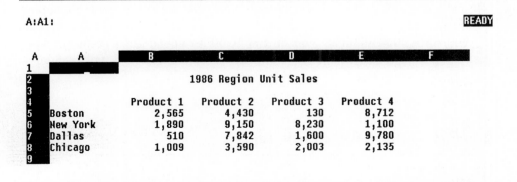

A:A1:   READY

A	A	B	C	D	E	F
1						
2			1986 Region Unit Sales			
3						
4		Product 1	Product 2	Product 3	Product 4	
5	Boston	2,565	4,430	130	8,712	
6	New York	1,890	9,150	8,230	1,100	
7	Dallas	510	7,842	1,600	9,780	
8	Chicago	1,009	3,590	2,003	2,135	
9						

Figure 11-11.   Regional sales data

For example, assume that you want to create a line graph using the data in Figure 11-11. Enter /**Graph Group**; 1-2-3 then prompts for the range that you want to divide into data ranges for the graph. You can enter the range by typing a range address, typing a range name, or pointing to the cells. Next, 1-2-3 asks if you want to divide the data for the graph according to columns or rows. For the data in Figure 11-11, you can select A5..E8 as the range and divide it by columns. This makes A5..A8 the X range, B5..B8 the A range, C5..C8 the B range, D5..D8 the C range, and E5..E8 the D range. The city names will be placed along the X axis. The sales for each product are thus assigned to different data ranges in the line graph.

An alternative approach would be to select B4..E4 as the range and divide it by rows. This makes B4..E4 the X range, B5..E5 the A range, B6..E6 the B range, B7..E7 the C range, and B8..E8 the D range. In this case, the product names are placed along the X axis, and the sales for each city are plotted as different ranges in the line graph.

Using /Graph View

Let's look again at the basic graph defined for the data in Figure 11-11. If you select View from the main Graph menu, you see a display like the one in Figure 11-12. This is all that is required to create a basic graph. It is wise to view the graph before proceeding further. This gives you the opportunity to spot problems, such as when the data ranges you have selected are too dispersed to be shown on one graph. An extreme example would be a pie chart where one section comprised 99% of the total and several others split the remaining 1% between them. In a bar or line graph showing multiple data sets, you would encounter a similar problem if one data set had values in the hundreds and others had values in the millions. You do not want to spend time creating titles, legends, and other enhancements if your basic graph is not usable, so check it with /Graph View first.

Enhancing the Basic Graph Type

While Release 3 has only seven basic graph types, there are many enhancements that make it seem as though you have more. Some of the

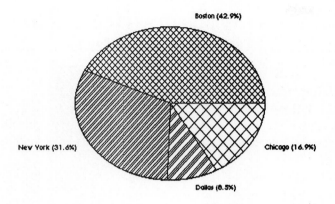

Figure 11-12.   Basic pie chart

changes you can make to the basic graph types are: rotating the axes, stacking data ranges, adding a second Y axis, and displaying the data ranges as a percentage of the total. These features are available through the /Graph Type Features menu, which is shown here.

AiA1:   ⬛XENU
⬛Vertical⬛ Horizontal Stacked 100% 2Y–Ranges Y–Ranges Quit
Draw the graph upright

Setting the Orientation of the Axes

All the graphs, except pie charts, start with the X axis on the bottom of the graph and the Y axis on the left side of the graph. You can switch these two axes and make the Y axis horizontal and the X axis vertical. To rotate the axes, select Horizontal from the /Graph Type Features menu. Figure 11-13 shows a graph without the axes rotated. After rotation, the appearance and emphasis of the graph is quite different, as shown in Figure 11-14. If you decide you want the X axis on the bottom of the graph again, use the /Graph Type Features Vertical command.

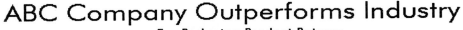

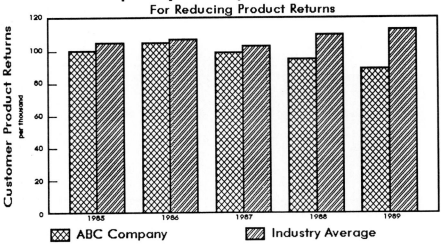

Figure 11-13.   Upright graph

Stacking the Data Ranges

The Stacked bar graph type option creates a graph with the values placed on top of each other, instead of next to each other, or in the same area like in a line graph. Previous releases of 1-2-3 supported stacked bar graphs, but with Release 3 you can also stack the values for the other graph types. When the Stacked option is selected, 1-2-3 prompts for a Yes or No selection. If you select Yes, 1-2-3 stacks the data range values for bar, line, mixed, and XY graphs. To discontinue stacking, enter /**Graph Type Features Stacked** and select No.

Figure 11-15 shows a line graph with stacked values. 1-2-3 first graphs the A data range, and then the B data range. The value of the B data range determines the distance between the A data range and the B data range.

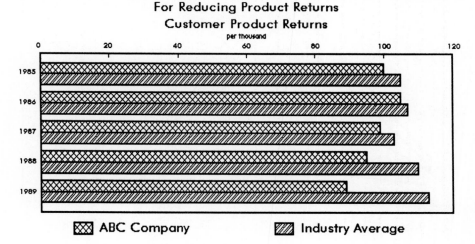

Figure 11-14.   Graph with axes rotated

Displaying Data Ranges As Percentages

In prior releases of 1-2-3, if you wanted to graph the data values as a percentage of the whole, you had to first create a table in the worksheet to compute the percentage for each value, for example, as shown in Figure 11-16. With Release 3, you can now display data values as percentages of the total value, without this extra work.

To use this special display for a bar, line, mixed, stacked bar, or XY graph, select 100% from the /Graph Type Features menu. When this option is selected, 1-2-3 prompts for a Yes or No selection. If you select Yes, 1-2-3 displays the data values as the percentage of their total value; the Y scale shows the percentages. Figure 11-17 shows a 100% bar graph.

If you create this same graph in Release 2, you must use the data in the range B11..E15 from Figure 11-16. With the 100% feature, you can use the data in the B4..E8 range, saving the time required for the additional computation and the worksheet space for other entries.

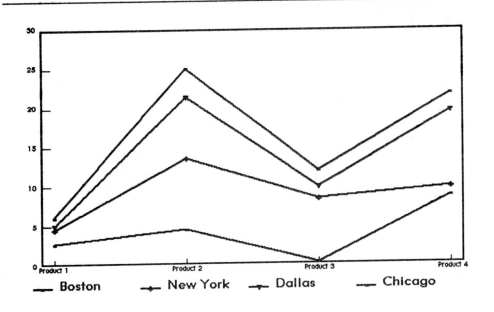

Figure 11-15.   Stacked data ranges on a line graph

To return to the default setting of not showing the data in percentages, enter /**Graph Type Features 100%** and select No.

Using Two Y Axes

Initially, a graph uses a single Y range. However if you are graphing different types of data together, one Y axis may not allow you to combine the data on one graph. You may want to include two axes—one for each measurement. Creating a second Y axis is as simple as assigning data ranges to the second axis, since 1-2-3 automatically creates the second axis when you assign data ranges to it.

To assign data to the second axis, select 2Y-Ranges under the Features option. 1-2-3 will prompt you for the graph ranges to assign to the second axis. Point to the range letter and press ENTER, or type the first range letter to be assigned to the second Y axis. You can continue

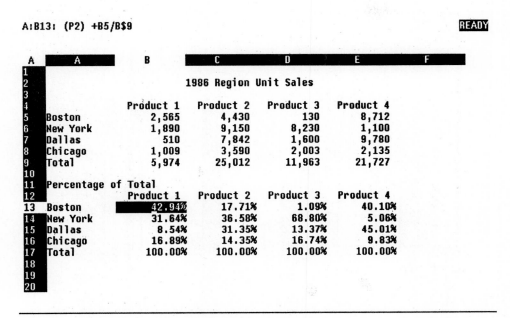

A:B13: (P2) +B5/B$9   READY

	A	B	C	D	E	F
1						
2			1986 Region Unit Sales			
3						
4		Product 1	Product 2	Product 3	Product 4	
5	Boston	2,565	4,430	130	8,712	
6	New York	1,890	9,150	8,230	1,100	
7	Dallas	510	7,842	1,600	9,780	
8	Chicago	1,009	3,590	2,003	2,135	
9	Total	5,974	25,012	11,963	21,727	
10						
11	Percentage of Total					
12		Product 1	Product 2	Product 3	Product 4	
13	Boston	42.94%	17.71%	1.09%	40.10%	
14	New York	31.64%	36.58%	68.80%	5.06%	
15	Dallas	8.54%	31.35%	13.37%	45.01%	
16	Chicago	16.89%	14.35%	16.74%	9.83%	
17	Total	100.00%	100.00%	100.00%	100.00%	
18						
19						
20						

Figure 11-16.   Worksheet for 100% graph

assigning ranges to the second Y axis, select the 2Y-Ranges Graph
option to assign all ranges to the second Y axis, or select Quit to return
to the /Graph Type Features menu. If you then decide to reassign a
range to the first Y axis, select Y-Ranges and execute the same steps
that you would execute with the 2Y-Ranges selection. If a graph does
not have any ranges assigned to the second axis, the second axis does
not appear.

Figure 11-18 shows a mixed graph with two axes. A mixed graph
frequently uses one Y axis for the bar graph values and the other Y axis
for the line graph values. The HLCO graph automatically assigns the E
range to the second Y axis.

If you rotate the X and Y axes for a graph that has two Y axes,
1-2-3 puts the first Y axis on top and the second Y axis on bottom; this is
demonstrated in Figure 11-19, where the data range/line graph is assigned to the second Y axis.

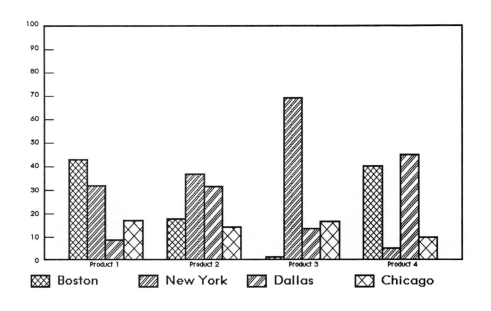

Figure 11-17.   100% bar graph

Enhancing the Basic Display

Once you are sure that your data can be shown effectively with the graph type you selected, you will most likely want to make some changes to improve its appearance. 1-2-3 offers plenty of enhancement options, from colors and hatch patterns, to exploding a pie chart, to adding titles and legends on any type of graph.

Before selecting these options, you will need to remove your graph from the screen and return to the Graph menu by pressing any key. (You can recall the graph display at any time by pressing F10 (GRAPH).) Most of the commands needed to produce graph enhancements are shown on the Graph Options menu, which follows; others are options on the main Graph menu.

A:A1:   MENU
Legend Format Titles Grid Scale Color B&W Data-Labels Advanced Quit
Create data-range legends

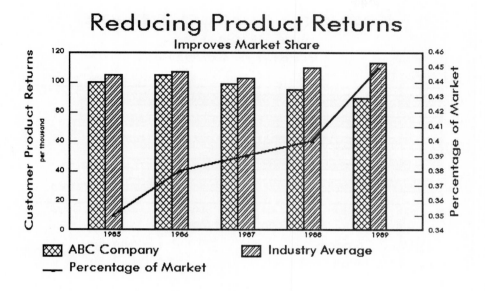

Figure 11-18. Graph with two Y axes

Pie Chart Options

Normally the B graph data range is used to specify a second set of data for your graph. With a pie chart, however, the B range can be used to specify the color or hatch pattern for the individual pieces of the pie. The B range offers code numbers from 1 through 14 representing different colors or hatch patterns. For example, Figure 11-20 shows the hatch patterns 1-2-3 uses for each of the 14 hatch pattern values. These hatch patterns are useful for a monochrome display, and for printing to a printer that cannot print colors. The same numbers (1 through 14) represent available colors when 1-2-3 can display or print the graph in color.

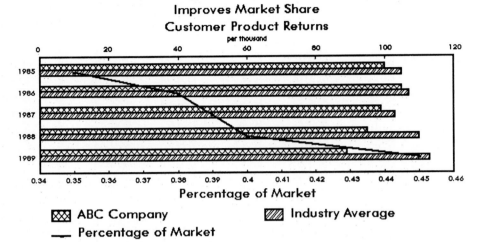

Figure 11-19.   Rotated graph with two Y axes

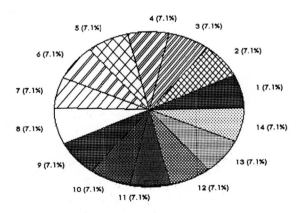

Figure 11-20.   The 14 hatch mark patterns

In a pie chart, the B data range assumes a special function, in addition to determining color or hatch mark patterns: it can also be used to explode or hide a section from the pie. Any pie slice can be exploded by adding 100 to the color or hatch pattern code number for the slice. A pie segment can be hidden by designating a negative, instead of a positive hatch or color pattern number.

Figure 11-21 shows the same data found in Figure 11-11, except that an extra column is added for the hatch pattern codes to be specified as the B data range. These codes are stored in F5 through F8; each set of data values to be shown in the pie chart has a hatch pattern code. When the B range is selected and F5..F8 is used as the range, the pie chart in Figure 11-12 will change its appearance, as you would see if you chose View again.

Figure 11-22 shows the pie chart exactly as it would appear in your display after the addition of these hatch pattern codes. Notice that the section for Dallas is pulled away from the center, or exploded; this is accomplished by using 103 for the B range value for this pie slice. Also, the segment for Chicago does not appear; it is hidden by using a negative number for the B range value.

Pie chart segments can also be displayed without their percentage values, using the C data range. To hide a percentage for any slice, put a zero in that segment's C range cell. Leave the other cells in the C range blank. For example, using the data in Figure 11-21 and the graph in Figure 11-22, define a C range as G5..G8 and put a 0 in G5. Leave

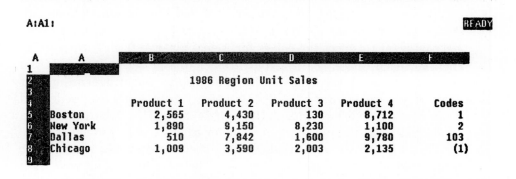

Figure 11-21.   Hatch mark pattern codes added in column F

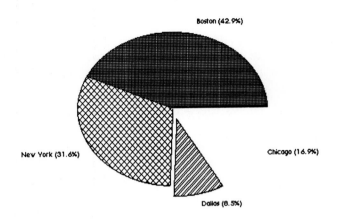

Figure 11-22.   Shaded pie chart

G6 through G8 blank. When 1-2-3 displays the graph, the percentage for Boston will not appear.

Selecting Colors for Graph Ranges

If your monitor can display graphs in color, or if your printer can print colors, you may want to select the colors 1-2-3 uses for the data ranges for all graph types.

To select the color for a data range, use the /Graph Options Advanced Colors command. When 1-2-3 prompts you for the data range that you want to select the colors for, select a range from A through F. Then, for each range, select a color from 1 to 8 or select Range. If you select a number 1 through 8, 1-2-3 will display the range using that color. If you select Range, 1-2-3 prompts you to supply a predefined range containing color codes 1 through 14 for each of the graph data values. Selecting Range selects a color for each value in a range.

Figure 11-23 shows worksheet data used for a graph, with a color range used for the graph data ranges. The color associated with each color value depends on your monitor. The color the graph prints depends on your printer or plotter. If you are using a plotter, the actual

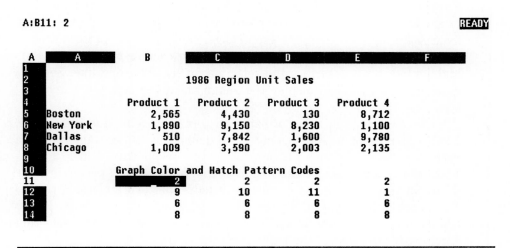

Figure 11-23.   Worksheet with color and hatch mark pattern codes

colors depend on the pens in the plotter. If your printer cannot print colors, changing the color 1-2-3 uses when displaying the ranges has no effect on how the printer prints the graph.

Once you select a color or a color range, 1-2-3 returns to the menu, and you can select another data range for color customization. You may want to change a data range's color to make it appear different from the surrounding data ranges. You can assign different colors to a data range's values when you want to emphasize the values of a particular data range. To return to the previous menu, select Quit. The /Graph Options Advanced Colors command only selects colors for pie slices (the A range) when a B range is *not* selected.

Selecting Hatch Patterns for Graph Ranges

1-2-3 can also differentiate the appearance of graph data ranges using hatch patterns. Hatch patterns are line patterns 1-2-3 uses for pie slices, bars, and areas. 1-2-3 has fourteen different hatch patterns that are shown in Figure 11-20. 1-2-3 can select the hatch patterns for you, or you can select them using the /Graph Options Advanced Hatches command.

To select the hatch patterns for a data range, use the /Graph Options Advanced Hatches command. 1-2-3 prompts you for the data range for which you want to select the hatch pattern; select a range from A through F. Then, for each range, select a hatch pattern from 1 to 8 or select Range. When each hatch pattern number (1 through 8) is highlighted, 1-2-3 describes the selection on the following line. Select a number, and 1-2-3 will display the range using the selected hatch pattern.

Choose Range to select a hatch pattern for each value in a range. 1-2-3 will prompt you to supply a predefined range containing hatch pattern codes 1 through 14 for each of the graph data values. Figure 11-23 shows a worksheet used for a graph, with a hatch pattern range. (You can use the same range for both hatch pattern and color codes.) The graph will display and print using the same hatch pattern. If you are using a color monitor and displaying the graph in color, selecting hatch patterns displays the hatch patterns in color.

Once you select a hatch pattern or a hatch pattern code range, 1-2-3 returns to the menu. You may then select another data range. You may customize a data range's hatch pattern to make it appear different from the surrounding data ranges. You can assign different hatch patterns to a data range's values, to emphasize each one. The /Graph Options Advanced Hatches command can select the hatch patterns for pie slices (the A range) when you want to combine colors with hatch patterns, or if a B range is *not* selected for a monochrome display. To return to the previous menu, select Quit.

Adding Descriptive Labels

Figure 11-24 shows a bar graph created by selecting Bar from the Graph Type menu. This graph has been enhanced with titles at the top, values along the Y axis, X axis data labels, legends, and a note at the bottom. Adding this type of extra description to a chart makes it convey your message more effectively. Additional text options let you select the color, font, and size of the text.

The data used to create this graph is shown in Figure 11-25. Of the data in the worksheet, only Salaries, Building Operations, and Travel are selected to be shown. This was done by assigning the numeric values for the January through June columns to the A, B, and C data ranges, respectively. The months are assigned to the X range. You can select all

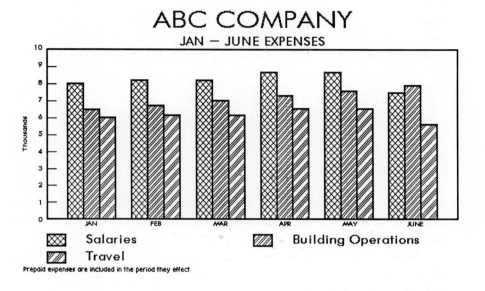

Figure 11-24.   Bar graph with titles and legends added

of the ranges at once by entering the /Graph Group command, selecting D4..J7 as the range, and selecting Rowwise to divide D4..J7 into graph data ranges according to rows.

Adding Legends

A legend provides a description for each of the ranges shown on a graph. (You saw an example in Figure 11-24.) If you create a line graph with symbols marking the data points in the range, the legend defines these symbols at the bottom of your chart. If you create a graph with hatch patterns, the legend defines each hatch pattern by placing a small box filled with the hatch pattern at the bottom of the chart, and adding a description next to the box.

Legends are added using the /Graph Options Legend command, which offers the menu shown here:

```
A:A1:                                              MENU
A  B  C  D  E  F  Range
Assign first data-range legend
```

A	A	B	C	D	E	F	G	H	I
1						ABC Company			
2									
3									
4				JAN	FEB	MAR	APR	MAY	JUNE
5	Salaries			$8,000	$8,200	$8,200	$8,700	$8,700	$7,500
6	Building Operations			6,500	6,760	7,030	7,312	7,604	7,908
7	Travel			6,000	6,150	6150	6,525	6,525	5,625
8	Supplies			500	500	500	500	500	500
9	Depreciation			1,200	1,200	1,200	1,200	1,200	1,200
10	Equipment Maintenance			750	750	750	750	750	750
11	Shipping Expense			400	400	400	400	400	400
12	Data Processing Costs			2,100	2,100	2,100	2,100	2,100	2,100
13	Printing & Duplicating			640	640	640	640	640	640
14	Other			1,030	1,030	1,030	1,030	1,030	1,030
15	Total Expenses			$27,120	$27,730	$28,000	$29,157	$29,449	$27,653

Figure 11-25.   ABC Company data

Enter the letter corresponding to the data range for which you want to specify a legend. Or select Range if the text that you want for all of the legends is predefined in a range in the worksheet.

When you enter a range letter, 1-2-3 prompts you for the legend description to be stored for that data range. The legends used for Figure 11-24 were Salaries, Building Operations, and Travel for the A, B, and C ranges respectively. If the legend you wish to use appears in a worksheet cell, you have an alternative entry method. Rather than typing the legend at the prompt, you can enter a backslash (\) and the address of the cell containing the legend data. For example, entering \A5 tells 1-2-3 to use the text in cell A5 as the legend. While 1-2-3 does not limit the number of characters you can enter for a legend, the legend text that appears in the graph is limited by the amount of space used for the other legends.

If you select Range, 1-2-3 prompts you for the worksheet range containing the predefined legends. You can enter this range by typing a range address or name, or by pointing to the cells you want to use. For example, for the legends in Figure 11-24, you could have selected Range and entered A5..A7. 1-2-3 assigns the first cell as the A range legend, the second cell as the B range legend, and so on, until it runs out of cells or graph data ranges.

You can also add legends to pie charts, to label the first six slices. To label pie slices, select Legend Range and enter the range address containing the predefined legends for the pie slices. 1-2-3 assigns the first cell in the legend range to the first slice, and continues assigning cell contents to pie slices until it uses all the cells in the legend range, or the sixth pie slice is assigned a legend, or the last pie slice is assigned a legend.

Tip: Combine pie slice legends with hatch patterns. If you want to group pie slices in a pie chart, assign the same hatch pattern to each group. Also, have one slice of each group in the beginning of the data range. Then assign legends describing the group to the first pie slice of each group. The resulting graph will show each group with the same hatch pattern and the legend identifying the group. Each slice is still individually labeled using the X range labels.

Adding Titles

1-2-3 has seven title options, all accessible through the /Graph Options Titles command. Titles appear at the top of the chart, or along the X, Y, or second Y axis. Notes appear at the bottom of the graph. The menu you see when you enter **/Graph Options Titles** is shown here.

```
A:A1:                                                                    MENU
First  Second  X-Axis  Y-Axis  2Y-Axis  Note  Other-Note
Assign first line of graph title
```

The first title appears at the top of the graph. For example, the first line title of the graph in Figure 11-24 was generated by entering /**Graph Options Titles First**, and then **ABC COMPANY**. (If this label were already somewhere in your worksheet, you could enter a backslash (\) and a reference to the cell containing the label.)

A line for a second label is also reserved at the top of the graph. To place an entry in this location, enter **/Graph Options Titles Second**. The entry JAN—JUNE EXPENSES was typed at the prompt for the second line title in our example. This second title can also be supplied from the worksheet, with a backslash (\) and a reference to the cell address. Either method lets you enter a title up to 512 characters long, although the number of characters that are displayed and printed depends on the monitor's resolution and on the printer.

Titles can also be given to the X or Y axis. These labels normally describe the quantities being measured. The Y axis title might be Dollars and the X axis title might be Sales, for example. If you enter a value for the Y axis title, it is placed vertically on the graph to the left of the Y axis. An X axis title is placed horizontally below the X axis. A graph containing a second Y axis can also have a label on the second Y axis; enter **/Graph Options Titles 2Y-Axis** and the label text, or a backslash and a reference to a cell containing the label.

A new feature of Release 3 allows you to add two lines of note text at the bottom of the graph. You can use these two lines to identify the data source or to add descriptions about what the data represents. For example, the note at the bottom of the example in Figure 11-24 is added by entering **/Graph Options Titles Note** and then the text for the note. A second line can be added with **Titles Other-Note**. If suitable text for a note is already in your worksheet, you can enter a backslash (\) and a reference to the cell containing the text.

Changing the Text Characteristics

New options in Release 3 let you select the color, font, and size of the text in a graph by using the /Graph Options Advanced Text command.

1-2-3 divides the text of a graph into three groups. The first text group includes the first title. The second group includes the second title, axes titles, and legend text. The third group includes the scale indicators, axes labels, data labels, and footnotes. The /Graph Options Advanced Text command can set the characteristics for any of these three groups. When this command is executed, 1-2-3 prompts you to specify the text group you want to change. Then it prompts for the text characteristic that you want to change. When you have set the text group's characteristics, select Quit to return to the previous menu.

Selecting a Font   You can choose a particular font for a text group. The various fonts have characters with different sizes, shapes, and thicknesses. When you select the Font option, 1-2-3 prompts you for the font number (1 through 8) or Default, which uses the default for the text group. The default for the first text group is font 1, and the default for the second and third group is font 3. The font selections of 1 through 8 match the /Print Printer Options Other Advanced Fonts selections.

This Font option only changes how 1-2-3 *prints* the graph's text, since it always uses the same predetermined font for *displaying* the graph. 1-2-3 will only display the graph using the selected font if a utility program adds display fonts. Although currently no utility programs are developed for adding fonts to 1-2-3's graph display, you can explore programs like Bitstream, which has font support for other Lotus products and may later include support for Release 3. The way the fonts print depends upon the printer.

Selecting the Text Color   If your monitor and printer can display and print graphs in color, you may want to experiment with the colors 1-2-3 makes available for displaying and printing graph text. You may also want to hide part of the text. The Color option either selects a color for the text group, or hides it. The color selections 1 through 8 match the /Graph Options Advanced Colors selections. The actual colors available depend on the monitor and printer. If your printer cannot print colors, changing the color option on 1-2-3 has no effect on how the printer prints the graph.

Choosing the Hide option hides the text group. This option works for both displaying and printing the graphs in color. On a monochrome printer or monitor, this command can only hide text groups.

Selecting the Text Size   You may wish to set the size of the text groups, for example, to enlarge some text groups so they are visible from a distance. This option selects the character size 1-2-3 uses for the text groups.

Choose this option, and 1-2-3 prompts for the character size (1 through 9) or Default, which uses the default for the text group. Since 1-2-3 only has three text sizes for displaying graphs, it displays graphs with the text sizes 1 to 3 as small-sized characters, text sizes 4 to 6 as medium-sized characters, and 7 to 9 as large-sized characters. The way the character sizes print depends on the printer and the font.

The default for the first text group is 7, the default for the second group is 4, and the default for the third group is 2. 1-2-3 automatically reduces the text size if it needs to fit more text on the graph, and then truncates text that still does not fit.

Enhancing an XY Graph

Data for the volume projections for XYZ Company is shown in Figure 11-26. An XY graph can be used to plot the unit sales at different prices. To produce such a graph, you first enter **/Graph Type XY**. Then enter **/Graph X** and specify B6..G6 as the X axis values, and B5..G5 as the A data range.

After viewing the graph, you might want to add first and second line titles like the ones shown in Figure 11-27. Enter the first line title with **/Graph Options Titles First** followed by **\C1**, and handle the second line title in the same way, using the Second option and **\C2**. This graph also has X axis and Y axis titles. To create these, enter **/Graph Options Titles Y-Axis** and then enter **Units Sold** from the keyboard. This title is displayed vertically, as shown in the figure. Similarly, enter the X axis title of **Price ($)** from the keyboard after selecting /Graph Options Titles X-Axis. Both of these titles could be taken from worksheet cells by entering a backslash and the address of the cell containing the entry, in response to the prompt.

Adding Grid Lines

If you have a number of points on a graph, it may be difficult to identify the exact X and Y values for each point on the line. To make such identification easier, 1-2-3 allows you to add vertical and horizontal lines that originate at the axis markers and extend upward and to the right. These lines are called *grid lines,* since using them in both directions forms a grid pattern across your graph.

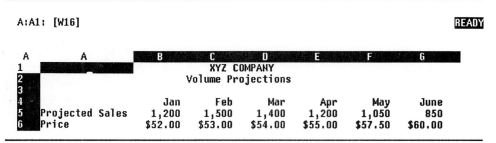

Figure 11-26.   Worksheet for XY graph

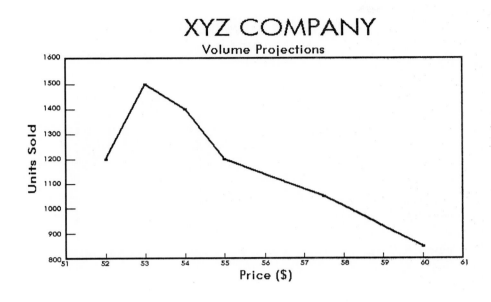

Figure 11-27.   XY graph

The menu for Grid is obtained by entering /Graph Options Grid. The Grid options can be used with all graph types except the pie chart, since grid lines across a pie chart would detract from your ability to interpret the graph. The Grid menu contains these five options:

```
A:A1:                                                          MENU
Horizontal  Vertical  Both  Clear  Y-Axis
Draw grid lines across the graph
```

Choose the first option to add horizontal lines across the graph. This is especially effective for bar graphs, since it enables you to more accurately interpret the tops of the bars. Figure 11-28 presents a bar graph to which horizontal lines were added by entering /**Graph Options Grid Horizontal.**

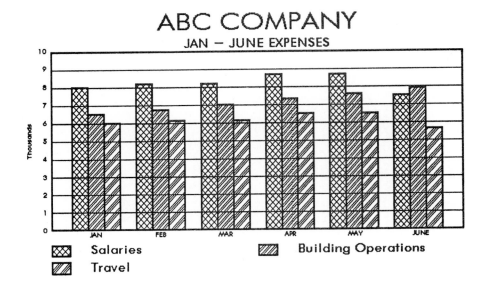

Figure 11-28.   Horizontal grid lines

Vertical bars extend upward from the X axis points. They are more effective on a line or XY graph than on a bar graph. They are added using /**Graph Options Grid Vertical.**

To add grid lines in both directions, enter /**Graph Options Grid Both.** Figure 11-29 shows a line graph with grid lines in both directions.

Since Release 3 graphs can contain two graph axes, you must specify which Y axis is to be used for grid lines when the graph uses Horizontal or Both grid line options. To select the Y axis for grid line use, enter /**Graph Options Grid Y-Axis.** 1-2-3 displays the selections Y Axis (the first Y axis), 2Y-Axis (the second Y axis), and Both.

You can remove grid lines without changing the rest of your graph, simply by entering the command sequence /**Graph Options Grid Clear.**

The grid lines start at a specific axis. If you rotate the axes, the grid lines rotate as well. For example, horizontal grid lines begin at the first or second Y axis. Rotating this graph also rotates the grid lines, so they will appear as vertical lines starting from the first or second Y axis.

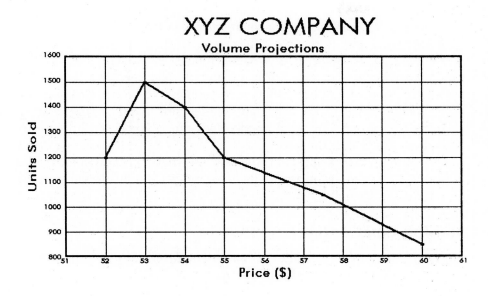

Figure 11-29.   Grid lines in both directions

Choosing Line and Symbol Options

1-2-3 allows you to show line graphs and XY graphs in a variety of formats by using the options under /Graph Options Format. You can show the graph as a smooth line connecting the points, or as symbols marking the points with lines connecting them, or just as symbols. Or you can fill in the area between the data ranges with different hatch patterns. The options are shown in the following menu:

```
A:A1:                                                        MENU
Lines  Symbols  Both  Neither  Area
Connect data points with lines
```

Before you select a line and symbol option, you must first specify the range for the graph application, as either Graph (everything on the graph) or one of the range letters, A through F.

The first Format option, Lines, connects the points for a data range with a line. The points are not marked by symbols when this option is chosen. The Symbols option omits the line and just marks the data points with one of the six different symbols that 1-2-3 provides. The third option is Both. As the name implies, it provides both lines and symbols for your display. The last option, Neither, may seem useless, since it means that neither lines nor symbols are shown. However, it can be used with the Data-Labels option (described later in this chapter) to mark the points with actual data values. The default setting for /Graph Options Format is Both.

A new Format option in Release 3 is Area. This option creates *area graphs*. An area graph stacks the data ranges and fills the area between the data ranges with a hatch pattern. Figure 11-30 shows an area graph.

Choosing Color or Black and White

If you have a color monitor, 1-2-3 automatically displays the graphs in color. If you have a monochrome monitor, 1-2-3 automatically displays

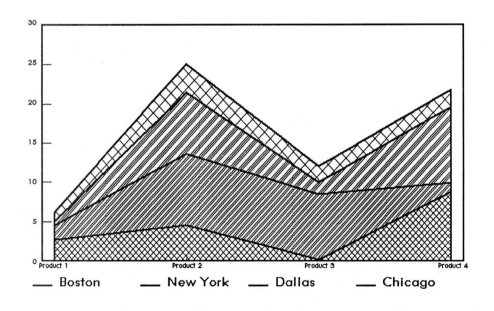

Figure 11-30.   Area graph

the graph in a monochrome. You can change the way 1-2-3 displays your graph with /Graph Options Color and /Graph Options B&W.

Unlike previous releases of 1-2-3, with Release 3 you do not have to change a color graph display to B&W in order to print the graph using a printer that cannot print colors. 1-2-3 automatically translates color graphs to monochrome graphs so it can print them using a single color (black). You will want to change the display to color if you are using a monochrome monitor but are printing on a printer that can print colors. Since you cannot view a color graph on a monochrome screen, wait to change the graph display until after you have finished viewing the graph and are ready to print it.

The colors 1-2-3 uses depends on the monitor selected during the Install program. For example, if you are using a Color Graphic Adapter screen, 1-2-3 uses three colors. If you are using an Enhanced Graphic Adapter, 1-2-3 uses sixteen colors.

Selecting Scaling Options

1-2-3's scaling options let you override the scaling selections that 1-2-3 makes when constructing a graph. You always have the option of letting 1-2-3 make the decisions, and you will seldom need to use the Scale option to improve upon the selections made by 1-2-3. You can use this command to change the scaling for the X, first Y, or second Y axis, or to specify a skip factor for X-axis data labels. The selections made for the X axis only affect XY graphs. /Graph Options Scale Skip was discussed earlier in this chapter in the section called "Labeling the X Axis."

Specify the scale to be changed by choosing /Graph Options Scale X-Axis, /Graph Options Scale Y-Axis, or /Graph Options Scale 2Y-Axis. The menu presented for any of these selections looks like this:

```
A:A1:                                                              MENU
Automatic  Manual  Lower  Upper  Format  Indicator  Type  Exponent  Width  Quit
Scale automatically based on data ranges
```

The Automatic option is the default setting. It is also the method for returning to automatic scaling after requesting Manual. 1-2-3 remembers the settings you have made for a manual axis in case you decide to switch to a manual axis later.

Manual permits you to decide what the upper and lower limits of your scale will be. If you choose this option, plan also to choose Upper and Lower to define the limits of your scale. With a manual setting, 1-2-3 does not display values outside the established limits. In a bar or stacked bar graph, 1-2-3 displays a bar stretching the height of the graph for values over the established limits and an empty space for values under the established limits. In a line graph, the line connecting the points discontinues at the top or bottom of the graph to indicate values outside the established limits.

The Format option on the Scale menu allows you to use any of the numeric formats on the scale markers for the X and Y axis. You can format the numbers as Currency, Percent, or any of the other formats acceptable for the /Range Format command covered in Chapter 5.

The Indicator option permits you to turn off the label indicator that specifies size, or create a new one. As an example, say you are showing sales in thousands of dollars, and 1-2-3 generates the label "Thousands" for use along the Y axis. If you do not wish this to appear, request Indicator None. If you want to use a different indicator, select Manual and enter the label you want as an indicator. You can reference a cell's contents by typing a backslash and the cell address. Yes is the default setting for this option.

With the Type option, you can select the type of scaling 1-2-3 uses for the axes. The two choices are Standard and Logarithmic; Standard is the default. Logarithmic increases the scale by powers of 10. You may want to change the type of scaling if you want to emphasize a trend. For example, Figure 11-31 shows a graph using the standard scaling. Since the numbers grow so rapidly, it is difficult to see any trend. Figure 11-32 shows the same graph after the type of scaling is changed to logarithmic. This graph shows a more definite trend.

The Exponent option lets you set the order of magnitude for a scale. The default, Automatic, lets 1-2-3 determine if the data should be scaled by thousands, millions or another power of 10. The other selection, Manual, allows you to select the power of 10 factor used to graph the numbers. 1-2-3 allows any integer between -95 and $+95$ as options for setting the order of magnitude.

The Width option permits you to set the width of the scale numbers. The default, Automatic, lets 1-2-3 determine the correct width for displaying the numbers. The other selection, Manual, lets you select the

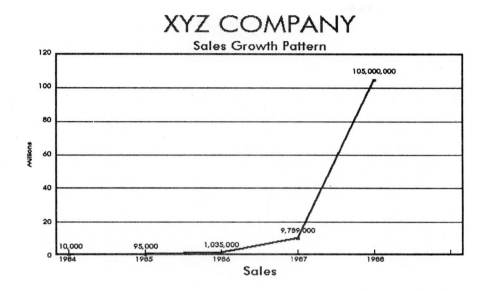

Figure 11-31.   Graph using standard Y axis scale

width. 1-2-3 prompts you for a number between 1 and 50 for the width. Numbers larger than the specified width appear as asterisks.

When you are finished with the Scale menu, enter /**Graph Options X-Axis** or **Y-Axis Quit**. This returns you to the Graph Options menu.

Tip: Use a manual axis scale indicator when the graph data produces an erroneous label. When a graph uses data with an order of magnitude other than 0, such as financial data listed in the thousands, you may want to change the scale indicator to reflect what the numbers actually represent. Select the Manual option for the indicator and enter an appropriate label, such as thousands.

Using Data to Label Your Graph

You can use the contents of worksheet cells to label the points or bars in a graph. 1-2-3 lets you assign data labels to any one of the data ranges involved in your graph.

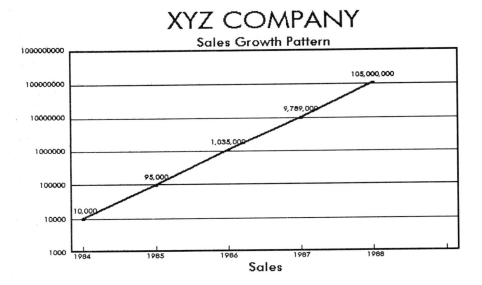

Figure 11-32.   Graph using logarithmic Y axis scale

Simply choose /Graph Options Data-Labels; then enter the letter of your range choice (A through F). Or choose Group to enter the data labels for all the data ranges at once. Then 1-2-3 prompts you for a range containing the data labels. The labels range must contain as many cells as there are data points in the range or ranges to which you are assigning labels. Enter the labels range by typing the range address or the range name, or by pointing to the cells. If you are assigning data labels to the A through F data ranges, you must choose whether 1-2-3 divides the cells into the data labels for each data range according to columns or rows.

After entering the range of cells containing the labels, you will need to choose the location for the data labels relative to your data points. Your options are Center, Left, Above, Right, and Below. Figure 11-33 presents a bar chart where labels are shown above the data points to provide a clear description of the height of each bar. On bar graphs, the Center, Left, and Right selections produce the same result as Above. On stacked bar graphs, 1-2-3 puts the data inside the stacked bar regardless of the position selected.

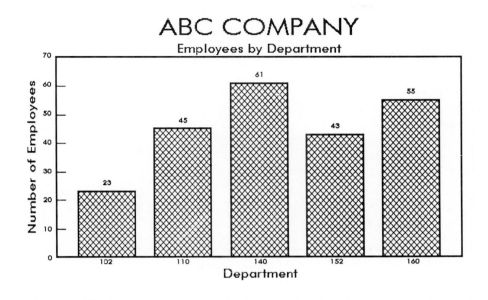

Figure 11-33. Data points marked with data labels

To use data labels as the only marker on a graph, create a line graph. Then enter /**Graph Options Format Neither**, which will keep lines and symbols from being displayed. Then center the data labels at each point on the chart with /**Graph Options Data-Labels Center** to create a display similar to Figure 11-34.

Resetting Graph Options

After specifying particular options for a graph, you might change your mind about some of them. Individual labels can be erased by reentering the appropriate command and deleting the label from the prompt. As an example, if you wish to remove the first line title, "ABC COMPANY," enter /**Graph Options Title First** and delete the title "ABC COMPANY" from this entry. If a cell reference was used to supply the label, just delete the cell reference and backslash from the entry.

If you want to eliminate all the graph settings, however, use /Graph Reset Graph. This command eliminates all graph settings, including ranges. It lets you redefine a new graph from the beginning.

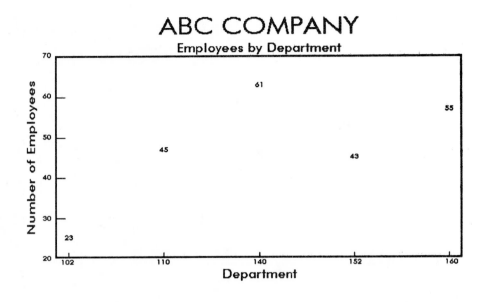

Figure 11-34.   Data labels displayed without lines or symbols

A:A1:
Graph   X   A   B   C   D   E   F   Ranges   Options   Quit
Clear all current graph settings

The Reset command also allows you to remove just some of the graph settings. The following menu provides a number of options for removing particular settings. You can remove the X data range by choosing X, or any of data ranges (A through F) by choosing the letter of the range you wish to eliminate. You can remove all of the ranges by choosing Ranges. To delete the selections made with the /Graph Options menu, choose Reset Options.

Since the Reset menu remains displayed after you make a selection, you will have to choose Quit or press ESC when you want to exit from this command.

Redrawing Graphs

You can make graphics an integral part of your "what-if" analysis with the F10 (GRAPH) key. Once you have defined your graph, return to READY mode by choosing Quit from the Graph menu. In READY mode, you can make changes to your worksheet. Then, to see how these changes affect your graph, simply press F10 (GRAPH). Your graph will be redrawn on the screen with the new data values shown.

The F10 key provides an effective way to toggle between graphics and the worksheet. With a graph on the screen (via /Graph View), press ESC twice and return to READY mode; this lets you review the detail behind the graph. If you want to view the graph from the worksheet, press F10. Then just press any key once to return to the worksheet. When you are ready to return to the graphics display, just press F10 again. This takes you from the worksheet READY mode to the graph display, where current worksheet figures are reflected in the graph. The F10 (GRAPH) key can be used from the READY mode or while you are using 1-2-3's menus.

Storing and Using Graphs

Each of the graphs created up to this point has been the current graph for the worksheet file. 1-2-3 limits the worksheet file to have only one current graph at a time. To include multiple graphs in your worksheet you must name a current graph before you create a new one. Once a graph is named, it can become the current graph at a later point. Another option for storing the graph once you create it is saving it to a file. 1-2-3 can save graphs to files that you can use with other software packages such as WordPerfect and Lotus Manuscript.

Naming Graphs for Later Use

1-2-3 uses all the settings you enter for a graph to define the current graph. Since only one graph can be current at a time, you will lose the original settings if you start choosing different ones for a new graph. If you want to retain the definition of the current graph while you begin a new graph, first save the current one with /Graph Name Create. When 1-2-3 prompts you for the name of the graph to create, you can enter any name up to 15 characters in length. To eliminate all of the settings after saving the graph, use /Graph Reset Graph. You can then start defining a new graph, and, when the definition is complete, you can name it, too. When you save your worksheet, all the graph names and definitions will be saved along with the other data.

A graph whose settings have been saved can be used again. To use the settings of a named graph, enter **/Graph Name Use** and specify the name you assigned previously with /Graph Name Create. The settings that were current at the time the graph was saved will be activated, and pressing View will recreate the graph on your screen.

1-2-3's ability to name and save graphs lets you create a number of graphs in one worksheet file. You can define and name all the graphs you need for a single application. Then, when you update your worksheet figures, you can create an up-to-date slide show of graphic results by using and viewing each of the named graphs. You will not have to recreate the graphs, because their settings are saved with the worksheet.

Once you have created the graphs, you may need to list them. The /Graph Name Table command lists a worksheet's defined graphs in a table in the worksheet file. When you execute this command, 1-2-3 prompts you for a location to start the graph name table. Specify an area three columns wide, and with as many rows as the worksheet file has named graphs. The table will contain the graph names, the graph types, and the first title line, if any. Figure 11-35 shows a graph name table.

Tip: 1-2-3 does not keep the setting and option changes that you make to a named graph unless you save it again with the /Graph Name Create command. This command saves the named graph with the other worksheet data. To use this graph in another 1-2-3 session, save the worksheet file with /File Save.

Deleting Graphs

The /Graph Name Delete command permits you to eliminate stored graph settings that you no longer need. When you enter this command,

A:A1: [W16] 'ABC_STOCK   READY

	B	C	D	E	F	G
ABC_STOCK	HLCO	ABC Company				
LINE	Line					
PIE	Pie					
PROD_1_DISTRIB	Pie	ABC COMPANY				
PROD_RETURNS	Mixed	Reducing Product Returns				
SALES_YEARS	Line	Seasonal Trend of Sales				
THREE_HIGH_EXP	Bar	ABC COMPANY				

Figure 11-35.   Table listing named graphs

1-2-3 prompts you with a list of all existing graph names. Selecting a name from the list or typing in a name causes all the settings for that graph to be eliminated. If you change your mind and wish to reproduce the graph, you must reenter all the options.

1-2-3 also provides a quick delete feature. Use it with caution, because it eliminates all saved graph names in the current file. If you do want to eliminate all the current graph names and their associated settings, enter /**Graph Name Reset**. Since 1-2-3 does not provide a confirmation step for this command, be sure you do not accidentally press R while working with the /Graph Name menu.

Tip: Check the graphs in your file before you reset them. Unless Undo is enabled, you cannot recover named graphs that you have reset. If multiple files are open, observe which worksheet file is active before you execute the /Graph Name Reset command, so you do not accidentally delete the wrong graphs. A good habit is to list the graphs in the current worksheet file with the /Graph Name Table command before resetting them.

Saving Graphs to an External File

The graphs created in a worksheet file are part of the worksheet file. The graphs in a worksheet file cannot be used in other programs, such as word processors. You can, however, extract a graph to an external file and use the external file in other programs. For example, once you have saved a graph to a .PIC file, you can incorporate it into a WordPerfect 5 document.

Release 3 saves graphic images in two formats. One format is the PIC format, which stores graphs in the same format that earlier versions of 1-2-3 used. Several word processors with graphics capabilities can incorporate .PIC files into a document. Release 3 can also save the file in a Metafile format, which is used in some word processors (such as Lotus' Manuscript) to create sharper graphics images than are available in .PIC files. Metafile follows the ANSI standard for graphic images. The /Worksheet Global Default Graph command selects which format 1-2-3 uses to save graphs. When Metafile is selected, 1-2-3 saves the graphs with a .CGM file extension. When PIC is selected, 1-2-3 saves the graphs with a .PIC file extension. This command also sets the format of graph files 1-2-3 uses for the /File Erase Graph and /File List Graph commands.

Once you have selected the external graph file format, you are ready to save a file. To create a graphic image file, enter /**Graph Save**. Then provide a filename up to eight characters in length. 1-2-3 will save the current graph as a .PIC or .CGM file. If you enter an existing filename, 1-2-3 prompts you to choose between canceling the command or saving the graph over the existing file. If you want to save a graph other than the current graph, you must first make the desired graph current with /Graph Name Use.

A graph that is saved to an external file cannot be read by a worksheet file. Also, the external graphic image file contains the graph as it existed when you saved it. The graphic image file is not updated if you update the graph data.

Quitting the Graph Menu

The main Graph menu and several of its submenus remain on your screen until you choose the Quit option when you are finished with the menu. Your other option for quitting is to press ESC the number of times required to return to READY mode.

Printing Graphs

Release 3 lets you print your graphs directly from 1-2-3. With previous releases, you had to save the graph to a file, exit 1-2-3, and enter the

PrintGraph program. With Release 3 this is not necessary; you can use the /Print menus to print your graphs. You only need to learn a few new 1-2-3 commands, because the graphics features from the PrintGraph program are now set with the /Graph and /Print commands. You can also print your graphs in combination with worksheet ranges. In addition to printing directly to the printer, you can also print to an encoded file. 1-2-3 cannot print graphs to a text file.

1-2-3 must have the correct printer selected when 1-2-3 was configured. If it is not, you will need to return to Install and add the necessary drivers to the program. Appendix A provides instructions for this.

Printing a Sample

Before you print your graphs, you will want to know how 1-2-3 can use the different features of your printer. Since each printer offers its own unique bells and whistles, the 1-2-3 /Print Printer Sample command to print a sample worksheet and a sample graph, so you can see how 1-2-3 will use the printer's features. The sample graph demonstrates the current image size, rotation, and pring density settings. It also shows how 1-2-3 will print the different colors, fonts, and text sizes that you have selected. If your printer cannot print some of these features, the sample will show how 1-2-3 will approximate them. Once you have entered the command and specified the graph, select Go to start printing the sample.

Tip: View the graph before printing it. This view displays most of the graph as it is set to print and gives you a last chance to check that the graph appears as you want it.

Selecting Graphs to Print

The first step in printing a graph is selecting the graph to print. You can use either the /Print Printer Image or the /Print Printer Range command.

If you only want to print a graph, use /Print Printer Image. Enter **/Print Printer Image** and indicate if you want to print the current graph or another named graph. When you select Current, 1-2-3 prints the graph that appears when you press F10 (GRAPH). When you select Named, 1-2-3 prompts you for the name of a graph to print, and provides a list the named graphs in the active worksheet files.

If you have multiple graphs to print, or you want to also include a worksheet range in the print range, you probably want to use the /Print Printer Range. Enter **/Print Printer Range** and specify the print range. (1-2-3 displays the last selected print range.) To include a graph in a print range, enter an asterisk followed by the graph name. When you select multiple graphs and multiple worksheet ranges, each graph name and worksheet range should be separated by a semicolon or the argument separator set with /Worksheet Global Default Other International Punctuation. Some valid print ranges are *LINE;*LOG;*STAND, and A1..G10;*LINE_GRAPH;A11..G25. When the print range includes multiple graphs and ranges, 1-2-3 prints them in the order specified by the /Print Printer Range command.

Print Menu Commands for Graphs

A few of the Print menu commands only apply to graphs, and were not covered in Chapter 6, "Printing." The /Print commands specific to graphs are for setting the rotation, the image size, and the density 1-2-3 uses to print graphs. These settings do not affect worksheet print ranges. The graph printing options are in the /Print Printer Options Advanced Image menu shown here:

```
A:A1:                                                        MENU
Rotate  Image-Sz  Density  Quit
Print the graph sideways on the page
```

Once you have finished with the /Print Printer Options Advanced Image menu, select Quit to return to the previous menu level.

Selecting the Image Size

The Image-Sz option provides the settings for the size of the graphs. You may want to change the graph's size so it fits on the same page with other print ranges. When you execute this command, 1-2-3 presents three choices: Margin-Fill, Length-Fill, and Reshape. The first two keep the width-to-height ratio at 4 : 3.

- For Margin-Fill, 1-2-3 expands the graph to stretch across from the left to right margin, and adjusts the height so the width-to-height ratio remains the same. This is the default setting.

- For Length-Fill, you must provide the height that 1-2-3 uses to create the graph. 1-2-3 expands the graph from top to bottom to stretch down the number of lines on the page that you specify, and adjusts the width so the width-to-height ratio remains the same.

- The Reshape option prompts for the graph width and height that 1-2-3 stretches the graph to fill. This option changes the width-to height ratio.

The Rotate option rotates the graph within the area specified by the Image-Sz option.

1-2-3 may change the graph's size within the area selected. For example, if you select Image-Sz Length-Fill and want the graph to occupy 33 page lines (about half a page), the graph will be about 7 1/3 inches wide. If you rotate the graph, the 5 1/2 inch graph length becomes the graph width. 1-2-3 keeps the same aspect ratio, and makes the graph's height 4 1/8 inches.

Tip: Do not change the image size drastically when you reshape a graph. If you alter the width-to-length ratio drastically, the graph will appear elongated or compressed. The image will appear correctly on the screen, but it will have a somewhat bizarre appearance when printed. Changes in the width-to-height ratio are especially noticeable in pie charts.

Rotating the Image

The Rotate option lets you rotate the graph within the area you selected with the Image-Sz option. Figure 11-36 shows a graph that is rotated and one that is not rotated. Both graphs are printed on the same page by printing them in separate print requests, and not forwarding the

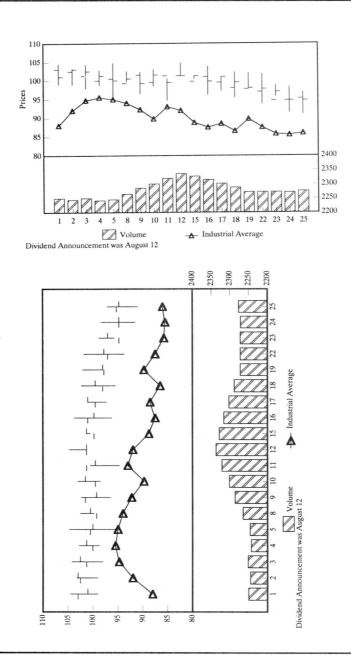

Figure 11-36. Two graphs with different rotation

page after printing the first graph. To rotate a graph like the first one in the example, you could request Rotate Yes. No is the default setting for this option. It is the selection made for printing the second graph in Figure 11-36.

Setting the Print Quality

Some printers can use different quality print levels. For example, a printer may have a draft print mode that prints quickly but does not produce the clearest image. The same printer may have a final print mode which takes longer to print but creates clearer images.

When you are creating your initial graphs, you may want to change to the draft print mode so you can print your graphs more quickly. Use the Density option to set the printer quality of the graphs. To print more quickly although not as clearly, request Draft. To print clearly although more slowly, request Final. When you execute this command using a printer that has only one print quality, the command has no effect.

Printing Selected Graphs

When 1-2-3 returns to the /Print menus, you may need to make other menu selections before selecting Go to print the graph. Once you have selected the graph you want to print (with /Print Printer Image or /Print Printer Range), and used any needed /Print Printer Options Advanced Image options, you are almost ready to print your graph. The final steps involve the other /Print commands that you learned about in Chapter 6, "Printing."

For example, if you want different margins around the graph, you must use the /Print Printer Options Margins command to set the margins the graph uses. Table 11-1 lists several /Print commands that you will use with graphs to control the output.

Finally, after you select the graphs and all their options, 1-2-3 will begin printing when you choose the Go option from the /Print Printer menu. Because Release 3 uses background printing, you can start creating your next print job as soon as Go is selected.

Moving Beyond 1-2-3's Graph Features

With Release 3's many new graphics features, you may not need any further enhancements. If you do want to explore other possibilites, there

Command	Task Performed
/Print Encoded	This command prints to a disk file containing printer-specific codes.
/Print Printer	This command prints to the printer.
/Print Printer Align	This command starts a new page at the printer's current position.
/Print Printer Clear	This command eliminates some or all of the print settings.
/Print Printer Go	This command starts printing to the printer or to a disk file.
/Print Printer Line	This command generates a line feed.
/Print Printer Options Advanced Device	This option selects which printer 1-2-3 uses.
/Print Printer Options Advanced Priority	This option assigns a priority level to the current print job.
/Print Printer Options Footer	This command adds a footer to the bottom of each page.
/Print Printer Options Header	This command adds a header to the top of each page.
/Print Printer Options Margins	This command sets the amount of blank space at the top, bottom, and sides of a printed page.
/Print Printer Options Name	This command handles named print settings that are saved with the file.
/Print Printer Options Pg-Length	This option determines the number of lines in a page of output.
/Print Printer Page	This command advances the paper to the top of the next form.
/Print Printer Range	This command determines which graphs and worksheet ranges are printed.
/Print Printer Sample	This command prints a sample worksheet and graph using the current print settings.

Table 11-1.   Print Commands Used with Graphs

are two other Lotus packages that support 1-2-3's graph definitions and offer additional enhancements. Lotus Graphwriter II offers a production feature for graphs, allowing you to define each graph once and then produce it periodically as your 1-2-3 worksheet files are updated for the current period. Although the package offers some additional graphics features, its greatest contribution is its ability to store information on all the graphs you need from many worksheet files and to produce them for you automatically, grouping as many as 100 charts in one production run.

The Lotus FreeLance Plus package provides graphics enhancements of a different sort. It lets you further customize graphs using arrows, a corporate logo, or tailoring the composite of any element of the graph. As an example, you can customize a corporate headcount report created with 1-2-3, to show the company logo. You can also change the bars representing the headcount to be composed of people figures stacked one on top of the other, where the total number of people in the stack represent the relative size of the data entry.

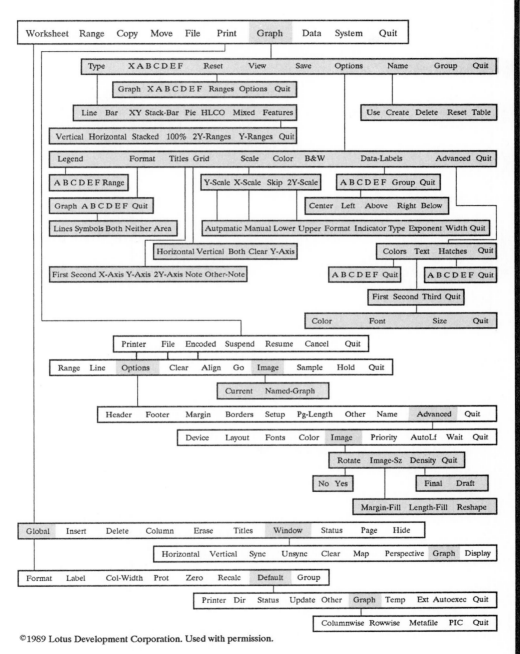

/Graph A B C D E F

Description

This is actually six different commands. Each one assigns one data range to be displayed on a graph. For instance, you would enter /**Graph A** and then specify the first graph data range, by entering or pointing to the range, or entering a range name.

Options

These commands allow you to use from one to six data ranges in your graph. To use all six data ranges, enter each of the range letters from A through F one by one and reference the data you want assigned to each one. If you are using only one data range (in a pie chart, for example), assign it to option A.

/Graph Group

Description

This command is used instead of /Graph A B C D E F when the data for the graph is in adjacent cells. This command assigns the first row or column as the X range, the second row or column as the A range, the third row or column as the B range, and so forth until the command runs out of worksheet data or graph data range names. When this command is executed, 1-2-3 prompts for the worksheet data that you want divided into graph data ranges. You can enter the range addresses a range name, or point to the cells you want to include.

Options

This command has two options, Columnwise and Rowwise which determine whether the worksheet data is divided into graph data ranges according to columns or rows.

/Graph Name Create

Description

The /Graph Name Create command assigns a name to the current set of graph settings and stores them with your worksheet. If you want this name and its settings available during your next 1-2-3 session, be sure to save the worksheet with /File Save. This command is used for creating a new named graph, and for saving the updates made to a named graph.

Options

Your only option for this command is the name you select. The name follows the rules for range names rather than filenames; you can use up to 15 characters. If you want to save the graph in another worksheet file, include the filename delimiters (< < > >) and the worksheet filename before the graph name. A graph created with this command is saved with the worksheet when the /File Save command is executed.

Note

1-2-3 does not warn you if you select a name that has already been assigned to another graph. If you do this, it will overwrite the existing settings with the current settings without asking you.

/Graph Name Delete

Description

The /Graph Name Delete command removes unneeded graph names one by one from the worksheet. Since this process frees up some memory space, it is wise to purge graph names and their associated settings when you no longer need them.

Options

Your only option for this command is the name you select to delete. 1-2-3 lists the current graph names below the prompt. You can select one of these names or type a name.

/Graph Name Reset

Description

This command removes all graph names and their settings from a worksheet file. Since there is no cautionary prompt before the deletion, you risk losing all your graph definitions if you accidentally choose Reset from the Graph Name menu. Be careful not to accidentally press R when you are working within the /Graph Name command.

Options

There are no options for this command.

/Graph Name Table

Description

This command creates a worksheet table that lists the named graphs in the current file. For each named graph it also lists the graph type and first line title, if any.

Options

The only option for this command is the location of the table the command creates. When this command prompts you for a location for the graph name table, enter or point to any cell in an active file where you want the table. This command creates the table starting at the selected cell, writing over existing information.

/Graph Name Use

Description

The /Graph Name Use command allows you to choose a graph name from the list associated with the current worksheet file. The graph selected becomes the current graph and appears on the screen.

Options

You can either type the graph name or point to it in the list that 1-2-3 displays.

/Graph Options Advanced Colors

Description

The /Graph Options Advanced Colors command specifies the color for a data range, or hides a range. If the printer can print colors, this command sets the colors the printer uses. If this command is not used to select the colors, 1-2-3 uses the colors 2 through 7 for the ranges A through F.

Options

When this command is executed, it displays the letters A through F, representing the six data ranges for which you can select colors. After you enter the data range, you can select one of the options discussed below. Then 1-2-3 returns to the /Graph Options Advanced Colors menu. Select Quit to return to the /Graph Options Advanced menu.

1 — 8   This option selects the color for the entire range that you named. The actual colors available depend on the monitor.

Hide   This option hides the data range selected. To redisplay a hidden range, assign a color to the range.

Range   Use this option to select the colors for the individual data values in a range. When this option is selected, 1-2-3 prompts you for the cells containing the color range. You can enter the color range by entering the range address or a range name, or by pointing to the cells. The color range contains as many cells as the data range, and contains color code values 1 to 14. If a value in a color range is negative, the corresponding value in the data range is hidden. This Range option has six more color selections than the other /Graph Options Advanced Colors command options. The first value in the color range sets the color of the legend for the data range. If the graph is a pie chart, 1-2-3 only uses the settings for this command when a B range is not selected and the graph is displayed in color.

/Graph Options Advanced Hatches

Description

Use the /Graph Options Advanced Hatches command to specify the hatch pattern for a data range in area, bar, stacked bar, HLCO, and mixed graphs, or for data values in pie charts. If the printer cannot print colors, this command is not used to select the hatch patterns the printer uses. If this command does not select the hatch patterns, 1-2-3 uses the hatch patterns 2 through 7 for the ranges A through F. When this command is combined with /Graph Options Advanced Colors, it displays (and prints if possible) the hatch patterns in colors.

Options

When this command is executed, it displays the letters A through F, representing the six data ranges for which you can select a hatch pattern. Once you enter the data range, you can select one of the options discussed below. Then 1-2-3 returns to the /Graph Options Advanced Hatches menu. Select Quit to return to the /Graph Options Advanced menu.

1 — 8   This option selects the hatch pattern for the entire range that you named. As each option is highlighted, 1-2-3 displays a description of the hatch pattern name on the next line.

Range   Use this option to select the hatch patterns for the individual data values in a range. When this option is selected, 1-2-3 prompts you for the cells containing the hatch range. You can enter the hatch range by entering the range address pattern or a range name, or by pointing to the cells. The hatch range contains as many cells as the data range, and contains hatch code values 1 to 14. If a value in a hatch pattern range is negative, the corresponding value in the data range is hidden. This Range option has six more hatch patterns selections than the other /Graph Options Advanced Colors command options. The additional 6 hatch patterns are grey scales. The first value in the hatch pattern range sets the hatch pattern of the legend for the data range. If the graph is a pie chart, 1-2-3 only uses the settings for this command when a B range is not selected and the graph is displayed in hatch pattern.

/Graph Options Advanced Quit

Description

The /Graph Options Advanced Quit command leaves the /Graph Options Advanced sticky menu and returns to the /Graph Options menu.

Options

There are no options for this command.

/Graph Options Advanced Text

Description

The /Graph Options Advanced Text command selects the color, fonts and sizes of text for various locations in a graph. This command divides the text in a graph into three groups. The first group includes the first line of the graph title. The second group includes the second line of the graph title, the axis titles, and the legend text. The third group includes the scale indicators, axes labels, data labels, and footnotes.

Options

When this command is executed, it prompts for the text group for which you want to set the text color, font, or size. Once the data range is selected, this command has the following options.

Color This option specifies the color for the text group or hides it. The selections of 1 through 8 match the color selections of the /Graph Options Advanced Colors command. The actual colors available depend on the monitor. Choose the Hide selection to hide the text group. Hide works whether the graph displays in color or monochrome.

Font This option specifies the font for the text group. When this option is selected, 1-2-3 prompts for the font number (1 through 8) or Default, which uses the default for the text group. The default for the first text group is font 1; the default for the second and third group is font 3. The selections of 1 through 8 match the /Print Printer Options Other Advanced Fonts command. This option only changes how 1-2-3 prints the graph's text, since it always uses the same predetermined font for displaying the graph. The way the fonts print depends upon the printer.

Size This option selects the character size 1-2-3 uses for the text groups. When this option is selected, 1-2-3 prompts for the size number (1 through 9) or default, which uses the default for the text group. The default for the first text group is 7, the default for the second text group is 4, and the default for the third text group is 2. Since 1-2-3 only has three text sizes for displaying graphs, it displays graphs with the text sizes 1 to 3 as small-sized characters, text sizes 4 to 6 as medium-sized characters, and 7 to 9 as large-sized characters. The way the character sizes print depends on the printer and the font. 1-2-3 automatically reduces the text size if it needs to fit more text on the graph, and truncates what still does not fit.

Quit This option leaves the sticky menu and returns to the /Graph Options Advanced Text menu.

/Graph Options B&W

Description

This command displays graphs in one color. To differentiate between the bars on a bar chart, 1-2-3 automatically adds hatch mark patterns when the B&W option is in effect. You can elect to choose hatch mark patterns for a pie chart by adding the codes for the patterns you wish to use. The codes should be placed on the worksheet and referenced as the B data range. To print a graph in color, even when the monitor is monochrome, you must use the /Graph Options Color command. If the printer can only print in one color, you do not need to change the color setting to print the graph.

Options

There are no options for this command.

/Graph Options Color

Description

This command displays your graphs in color. If your printer cannot print the graph in color, 1-2-3 converts the colors to hatch patterns automatically.

Options

There are no options for this command.

/Graph Options Data-Labels

Description

The /Graph Options Data-Labels command permits you to add specific labels to a range of data points. 1-2-3 will obtain these data labels from the range of worksheet cells you specify.

Options

You can choose where to place the data labels in relation to your data points. Your options are Center, Above, Left, Right, and Below. First 1-2-3 prompts for the name of the data range to which you want to assign labels; the range choices are A through F, or Group. If Group is selected, this command assigns data labels one by one to data ranges A through F until the command runs out of label data or graph data names. When you specify the data range name, you are prompted for the range containing the data labels. The labels range should contain the same number of cells as the data values selected for the graph data range. After you enter the labels range, the command prompts for the labels' placement relative to the data point. For line graphs, the choices are Center, Left, Above, Right and Below; for bar graphs, the choices are Above and Below. The other selections are equivalent to Above. When you are finished assigning data labels, select Quit to return to the /Graph Options menu.

Note

In a line graph, you can use data labels as the only markers for your data points. To do this, choose /Graph Options Format Neither to remove lines and symbols.

/Graph Options Format

Description

The /Graph Options Format command lets you select the type of line or XY graph you will create. You can also choose whether data points are shown as symbols, are connected with a line, or are marked with both symbols and a line (or neither). An additional option makes a line graph an area graph.

Options

Your first choice is the range that the format will apply to. Specify Graph as the range if you want your selection used for all ranges on the graph. Or select a specific data range by entering a letter from A through F. Then select among the following options:

Lines   This option shows the data points connected by a line without marking the data points.

Symbols   This option shows only symbols, with no connecting line. 1-2-3 uses a different symbol for each of the ranges.

Both   This option shows both the symbols and a connecting line.

Neither   This option shows neither lines nor symbols. This option is used in conjunction with the Data-Labels option when you center a data label to mark a point and do not want any other marking on the graph.

Area   This option creates the graph with lines. It fills the space between the lines (for each data range and the X axis) with a different color or hatch pattern. If more than one data range is formatted, 1-2-3 stacks the data—even if /Graph Type Features Stacked is set to No. An area graph treats negative numbers as 0.

/Graph Options Grid

Description

The /Graph Options Grid command adds vertical lines, horizontal lines, or both to a graph. These lines start at the markers on the X or Y axis and extend upward or to the right, depending on whether you choose Vertical, Horizontal, or Both. Additional options clear the existing grid lines or set the origination point for horizontal grid lines. The lines can greatly aid in the interpretation of points on the graph.

Options

The options for /Graph Options Grid determine whether the grid lines are generated in one or both directions.

Horizontal

This option adds horizontal lines that extend across from the Y axis. These lines are effective with bar graphs, since they help you interpret the value for the top of each bar. Horizontal grid lines originate from the Y axis, the second Y axis, or both, depending upon the Y-Axis setting.

Vertical   This option adds vertical lines that start at the X axis and extend upward. They are most effective with an XY or line graph; they tend to detract from the clarity of a bar graph.

Both   This option adds lines in both directions at once. The lines form a grid pattern on the graph. Horizontal grid lines will originate from the Y axis, the second Y axis, or both depending upon the Y-Axis setting. Vertical lines start at the X axis.

Clear   This option eliminates grid lines that you have added to a graph.

Y-Axis   This option determines whether the horizontal lines created with the Horizontal or Both options originate from the first Y axis, the second Y axis, or both. The default is the first Y axis.

Note

Rotating the graph axes rotates the grid lines. If a graph is rotated, this command starts grid lines from the X and Y axis as set with this command, although the horizontal line setting appears vertical and the vertical line setting appears horizontal.

/Graph Options Legend

Description

This command displays legends at the bottom of your graph to describe the data represented by the different graph data ranges.

Options

You can choose any one of the ranges (A through F) each time you request this command. If you select Range, you will select the legends for all data ranges. You can either type in a legend or reference a cell address containing the legend you wish to use. With the Range option, you must select a legend range containing up to six legends for the six data ranges. While this command does not limit the number of characters that you can enter for a legend or in a cell referenced for the legend, the practical limit on the legend size is based on what 1-2-3 can fit in the graph. The number of characters a legend can contain depends on the number of legends, and the amount of text in each legend.

Note

The /Graph Options Legend Range command can also be used to assign legends to the first six pie slices in a pie chart. The first cell in the legend range is assigned to the first slice. One by one, cell contents are assigned to pie slices until all the cells in the legend range are used, or the sixth pie slice is assigned a legend, or the last pie slice is assigned a legend.

/Graph Options Quit

Description

The /Graph Options Quit command leaves the /Graph Options sticky menu and returns to the /Graph menu.

Options

There are no options for this command.

/Graph Options Scale Skip

Description

This command permits you to remove the congestion that can occur when you assign labels to be displayed along the X axis. The skip factor you specify lets you use only some of the labels in the range. If you specify a skip factor of 3, for example, only every third label will be used.

Options

You can specify any number from 1 to 8192 for the skip factor. The default is 1, meaning that 1-2-3 uses every label in the range.

/Graph Options Scale X-Scale

Description

This command permits you to let 1-2-3 choose the scale for the X axis or, alternatively, to choose the scale yourself. These options only affect XY graphs.

Options

The options for the /Graph Options Scale X-Scale command are as follows:

Automatic   This setting is the default. It lets 1-2-3 determine the proper lower and upper range of the X axis.

Manual   This option informs 1-2-3 that you want to determine the scale range.

Lower   This is the lower limit or the smallest value that can be shown on your scale. You must define it when you select Manual.

Upper   This is the upper limit or the highest value that can be shown on your scale. You must define it when you select Manual.

Format   This option allows you to select a display format (Currency, Percent, or the like) for the numeric values represented on the scale.

Indicator   This option permits you to turn off the size indicator for the scale or create your own. The default is Yes, allowing 1-2-3 to display indicators like "Thousands." Another choice, None, hides the indicator. The third choice, Manual, prompts for a different indicator, which you can type in or specify with a backslash and a cell address containing the text you want as the indicator.

Type   This option selects a linear or logarithmic scale for the X axis. The default is Standard, or linear. Select Logarithmic when you want the scale increments to increase by the power of 10. For example, the first increment is 1, the second increment is 10, and the third increment is 100.

Exponent   This option selects an order of magnitude for a scale. The order of magnitude is the power of 10 by which you multiply the numbers in the X axis to determine the values they represent. For example, if the scale has an exponent of 6, the numbers on the X axis scale must be multiplied by one million (10 to the sixth power) to determine the number they represent. This option has two selections. When Automatic is selected, 1-2-3 automatically determines the appropriate exponent for the graph. When Manual is selected, 1-2-3 prompts for the power of 10 for the exponent. 1-2-3 accepts any number between −95 and +95. If the order of magnitude is not 0, 1-2-3 adds an indicator that appears if /Graph Options Scale X-Scale Indicator is set to Yes.

Width   This option sets the maximum width of the X axis scale numbers. This option has two selections. Automatic lets 1-2-3 set the width for the X axis scale numbers. Manual prompts you for a number between 1 and 50 for the X axis scale number width. 1-2-3 displays the scale numbers as asterisks when the width is insufficient for the scale numbers, or when the scale numbers would extend for more than one-third of the graph's area.

Quit   This option returns you to the Graph Options menu.

/Graph Options Scale Y-Scale

Description

This command permits you to let 1-2-3 choose the scale for the Y axis or, alternatively, to choose the scale yourself.

Options

The options for the /Graph Options Scale Y-Scale command are as follows:

Automatic   This setting is the default. It lets 1-2-3 determine the proper lower and upper range of the Y axis.

Manual   This option informs 1-2-3 that you want to determine the scale range.

Lower   This is the lower limit or the smallest value that can be shown on your scale. You must define it when you select Manual.

Upper   This is the upper limit or the highest value that can be shown on your scale. You must define it when you select Manual.

Format   This option allows you to select a display format (Currency, Percent, or the like) for the numeric values represented on the scale.

Indicator   This option permits you to turn off the size indicator for the scale or create your own. The default is Yes, allowing 1-2-3 to display indicators like "Thousands." Another choice, None, hides the indicator. The third choice, Manual, prompts for a different indicator, which you can type in or specify with a backslash and a cell address containing the text you want as the indicator.

Type   This option selects a linear or logarithmic scale for the Y axis. The default is Standard, or linear. Select Logarithmic when you want the scale increments to increase by the power of 10. For example, the first increment is 1, the second increment is 10, and the third increment is 100.

Exponent   This option selects an order of magnitude for a scale. The order of magnitude is the power of 10 by which you multiply the numbers in the Y axis to determine the values they represent. For example, if the scale has an exponent of 6, the numbers on the Y axis scale must be multiplied by one million (10 to the sixth power) to determine the number they represent. This option has two selections.

When Automatic is selected, 1-2-3 automatically determines the appropriate exponent for the graph. When Manual is selected, 1-2-3 prompts for a integer between −95 and +95 representing the power of 10 for the exponent. If the order of magnitude is not 0, 1-2-3 adds an indicator that appears if /Graph Options Scale Y-Scale Indicator is set to Yes.

Width   This option sets the maximum width of the Y axis scale numbers. This option has two selections. Automatic lets 1-2-3 set the width for the Y axis scale numbers. Manual prompts you for a number between 1 and 50 for the Y axis scale number width. 1-2-3 displays the scale numbers as asterisks when the width is insufficient for the scale numbers or when the scale numbers would extend for more than one-third of the graph's area.

Quit   This option returns you to the Graph Options menu.

/Graph Options Scale 2Y-Scale

Description

This command permits you to let 1-2-3 choose the scale for the second Y axis or, alternatively, to choose the scale yourself.

Options

The options for the /Graph Options Scale 2Y-Scale command are as follows:

Automatic   This setting is the default. It lets 1-2-3 determine the proper lower and upper range of the second y axis.

Manual   This option informs 1-2-3 that you want to determine the scale range.

Lower   This is the lower limit or the smallest value that can be shown on your scale. You must define it when you select Manual.

Upper   This is the upper limit or the highest value that can be shown on your scale. You must define it when you select Manual.

Format   This option allows you to select a display format (Currency, Percent, or the like) for the numeric values represented on the scale.

Indicator   This option permits you to turn off the size indicator for the scale or create your own. The default is Yes, allowing 1-2-3 to display indicators like "Thousands." Another choice, None, hides the indicator. The third choice, Manual, prompts for a different indicator, which you can type in, or specify with a backslash and a cell address containing the text you want as the indicator.

Type   This option selects a linear or logarithmic scale for the second Y axis. The default is Standard, or linear. Select Logarithmic when you want the scale increments to increase by the power of 10. For example, the first increment is 1, the second increment is 10, and the third increment is 100.

Exponent   This option selects an order of magnitude for a scale. The order of magnitude is the power of 10 by which you multiply the numbers in the second Y axis to determine the values they represent. For example, if the scale has an exponent of 6, the numbers on the second Y axis scale must be multiplied by one million (10 to the sixth power) to determine the number they represent. This option has two selections. When Automatic is selected, 1-2-3 automatically determines the appropriate exponent for the graph. When Manual is selected, 1-2-3 prompts for a number between −95 and +95 which represents the power of 10 for the exponent. If the order of magnitude is not 0, 1-2-3 adds an indicator that appears if /Graph Options Scale 2Y-Scale Indicator is set to Yes.

Width   This option sets the maximum width of the second Y axis scale numbers. This option has two selections. Automatic lets 1-2-3 set the width for the second Y axis scale numbers. Manual prompts you for a number between 1 and 50 for the second Y axis scale number width.

1-2-3 displays the scale numbers as asterisks when the width is insufficient for the scale numbers, or when the scale numbers would extend for more than one-third of the graph's area.

Quit   This option exits the command and returns you to the Graph Options menu.

/Graph Options Titles

Description

This command permits you to add titles to your graph to improve its clarity and readability. Your titles will be limited to the characters 1-2-3 can fit on the graph. Referencing a stored title requires that you enter a backslash (\) and a cell address containing the title.

Options

You can add titles at the top of your graph, along the axes, or at the bottom of your graph with the options available. Your choices are as follows:

First   The label you enter after this choice will be centered at the top of your graph.

Second   Your label entry for this option will be centered and placed immediately below the label shown by the First option.

X-Axis   This option places a title below the X axis.

Y-Axis   This option places your entry vertically to the left of the Y axis.

2Y-Axis   This option places your entry vertically to the right of the second Y axis.

Note   This option places your entry below the graph, starting at the left side of the graph area.

Other-Note   This option places your entry below the text entered for the Note option.

Quit   This option returns to the /Graph Options menu.

/Graph Quit

Description

This command exits the Graph menu and returns you to the worksheet READY mode.

Options

There are no options for this command.

/Graph Reset

Description

The /Graph Reset command cancels graph settings in a worksheet file that you selected in a previous session.

Options

You can choose to cancel all or some of the graph settings with the options for this command. Your choices are as follows:

Graph   This option cancels all graph settings.

X   This option cancels the X data values.

A-F   Choosing one of this set of letter options cancels the data range for the letter selected.

Ranges   This option cancels the data ranges and data label settings for the X, A, B, C, D, E, and F data ranges.

Options   This option cancels the selections made with /Graph Options commands.

Quit   This option tells 1-2-3 that you have canceled all the settings you want to eliminate and returns you to the previous menu.

/Graph Save

Description

The /Graph Save command saves the current graph picture in a .CGM or .PIC file separate from your worksheet. It can be used by other programs, but not by 1-2-3. The extension this command uses is set by the /Worksheet Global Default Graph command.

Options

After selecting this command, you have the choice of entering a filename or choosing one from the list that 1-2-3 presents. If you choose to use an existing .CGM or .PIC filename, 1-2-3 prompts you to confirm that you do want to reuse (and therefore overwrite) that file, or else to cancel your request. If you want to use an extension other than .CGM or .PIC, specify it with the filename.

/Graph Type

Description

The /Graph Type command lets you pick from seven different formats for displaying your graph data. You can easily change from one format to another without any alterations other than selecting another type. If you do not select a graph type, 1-2-3 uses a line graph. Use the other selections in this command to add graph enhancements. By selecting a graph type without selecting graph data, and then moving the cell pointer to the upper left corner of the data that you want to graph, you can create an automatic graph if your data is in the proper format. To view the automatic graph, press F10 (GRAPH) or use the /Graph View command.

Options

This command provides seven basic graph types, and a Features option to add other enhancements to the basic graph. These options are as follows:

Line   This graph plots the points of a data range and connects them with a line. The default is to use both symbols and a line on the graph. Symbols mark each point, and a line joins the data points. You can use the /Graph Options Format command to change the display so that it uses just a line or just symbols if you prefer. Up to six separate lines, displaying six data ranges, can be generated on one graph. A line graph can also become an area graph (one that fills the area between the data values with a color or hatch pattern) if you select the Area option under the /Graph Options Format command.

Bar   This graph uses up to six sets of vertical bars to represent the data ranges selected. 1-2-3 uses hatch mark patterns or colors to distinguish the different data ranges.

XY   This graph pairs X range values with values from the A through F data ranges. You can use the /Graph Options Format command to connect the points with a line or display them as symbols. With this kind of graph, 1-2-3 generates a numeric scale for the X, as well as the Y axis.

Stacked-Bar   For one data range, a stacked bar graph will appear the same as an ordinary bar graph. Graphing several data ranges lets you compared them differently. Rather than adding the second set of bars to the right of the first, the stacked bar graph option stacks the second set on top of the first, the third on top of the second, and so on. The total height of a bar thus indicates the total of the values for that category. The different bars in a stack are distinguished by hatch patterns or colors.

Pie   A pie chart is used to compare the size of each of several categories relative to the whole. Each category shown in the pie will be represented by a wedge whose size is proportional to its value compared with the values for the other categories shown in the chart. Only one set of data, the A range, can be shown. A B range can be used to indicate a range of colors or hatch patterns with number codes from 1 to 14, or wedges that are hidden, or wedges that are exploded (removed from the pie and shown as a separate slice). If 100 is added to the code in the B range, the pie slice represented by that code is exploded. A negative number in the B range hides the wedge. A C range can be added to remove the percentages from the pie slice labels.

HLCO   A HLCO chart creates a High-Low-Close-Open graph used to graph financial commodities over time. For each set of data values (such as each day you are recording stock prices), the HLCO has a line from the high to the low value. A projection to the left indicates the open value; a projection to the right indicates the close value. 1-2-3 uses the A data range as the high values, the B data range as the low values, the C data range as the close data range, and the D data range as the open data range. The E range appears as a bar graph below the HLCO graph for the A, B, C, and D ranges, and is assigned to the second Y axis. The F range is graphed as a line graph with A through D ranges. An HLCO graph must have at least an A and B range, or an E and F range. While this graph is primarily for financial commodities, it can also be used for graphing ranges such as statistical data showing the high, low, and average values for X range values.

Mixed   A mixed graph displays the A, B, and C data ranges as bar graphs, and the D, E, and F data ranges as line graphs. The bar graph data uses different hatch patterns or colors to distinguish the data ranges; the line graph data uses lines and symbols to indicate the data ranges. The colors, hatch patterns, lines, and symbols can be changed with the /Graph Options commands.

Features   This option is not a graph type. It creates variations of the other basic graph types. The Vertical feature orients the graph axes so the X axis is horizontal and the Y axes are vertical; this is the default orientation. The Horizontal feature orients the graph axes so the X axis is vertical and the Y axes are horizontal. The Stacked feature, if set to Yes, stacks the data ranges of line, bar, mixed, and XY graphs on top of each other; the default is No. The 100% feature displays the data values as the percentage of their total value, and the Y axis markings as percentages, if set to Yes; the default is No. The 2Y-Ranges feature assigns ranges to the second Y axis range. The Y-Ranges feature assigns ranges to the first Y axis range. For both 2Y-Ranges and Y-Ranges you must select a graph range (A-F) or all of the graph ranges (Graph). Ranges belong to the first Y axis unless assigned to the second Y axis. Selecting Quit returns you to the /Graph Type Features menu; selecting Quit again returns to the /Graph menu.

/Graph View

Description

The /Graph View command displays the graph that you have defined by selecting data ranges and a graph type. If you have not defined data to graph and you invoke /Graph View, 1-2-3 attempts to create an automatic graph using the worksheet data, starting with the cell pointer's position. If 1-2-3 cannot create an automatic graph, the screen appears blank when you select this command. To return to the Graph menu when you are through with the View option, press any key. You can also view the graph by pressing F10 (GRAPH). Using the F10 (GRAPH) function key lets you see the graph at any time, including while you are using other Graph menus. Pressing any key returns you to where you were before you pressed F10 (GRAPH).

Options

This command does not have any options.

Note

If your 1-2-3 package is installed for a graphics device that your monitor cannot support, your screen will appear blank when you invoke /Graph View. To correct the problem, go back to the installation process described in Appendix A, "Installing 1-2-3." Similarly, if you attempt to use the package on a system without graphics support, entering /Graph View will cause the screen to appear blank. In both cases you can press any key to return to the Graph menu.

/Graph X

Description

The /Graph X command is used to label the points on the X axis for a line or bar graph. For a pie chart, the X values provide labels for the pie segments; for an XY chart they provide values to plot against the Y values. The labels assigned to the points must be stored in worksheet cells and specified with a range name or a range address, or by pointing to the cells you wish to use.

Options

There are no options for this command. If the labels you choose contain too many characters, 1-2-3 uses two rows to display the X labels, alternating the X labels between the rows. If the labels still have too many characters, 1-2-3 truncates the X labels. You can use /Graph Options Scale Skip to tell 1-2-3 not to use every label.

/Print Printer Image

Description

This command selects a graph to print. Once a graphics image is selected, you can use the other /Print commands to control how 1-2-3 prints the graph. Most of the /Print commands have the same effect for graphs as for worksheet ranges. If the current printer cannot print graphs, 1-2-3 leaves the space for the graph blank. Once a graph is selected to print, 1-2-3 keeps the graphics image in memory so you can print the graph again without reselecting it. Graphs can be printed to encoded files and to the printer, but not to text files.

Options

This command has two options: Current and Named-Graph. The Current option prints the current (active) graph. The Named-Graph option prompts you for a graph name and displays the named graphs in the current worksheet file. You can select a listed graph name or type a different one.

Note

You can also print a graph by entering an asterisk and the graph name after invoking the /Print Printer Range command. This option is for printing a combination of worksheet ranges and graphs.

/Print Printer Options Advanced Image Density

Description

This command sets the density of the points that 1-2-3 uses to print the graph. This command sets the printer quality, in order to change the speed at which the printer prints the graphs.

Options

This command has two options: Final and Draft. Final prints a higher quality graph, but takes longer. Draft prints a lower quality graph, but prints more quickly. If a printer can only print using one quality level, this command has no effect.

/Print Printer Options Advanced Image Image-Sz

Description

The /Print Printer Options Advanced Image Image-Sz command determines the size of the printed graph. The graph can be sized according to the height or width, while maintaining the same height-to-width ratio. This command can also set the height and width, which can change the height-to-width ratio.

Options

This command has three options: Length-Fill, Margin-Fill, and Reshape. If the values for the height and width exceed the printer's capabilities, 1-2-3 automatically resizes the graph to fit within the printer's width. The graph's default width-to-length ratio is 4:3, although the Reshape option will change it.

Length-Fill   This option expands the graph down to fill the graph length you specify, and adjusts the width to have the same length-to-width ratio. This option prompts you for the number of standard lines that the graph should use. Entering a number greater than the page length will use the number of lines per page for the graph, and will center the graph horizontally and vertically on the page.

Margin-Fill   This option expands the graph to fill the area between the left and right margin. This option adjusts the length to have the same length-to-width ratio. 1-2-3 centers the graph horizontally on the page. This option is the default.

Reshape   This option expands the graph to fill the length and width you specify. This option changes the length-to-width ratio. You are prompted for the number of standard lines and the number of characters across that the graph should use. Entering a higher number than can fit on a page will center the graph horizontally and vertically on the page.

/Print Printer Options Advanced Image Quit

Description

This command returns you to the /Print Printer Options Advanced menu.

Options

There are no options for this command.

/Print Printer Options Advanced Image Rotate

Description

The /Print Printer Options Advanced Image Rotate command rotates the entire graph. This is different from the /Graph Type Features Vertical and /Graph Type Features Horizontal command which select the orientation of the X axis and the Y axes in a graph. If a graph is rotated, 1-2-3 changes the image size, since the width and length of the graph are perpendicular to the width and length of the paper. If the printer cannot rotate graphs, this command has no effect.

Options

When the No option is selected (the default) the top of the graph is parallel to the top of the page. When the Yes option is selected, the top of the graph is parallel to the left side of the page.

/Worksheet Global Default Graph

Description

This command provides two different sets of features. First, it lets you decide the default graphic image file extension. This is the extension used by the /Graph Save, /File List Graph, and /File Erase Graph commands. Second, this command lets you determine how 1-2-3 uses worksheet data to create automatic graphs.

Options

This command has five options: Columnwise, Rowwise, Metafile, PIC, and Quit. The first four options form two pairs, with each member of the pair having an effect opposite to that of the other.

Columnwise   This option divides a worksheet data range into graph data ranges according to columns. This is the default.

Rowwise   This option divides a worksheet data graph range into graph data ranges according to rows.

Metafile   This option sets the default graphic image file extension to .CGM and saves graphic images in a Metafile format.

PIC   This option sets the default graphic image file extension to .PIC and saves graphic images in a picture file format. This is the default.

Quit   This option returns to the /Worksheet Global Default menu.

/Worksheet Window Graph

Description

This command splits the display screen in half. In the left half, 1-2-3 displays the current worksheet. In the right half, 1-2-3 displays the current graph. As the worksheet data changes, 1-2-3 updates the graph concurrently. The Graph window remains in effect for all worksheets and active files until another /Worksheet Window, or /File Retrieve, or /Worksheet Erase command is executed.

Options

There are no options for this command.

Note

Creating a Graph window does not create an automatic graph. To create an automatic graph, you must position the cell pointer and use the /Graph View command or F10 (GRAPH) key. When you return to the worksheet, the automatic graph will appear in the Graph window.

Keyboard Macros

Many people are intimidated by macros because they have tried unsuccessfully to work with them. Macros, however, are a powerful and flexible feature of 1-2-3. They can be quite simple to master if you use a step-by-step approach and learn the most basic macros first, before attempting the more sophisticated variety. The new Release 3 keystroke recorder feature and other macro enhancements make mastery of macros easier than ever. You will also be able to improve your success ratio if you follow the procedures for creating macros outlined in this chapter and Chapter 13, "Command Language Macros."

Types of Macros

1-2-3's *keyboard alternative macros* can be used to automate printing, formatting, or any other task that is accomplished with menu selections. This type of macro provides an alternative to typing from the keyboard. Keyboard macros are good to begin with if you are new to macros, since they contain familiar keystroke commands. They can also provide a wealth of time-saving features. If you follow the instructions in this chapter, you will find yourself creating keyboard alternative macros that are successful the first time you try them.

The second type of macro uses commands beyond menu selections. These commands are available as keyword options from 1-2-3's macro command language. With *command language macros* you can read and write records to a file, create your own menus, utilize iterative loops, and alter the order in which commands are processed. 1-2-3's command language is a full programming language that functions like other programming languages, to allow you to develop complete applications. With new Release 3 macro commands, you will even be able to create data entry forms for your 1-2-3 database applications. Chapter 13 will cover all the features of 1-2-3's command language.

Both types of macros can be stored in the worksheet file where they are used, or in a separate file if you want to create a library of macros for use with many worksheets. At a minimum, macros should be placed on a separate sheet of the file to minimize the risk of change due to alterations in the remainder of the worksheet entries. With Release 3, you can easily build macro library files that support many applications. Since 1-2-3 can access macros in any sheet in memory, you can open a macro library at the beginning of a session and utilize it throughout.

Keyboard Macros

Like all macros, a keyboard alternative macro is nothing more than a column of label entries that have a name assigned to them. The contents of the labels are the sequence of keystrokes that you want 1-2-3 to execute for you.

After all your label entries are stored in a column, you will name the top cell in the column with the /Range Name Create or the /Range Name Labels command. You can use any name to name a macro in Release 3, as long as it conforms to the rules of range names and falls within the 15-character limit. The special names consisting of a backslash and a single letter that were required in earlier releases are still accepted. These special names allow you to execute a keyboard macro by pressing the ALT key in combination with the letter used as the macro's name, but these letters are not very descriptive.

To execute a macro without the special backslash-letter combination name, press ALT-F3 (RUN) and highlight the macro name in the list or type the name. In both cases you will need to press ENTER to start macro execution. The steps for creating and executing keyboard macros are summarized for you in the box entitled "The ABCs of Keyboard Macros."

The ABCs of Keyboard Macros

1. Plan the task you want the macro to perform.

2. Erase the keystroke recorder with ALT-F2 (RECORD) Erase. Execute the steps required for your task and enter ALT-F2 (RECORD) Copy. To copy the keystrokes to your macro, move to the entry in the recorder screen, press the TAB key, move to the last keystroke, and press ENTER. Move to a cell at the top of an empty column in the worksheet and press ENTER. (If you prefer, you can simply type the macro keystrokes you want into a series of labels in a column of worksheet cells.)

3. Edit the label entries in the macro column and make any required changes.

4. Record the macro name one cell to the left of the top cell in the macro column. Use the backslash key and a single letter if you want to execute the macro with a single key combination. Or you can use any valid range name.

5. Use /Range Name Labels Right to apply the name to the macro.

6. Save the worksheet containing the macro.

7. Execute the macro using the ALT key plus the macro letter name, like \s. If you used a range name, use ALT-F3 (RUN), highlight the name, and press ENTER.

Tip: Avoid macro names that duplicate cell addresses, existing range names, and 1-2-3's keywords. Stay away from macro names like A10, @SUM, and {DOWN}. With so many other meaningful names from which to select, it is easy to avoid names that will cause confusion.

Recording the Keystrokes

There are several options for storing macro keystrokes in Release 3. You can type them in a cell as label entries, or you can use the entries in 1-2-3's buffer, which records your keystrokes. To utilize any of the 512 characters that 1-2-3 records in the keystroke recorder, you must first copy them to a cell or play them back directly from the buffer. First, you will look at the typing alternative. You will need this technique to modify existing macros, and the procedure will give you an appreciation for the work that the new keystroke recorder does for you.

Typing the Required Keystrokes

When you want to store a menu request in a macro, begin the sequence with a single quotation mark, so it will be treated as a label. This prevents 1-2-3 from executing a menu request immediately. Then enter the keystrokes. Indicate the request for a menu command with a slash, and record each of the menu commands by entering the first letter of the menu choice. For instance, to enter the keystrokes necessary to view a Worksheet Status screen, type '/ws or '/WS in the cell (case is not important).

Tip: If you make a mistake throughout a long macro repeatedly, the quickest correction method is the Replace option of /Range Search.

In addition to specifying menu selections, you will sometimes have to indicate an ENTER key press. The ENTER key is represented in a macro by the tilde mark ($\sim$).

Filenames or range names should be entered in full. As an example, to store the characters needed to retrieve a file named SALES from the default drive, enter **'/FRSALES˜** or **'/FRsales˜** in the macro cell. Although you can use all upper- or lowercase for the keystroke entries, a consistent combination can help to clarify range names, filenames, cell addresses, and menu selections.

Tip: Beware of missing tildes. The single most frequent cause of mistakes in macros created by novice users is missing tildes. After recording the correct menu selections, it is easy to forget that you press ENTER at certain points when executing a command sequence from the keyboard. Even one missing tilde will cause the macro to malfunction.

To correct a macro once it is entered, you can use the F2 (EDIT) key with the cell pointer on the cell containing the macro code. Since the macro code is nothing more than a label entry, special techniques are not required for making changes.

Recording Special Keys

There are a number of special keyboard keys, like the function keys and cell pointer movement keys, that you will want to include in your macros. These keys and the macro keywords that stand for them are listed in the box called "Special Keys in Macro Commands." Note that all the keywords are enclosed in curly brackets or braces ({ }). There are many new keys in this list when compared against prior releases, due to Release 3's ability to work with multiple worksheets and multiple files. Whether you use the keystroke recorder feature to enter your macros or type them in, you will need to be familiar with the effect of each of these keys so that you can make intelligent modifications to existing macros.

There is no keyword for the NUM LOCK or SCROLL LOCK key, because it must be requested from outside a macro. CAPS LOCK is not represented either, since cell entries are typed right into a macro and you have your choice of typing either uppercase or lowercase letters. Case is also unimportant in operator entries made while a macro is executing, unless you are storing these entries on the worksheet and have preference for

**1
2
3**

Special Keys in Macro Commands

1-2-3 has a macro keyword to represent each of the special keyboard keys, except for NUM LOCK, SCROLL LOCK, CAPS LOCK, ALT-F1 (COMPOSE), ALT-F2 (RECORD), ALT-F3 (RUN), ALT-F4 (UNDO), SHIFT, and PRINT SCREEN.

Cell Pointer Movement Keys	Keywords
UP ARROW	{UP} or {U}
DOWN ARROW	{DOWN} or {D}
RIGHT ARROW	{RIGHT} or {R}
LEFT ARROW	{LEFT} or {L}
HOME	{HOME}
END	{END}
PGUP	{PGUP}
PGDN	{PGDN}
CTRL-RIGHT or TAB	{BIGRIGHT}
CTRL-LEFT or SHIFT-TAB	{BIGLEFT}
CTRL-END-CTRL-PGUP (next file)	{NEXTFILE}, {NF}, or {FILE}{NS}
CTRL-PGUP (next sheet)	{NEXTSHEET} or {NS}
CTRL-PGDN (prev sheet)	{PREVSHEET} or {PS}
CTRL-END-CTRL-PGDN (prev file)	{PREVFILE}, {PF}, or {FILE}{PS}
CTRL-END (file)	{FILE}
CTRL-HOME (first cell)	{FIRSTCELL} or {FC}
CTRL-END-HOME (first file)	{FIRSTFILE}, {FF}, or {FILE}{HOME}
END-CTRL-HOME (last cell)	{LASTCELL} or {LC}
CTRL-END-END (last file)	{LASTFILE}, {LF}, or {FILE}{END}

Editing Keys

DEL	{DEL} or {DELETE}
INS	{INS} or {INSERT}
ESC	{ESC} or {ESCAPE}
BACKSPACE	{BACKSPACE} or {BS}

Function Keys

F1 (HELP)	{HELP}
F2 (EDIT)	{EDIT}
F3 (NAME)	{NAME}
F4 (ABS)	{ABS}
F5 (GOTO)	{GOTO}
F6 (WINDOW)	{WINDOW}
F7 (QUERY)	{QUERY}
F8 (TABLE)	{TABLE}
F9 (CALC)	{CALC}
F10 (GRAPH)	{GRAPH}
ALT-F6 (ZOOM)	{ZOOM}
ALT-F7 (APP1)	{APP1}
ALT-F8 (APP2)	{APP2}
ALT-F9 (APP3)	{APP3}
ALT-F10 (ADDIN)	{ADDIN} or {APP4}

Special Keys

Input from keyboard during macro	{?}
ENTER key	~
Tilde	{~}
{	{{}
}	{}}
/ or <	/, <, or {MENU}

the case of the entry. Other keys not supported are ALT-F1 (COMPOSE), PRINT SCREEN, ALT-F2 (RECORD), ALT-F3 (RUN), ALT-F4 (UNDO), and the SHIFT key.

Tip: Check the spelling of the special key names carefully. In a macro, your entries must be exact. A small mistake is just as serious as a large one, since 1-2-3 only recognizes entries that exactly match the defined set of options.

Cursor Movement Keys

In a macro, movement of the cell pointer to the right is represented by {RIGHT}. Movement to the left is {LEFT}, movement down is {DOWN}, and movement up is {UP}. If you want to move the cell pointer up three times in Release 3, use {UP}{UP}{UP} or the shortcut entry {UP 3}. When this key sequence is stored by the recorder, it is even more abbreviated as {U 3}. All three representations have the same effect; they all move the cell pointer three cells above its current location, if three cells exist above the current position of the cell pointer.

The effect of specifying {HOME} for a worksheet or a cell depends on whether the macro is in READY mode or EDIT mode. If in READY mode, it returns you to A1. If in EDIT mode, it moves you to the beginning of your entry.

The END and arrow key combination is supported in macros. You can enter {END}{RIGHT} to have the macro move the cell pointer to the last occupied cell entry on the right side of the worksheet. {BIGLEFT} and {BIGRIGHT} are also supported under Release 3. They will shift you a whole screen to the left or the right, respectively. To specify paging up and paging down, use the entries {PGUP} and {PGDN}.

All of the special Release 3 entries that relocate the cell pointer to different sheets or files are also supported. The entries {NEXTFILE}, {NF}, and {FILE}{NS} move the cell pointer to the next file. The cell pointer will be placed in the first cell in the current file if you enter {FIRSTCELL} or {FC}.

Function Keys

With the exception of ALT-F1 (COMPOSE), ALT-F2 (RECORD), ALT-F3 (RUN), and ALT-F4 (UNDO), all the function keys can be represented by special macro keywords.

- To represent F2 (EDIT), enter {EDIT}.

- For the F3 (NAME) key, enter {NAME} in the macro.

- {ABS} is used to convert the reference type of a formula entry while the formula is being constructed and is equivalent to F4 (ABS).

- The F5 (GOTO) key is used frequently to control cell pointer movement while the macro is executing and is represented by {GOTO}.

- To move the cell pointer into the opposite window, use {WINDOW}, which stands for F6 (WINDOW).

- Zooming to a full-screen view of the current window requires ALT-F6 (ZOOM), represented by {ZOOM}.

- {QUERY} will reexecute the last query operation as long as your input range and criterion are the same size. This keyword takes the place of F7 (QUERY).

- F8 (TABLE) is synonymous with {TABLE}.

- To recalculate your worksheet you can press F9 (CALC); using {CALC} in a macro performs the same function. In both cases, if you are in EDIT mode, {CALC} performs the calculation on the current worksheet cell and eliminates the formula when you press ENTER.

Edit Keys

In addition to F2 (EDIT), which places you in the EDIT mode, there are several special keys that you use when correcting worksheet entries. The ESC key can remove an entry from a cell and delete a menu default, such as a previous setup string, so you can make a new entry. The ESC key is represented as {ESC} or {ESCAPE} in macros.

Release 3 offers another macro entry to remove existing data from the Edit line: {CLEARENTRY} or {CE}. Although it is similar to {ESC}, there are important differences. This command is unique because it is the only keystroke command that does not have a single keyboard equivalent. When there is one entry in the Edit line, {CE} functions identically to {ESC} and eliminates the entry. When there are multiple entries on the Edit line for a command, {CE} offers an advantage; one {CE} instruction eliminates all the entries, whereas you must include {ESC} once for each entry. If the command is /Data Fill, there can be one, two, or three entries on the Edit line that you want to eliminate; one {CE} instruction can handle the task.

The {CE} instruction is also handy when you are not certain if there is an entry on the Edit line. Where {ESC} returns 1-2-3 to the previous command level, {CE} always remains in EDIT mode. Compare {ESC} and {CE} in the context of the /Print command, and the difference is clearer. If a macro includes the entry /PPR, there may or may not be a range highlighted on the screen. If there is one, {ESC} will unlock the range and show the beginning of the range as a cell reference. If there is no range, {ESC} places you in the main Print menu. The {CE} entry remains in the Print Range entry regardless of whether there are any entries. With {CE} you can proceed to enter a new range. With {ESC} your ability to do so is dependent on the existence of a predefined range.

To delete the character in front of the cell pointer while in EDIT mode, or to delete the last character entered, you can use the BACKSPACE key when making your entries from the keyboard. To represent this key in a macro, use {BS} or {BACKSPACE}.

The DEL key deletes the character above the cell pointer while you are in EDIT mode. This is represented in a macro as {DEL} or {DELETE}. As an example, you can request a change of a label prefix to center justification with the following sequence of macro entries:

{EDIT}{HOME}{DEL}^~

The repeat factors can also be used with the editing keys in Release 3. {DELETE 4} deletes the character above the cursor and the next three characters. {BACKSPACE 7} deletes seven characters to the left of the cursor. You can even use a range name, as in {DELETE rows}, where the value of the named range "rows" controls the number of rows deleted.

Other Special Keys

As mentioned earlier, the tilde represents ENTER. To use a macro to place an actual tilde in a cell, type {~}. To use a macro to place curly brackets (braces) in a cell, enter either {{} or {}}. These features can be useful in a macro that builds another macro.

The symbol {?} can be used in a macro to let 1-2-3 know that you want the operator to input something from the keyboard. 1-2-3 will then wait for the entry to be made and ENTER to be pressed. Chapter 13 covers two additional methods for indicating keyboard input that offer greater sophistication, in that they allow you to present a message to the operator regarding the data you wish to have entered.

Typing a Keyboard Macro

The following procedure for entering a macro is not the fastest way, but it should more than pay for itself in time savings during the testing and debugging phase, as you are trying to get your macro to execute correctly.

- The first step in creating a keyboard macro is planning the task you wish to accomplish. Without a plan, you are not likely to create a macro that is well organized and successful.

- After you have made your plan, test it by entering the proposed keystrokes for immediate execution by 1-2-3. As you enter each keystroke directly into the menus, record it on a sheet of paper. Later you will learn to capitalize on these written entries and actually turn them into the macro code. For now, you will want to type at least a few for a firsthand look at what each keystroke represents.

- If the menu selections handled your task correctly, use your sheet of paper as a script when you record the keystrokes as labels in the macro cells.

- Choose a location on your worksheet, or a macro library worksheet for recording your macro. With Release 3, you might want to use a separate worksheet in the current file, or even a separate file; Release 3 can access all the macros in memory as long as they each have a unique name.

- Where possible, use range name references rather than cell addresses as you build your macro. 1-2-3 will adjust to a change in the range name location, but it will not adjust for changes in the location of cell addresses.

- You can record up to 512 keystrokes in one label cell, but it would not be advisable to do so, since you could never read the entire entry at one time without editing the cell. At the other extreme, you can enter each single keystroke of the entry in a separate cell of the column. 1-2-3 will read down the column until it reaches a blank cell. However, this second approach is also not advisable because you would need so many cells to create even a short macro. The best approach is to select some reasonable upper limit for the number of characters to be entered in one macro cell and then, within that limit, move to a new cell whenever you reach a logical breaking place in your keystroke entries.

• Use file references if you need to refer to cells or ranges outside the current worksheet.

Tip: Remember to enter all your macro instructions as labels. Start them with a label indicator if the first character is a number or one of these characters: / + − @ . # $. Another option is to format the macro instruction cells with the Label format.

Using the Keystroke Recorder Feature

Release 3's automatic keystroke recorder can save you a significant amount of time in macro entry. It makes the creation of macros easy, because you can execute a task without needing to remember the representations for the special keys; 1-2-3 will record the proper entries. The special keyboard buffer that 1-2-3 uses can hold up to 512 characters. You can create longer macros, but you must copy the keystrokes from the buffer before the limit is exceeded and begin recording a new group of keystrokes to add to the macro.

Copying Recorder Entries to the Worksheet

There is no need to invoke the macro recorder; it automatically, continually records your keystrokes. However, it is a good idea to empty the buffer if you know that you are beginning to record a macro. At any time during a macro session, you have the option of converting any or all of the last 512 keystrokes to macro entries.

Before looking at the buffer, let's make a few entries so you will have at least a few keystrokes recorded, even if you just started your 1-2-3 session. First, enter **/Range Format Currency** and press ENTER twice. Next, enter **/Worksheet Column Set-Width 18** and press ENTER.

As you know, these entries have formatted the current cell as Currency and extended the width of the current column to 18.

To work with these entries in the keyboard buffer, press the ALT-F2 (RECORD) key to see this menu:

```
A:A1:                                                    MENU
Playback  Copy  Erase  Step
Select keystrokes to play back
```

If you select the Copy option, you will see the last keystrokes (up to 512) entered in the current session. They may look something like the entries in Figure 12-1, depending on the type of entries that you have made.

Notice that the recorder translates your entries to uppercase and uses the abbreviated form for the keyword wherever possible. For consistency, uppercase is used for all the macros in this book, even the ones that are entered from the keyboard. Range names and cell addresses are in lowercase, since the recorder does not convert these entries to uppercase for you. Comments start with an initial capital letter. You can use the arrow keys, the END key, and the HOME key to move within the recorder screen.

Despite any preceding entries you have made, you should be able to see the entries representing the /Range and /Worksheet commands you just entered. Move the cursor to the / that precedes the R representing the /Range command (the second / from the end of the last line). Press the TAB key to mark this keystroke as the place where you want to begin copying keystrokes. Use the RIGHT ARROW key to move to the final tilde ($\sim$) and press ENTER. Supply an address on any active sheet where you

```
A:A1: (C2) [W18]                                         EDIT
Select keystrokes to copy:
TOTAL SALARIES{RIGHT 2}~{D}'@SUM(E2..E17)~~{D}'/RFC)~E2..E19~~{D}{HOME}~/WCS{R 1
6}~{U 11}{R}/WCS{R 29}{L}{R}~Move cell pointer to A1{D}Enter Last Name & move ri
ght{D}Enter First Name & move right{D}Enter "SS# & move right{D}Enter Job Code &
 move right{D}Enter "Salary & move right~{D}Enter Location & press ENTER{D}Move
to C19~~{D}Enter TOTAL SALARIES & move right{D}Enter @SUM formula{D}Format salar
ies as currency{D}Move to A1~{HOME}/FS{CE}C:\123R3\c:\disk3\fig12_1~{ESC}C:\disk
3\fig12_1~/FS~R/WEY/RFC~~/WCS18~
 A       A          B       C       D       E       F o     G
1
```

Figure 12-1.   Keystrokes stored with macro keystroke recorder

want 1-2-3 to record these keystrokes. You can use the pointing method or type in the cell address where you want the first group of these keystrokes copied. Then enter the output range, including the columns that you want the macro instructions to stretch across. Be sure the cells specified are empty, since 1-2-3 will write over any entries they contain. After pressing ENTER to finalize, the entries are copied.

Figure 12-2 shows a large number of keystrokes copied by the recorder feature. Notice how the keystrokes are split up into manageable groups. While each cell's contents are in the output range's first column, the contents use the width selected by the number of columns you chose for the range. When you copy your own entries, follow this procedure to ensure that keywords enclosed in curly braces begin and end in the same cell.

Tip: Keywords in a macro are easier to understand when they are spelled out. Use /Range Search with the Replace option to locate entries like {D} and change them to {DOWN}. You can even develop a macro that will handle this task if you specify the search range it should use.

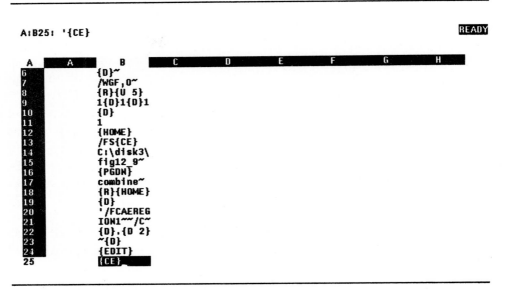

Figure 12-2. Recorded keystrokes copied to a worksheet

Other Recorder Menu Options

Other options on the keystroke recorder menu include Erase, which empties the buffer. Invoke the recorder feature with ALT-F2 (RECORD) and select Erase. Remember to do this before beginning a sequence of keystrokes you plan to record as a macro. The Playback feature allows you to reexecute the keystrokes in the buffer.

Step turns on the STEP mode of execution, so that each macro instruction executes at your request as you press the SPACEBAR. You will see an indicator at the bottom of the screen telling you when STEP mode is on. To turn off STEP mode, enter ALT-F2 (RECORD) a second time and choose Step again. In prior releases of 1-2-3, pressing ALT-F2 alone controlled STEP mode, since there was no recorder feature.

Naming Your Macro

Once you have entered or copied all the macro keystrokes, you are ready to name your macro. Before doing this, position your cell pointer on the top cell in the macro, since this is the only cell that will be named. Then enter /**Range Name Create**. At the prompt for the range name, enter a backslash and any single alphabetic character before pressing ENTER if you want to be able to execute the macro with a single key combination. An alternative is to type any valid range name and press ENTER to execute the macro with the ALT-F3 (RUN) option. Since you positioned your cell pointer before requesting the /Range command, simply press ENTER in response to the prompt for the range address. When you save the worksheet, the macro and its name will be saved as well and will be available whenever you retrieve the worksheet.

The naming conventions for 1-2-3's macros allow you to create an unlimited number of macros. You can also create 26 unique macro names using the backslash and the letters of the alphabet, such as \t; these macros can be executed with the ALT key in combination with the letter used in the macro name. 1-2-3 does not distinguish between upper- and lowercase characters in a macro name.

Tip: Choose a special character or letter as the first entry in all macro names. When you use the F3 (RUN) option, 1-2-3 displays a list of all valid range names. To help distinguish macro names from other range names, start all of them with the same character. Using a special symbol like # will place them at the front of the list.

You can obtain a list of all your current macro names and the range addresses to which they are assigned with the /Range Name Table command. Enter /**Range Name Table** and respond to 1-2-3's prompt for a table range by entering the address of the upper left cell in any blank section of the worksheet where 1-2-3 can write the macro name assignments. This command is described more fully in Chapter 5.

Documenting Your Macro

As you create a macro, you are aware of the name you have assigned to it and the function of each of its steps. A month from now, however, when you look again at the macro cells, it may take some thought to remember what you were attempting to accomplish. It is therefore a wise move to document information like the macro name and the function of each step on the worksheet as you create the macro. The time investment involved in this extra step will more than pay for itself later on.

A good documentation strategy is placing the macro name in the cell immediately to the left of the top macro cell. If the macro is named Currency, type **currency** in the cell immediately to the left of the top macro cell. If the macro is named \a, you would enter '\a in the name cell. (The ' is needed to prevent 1-2-3 from interpreting the backslash as the repeating label indicator and filling your cell with the letter a.) The cell to the left of your top macro cell is an especially appropriate choice because, if you have already placed the macro name there before actually naming the macro range, you can use the /Range Name Labels Right command to name the macro cell without typing the name in again. In other words, you can type the macro steps, then type the macro name in the empty cell to the left of the macro, leave the cell pointer on the name, enter /**Range Name Labels Right**, and press ENTER.

A good area to use for documenting macro instructions is a column of cells to the right of the instructions. Depending on the length of your macro entries, you can widen the column containing the macro instructions or move several cells to the right of the macro column for the documentation entries. A brief description of every command will make each step's function clearer and will save a significant amount of time if it is necessary to modify the macro later. Figure 12-3 shows a macro with documentation entries for the individual macro instructions.

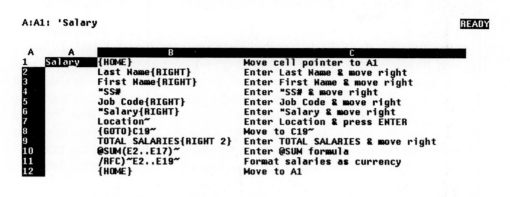

A:A1: 'Salary   READY

A	A	B	C
1	Salary	{HOME}	Move cell pointer to A1
2		Last Name{RIGHT}	Enter Last Name & move right
3		First Name{RIGHT}	Enter First Name & move right
4		"SS#	Enter "SS# & move right
5		Job Code{RIGHT}	Enter Job Code & move right
6		"Salary{RIGHT}	Enter "Salary & move right
7		Location~	Enter Location & press ENTER
8		{GOTO}C19~	Move to C19~
9		TOTAL SALARIES{RIGHT 2}	Enter TOTAL SALARIES & move right
10		@SUM(E2..E17)~	Enter @SUM formula
11		/RFC)~E2..E19~	Format salaries as currency
12		{HOME}	Move to A1

Figure 12-3.   Macro with documentation

Executing Your Macro

Once you have entered and named a macro, you can use it whenever you wish. Release 3 supports macro execution from READY mode or within a command. Macros can supply entries like graph titles or print headers. If your macro requires the cell pointer to be positioned in a certain cell, put the cell pointer there before executing the macro. The cell pointer does not need to be on the macro cell to execute the macro.

If the macro is named with a backslash-letter combination, you can execute the macro in several ways. The short-cut approach is to press the ALT key and, while the key is pressed, touch the letter key that you used in your macro name; then release both keys.

The other approach can be used regardless of the macro's name. Press the ALT-F3 (RUN) key, and 1-2-3 displays the names of all the range names in active files, including macro names. Highlight the name you want to use and press ENTER; or type the desired name.

Tip: Save the worksheet where you recorded the macro before trying it. If the macro contains mistakes, saving it will prevent you from losing your work if the macro writes over its own instructions or locks up your system. If the macro sheet contains other entries, you might want to use the /File Save Backup feature to maintain the integrity of the existing file until after macro testing.

Using the Playback Feature of RECORD

When you want to repeat a sequence of keystrokes without saving it, the Playback option of the keystroke recorder is the best solution. It allows you to repeatedly tailor the format of cells, change the width settings for columns, or alter the Protection status of ranges of cells—without having to name the macro instructions or document them. First erase the keystroke buffer and enter the commands the first time. You can then repeat ALT-F2 (RECORD) Playback as many times as you need the instruction repeated. When you are through, you can erase the buffer.

To use the Playback feature to format selected columns that are evenly spaced on a worksheet, follow these steps.

1. Press ALT-F2 (RECORD) and type an **E** for Erase.

2. Move to the top of the first column that you want to format. Enter **/RF**. Type the letter corresponding to the format you want. If it requires you to supply a number of decimal digits, type the number and press ENTER. If you are working with a solid column of numbers, you can move to the bottom by pressing END followed by the DOWN ARROW.

3. Move to the top of the next column to be formatted.

4. Press ALT-F2 (RECORD), and type a **P** for Playback. Move to the first keystroke in the buffer that you wish to execute. (If you emptied the buffer before starting, you should be able to do this with the HOME key.) Press TAB to lock in the beginning of the repeated block; then move to the last instruction you want to repeat, and press ENTER. 1-2-3 will format the column and move to the next column to be formatted.

Tip: Use Playback to perform repetitive tasks where exact duplication is needed. The Playback feature is not designed to allow you to make extensive changes from iteration to iteration. Reserve it for occasions like widening columns, or formatting rows and columns of the same length with the same format options.

Creating a Macro Library

A macro library is simply a worksheet file that contains all of your macros. With Release 3 you can really use this concept effectively, since the macros and the files they work on can be different—as long as the macros are in an active file.

Your separate macro library file can be in any worksheet in the file. You might want to start in sheet A at the beginning of the file, since the file will not contain other types of data. You can also group the macros, using different sheets to group a single type of macros—like formatting macros, data entry macros, and print and graph macros. An organized storage method makes it easy to find the macro when you need it for use, or when it is time to make modifications. If you decide to create some specialized macros in a worksheet file with a model or a database, you will want to store the macros on a separate sheet. This minimizes the risk of damage to the macro when changes are made to the application area of the file.

If you use the macro library concept, you must load the library into memory before using any of its macros. If your application file is already in memory, you can use the /File Open command.

When you wish to add a new macro to your library file, make the macro library file the current file. Enter the new macro, and it will be available in all your other active files. Save the macro library file under its original filename. To add a macro from another worksheet to the library, use the /File Xtract command to extract the macro from the other sheet, saving it to another file temporarily. Then retrieve your macro library file and use the /File Combine Copy command to place the new macro in the library. This approach also works for copying a single macro from the macro library to any of your other worksheets. Be sure to name the entire range for each macro, including the documentation to the right and left of the macro. Then, when you use /File Combine, you can specify the Named-Range option and copy in just the one macro.You will need to name the macro again once it is on the new worksheet, since the range name used for the macro on the disk file will not be copied.

Tip: Be careful of multiple-sheet and external file references. Cell or range addresses consisting of nothing more than column and row references are always assumed to reference the current sheet. To reference a different sheet, use the level indicator, as in B:A10. Even with a level indicator, the reference is assumed to be in the current file. To reference an external file, use the angle brackets around the filename, as in < <ACCT.WK3> >B:A10.

Debugging Macros

The debugging process involves testing and correcting macros to ensure that you obtain the desired results. One of the most common mistakes made when creating keyboard macros is forgetting to enter the tilde mark to represent each time the ENTER key needs to be pressed.

1-2-3 has a STEP mode that executes a macro one keystroke at a time so you can follow its progress and spot any area of difficulty. STEP mode is available from the Record menu activated with ALT-F2 (RECORD). Once you activate the menu you can highlight Step and press ENTER, or type an S. Step is a toggle operation, so selecting Step a second time turns STEP mode off again. When this mode is operational, you will see "STEP" on the bottom line of your screen.

When the STEP indicator is on, any macro you invoke will be executed one instruction at a time. Press the SPACEBAR whenever you are ready to move on to the next instruction. The macro steps will display in the control panel to provide information on the operation of the macro, but you will not be able to enter direct commands while the macro is executing. While the macro is executing, "SST" will appear in place of STEP at the bottom of the screen.

To stop a malfunctioning macro, press the CTRL and BREAK keys simultaneously. This cancels macro operation immediately, and presents an ERROR indicator at the upper right corner of the screen. Pressing ESC will return you to READY mode so you can make corrections to your macro.

Automatic Macros

1-2-3 has a unique feature that allows you to create an automatic macro for a worksheet. Every time a worksheet containing an automatic macro is retrieved, 1-2-3 immediately executes this macro. This feature has more application with the advanced macro commands discussed in Chapter 13. However, there may be situations where you want to execute, say, a /File Combine or a /Range Erase command as soon as a worksheet is retrieved. 1-2-3 also can suspend execution of automatic macros; you will want to be familiar with this command, too.

Creating an Automatic Macro

The only difference in creating an automatic macro and a normal executable macro is in the macro name. There can be only one automatic macro on a worksheet, and it must have the name \0 (backslash zero).

Figure 12-4 shows an automatic macro designed to erase a range of input cells in the worksheet in Figure 12-5, every time the worksheet is retrieved. That way, each new operator can enter new values for the principal, monthly or yearly payments, and term. To create this macro, place your instructions into a column of worksheet cells on the sheet that will trigger its execution, and assign the special \0 name to the name cell. Then save the worksheet file with /File Save. The next time the worksheet is retrieved, the macro executes immediately.

Tip: An automatic macro in a library worksheet executes when you retrieve the library sheet. An automatic macro must be stored in the file whose retrieval you want to trigger execution of the macro.

Disabling Automatic Macros

If you change the setting for /Worksheet Global Default Automatic to No, 1-2-3 will not execute automatic macros when you retrieve a file that

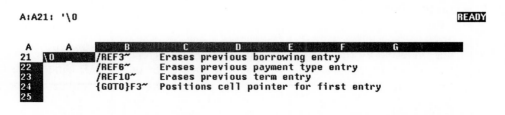

Figure 12-4.   Automatic macro to erase worksheet cells

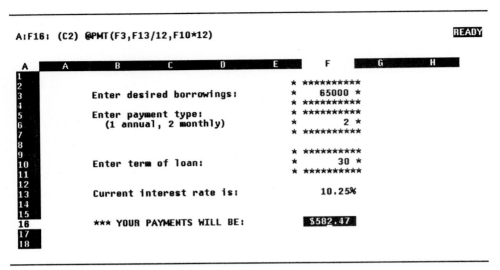

A:F16: (C2) @PMT(F3,F13/12,F10*12)   `READY`

```
A        A        B        C        D       E        F        G        H
1
2                                                     * **********
3           Enter desired borrowings:                *   65000 *
4                                                     * **********
5           Enter payment type:                       * **********
6             (1 annual, 2 monthly)                   *       2 *
7                                                     * **********
8
9                                                     * **********
10          Enter term of loan:                       *      30 *
11                                                    * **********
12
13          Current interest rate is:                    10.25%
14
15
16          *** YOUR PAYMENTS WILL BE:                   $582.47
17
18
```

Figure 12-5.   Worksheet example with cells that macro erases

contains one. When you first install 1-2-3, the default setting for this command is Yes. To make a permanent change to this setting, you have to use /Worksheet Global Default Update to save the change to the configuration file.

With Release 3's multiple file capabilities, you can have nested automatic macros. For instance, if an executing macro in file A contains an instruction that opens file B, and file B contains an automatic macro, the setting for /Worksheet Global Default Automatic determines which macro will execute first. If the setting is No, the automatic macro in File A will continue. If the setting is Yes, the automatic macro in File B will begin execution.

Ready-to-Use Macros

The macros in the following paragraphs are ready to use; they are complete macros designed to perform the tasks described. Since it is likely your data will be located in files, sheets, or cells different from the data on the worksheets used to create these examples, you probably will have to make minor modifications to the cell addresses referenced in the macros. Each macro description will include guidelines for its use, and a section on potential modifications.

The same conventions have been used for all the macros. The name used for the macro is shown in column A, line 1, to the left of the top cell in the macro. The macro is written in column B as a label. A description is placed in column C, often extending into the columns to the right of column C. Uppercase characters are used for the all the macro entries, including menu selections, responses to menu prompts, filenames, special key indicators such as {HOME} and {ESC}, and range names.

Worksheet Macros

Many repetitive worksheet tasks are candidates for macros. Examples are changing the global format, checking the worksheet status, moving between worksheets or between files, and changing default settings like the printer interface. You can even have a macro do some of your typing in worksheet cells. For example, you can create a date macro that enters the repetitive keystrokes while you supply the essential year, month, and day information. You can have a macro make changes to an entry to enhance it, or to cover up existing errors.

A Macro to Display Formulas

1-2-3 prints the formulas behind your worksheet results when you specify /Print Printer Options Other Cell-Formulas, but it creates one line of printed output per cell. If you would like to display or print out formulas while maintaining the integrity of your worksheet design, you will have to change the format of each formula cell to text. The steps involved can be placed in a macro to simplify the task.

```
     A     B          C
1    \t    /WGFT      Request global format as text
2          /RFR       Request range format reset
3          A1..Z60~   Specify range as A1..Z60 in current sheet
```

The instructions in the first line request /Worksheet Global Format Text. If there were no range formats for your worksheet cells, you could end the macro at this point. Since most worksheets do use a range format to override the global setting, our macro is designed to operate under this condition. It uses /Range Format Reset to make all the cells conform to the global format setting of Text. This command is specified in B2. It is followed by a range that contains all the entries on the worksheet with which the macro is designed to work.

Guidelines for Use   It is important that you save your worksheet before executing this macro. You will not want to save your worksheet afterward, since all your regular formats will have been superceded.

Modifying the Macro   You may want to add an instruction at the beginning to save your current worksheet file, so that you do not lose your established formats. The only risk with this addition is that you might execute the macro a second time and overlay your existing file with the Text formatted version.

Another option is adding the commands necessary to print the file. These instructions could be placed at the end of the macro. You could add a /Worksheet Erase command after the /Print commands so that the text formatted version is not saved to disk after the macro ends. You could also add a command to increase the column width so that complete formulas can display. You can alter the macro to select the range with a specification of {CE}{HOME}.{END}{HOME}. This approach selects A1 as the first cell in the range, and the last cell in the sheet is used as the last cell in the range.

A Macro to Insert Blank Rows

Many people do not like 1-2-3's requirement that you not leave blank rows between column headings and data if you wish to perform /Data Query operations. You can, however, create macros that will add and delete blank rows for you. When you use the worksheet for calculations and printed reports, use the macro that inserts blank rows. When you perform a query, you can invoke the macro that deletes the blank rows. In fact, this latter macro could be made a part of a /Data Query macro.

The macro that follows will insert blank rows.

	A	B	C
1	INSERT	/WI	Request worksheet insert
2		R	Specify rows
3		{DOWN}{DOWN}~	Move down to insert 3 rows

The macro as shown adds three blank rows, but it can easily be modified to add any number you choose. The first macro instruction, in B1, requests Worksheet Insert. The next instruction specifies that rows rather than columns should be inserted. The third instruction expands the insertion to three rows. You can use the shortcut approach for moving the cell pointer and write this instruction as {DOWN 2}~.

Guidelines for Use   This macro requires that you place your cell pointer where you want to insert the blank rows, since they are added above the cell pointer. When you invoke the macro, the cell pointer row is shifted down to make room for the new rows. Just as with a keyboard entry of the same command, your formulas are adjusted to reflect the addition, but insertions at the top or bottom of a range do not expand the range.

Modifying the Macro   By changing the entry in B2, you could create a macro that inserts columns or sheets. If you choose to add sheets, an additional modification will be required to indicate that you want the sheets inserted either before or after the current sheet by including a *B* or an *A* after the 5 in B2. You may also wish to modify the last instruction, to allow for the addition of extra rows, columns, or sheets. A third option is to end the macro after line 2 and allow the operator to specify the number of rows, columns, or sheets to be added. You can use a range name to specify the number.

A Macro to Change the Global Default Directory

When you are working with completed worksheet models, you may want your directory set at drive C if all your completed models are stored on the hard drive. If you have a number of new models to create and wish to store them on a floppy disk, you may want the directory set at drive B. You may also wish to change the directory if you use 1-2-3 on two systems that have different configurations. Changing the drive with a macro eliminates the need for remembering the command path required.

The following macro changes the existing directory to drive B:\.

```
    A           B       C
1   CHG_DIRB    /WG     Request worksheet global change
2               D       Specify a default change
3               D       Specify directory
4               {CE}    Clears existing directory entry
5               B:\~    Sets new directory
6               Q       Quits default menu without saving
```

The first instruction requests a /Worksheet Global change. A default change and directory change are specified in the next two instructions. B4 causes the macro to remove the current directory setting. The instruction in B5 generates the new directory setting and finalizes it, and the last instruction leaves the Default menu and returns to READY mode.

Guidelines for Use   When you change the directory, both the old and the new directories must be available on the system you are using to change the settings. If you are changing the directory to a floppy drive, place a data disk in the drive before executing the macro, since 1-2-3 attempts to read the directory for the selected device. You can also use this macro to change the subdirectory for model storage and retrieval if you are using a hard disk.

Modifying the Macro   B5 is the instruction you are likely to want to modify in this macro. B5 should contain the pathname of the device and directory you plan to use for data storage. As an example, if you are currently using drive A and want to change to a subdirectory on drive C, you might change this instruction to read C:\123\Dallas\Sales\.

A Macro to Set the Window to Perspective and Move to the First Sheet

When you are working with multiple sheets or files, Release 3's Perspective window makes it easier to work with your data. If you change frequently from a consolidation sheet to one of the detail sheets, you might want several macros to handle some of these changes for you. For example, this macro creates a Perspective view and then moves to the first sheet:

```
      A       B       C
1     \w      /WWP    Use perspective window
2             {FS}    Move to the first sheet
```

The consolidated sheet might look something like Figure 12-6 before invoking the macro. The first instruction sets the screen to a three-window perspective, and the second moves the cell pointer to the first sheet in the current file, providing the display in Figure 12-7. Although the macro only saves a few keystrokes, it can still save time if you need to execute the task frequently. Having the required keystrokes in a macro also frees you from having to remember anything other than the name of the macro.

Guidelines for Use   You can use this macro regardless of the sheet you are on when you decide you need to see a Perspective view. You can also use this macro when the current worksheet only contains one sheet, and other files are open in memory, since the other worksheet files will display in the other windows.

Modifying the Macro   You can modify the macro to generate a Map window, or a horizontally or vertically split screen. You can also choose to make one of the other sheets active instead of the first sheet.

AιA1ι   READY

A	A	B	C	D	E	F	G
1			Total	1989 Advertising Expenditures			
2			Q1	Q2	Q3	Q4	
3		Product 1					
4		Radio	30,000	45,000	21,000	18,000	
5		TV	125,000	215,000	295,000	350,000	
6		Magazine	25,000	50,000	25,000	75,000	
7		Product 2					
8		Radio	56,000	78,000	132,000	98,000	
9		TV	250,000	500,000	345,000	400,000	
10		Magazine	250,000	300,000	175,000	225,000	
11		Product 3					
12		Radio	15,000	45,000	75,000	100,000	
13		TV	0	200,000	350,000	125,000	
14		Magazine	25,000	55,000	65,000	70,000	
15							

Figure 12-6.   Worksheet before macro is performed

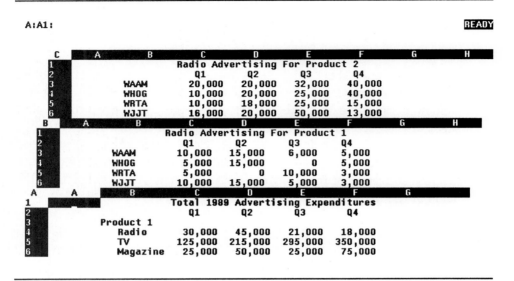

Figure 12-7. Macro setting a Perspective window display

A Macro to Change the Global Printer Default Setup

When you install your 1-2-3 package, you have the option of installing more than one printer. You may have both a dot matrix and a letter quality printer coupled to your system. You may want to use the letter quality printer for printing most worksheets, and the dot matrix for printing graphs or quick drafts of a model.

If you want to change the default printer that 1-2-3 uses when you request /Print, but your second printer is cabled to another port, you will have to change both the printer requested and the interface. The printer will be the device requested, and the interface specification will tell 1-2-3 whether you have it cabled to a serial or parallel device, or wish to access one of the operating system devices on your local area network.

A macro for changing the default printer is as follows:

```
     A      B                      C
1    \s     /WG                    Request worksheet global change
2           D                      Specify default
3           P                      Choose printer
```

```
4         I1                          Set interface to parallel 1
5         N1                          Set name to first printer installed
6         S\027\040\048\071~          Create default setup string for HP
                                      LaserJet as HP German
7         Q                           Quit printer default menu
8         Q                           Quit default menu
```

The first line requests a /Worksheet Global change. The next two lines tell 1-2-3 that you wish to use the Default Printer option. The instruction in B4 tells 1-2-3 to set the Interface option to the first parallel interface. The Name option is selected next, and the first name in the list of printers is specified. In this example this was a Hewlett Packard LaserJet II printer.

It is possible to change other default print settings at the same time you change the specified printer. Although you can now select many print options from 1-2-3's Print menus where setup strings were required in earlier releases, there are still many specialized setup strings that are not part of the menus. For instance, to have the default character set as HP German on the printer, you would need a setup string. B6 contains this setup string of \027\040\048\071 on the Hewlett Packard LaserJet II. This entry is correct for a first use of the setup string. However, if the worksheet already has a setup string, B6 in the macro should be changed to read S{ESC}\027\040\048\071~ or S{CE}\027\040\048\071. The {CE} option is best because the macro will work regardless of whether there is an existing setup string entry. The last two instructions quit the Default Printer submenu and the Default menu.

Guidelines for Use   Before creating this macro, you will need to familiarize yourself with the settings for the nine Default Printer interfaces. Interfaces 1 and 3 are parallel interfaces, and 2 and 4 are serial. The other five options are the operating system devices LPT1, LPT2, LPT3, COM1, and COM2.

The printer names you use in the macro depend on the options you selected during installation. You cannot access printer types that were not installed, since the necessary driver files will not be available. If you plan to use a new printer device, you must go back to the installation program and add it there.

Modifying the Macro   B4 would be modified to I2 or I4 if you planned to use a serial connection for your printer. For a serial printer, you would also need a macro instruction to select the baud rate. If you wanted a different setup string, you would modify the string in B6.

You could also expand this macro to include a change to the default settings for other print characteristics, such as margins and page length. If you wanted to have these new settings available the next time you used the package, you would have to add a command to select the Global Default Update option after exiting the Default Printer menu. Then you could save your changes to the file 123.CNF.

A Macro to Enter a Date in a Worksheet Cell

You have learned to enter dates in worksheet cells as values. If you enter a date as a label, you cannot use it in date arithmetic operations unless you use @DATEVALUE to convert the string to a date serial number. Otherwise, the cell does not have an internal serial date number behind the date displayed. Although you can enter a date directly, previous releases require that you use the @DATE function. With the @DATE function, a substantial number of additional keystrokes are required. A macro can solve this problem by making most of the entries for you, including @DATE, the parentheses, and the argument separators. The only entries you have to make are the year number, the month number, and the day number.

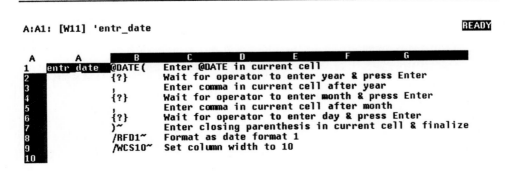

Figure 12-8.   Macro to enter dates

A macro to enter dates is shown in Figure 12-8. It is designed to make its entries in the current cell and begins by entering the keystrokes @**DATE**(. When the macro executes the first input instruction, {?}, it waits for you to make an entry and stores your keystrokes in the cell. It then adds a comma to the cell and waits for additional input. Another comma is added next, after which the third input instruction is executed. The cell entry is completed with an entry of the closing parenthesis.

B8 contains the /Range Format Date 1 request for the cell in which the date entry was just made. The column that contains the cell is set to a width of 10 via a request for /Worksheet Column Set-Width 10. The result of using the macro three times to enter dates in worksheet cells is shown in Figure 12-9.

Guidelines for Use   The {?} method of input does not provide a message prompt telling the operator what it is waiting for. It is important that the operator knows to enter the year number and press ENTER, then the month number and press ENTER, and then the day number and press ENTER, since that is the argument order that the @DATE function requires. In Chapter 13 you will learn how to use the {GETLABEL} macro command to create prompts for the user.

Modifying the Macro   This macro can be modified to use any of 1-2-3's built-in @functions. Just begin the macro with a different

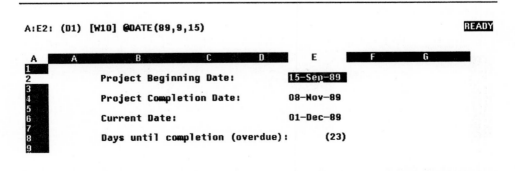

Figure 12-9.   Worksheet with dates entered

keyword. The number of input statements will depend on the number of arguments in the particular @function.

In Chapter 13, you will learn how you can make a macro like this display prompts as it fills a complete column of cells. As it exists now, you would have to move to another cell and reexecute the macro if you wished to enter additional dates.

A Macro to Round Formulas

When you format worksheet cells, you may choose a format that displays less than the full number of decimal places in a number. 1-2-3 will round the displayed number to the number of decimal places you specify. The internal storage of the number is not changed and still retains its full accuracy, however. Calculations will use the stored number, not the displayed one. This can result in a total at the bottom of a column that seems not to be in agreement with the figures in the cells above it.

The @ROUND function handles this problem by rounding the internally stored number to the number of decimal places you specify. The catch is that you have to enclose your numbers or formulas in the @ROUND function arguments, and supply the position in the entry at which rounding should take place. When a number of formulas are involved, this can be a tedious process. You can create a macro to make most of the entries for you.

A sample macro is shown in Figure 12-10. The first instruction enables the EDIT mode for the current cell. The cell pointer is moved to the front of the entry. The keystrokes @**ROUND(** are added at the

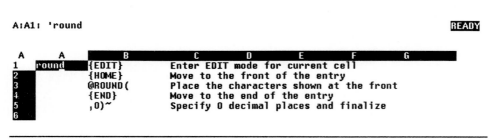

Figure 12-10. Rounding macro

front of the entry. The pointer is then moved to the end of the entry with the instruction in B4. The keystrokes ,0) are placed at the end of the entry to complete the arguments for @ROUND, and the entry is finalized with the tilde (~).

Guidelines for Use   This macro is position dependent. It rounds only the formula or number at the cell pointer location to the specified number of decimal places. You must move the cell pointer and reexecute the macro to round additional cells.

Modifying the Macro   The macro can be easily modified to round to any number of decimal places. Simply change the number in B5 to reflect the place at which you want rounding to occur. The places for rounding are described under the @ROUND function in Chapter 7.

You could also change this macro so that it uses the input statement {?} to allow the operator to enter the place of rounding each time it is executed. The operator types the number and presses ENTER to have 1-2-3 include it in the instruction.

When you learn in Chapter 13 how to create a loop with the macro instructions, you can modify this macro to round a whole column of numbers with one execution of the macro.

A Macro to Handle Data Entry Errors

Macros can be used to correct a variety of data input errors. They are especially valuable since 1-2-3 gives you access to all the string functions.

For example, if you had employees' names entered in the following format in your database:

Jeff Jones

it would be considered "proper case," since only the first letter of each word is capitalized. Some string functions such as @EXACT, @HLOOKUP, and @VLOOKUP are case sensitive, so if someone else updates your database and enters names as BOB BROWN or bill smith, you are likely to have trouble with these functions. It could be time consuming to make corrections so that all the entries match in format. However, you can create a macro that will change any entry into proper case. It is shown in Figure 12-11.

The macro begins by preparing to edit the current cell. It then moves to the first position and deletes the label indicator in the first position. The @PROPER function is entered, followed by a (and ", since the string entry from the current cell must be enclosed in double quotes. The instruction in B4 moves the cell pointer to the end of the entry. The last instruction adds the " at the end and follows it with a). Before finalizing the entry, the macro calculates the formula so it can be stored in the cell as a label rather than as a formula.

Guidelines for Use   This macro is position dependent. It changes only the label entry at the cell pointer location to proper case. You must move the cell pointer and reexecute the macro to change additional cells.

Modifying the Macro   If you want your data in uppercase, you can use the @UPPER function in place of @PROPER. For lowercase, use @LOWER.

A Macro to Enter a Worksheet Heading

If you need to create a whole series of worksheets that use the same heading, you can place the heading instructions in a macro and use the macro in each worksheet. Since the macro is designed to begin the

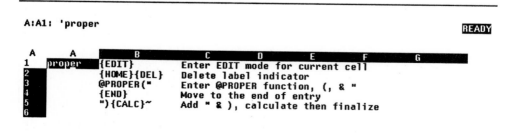

Figure 12-11.   Proper case macro

heading at the cell pointer location, the headings need not start in the same position in each worksheet.

The following macro places headings for the quarters of the year across a worksheet:

```
      A            B                C
1     heading      ^QTR1{RIGHT}     Enter QTR1 and move 1 cell right
2                  ^QTR2{RIGHT}     Enter QTR2 and move 1 cell right
3                  ^QTR3{RIGHT}     Enter QTR3 and move 1 cell right
4                  ^QTR4{RIGHT}     Enter QTR4 and move 1 cell right
5                  ^TOTAL~          Enter TOTAL and press ENTER
6                  {END}{LEFT}      Move to the leftmost entry
7                  {DOWN}           Move down 1 cell
```

Each of the first four macro instructions center justifies one of the quarter headings in a worksheet cell, and moves one cell to the right. The instruction in B5 places the heading TOTAL in a cell and finalizes the entry with ENTER. The cell pointer is then moved to the left of this section of the worksheet. It will be on the first heading if the cell to its left is blank, or it will be in column A. The last instruction moves the cell pointer down one cell.

Guidelines for Use   The macro places the first heading at the cell pointer location and moves to the right with subsequent entries, so it is important that you position your cell pointer before executing the macro.

Modifying the Macro   The macro can be modified to create any series of headings, like the months of the year, weeks of the month, multiple years, or account numbers. All you need to change are the headings themselves. You can easily modify the label prefix that begins each heading entry as well, if you wish different justification.

This macro can be modified to create account names down a column. The only difference is that the cell pointer would be moved down after each entry and the caret symbol (^) for center justification would not be used.

Range Macros

You can create macros for all the /Range commands you use frequently. They can be either open-ended macros or closed ones. An open-ended macro is one that returns control to the operator before the range is selected. As an example, if you wanted a macro to format cells as Currency with zero decimal places, you would record the following keystrokes:

/RFC0~

If you end the macro at this point, it is open-ended, since the operator can complete the range specification.

It would be a closed macro if you supplied the range as part of the formula, for example:

/RFC0~{DOWN 5}~

or

/RFC0~a1..d12~

Closed macros are more limited in their application, since they function only under one particular set of circumstances.

If you are developing macros for yourself, open-ended macros add flexibility. If you are developing them for someone else and want to maintain as much control over the application as possible, try closed macros.

A Macro to Create a Range Name Table

The /Range Name Table command lists all the range names and their cell addresses in a table on your worksheet. This table is not updated automatically as you add new range names, however; you must execute the command sequence again to have 1-2-3 update the table. A macro can easily handle this task for you.

The short macro needed reads as follows:

```
      A       B                 C
1     \z      {GOTO}G5~         Position cursor at range table
2             /RNT~             Request range name table at current
                                  location
```

The first instruction in the macro positions the cell pointer in the upper left corner of the area where you wish your table to appear—cell G5, in this example. The second instruction requests the /Range Name Table command.

Guidelines for Use   Before executing this macro, make sure the area to the right and below G5 (or wherever you send the cell pointer) is empty, since the macro overwrites any data that is stored there. If you plan to print the table of range names, you will always want to execute this macro before printing, to ensure that your table of names is current.

Modifying the Macro   The macro can be modified to supply a complete range address or range name for the table. If a range address is supplied instead of the upper left cell, 1-2-3 will use only the specified range area for the table and will truncate what it can't find room for. Specifying the upper left cell allows 1-2-3 to use as much space as it needs below the cell specified. When building the table of range names, 1-2-3 will always use the column of cells to the right of the cell specified, whether the /Range Name Table command is executed through a macro or from the keyboard.

File Macros

You can automate any of the /File commands with a macro. Although /File Save and /File Retrieve do not require a significant number of keystrokes, they are still possible candidates for a macro because they are used so frequently. Other /File commands, such as Combine and Xtract, also can be automated. This may cut down on typing errors, since the same keystrokes are executed each time.

A Macro to Save Files

A /File Save does not require many keystrokes, but it should be done frequently so you do not risk the loss of your data. A macro can be created to save your file with one keystroke, as follows:

```
     A      B      C
1    \s    /FS    Request file save
2           ~     Specify existing file name
3           R     Replace file
```

The first line of the macro invokes the /File Save command. The tilde (~) in line 2 indicates that you want to retain the file's existing name. The final line tells 1-2-3 to replace the file on disk with the current contents of memory.

Guidelines for Use   This macro is designed to save a file that has been saved previously. It cannot be used if a file has never been saved to disk or if you want to use a new name for the file.

Modifying the Macro   The macro can easily be modified to allow your input of the filename. Simply use an input statement between line 1 and line 2 of the macro. If you prefer, a predetermined filename can be placed in the macro in the same location.

A Macro to Retrieve Files

The /File Retrieve macro that follows calls a new file into memory. The worksheet file that is active when you execute this macro will no longer be resident in memory when the retrieve operation is completed. Such a macro is normally used as part of a larger macro that chooses the task you wish to have performed and retrieves the appropriate file.

A Retrieve macro might look like this:

```
     A      B        C
1    \r    /FR      Request file retrieve
2          SALES~   Specify SALES file
```

The first line of the macro issues the request to retrieve a file. The second line contains the filename and the tilde (~) to finalize the filename entry.

Guidelines for Use   The macro erases the active worksheet file when the macro is executed. If you made changes to the current worksheet, you will want to save it before executing this macro.

Modifying the Macro   You can modify the macro to add a /File Save before the /File Retrieve. You can also change the name of the file being saved.

If you want, you can modify the macro so it has a name of \0. This causes it to do an immediate retrieve of a second file as soon as the first one is retrieved. In this situation you will probably want to add some other macro instructions at the beginning, to perform a few tasks in the current file before retrieving the new file.

A Macro to Extract Files

The /File Xtract command is used to save a section of a worksheet in a separate worksheet file. This process can be used to transfer end-of-period totals to a new worksheet for the next period, for example. If you need to extract files frequently, consider the time-saving features of a macro that does the job.

Our macro is as follows:

```
   A            B                   C
1  extract      /FXV                Request value extract
2               TOTALS~             Specify filename TOTALS
3               year_end_total~     Enter range name to extract
4               R                   Select replace
```

The first line contains a request to perform a /File Xtract Values operation to save the values from the original file. The next step contains the name of the file in which you want the new material saved. In this macro, the filename is TOTALS. The next instruction tells 1-2-3 what to place in the new file; you can specify a range address or a range name. This macro uses the range name **year_end_total**. The *R* in the last instruction tells 1-2-3 to replace the TOTALS file with the current contents of year_end_total.

Guidelines for Use   This macro operates on two assumptions. First, it assumes that the range name **year_end_total** has already been created. Second, it assumes that the file TOTALS has already been created, since it requests that 1-2-3 replace it.

Modifying the Macro   The macro can be modified easily to use a range address rather than a range name for the extract area. The

```
A:A21:  'combine                                                    READY

 A      A        B            C         D       E       F       G
21  combine  {HOME}        Move to A1
22            /FCAEREGION1~  Request file combine add for region 1
23            /FCAEREGION2~  Request file combine add for region 2
24            /FCAEREGION3~  Request file combine add for region 3
25            /FCAEREGION4~  Request file combine add for region 4
```

Figure 12-12.   Macro to combine files

filename used can also be modified. Either of these can be entered by the operator while the macro is executing if you use an input instruction.

A Macro to Combine Files

The /File Combine command allows you to add data from files on disk to the current worksheet, without erasing the current worksheet as a /File Retrieve operation would do. A macro to handle the combining operation is shown in Figure 12-12. The final product of the macro is shown in Figure 12-13, where each figure represents the combined totals of each of the four company regions.

Each of the detail worksheets contains a 1 in column H in the row number that corresponds to the region number. After the macro has added all four regions to the consolidated company template, the four cells in column H should each contain a 1, as they do in Figure 12-13.

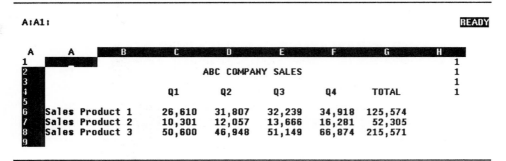

```
A:A1:                                                              READY

 A      A        B           C          D        E       F         G        H
1                                                                           1
2                              ABC COMPANY SALES                            1
3                                                                           1
4                           Q1         Q2       Q3      Q4      TOTAL        1
5
6  Sales Product 1        26,610     31,807   32,239  34,918   125,574
7  Sales Product 2        10,301     12,057   13,666  16,281    52,305
8  Sales Product 3        50,600     46,948   51,149  66,874   215,571
9
```

Figure 12-13.   Worksheet after combining files

These 1's are your confirmation that each detail sheet has been combined with the total worksheet only once, since each detail sheet has a 1 in a different location. In addition to saving keystrokes, this macro ensures that the combining process is handled consistently and accurately. When you are entering /File Combine commands from the keyboard to consolidate many worksheets, it is easy to forget which combining operations have been completed.

After moving to A1 to ensure correct cell pointer placement, the macro executes the /File Combine instructions that follow. The four Combine instructions are the same except for the filenames being combined. Each requests a /File Combine Add Entire-File operation for the appropriate region file.

Guidelines for Use   The region files are assumed to be in the current directory at the time you execute this macro. Each of the region files is also assumed to have a format identical to that of the file in memory. The region file should contain a 1 in column H in the row that corresponds to the region number (rows 1 through 4). As previously noted, these serve as flags to indicate that each region has been combined into the total worksheet. This is a good strategy to use with /Combine Add even when you are not using a macro.

Modifying the Macro   The macro can be modified to combine any number of files. Although each of the region files is combined with the Add option in this case, you can easily change the macro to use the Subtract option instead.

After you learn to add more sophistication to macros in Chapter 13, you may want to return to this macro and make it check for the 1's in column H using the {IF} and {BRANCH} instructions.

With 1-2-3's ability to handle multiple sheets in one file, you might want to revise the macro to load the detail for each region on a separate sheet in the file and use formulas that span sheets to create the consolidation report.

Print Macros

Since 1-2-3 can retain only one set of print specifications at a time, and since many worksheets contain more than one printed report, you may find that you are reentering print specifications each month as you print your worksheet reports. This wastes time and can lead to errors that might require the reprinting of a report.

You can avoid such problems by using macros to record the commands needed to print your reports. Once you have worked out the details, a macro can print as many reports as you like with one keystroke. Also, since the macro is tested, you will not have to reprint reports because of errors in print specifications.

A Macro to Create Printed Reports

Most of your reports are likely to be sent directly to the printer. It is possible that the margins, setup strings, header, and other specifications for the printed page may differ between two reports printed from the same worksheet. If you store the different print specifications in a macro, you need only position your paper at the top of a form and turn your printer on. 1-2-3 can handle everything else.

The macro shown here will print two different reports from one worksheet.

```
      A     B                       C
 1    \p    /PP                     Request print
 2          RA1..C15~               Specify range
 3          OML20~                  Request options and left margin of 20
 4          MR55~                   Request right margin of 55
 5          MT15~                   Request top margin of 15
 6          H¦¦Today's Date:@~      Create header with date
 7          Q                       Quit options
 8          G                       Print
 9          PA                      Page & align
10          RA1..H20~               Specify range
11          OML5~                   Left margin 5
12          MR75~                   Margin right 75
13          S\027\040\049\071~      Change character set
14          Q                       Quit options
15          G                       Print
16          PA                      Page & align
17          Q                       Quit print
```

The first instruction in the macro tells 1-2-3 that you want the /Print commands and would like your output sent directly to the printer. The first print range, A10..C15, is requested in B2.

The Options changes come next. The first request is to change the left margin to 20. Next, the right margin is set to 55. The top margin is set to 15. B6 specifies the header to be used at the top of each page of the report. There is no entry on the left or in the center of the header, so the line contains only two vertical bars to mark the positions. The rightmost portion of the header contains the constant "Today's Date:". It also contains an @ sign, which will cause 1-2-3 to substitute the current date. Since this is the last change through the Options menu, a *Q* is used to quit this menu. Printing is requested with the *G* for Go in the next cell.

The Page and Align request will be processed as soon as 1-2-3 finishes printing. This request causes 1-2-3 to page to the top of the next form and align its internal line count with the appropriate setting for a new page.

B10 contains the first instruction for the second report. Since the Print menu remains on the screen until you choose Quit, there is no need to make a new request for this menu. The first Options request for the second report is found in B11. The left margin is set at 5 and the right margin is set at 75.

B14 quits the Options menu. The second report is printed by the *G* in B15. Page and Align are issued again to position the paper and 1-2-3's line count for your next Print request, and the Print menu is exited with the *Q* in the last macro instruction.

Guidelines for Use   The critical success factor for use of the macro is positioning your paper before turning your printer on. The position of your paper when you turn on your printer is where 1-2-3 assumes the top of the form to be. The macro assumes that the paper is at the top of a form when you start.

Modifying the Macro   You will want to modify this macro to conform to the specific ranges you need to print your report. These instructions are found in B2 and B10; they can be edited to supply a new range. Depending on the range you select and your exact printing requirements, you may need to modify Options parameters such as margins and setup strings. You may also wish to add print options besides those listed in this macro. If you have additional reports to create, you can insert their specifications on new lines ahead of line 17. This way you will be able to have one macro print all your reports.

You can also modify this macro to clear all the print options between reports, depending on how much your specifications change from report to report. If they stay almost the same, you might prefer to change just one or two options by including the appropriate commands and new values in your macro. On the other hand, if there are substantial changes, you might want to include /Print Printer Clear All in the macro. This could be accomplished by adding CA (for Clear All) after the *G* in B8.

A Macro to Store Print Output in a File

If you have never printed to a file, you may wonder why anyone would want to store printed output on a file. There are several good reasons. First, your printer may be out for repair, and you may want to save the printed output until later. Or you may simply want to continue with your current task and wait until later to print. Perhaps you want to use the worksheet data in another package, and you need to supply that program with print output stored on a .PRN file.

The macro presented here will write worksheet formulas to a file with one formula per line. The macro reads as follows:

	A	B	C
1	formulas	/PF	Request print to file
2		FORMULAS~	Write to file FORMULAS
3		RA1..C20~	Specify range A1..C20
4		OO	Request options other
5		U	Request unformatted
6		OC	Request other cell formulas
7		Q	Quit options menu
8		G	Write requested file
9		CA	Clear all print specifications
10		Q	Quit print menu

The first line in the macro requests the Print menu and selects File as the output destination. B2 contains the filename that will be supplied in response to 1-2-3's prompt. The range to be printed is shown next and includes the cells in A1..C20.

The Options menu is requested next, and the Other selection from this menu is chosen. Unformatted output is requested to remove any formatting specifications in the current print settings. While still in the

Options menu, the macro requests Other again, and Cell-Formulas is chosen to print each cell in the range on a line by itself and print the formulas. B7 contains a request to quit the Options menu, and the next instruction writes the output to disk. All print specifications are cleared with the CA in B9, and the Print menu is exited via the *Q* in B10.

Guidelines for Use   When your computer writes to disk files, it writes data to the disk in blocks. When you request Go, most of your print output is written to the disk. It is not until you request Quit from the Print menu that you can be sure that all of your output is written to the file, however. Also, the end-of-file indicator is not placed on the file until after you choose Quit. Be sure to quit the Print menu with Quit rather than pressing ESC, and make sure you leave your disk in the drive until after quitting, to ensure that all your data is in the file.

Modifying the Macro   This macro will work for any set of reports. You should eliminate the request for Other Cell-Formulas from B6 if you want the worksheet printed as displayed rather than as the formulas the macro requests. The range in B4 can be modified to print other reports.

If you want to print multiple reports to one file, you can begin the range specification process again after B8 or B9, depending on whether or not you want the existing print parameters cleared. If you want the output in a second file, place your second request after B10, and begin again with /Print File so you can request a new filename.

Graph Macros

Graphs normally require numerous settings. You have to add titles, data labels, grid lines, legends, and other options to create appealing graphs. You can save time and reduce errors by capturing the required keystrokes in a macro and making it available for use with departmental budgets or other worksheets where a number of managers are using the same formats.

A Macro to Create a Bar Graph

The following macro is designed to work with the sales worksheet used with the /File Combine macro example shown earlier in the chapter

(Figure 12-13). It can be used for any of the regional budgets or the total company worksheet. The only change you may wish to make is in the first line title.

The macro looks like this:

```
        A          B                    C
1    graph      /GRG                  Request graph and reset all options
2               TB                    Select bar type graph
3               XC4..F4~             X range for labels below axis points
4               AC6..F6~             First data range
5               BC7..F7~             Second data range
6               CC8..F8~             Third data range
7               OGH                   Select horizontal grid lines from
                                         Options menu
8               TF\D2~               First line title from D2
9               TY$ Sales~           Y axis title
10              LAProduct 1~         Legend for first product
11              LAProduct 2~         Legend for second product
12              LAProduct 3~         Legend for third product
13              CQ                    Request color and quit options
14              V                     View graph
```

The macro begins in line 1 with a request for the Graph menu. This instruction also resets all the graph values. A bar graph is selected in the next instruction, after which the ranges for the different series used to create the graph are specified. The labels below the X axis will be the entries in cells C4..F4. The next three instructions assign values to data ranges A, B, and C.

The /Graph Options menu is requested next, and horizontal grid lines are added by the instruction in B7. The first line title is set to use the contents of cell D2. A Y axis title of $ Sales is entered next. Legends for data ranges A, B, and C are then added. Color is requested as the last option, and the Options menu is exited. The graph is viewed with the V in B14.

Guidelines for Use   This macro can be used every time you update your worksheet. Of course, if you have just displayed a graph and simply want to see it again, the F10 (GRAPH) key is a quicker approach, since the graph specifications will not be changed. This macro is useful when you are in a new 1-2-3 session and find that someone else has been using the graphics features and has deleted the definition of your graph.

Modifying the Macro   This macro can be modified to save the graph specifications under a graph name. A second, shorter macro could issue a /Graph Name Use command to make the specifications current at a later time.

The macro can also be modified to specify settings for any type of graph you wish. You can use as many options as you need to enhance your basic data.

Data Macros

Macros can also save you time when used to automate functions in the data environment. Most of the /Data commands require that you make a number of selections before you complete your task. Some, like /Data Table, require that you complete preliminary steps before requesting the command. Also, since you must reissue the /Data commands if you want a sort, Data Table, frequency analysis, regression analysis, or /Data Fill operation performed again, you could be executing them frequently. With the macro approach, you can enter them once and check their accuracy, then store them in worksheet cells and use them as much as you want.

A Macro to Create a Data Table

A data table can perform a sensitivity analysis for you by systematically plugging values into your input variables. Before you ask 1-2-3 to perform this analysis, you must build a table shell on the worksheet. Since a macro to do this is a little more complicated than our other macros, you will want to take a look at the worksheet in Figure 12-14 before you study the next macro listing. Projections for Products A and B use the growth rates in C10 and C11 and the previous years' sales to project future periods. Product C is calculated as a percentage of Products A and B sales. The completed table is shown in Figure 12-15.

The rules for working with tables are found in Chapter 10; you will want to look at this chapter if you are not familiar with the /Data Table command. The table in our macro is calculated by having 1-2-3 substitute the values in column B for the growth of Product A in C10 each time the table performs a new calculation. The percentages in row 22

A:A1:   READY

```
 A    A        B        C        D        E        F        G        H
 1                              Sales Projections
 2
 3                            1989     1990     1991     1992     1993
 4          Product A        1,000    1,080    1,166    1,260    1,360
 5          Product B        2,000    2,240    2,509    2,810    3,147
 6          Product C          700      780      869      969    1,080
 7          TOTAL            3,700    4,100    4,544    5,038    5,588
 8
 9
10          % Growth A        8.00%
11          % Growth B       12.00%
12
```

Figure 12-14.   Worksheet for use with /Data Table

will be substituted as new growth factors for Product B. The table contains the result of the formula in G7, which is the total sales in 1990. The first macro instruction is found in B1, as shown here:

```
     A       B                  C
 1   \t      /DF                Request Data Fill
 2           B23..B31~          Set fill range
 3           .05~               Enter start value
 4           .01~ ~              Enter increment & accept stop value
 5           /DF                Request Data Fill
 6           C22..H22~          Set fill range
 7           .09~               Enter start value
 8           .01~ ~              Enter increment & accept stop value
 9           /DT2               Request Data Table 2
10           B22..H31~          Set range
11           C10~               Set input value 2
12           C11~               Set input value 1
13           {GOTO}A21~         Move cell pointer to view table
```

This starting location may seem to conflict with the table data, except that the table macro is on sheet B but the macro is executed on sheet A. This first instruction requests /Data Fill to start building the shell for the table. A fill range is established with the second instruction. Then a start value of .05 and an increment of .01 are specified. When the stop value prompt is displayed, the second tilde in B4 will accept the default, since it is greater than the stop value needed.

The second /Data Fill operation supplies the values across row 22. A start value of .09 is used, along with the same increment as the first range. The default stop value is accepted again.

A:A21:   READY

A	A	B	C	D	E	F	G	H
21					PRODUCT B			
22		+H7	9.00%	10.00%	11.00%	12.00%	13.00%	14.00%
23	P	5.00%	5,007	5,144	5,284	5,428	5,576	5,728
24	R	6.00%	5,059	5,195	5,336	5,480	5,628	5,780
25	O	7.00%	5,112	5,249	5,389	5,533	5,681	5,833
26	D	8.00%	5,167	5,303	5,444	5,588	5,736	5,888
27	U	9.00%	5,223	5,359	5,500	5,644	5,792	5,944
28	C	10.00%	5,281	5,417	5,557	5,702	5,850	6,002
29	T	11.00%	5,340	5,477	5,617	5,761	5,909	6,061
30		12.00%	5,401	5,538	5,678	5,822	5,970	6,122
31	A	13.00%	5,464	5,600	5,741	5,885	6,033	6,185
32								

Figure 12-15.   Completed table

The request for the /Data Table 2 command is made in B9. The table location is defined in B10 as B22..H31. The first input value is the value for the growth factor for Product A, stored in C10. The second input value is the growth factor for Product B, which is stored in C11. When this second input value is entered, the macro calculates the new values for G7 and places them in the table.

Guidelines for Use   This macro is designed to handle most of the table setup, as well as the call for /Data Table to do the calculations. The only tasks it does not perform are the entry of the formula in cell B22 on the sheet containing the table, and the formatting of the table cells. This is to ensure that the values you want are always placed in the table as input values. Be sure not to store information in the cells the table uses, since executing the macro would overlay these cells.

Modifying the Macro   The macro can be modified to create a table of a different size or with different input values generated by the /Data Fill operation. You could also modify the instructions in B3, B4, B7, and B8 to contain {?}, so that the operator can enter the fill parameters, and therefore the input values, every time the macro is executed.

You can also modify the macro to handle the remaining preliminary steps for preparing the table. It would be easy to include instructions for the entry of the formula in B22 on the table sheet and the /Range Format statements required to display the table as shown.

A Macro to Sort a Database

Sorting a database requires the definition of the data range. This does not have to be done every time you sort, but it must be done if you have added a new field or new records to your database. Since it is easy to forget to do this, you can have a macro handle this precautionary step to ensure that you do not sort just a section of your database.

The database this example will use is shown in Figure 12-16. Notice that the names are in random sequence. The macro will sort the file into sequence by last name and use the first name as a secondary key. The result of using the macro is shown in Figure 12-17.

The macro shown here begins in B1 with a request for /Data Sort Data-Range.

```
     A       B                  C
1    sort    /DSD               Request data sort data-range
2            {CE}               Clear entry of existing data range
3            {HOME}{DOWN}       Set A2 as beginning of the range
4            .                  Lock beginning of range
5            {END}{DOWN}        Move to last entry in first field
6            {END}{RIGHT}       Move to last field on right
7            PA2~A~             Set last name as primary ascending key
8            SB2~A~             Set first name as secondary ascending
                                key
9            G                  Complete sort
10           {HOME}             Move to A1 to view sorted records
```

Here the macro is stored on a different sheet from the data. Since the range is set from the previous use, {CE} is needed to unlock the beginning of the range. The cell pointer is moved to A1 with the HOME key, and then down one row to A2. This cell is locked in place as the beginning of the sort range by typing a period. The cell pointer is moved to the last entry in the column and then is moved across to the last column to complete the range specification.

A2 is defined as the primary key, on which the records will be sorted in ascending sequence. The secondary key is B2, the first name, which will also be applied in ascending sequence. The *G* in B9 on the macro sheet requests that the sort begin. The macro ends by moving to A1 so you can review your results.

AɪA1ɪ [W12] 'Last Name   READY

A	A	B	C	D	E
1	Last Name	First Name	SS#	Job Code	Salary
2	Chambers	Sally	817—66—1212	15	$54,600
3	Wilkes	Caitlin	670—90—1121	21	$27,600
4	Stephens	Tom	659—11—3452	14	$19,800
5	Smythe	George	569—89—7654	12	$32,000
6	Samuelson	Paul	560—90—8645	15	$65,000
7	Preverson	Gary	560—55—4311	14	$23,500
8	Patterson	Lyle	543—98—9876	23	$12,000
9	Parker	Dee	459—34—0921	23	$32,500
10	Miller	Lisa	431—78—9963	17	$41,200
11	McCartin	John	313—78—9090	15	$31,450
12	Lightnor	Peggy	312—45—9862	12	$32,900
13	Larson	Mary	219—89—7080	23	$28,900
14	Kaylor	Sally	219—78—8954	15	$17,800
15	Justof	Jack	215—67—8973	21	$19,500
16	Hawkins	Mark	214—89—6756	23	$18,700
17	Hartwick	Eileen	213—76—9874	23	$23,000
18	Deaver	Ken	212—11—9090	12	$21,500
19	Campbell	David	198—98—6750	23	$24,600
20	Campbell	Keith	124—67—7432	17	$15,500

Figure 12-16.   Unsorted database

AɪA1ɪ [W12] 'Last Name   READY

A	A	B	C	D	E
1	Last Name	First Name	SS#	Job Code	Salary
2	Campbell	David	198—98—6750	23	$24,600
3	Campbell	Keith	124—67—7432	17	$15,500
4	Chambers	Sally	817—66—1212	15	$54,600
5	Deaver	Ken	212—11—9090	12	$21,500
6	Hartwick	Eileen	213—76—9874	23	$23,000
7	Hawkins	Mark	214—89—6756	23	$18,700
8	Justof	Jack	215—67—8973	21	$19,500
9	Kaylor	Sally	219—78—8954	15	$17,800
10	Larson	Mary	219—89—7080	23	$28,900
11	Lightnor	Peggy	312—45—9862	12	$32,900
12	McCartin	John	313—78—9090	15	$31,450
13	Miller	Lisa	431—78—9963	17	$41,200
14	Parker	Dee	459—34—0921	23	$32,500
15	Patterson	Lyle	543—98—9876	23	$12,000
16	Preverson	Gary	560—55—4311	14	$23,500
17	Samuelson	Paul	560—90—8645	15	$65,000
18	Smythe	George	569—89—7654	12	$32,000
19	Stephens	Tom	659—11—3452	14	$19,800
20	Wilkes	Caitlin	670—90—1121	21	$27,600

Figure 12-17.   Sorted database

Guidelines for Use   The macro makes one assumption about the worksheet. The macro assumes that the first and last data fields will have values for every record. The instructions in B5 and B6 would not work if some of the fields were blank.

Modifying the Macro   The macro can be modified to sort on any field. You can enter the range address for the macro, though this approach would require modification to the macro as the database expands.

Command Language Macros

**Differences Between Command Language Macros
and Keyboard Macros
Constructing and Using Command Language Macros
Macro Commands**

Command language macros are even more powerful than the keyboard alternative macros described in the last chapter. Command language macros allow you to perform repetitive tasks with ease, and automate applications so that even novice users can handle complex worksheet tasks. They also allow you to use features that are not part of the 1-2-3 menu structure.

The macro command set in Release 3 provides a number of new options—especially in support of data management activities. The Release 1A macro commands are located in the /X command section near the end of this chapter. Although these commands are still supported in Release 3 for compatibility, there are Release 3 commands that support all these features. When writing new macros, always use the new commands since they are more descriptive. With both sets of commands, you can alter the execution flow of a macro by branching to a new location. You can also create your own custom menus patterned after 1-2-3's.

Command language macros are not for everyone, however. They are built with 1-2-3's command language, which is essentially a programming language. As with any programming language, you are likely to have moments of frustration and exasperation as you strive to make 1-2-3 understand your needs. To be successful in creating command language macros, you must be willing to work at the detail level in defining your needs exactly. You will need blocks of uninterrupted time so you can concentrate fully on these details. Finally, you will need persistence to stick with the task until the macro works correctly. Given these efforts, you can learn to create macros you will be proud of.

This chapter is designed to provide strategies for creating command language macros with as little pain as possible. The first part of the chapter offers some general strategies for creating macros, and discusses specific techniques used by programmers working in other programming languages to ensure the correct operation of their programs. Since the 1-2-3 macro command language is also a programming language, you are likely to find some of these techniques helpful when writing your macros. The second section of this chapter describes each macro command separately. It provides a description and a working example that incorporates the macro command.

Differences Between Command Language Macros and Keyboard Macros

Command language macros are entered in the same way as the keyboard variety covered in Chapter 12. Like keyboard macros, they are label entries stored in a column of worksheet cells, named with a backslash and a single letter key. Just as you needed to follow rigid rules when entering a keyboard menu selection sequence, you also have to follow rules when entering instructions from 1-2-3's macro command language. The command keyword and any arguments it requires must always be enclosed in curly braces{ }—for example, {BRANCH A9}. Arguments must always be entered in the prescribed order.

How will you know when to use command language macros and when to use keyboard macros? It is really quite easy. When a keyboard macro will work, use it. When you want to accomplish things that menu commands cannot handle, however, it is time to look beyond keyboard macros.

Your first command language macros may use only a few statements, as in the following macro, which enters a date all the way down a column.

```
1   \d       {LET z1,0}

2   top      {IF z1=5}{BRANCH finish}

3            @DATE(

4            {?}
```

5		,
6		{?}
7		,
8		{?}
9		)~
10		{DOWN}
11		{LET z1,z1+1}
12		{BRANCH top}
13	finish	{QUIT}

After you master the simpler variety of command language macro, you can begin to think of more sophisticated tasks you would like to delegate to 1-2-3. Many of these will require the use of command language instructions, but they are likely to employ the familiar built-in functions, formulas, and menu options, as well. As long as you are working with the 1-2-3 package, you will want all its features at your disposal.

Constructing and Using Command Language Macros

A command language macro normally consists of a number of detailed steps that must be executed in a logical order. When you communicate instructions to another person, you can often be less than fully specific and still get the desired results. That is because human beings can interpret directions and make assumptions about the exact way a task should be performed. If someone knows your way of doing business and has worked for you in the past, his or her interpretations and assumptions about the way you want a particular task done are likely to be correct.

When you ask a computer to do your bidding, however, there will be no interpretation and no assumptions. You will get exactly what you ask for, whether or not it is what you want. If you leave out a step or provide the steps in the wrong sequence, you will get results different from what you expect.

Since you can't change the way computers do their processing, you must learn to set up tasks in a way that a computer can handle. You need to create a road map showing what you want the computer to do for you. If you create this road map on paper, it will be easy to separate logic and syntax. *Logic* refers to the steps in the task you wish the computer to perform, and *syntax* refers to the detailed instructions in the 1-2-3 macro command language, and the arguments they need to execute successfully. If you do not have all the logic of your macro worked out, you will never be able to solve the problem by entering specific instructions. You need to know where you are going and the general route you plan to follow before you start.

Planning Command Language Macros

You can use a variety of techniques to map out your logic flow. Programmers frequently use *flowcharts* or *pseudocode* (statements written in something like computer code but without concern for precise syntax) to map out their programs. The following subsections describe these techniques in more detail. You can use one of them, or you can develop your own technique. The important thing is to completely think through the steps needed to complete your tasks before you get involved with the command language syntax. If you attempt to tackle both logic and syntax at once, and your macro does not work, you will not know where to begin the correction process.

Flowcharts

Flowcharts are diagrams of the detailed logic in a macro or other program; they are constructed with special symbols. These symbols are joined with lines to form a pictorial representation of the logic flow. A standard set of symbols is used so that any programmer can understand a flowchart created by another individual. In fact, a programmer often asks another programmer to review the flowchart of a problem solution before it is coded, to help identify logic errors early in the testing process.

In most flowcharts, the diamond represents a decision to be made, the small circle is a connector, the parallelogram marks input and output operations, and the rectangle indicates arithmetic operations and other processes. Figure 13-1 presents a flowchart using these symbols. It describes the logic required to combine a variable number of region files into one worksheet. This would allow someone to create division or total company reports with one worksheet. Ctr1 and Ctr2 are counters.

If you use flowcharts for mapping your program logic, there is no need to buy a special flowchart template to create the special symbols. Drawing them by hand is just as effective. You can even use a different set of symbols if you prefer.

Pseudocode

Pseudocode is a shortcut method of documenting your logic with every-day English words. It is quicker to use than flowcharts, since there are no figures to be drawn, and it is closer to the final form of program code that you will use. When writing pseudocode, don't concern yourself with spelling, grammar, or complete sentences; phrases are best, in fact, as long as they are clear.

The following lines of pseudocode describe the same process that was pictured in the flowchart in Figure 13-1. The first column represents labels that the macro uses to branch to. The second column shows the steps the macro performs.

	Initialize Ctr2 to 1
	Position cursor
	Enter number of regions to combine
	Set Ctr1 = # regions
Combine	Use/File Combine Add
	If Ctr1 = Ctr2 branch to End
	Add 1 to Ctr2
	Branch to Combine
End	Quit

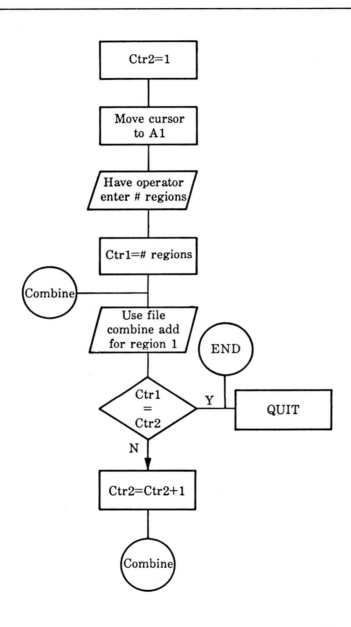

Figure 13-1.   Flowchart for combining files

Strategies for Designing Complex Macros

A three- or four-line command language macro is no more difficult to create than a keyboard macro. It is so small that you can keep track of its entire logic flow mentally. More sophisticated command language macros, however, need more careful structuring and planning.

Branching Versus Straight-Line Code

It is easy to create macro code that branches all over the place; programmers refer to this as "spaghetti bowl" code. It usually results from lack of planning. New instructions are simply added as the programmer thinks of them. If there is not enough room to insert all the instructions needed, the program branches away to a blank location and then branches back again to execute the remaining instructions. The result is confusion. It may be faster to code a program or a macro in this fashion, but making it work correctly is something else again.

Straight-line code is at the opposite end of the spectrum. Wherever possible, it proceeds from the top to the bottom of the logic flow without branching. Of course, branching need not be forbidden entirely. A little common sense can go a long way in creating macros that are both workable and correct. Straight-line code, however, offers the advantage of allowing you to read from the top to the bottom of the code and get a picture of what it is accomplishing.

Main Code and Subroutines

You can write a large macro that contains, say, 400 instructions, and list them consecutively down a column on your worksheet. To get a picture of what this macro is designed to accomplish, one would have to read all 400 lines of code. A better approach is to separate your macros into a mainline code section and subroutines. Properly planned, this structure combines the advantages of branching and straight-line code.

A manageable upper limit for the length of the main section is considered to be 50 lines. Detail tasks are taken out of this section and placed in subroutines, which are referenced by instructions in the main section. Because the main section is short, it can be scanned quickly to learn the essence of the macro. This form of organization also makes it easier to test the macro a section at a time and thereby trace errors to particular sections of code.

When a main program calls a subroutine, the subroutine instructions will be executed until a {RETURN} is encountered or the end of the subroutine is reached. At that time, control will return to the main program that called the subroutine. The instruction immediately following the subroutine call will be executed next. A subroutine call is always indicated by enclosing the subroutine name in curly braces. To call a subroutine named Print, for example, you would enter {**Print**}.

The following example shows how a main program and its subroutines might be structured.

```
Main Routine
        . . .
        . . .
        {update}
        {print}

Subroutines
update
        . . .
        . . .
        . . .
        . . .
        {RETURN}
print   . . .
        . . .
        {RETURN}
```

The . . . entries represent macro instructions appropriate for the routines. Note that with this structure, you can read down the main code and see that an update operation will be performed, followed by a print operation. You need not read the precise instructions in either subroutine to understand the program's basic structure.

When you call a subroutine, you can pass arguments to it. This allows you to tailor the routine to each particular situation. Passing arguments to a subroutine requires that the arguments be included in the instruction that calls the subroutine. In addition, the subroutine must contain a {DEFINE} instruction that provides a storage location for each argument passed to it. Release 3 supports a maximum of 31 arguments for each subroutine.

When it encounters a {RETURN} statement, 1-2-3 returns to the subroutine calling location and executes the instruction immediately following the subroutine call. If 1-2-3 encounters a second subroutine call before a {RETURN} instruction, it begins executing the code in the second subroutine. Adding various levels of subroutine calls within a macro is referred to as *stacking* or *nesting* subroutine calls. The number of levels of stacked subroutines that you can use is limited by available memory, although you may reach a practical limit well before you run out of memory.

Tip: Limit nested subroutines to three levels. It can be difficult to decipher the logic of a program when it contains nesting of subroutines that exceed three levels.

You can have a main program that calls the same subroutine multiple times and passes different arguments to it each time. For example, you might want to print your worksheet with three different setup strings, using an argument to pass a setup string to the print subroutine. Your main program might appear as follows:

```
{print k1}
{print k2}
{print k3}
```

Each time a call is executed, whatever is stored in the specified cell (that is, K1, K2, K3) is passed to the subroutine.

The print subroutine would require a storage place for only one argument, since only one argument is passed to it each time it is executed. Assuming Setup was defined as a range name, the print subroutine might appear like this:

```
print {DEFINE Setup:string}
     . . .

     . . .
{RETURN}
```

Setup is defined as a string argument; it will contain the value of K1, K2, and K3 from each execution of the Print routine. You must include a location argument in the {DEFINE} command for each argument passed by the subroutine call.

The location arguments in a {DEFINE} command support the addition of :*string* or :*value*. If you use :*string*, 1-2-3 will store the argument that is passed to the location argument as a left aligned label. When :*value* is used, 1-2-3 stores the entry if it is a number, or evaluates the argument if it is a formula. When a cell address or range name is supplied as argument, 1-2-3 evaluates the cell reference and stores the contents based on the type of entry it finds. The way the result is stored depends on the type of formula evaluated. String formulas return labels, and numeric formulas return numbers. If you omit the argument, 1-2-3 uses :*string*.

Entering Command Language Macros

Having mapped out a plan for your macro, you are ready to begin entering actual code. Command language macros are entered in the same manner as keyboard alternative macros. As with keyboard macros, you can enter them in a separate file to create a macro library or as part of a file that contains worksheet or data management entries. If you enter them within an existing file, consider using a separate sheet. If a separate sheet does not meet your needs, it is a good idea to place command macros in an out-of-the-way location that has room for a blank column on both sides of the macro instructions column. Then you can use the column to the left of the macro for the macro name and any range names you might assign to different sections of the macro. You might want to consider a location diagonally opposite from your data. This way, if you insert rows or columns in the data portion of the sheet, the macro will not be affected.

You can use either upper- or lowercase for macro commands, argument names, cell address references, keyboard commands, and macro names. You must follow the command syntax exactly, using the curly braces around each command entry, and the exact spelling for each command keyword.

You can have 1-2-3 do some of the work for you: Type the curly brace { once, and press F3 (NAME) twice. 1-2-3 will list all the macro key names and commands; you can highlight the one you want, and press ENTER to have 1-2-3 add it for you. Since most of the commands expect arguments to define the specific use of the command, a space is left after the keyword, and each of the arguments is entered with commas as separators. You must then supply the proper type of data for each type of argument. Although you can use the specified type of entry within the macro, you can also use range names, cell addresses, or an appropriate formula to supply the necessary argument information. Only commas may separate the arguments. A closing brace follows the last argument entry.

Arguments that are literal strings sometimes require quotation marks around them. Quotation marks are needed when the string contains 1-2-3's separator characters (a comma, a semicolon, a colon, or a period).

Each cell in the column where you make your macro entries can contain up to 512 characters, since each macro instruction is entered as a label. It is not recommended that you use entries that even approach this upper limit, however. Forty or fifty characters is a reasonable upper limit if you want your macros to be readable. Try to complete each macro instruction in the same cell where you begin entering it.

Naming Command Language Macros

Command language macros are named in the same fashion as keyboard macros. The name of any command language macro that you wish to execute directly from the keyboard should consist of a single letter preceded by a backslash (\). This naming convention affords a quick keyboard execution of the macro, or use any valid range name if a quick entry alternative is not required. Upper-and lowercase are equivalent, so you can have 26 unique macros that can be executed from the keyboard. Remember that you can also have one special automatic macro in each file, that will begin execution as soon as the worksheet containing it is retrieved. This assumes that the /Worksheet Global Default Autoexec command is set to yes. This macro must have the special name of \0.

Since command language macros have branching instructions as well as subroutine calls to execute other macros, you can have macros named with regular range names. These macros will be able to be executed when invoked by another macro or by pressing ALT-F3 and selecting the macro name.

In all cases, you will need to name only the top cell in a macro. 1-2-3 considers a macro to continue until a blank cell or a {QUIT} instruction is encountered.

Creating a Macro Shell

If you like, you can code all your macro instructions at once. It often works better, however, to code just the major instructions first. As an example, if you have a macro that branches to one of four principal subroutines depending on an operator input, first code only the instructions to process the operator's input and the beginning instructions for each of the four subroutines. At the beginning of each subroutine, place an instruction that informs you that you have reached that particular routine. In this manner you can check out the upper-level logic of your macro without investing time in creating detailed code. This kind of "framework" code is called a *macro shell*.

This approach to program construction is referred to as top-down programming. It can save considerable time by allowing you to detect major logic problems before you proceed with detailed coding. If a problem occurs, there will be far fewer instructions at this point to change or move.

You might construct a shell that consists of little more than subroutine calls and instructions to display messages, for example. You can use a "dummy" input statement with the {GETNUMBER} or {GETLABEL} command with the sole purpose of displaying a message on the screen. The {INDICATE} instruction is another option to inform you of a macro's progress.

This method speeds up your testing process significantly, since you can test the program's basic logic by invoking each subroutine and checking the special message it displays. Once you check the execution flow, you can add the detailed code needed to complete the subroutines.

Figure 13-2 provides an example of this shell structure. Here, each subroutine contains only an instruction to let you know that you have arrived at that location in the macro. Once this program pattern checks out as correct, you can add instructions for each routine.

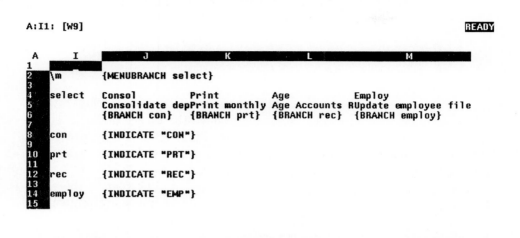

Figure 13-2.   Macro shell for a menu

Creating Interactive Macros

Interactive macros are macros that change as they are executed. They can change logic flow in response to entries by the operator. They can even change entries in instructions, such as filenames.

Macros That Respond to Operator Input

As you look through the various macro commands in this chapter, you will find several that accept operator input. These include {?}, {GETLABEL}, {GETNUMBER}, {GET}, and {LOOK}. You can use the information obtained from these entries to control {BRANCH} instructions and subroutine calls, as well as other processing within the macro.

Dynamically Altered Macros

Dynamically altered macros store information that is input or calculated during execution as part of the macro itself.

For example, in a file retrieve instruction, you might want to change the file retrieved depending on the application you are working on. To do this, use a menu selection to determine the application and have this instruction alter the following macro instruction sequence:

/fr
blank

~

In this example, the macro cell that contains the word "blank" would actually be an empty cell. You want to have the macro make an appropriate entry in this cell, using either a {PUT} or a {LET} instruction. Thus the macro would be altering itself to perform the exact action you want.

A simpler form of this dynamic alteration will be seen in the example of the {GETLABEL} command, where dates are being temporarily entered in macro cells for later storage in a different area of the worksheet. Depending on your entries, the macro is altered to create a variety of date entries. Release 3's ability to accept @functions as arguments in Release 3 macros allows you to perform many calculations from within a macro instruction.

Documenting Command Language Macros

Macro documentation consists of comments added to the worksheet to explain the macro. Its main purpose is to make each macro step clear to someone who was not involved in the macro's creation. However, you also are likely to find it helpful when you look back at a macro you wrote, say, three months previously.

Variables in a macro should be given meaningful names. This will minimize the need for supplemental documentation and will make formulas in the macro easier to read.

You can document the name of your macro by placing it in the column to the left of the top macro instruction. When naming subroutines, place the name to the left of the top cell in each subroutine. Macro instructions should be documented by writing a description to the right of each instruction. Be as brief as possible, but make sure you clearly describe all formulas or other entries that might not be clear at a later time.

Since macro instructions are label entries, any references to cell addresses they contain will not be updated if referenced cells are moved or deleted. You may want to flag macro cells containing cell address references with an asterisk to the far left or right of the macro column, to make sure you check these entries any time you reorganize the worksheet.

Consider also the use of section names within your macro. Section names are names placed in the column to the left of a macro; they simply name sections of the macro. Even when you have not created range names for these locations, section names can make your macro more readable.

If you are like most people, you probably will not want to bother with the documentation step. Learn to think of documentation as a worthwhile investment that can save you time in the future, and make it possible to delegate the maintenance of your applications to others as you move on to new responsibilities. A few extra minutes spent documenting a macro when you have just finished creating it can pay off in hours of time saved later.

Testing Command Language Macros

Do not assume that a macro will work correctly unless you have tested it. A multiple-step testing process is the most efficient and will ensure that your macro works under all conditions. Here are macro testing guidelines.

1. Your first test should be an easy one. If the macro performs calculations, use even numbers so you can check its answers mentally. If you choose a complicated number, you might make arithmetic mistakes yourself while testing it.

2. If your macro is an iterative one (one that is executed numerous times), test only two or three iterations of its cycle. This saves time and makes it easier to check results.

3. Next try to see what the macro does with exceptions or unusual conditions that occur only sporadically.

4. Check for error conditions next. If the macro prompts you for the number of times you wish to execute a certain routine, respond with −25. If it asks for a number of vacation days, respond with

560. If it asks for a salary increase, respond with 1500%. See whether it responds to the error conditions as you would expect.

5. If your macro fails at any step along the way, correct the error condition and go back to the first step for a quick recheck after the change. Never assume that a change to one part of a macro will not affect another part. It often does, and the only way you will know for sure is to test it.

6. If your macro will be used by others, involve them in the testing process. No one knows better the type of data that will be entered into the macro than the person who will use the program every day. This approach will also help you discover if you have to change the macro because you have misinterpreted the user's needs. For instance, you may have allowed for the entry of an invoice amount, whereas the user expected the macro to compute a total invoice amount based on entry of detail figures.

7. If you are designing a macro to work in multiple files, you must test its operation in more than one file.

Tip: Turn on the Undo feature with /Worksheet Global Default Other Undo Enable, before testing a macro. Then you can press ALT-F4 (UNDO) to eliminate all the effects of the macro if it causes errors in the worksheet.

Executing Command Language Macros

Executing a completed command language macro is easy. Just like a keyboard macro, simply press the ALT key and the letter key of the macro's name simultaneously. An alternative is to press ALT-F3 and select the name of the macro you want to execute. There are several other things you should be aware of before executing a macro, however.

Using Undo While Running Macros

As indicated in the last Tip, if you run a macro with Undo enabled, you can press ALT-F4 (UNDO) to cancel all the effects of the macro on the worksheet. Undo eliminates the effect of menu selections and macro commands within the normal scope of its capabilities; (that is, the action of Undo is confined to the worksheet and cannot eliminate /File Saves and print operations that have been completed. If 1-2-3 does not have sufficient memory to run the macro with Undo turned on, it will prompt you before turning Undo off.

Updating the Worksheet

As you begin using macros, you will find that some of the macro commands update worksheet cells. They do not always update these cells immediately, and sometimes the worksheet must be recalculated before the update takes place. For some commands, pressing the ENTER key may be sufficient to cause the updating. You will want to follow these commands with a tilde ($\sim$) if immediate update is critical to the successful execution of the macro. Other commands require that the worksheet be recalculated.

The following commands will update the worksheet if you follow them with a tilde ($\sim$) or {CALC}:

    {CONTENTS}
    {DEFINE}
    {FILESIZE}
    {FOR}
    {GET}
    {GETLABEL}
    {GETNUMBER}
    {GETPOS}
    {LOOK}
    {ONERROR}
    {PUT}
    {READ}
    {READLN}
    /XL
    /XN

Stopping a Macro

Unless you have disabled the BREAK key by including {BREAKOFF} in your macro, you can interrupt a macro in midstream simply by pressing

CTRL-BREAK. This displays an ERROR indicator on the screen. If you then press ESC, you can leave the macro and return to READY mode. {BREAKOFF} is described in the "Macro Commands" section of this chapter.

Macro Commands

Syntax of Macro Commands

1-2-3's command language has two separate types of macro commands: commands without arguments and commands with arguments. Both types include a keyword in braces. Subroutine calls are exceptions to these rules. See the box named "The Macro Language Commands" for a list of macro commands and their functions.

The format of a command without arguments is nothing more than a keyword enclosed in braces. Examples are {RETURN}, {RESTART}, and {QUIT}.

The format of a command with arguments consists of the keyword followed by a blank space and a list of arguments separated by commas. As with @function arguments, no spaces are allowed between or within arguments. The entire entry is enclosed in braces. Here are two examples:

```
{GETLABEL "Enter your name :",A2}

{FOR Counter,1,20,1,Loop}
```

The following discussion describes all the arguments for each command and specifies which of the arguments are optional.

Conventions for Macros in This Chapter

The same conventions have been used for all the example macros whenever possible. The macro name is shown in column A to the left of the top cell in the macro. Subrouting names are also in column A. The macro

The Macro Language Commands

Macro Command	Function	Type of Macro
{?}	Accepts keyboard input	Interactive
{APPENDBELOW}	Appends one or more rows of data below an existing database	Data
{APPENDRIGHT}	Appends one or more columns of data to the right of an existing database	Data
{BEEP}	Sounds bell	Screen
{BLANK}	Erases cell or range	Data
{BRANCH}	Changes execution flow to a new routine	Flow
{BREAKOFF}	Disables BREAK key	Interactive
{BREAKON}	Restores BREAK key function	Interactive
{CLOSE}	Closes an open file	File
{CONTENTS}	Stores the numeric contents of a cell as a label in another cell	Data
{DEFINE}	Specifies location and type of arguments for a subroutine call	Flow
{DISPATCH}	Branches to a new location indirectly	Flow
{FILESIZE}	Determines number of bytes in a file	File
{FOR}	Loops through a macro subroutine multiple times	Flow
{FORBREAK}	Cancels current {FOR} instruction	Flow
{FORM}	Allows you to use a form for input. Can monitor keystrokes and execute subroutines	Interactive
{FRAMEOFF}	Turns off the worksheet frame	Screen
{FRAMEON}	Restores the worksheet frame	Screen
{GET}	Halts macro to allow single-keystroke entry	Interactive
{GETLABEL}	Halts macro to allow label entry	Interactive
{GETNUMBER}	Halts macro to allow number entry	Interactive
{GETPOS}	Returns to pointer position in a file	File
{GRAPHOFF}	Restores graph settings to before {GRAPHON}	Screen
{GRAPHON}	Displays a graph or makes a set of graph settings active	Screen
{IF}	Causes conditional execution of command that follows	Flow
{INDICATE}	Changes mode indicator	Screen
{LET}	Stores a number or label in a cell	Data
{LOOK}	Checks to see if keyboard entry has been made	Interactive

Macro Command	Function	Type of Macro
{MENUBRANCH}	Allows the construction of a custom menu	Keyboard
{MENUCALL}	Executes a custom menu as a subroutine	Interactive
{ONERROR}	Branches to an error processing routine	Flow
{OPEN}	Opens a file for read or write access	File
{PANELOFF}	Eliminates control panel updating	Screen
{PANELON}	Restores control panel updating	Screen
{PUT}	Stores a number or label in one cell of a range	Data
{QUIT}	Ends the macro and returns to READY mode	Flow
{READ}	Reads characters from file into cell	File
{READLN}	Reads a line of characters from a file	File
{RECALC}	Recalculates formulas in a range row by row	Data
{RECALCCOL}	Recalculates formulas in a range column by column	Data
{RESTART}	Clears subroutine pointers	Flow
{RETURN}	Returns to the instruction after the last subroutine call or {MENUCALL}	Flow
{*routine*}	Calls the subroutine specified by *routine*	Flow
{SETPOS}	Moves file pointer to a new location in the file	File
{SYSTEM}	Executes an operating system command	Flow
{WAIT}	Waits until a specified time	Keyboard
{WINDOWSOFF}	Suppresses window updating	Screen
{WINDOWSON}	Restores window updating	Screen
{WRITE}	Places data in a file	File
{WRITELN}	Places data in a file and adds a carriage return/line feed at the end	File
/XC	Calls a subroutine	/X
/XG	Branches to a new location	/X
/XI	Tests a logical condition	/X
/XL	Gets a label entry from the keyboard	/X
/XM	Creates a user-defined menu	/X
/XN	Gets a number from the keyboard	/X
/XQ	Quits the macro	/X
/XR	Returns control to the main macro code from a subroutine	/X

instructions are written in column B as labels, except for menu macros, which extend to the right into additional columns. The columns on the sheets where the macros were entered were widened to allow for the complete entry of each element.

When possible, documentation has been placed in column C. Each description extends to the right and sometimes displays in the columns to the right of column C or in a widened column C. In this book, the display of the documentation entries sometimes continues to a second line. However, you should keep documentation entries in your macros all on one line on the worksheet. The documentation entry is split in these examples due to the restrictions of printing. Also, it is sometimes not possible to show complete macro documentation in the book due to width restrictions. Macros that lack descriptions in the book should be documented on your worksheet.

Lowercase characters are used for menu selections and responses to menu prompts. Filenames, command keywords, and special key indicators, such as {HOME}, {ESC}, {IF}, and {MENUBRANCH} are shown in uppercase. Range names, which also serve as subroutine names, are shown in lowercase. When used within the text, these names are bold-faced to indicate their special use. Arguments in the text are shown in italics.

The macro commands in the sections that follow are grouped according to the categories in which they are placed in your 1-2-3 manual: commands that affect the screen, commands that interact with the keyboard operator, commands that control the flow of execution within a macro, a group of Release 1A macro commands that are included for compatibility, commands that affect data entry, and commands that access file data. For each command you will find a description, format rules, descriptions of arguments (if any), suggestions for use, and an example. Special setup procedures are also described, if any are required.

Macro Commands That Affect the Screen

Macro commands that affect your screen can handle such tasks as updating the Window option and control panel. If the macro commands display as they execute you have an indication of where the macro is at any particular moment, but the macro's quick progress can cause a flicker as the screen is updated. These macros also provide the ability to create your own mode indicator, and to sound your computer's bell to get the operator's attention.

{BEEP}

The {BEEP} command sounds your computer's bell.

Format   The format for the {BEEP} command is

{BEEP *number*}

where *number* is an optional argument to set the tone of the bell. The *number* argument can have any value from 1 to 4, with 1 as the default when no number is specified.

Use   You can use the beep to alert the operator to an error, indicate that you expect input, show periodically that a long-running macro is still functioning, or signify the conclusion of a step. In this example, it is used to indicate that an input instruction follows.

```
{BEEP 3}
{GETNUMBER "Enter your account number",F2}
```

This {BEEP} instruction will cause the computer's bell to ring with tone 3 right before the input message is displayed.

Tip: Switching the Beep tone off causes the macro to have no audible effect.

If you set /Worksheet Global Default Other Beep to No, the {BEEP} command will not cause a beep sound.

Example   The following macro uses the {BEEP} instruction to alert the operator that a significant response is being requested.

```
            A                                B
1   \b               {GETLABEL "Do you wish to erase your work?",h1}

2                    {IF h1="Y"}{BRANCH erase}

3                    {QUIT}

4

5   erase            {BEEP}

6                    {GETLABEL "Confirm erase request by typing a Y",h2}

7                    {IF h2="Y"}/wey

8                    {QUIT}
```

The worksheet is about to be erased, and this macro requests confirmation that this significant action is desired. The first macro instruction uses {GETLABEL} to request a response concerning whether or not the worksheet should be erased. If the operator responds with a Y, the condition test {IF h1 = "Y"} will be true, and the instruction from the same line that branches to the **erase** subroutine will be executed. If any other response is provided, the macro quits. The blank line between the two macros separates them so 1-2-3 does not execute the second macro when it finishes the first.

When **erase** is executed following the {BRANCH} instruction, its first step is to issue the {BEEP} warning. It then asks for confirmation of the erase request. If the request to erase is confirmed, the macro erases the worksheet and then quits.

Note: Beep without an argument is equivalent to {BEEP 1}. When you use a tone argument other than 1 through 4, 1-2-3 divides the number by 4 and uses the remainder for the tone value.

{FRAMEOFF}

The {FRAMEOFF} command allows further customization of the screen by turning off the display of the worksheet frame.

Format   The format for the {FRAMEOFF} command is {FRAME-OFF}. This command has no arguments.

Use   This command allows you to create a help display or data entry form without the distraction of the frames containing column letters and row numbers. The frame will not be restored to the display until a {FRAMEON} instruction is encountered.

Example   The screen in Figure 13-3 is created with text entries and format commands. The {FORM} command displays the form and controls input within the defined input area. If the {FRAMEOFF} command is added to the macro code before executing the {FORM} command, the row and column headings are eliminated and the screen looks like Figure 13-4.

{FRAMEON}

The {FRAMEON} command allows you to restore the display of the worksheet row and column frame after it has been disabled with {FRAMEOFF}.

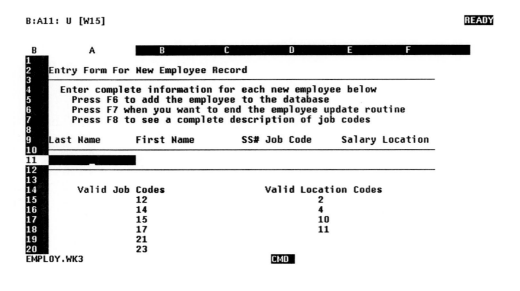

Figure 13-3.   Data entry form with a frame

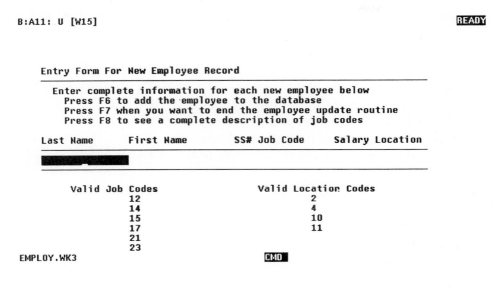

B:A11: U [W15]   READY

Entry Form For New Employee Record
⎯⎯⎯
   Enter complete information for each new employee below
     Press F6 to add the employee to the database
     Press F7 when you want to end the employee update routine
     Press F8 to see a complete description of job codes

Last Name   First Name   SS# Job Code   Salary Location
⎯⎯⎯

        Valid Job Codes   Valid Location Codes
               12   2
               14   4
               15   10
               17   11
               21
               23
EMPLOY.WK3   CMD

Figure 13-4.   Data entry form after {FRAMEOFF} is executed

Format   The format of the command is {FRAMEON}. This command
has no arguments.

Use   You can use the {FRAMEON} command to restore the display
of the frame when a task requiring cell pointer positioning is required.
You might remove the frame to display a help screen or a data entry
form. If the next required task is completing data entry in a group of
cells you might want to restore the frame.

Example   The following code illustrates the restoration of the frame
after the execution of the {FORM} command:

```
        A                B                    C
1   addrec          {FRAMEOFF}        Eliminate frame

2                   {FORM custadd}    Use custom form for add

3                   {FRAMEON}         Restore frame
```

Setup   You must create the range name **custadd** before invoking this macro. The range should have its Protection status removed, as this is the area where entries can be made on the form.

{GRAPHOFF}

The {GRAPHOFF} command eliminates the effect of the {GRAPHON} command. It restores graph settings that were current before {GRAPHON} and eliminates the graph display from the screen.

Format   The format of the command is {GRAPHOFF}. The command has no arguments.

Use   You can use this command to eliminate the effect of a {GRAPHON} command that you executed. You may display a graph with {GRAPHON} for a fixed amount of time or allow the user to make an entry that will remove it. Either way, when you want the graph eliminated from the screen, use {GRAPHOFF}.

Example   The following macro code will display and remove a graph:

	A	B	C
1	dispgrph	{GRAPHON piel}	Display pie graph
2		{WAIT @NOW=@TIME(0,0,20)}	Wait 20 seconds
3		{GRAPHOFF}	

The graph will remain on the display for the 20 seconds generated by the {WAIT} instruction. Next, it will be removed with the {GRAPHOFF} command.

{GRAPHON}

The {GRAPHON} command makes a specific graph current and displays this graph or the current set of graph definitions on the screen.

Format   The format of this command depends on the specific action desired. {GRAPHON} with no arguments displays the current graph on the screen. To make another graph current and display it on the screen, the format of the command is {GRAPHON *named-graph*} where *named-graph* is a set of graph definitions. Another format of this command is {GRAPHON *named-graph,no-display*}. Although the named graph is still made current, it is not displayed on the screen.

Use   You can use this command to display a graph on the screen for the user. Since the macro continues to process commands, you can use {GETLABEL} instructions and make customization changes available without the user needing to know the commands required to make enhancements to the graph. Since the graph remains on the screen, you can make changes based on the user's response and display the new results immediately.

You can also use this command to make a set of graph specifications current, yet not display them immediately. This allows you to provide a menu of options for the user that will affect the graph. When the selections are made, you can issue the {GRAPHON} command again without the *no-display* argument, and the graph will display with the changes made from the user's selections.

Example   You can use this command to create a slide show of graphs. The following example displays four graphs for 30 seconds each:

	A	B	C
1	slides	{GRAPHON pie1}	Displays graph pie1
2		{WAIT @NOW+@TIME(0,0,30)}	Wait 30 seconds
3		{GRAPHON bar1}	Displays graph bar1
4		{WAIT @NOW+@TIME(0,0,30)}	Wait 30 seconds
5		{GRAPHON pie2}	Displays graph pie2
6		{WAIT @NOW+@TIME(0,0,30)}	Wait 30 seconds
7		{GRAPHON bar2}	Displays graph bar2
8		{WAIT @NOW+@TIME(0,0,30)}	Wait 30 seconds

Since the macro continues to execute, you can use commands that display prompts in the control panel and accept user input that will affect the graph. The graph continues to appear until a {GRAPHOFF}, another {GRAPHON}, a {?}, an {INDICATE}, or other macro command displays a prompt or menu in the control panel (like {GETLABEL}, {GETNUMBER}, {MENUCALL}, {MENUBRANCH}, /XL, /XM, or /XN).

The following code displays a bar graph and prompts the user about the addition of grid lines to the graph:

```
          A                    B                           C
1       dispbar         {GRAPHON bar1}            Display graph bar1

2                       {WAIT @NOW+@TIME(0,0,10)}

3                       {GETLABEL "Do you want to add gridlines to

                        the graph? Enter Y or N ",answer}

4                       {IF answer="Y"}/goghqq     Add gridlines if Y

5                       {GRAPHON}

6                       {GRAPHON}

7                       {WAIT @NOW+@TIME(0,0,10)}

8                       {GRAPHOFF}
```

Note that some of these instructions are on two lines for purposes of this book; but unless a new row number is shown, the entire instruction should be placed in one cell. The graph **bar1** is displayed by the first instruction. The first {GETLABEL} instruction removes the graph from the screen, and then determines if the user wants to add gridlines. The {IF} statement causes them to be added, if appropriate. The two {GRAPHON} instructions redisplay the graph for ten seconds. The graph is then removed with the {GRAPHOFF} command.

{INDICATE}

The {INDICATE} command provides the ability to customize the mode indicator in the upper right corner of the screen.

Format   The format of the {INDICATE} command is

{INDICATE *string*}

where *string* is any character string. The string supplied is displayed in place of 1-2-3's regular indicator. Using an empty string, that is, {INDICATE ""}, removes the indicator light from the control panel. Using no string, that is, {INDICATE}, returns the indicator to READY mode. Although the normal mode indicators are limited to five characters, with {INDICATE} your only limit is the number of characters that will fit in the control panel.

Use   The indicator you select with this command will remain until you use the command again to establish a new setting. The setting will continue beyond the execution of the macro. If you set the indicator to be FILE, FILE will remain on the screen even if you are in READY mode. Remember to include {INDICATE} without an argument at the end of any macro that has used this instruction. Doing so will restore 1-2-3's normal indicator display at the conclusion of the macro.

The {INDICATE} command is useful when you are designing automated applications. If you have a series of menu selections for the operator to use, you can have an {INDICATE} instruction for each path that will supply a string related to the selection the operator has made. This command is also useful in testing macro shells. Each subroutine can be represented initially by nothing more than an {INDICATE} with a suitable character string, to allow you to check the logic flow. If you have a budget subroutine, for example, you might represent it in your shell with {INDICATE "BUDGET SUBROUTINE"}.

Example   The macro shown here will change the mode indicator several times.

	A	B	C
1	\i	{INDICATE "SETUP"}	Change indicator to SETUP
2		/wcs15~	Change column width to 15
3		/rfc0~{DOWN 5}~	Format as currency 0 decimals
4		{INDICATE "SPLIT"}	Change indicator to split
5		{DOWN 5}	Move down 5 cells

6	/wwh	Create horizontal window
7	{INDICATE}	Eliminate indicator setting

You may want to try this macro in STEP mode, since it does not remain in any one mode for very long. You will just see the indicators flash on the screen briefly, unless you slow the macro down.

The first step in the macro changes the indicator to SETUP. The macro then performs worksheet commands to set up the worksheet with a new column width adjustment and Currency format.

The instruction in B4 changes the indicator to SPLIT. A horizontal second window is then created. Finally, the {INDICATE} command is used without an argument to return to the default setting of READY mode when the macro ends. Without this last instruction, the mode indicator would still read SPLIT after the macro executed. This indicator instruction is most useful in a long macro when you stay in a set mode for a large section of the macro.

Note: If you want to include symbols like commas, semicolons, colons, or periods in the indicate string, enclose the string in quotation marks.

{PANELOFF}

The {PANELOFF} command prevents 1-2-3 from redrawing the control panel while the command is in effect.

Format   The format for the {PANELOFF} command is

{PANELOFF} or {PANELOFF clear}

When the second form is used, the control panel is cleared before freezing it.

Use   This command reduces the flicker that can occur when macro instructions are executed. It is also useful if you do not want the operator to be aware of the exact instructions being executed. Even if the operator turns the STEP mode on to slow down the operation of the instructions so they can be read, the control panel is not updated while

{PANELOFF} is in effect. This command affects only the execution of menu commands, since 1-2-3 does not use the control panel for advanced macro commands like {BRANCH} and {IF}.

Example   The following macro lets you determine whether you want the control panel updated as you execute the macro.

```
     A                          B
1   \p          {GETLABEL "Update Control Panel?",update}

2               {IF Update="Y"}{BRANCH yes}

3               {PANELOFF}

4               {BRANCH finish}

5   yes         {PANELON}

6   finish      {GOTO}d1~

7               /RFC2~~

8               /WCS12~

9               {GOTO}f3~

10              /rfp3~{DOWN 3}~

11              {QUIT}
```

This macro lets you see the effect of updating the panel instead of disabling it. The first instruction expects a Y if you want to update the control panel and an N if you do not. The entry you make is stored in a range (cell) called **update**, which is checked by the {IF} statement in B2. If the entry in Update is a Y, control passes to B5. If it is any other value, control passes to B3, where {PANELOFF} disables updating of the control panel. B4 branches to the subroutine called **finish** to bypass the instruction that turns the control panel on. The remainder of the macro moves the cell pointer to D1, then invokes a /Range Format and a /Worksheet Column Set-Width command. The cell pointer is moved to F3, and another format instruction is issued before the {QUIT} instruction ends the macro.

Using this macro with the two alternative responses shows you what both ways look like to the user. You can then select the approach you think would be most appropriate for your application.

Setup   In addition to entering the macro instructions and naming the macro \p, you must select a cell to contain the response to the {GETLABEL} instruction. This cell should be assigned the range name **update**. Range names must also be assigned to two sections of the macro. B5 is assigned the range name **yes**, and B6 is assigned the range name **finish**. You may wish to enter these labels in column A as documentation and assign the names with /Range Name Labels Right.

{PANELON}

The {PANELON} command restores the default setting of having 1-2-3 update the control panel with each instruction executed.

Format   The format for the {PANELON} command is

      {PANELON}

This command has no arguments.

Use   This command is useful when you want to reactivate control panel updating in the middle of a macro.

Example   The example for the {PANELOFF} instruction shows the effect of both {PANELOFF} and {PANELON} on the control panel.

{WINDOWSOFF}

The {WINDOWSOFF} command freezes the entire screen, with the exception of the control panel.

Format   The format for the {WINDOWSOFF} command is

      {WINDOWSOFF}

The command has no arguments.

Use   Using this command reduces the flicker that occurs on the screen with each new macro instruction executed. Without this command, you see the screen flicker as ranges are selected, the cell pointer is moved, and entries are generated for worksheet cells. This flicker can be annoying to the operator and is best eliminated. Eliminating window updating also reduces execution time for long macros, since it means that 1-2-3 does not have to redraw the screen every time you move the cell pointer or manipulate data.

Like {PANELOFF}, {WINDOWSOFF} is also useful when you do not want the operator to be aware of each activity performed. You can change the mode indicator to WAIT and resume window updating (with {WINDOWSON}) at an appropriate point in the macro.

Example   The following macro will allow you to monitor the effects of updating the window or freezing it during the execution of the macro.

```
        A                           B
1   \w              {GETLABEL "Do you wish to have window updated?"

                    ,update}

2                   {IF update="Y"}{BRANCH yes}

3                   {WINDOWSOFF}

4                   {BRANCH finish}

5   yes             {WINDOWSON}

6   finish          {GOTO}d1~

7                   /rfc2~~

8                   /wcs~

9                   {GOTO}f3~

10                  /rfp3~{DOWN 3}~

11                  {QUIT}
```

With just one entry in response to a prompt message you can change the window updating option, enabling you to see the difference between updating and freezing.

The first instruction expects a Y if you want to update the screen while the macro executes and an N if you do not. The entry you make is stored in the cell range **update**, which is checked by the {IF} statement in B2. If the entry is a Y, control passes to B5, where {WINDOWSON} is executed. If it is any other value, control passes to B3, where {WINDOWSOFF} disables updating of the window portion of the screen. B4 branches to the subroutine called **finish** to bypass the instruction that turns window updating on. The remainder of the macro moves the cell pointer to D1, then invokes a /Range Format and a /Worksheet Column Set-Width command. The cell pointer is moved to F3, and another format instruction is issued before the {QUIT} instruction ends the macro.

Using this macro with the two alternative responses shows you what both ways look like to the user. You can then select the approach you think would be most appropriate for your application.

Setup   In addition to entering the macro instructions and naming the macro \w, you must select a cell to contain the response to the {GETLABEL} instruction. This cell should be assigned the range name **update**. Range names must also be assigned to two sections of the macro. B5 is assigned the range name **yes**, and B6 is assigned the range name **finish**. You may wish to enter these labels in column A as documentation and assign the names with /Range Name Labels Right.

{**WINDOWSON**}

The {WINDOWSON} instruction returns to the default setting of having the screen updated with each instruction.

Format   The format of the {WINDOWSON} command is

{WINDOWSON}

This command has no arguments.

Use   You would use this command when you want to reactivate screen updating. It could be inserted near the end of a macro to have the screen updated with the current results.

Example   The example found under {WINDOWSOFF} provides a look at the {WINDOWSON} command, as well. Take a look at this example to see the impact of both settings on the execution of a macro.

This extract from a macro shows how {WINDOWSOFF} can be used at the beginning of a macro in which entries for labels are made in a number of cells.

	A	B	C
1	\w	{WINDOWSOFF}	Turn off window updates
2		{GOTO}k1~	Move cursor to K1
3		/wcs20~	Set column to 20
4		Cash~	Enter title in K1
5		{DOWN}	Move cursor down
6		Accts. Receivable	Enter next title
7		{DOWN}	Move cursor down
8		Mkt. Securities	Enter title
9		{DOWN 2}	Move down 2 cells
10		Total Current Assets~	Enter title
11		{GOTO}l1~	Move cursor to L1
12		{WINDOWSON}	Turn window updating on

The macro produces a considerable amount of movement on the screen, which would show as a flicker to a watching operator. {WINDOWSOFF} turns this off. Once the instruction in B11 is completed, the screen will look like Figure 13-5. There will not be a significant amount of movement again, so window updating is turned back on in B12 before the macro proceeds.

Interactive Macro Commands

{?}

The {?} command is actually an advanced macro instruction, although it was introduced in Chapter 12, "Keyboard Macros." As you know, it is used to allow the operator to enter information from the keyboard.

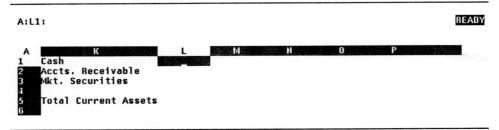

Figure 13-5.   Completed screen for {WINDOWSON} example

Format   The format for the {?} command is

{?}

This command has no arguments.

Use   The {?} command is useful when you need to obtain a few pieces of information from the operator. If you have more extensive needs, {GETNUMBER} and {GETLABEL} are more useful, since they allow you to supply prompts as part of the instruction, to clarify the exact information you want.

If you do use the {?} instruction, you can precede it with an instruction to place a prompt message in the current cell, as follows:

Enter your department number~

{?}

The number entered by the operator would replace the message placed in the current cell by the previous instruction.

Example   Let's enhance a macro from the last chapter that allowed you to enter a date in a cell. Frequently when you need to enter dates in cells, you want to enter an entire column of dates. The basic macro shown in Chapter 12 under the {?} command description can be enhanced to add a loop for a fixed number of iterations. It might then appear as follows:

A	J	K
1 \d	{LET a1,0}	Initialize A1 to 0\
2 top	{IF a1=10}{BRANCH end}	Check for max value in counter
3	{LET a1,a1+1}	Increment counter
4	@DATE(	Enter first part of function
5	{?}	Pause for the entry of year
6	,	Generate comma separator
7	{?}	Pause for the entry of month
8	,	Generate comma separator
9	{?}	Pause for the entry of day
10	)~	Generate close and finalize
11	{DOWN}	Move cursor down 1 cell
12	{BRANCH top}	Begin loop again
13 end	{QUIT}	End macro after 10 entries

This macro follows the basic format of the earlier one, but shows how the {?} can be enhanced with the use of other instructions to produce multiple dates rather than a single entry. The {?} command will appear again in the example for {GETNUMBER}, where further flexibility will be provided by letting you enter the number of dates you wish to produce each time the macro is executed.

Setup   In addition to entering the macro instructions and a macro name assignment of \d, you will need to assign the range names **end** and

top to two sections of the macro. Assign these range names to the appropriate cells with either /Range Name Create or /Range Name Labels Right.

{BREAKOFF}

The {BREAKOFF} command is used to disable the BREAK key function, thereby preventing the interruption of a macro.

Format   The format of the {BREAKOFF} command is

{BREAKOFF}

This command has no arguments.

Use   Normally, CTRL-BREAK can be used to stop a macro. It will display ERROR as a mode indicator. When you press ESC, you can proceed to make changes to the worksheet from READY mode. However, when you have designed an automated application and want to ensure its integrity by maintaining control throughout the operator's use of the worksheet, you can disable the Break feature by placing {BREAKOFF} in your macro. Be sure you have tested the macro before doing this, since a macro that contains an infinite loop and {BREAKOFF} can be stopped only by turning off the machine.

Example   Since the {BREAKOFF} command disables the ability of the CTRL-BREAK sequence to stop a runaway macro, it can be dangerous. It is even more dangerous in a \0 macro that executes automatically, since there is then no way to interrupt the macro.

This may be exactly what you want if you have enabled the Protection feature and wish to ensure that the operator's entries are restricted to the cells you choose. With Worksheet Protection, you can prevent accidental destruction to the contents of cells, but you cannot prevent malicious destruction, since an operator can turn Protection off. However, if you allow worksheet updating only through a controlled access macro with /Range Input statements, disable Break, and save the file at the end before erasing the worksheet, the operator cannot do anything other than what you have established. The only problem is that your access also is limited but a solution to that problem will be presented later, after a discussion of what is needed to lock the operator out of illegal changes.

The macro reads as follows:

```
     A                          B
23   \0          Insert {BREAKOFF} here

24               {GETLABEL "Do you wish to update employee names?"
                 ,r1}

25               {IF r1<>"Y"}{BRANCH address}

26               /ria2..b20~

27   address     {GETLABEL "Do you wish to update employee
                 addresses?",r2}

28               {IF r2<>"Y"}{BRANCH phone}

29               /ric2..f20~

30   phone       {GETLABEL "Do you wish to update employee phone
                 numbers?",r3}

31               {IF r3<>"Y"}{BRANCH salary}

32               /rig2..g20~

33   salary      {GETLABEL "Enter password to update salaries",r4}

34               {IF r4=z1}{BRANCH update}

35   end         {BREAKON}{QUIT}

36

37   update      /rih2..h20~

38               {BREAKON}{QUIT}
```

The first instruction, in B23, will eventually contain {BREAKOFF}, but it is best not to add this until you have tested the macro. From here the macro controls the updating of various sections of an employee database. Certain fields cannot be changed, others can be changed as desired, and salaries are updatable only with the correct password.

The {GETLABEL} instruction in B24 checks to see if the operator wishes to update the section of the database that includes employee names. If the response is Y, the macro proceeds to the /Range Input instruction in B26. The names in the database for our example are located in worksheet columns A and B, and this instruction allows the operator to change any of them.

If the operator does not wish to alter any names and responds with N, the **address** section of the macro is executed next. Again the operator will respond to the {GETLABEL} prompt, and if updates are needed, a new Range Input instruction is established.

The next section is **phone**, which allows the updating of phone numbers in the same manner. When the operator is finished with this section, **salary** is next. This section functions a little differently, in that the {GETLABEL} instruction expects a password. This password must match the one stored in cell Z1. Since BREAK is disabled, the operator must know the password, because it is impossible to interrupt the macro to look at the contents of Z1. If the operator's entry matches Z1, the macro branches to **update** and allows updates to the section of the worksheet where salaries are stored. In our example, this is H2..H20, but of course it could be changed to any appropriate range.

{BREAKOFF} is then canceled with {BREAKON} before the macro ends, although this is not mandatory, since ending a macro automatically disables {BREAKOFF}. This macro leaves the worksheet vulnerable to unauthorized changes after the update is completed, because the worksheet is still on the screen. To prevent this, the two {BREAKON}{QUIT} instruction sequences can be replaced with **/fsemploy~r/wey** to both save the worksheet and erase memory. If you do this, you have forever locked both the operator and yourself out of this worksheet unless Undo is enabled.

A fix for this problem is to store another password in a different cell and request the password right before the /File Save. If the password is entered correctly, {BREAKON} is executed and another instruction asks if you have further changes. The changed ending for the macro might look like this:

```
{GETLABEL "Enter special password for further updates ",r10}

{IF r10<>z2}/fsemploy~r/wey
```

```
{BREAKON}

{QUIT}
```

Setup   There are a number of steps to be completed in addition to the entry and naming of the macro.

- The cells where you wish to allow entries must be unprotected with /Range Unprot.

- Worksheet Protection must be enabled with /Worksheet Global Prot Enable.

- Range names of **address, phone, salary, end**, and **update** must be assigned to B27, B30, B33, B35, and B37 respectively.

- The password to allow salary updates must be stored in Z1. Although you can assign any password you wish, LOCK was used for our macro.

- You may wish to freeze titles on the screen, since this will affect the display when the /Range Input statements are executed. Test the macro once and then decide. If you wish to make this change, use the command /Worksheet Titles. You may decide to incorporate this command into the macro to allow the area of frozen titles to change for each section.

{BREAKON}

The {BREAKON} command restores the BREAK key function so that you can press CTRL-BREAK to interrupt a macro.

Format   The format of the {BREAKON} command is

{BREAKON}

This command has no arguments.

Use   You may elect to disable the BREAK function during part of a macro and then restore its operation for a later section, for printing or data entry. BREAK is always restored at the end of a macro.

Example   The example found under {BREAKOFF} contains an explanation and example of the {BREAKON} instruction. {BREAKON} is the default setting, and is needed only to restore the default after using {BREAKOFF}.

{FORM}

The {FORM} command suspends macro execution, allowing you to enter data in an unprotected range. Although the concept is similar to /Range Input, {FORM} offers more flexibility because you may define either included or excluded keystrokes. You may also define keys that will invoke subroutines during the execution of the {FORM} instruction.

Format   The basic format of the command is

   {FORM *input-location*}

where *input-location* is a range of unprotected cells where you want to make entries. Normally *input-location* is an area on a form which you have designed for data entry purposes. Since {FORM} is frequently used with {APPENDBELOW} in adding records to a database, the input-location is likely to be a row.

   The {FORM} command has three optional arguments. The full set of possibilities are:

   {FORM *input-location,call-table,include-list,exclude-list*}

Input-location is used as described in the preceding paragraph.

Call-table allows you to equate keystrokes like function keys or other entries to a subroutine. It is supplied as a range address or range name. The entries in this range are expected to be placed in two adjacent columns. The first column lists the keystroke, and the column to the immediate right of the keystroke contains the subroutine commands that will be executed in response to the keystroke. The keystroke entries are case sensitive; *A* is a different request from *a*. These assignments are only effective while the form is active.

The remaining two arguments are also optional. When you choose to use *include-list,* do not specify *exclude-list* since 1-2-3 will ignore it. You can use *include-list* when you wish to limit the keys that can be used while the form is active. Any key not listed will be disabled. You can include typewriter keys, pointer movement keys, and function keys in the list. *Include-list* is specified as a range address or range name where these keystrokes are stored. The *exclude-list* allows you to list the keys that you wish to be inactive. Any keys not in this list are enabled. Keys in the list will not function. The *exclude-list* argument is provided as a range address or range name where these keys are stored. Like *call-list,* both *include-* and *exclude-list* are case sensitive.

Use   You can use the {FORM} command to improve data entry. Rather than entering information directly into a database, with the distraction of the records above your entry, you can make your entry on a form and then transfer it to the database with {APPENDBELOW}. The {FORM} command offers other options, like specifying a table of subroutine calls. Or you may take the approach of allowing all keyboard entries during input by not using either an include- or an exclude list; this makes all keys available to you. The keys will function as they do when /Range Input is being used.

Example   Figure 13-6 shows a form that was developed for entering new employee information. The range A11..F11 was unprotected with /Range Unprot. This allows you to enable Worksheet Protection yet continue to make entries in these cells. Any input range on an entry form should always be unprotected. This will focus attention on newly entered information, because unprotected ranges display in green on a color monitor or are highlighted on a monochrome display. The input range is named **newrec**.

Next, the macro code in Figure 13-7 is entered. The first instruction activates the form and allows for input in the range **newrec**. Subroutines which you want invoked can be defined with an optional argument *call-table.* For this instruction the call table is a two-column range named **subrtns** located in K3..L5. The keys are recorded using standard macro representation like {WINDOW} for the F6 key. Actions assigned to each of these keys are noted on the form for the operator, and they

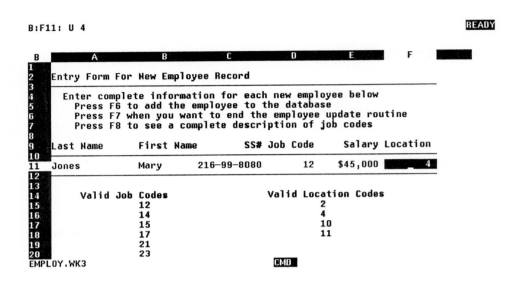

Figure 13-6.   Data entry form displayed with {FORM}

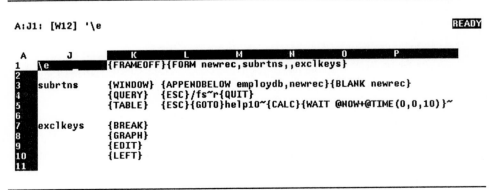

Figure 13-7.   Macro code using {FORM} with a call table and excluded keys

are placed in the table. The optional argument for *include-list* is not supplied, so an extra comma is used to separate *exclude-list* from *call-table*. The exclude list is named **exclkeys**. It is located in K7..K10. The keys in this list will not be operational when {FORM} is active.

Tip: Be careful not to make your *exclude-list* an *include-list*. Remember the extra comma separators to replace unused optional arguments. If you forget this comma, 1-2-3 will misinterpret your {FORM} command entries.

If the user presses F6 (WINDOW), F7 (QUERY), or F8 (TABLE), special actions occur. F6 appends the input information to the area below the database named **employdb**. It then blanks the range named **newrec**. Once the subroutine is finished, 1-2-3 automatically branches to the top of the macro for the entry of another form. This loop continues until the user presses F7 (QUERY) or F8 (TABLE). F7 (QUERY) saves the file and quits the macro. F8 (TABLE) displays a special help screen (like the one shown in Figure 13-8) for 10 seconds and returns to the form entry. The {ESC} in the second and third subroutines leaves the restricted input of the {FORM} command. Another possibility for this macro is to use a {GETLABEL} to let the user determine the length of the display. Or use a horizontal window split with the help information always in the bottom window while the operator works on the form in the top window.

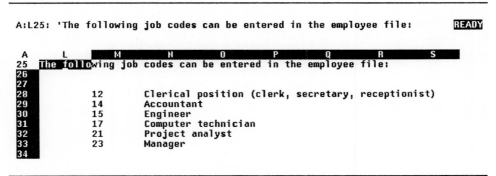

```
A:L25: 'The following job codes can be entered in the employee file:        READY


 A      L       M       N       O       P       Q       R       S
25 The following job codes can be entered in the employee file:
26
27
28         12           Clerical position (clerk, secretary, receptionist)
29         14           Accountant
30         15           Engineer
31         17           Computer technician
32         21           Project analyst
33         23           Manager
34
```

Figure 13-8.   Job code help screen invoked with F8

Setup   In addition to naming the macro before invoking it, the example requires establishment of the range names **newrec**, **subrtns**, and **exclkeys**.

{GET}

The {GET} command is designed to accept the entry of a single character from the keyboard.

Format   The format of the {GET} command is

{GET *location*}

where *location* is the storage location for the single character you enter from the keyboard. Your entry can be an alphabetic character, a numeric digit, or any other key, including one of the special function keys such as F9 (CALC) or F2 (EDIT).

Use   This command provides another option for keyboard input. It offers an advantage over commands like {?}, {GETLABEL}, and {GETNUMBER} in that it can restrict the keyboard response to a single character. However, it lacks the ability to display a prompt message as {GETNUMBER} and {GETLABEL} can. {GET} is the ideal solution for situations where you wish to build your own full-screen menu and expect a one-letter code for each selection.

Example   The screen in Figure 13-9 presents a full-screen menu that offers selections in Smith Company's accounting application. Letter selections represent a budget update, aging of receivables, and other accounting functions. Instructions at the bottom of the screen tell the operator to enter the letter representing a menu choice.
    The following macro works with this menu.

	J	K
1	\g	{BLANK a20}
2		{INDICATE}
3		{GOTO}a1~
4		{GET choice}

```
5            {IF choice="B"}{BRANCH budget}

6            {IF choice="R"}{BRANCH rec}

7            {IF choice="I"}{BRANCH inv}

8            {IF choice="U"}{BRANCH payroll}

9            {IF choice="P"}{BRANCH report}

10           {INDICATE "ERROR"}

11           {LET a20,"Incorrect entry re-execute macro"}{CALC}

12

13  budget   {GOTO}ql~

14           {GETLABEL "Budget routine",zl}

15           {CALC}

16

17  rec      {GOTO}ql~

18           {GETLABEL "Receivables Routine",zl}

19           {CALC}
```

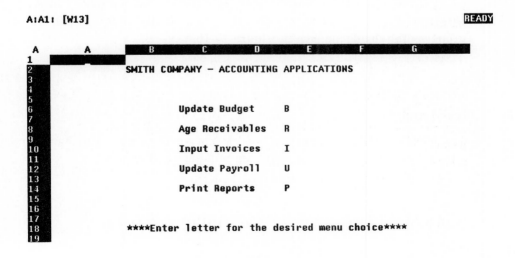

Figure 13-9.   Menu for {GET} example

The macro begins with a {BLANK} instruction makes sure A20 has been erased. This cell must be erased because it will be used to present an error message to the operator when incorrect entries have been made. You must start each new selection process with no entry in this cell.

The {INDICATE} instruction in line 2 ensures that the mode indicator is in its default state, without any previous displays in this area of the screen. Again, this is necessary so that the mode indicator can be set to ERROR if an incorrect response is made.

The cell pointer is next moved to A1 to allow the display of the entire screen. The {GET} instruction accepts a single-character response and stores it in a cell that has previously been assigned the range name **choice**.

The next five instructions check the value of **choice** and then branch to appropriate subroutines. Only two of these subroutines are shown in the listing, but they all follow the same pattern. They have been established as shell routines that do nothing more at this time than move the cell pointer and display a message letting the operator know what routine has been reached. These shells can be expanded later to include a full set of instructions to do the appropriate processing.

If none of the branches is taken, this means that the operator entered an unacceptable character. When this happens, the mode indicator is set to ERROR in line 10, and an error message is placed in A20 with the {LET} instruction, which assigns a string value to A20. This produces the display shown in Figure 13-10.

{GETLABEL}

The {GETLABEL} command is used to permit the entry of a character string from the keyboard in response to a prompt message.

Format   The format for the {GETLABEL} command is

{GETLABEL *prompt-message,location*}

The argument *prompt-message* is a string that must be enclosed in double quotation marks if it contains a character that can be used as an argument separator (a comma, colon, semicolon, or period), or a cell reference, range name, or formula that produces a string. The string displays in the control panel. Its length is limited to the 72 characters at the top of the control panel. If you supply a longer string, it scrolls off the screen.

The argument *location* is a reference to a cell, range, or range name where the information entered from the keyboard is stored. Up to 80 characters will be accepted as input. If a range is supplied for the argument, the character string entered is stored in the upper left cell of the range.

Use   The {GETLABEL} command stores your entry as a left justified label in the location specified. This feature makes the command

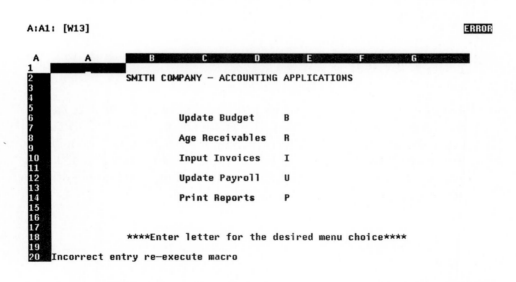

Figure 13-10.   Error message due to incorrect entry

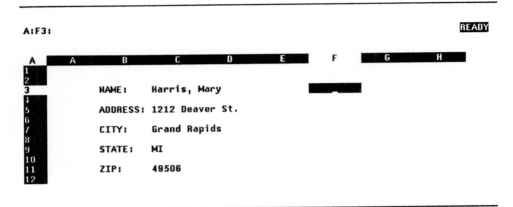

Figure 13-11.   Data entry screen for {GETLABEL} example

appropriate for numeric entries, as well, when you want them placed at the left edge of the cell so they can be read as macro keystrokes.

You might use this command to obtain the name of a vendor with the following instruction:

{GETLABEL "Enter Vendor Name...",a2}~

The name you enter will be stored as a left justified label in A2 in this instance.

Example   Figure 13-11 shows a screen that might be used to capture data entry information. Although you cannot use {APPENDBELOW} when you use this type of form, it may seem a little more familiar to your users than entering record information across a row. The following instructions are an extract from a macro that might be used with this data entry screen.

```
     J           K
 1   \e          {GOTO}c3~

 2               {GETLABEL "Enter Name (Last, First)",c3}

 3               {GOTO}c5~

 4               {GETLABEL "Enter Street Address",c5}
```

5	{GOTO}c7~
6	{GETLABEL "Enter City",c7}
7	{GOTO}c9~
8	{GETLABEL "Enter State",c9}
9	{GOTO}c11~
10	{GETLABEL "Enter Zip",c11}~

The first macro instruction moves the cursor to C3. Then the {GETLABEL} instruction presents a prompt and stores the response in C3. The cell address was added for clarity. The remaining instructions all follow the same pattern, providing a prompt for each new piece of information required and storing it in the current cell. At the end of these instructions, you might wish to add further instructions to move this data to the next available database record within the worksheet or perform some additional manipulations with the data.

The second example for the {GETLABEL} command shows its use with numeric data that you wish stored as a left justified label. The macro reads as follows:

	A	B
18	\1	{LET p1,0}
19		{GETNUMBER "How many dates would you like to enter?"
		,p2}
20	begin	{IF p1=p2}{BRANCH end}
21		{LET p1,p1+1}
22		{GETLABEL "Enter month number",b28}
23		{GETLABEL "Enter day number",b30}
24		{GETLABEL "Enter year number,e.g. 89",b26}
25		@DATE(
26		89
27		,
28		1
29		,

```
30              12
31              )~
32              {DOWN}
33              {BRANCH begin}
34    end       {QUIT}
```

The first instruction initializes a counter to zero. Then the {GETNUMBER} instruction asks how many dates you wish to enter. The response you make controls the number of iterations performed by the macro. As soon as the counter is equal to the number of iterations you have requested, the {IF} instruction in the third line will branch to **end**.

Until then, each cycle will increment the counter by one. The cycle includes three {GETLABEL} instructions that you can use to obtain the date components in a convenient sequence. Since you are storing these components in worksheet cells, you are not restricted to the year, month, and day sequence required by the @DATE function. The current instructions obtain month, day, and year, respectively. These pieces of information are stored in a different sequence than how they are entered, so they will be in the correct order for the @DATE function. The macro then enters a date into a cell. The cells referred to in the macro (B26, B28, and B30) show the year, month, and day number from the last time the macro was executed.

After the date entry is finalized, the cell pointer is moved down one cell, and control branches to the top of the loop, which is named **begin**. The macro ends when the {IF} instruction at the top of the loop encounters the equal condition and branches to **end**, which executes {QUIT}.

Setup   The first macro example requires a predefined menu. The macro also assumes that the cell pointer is positioned in A1 before the macro begins. You could add a {GOTO} instruction at the top of the macro to eliminate this assumption if you choose.

The second macro requires that range names be established for **begin** and **end** subroutines before the macro is executed.

{GETNUMBER}

The {GETNUMBER} command is used to permit the entry of numeric information from the keyboard in response to a prompt message.

Format   The format for the {GETNUMBER} command is

{GETNUMBER *prompt-message,location*}

The argument *prompt-message* is a string that must be enclosed in double quotation marks if it contains a character that can be used as an argument separator (, : ; or .) or a cell reference, range name, or formula that produces a string. The string displays in the control panel. Its length is limited to the 72 characters at the top of the control panel. If you supply a longer string, it scrolls off the screen.

The argument *location* is a reference to a cell, range, or range name where the information entered from the keyboard is stored. A numeric value, formula, or range name referencing a numeric value can be entered. If a range is supplied for the argument, the numeric value entered is stored in the upper left cell of the range.

Use   You might use this pair of instructions to obtain the price and quantity for a purchase order:

{GETNUMBER "Enter the price. . ...",price}~
{GETNUMBER "Enter the quantity. . . . .",quantity}~

The values you enter in response to these two instructions would be stored in the cells with the range names **price** and **quantity**.

Example   The following macro is another macro that can be used to enter a built-in function like @DATE.

	H	I
1	\d	{LET p1,0}
2		{GETNUMBER "How many dates would you like to enter?"
		,p2}
3	top	{IF p1=p2}{BRANCH end}
4		{LET p1,p1+1}
5		@DATE(
6		{?}
7		,

8		{?}
9		,
10		{?}
11		)~
12		{DOWN}
13		{BRANCH top}
14	end	{QUIT}

This macro uses the {?}, which does not provide prompts. You can still choose the number of iterations you want, however. The first instruction initializes a counter. Next, the number of iterations is determined by requesting input from the operator. The iterative section or loop begins with the label **top**. An {IF} instruction checks for equality between the counter and the number of iterations requested. If they are equal, a branch to **end** executes a {QUIT} to stop the macro.

Until the equal condition is reached, the macro stays within the loop and enters the @DATE function in worksheet cells. The operator provides the year, month, and day numbers, and the macro adds the fixed characters needed for each function. At the end of the loop, the cursor is moved down a cell, and control branches to the top of the macro.

{LOOK}

The {LOOK} command checks the keyboard buffer for characters and places the first character in this buffer as an entry in the range identified by the *location* argument. It is similar to {GET}, except that with {LOOK} the operator can type the entry ahead and the macro will still find it.

Format   The format of the {LOOK} command is

    {LOOK *location*}

where *location* is a cell address or range name used to store the character from the type-ahead buffer. If {LOOK} finds the buffer blank, it erases the *location* cell.

Use   {LOOK} does not suspend macro execution while waiting for an entry, as the {GET} instruction does. Normally you will use {LOOK} within a loop, allowing a certain amount of time for an entry before canceling the instruction. You may or may not wish to update the file before canceling.

Example   The following macro uses the {LOOK} instruction to process a menu request from the same application designed for {GET} earlier in this section.

```
           I                     J
1  \l                 {INDICATE}{GOTO}a1~

2                     {LET time,@NOW}

3  keep_looking       {LOOK selection}

4                     {IF selection<>""}{BRANCH process}

5                     {IF @NOW<(time+@TIME(0,10,0))}{BRANCH

                      keep_looking}

6                     {INDICATE "ERROR"}

7                     {LET a20,"No selection made -

                        Reexecute macro"}

8                     {QUIT}

9

10 process            Macro instructions to process menu selection
```

Unlike the example with {GET}, this macro does not wait beyond a specific amount of time. It uses a loop to control the time it will wait if the selection is not in the type-ahead buffer.

The macro begins by setting the indicator to its default setting and moving the cursor to A1. It then places the current date and time in a cell named **time**.

The next instruction begins the loop for checking the type-ahead buffer. {LOOK} is executed and stores the first character from the type-ahead buffer, if present, in **selection**. The next instruction, in line 4, checks to see if anything has been placed in **selection**. If anything is stored there, the macro branches to **process**. If the cell is empty, the macro continues to the {IF} instruction in line 5. This {IF} instruction compares the current time against the time stored at the beginning (in **time**) plus an acceptable wait interval. For this example, the wait time was set at 10 minutes. If the current time is less than 10 minutes after the beginning time, the macro continues to look for an entry by branching to the **keep_looking** subroutine. If the chosen time interval has elapsed, the macro sets the indicator to ERROR and displays an error message in A20. Alternative strategies might be to save the file, clear memory, and quit 1-2-3. The **process** section of this macro is not shown, but would contain instructions similar to those in the {GET} example shown earlier.

Setup The example macro requires that cells for the storage of variables be named **time** and **selection**. The range names **keep_looking** and **process** must be assigned to locations in the macro as shown.

{MENUBRANCH}

The {MENUBRANCH} command allows you to branch to a location containing information required to build a customized menu. Once this branch occurs, the macro executes instructions based on your menu selections.

Format The format of the {MENUBRANCH} command is

{MENUBRANCH *location*}

where *location* is a cell address or range name that represents the upper left cell in the area for menu storage. This area must be a minimum of three rows deep and two columns wide. You may have up to eight columns of menu information.

Use Information for the customized menu must be organized according to specific rules.

• The top row of the menu area will contain the menu selection words that you wish to use. Each of these words should begin with a different character, just as in 1-2-3's menus. This allows the operator to enter the first letter of an option to represent its selection, or to point to the option. Menu selection words are entered one to a cell and must not exceed eight characters each. You may use up to eight cells across, providing eight menu options.

• The second row of the menu area contains the expanded description for each menu choice that will display when you point to the menu selection. As you make one label entry in each cell and move across, it is likely that the entries will appear truncated, since they are long labels. Although you will want to keep your descriptions brief, do not be concerned about this apparent overlap. Place description in the appropriate column for the menu choice.

• Place the remainder of the macro instructions appropriate for each choice in the column with the menu item and expanded description. Begin these instructions in the cell immediately under the expanded description, and extend as far down the column as you need. You may include a branch to a subroutine.

Example   Figure 13-12 shows a menu. There are four different selections in the menu, and it is duplicated four times in the figure so that you can see the expanded description for each of the four choices.

The macro that created this custom menu is shown in Figure 13-13. The macro begins with the {MENUBRANCH} instruction and has all the menu options stored at a location named **select**. The cell J3 is the one to which this name was attached, although the menu selections and descriptions extend down from there and to the right.

The menu selections shown in J3..M3 are the words "Consol," "Print," "Age," and "Employ." As required, each word begins with a different letter. The expanded descriptions appear in cells J4..N4. They are as follows:

J4	Consolidate department budgets
K4	Print monthly reports
L4	Age accounts receivable

M4   Update employee file

As you enter the second through the fourth descriptions, it will appear that you are writing on top of previous ones, but you need not be concerned. Each description is stored as a label in the appropriate cell.

  The last step in creating a menu macro is to fill in the cells underneath the descriptions with all the instructions for each choice. In our example, these instructions occupy only row 5, but internally the entries could extend down in the columns to row 50 or longer.

  In this macro, each option has a branch to a different subroutine. At this point the routines are simply shells to allow you to check the logic. The only action taken in each shell is to change the indicator to the entry specified.

```
A:03:                                                    MENU
Consol   Print  Age  Employ
Consolidate departmental budgets




A:K4: 'Print monthly reports                             MENU
Consol  Print  Age  Employ
Print monthly reports




A:K4: 'Print monthly reports                             MENU
Consol  Print  Age  Employ
Age Accounts Receivable




A:M4: 'Update employee file                              MENU
Consol  Print  Age  Employ
Update employee file
```

Figure 13-12. Custom menu with expanded descriptions

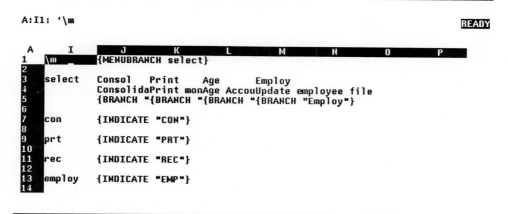

Figure 13-13.   Macro for creation of custom menu

Setup   The entire menu section must be entered before a macro like this can be tested. It is the only example of a macro that can extend across as many as eight columns. Actually, it is eight individual macros in adjacent columns.

All the names listed in column I must be assigned to the respective cells in column J. /Range Name Labels Right is the easiest way to handle this task.

{MENUCALL}

The {MENUCALL} command displays a custom menu as does {MENUBRANCH}, but it executes the menu as a call rather than as a branch. This affects the execution flow at the end of the menu processing. With {MENUBRANCH}, the macro ends when the code for the selected option completes. With {MENUCALL}, control returns to the statement following {MENUCALL} in the main code for the macro, and execution begins again at that location.

Format   The format of the {MENUCALL} command is

{MENUCALL *location*}

where *location* is a cell address or range name that represents the upper left cell in the area for menu storage. This area must be a minimum of three rows deep and two columns wide. You may have up to eight columns of menu information.

Use   Information for the menu must be organized according to specific rules:

> • The top row of the menu area will contain the menu selection words that you wish to use. Each of these words should begin with a different character, just as in 1-2-3's menus. This allows the operator to enter the first letter of an option to represent its selection or to point to the option. Menu selection words are entered one to a cell, and must not exceed eight characters each. You may use up to eight cells across, providing eight menu options.

> • The second row of the menu area contains the expanded description for each menu choice that will display when you point to the menu selection. As you make one label entry in each cell and move across, it is likely that the entries will appear truncated, since they are long labels. Although you will want to keep your descriptions brief, do not be concerned about this apparent overlap. Place each description in the appropriate column for the menu choice.

> • Place the remainder of the macro instructions appropriate for each choice in the column with the menu item and expanded description. Begin these instructions in the cell immediately under the expanded description, and extend as far down the column as you need. You may include a branch to a subroutine.

Example   An example of {MENUCALL} would be exactly the same as the one for {MENUBRANCH}, except that you would expect to see statements after {MENUCALL} in the main code. These would be executed after the menu processing had completed.

{WAIT}

The {WAIT} command will halt the execution of a macro until a specified time.

Format   The format of the {WAIT} command is

{WAIT *time_serial_number*}

where *time_serial_number* is a decimal value that represents the serial time number for the time of day when you wish execution to continue. This value can be computed by adding a time value to the value computed with @NOW to create a fixed delay. You may, for example, want to display information on the screen for 30 seconds to allow time for it to be read, like this:

{WAIT @NOW + @TIME(0,0,30)}

This adds 30 seconds to the current time and waits until that time is reached before continuing execution. While 1-2-3 is waiting, the mode indicator will say WAIT.

Example   If you want an operator to read the instruction screen shown in Figure 13-14, you have several choices for proceeding after the information is displayed. You can have the operator enter a character to proceed and use the {GET} instruction to process this. In this situation,

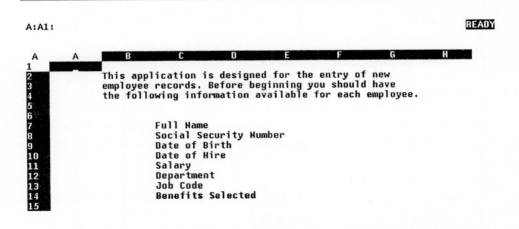

Figure 13-14.   Instruction screen for {WAIT} example

the operator may move hurriedly past the screen without reading it. An alternative is to include a {WAIT} instruction in the macro. This allows you to freeze the displayed screen for a period of time, increasing the chance that the information will be read. If you elect to use this approach, these instructions might appear in your macro:

```
{GOTO}a1~                      Position cellpointer at the display

{WAIT @NOW+@TIME(0,0,25)}      Wait 25 seconds before proceeding

...
                               Macro instructions to be executed

                               after wait

...
```

Macro Commands That Affect Flow of Execution

{BRANCH}

The {BRANCH} command allows you to move the flow of execution in your macro to a new location.

Format   The format of the {BRANCH} command is

{BRANCH *location*}

where *location* is a cell address or a range name that tells 1-2-3 the location of the next keystroke to be executed. If you specify a range name that refers to a range of cells, 1-2-3 will begin execution with the keystrokes in the upper left cell of the range.

Use   {BRANCH} is frequently used with a condition test to change the flow of execution. As an example, you might have the following entry in your macro:

```
      {IF A1>10}{BRANCH end}

  ..

  ..

end   {QUIT}
```

In this case you may have been using A1 as a counter, and when A1 exceeds 10, your task is finished. This sequence of instructions would then branch to **end** and execute the {QUIT} instruction stored there.

Example   The following listing is an excerpt from a macro that combines the data in four files.

	A	B
1	\c	{GETLABEL "Begin combine?",h21}
2		{IF h21<>"Y"}{BRANCH stop}
3		{HOME}
4		/fcaeREGION1~
5		/fcaeREGION2~
6		/fcaeREGION3~
7		/fcaeREGION4~
8	stop	{CALC}{QUIT}

The excerpt begins by asking the operator whether to proceed with the consolidation. The logical {IF} in the next line checks for any value other than Y and uses the {BRANCH} instruction to alter the execution flow to **stop** if such a value is found. Stop recalculates the worksheet and ends the macro.

Assuming a Y was entered, the cursor is moved to the Home position, and the four files are combined with the /File Combine Add Entire-File command. The worksheet is then recalculated, and the macro ends.

Note: {BRANCH} is frequently confused with {GOTO}, but they are not the same. {GOTO} repositions the cursor without affecting the execution of the macro. {BRANCH} alters the macro's execution flow but does not move the cursor.

{DEFINE}

The {DEFINE} command allocates space for arguments to be passed to subroutines and establishes the type of information they will contain.

Format   The format of the {DEFINE} command is

{DEFINE *location1:type1,location2:type2,...locationn:typen*}

The argument *location* is a cell where the value being passed to the subroutine is to be stored. This cell can be specified with a cell address or a range name. A range name is preferable, since it will automatically be updated when the worksheet is restructured. If you specify a range name that references a group of cells, the upper left cell in the range will be used for storage.

The argument *type* tells 1-2-3 whether value or string data is to be passed to the subroutine. *Type* may be entered as either value or string, like this:

{DEFINE Price:value,supplier:string}

where **price** and **supplier** are range names that will be used for passing the arguments to the subroutine. **Price** will contain value data, and **supplier** will contain strings. String is the type default.

Example   If you want to call a subroutine and pass it three numeric arguments, the subroutine will require a {DEFINE} statement to specify storage locations for the three arguments. Since you want these arguments treated as values, you must specify the *type*, because string is the default. If you specify nothing for *type*, the values will be placed in their locations as strings. Your {DEFINE} statement for this example might appear as follows:

{DEFINE z1:value,z2:value,z3:value}

If any of the arguments passed to these locations are arithmetic formulas, they will be evaluated before storage, since the value type has been specified.

For an additional example, look at the description of *{routine}* later in this section.

{DISPATCH}

The {DISPATCH} command allows you to use the contents of a cell to determine the branch location.

Format   The format of the {DISPATCH} command is

{DISPATCH *location*}

where *location* is a cell address or a range name that refers to a single cell. This cell in turn must contain a cell address or a range name of another cell. {DISPATCH} will read this information from the cell and branch to the location represented by its contents.

Use   This command is useful when you need to set up a variable branching situation based on the contents of data fields or other worksheet results. It differs from the {BRANCH} command in that {BRANCH} immediately executes the instructions in the cells beginning at location, whereas {DISPATCH} first reads the location cell to determine the final branch location at which it will execute instructions.

Example   The macro shown here provides an example of {DISPATCH}.

```
      A                          B
1   \d          {IF due_date>@NOW}{LET routine,"not_due"}

2               {IF due_date<=@NOW}{LET routine,"over_due"}

3               {CALC}{DISPATCH routine}

4
```

```
5   not_due    {GETLABEL "Account not yet due",a18}

6

7

8   over_due   {GETLABEL "*** Account Overdue***",a18}
```

The macro is designed to take two different paths, depending on whether the date in **due_date** is greater than today's date. The first instruction checks **due_date** against @NOW. If **due_date** is greater, it places the value **not_due** in the cell named **routine**. If the opposite condition is true, the value **over_due** is placed in **routine**.

The worksheet is calculated to place these values in **routine**, so you can see them display if you use the STEP mode for this macro. {DISPATCH} is the next instruction. It reads the entry in **routine** and then branches to the appropriate location. Again the two subroutines have been set up in the example as shells, but they can be expanded easily to handle whatever tasks you require.

{FOR}

The {FOR} command permits you to execute the code at a given location numerous times through a loop that it establishes.

Format   The format of the {FOR} command is

{FOR *counter,start,stop,increment,starting_location*}

The argument *counter* is a location within the worksheet that the {FOR} instruction can use to count the number of iterations performed. {FOR} initializes this location with the value you specify for *start*.

The argument *start* is the initial value for counter.

The argument *stop* is the end value for *counter. Counter* will never exceed this value.

The argument *increment* is the amount that should be added to *counter* for each iteration of the loop.

The argument *starting_location* is a cell address or range name that specifies the location of the routine to be executed repetitively.

None of these values should be altered from within the subroutine. *Start, stop,* and *increment* are maintained internally by 1-2-3.

Use   You have seen examples earlier in this chapter of loops created without the {FOR} statement. Using {FOR} can make looping tasks easier, since it automatically handles initialization of the counter, increments it with each iteration, and checks for the last execution of the loop. When you create an iterative process outside of {FOR}, you must manage these tasks yourself.

The rules used by {FOR} in processing a loop are as follows:

- Before each pass through the loop, {FOR} compares *counter* and *stop.* If *counter* is less than or equal to *stop,* the loop is processed. If *counter* is greater than *stop,* control passes to the instruction following {FOR}.

- At the end of the *start* routine or at a {RETURN}, control passes to the top of the loop. At this time, *counter* is increased by *increment.*

- If *stop* is less than *start,* the loop is not executed. A loop with an *increment* of 0 is an infinite loop; it can be stopped only by pressing CTRL-BREAK.

- If {QUIT} or {FORBREAK} is used at the end of the loop rather than {RETURN}, the loop ends after the first pass.

Example   The following macro is designed to enter a column of numbers from the numeric keypad and to sum the numbers once they are entered. An arbitrary limit of 20 numbers was established, but if you want to stop sooner, enter **z**.

The macro instructions are as follows:

```
      A                      B
1   \f              {FOR counter,1,20,1,numbers}

2                   /re~

3                   @SUM(

4                   {UP}{END}{UP}.{END}{DOWN}
```

```
5              )~

6

7   numbers    {?}~

8              {IF @CELLPOINTER("contents")="z"}{FORBREAK}

9              {DOWN}
```

The first instruction sets up the loop with an initial value of 1, an *increment* of 1, and a *stop* value of 20. A cell named **counter** is used to store the number of iterations performed, and **numbers** is the location of the code that begins the loop.

Numbers will be executed next. In every iteration, it will expect you to enter a value. You may use the numeric keypad if you disable the movement keys with NUM LOCK.

The next instruction checks to see whether the current cell contains a z. If it does, the {FOR} loop ends (via {FORBREAK}), regardless of the number of iterations completed, and control returns to line 2. If a z was not entered, the cell pointer moves down one cell. The *counter* is incremented by 1, and the loop begins again.

When control returns to B2, the current cell is erased. It will either be blank already or contain a z, depending on how the loop ended. The @SUM instruction is added to this cell. The complete list of numbers you entered will then be added and the @SUM function finalized.

Setup   The range name **numbers** must be assigned to line 7. You must also assign a range name to *counter*. Before executing the macro, position your cell pointer in the desired location for the column of numbers to be entered, and turn on NUM LOCK, since this cannot be done from the macro.

{FORBREAK}

The {FORBREAK} command cancels processing of a {FOR} loop before the stop value is reached.

Format   The format of the {FORBREAK} command is

{FORBREAK}

This command has no arguments.

Use   Normally {FORBREAK} is used in conjunction with an {IF} statement that checks the value of a variable and, on a certain condition, exits the loop. As an example, say you want to process a loop 20 times, or until the account balance is zero. {FORBREAK} can be executed based on a test of the account balance.

Example   The {FOR} example also contains an example of a {FORBREAK} instruction that can end the loop early, based on the contents of a cell.

{IF}

The {IF} command will conditionally execute the command on the same line with {IF}.

Format   The format of the {IF} command is

{IF *condition*}

where *condition* is any expression with either a numeric or a string value.

Use   The statement on the same line as the {IF} statement is treated as a THEN clause: "IF the expression is true, THEN the instruction following is executed." Any numeric expression is considered true as long as it is not the numeric value zero. A false condition, blank cells, ERR, NA, and string values all evaluate as zero.

The instructions on the line after {IF} are regarded as the ELSE clause. Normally the THEN clause contains a {BRANCH}; otherwise, the macro executes the instructions in the ELSE clause after completing the THEN instructions.

Example   The macro shown here provides an example of the {IF} command.

	A	B	C
1	\h	{GOTO}i1~	Move cell pointer to read directions
2		{GET k1}	Get type
3		{IF k1="C"}{LET c15,i20}	Check Budget Year/Set heading
4		{IF k1="P"}{LET c15,i19}	Set heading for previous year
5		{GOTO}b16~	Move to B16
6		^QTR 1	Enter ^QTR 1
7		{RIGHT}^QTR 2	Move cell pointer right and enter ^QTR 2
8		{RIGHT}^QTR 3	Move right and enter ^QTR 3
9		{RIGHT}^QTR 4	Move right and enter ^QTR 4
10		{RIGHT}^TOTAL	Move right and enter ^TOTAL
11		{END}{LEFT}	Move to end on left (i.e. B16)
12		{DOWN}	Move down 1 cell

This macro establishes a heading for a budget report and uses the {IF} command to determine which budget year to print at the top of the report.

At the beginning of the macro the cell pointer is moved to cell I1, where directions are displayed. Then {GET} waits for a single-character entry of *C* for current or *P* for previous.

The {IF} statements in lines 3 and 4 check the character entered to determine the proper heading to use; then it is placed in C15. The statement following each {IF} on the same line will be executed only if the condition shown for that {IF} is true.

The macro then proceeds to complete the remainder of the heading after the year is entered. The year is selected by the {IF} command as described in the previous paragraph. At the end of the macro, the cell pointer is positioned immediately beneath the first quarter heading to be ready for the operator's first entry.

Setup   The macro expects to find headings for the previous and current budget years in I19 and I20, respectively.

{ONERROR}

The {ONERROR} command allows you to intercept errors, or process them yourself, during macro execution.

Format   The format of the {ONERROR} command is

{ONERROR *location,message-location*}

The argument *location* is the location to which 1-2-3 branches for error processing when an error is encountered.

The argument *message-location* is a cell containing the message that 1-2-3 displays at the bottom of the screen when an error occurs. This argument is optional, but if you do not supply it, you will not be able to determine what type of error occurred.

Use   Since the {ONERROR} command is not effective until 1-2-3 has executed it within the flow of the macro, you will want to place it near the beginning of your macro. It remains in effect until either another {ONERROR} command is executed, an error is encountered, CTRL-BREAK is pressed, or the macro ends. Since CTRL-BREAK registers as an error, you can use {ONERROR} to intercept BREAK requests without using {BREAKOFF}. Once {ONERROR} is used to intercept an error, it will not normally be available again in the same macro. If you want to reinstate {ONERROR} after using it, the routine at *location* should contain another {ONERROR} command.

The following macro shows the macro and message 1-2-3 uses when an error occurs. This macro automatically executes when the file is retrieved. The {ONERROR} command directs 1-2-3 to execute the macro starting at the cell called **start_over** if an error occurs while 1-2-3 executes the {Update_pay} macro. If an error occurs, 1-2-3 displays the message in the cell labeled **message** for ten seconds before retrieving the file again so you can start over. This type of error processing would occur when you want an all-or-none transaction processing. If the macro cannot perform all of the changes and save the modified file, it does not save any changes. In a payroll example, you would not want to perform payroll computations for only half of your employees. You would want to make the computations for all of them or none of them.

	A	B	C
1	\0	{ONERROR start_over, message}	If error, restarts transaction
2		{update_pay}	Updates payroll
3		/fs~r	Saves results
4			
5	start_over	{WAIT @NOW+@TIME(0,0,10)}	Displays message for 10 seconds
6		/frPAYROLL~	Retrieves the file to start over
7			
8	message	Unable to complete process, starting over	

{QUIT}

The {QUIT} command is used to terminate a macro.

Format   The format of the {QUIT} command is

     {QUIT}

This command has no arguments.

Use   The {QUIT} command can be used as a value at the end of a condition test, for example, {IF a1 > 10}{QUIT}. When the condition evaluates as true, the macro, including all its subroutines, will end.

{RESTART}

The {RESTART} command cancels the execution of the current subroutine and eliminates all pointers to routines that called it, so it cannot return.

Format   The format of the {RESTART} command is

{RESTART}

This command has no arguments.

Use   When you include this command anywhere within a called subroutine, it will immediately cancel the call, complete the routine, and continue executing from that point downward. All upward pointers to higher-level routines are canceled.

{RETURN}

The {RETURN} command is used to return from a subroutine to the calling routine. It is used in conjunction with {MENUCALL} and {*routine*}. A blank cell or one containing a numeric value have the same effect as {RETURN} when it is encountered in a subroutine.

Format   The format for the {RETURN} command is

{RETURN}

This command has no arguments.

Use   Placing {RETURN} anywhere in a called subroutine sends the flow of control back to the instruction following the one that called the subroutine. Unlike {RESTART}, {RETURN} does not cancel upward pointers. Check the example under the {*routine*} command for further information on the use of {RETURN}.

Note: Do not confuse {RETURN} with {QUIT}. {RETURN} continues processing after returning to the calling routine. {QUIT} ends the macro. With {QUIT}, no further instructions are processed.

{routine}

This command calls the subroutine it specifies. Its format is different from that of all the other macro commands, in that it contains no keyword, but only the argument *routine* and any optional value arguments you may choose to use.

Format   The format of the *{routine}* command is

{routine argument1,argument2,argumentn}

The *routine* is a range name assigned to a single cell. This name
must not be the same as any of the function key or cursor movement
key names, such as {UP}, {EDIT}, or {CALC}.

The *arguments* are optional values or strings passed to the subroutine. They must have corresponding entries in a {DEFINE} statement.

Example   The following macro provides an example of the use of a
subroutine call.

```
        A                    B
1    \r          {GETNUMBER "How many items did you buy?",k1}

2                {LET counter,0}

3                {LET k5,0}{LET k6,0}

4                {purchase k1}

5                {INDICATE "DONE"}

6                {GOTO}q1~The total purchased is :~

7                {RIGHT 3}+k6~/rfc2~~

8                {QUIT}

9

10   purchase    {DEFINE k2:value}

11               {IF counter=k2}{BRANCH end}

12               {GETNUMBER "Enter Purchase Amount"}

13               {LET k6,k6+k5}

14               {LET counter,counter+1}

15               {BRANCH purchase}

16   end         {RETURN}
```

This macro allows you to enter as many purchase amounts as you wish,
and totals them for you.

The first instruction prompts you for the number of items purchased. This number is stored in cell K1. The next two instructions do some housekeeping by zeroing counters that the macro will use.

The subroutine call is in line 4. Notice that the optional argument is used to pass the value in K1 to the subroutine.

The subroutine that begins in line 10 first uses a {DEFINE} statement to set aside K2 for the information passed to it, and declares this information to be a numeric variable. It uses **counter** to loop within the subroutine until **counter** is equal to the number of purchases specified. Until that time, it increments cell K6 by the purchase amount each time, increments **counter** by 1, and then branches back to the top of the subroutine.

When all purchases are processed, the subroutine branches to **end**, where a {RETURN} statement is located. This statement returns control to line 5 in the main routine. The mode indicator is then changed to DONE, and the total amount purchased is displayed.

{SYSTEM}

The {SYSTEM} command allows you to temporarily suspend your work with 1-2-3 and execute an operating system command.

Format   The format for the {SYSTEM} command is

{SYSTEM command}

The argument command is the name of a batch file or an operating system command or a string formula that evaluates to a command or a batch file name. The entry should be enclosed in quotation marks unless it is a range name or cell address where this information is stored.

Use   You can use this command any time you want to suspend 1-2-3's execution to run operating system commands. When running under DOS you should not attempt to invoke a memory resident program with this method since it may overlay some of 1-2-3's memory space and not allow you to resume execution of the macro. When the operating system command completes execution, the macro execution will resume.

Example   You can format a new disk during macro execution with an entry of {SYSTEM "FRMTA.BAT"} if the batch file FRMTA contains the operating system command to format a disk.

Release 1A Macro Commands

The /X commands and {?} are the only macro commands available in Release 1A. These commands are also still available in Release 3 for compatibility, but all of them have corresponding keyword commands in the new Release 3 macro language. This section contains a brief description and example for each of the /X commands. In addition, you will find a reference to the corresponding Release 3 keyword command. Refer to that command's description for an expanded example of its use. You may substitute the /X command in the example if you are using Release 1A. If you have Release 3, however, you will want to use the keyword commands, since they are self-documenting.

Note that the /X commands, unlike the keyword commands, are preceded by a slash and are not enclosed in braces. Note too, that there is no space between the command and its arguments.

/XC

The /XC command corresponds to the {*routine*} command, which is described in the section, "Macro Commands That Affect Flow of Execution."

Format   The format for the /XC command is

/XC*location*~

where *location* is the address or range name of a cell containing a subroutine that you wish executed.

Use   After /XC executes the routine, or when it encounters the /XR or {RETURN} statement at the end of the routine, control will return to the line following the /XC instruction.

An excerpt from a macro using the /XC command might look like this:

```
/XCTotal~

/pprA1..F20~

gpaq
```

These lines would appear in the main macro. You would also need a subroutine named Total with an /XR or {RETURN} at the end of it, as follows:

```
Total {GETLABEL "Enter first amount",b5}

/XR
```

When the /XR instruction is executed, control returns to the /Print instruction following the initial call.

/XG

The /XG command alters the execution flow in a macro by branching to a new location. This new location contains the keystrokes that will be entered next.

Format   The format of the /XG command is

/XG*location*~

where *location* is the cell address or range name containing the keystrokes that you want executed next. If a range name is used, and it refers to a range of cells, the upper left cell in the range will be executed first.

Use   You might use this instruction with a condition test, like this:

/XIcounter > 10 ~ /XGs3 ~

The instruction transfers control to cell S3 only if the condition counter > 10 is true. If this condition is false, control passes to the macro instruction in the cell below the condition test.

The /XG command is equivalent to the Release 3 macro command {BRANCH}. {BRANCH} is described in the section "Macro Commands That Affect Flow of Execution."

/XI

The /XI command allows you to test a condition and take one action if it is true and another if it is false.

Format   The format for the /XI command is

/XI*condition ~ keystrokes for true condition*
      keystrokes for false condition

The argument *condition* is a comparison of two values in cells or a formula.

The argument *keystrokes* is any valid macro instruction. It can be a menu selection, an /XG instruction, or any other instruction you wish executed.

Use   You might use this instruction to check for the end of a repetitive operation by checking the value of a counter, like this:

```
         /XIcounter<>10~/XGcontinue~

         /XGend~

continue  ...

         ...

end       /XQ
```

This command is equivalent to the {IF} command in the Release 3 macro commands, as described in the section, "Macro Commands That Affect Flow of Execution."

/XL

The /XL command causes 1-2-3 to wait for the operator to input a character string from the keyboard and then stores the entry in a specified location.

Format   The format for the /XL command is

/XL*prompt message~location~*

The argument *prompt message* is a message of up to 39 characters that prompts the operator for the information you expect to be entered.

The argument *location* is an address or range name for a cell that will contain up to the 240-character limit that the instruction permits the operator to enter from the keyboard. If the range name supplied pertains to a range of cells, the information will be stored in the upper left cell in the range.

Example   An example of this command might look like this:

/XLEnter your name :~A10~

This instruction displays the prompt "Enter your name :" and then waits for the operator to enter something and finalize it with the ENTER key. The entry is stored in A10. If you wish, you can omit the location, and 1-2-3 will store the entry in the current cell, as in the command /XLEnter your name :~ ~ .

This command is equivalent to the {GETLABEL} command in the Release 3 macro commands. It is described in the section, "Macro Commands That Manipulate Data."

/XM

The /XM command permits you to construct a custom 1-2-3 menu at the top of the screen, with up to eight menu choices and the same expanded descriptions that 1-2-3 provides when you point to a selection.

Format   The format of the /XM command is

/XM*location* ~

where *location* is the range name or address of the cell that begins the description of the menu. Specify the upper left cell in the menu area.

Use   The location that contains the menu conforms to the area used by the {MENUBRANCH} command, which is the Release 3 equivalent to /XM. {MENUBRANCH} is described in the section, "Interactive Macro Commands."

/XN

The /XN command causes 1-2-3 to wait for the operator to input a numeric value from the keyboard and then stores the entry in a specified location.

Format   The format for the /XN command is

/XN*prompt message* ~ *location* ~

The argument *prompt message* is a message of up to 39 characters that prompts the operator for the information you expect to be entered.
The argument *location* is an address or range name for a cell that will contain up to the 80-character limit that the instruction permits the operator to enter from the keyboard. If the range name supplied pertains to a range of cells, the information will be stored in the upper left cell in the range.

Use   You may specify numeric values, range names referencing numeric values, formulas, or built-in functions in response to the prompt.
An example of the use of the /XN command is:

/XNEnter your age : ~ a10 ~

This instruction would display the prompt "Enter your age :" and then wait for the operator to enter something and finalize it with the ENTER key. The entry would be stored in A10. If you wish, you can omit the location, and 1-2-3 will store the entry in the current cell, as in the command /XNEnter your age :~ ~ . This command is equivalent to the Release 3 {GETNUMBER} command. It is described in "Macro Commands That Manipulate Data."

/XQ

The /XQ command stops execution of a macro.

Format   The format for the /XQ is

/XQ

This command has no arguments.

Use   This command is equivalent to the Release 3 {QUIT} command, described in the section, "Macro Commands That Affect Flow of Execution."

/XR

The /XR command causes a return from the execution of a macro subroutine. An /XR instruction must have a corresponding /XC instruction in the main macro program in order to function.

Format   The format for the /XR command is

/XR

This command has no arguments.

Use   This command may be used as follows:

```
Main Routine

    ...

    ...

    /XCsub~

    /XLEnter next selection :~a1~

Subroutine

sub  ...

    ...

    ...

    ...

    /XR
```

When the /XC instruction calls **sub**, this subroutine will be executed until /XR is reached. Control will then return to the /XL statement following /XC in the main routine.

The /XR statement is equivalent to the {RETURN} statement in Release 3. {RETURN} is described in the section, "Macro Commands That Affect Flow of Execution."

Macro Commands That Manipulate Data

The macro commands in this section allow you to manipulate values and strings stored in worksheet cells. You can use these commands to blank out a section of the worksheet or store a value or string in a cell. Commands from this section can also be used to recalculate the worksheet in row or column order.

{APPENDBELOW}

The {APPENDBELOW} instruction allows you to add information across a row in a worksheet to the end of an existing database. It extends the range of the database to include the extra row that it adds.

Format   The format of {APPENDBELOW} is

{APPENDBELOW *target-location,source-location*}

Target-location is a range or range name that references an existing database. *Source-location* is the range of entries across a row or rows, for one or more records, to be added to the existing database. The number of rows in the source location cannot exceed the number of available rows in the worksheet below the target location. 1-2-3 will not write over existing entries when executing this command.

Use   You can use this command to enter new records in a database. It is normally used in conjunction with /Range Input or {FORM} to add the information as a new record in the database. It can also be used to join the contents of two database tables with an identical format.

Example   Figure 13-15 shows an employee database with 19 records. You can use a custom input form and have 1-2-3 automatically add new records to the end of this database; Figure 13-16 shows the Entry Form that was designed for this purpose. The form in the example was invoked with {FORM} and will accept entries in much the same way as /Range Input. When the user presses F6 (WINDOW), the {FORM} instruction executes an {APPENDBELOW} instruction, which adds the new record to the database as shown in Figure 13-17. The Unprotect attribute moves to the database with the new entry and causes it to appear green or highlighted depending on your monitor. You can continue to add records, and each one will be added to the end of the database as shown in Figure 13-18.

{APPENDRIGHT}

The {APPENDRIGHT} command is used to add fields of data to an existing database. It will extend the range of the database to include the new columns of information.

Format   The format of the {APPENDRIGHT} command is

{APPENDRIGHT *target-location,source-location*}

A:A1: [W12] 'Last Name   `READY`

A	A	B	C	D	E	F
1	Last Name	First Name	SS#	Job Code	Salary	Location
2	Wilkes	Caitlin	124-67-7432	17	$15,500	2
3	Campbell	David	213-76-9874	23	$23,000	10
4	Parker	Dee	659-11-3452	14	$19,800	4
5	Hartwick	Eileen	313-78-9090	15	$31,450	4
6	Preverson	Gary	670-90-1121	21	$27,600	4
7	Smythe	George	560-90-8645	15	$65,000	4
8	Justof	Jack	431-78-9963	17	$41,200	4
9	McCartin	John	817-66-1212	15	$54,600	2
10	Campbell	Keith	569-89-7654	12	$32,000	2
11	Deaver	Ken	198-98-6750	23	$24,600	10
12	Caldor	Larry	459-34-0921	23	$32,500	4
13	Miller	Lisa	214-89-6756	23	$18,700	2
14	Patterson	Lyle	212-11-9090	12	$21,500	10
15	Hawkins	Mark	215-67-8973	21	$19,500	2
16	Larson	Mary	543-98-9876	23	$12,000	2
17	Samuelson	Paul	219-89-7080	23	$28,900	2
18	Lightnor	Peggy	560-55-4311	14	$23,500	10
19	Kaylor	Sally	312-45-9862	12	$32,900	10
20	Stephens	Tom	219-78-8954	15	$17,800	2

EMPLOY.WK3

Figure 13-15.   Employee database with 19 records

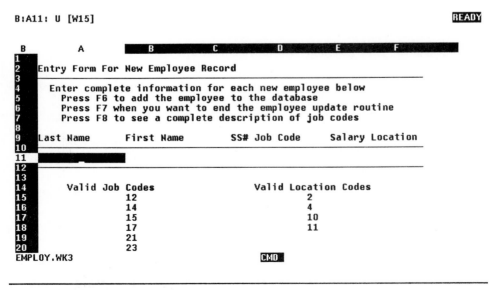

B:A11: U [W15]   `READY`

B	A	B	C	D	E	F
1						
2	Entry Form For New Employee Record					
3						
4	Enter complete information for each new employee below					
5	Press F6 to add the employee to the database					
6	Press F7 when you want to end the employee update routine					
7	Press F8 to see a complete description of job codes					
8						
9	Last Name	First Name	SS#	Job Code	Salary	Location
10						
11						
12						
13						
14	Valid Job Codes			Valid Location Codes		
15		12			2	
16		14			4	
17		15			10	
18		17			11	
19		21				
20		23				

EMPLOY.WK3   `CMD`

Figure 13-16.   Entry form for new employee record

A:A21: U [W12] 'Jones   READY

	A	B	C	D	E	F
1	Last Name	First Name	SS#	Job Code	Salary	Location
3	Campbell	David	213-76-9874	23	$23,000	10
4	Parker	Dee	659-11-3452	14	$19,800	4
5	Hartwick	Eileen	313-78-9090	15	$31,450	4
6	Preverson	Gary	670-90-1121	21	$27,600	4
7	Smythe	George	560-90-8645	15	$65,000	4
8	Justof	Jack	431-78-9963	17	$41,200	4
9	McCartin	John	817-66-1212	15	$54,600	2
10	Campbell	Keith	569-89-7654	12	$32,000	2
11	Deaver	Ken	198-98-6750	23	$24,600	10
12	Caldor	Larry	459-34-0921	23	$32,500	4
13	Miller	Lisa	214-89-6756	23	$18,700	2
14	Patterson	Lyle	212-11-9090	12	$21,500	10
15	Hawkins	Mark	215-67-8973	21	$19,500	2
16	Larson	Mary	543-98-9876	23	$12,000	2
17	Samuelson	Paul	219-89-7080	23	$28,900	2
18	Lightnor	Peggy	560-55-4311	14	$23,500	10
19	Kaylor	Sally	312-45-9862	12	$32,900	10
20	Stephens	Tom	219-78-8954	15	$17,800	2
21	Jones	Mary	216-99-8080	12	$45,000	4

EMPLOY.WK3

Figure 13-17.   Record appended below the existing database records with {APPENDBELOW}

A:A26: U [W12] 'York   READY

	A	B	C	D	E	F
1	Last Name	First Name	SS#	Job Code	Salary	Location
19	Kaylor	Sally	312-45-9862	12	$32,900	10
20	Stephens	Tom	219-78-8954	15	$17,800	2
21	Jones	Mary	216-99-8080	12	$45,000	4
22	Lester	Jeff	217-22-9801	21	$54,500	11
23	Harris	Mark	987-66-5412	14	$32,140	10
24	Kaylor	Jim	321-56-9980	15	$12,500	4
25	Unger	Stewart	787-66-1892	21	$23,500	11
26	York	Marcy	342-12-8976	15	$15,000	4
27						

Figure 13-18.   Additional records appended to employee database

where *target-location* is a range name that references an existing data-base. *Source-location* is a range name referring to one or more columns that you want to append to the right edge of the existing database. The number of columns in the source location should not exceed the number of columns to the right of the target location. 1-2-3 will not write over existing entries when executing this command.

Use   If you have two databases that are in the same table sequence and contain information about identical objects, you can use {APPENDRIGHT} to add several columns of one database to another, and maintain a single database. You might want to add information from the employee benefits database to the salary database, for example.

Example   Figure 13-19 shows records from an employee salary data-base. Other information on the exact same employees is recorded in the personnel database on another sheet in the same file (Figure 13-20). Notice that the employees are listed in the same order. You can use

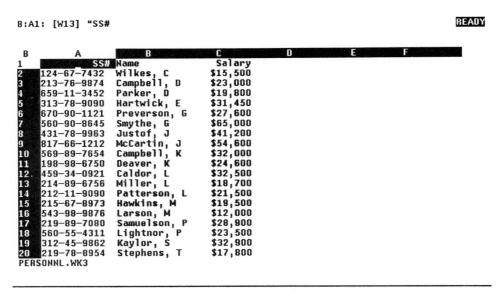

Figure 13-19.   Salary information

{APPENDRIGHT} to join the last two columns of information in the personnel database to the employee database.

As a precaution, you might want to initially append all three personnel database columns, as shown in Figure 13-21. Then add a formula temporarily to verify that the two columns of social security number entries are identical. You might use a formula like @IF(A2 = D2, "","SS#'s DO NOT MATCH ERROR"). This formula could be copied down another column of the combined worksheet to verify a match on all records. Assuming no errors displayed, column D could be deleted and the database size would automatically readjust. The column range containing the @IF formula could also be deleted.

The result of joining the two database tables with {APPENDRIGHT} is shown in Figure 13-21. If the employee database is named **employdb** and the personnel database is named **personnl,** the append instruction {APPENDRIGHT employdb,personnl} can handle the task.

{BLANK}

The {BLANK} command is functionally equivalent to /Range Erase; it erases a range of cells on the worksheet.

Format   The format of the {BLANK} command is

{BLANK *location*}

where *location* is a range of cell addresses or a range name associated with one or more worksheet cells.

Use   This command can be used to clear data from previous uses of the worksheet. You might want to clear a data entry area with this command.

Example   Figure 13-22 presents a data entry screen to be used with a macro. The screen shown contains the data from the previous entry, which may confuse an operator ready to enter a new record. To clear the screen, add these lines of code to an existing macro, placing them so they will be executed following the processing of the current record.

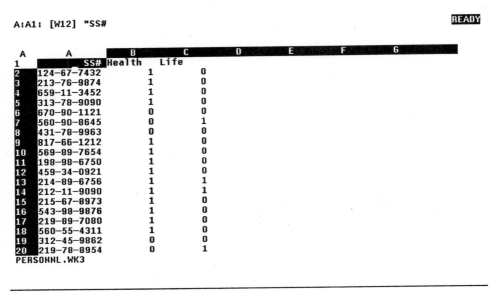

Figure 13-20.   Personnel information

B	A	B	C	D	E	F
1	SS#	Name	Salary	SS#	Health	Life
2	124-67-7432	Wilkes, C	$15,500	124-67-7432	1	0
3	213-76-9874	Campbell, D	$23,000	213-76-9874	1	0
4	659-11-3452	Parker, D	$19,800	659-11-3452	1	0
5	313-78-9090	Hartwick, E	$31,450	313-78-9090	1	0
6	670-90-1121	Preverson, G	$27,600	670-90-1121	0	0
7	560-90-8645	Smythe, G	$65,000	560-90-8645	0	1
8	431-78-9963	Justof, J	$41,200	431-78-9963	0	0
9	817-66-1212	McCartin, J	$54,600	817-66-1212	1	0
10	569-89-7654	Campbell, K	$32,000	569-89-7654	1	0
11	198-98-6750	Deaver, K	$24,600	198-98-6750	1	0
12	459-34-0921	Caldor, L	$32,500	459-34-0921	1	0
13	214-89-6756	Miller, L	$18,700	214-89-6756	1	1
14	212-11-9090	Patterson, L	$21,500	212-11-9090	1	1
15	215-67-8973	Hawkins, M	$19,500	215-67-8973	1	0
16	543-98-9876	Larson, M	$12,000	543-98-9876	1	0
17	219-89-7080	Samuelson, P	$28,900	219-89-7080	1	0
18	560-55-4311	Lightnor, P	$23,500	560-55-4311	1	0
19	312-45-9862	Kaylor, S	$32,900	312-45-9862	0	0
20	219-78-8954	Stephens, T	$17,800	219-78-8954	0	1

PERSONNL.WK3

Figure 13-21.   Result of joining two tables with {APPENDRIGHT}

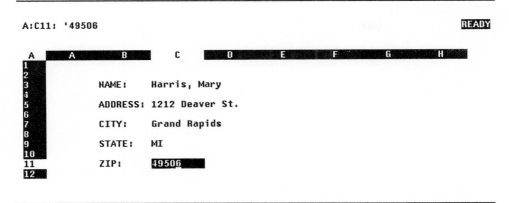

Figure 13-22.   Data entry screen containing old data

```
     P                  Q
1    \b          {BLANK c3..c11}

2                {CALC}
```

The lines are shown with a macro name, so they could be executed from the keyboard without incorporating them into another macro if desired. The first line requests that the range C3..C11 be erased. The second line calculates the worksheet to ensure that these cells are blanked immediately, as shown in Figure 13-23.

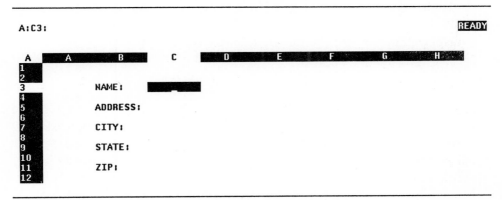

Figure 13-23.   Data entry screen cleared with {BLANK}

{CONTENTS}

The {CONTENTS} command stores a numeric value in a cell as a label with a specified format.

Format   The format for {CONTENTS} is

{CONTENTS *destination,source,width,format*}

The argument *destination* is the location where you wish the label to be stored. You may specify it as a cell address or a range name.

The argument *source* is the location of the value entry you want stored in *destination* as a string (label). You may specify this location as a cell address or a range name.

The argument *width* is an optional argument unless you choose to specify *format,* in which case *width* is required. *Width* determines the width of the string entry. If you do not specify width, it is obtained from the *source* location.

The argument *format* is an optional argument that allows you to determine the exact manner in which the *source* value is formatted in the destination string. Figure 13-24 shows a list of the values you may select for this argument.

Example   If you ever want to display the formula behind a cell at a given location, the {CONTENTS} command allows you to do this. Let's say that the *source* location is D1, and it contains the formula +Z1*Z3, although a 30 displays in the cell. The formula behind D1 can be displayed in D5 with the following macro statement:

{CONTENTS D5,D1,9,117}~

In this statement, D5 represents the *destination* location and D1 represents the *source*. A *width* of 9 is established, and the *format* represented by 117 is selected. The number 117 specifies Text display, so the formula behind D1 will display in D5. Remember that it is no longer a formula but a string once it is stored in the *destination* location.

0 to 15	Fixed format with 0 to 15 decimal places, depending on the number. 0 means zero decimal places and 15 means 15
16 to 32	Scientific format with 0 to 15 decimal places
33 to 47	Currency ($) format with 0 to 15 decimal places
48 to 63	Percent (%) format with 0 to 15 decimal places
64 to 79	Comma (,) format with 0 to 15 decimal places
112	+/− format
113	General format
114	Date format 1 (DD-MMM-YY)
115	Date format 2 (DD-MMM)
116	Date format 3 (MMM-YY)
117	Text display
118	Hidden
119	Date format 6 (HH:MM:SS AM/PM)
120	Date format 7 (HH:MM AM/PM)
121	Date format 4 - Full International date display
122	Date format 5 - Short International date display
123	Date format 8 - Full International time display
124	Date format 9 - Short International time display
127	Default Numeric display format for the worksheet

Figure 13-24.   Codes and associated formats for the {CONTENTS} command

{LET}

The {LET} command permits the assignment of a number or a string to a location on the worksheet.

Format   The formats for the {LET} command are

{LET *location,number*}

or

{LET *location,string*}

The argument *location* is the address or range name of the cell in which you wish to store the value or label. If you specify *location* as a range, only the upper left cell in the range will be used.

The argument *number* is a numeric value or a formula that evaluates to a numeric value.

The argument *string* is a string or a string formula.

Use   This command is useful whenever you wish to control the value in a worksheet cell. It can be used with a loop to increment a counter. Since it can be used with either strings or values, it is extremely flexible. Here are several examples.

- {LET a1,10}~ stores 10 in cell A1.

- {LET a1,a1 + 1}~ increments cell A1 by 1.

- {LET a1,"ABC "&"COMPANY"}~ places ABC COMPANY in cell A1.

You also have the option of using an indicator for numeric values that tells 1-2-3 whether you wish them treated as numbers (values) or as strings. The examples that follow show the proper format:

- {LET a1,5 + 1:value} places a 6 in cell A1.

- {LET a1,5 + 1:string} places '5 + 1 in cell A1.

Example   The {LET} command can be used to initialize and increment a counter when you want to set up your own loops. The following
shell shows the format of a loop using {LET} in this way.

```
\s        {LET counter,1}

top_loop  {IF counter>stop}{BRANCH end_loop}

          . . .

          . . .

          . . .

          {LET counter,counter+1}

          {BRANCH top_loop}

end_loop  {QUIT}
```

If you choose to build your own loop rather than use the {FOR}
instruction, you will always need to initialize your counter, increment it,
and test it to see that it is within an acceptable range. In this example,
stop is a range name used to contain the ending value for this range.

{PUT}

The {PUT} command allows you to put a value in a location within a
range. Unlike {LET}, which accepts only a cell address, {PUT} lets you
select a row and column offset within a range.

Format   The formats for the {PUT} command are

{PUT *location,column,row,number*}

or

{PUT *location,column,row,string*}

The argument *location* is a range of cells identified by cell addresses or a range name.

The argument *column* is the column number within the *location* range. The first column in the range is column 0.

The argument *row* is the row number within the *location* range. The first row in the range is row 0.

The argument *number* is the value you wish to have stored at the specified *location*.

The argument *string* is the string you wish to have stored in the specified *location*.

Use   This command is similar to {LET} but has additional flexibility, since it lets you store values within a range. A few examples and their results follow:

- {PUT a1..b5,0,3,4} places a 4 in cell A4.

- {PUT a1..b5,1,0,3} places a 3 in cell B1.

- {PUT a1..b5,0,15,0} causes an error, since a row number of 15 is not within the range specified.

Example   This command could be used to supply the values for a table. You might have entries like this in your macro:

- {PUT table,0,0,100}~

- {PUT table,0,1,d5/2}~

The tilde at the end of each instruction causes the table entry to be updated immediately.

Note: The row and column offsets must be within the range you establish with the location argument. When they are not, an error occurs. This error cannot be processed with {ONERROR}.

{RECALC}

The {RECALC} command recalculates the formulas within the range you specify, proceeding row by row within this range.

Format The format for the {RECALC} command is

{RECALC *location,condition,iteration*}

The argument *location* is the range of the worksheet that you wish to have recalculated.

The optional argument *condition* specifies a condition that must be true before the *location* range selected is no longer recalculated. As long as the condition is false, 1-2-3 will continue to recalculate the worksheet. This argument is used in conjunction with *iteration*, which specifies a maximum number of iterations.

The optional argument *iteration* specifies the number of times that formulas within the location range will be recalculated as long as condition is false. When *condition* is true, recalculation stops, even though you may not have used all the iterations. With each iteration the count is reduced by 1. When it is zero, no further recalculations will occur.

Use When you use {CALC}, the entire worksheet is recalculated. This can be unnecessarily time-consuming if you need just a section of it recalculated. The {RECALC} and {RECALCCOL} commands are designed for this purpose. Use {RECALC} when the area you are recalculating is below and to the left of the cells referenced by the formulas in this area. Use {RECALCCOL} when the area you are recalculating is above and to the right of the cells referenced by the formulas in this area. If the formula is *both* above and to the left of cells with new values, you must use {CALC} and recalculate the entire worksheet.

Example If you have a macro that changes the value of cell AB10 and you are interested in the value of cell Z12, which is affected by AB10, you can use a {RECALC} instruction in your macro, as follows:

{RECALC z1..ab12}

1-2-3 will recalculate row by row to obtain the correct result of AB10 and thus for Z12. You can also add a condition and iteration count to this instruction:

{RECALC z1..ab12,z3 > 20,10}

The recalculation of the specified range will now continue until either Z3 is greater than 20, or 10 iterations are performed.

{RECALCCOL}

The {RECALCCOL} command recalculates the formulas within the range you specify, proceeding column by column within this range.

Format   The format for the {RECALCCOL} command is

{RECALCCOL *location,condition,iteration*}

The argument *location* is the range of the worksheet that you wish to have recalculated.

The optional argument *condition* specifies a condition that must be true before the *location* range selected is no longer recalculated. As long as the condition is false, 1-2-3 will continue to recalculate the worksheet. This argument is used in conjunction with *iteration*, which specifies a maximum number of iterations.

The optional argument *iteration* specifies the number of times that formulas within the location range will be recalculated as long as condition is false. When *condition* is true, recalculation stops, even though you may not have used all the iterations. With each iteration the count is reduced by 1. When it is zero, no further recalculations will occur.

Use   When you use {CALC}, the entire worksheet is recalculated. This can be unnecessarily time consuming if you need just a section of it recalculated. The {RECALC} and {RECALCCOL} commands are designed for this purpose. Use {RECALC} when the area you are recalculating is below and to the left of the cells referenced by the formulas in this area. Use {RECALCCOL} when the area you are recalculating is above and to the right of the cells referenced by the formulas in this area. If the formula is *both* above and to the left of cells with new values, you must use {CALC} and recalculate the entire worksheet.

Example   {RECALCCOL} follows the same syntax rules as {RE-CALC}. Select one or the other depending on whether a row or a column order of recalculation fits best with your application. Refer to the example under {RECALC} for additional information.

Macro Commands That Handle Files

The file macro commands provide sequential file handling capabilities equivalent to the ones you find in the BASIC programming language. You can use these commands in macros to read and write records to text files. If you have never worked with files, you will want to review a section from a data processing text that overviews records, file size concepts, file input and output procedures, and other basic terminology connected with the use of files before you try to use these macros.

The commands in this section are interdependent. For example, it is not possible to use {READLN}, {READ}, {WRITE}, or {WRITELN} unless you have first opened the file with {OPEN}. Short examples dealing with the syntax are provided with each command. Examples showing commands used in context with other required commands are found under {WRITE}, {WRITELN}, {READ}, {READLN}, and {FILESIZE}.

{CLOSE}

The {CLOSE} command closes the file you opened with the {OPEN} command. You must close one file before opening a second one.

Format   The format for the {CLOSE} command is

    {CLOSE}

This command has no arguments.

Use   If you use this command when there are no open files, 1-2-3 will ignore it.

{FILESIZE}

This command allows you to determine the number of bytes or characters in your file.

Format   The format for the {FILESIZE} command is

{FILESIZE *location*}

where *location* is the cell address or range name of the cell where you want 1-2-3 to store the number representing the length of your file.

Use   The file must be open before you use this command. Remember, too, that the character for the end-of-file condition will be included in the count for {FILESIZE}. If you know the length of the records on the file, you can use {FILESIZE} to determine how many records the file contains.

Example   The following macro uses the {FILESIZE} command:

```
       A                B
22   \f            {OPEN "B:TEST.PRN",R}

23                 {FILESIZE g21}

24                 {CALC}

25                 {CLOSE}
```

The first step in the macro is to open the file, since a file must be opened before {FILESIZE} can be used. The entry in line 23 determines the number of bytes in the file and places this number in cell G21. A {CALC} is included to update the worksheet cell immediately, after which the file is closed.

{GETPOS}

The {GETPOS} command determines the current position in a file.

Format   The format for the {GETPOS} command is

{GETPOS *location*}

where *location* is the address or range name of the cell where you wish the current position number stored. Remember that the first character in a file is considered position 0.

Example   You can use this command to monitor your progress through a file, comparing the current position to the file size so that you do not attempt to read beyond the end of the file. After reading a record, you might include a {GETPOS} instruction, like this:

{READLN a10}

{GETPOS current}

You could then compare **current** and the result from the {FILESIZE} command and determine the number of records yet to read.

{OPEN}

The {OPEN} command allows you to open a file and specify whether you plan to read the file, write to it, or do both.

Format   The format for the {OPEN} command is

{OPEN *file,access*}

The argument *file* is a string or range name referring to a single cell that contains a string or string formula that references the name of the file you want to open. The cell string has an upper limit of 64 characters and can include the entire pathname and subdirectory, as well as the filename extension.

The argument *access* is a single character that controls the type of access you have to the file. The possible code characters are as follows:

R means read-only. You cannot write to the file if your access mode is R.

W means write-only. This argument opens a new file or recreates an existing file. You cannot read from a file if the access mode is W.

M allows modifications to the file, permitting both read and write access. It can be used only on existing files.

A means append. This argument opens the existing file and adds data written to it at the end of the file. You can both read and write data.

Use   If you wish to use an error routine in the event {OPEN} fails, you can place it on the same line as {OPEN} as a subroutine call—for example, {OPEN SALES,R}{fix_err}.

{READ}

The {READ} command reads the number of characters specified into the location you define, starting at the file pointer's present location.

Format   The format for the {READ} command is

{READ *byte-count,location*}

The argument *byte-count* is the number of characters you wish to have read from the file, beginning at the current position in the file. If the number of bytes is larger than the number of remaining characters in the file, {READ} will take the amount of data remaining. *Byte-count* must be a numeric value or an expression that evaluates to one. The number should be between 0 and 512; if it is negative, use 512.

The argument *location* is the address or range name for the cell where you would like the string of characters to be stored. The data will be stored in this location as a left justified label.

Example   The following macro shows the use of the {READ} instruction:

	A	B
30	\r	{OPEN "B:TEST.PRN",R}
31		{SETPOS 6}
32		{READ 9,g22}

```
33          {CALC}

34          {CLOSE}
```

The file is opened for reading in the first instruction. The file pointer is then set at 6, which would be the seventh character in the file. Nine bytes (characters) are read from the file and stored in cell G22. The worksheet is recalculated immediately to show this entry, after which the file is closed.

{READLN}

The {READLN} command copies a line of characters (a record) from a file and places it at the location specified.

Format   The format for the {READLN} command is

{READLN *location*}

where *location* is the cell address or range name that specifies the cell where you wish the line of data stored.

Use   The {READ} command works based on the number of bytes. {READLN}, by contrast, looks for a carriage return/line feed to know how many characters to read. Like {READ}, it uses the current file pointer position as the starting point and can be used with {SETPOS}.

Example   The following macro will read one line from a text file.

```
      A                B
1    \z      {OPEN "B:TEST.PRN",R}

2            {READLN place}

3            ~

4            {RIGHT}

5            {CLOSE}
```

The file is first opened. {READLN} then reads the first line from the file and places these characters in **place**. A tilde rather than {CALC} is used to update the worksheet, since the tilde is just as effective and more efficient. The cell pointer is moved to the right, and the file is closed.

{SETPOS}

The {SETPOS} command positions the file pointer at the location you specify.

Format   The format for the {SETPOS} command is

{SETPOS *number*}

where *number* is a numeric value or expression that results in a numeric value that tells 1-2-3 which character you want the pointer set on. Remember that the first character in the file is considered to be position 0.

Use   1-2-3 does not prevent you from setting the pointer at a location beyond the end of the file. You should always use {FILESIZE} to ensure that this does not occur.

Example   Given the following information stored in a file:

ABC Company, LaCrosse, MI

setting the pointer to 4 would place it on the *C* in "Company."

{WRITE}

The {WRITE} command places a set of characters in a file that you have opened.

Format   The format for the {WRITE} command is

{WRITE *string*}

where *string* is a character string, an expression evaluating to a character string, or a range name assigned to a single cell that contains a string.

Use   When you use this command, 1-2-3 writes a string to the file at the current location of the file pointer. It then moves the pointer to the end of this entry to place it in position for writing the next set of characters.

Example   If you have a column of worksheet cells that contains the days of the week, use this command to write this list of names to a file. If you use {WRITE}, they will all be in one line (record) of the file.

Assuming that you position your cell pointer at the top of the list, the macro that follows will write all seven names for you.

```
      A              B
1     \z            {OPEN "B:TOGETH.PRN",W}

2                   {LET ctr,1}

3     top           {IF ctr>7}{BRANCH end}

4                   {WRITE @CELLPOINTER ("contents")}

5                   {DOWN}

6                   {LET ctr,ctr+1}

7                   {BRANCH top}

8     end           {CLOSE}
```

The file is opened for write access in the first instruction. A counter is initialized in line 2. The first statement in the iterative loop of the macro checks the counter to see whether it is greater than 7. If it is, the macro ends by closing the file.

If the counter is not greater than 7, the loop continues. The contents of the current cell are written to the file using the built-in function @CELLPOINTER. The pointer is moved down, and **ctr** is incremented. The execution flow then branches to the top of the loop. The macro continues in this cycle until it has written all seven entries to the file.

Since entries are written sequentially on the same line, the result of using this macro would be

MondayTuesdayWednesdayThursdayFridaySaturdaySunday

assuming that the first cell contained Monday and the days proceeded in order throughout the week as you moved down the column.

Setup   The macro requires that the range names **top, end,** and **ctr** be assigned to appropriate cells. Also, the days of the week must already be in the worksheet, and your cell pointer must be positioned on the first one before you execute the macro.

{WRITELN}

The {WRITELN} command places characters in an open file. In contrast to {WRITE}, it adds a carriage return/line feed to the end of each character string written, so a new line or record is created in the file each time the command is used.

Format   The format for the {WRITELN} command is

{WRITELN *string*}

where *string* is a character string, an expression evaluating to a character string, or a range name assigned to a single cell that contains a string.

Use   When you use this command, 1-2-3 writes a string to the file at the current location of the file pointer. It then moves the pointer to the beginning of the next line to place it in position for writing the next set of characters.

Using {WRITELN ""} generates a carriage return/line feed at the current position in the file. You might want to build a record with a series of {WRITE} commands, and then use {WRITELN} to add a line feed before beginning the next record.

Example   Let's look at two examples. The first writes a series of string literals to a file named DAYS. It reads as follows.

	A	B
1	\z	{OPEN "B:DAYS",W}
2		{WRITELN "Monday"}
3		{WRITELN "Tuesday"}
4		{WRITELN "Wednesday"}
5		{WRITELN "Thursday"}
6		{WRITELN "Friday"}
7		{WRITELN "Saturday"}
8		{WRITELN "Sunday"}
9		{CLOSE}

The file is first opened. Seven individual {WRITELN} statements are then used to write character strings to the file, after which the file is closed.

If you import the text file created with this macro into the worksheet with your cell pointer in Z1, Z1..Z7 will contain the following:

Monday
Tuesday
Wednesday
Thursday
Friday
Saturday
Sunday

Since each day was written to a separate line when the file was imported, each record is written to a different cell.

A second macro that achieves the same end results is this:

	A	B
1	\z	{OPEN "B:TOGETH.PRN",W}
2		{LET ctr,1}
3	top	{IF ctr>7}{BRANCH end}
4		{WRITELN @CELLPOINTER("contents)"}
5		{DOWN}

```
6              {LET ctr, ctr+1}

7              {BRANCH top}

8      end     {CLOSE}
EL
```

This macro uses a loop construction and writes the days of the week, which are stored in worksheet cells, to the file. It follows the same format as the example discussed under {WRITE}, except that each day of the week appears in a separate line (record) of the file.

Using 1-2-3 on a Network

Release 3 fully supports the use of 1-2-3 on a *local area network*. This means you can design applications for use on a single user system, or network applications that access shared files. You will use the same familiar commands and features in both environments. In addition, Release 3 includes new commands in its menu structure that provide support for network applications; these commands will be described in this chapter. You will also be introduced to some important network concepts and design strategies that will prepare you to work with network applications.

Limitations of Single User Worksheet Applications

When 1-2-3 was first introduced, business users were delighted to have a flexible tool that could be used for a variety of applications, like budgeting, cash flow analysis, and sales projections. Networks were not yet prevalent in the business environment, and users shared 1-2-3 information by printing copies of the final output or making a copy of the diskette containing the model.

Applications for 1-2-3 quickly evolved, as the popularity of the package grew and its use was no longer limited to monthly and annual projection applications. Users developed 1-2-3 models for project cost-ing, leases, inventory control, invoices, and client information. The up-date cycle for some of these applications was much more frequent, with some models being refreshed continuously throughout the day. Another change that occurred in applications development was the spread of 1-2-3 from corporate administration areas to subsidiary operations and into many levels throughout the company. With this dispersion of data, there was an increased need to provide consolidated reporting using standard models. In addition to the conventional computations provided by the models, standard lists of information like corporate accounts codes were also needed to ensure consistency between operations.

Since a special networked version of 1-2-3 was not available, even users in the same location could not share files easily, because there was no way to reserve a file for exclusive use while it was being updated. If a user chose to install 1-2-3 on a network, there was a risk that several users could simultaneously obtain the same file for update, and one set of changes would overlay another set, without either user being aware of the problem. Two less-than-optimal alternatives have been used in lieu of network support: users distributed worksheet files or maintained a number of separate models.

Distributing Updated Files

Organizations maintaining a central database of 1-2-3 transactions often distributed copies of the updated worksheet file at the beginning of the day. Users in close proximity might receive new diskettes. Others could receive models transmitted via modems and phone lines in other loca-tions. Figure 14-1 shows the flow of information between several users needing to transfer data back and forth. It is a system that requires constant intervention and contains a good potential for error, as when incorrect files are sent or needed data is forgotten.

Users receiving the new models would use them throughout the day for current information on the status of an account, leases on managed properties, or any other application. Since users such as these need up-to-date information on a read-only basis, those in close proximity would benefit from access to a network file of information that is updated many times throughout the day.

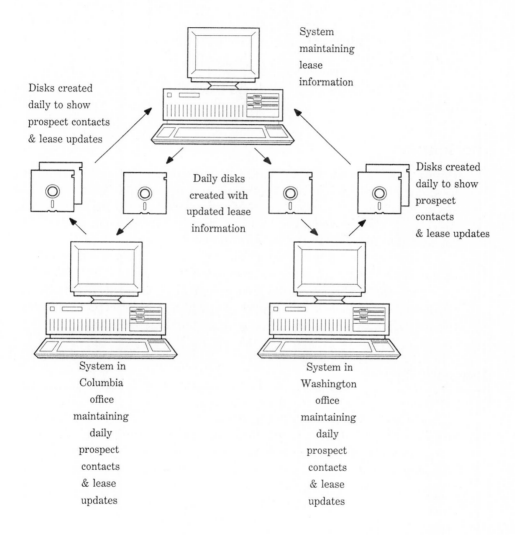

Figure 14-1.   Users transferring information without the benefit of a network

Maintaining Separate Files

Another approach used in lieu of a network was the maintenance of separate 1-2-3 worksheet files, split to allow different users to access different sections of the file. There might be a file for each branch, region, or operating unit. For consolidation purposes, the files could be combined with /File Combine before reports were produced periodically. Figure 14-2 shows the information from several subsidiaries flowing to one point for consolidation. Although tolerable on a once-a-month basis, this procedure is too time-consuming for a daily update process.

The Solution

Unless there is a need for constant updates to each of several separate files, one single file can be maintained in a networked version of 1-2-3. Throughout the day various users can make changes to the model. With Release 3, the consolidation can be performed automatically as the consolidated file, containing links to the individual files, is retrieved.

Before exploring network options with 1-2-3, study the next section on network basics. It contains some of the terminology pertinent to networks and the components that comprise a network. Although you need not become a network expert, you will feel more comfortable with the migration to a network if you understand a few key principles.

Network Basics

Local area networks (LANs) are not as complex as they seem. Most of their mystique is due to users' lack of understanding about basic network concepts. In this section you will learn about standard network components and the ways in which various components can be connected.

Network Components

Personal computers are the basic building blocks used to set up a network. These computers are linked together with cabling, so that they can communicate with each other and share common files and network

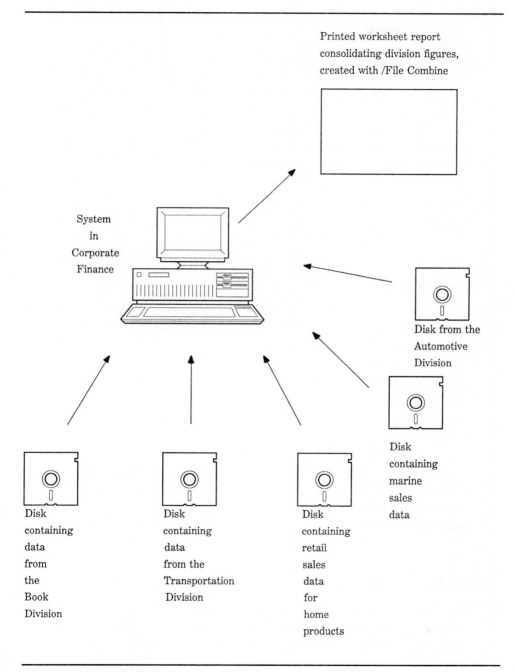

Printed worksheet report
consolidating division figures,
created with /File Combine

System
in
Corporate
Finance

Disk from the
Automotive
Division

Disk
containing
marine
sales
data

Disk
containing
data
from
the
Book
Division

Disk
containing
data
from the
Transportation
Division

Disk
containing
retail
sales
data
for
home
products

Figure 14-2.   Consolidating data without a network

devices. The computers used in the network do not need to be identical. Some may have their own fixed disk space; others may have only floppy disks. At least one of the computers must have fixed disk space. This one functions as the *file server* for the network. All the other network systems will be able to access this fixed space when they are logged onto the network.

In addition to the computers, other network components are the cabling to link the computers, special network cards placed in an expansion slot inside each of the computers, and network software.

The selection of network software and a file server are two of the most critical decisions in designing a LAN. Although you may have more than one file server in a more sophisticated network design, for our purposes one file server is assumed. Normally, the file server will be the computer with the largest hard disk system and the fastest clock speed. In other words, if you must choose between using an IBM XT with 20MB hard disk, and an IBM PS/2 with a 130MB hard disk, the decision is easy; the PS/2 will service the network requests much better. Other resources, like a network printer, may be attached to the file server to service network printing requirements or a separate print server system may be designated.

The network software decision is an important one because it defines the capabilities of the network. It determines how many *workstations* (PCs) can be part of the network, and manages all shared network resources including disk space and print capability. The network software will provide security for network and file access in addition to whatever security is offered by 1-2-3 and other programs used by the network. The choice of software also determines the utilities that are available for administrative tasks on the network.

Network cards and cabling are the last components of the network. Network throughput objectives, participating machines, the operating system, geographic distribution of workstations, and other factors will be used in making these selections. Some of the options for network cards are Ethernet or Arcnet, which match the architecture of the networks (discussed later). Cabling choices include twisted pair, broadband, fiber-optic, and coaxial cable. It is likely that you will obtain both cards and cabling from the same vendor to ensure compatible selections.

Network Topology

Topology is the way the network is built; it is the network's architectural design. A network topology determines how each of the workstations are connected to the network. Some network vendors support many architectures, and others only one.

Some of the popular network designs are shown in Figure 14-3. The workstations, or *nodes,* in a ring architecture like IBM's Token Ring are connected in a circle, with data traveling in this circle to reach a designated node. The star topology has a file server at the center with other nodes attached and located at the points of the star. The Arcnet structure was originally developed by Datapoint and uses one or more passive hubs. Both workstations and the server are attached like spokes to the hub. The Ethernet structure uses a single bus structure for connecting each of the nodes. Rather than joining the two ends of the cable, as in the ring design, terminators are placed on each end. Since 1-2-3 will run regardless of the topology selected, other factors (mentioned in the previous section) will serve as determining factors for the topology of a network using 1-2-3.

Depending on the network software selected, you may be able to connect two networks via a bridge. Although the connected networks do not have to be identical, individual network vendors each support a limited realm of options. Workstations are used to serve as the bridge and may be dedicated to this function or serve as a workstation as well.

Network Vendors

1-2-3 will run on the network software of a number of vendors. Novell and 3COM are two of the more popular vendors marketing network software and hardware. Each of these vendors market several network software products that determine the structural possibilities for the network, the number of users supported, and sophistication of the software in terms of failure recognition and security.

You will not purchase your network software and hardware directly from the manufacturer in most cases but from authorized resellers. The reseller should supply installation support and may provide training to the individual designated to administer the requirements of the network,

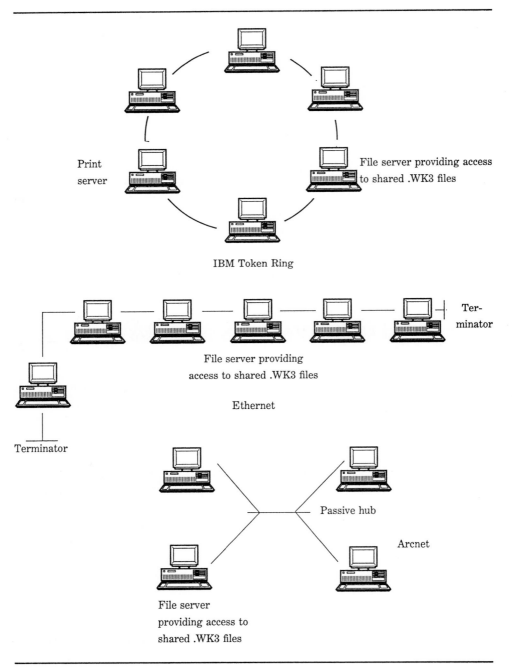

Figure 14-3.   Popular network topologies

such as assigning network passwords. Most resellers will also provide a short class for the end-user of the network, although it is frequently offered at an additional fee.

1-2-3 Requirements

Lotus offers special packaging options of 1-2-3 for network users. In addition to a Standard edition of 1-2-3 for use on stand-alone systems, there is a Server edition and a Node edition. The Server edition includes a copy of 1-2-3 software and documentation, a network administrator's guide, and special network software. The network administrator's guide provides guidance for installation and other administrative tasks. The Node edition is offered at a reduced price and includes authorization for another user and documentation.

Advantages of Using 1-2-3 on a Network

Using a network version of 1-2-3 offers several advantages. When 1-2-3 is used on a network, users can share files easily. On low-activity applications, this eliminates the need to maintain separate databases. It also eliminates the problems caused by distributing models, since any model can be accessed by a network user who has the proper network access level and 1-2-3 password. When a model is reserved for update, 1-2-3's file reservation system guarantees that other users will not be able to update the file, thereby eliminating the problem of simultaneous updates to a single file.

Network use of 1-2-3 provides additional security, better utilization of hardware, and the opportunity to support applications that are not practical with a series of stand-alone computers. Some of the network features discussed in this section depend on the individual capabilities of the network software which you select. Specific examples of options are provided using Novell Netware as an example of these capabilities.

Increased Security

1-2-3 offers several features to protect the investment you have made in developing models with 1-2-3. You can choose to assign a password to a file as you save it, thereby preventing other users from accessing the file without the password. Within a single worksheet, you can use Worksheet Protection features to prevent accidental destruction of important formulas once a worksheet is in memory. A new network command, /File Admin Seal, described later in this chapter, lets you seal a file with a password to prevent changes to unprotected cells, access status for a file, or file settings.

Most of the popular network software offers security features that supplement the options currently built into 1-2-3. Since it is not possible to look at the specifics of each vendor product, the features available in the popular Novell Netware software will serve here as an example of the types of options available.

The first level of security check for a user of 1-2-3 on a Novell network is access to the network. Login or password security is available at this level and will not allow the user to log in to the network without a valid access name and password. Repeated attempts to use invalid passwords will lock the account on the server, to prevent repeated attempts at unauthorized access.

With a product like Novell, access can be controlled by time of day, if you wish to restrict use to an 8-to-5 business day. An optional time accounting system can also restrict a user who has already used his/her allotted time on the system. Users who do not meet password validity checks, time of day restrictions, or who overrun allotted system time are denied access to the network and thus the use of 1-2-3 on this network. Even if they have a copy of 1-2-3 on their own system, they will not be able to use network files without access to the network.

Novell provides trustee assignments as the next level of security. These assignments define read, write, open, create, delete, search, and modification rights for files in a directory. In addition, a parental rights category controls the creation and deletion of subdirectories. Although these rights can be assigned to individual users, they are normally assigned to groups of users—making it possible to administrate users' access options based on the directory in which they are working.

Directory rights can also be assigned with Novell's network. These rights control the same activities as trustee assignments, except they automatically include all users and have precedence over trustee assignments. This means that you cannot grant trustee assignments at a level higher than what is allowed by the directory rights for the file. This combination of trustee assignments for a user and directory rights for a directory defines a user's effective rights to any file in the directory. For example, an individual user might be authorized to retrieve files in the ACCOUNT subdirectory, but not to save or create files in this directory, because the user's effective rights might not allow these latter two activities. This same user may have the appropriate effective rights to delete or save files in another directory.

A user's effective rights can be further limited by the use of 1-2-3 passwords when a file is saved or sealed. In addition, Novell's Filer options can set file attributes. File attributes can be set to indicate read-only status for a file; this will not allow anyone to change it. A file can also be specified as nonshareable, through Filer, to limit its use to one user at a time.

Messaging Features

The messaging features provided by most network software packages allow you to send messages to either the entire group of network users or an individual user. For instance, if a group of users is working on various components of a budget or other "rush" activity, as soon as a user has completed one portion of the 1-2-3 models, that user can send a network message to the others on the project.

As an example, with Novell, the SESSION command is entered at the dot prompt, to send a message of up to 40 characters. The user name and send options are both selectable from the list of options which Novell presents. Novell also supports the SEND command. Although it is not menu driven like SESSION, the SEND entry is easy and might look like one of these:

SEND "Travel expense model complete" TO USER John
SEND "Travel expense model complete" TO GROUP Budget.

Better Hardware Utilization

It is impractical to attach expensive output devices like laser printers to each individual system unit; yet the fact remains that most users do prefer this output quality. Using a network allows the sharing of such high-quality output devices between systems attached to the network. Within the network, each 1-2-3 user can select the network laser printer when needed, and route their output to this device. Graphics output devices like plotters can be shared in the same way. Sharing these resources results in a significantly lower cost without a compromise in quality. In addition, less total space is required for each workstation, since most locations will only require a basic system unit.

Since Release 3 requires a system with an 80286 or 80386 architecture to run the program, older models of stand-alone systems like the IBM XT are insufficient, because their architecture is based on the 8088 chip. Installation of 1-2-3 on a network, however, makes it possible to utilize these older systems. They can run with a copy of the program on another network machine that is equipped to run the new version; and this is transparent to the user who is viewing a 1-2-3 worksheet on the screen of the older unit.

New Application Opportunities

Using a network version of 1-2-3 makes feasible some design applications that were not practical with earlier versions. Since files can be shared, information like tables of interest rates, account codes, customer databases, and other data needed by multiple users can be stored on the network and accessed by everyone. Templates for shared applications can also be stored on the network. This allows a project analyst working on a new project cost estimate to copy a template for the creation of a new estimate without jeopardizing the original model.

Consolidations are easy with networked 1-2-3. Each user can update a worksheet in a master file, or create an individual file. All the data is stored on the network and can be based on the format of a sample file that each user uses as a template. Then the consolidation can be automatically done using all the master file sheets, or accomplished quickly and accurately through the linked individual files.

Network Planning Considerations

Although on a network you will create models with all the same commands used with 1-2-3 on stand-alone systems, there are some important planning considerations if you want the migration to a network environment to go smoothly.

Implementation

1-2-3 is as easy to install on a network as on a stand-alone system, but if 1-2-3 is your first network application, your first task is to install the network software. This can be an exacting task for a business user (unless you are familiar with every aspect of your hardware), and you will probably want to invest in the services of a skilled network software specialist for installation.

The installation process for Novell Netware SFT takes approximately half a day for a small network of four to six workstations. If you are unfamiliar with your hardware and the specifications on the network cards in the expansion slots of each computer, it can take longer. The process requires formatting the hard drive of the file server, and making other selections to define your hardware and network configuration as the network software is copied to the newly formatted drive. If the file server was formerly used as a stand-alone system, you will need to back up all of its files before starting the new formatting.

The only installation required for each workstation is the insertion of the network card. Also, a batch file is normally created, giving the workstation access to the network. Although it is possible to type each of the network access commands every time you want to link to the network, the batch file approach is much more efficient.

Network Administrator

No matter how few workstations are on your network, one individual must be designated as the network administrator. This individual assigns passwords and determines security levels for files, directories, and user access.

The network supervisor has the highest authority of any user on the network. Although these duties are not a full-time responsibility, they should be assumed by one individual to coordinate network resources and maintain security.

Training

Users of a network version of 1-2-3 do not need extensive training in 1-2-3, since all the commands function the same as in the stand-alone version. New Release 3 network commands are found under /File Admin in the main menu. Since there are only a few commands in this menu, it will not require much time to learn their operation. Experienced 1-2-3 users can review the descriptions in the following section to gain sufficient familiarity with these new commands.

Although extensive 1-2-3 training is not required, most users who have not yet used a network will benefit from several hours of training on the basic network concepts, features, and utilities of interest to an end-user.

Application Design

Worksheets used in a network operation have the same basic row, column, and sheet organization as a single-user version of 1-2-3. The same basic design principles that are effective for single-user applications are appropriate for shared applications.

To make your network applications more efficient when used with shared files, you will want to minimize the different types of data stored in each file. A variety of different types of data in one file will be more likely to be needed by a variety of different users. As an example, the daily orders for several salespeople are more effectively stored in individual worksheet files to be combined later. Storing them in one sales order file would likely result in the file being frequently unavailable for updates; with a high volume of sales activity, several users might simultaneously need to enter sales data. With individual files stored on the file server, each user can be assured of his or her files being available.

1-2-3 Network Commands

1-2-3 has several special network commands. Also, some /File commands work differently on a network. The new file handling commands are found under the /File Admin menu. The most noticeable differences in existing commands are encountered when retrieving files, opening files, and printing on a network. You may also want to look at the /File Admin

Table Active and /File List Active commands in Chapter 8, which list the active files and show which files you have the reservation for.

Retrieving Network Worksheet Files

When you retrieve a file on a network with /File Retrieve or /File Open, you will notice several changes. These changes relate to selecting the path for the worksheet file, the file password, the file reservation, and how 1-2-3 treats non-Release 3 worksheet files in a network.

When you retrieve a worksheet file on a network server, you must often supply the path to the network directory. If you are using several files from the network, you may want to change the default directory to the network directory.

Many network files use passwords to restrict who can retrieve a worksheet file. If the file you retrieve requires a password, 1-2-3 prompts you for the password after you select a filename to retrieve. The password permits you to limit who can read the data from the file. Network software also has the ability to prevent users from reading data. A network administrator can limit read access to files through the network software. Either a network administrator or worksheet user can limit access to worksheets by assigning passwords.

To update a network file, you must have a *reservation* for the file. A reservation means you can save changes to a file using the same file-name. Normally, retrieving a file on a network causes 1-2-3 to automatically obtain a file reservation for you. If the file reservation setting for a file is set to automatic, but 1-2-3 cannot get the file reservation, 1-2-3 displays a Yes/No menu. Select Yes if you want to retrieve the file without the reservation; select No if you do not want to retrieve the file under this circumstance.

You may be unable to get a file reservation because another user has the reservation, or because the setting for file reservations is set to manual. (The /File Admin Reservation Setting command is described in the next section.) Without the file reservation, you will only be able to read the file, because the file access attribute is set to read-only. In this situation, 1-2-3 displays a RO indicator in the status line. Any changes that you make to this file cannot be saved to the same file until you get the file reservation.

File Reservations

You have learned that, for some files, you automatically obtain the file reservation when you retrieve the file. (You then release the file reservation by entering a command to retrieve another file, or a /Worksheet Erase, /Worksheet Delete File, /Quit, or /File Admin Reservation Release command.)

For other files, you must manually obtain and release the file reservation. To get a file reservation, use /File Admin Reservation Get. When you invoke this command, 1-2-3 tries to get the file reservation if the file has not changed since you last retrieved it. If 1-2-3 is successful, the RO indicator disappears. If not, 1-2-3 displays a message and leaves the RO indicator on the screen. If it cannot get the reservation because the data has changed, 1-2-3 displays an error message.

Tip: If you cannot get a file reservation because the data in the file has changed since you last retrieved it, remove the file from 1-2-3's memory and retrieve it again.

When you have a file reservation that you no longer need, you should release it immediately. To release a file reservation, use the /File Admin Reservation Release command. If you have made any changes to the worksheet that you want to save, save the worksheet file before releasing the reservation. When a reservation is released, 1-2-3 again displays the RO indicator on the status line.

Tip: If you have a file reservation and you do not plan to make any changes, release it so that other users who need to update the file can get the reservation.

There is a test you can perform to determine if you have a file reservation; use either the /File Admin Table Active or /File List Active command. /File Admin Table Active creates a table in which the last column contains a 1 if you have the reservation, or a 0 if you do not. With /File List Active, the last column of the file description is blank if you have the reservation, or contains RO if you do not.

Once you have the file reservation for a specific file, you can change the setting for when a file reservation is obtained, by using the /File Admin Reservation Setting command. When you execute this command, you can select between an Automatic or Manual setting. Selecting Automatic causes 1-2-3 to attempt to obtain the file reservation when the file is retrieved. Selecting Manual makes the file read-only when the file is retrieved, and forces you to request a reservation separately if you decide you want to update the file. The reservation can then only be obtained with the /File Admin Reservation Get command.

Use the Automatic setting when most of a worksheet file's users will need to change the file data. Use the Manual setting when few of the file's users need to change the data and usually only want to look at the file without updating it. Changing the reservation setting does not take effect until the worksheet file is saved; 1-2-3 will not let you change the setting if the file reservation is sealed.

Sealing File Reservations and Worksheet Settings

To protect your data, you can seal the file reservation and worksheet settings. Sealing a reservation prevents other users from changing the setting for the /File Admin Reservation Setting command. Sealing a worksheet prevents changes to the worksheet settings, although it still permits changes to the data.

When a reservation is sealed, only users who can supply the correct password can change the file reservation setting. You may want to seal a file reservation after you have changed the file reservation setting to Manual, to prevent users from monopolizing a worksheet file.

To seal the file reservation setting, use the /File Admin Seal Reservation-Setting command. 1-2-3 prompts you for a password; this is the password that you must provide to unseal the reservation setting. This password follows the same rules as the password for the /File Save command. It can be up to 15 characters, and cannot include any spaces. 1-2-3 displays your entry as asterisks. Next, reenter the password to confirm it. You must remember this password since you cannot disable the reservation seal without providing it. When 1-2-3 returns to the READY mode, save the file so the reservation setting is sealed to other users. This password is case-sensitive.

When a worksheet is sealed, a user can only change the cell pointer's position, the worksheet data, and the Window settings. You can further limit which cells are changed by unprotecting cells where changes are allowed, and then enabling Worksheet Protection before sealing the worksheet. Once the worksheet settings are sealed, the Protection status cannot be changed, and only the unprotected data cells can be modified. An example of this is the worksheet in Figure 14-4. In this worksheet, the cells C4..C11 are unprotected, global protection is enabled, and the worksheet settings are sealed. A user can only modify the cells in the C4..C11 range. Sealing the worksheet also seals the reservation setting.

To seal a worksheet, invoke the /File Admin Seal File command. The procedure for password entry is the same as with the /File Admin Seal Reservation-Setting option.

After you have created the file reservation or worksheet setting seals, you may want to temporarily or permanently remove them. To remove a seal, use /File Admin Seal Disable. 1-2-3 prompts you for the password that you entered when you sealed the file or reservation setting. If it is correct, 1-2-3 unseals the file. You can also use this command to change the password, by disabling the seal, then reestablishing it, and then providing a new password.

Tip: Get the file reservation before changing the worksheet setting or reservation seals. Since you cannot save the worksheet without the file reservation, and you need to save the file to maintain the worksheet or reservation seal, get the file reservation before sealing the file.

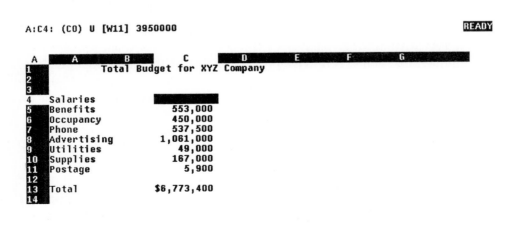

Figure 14-4.   Worksheet allowing entries in C4..C11

Saving a Worksheet File on a Network

When you finish using a worksheet file, you will want to save it. You will also want to save it immediately after executing the /File Admin Reservation or /File Admin Seal command. Saving a file on a network is a little different from saving a file in a single-user environment, because you must have the file reservation when you save the file. If you try saving the file without the file reservation, 1-2-3 displays an error message. Another difference is that files on a network are more frequently password-protected. This prevents users from reading files without authorized access. Most network software imposes similar restrictions by limiting which files a user can access.

1-2-3 allows you to save a worksheet file even if you do not have a file reservation, by letting you save the worksheet file to a different name. Another option is to copy a portion of the file to a new worksheet with /File Xtract. You do not want to copy the new file to the old file later, since it destroys the work done by others.

Printing on a Network

When you are using 1-2-3 in a network environment, you have several options for printing. Your own workstation may have a printer directly connected to it, and the network may also have one or more printers on the file server. You can select which printer you want to use.

Before you can print to a printer, the printer must be selected in a driver configuration file. If you have more than two printers to choose from, consider using more than one driver configuration file. For example, you may want one driver configuration file for the printers connected to the workstation computers and a second driver configuration file for the printers connected to the network.

Once a printer driver is included in a driver configuration file, you can select (activate) the printer name. The /Worksheet Global Default Printer Name command suggests the printer name that you have selected in the Install program. Next, you need to specify the printer port that connects the printer to the network printers. Use /Worksheet Global Default Interface, and select the appropriate printer port for the network printer. Most network printers use selections 5 (LPT1), 6 (LPT2), 7 (LPT3), 8 (COM1), and 9 (COM2). You can then make all your settings the default printer settings with the /Worksheet Global Default Update command. Consider making this adjustment if you normally print all your files to the same printer. These settings are not saved with the files that use them.

If you print certain files to certain printers, consider saving the printer settings with each file. To do this, use the /Print Printer Options Advanced Device Name and /Print Printer Options Advanced Device Interface commands, instead. The selections made for these commands are the same as the similar /Worksheet commands.

Once 1-2-3 knows the printer and the printer interface to use, you can enter the other /Print commands just as if you were printing to a printer attached to your workstation. A network sends print jobs to a print spooler, so the network does not start printing the print jobs until you either leave the /Print menus (except by using /Print Hold) or exit 1-2-3.

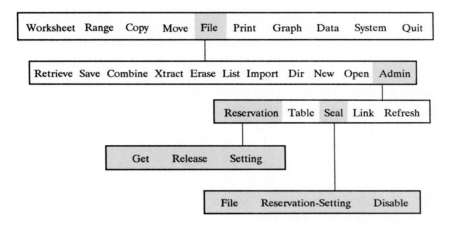

© 1989 Lotus Development Corporation. Used with permission.

/File Admin Reservation

Description

This command obtains or releases a file reservation for the current file. You need a file reservation for worksheet files shared on a network to change or save the file under the same filename. If you do not have the reservation, you cannot save the file.

Options

This command has three options: Get, Release, and Setting. These options select the task 1-2-3 performs.

Get   This option gets the file reservation for the current file if it is available and if the file has not changed since you last retrieved it.

Release   This option releases the file reservation for the current worksheet file. This allows another user to obtain the file reservation to modify the file.

Setting   This option determines whether 1-2-3 automatically attempts to obtain the file reservation when a file is retrieved with /File Retrieve or /File Open.
This option has two selections. Select Automatic to automatically get the file reservation when a file is retrieved. Select Manual if you want the file reservation to be obtained only with the /File Admin Reservation Get command. This setting is retained by the file when the file is saved.

/File Admin Seal

Description

The /File Admin Seal command seals the worksheet file or reservation settings for the current file. When a file is sealed, only the cell pointer's position, the worksheet data, and the Window settings can be changed.

You can further limit which cells are changed by protecting cells you want to remain intact, and then enabling global protection; 1-2-3 will not let the protected cells be modified.

When a reservation is sealed, the Automatic or Manual method for obtaining a file reservation is protected. A reservation is sealed to prevent users from monopolizing a worksheet file by setting the reservation setting to Manual.

The file or reservation seals are not effective until the file is saved with the /File Save command.

Options

This command has three options: File, Reservation-Setting, and Disable. These options select the task 1-2-3 performs. Once one of these options is selected, 1-2-3 prompts for a password. Like passwords for the /File Save command, the password can be up to 15 characters and cannot contain spaces. Like the /File Save command, the password appears as asterisks and is case sensitive. When you enter a password for the File or Reservation-Setting options, you must enter it a second time as a confirmation. This is the password that you must enter to disable the file or reservation seal. It is different from the file password.

File   This option seals the file settings for the current file.

Reservation-Setting   This option seals the reservation setting for the current file.

Disable   This option unseals the file and reservation settings for the current file.

Appendixes

PART THREE

Installing 1-2-3

Your Equipment
Installing 1-2-3
Using Install After Installing 1-2-3

This appendix introduces you to the Lotus Install program, which you use when you initially install 1-2-3. You will also use Install when you change the hardware attached to your computer, for instance, to add a new laser printer or upgrade to a monitor with higher resolution. You can also use Install to change the configuration settings for 1-2-3.

Before describing 1-2-3's installation procedure, this appendix introduces the hardware options for 1-2-3 and the various system components. It is not possible to successfully install 1-2-3 unless you have at least some general knowledge about the system you will be using. In order for the Install program to configure your copy of 1-2-3 to run with the specific hardware components you have, you must be able to tell the program what those components are.

Your Equipment

Release 3 is designed to run on a DOS-based 80286 or 80386 IBM-compatible computer. This includes ATs and the newer PS/2 machines. Since the compatible market is constantly changing, you will need to check with your dealer for the most up-to-date list of certified compatibles. If you are in doubt, have the dealer demonstrate 1-2-3 on the machine you are considering.

Throughout this appendix, the assumption is made that you have an IBM AT or PS/2. The keyboard for this machine is shown in Appendix B. If you have a certified compatible, locate the keys shown in Appendix B on the keyboard of your own system.

Minimum Configuration

Release 3 has minimum system requirements that are different from its 1-2-3 predecessors'. Release 3 requires a minimum of 1MB RAM. Most ATs that use 640K RAM for DOS applications have 1MB of RAM that 1-2-3 can use. If you are planning to use OS/2, you should have 4MB of RAM, which is the minimum required by OS/2 version 1.1. Release 3 can use expanded and extended memory, allowing you to take full advantage of the memory in PS/2s, as well as memory added to ATs with cards like Intel's Above Board card.

Unlike earlier versions, 1-2-3 Release 3 must be run from a hard disk. The hard disk needs at least 4MB of available space for the 1-2-3 files if the DOS or OS/2 operating system is used. If you plan to use both DOS and OS/2, 5MB of disk space is required.

The models you create are limited by the amount of memory on your system. While operating 1-2-3 at the lowest memory level possible, you can use all of the package's features, but you are restricted in the size of your data files, worksheet applications, and the number of files you have in memory. If you plan to build large models, you will want to consider expanding the memory of your machine. The DOS protected mode extension technology is built into the 1-2-3 product, allowing you to take advantage of all available memory. Network and TSR software can still be used within the conventional 640K limit for DOS while 1-2-3 utilizes extended memory. Release 3 can use up to 16MB of extended memory and 32MB of LIM 4 memory. With the LIM 4 memory board option and DOS, you can use up to 48MB of memory for 1-2-3 and your models. Under OS/2, the limit is 16MB of extended memory.

Release 3 also supports the addition of a math coprocessor. Both the 80387 and the 80287 coprocessor chips are supported and are automatically recognized once they are installed. Worksheet models with a significant number of calculations are calculated much more quickly with one of these chips added to the motherboard of your machine.

Printers

If you have both a dot-matrix and a letter-quality printer, you may want to use the letter-quality device for text and use the dot-matrix to print graphics. If you have both a dot-matrix printer and a laser printer, you the dot-matrix for draft copies and the laser for the final output.

On a network, you may have a variety of output devices from which to select, including a plotter for graphics and a laser printer for professional-looking text and graphics output.

To connect any of these printers to your system, you need a cable and an available port. It is possible to connect printers to either the parallel or serial port as long as they are compatible, but there are some special settings if you use a serial connection. First, you must set the printer's baud rate to control the speed of data transfer. At any baud rate except 110, also set 1 stop bit, 8 data bits, and no parity. With a speed of 110 there must be 2 stop bits. Once the program is loaded, use the Worksheet Global Default Printer Interface command and select the baud rate matching your printer's rate. This is done by typing /**WGDPI**, pointing to the baud rate you need, and pressing ENTER. Then save this change with the /Worksheet Global Default Update command (/**WGDU**). If you are purchasing your hardware system at the same time you acquire 1-2-3, your dealer will normally assist you with this installation.

A plotter provides another option for producing graphs. With most devices you can use either paper or transparencies in your plotter with the appropriate pens to create the display medium of your choice. Since 1-2-3 supports only a limited number of plotters, you will want to ensure that the one you are considering purchasing is on the acceptable list; otherwise it may not function with 1-2-3.

The Operating System

The operating system is the control program that resides in the memory of your computer, regardless of the software you are working with. It controls the interface between the various devices and establishes the format for data storage on disk. Release 3 can use the DOS or OS/2 operating system, or both. To use Release 3 with DOS, you must use at least a 3.0 version of DOS. For OS/2, you must use at least the 1.1 version of IBM OS/2.

Noting Your Equipment

You are now ready to proceed with the steps to install your 1-2-3 disks. First, however, make a note of the names of your monitor, your graphics card, and printer. For your monitor, you must note the type of screen it uses. For the printer, you must note the manufacturer and the model number.

Installing 1-2-3

One goal of installation is to tailor your 1-2-3 disks to run with your specific hardware configuration. If 1-2-3 only ran with one type of hardware, this step would not be necessary. Since it is, you should remember that it offers you an advantage: you can continue to use the package even if you change your hardware configuration to include a plotter, a new printer, or a different monitor.

Preliminary Steps

When you purchase 1-2-3, the package you receive contains an envelope with several diskettes, depending on the disk size. With 3 1/2-inch disks, you receive an Install disk, a System disk for DOS, a System disk for OS/2, two Driver disks, a Font disk, and a Translate disk. With 5 1/4-inch disks, you receive different disks, but they contain the same information.

The *Install Disk* contains the installation program, Install, which copies the necessary files to your computer. The *System Disks* for DOS or OS/2 contain the program files that 1-2-3 runs to execute 1-2-3. The *Font Disk* contains information that 1-2-3 uses to print and display fonts. The *Driver Disks* contain the driver files for all the equipment Lotus supports, including printer drivers, plotter drivers, and display drivers. When you run the Install program and indicate your equipment selection, the drivers will be copied from the driver disks to your computer. The *Translate Disk* contains 1-2-3's translation programs and sample files to use with 1-2-3. The translation programs allow you to use a recorded in another program, such as dBASE III or VisiCalc, by ﹍ting the data to a format that 1-2-3 can read.

Installing with a Hard Disk

1-2-3's installation program requires the same steps for the DOS operating system, the OS/2 operating system, or both DOS and OS/2. The instructions for this section assume that DOS or OS/2 is already on your hard drive and that you are using Release 3 of 1-2-3.

1. The first step in installing 1-2-3 is determining if the available disk space is adequate. To install 1-2-3 for DOS or OS/2, the computer must have 4MB of free disk space. To install 1-2-3 for both DOS and OS/2, the computer must have 5MB of free disk space.

2. To start the Install program, insert the Setup/Install disk into drive A. Type **A:** and press ENTER to make the drive current. (If you need to use drive B to install 1-2-3, insert the disk in drive B and type **B:**.) Then type **INSTALL** and press ENTER to start the installation program. If you need to leave the Install program for any reason, press ESC until the installation program asks if you want to exit the installation program; select Yes.

3. Install prompts you to register your name and the company's name. In the first line, enter your name. In the second line, enter your company name. If you do not have a company name to supply, reenter your name. Then press INS to finalize the entries. The Install program prompts for a confirmation, which you can supply by typing a **Y**.

4. Install displays the opening menu. After reading it, press ENTER. Then Install displays a menu to select the type of installation. Type a **1** to select Both DOS and OS/2, a **2** to select DOS, or a **3** to select OS/2. Press ENTER.

5. After 1-2-3 knows the operating system you will use with 1-2-3, Install displays the next menu and you must indicate if Install copies the translation and sample files. Type a **1** to copy both translation and sample files, a **2** to copy translation files, a **3** to copy sample files, or a **4** to skip copying these files. Press ENTER. Since 1-2-3 compresses these files, always use Install to copy these files. Install uncompresses them as it copies them. If you copy them directly from the disk, you must later use the Inflate program to uncompress them.

6. Next, 1-2-3 prompts for the disk drive 1-2-3 will use and displays C as the default. If you want to use 1-2-3 on a hard disk other than drive C, enter the drive letter. Press ENTER to accept the default of C or your new entry.

7. The program now prompts for the directory that 1-2-3 will use. It can be an existing directory or one that the installation program will create for you. Either use 1-2-3's suggested directory of \123R3, or supply a subdirectory name. Subdirectories have the same name conventions as filenames; they are limited to eight characters. Press ENTER to finalize the entry and continue with the next step.

a. If you provide an existing empty directory, 1-2-3 does not prompt for a confirmation, but immediately starts copying files from the Setup/Install disk.

b. If the directory you chose does not exist, the installation program displays a confirmation box, prompting you to type a **Y** to continue and create the subdirectory, or an **N** to return to the previous screen to select a new directory. Then press ENTER to return to the previous screen or to advance to the next installation step.

c. If the directory exists and contains files, the installation program prompts for a confirmation. Type a **Y** and press ENTER if the file contains Release 3 program files, which Install will replace. Type an **N** and press ENTER if the directory contains other files. You do not want Install to write over files you will later need. If you type an **N** and press ENTER, 1-2-3 returns to the screen for entering the file directory name so that you can enter a new directory name.

d. After you confirm an existing directory name or instruct 1-2-3 to create a directory, 1-2-3 starts copying files from the Setup/Install disk.

8. Most of the installation process involves copying files from the 1-2-3 disks to your computer. 1-2-3 now prompts for the following disks: Translate Disk if you are copying translation or sample files, Driver Disk 1, 1-2-3 System Disk (DOS) if you are installing for DOS or DOS and OS/2, and 1-2-3 System Disk (OS/2) if you are installing for OS/2 or DOS and OS/2. If you are using 5 1/4-inch

disks, Install will instruct you to insert different disks. For each of the disks that the installation program requests, insert the disk in drive A (or B) and press ENTER. Make sure to insert the disk fully into the disk drive and close the disk drive door. Also, do not remove a disk from the disk drive until the installation program prompts for the next disk.

9. Once Install has finished copying files to your hard drive, it displays the second part of the installation process: telling 1-2-3 the type of monitor and printer you will use. Press ENTER to continue to the next step.

10. The next screen lets you select First-Time Installation, Change Selected Equipment, or End Install Program. Since you are installing 1-2-3 for the first time, press ENTER to select First-Time Installation. Later, if you use the Install program again, you will use the Change Selected Equipment Option. At the end of the installation process, you may use the last option, End Install Program, to return to the operating system prompt.

11. Next Install displays a screen describing how to select a screen display. The program displays what it has identified as the correct screen display. For most monitors, it is correct. Unless you know that the suggestion is incorrect, make a note of this suggestion. Press ENTER to display the screen listing the available screen displays.

Move the highlight to the display that you want. In most cases this is the display 1-2-3 suggested on the previous screen. Press ENTER. Some monitor selections have a second menu that offers additional options for the resolution 1-2-3 will use when displaying your screen. The options may include available colors and the number of lines 1-2-3 uses. For example, 1-2-3 can display with 25, 34, or 60 lines for a Video Graphics Array monitor.

12. 1-2-3 next wants to know the printer that you will use. This enables 1-2-3 to print graphs directly and to include printer enhancements, such as fonts, in your graphs and worksheets. Unless you do not have a printer, select Yes. Then select the printer. The installation program lists most major manufacturers; if your printer is not listed, select one that is identical to yours, or select Generic. (If you select Generic you will not be able to print graphs.) For

each of the printer models, the installation program prompts for additional information about the printer. Highlight the option that is appropriate for your printer and press ENTER.

13. After all the selections for the first printer are made, the installation program prompts to indicate if you want to use a second printer with 1-2-3. You may want to select a second printer if your computer is linked to two printers or if the type of printer connected to your computer varies. If you select Yes, 1-2-3 takes you through the same steps that you performed for selecting the first printer. If you select No, 1-2-3 skips the second printer information requests.

14. After the printers are selected, 1-2-3 prompts to determine the name you want to use for the configuration file. The configuration file contains the information about the screen display, printer, and other information that 1-2-3 uses to execute. If you do not name the configuration file, the installation program names it 123.CNF. If you name the configuration file, you must provide a filename of up to eight characters and use .CNF for the filename extension.

15. Now that the installation program knows the printer and the screen display, it needs to copy additional files to your computer. 1-2-3 again asks for the disk drive letter, displaying A as a suggested selection. For most cases, press ENTER. If the installation program will read the files from another drive, type that drive letter and press ENTER. 1-2-3 then prompts you to insert the Driver disks based on the selections you have made. For each of the disks that the installation program requests, insert the disk in drive A (or B) and press ENTER. Make sure to insert the disk fully into the disk drive and to close the disk drive doors. Also, do not remove a disk from the drive until the installation program prompts you for the next disk.

16. Once 1-2-3 has copied the files it needs, it tells you that 1-2-3 is successfully installed. To continue, press ENTER. 1-2-3 displays a screen asking if you want to leave Install. If you select Yes, the installation program ends and you are returned to the system prompt. If you select No, the Install program main menu is redisplayed.

With Install completed, you are now ready to use 1-2-3. You can display graphs and interface with your printer or plotter. Changing between 1-2-3 programs will be easy, since all the Lotus files are stored on your disk.

Using Install After Installing 1-2-3

Once you have installed 1-2-3, you may need to use the Install program again. You will use the Install program if you want to create more than one driver set. You may need to change the hardware configuration to include another printer or screen display. You may also want to change the sort order 1-2-3 uses for the /Data Sort command.

Creating More Than One Driver Set

If you frequently alter the configuration of your system, you will want more than one driver set. This allows you to switch from one driver set to another without having to change the installation parameters each time.

If you use more than one driver set, pick a meaningful driver name for each, such as 2MONITOR, PLOTTER, or HOME. You can use up to eight characters for the first part of the name. You must avoid the following symbols:

, . ; : / ? * ^ + = < > [ ] \ '

1-2-3 adds a .DCF extension to the filename—for example, COLOR.-DCF.

Use the First-Time Installation option to create each driver set. Save each driver set under a different name. You may want to store these multiple drivers on a separate disk, if you want to use different drivers with the files in different directories.

Modifying the Current Driver

Install has two options for modifying the 1-2-3 driver files. They are First-Time Installation and Change Selected Equipment. The First-Time Installation option creates driver files. The Change Selected Equipment option changes a driver file.

To change a driver file, select Change Selected Equipment. To select the driver file to modify, select Make Another DCF Current and enter the driver name that you want to modify. If you do not select a driver file, Install uses 123.DCF. Then select Modify Current DCF. This selection has the following options: Return to menu, Change Selected Display, Change Selected Printer, and Change Selected Country. Select one of these options to change the display driver, printer driver, or sort sequence for the current driver file. When you are finished with this menu, select the Return to menu option.

Changing the Display

The Display driver may need to be changed if you want to change the initial display driver or add a second one. Several of the monitors can use more than one display driver. For example, if you are using a monitor with a VGA display, you may want to see how your graphs will look to someone with an EGA monitor. You can have two display drivers for a driver file.

To add or change a display driver, select Change Selected Display. The Install program lists the possible display drivers, with a "1" listed next to the display driver name that is selected. To add a second display driver or replace the first one, select the display driver you want to add or substitute. This selects the display driver that you added as the secondary display driver. For some selections you will need to make an additional choice. To replace the first display driver with the second display driver, select Change Selected Display again and highlight the display driver you want to remove. Press SPACEBAR. The 1 next to the highlighted selection disappears, and the 2 next to the selection you added becomes a 1. Press ESC to return to the Change Selected Equipment menu.

To select which display driver 1-2-3 uses, invoke the /Worksheet Window Display command. Then type a 1 or 2 to select which display driver to use.

Changing the Printer

The printer driver may need to be changed if you change the printer or add a second one. 1-2-3 allows up to two printer drivers in a driver configuration file. To add or change a printer driver, select Change Selected Printer. The Install program lists the supported printer manufacturers with a 1 next to the printer manufacturer that is selected.

To add a second printer driver or replace the first one, select the printer driver you want to add or substitute. Then make the additional menu selections appropriate for the printer. This selects the printer driver that you added as the secondary printer driver. To replace the first printer driver with the second printer driver, select Change Selected Display again and highlight the printer driver you want to remove. Press SPACEBAR. The 1 next to the highlighted selection disappears and the 2 next to the selection you added becomes a 1. Press ESC to return to the Change Selected Equipment menu.

To select which printer driver 1-2-3 uses, invoke the /Worksheet Global Default Printer Name command. Then type a 1 or 2 to select which printer driver to use.

Changing the Sort Order

The Change Selected Country option allows you to change the collating sequence for the existing driver set. Release 3 provides three options: Numbers First, Numbers Last, and the standard ASCII sequence. These options use the following sort orders:

- **Numbers Last**   Blank cells, label entries with letters in alphabetical order, label entries beginning with numbers in numeric sequence, labels beginning with special characters, then values

- **Numbers First**   Blank cells, labels beginning with numbers in numeric sequence, labels beginning with letters in alphabetical order, labels beginning with special characters, then values

• **ASCII**   Blank cells, followed by labels and values in ASCII order. Capitalization will affect the sort order with this choice. This selection also makes @functions case sensitive, and can have serious implications for formulas containing string functions that are used in computations or the Criteria area for /Data Query commands.

To change the collating sequence, select Change Selected Country from the menu and then choose the sort order you want from the sub-menu.

Saving the Driver Files

Once you have changed your driver file display, printer, and sort configurations, you need to save it, so the driver file will contain your new selections. To save the driver file, return to the Change Selected Equipment menu and select Save Changes. When 1-2-3 displays the filename, you can edit it if you want the new settings saved with a different filename. When the filename is correct, press ENTER to save the updated changes. Return to the Change Selected Equipment menu, and select End Install Program to leave Install, or continue using the other menu options.

Changing Other Configuration Parameters

Most of the hardware configuration options are specified in the installation process. However, two additional items that may require frequent change can be altered directly from 1-2-3. One is the disk drive assignment for data files, and the other is the printer settings.

The disk drive assignment can be changed from the default drive of C:\123R3 to another drive. From within 1-2-3, use /Worksheet Global Default Dir to do this.

Printer setting options can be changed with /Worksheet Global Default Printer. The changes made with this command can be saved with /Worksheet Global Default Update.

Preparing Data Disks

While 1-2-3 stores the program files on the computer's hard disk, you can use floppy diskettes for data storage. They will need to be prepared before you can store data on them. Use the formatting process described in your DOS or OS/2 manual (under FORMAT) before storing data on new diskettes.

1-2-3 Keyboard Guide

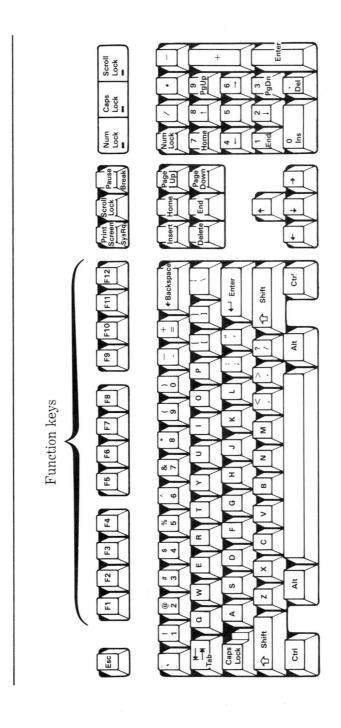

Figure B-1. IBM Enhanced keyboard guide

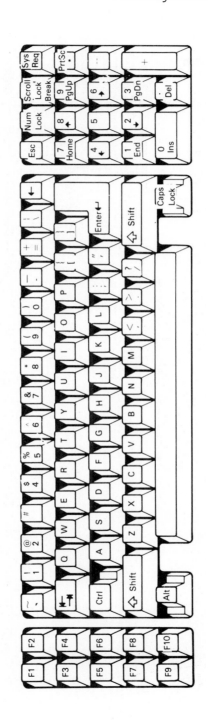

Figure B-2.   IBM Regular keyboard guide

A History of 1-2-3

Although the first computer was introduced in the 1940s, computers began to find their way into the business world only in the early 1960s. At this time large universities and corporations began to tap into the power of computers to automate business tasks such as payroll calculations, accounts payable, and record keeping.

Computers Enter the Business World

The first computers were big enough to fill a large room or even a small building. Even so, their capabilities were very limited compared to those of today's machines. These early machines often had memory sizes of 16K or less. Since most business systems of that era were oriented around punched paper cards and did little more than provide an ability to read and tabulate the data in these cards, that memory capacity was adequate. Error checking and correction in the early days consisted of a failed job, followed by the correction of the faulty punched card and a rerun of the entire job.

If business users wanted a new report from the data contained in their cards, they had to define their needs to someone in the business's data processing group. The technical guru from data processing then had to translate the users' needs into a language the computer could understand. Autocoder was one popular language of this era. One of a number of machine level languages, it had instructions that looked something like this:

SIO	Start I/O
MVC	Move character
LR	Load register

These assembly language instructions were combined with a reference to a machine register or a numeric address location to give instructions to the computer. It is easy to see that it must have been quite time-consuming to define a business problem and solution in this way. Furthermore, these programs often did not work correctly the first time they were executed. It was not unusual for a lengthy debugging process to be required to eliminate errors.

Obtaining desired output often meant changing the sequence of data or merging data in two different card files. Supporting equipment known as unit record devices was often used to reorganize the data files prior to reading the cards into the computer. To complete these sorting and merging operations, a data processing person had to rewire the boards of the unit record devices. In short, no computer-related processing could ever be completed by the business user. Users were completely dependent on technical experts to obtain the limited, inflexible output produced by the business programs of the 1960s.

Changes in the 1970s

The early to middle 1970s brought changes on some fronts in business computing, and adherence to the status quo on others. The size and price of computing power changed greatly, for example. Mainframe computers began to shrink in size and grow in capabilities and features. Cycle speed for computations became measurably shorter, and price /performance ratios fell rapidly. Replacing the punched paper cards of the past, magnetic tape units, large disk drives, and mass storage devices became the norm. Businesses placed more and more of their information in these new storage media as per-character storage costs continued to rapidly decline.

The location of equipment was also changing during this era. The centralized computer room of the 1960s evolved into increasing placement of computing equipment in the user's environment. Smaller computers called minicomputers were installed on the shop floor of manufacturing facilities and in some offices with specialized applications. Terminals were located throughout the business organization to allow users to enter data and access the files stored on a mainframe computer. Although these terminal devices did not have enough intelligence to handle application processing, they did have sufficient intelligence to check errors as the operator entered data. This improved accuracy control greatly reduced aborted processing caused by incorrect data entry. In some instances, data was processed on a real-time basis, and the mainframe files were updated immediately. In other, less time-critical applications, the data was stored so that files could be updated during off hours.

Software, as well, was growing more sophisticated. Users began to expect more than just a printed listing and total for their transactions. There was a demand for exception reporting to bring potential problems to management's attention, and also for the automation of complex tasks. Faster machines with larger memory lent popularity to programming languages like COBOL and PL/1. These languages were much closer to everyday English and escalated the application development process markedly. For example, a line from a COBOL program might look like this:

```
COMPUTE GROSS_PAY = HOURS * RATE
```

In addition to readable commands, COBOL provided a program structure with divisions for different functions and "paragraphs" within the main body of the program. These divisions made it easy to create a logical, well-organized program that others could follow as easily as the program's developer. This feature was especially important when modifications had to be made in a program.

Software packages to handle business functions such as accounts receivable, payroll, personnel, general ledger, and inventory control were being marketed by a number of vendors. If a package was flexible enough to meet a user's needs, a new system could be available in a matter of weeks — compared to the months that were required in earlier years — even if high-level languages were used.

Database management was also a popular focus for the 1970s. A number of mainframe packages for this purpose were introduced, such as IMS and Adabas. These packages allowed an organization to build a repository of corporate information. They also provided the ability to separate the data structure from the application programs. Alterations in file structures thus no longer required changes in application programs. In theory, this change eliminated the need for major program overhauls every time a new field was added. Unfortunately, building a corporate database took much longer than anyone had ever envisioned — in most companies, a period of years.

Throughout all these changes, the end-user's dependence on the data processing staff remained the same. Although the transition to a database environment helped, most new reports and all new calculations required the expertise of the programming staff to make necessary changes. Some organizations had as much as 80 percent of their data processing staff working on maintenance activities. This meant that few resources were available to implement new applications. Some organizations had a backlog of three years or more for new requests. By the time a new request made its way to the top of the backlog list, the user's needs had often changed.

Not surprisingly, users felt increasingly frustrated by the time lag between defining requirements and actually seeing the new or updated system in production. Users felt that, with all the computer claimed to offer, there should be a way for them to change storage requirements without major work, to query their data files at will, to create new reports on the spur of the moment, and to have flexible computation capabilities. Their current systems were not meeting these needs.

Users were aware of efforts to build corporate databases, and they had been promised that such databases would provide some of the options for which they were searching. Once a database was in place, query languages and report writers supposedly would allow users to tap into their information with only minimal involvement of data processing personnel. The problem was that this effort took much longer than most organizations had bargained for, and users were not seeing the results they had been promised. Although a solution seemed in sight, most users found it to be still out of reach, and many blamed the data processing staff for not delivering the tools the users needed.

The First Micros

Technology continued to bring down the size and cost of computing power, and the first microcomputer was introduced in 1974. This small machine could fit on a desktop like a terminal, yet, unlike a terminal, all its computing power was self-contained. The micro or personal computer even had data storage capabilities, so it could truly function as a stand-alone machine.

The early micros manufactured by Altair were not intended for the office. These machines were available only in kit form, for one thing. Even after they had been soldered and otherwise assembled, there was no software available for them. They were designed to be programmed with toggle switches on the front of the machines, or with assembly language, and thus required a time investment that was not practical in the business environment. At $400, the cost of these early micros was reasonable, but the time had not yet arrived for their introduction to business.

The Apple II was developed by Steven J. Jobs and Stephen W. Wozniak not too long after the Altair. The Apple II offered the advantage of preassembly and opened the possibility of owning a micro to many individuals. Tandy and countless other companies quickly followed Apple's lead, introducing micros like the TRS-80 and the Vector Graphic. The fact that these new machines could be programmed with a relatively easy-to-learn language like BASIC made them acceptable to at least a small group of end-users.

Since most business users did not have the time or inclination to become programmers even with BASIC, however, these early machines generally remained relegated to the computer hobbyist. Furthermore, data processing departments, already buried by requests for work on mainframes and minicomputers, tended to ignore micros in the hope that they would go away. Thus, users initially found little support within the data processing ranks for programming the micro. Besides, many data processing professionals thought of the microcomputer as merely a toy. Surely a "real computer" could not fit on a desktop!

Flexible, easy-to-use software was the missing component required for micros to make a significant contribution to the business world. Public domain software was free, but was useful only if you were interested in playing games or generating pictures of trees or cars on your computer screen. These programs certainly did not provide the tools business users were looking for. Users thus might purchase an Apple or TRS-80 for around $2,000—and then have to spend $5,000 or more to have someone develop a custom program for their application, since little or no commercial business software for micros existed.

VisiCalc: The First Generation

In 1978, VisiCalc, the first successful business software for microcomputers, entered the marketplace. Dan Bricklin, its creator, was more an end-user than a computer professional. Bricklin was motivated to develop a solution for the tedium of calculations involved in case studies in his program at the Harvard Business School. The solution he developed for his problems resulted in a tool that was soon welcomed by thousands of users.

VisiCalc was actually one of the first packages for any computer that offered complete flexibility in the tasks it could be used for. It was able to produce reliable computations—whether the user's needs were for loan amortization schedules, income projections for a legal practice, salary calculations, or a ratio comparison of potential investments.

Another advantage VisiCalc offered was that it operated with a limited instruction set that the user could control from menus at the top of the display screen. Although these menus were a bit cryptic, they were still easier to use than a programming language. Essentially, VisiCalc provided a large electronic sheet of paper that the user could work with in a variety of ways. Numbers, labels, and formulas could be placed anywhere on the sheet to create a model tailored to the user's exact needs. Other features such as windows, printing, and built-in functions made this product an even better solution for tasks that involved projections and calculations.

VisiCalc's commands were so easy to master that any user willing to learn them could escape dependence on data processing support. This was just as well, for in most organizations, data processing departments chose to ignore VisiCalc. In any case, they were so backlogged with work on mainframes and minis that they did not have the resources to get involved. Also, as with the microcomputer itself, many data processors felt that the VisiCalc innovation was only a passing fad.

Many microcomputers were purchased for the sole purpose of gaining access to VisiCalc software. In particular, VisiCalc gained immediate and widespread acceptance among accounting and finance professionals. Since these individuals were constantly making projections and doing other financial analyses, a package like VisiCalc saved them an immense amount of valuable time. The payback period for the cost of hardware, software, and model development became extremely short.

Before the availability of tools like VisiCalc, most financial projections were done with a pencil and paper. A change in one worksheet number meant that the entire worksheet had to be totaled and cross-footed again. This slow process made it difficult to evaluate a series of assumptions in a reasonable period of time. With VisiCalc, users could define the required calculations once and then have the software handle the recalculations whenever a number was changed. Since the recalculation normally required only a few seconds, users could evaluate dozens of assumptions in the time it formerly took to perform one recalculation by hand.

Although VisiCalc was adopted immediately by accountants and financial analysts, at first it found little support outside these professions in large corporations. In fact, accountants sometimes had to smuggle an Apple and a copy of VisiCalc into the office under the guise of purchasing a typewriter or a calculator. This secrecy was due to the fact that in most corporations the purchase of computer equipment or software had to be approved by a central committee, and such groups often doubted the usefulness of micros. More and more micros nonetheless came in "through the back door." Users were deciding what they needed and somehow finding money in their budgets to acquire these low-cost machines.

The Growth of Business Software for Micros

IBM was an established leader in the mainframe and minicomputer marketplace, and this company's entry into the personal computer market in the early 1980s convinced many organizations that micros were not merely a passing fad. IBM's action also encouraged third-party vendors to develop business software for microcomputers. A number of VisiCalc clones appeared, each providing some old and some new features.

New packages to handle word processing, data management, and graphics were introduced as well. Many were marketed by the same companies that were marketing spreadsheet packages. As an example, VisiCorp offered VisiFile for data management and VisiTrend/VisiPlot for statistics and graphics. Many of these new packages even allowed data transfer between the various software of a given company.

The biggest flaw in the design of these new offerings was the user interface. Users who had mastered one product felt that they were starting all over again when they attempted to learn a new package, because there was no consistency in the user interface from product to product, even when the products were manufactured by the same company. This frustration, along with the increasing sophistication of end-users, led to a demand for a second generation of microcomputer business software with additional sophistication and integrated features.

Integrated Packages: The Second Generation

The demand for additional features and sophistication, as well as the need to use multiple environments, led to the development of Lotus 1-2-3, Context MBA, and other integrated software packages. The computer memory needed to effectively utilize integrated packages was now reasonably priced; companies began offering add-on cards to boost the basic memory of a PC at a nominal cost.

Lotus 1-2-3 became the distinct leader among these second-generation offerings. It offered support for spreadsheet, data management, and graphics work in one package. It also possessed a consistent and easy-to-use user interface spanning all three environments.

Lotus had a strong management team with in-depth experience in the microcomputer field and the backing of financial leaders. The management team was headed by Mitch Kapor, a former VisiCorp employee and developer of the VisiTrend/VisiPlot package. Financial backers included heavyweights like Ben Rosen. The excellence of both management and support convinced corporate buyers that this new company was planning to be a major factor in microcomputer software then and in the years to come.

Reasons for 1-2-3's Popularity

Within just a few months of its introduction, Lotus 1-2-3 zoomed to the top of Softsel's best seller chart. Sales were spurred by a full-scale publicity campaign, with ads in the popular computer and business publications. Word of mouth was another strong sales factor. Business users who had tried the product were impressed with its features, and they did not hesitate to tell their associates about it. Corporations had been reluctant to adopt the products of many microcomputer firms, fearing that dependence on a small firm that might fail could result in later problems with updates and support. Because of its instant success, Lotus was able to convince the corporate decision makers that it had long-term viability. It was also one of the first software companies to provide online phone support at no additional fee. Whenever users had questions, they could call one of the support lines and have one of Lotus' staff provide quick answers.

Success in the corporate arena led to volume sales for the 1-2-3 product. Unlike Apple products, which were typically purchased by single users or small businesses, 1-2-3 was often bought by Fortune 500 companies that purchased hundreds or thousands of copies for their employees.

Lotus quickly began to plan enhancements to its original offering. Small changes were made between release 1 and release 1A. Release 2, introduced in the fall of 1985, made major enhancements to the product, including new options and commands that do everything from suppressing zero entries to performing regression analysis. These new features were the result of user requests and helped to keep the product current amid a sea of integrated packages.

In 1985 Lotus further strengthened support for the 1-2-3 package with several new products. The first is a monthly magazine called *Lotus Magazine*. It has a business emphasis and provides information about using Lotus products, and about microcomputers in general. A free six-month subscription is given with each purchase of 1-2-3 or Symphony.

Other new products to support the 1-2-3 user are 1-2-3 Report Writer and Lotus HAL. The Report Writer package allows users to produce a wide variety of reports from a 1-2-3 database or spreadsheet. The Lotus HAL product allows users to access 1-2-3's features without learning the menu sequences of 1-2-3. Using HAL's vocabulary in structuring requests, commands can be entered and executed immediately. Graphics products like Lotus' Freelance Plus and Graphwriter II provide graphics enhancements for 1-2-3 users among their other features.

Perhaps even more important is the addition of the Add-In Manager and a developer's kit that allows for the development of hundreds of add-in products. These third-party products can significantly enhance 1-2-3's capabilities, allowing for sideways printing, a wider screen display, spell-checking worksheet entries, and many other enhancements.

The Latest Releases

In 1989, Lotus announced two significant new releases of 1-2-3. Release 2.2 was announced for DOS users working within the limitations of 640K, and Release 3 was developed for users working with either DOS or OS/2 on the newer 286 and 386 machines.

Release 3's advanced worksheet features allow users to build three-dimensional worksheets containing as many as 256 individual sheets. Multiple files can be stored in memory at one time, and links to external files make it easy to consolidate information. Improved business presentation capabilities have been added, with new business graphics features and enhanced print support. Release 3 also adds database enhancements, including features of a relational database, like "joins." There is a new utility called DataLens, which allows users to link to external databases in mainframes, minicomputers, and PCs. New macro and @function options increase the level of sophistication that can be added to your models with this state-of-the-art product. A new developer's tool, code named LDE, will allow vendors to develop sophisticated, custom built-in functions and applications.

Shortly after the introduction of Release 3, Lotus announced Release 2.2. This release offers new graphics and print features, and comes with a copy of Allways for improving printed output. Eight new setting sheets make it easy to enter print, graph, and worksheet options. A search-and-replace option lets you quickly find and change a worksheet entry. Release 2.2 is a fast, compact upgrade to Release 2.01 that provides a substantial amount of new functionality and improved performance for users who are not yet ready to upgrade to Release 3.

Both new releases offer support for minimal recalculation, an Undo feature for correcting mistakes, and macro step recording. In addition, both packages support local area networks. Users can share worksheet files on a network, with the benefit of the new file locking and file reservation options. These features are compatible between the two new releases.

LMBCS Codes

Creating LMBCS Codes
Creating LMBCS Characters

You can use the Lotus Multibyte Character Set codes to create special characters within your worksheets. These special characters can create boxes or special letters used in various languages.

Creating LMBCS Codes

Use LMBCS codes to create characters unavailable on your keyboard. Each possible character has an LMBCS code. LMBCS characters are divided into groups of 256 characters. The first group, Group 0, omits the characters from 0 to 31. If you use them, 1-2-3 returns the characters for LMBCS codes 256 through 287.

Some monitors and printers cannot display all LMBCS characters. When a worksheet contains an LMBCS character that the monitor cannot display or the printer cannot print, 1-2-3 substitutes a different character for displaying and printing.

Table D-1 lists the LMBCS codes, the characters the codes create, and the key codes you use to create them.

Creating LMBCS Characters

You can create LMBCS characters five different ways. The method you use depends on the task you are performing when you want the LMBCS character.

• **Enter the character directly from the keyboard.** Many LMBCS characters such as letters, numbers, and common punctuation can be entered by pressing a key.

• **Use the** F1 (COMPOSE) **key.** Press F1 and type the Compose sequence. For example, to create a trademark symbol (™), press the F1 (COM-POSE) key and type a **T** and an **M**. 1-2-3 converts these entries into a trademark symbol.

• **Use extended Compose.** Press the F1 (COMPOSE) key twice and type the LMBCS group number, a hyphen, and the key code. For example, to create a trademark symbol (™), press the F1 (COMPOSE) key twice. Then type a **1** for the group number, a - and **118**. 1-2-3 converts these entries into a trademark symbol.

• **Use the** ALT **key.** Hold down the ALT key while you type the LMBCS code using the numeric keypad or the keyboard numbers above the letters. For example, to create a trademark symbol (™), hold down the ALT key while you type **374**. 1-2-3 converts these entries into a trademark symbol.

• **Use the @CHAR function.** Enter the appropriate LMBCS code for the function's argument. For example, to include the trademark symbol (™) in a note for a cell formula, enter **@CHAR(374)**. 1-2-3 converts the function into a trademark symbol. The @CHAR function is used within formulas especially when you cannot enter the character using another method, such as a double quote.

LMBCS Code	Character	Compose Sequence	Key Code	Description
Group 0				
32			032	Space
33	!		033	Exclamation point
34	"		034	Double quotes
35	#	++	035	Pound sign
36	$		036	Dollar sign
37	%		037	Percent
38	&		038	Ampersand
39	'		039	Close quote
40	(		040	Open parenthesis
41	)		041	Close parenthesis
42	*		042	Asterisk
43	+		043	Plus sign
44	,		044	Comma
45	-		045	Minus sign
46	.		046	Period
47	/		047	Slash
48	0		048	Zero
49	1		049	One
50	2		050	Two
51	3		051	Three
52	4		052	Four
53	5		053	Five
54	6		054	Six
55	7		055	Seven
56	8		056	Eight
57	9		057	Nine
58	:		058	Colon
59	;		059	Semicolon
60	<		060	Less than
61	=		061	Equal sign
62	>		062	Greater than
63	?		063	Question mark
64	@	aa or AA	064	At sign

Table D-1.   Lotus Multibyte Character Set (LMBCS) Codes

65	A	065	A,	uppercase
66	B	066	B,	uppercase
67	C	067	C,	uppercase
68	D	068	D,	uppercase
69	E	069	E,	uppercase
70	F	070	F,	uppercase
71	G	071	G,	uppercase
72	H	072	H,	uppercase
73	I	073	I,	uppercase
74	J	074	J,	uppercase
75	K	075	K,	uppercase
76	L	076	L,	uppercase
77	M	077	M,	uppercase
78	N	078	N,	uppercase
79	O	079	O,	uppercase
80	P	080	P,	uppercase
81	Q	081	Q,	uppercase
82	R	082	R,	uppercase
83	S	083	S,	uppercase
84	T	084	T,	uppercase
85	U	085	U,	uppercase
86	V	086	V,	uppercase
87	W	087	W,	uppercase
88	X	088	X,	uppercase
89	Y	089	Y,	uppercase
90	Z	090	Z,	uppercase
91	[	091	Open bracket	
92	\	092	Backslash	
93	]	093	Close bracket	
94	^	094	Caret	
95	_	095	Underscore	
96	`	096	Open single quote	
97	a	097	a,	lowercase
98	b	098	b,	lowercase
99	c	099	c,	lowercase
100	d	100	d,	lowercase
101	e	101	e,	lowercase
102	f	102	f,	lowercase
103	g	103	g,	lowercase

Table D-1. Lotus Multibyte Character Set (LMBCS) Codes *(continued)*

104	h	h, lowercase
105	i	i, lowercase
106	j	j, lowercase
107	k	k, lowercase
108	l	l, lowercase
109	m	m, lowercase
110	n	n, lowercase
111	o	o, lowercase
112	p	p, lowercase
113	q	q, lowercase
114	r	r, lowercase
115	s	s, lowercase
116	t	t, lowercase
117	u	u, lowercase
118	v	v, lowercase
119	w	w, lowercase
120	x	x, lowercase
121	y	y, lowercase
122	z	z, lowercase
123	{	Open brace
124	|	Bar
125	}	Close brace
126	~	Tilde
127		Delete
128	Ç	C cedilla, uppercase
129	ü	u umlaut, lowercase
130	é	e acute, lowercase
131	â	a circumflex, lowercase
132	ä	a umlaut, lowercase
133	à	a grave, lowercase
134	å	a ring, lowercase
135	ç	c cedilla, lowercase
136	ê	e circumflex, lowercase
137	ë	e umlaut, lowercase
138	è	e grave, lowercase
139	ï	i umlaut, lowercase
140	î	i circumflex, lowercase
141	ì	i grave, lowercase
142	Ä	A umlaut, uppercase

Table D-1.   Lotus Multibyte Character Set (LMBCS) Codes (*continued*)

Code	Char	Symbol	Description
143	Å	A*	A ring, uppercase
144	É	E'	E acute, uppercase
145	æ	ae	ae diphthong, lowercase
146	Æ	AE	AE diphthong, uppercase
147	ô	o^	o circumflex, lowercase
148	ö	o"	o umlaut, lowercase
149	ò	o`	o grave, lowercase
150	û	u^	u circumflex, lowercase
151	ù	u`	u grave, lowercase
152	ÿ	y"	y umlaut, lowercase
153	Ö	O"	O umlaut, uppercase
154	Ü	U"	U umlaut, uppercase
155	ø	o/	o slash, lowercase
156	£	L= 1= L- or 1-	British pound sterling symbol
157	Ø	O/	O slash, uppercase
158	×	xx or XX	Multiplication sign
159	ƒ	ff	Guilder
160	á	a'	a acute, lowercase
161	í	i'	i acute, lowercase
162	ó	o'	o acute, lowercase
163	ú	u'	u acute, lowercase
164	ñ	n~	n tilde, lowercase
165	Ñ	N~	N tilde, uppercase
166	ª	a_ or A_	Feminine ordinal indicator
167	º	o_ or O_	Masculine ordinal indicator
168	¿	??	Question mark inverted
169	®	RO or ro	Registered trademark symbol
170	¬	-]	End of line symbol/Logical NOT
171	½	12	One half
172	¼	14	One quarter
173	¡	!!	Exclamation point, inverted
174	«	<<	Left angle quotes
175	»	>>	Right angle quotes
176	░		Solid fill character, light
177	▒		Solid fill character, medium
178	▓		Solid fill character, heavy
179	│		Center vertical box bar
180			Right box side
181	Á	A'	A acute, uppercase

Table D-1.   Lotus Multibyte Character Set (LMBCS) Codes *(continued)*

Code	Char	Alt	Code	Description
182	Â	A^	182	A circumflex, uppercase
183	À	A`	183	A grave, uppercase
184	©	CO co or co	184	Copyright symbol
185	╣		185	Right box side, double
186	║		186	Center vertical box bar double
187	╗		187	Upper right box corner double
188	╝		188	Lower right box corner double
189	¢	c| c/ c| or c/	189	Cent sign
190	¥	Y= y= Y- or y-	190	Yen sign
191	╜		191	Upper right box corner
192	╛		192	Lower left box corner
193	┐		193	Lower box side
194	┴		194	Upper box side
195	├		195	Left box side
196	─		196	Center horizontal box bar
197	┼		197	Center box intersection
198	ã	a~	198	a tilde, lowercase
199	Ã	A~	199	A tilde, uppercase
200	╚		200	Lower left box corner, double
201	╔		201	Upper left box corner, double
202	╩		202	Lower box side, double
203	╦		203	Upper box side, double
204	╠		204	Left box side, double
205	═		205	Center horizontal box bar double
206	╬		206	Center box intersection, double
207	¤	XO or xo	207	International currency sign
208	ð	d-	208	Icelandic eth, lowercase
209	Ð	D-	209	Icelandic eth, uppercase
210	Ê	E^	210	E circumflex, uppercase
211	Ë	E"	211	E umlaut, uppercase
212	È	E`	212	E grave, uppercase
213	ı	i (space)	213	i without dot (lowercase)
214	Í	I'	214	I acute, uppercase
215	Î	I^	215	I circumflex, uppercase
216	Ï	I"	216	I umlaut, uppercase
217	┘		217	Lower right box corner
218	┌		218	Upper left box corner
219	■		219	Solid fill character
220	■		220	Solid fill character, lower half

Table D-1.   Lotus Multibyte Character Set (LMBCS) Codes (*continued*)

Code			Description
221	¦	/ (space)	Vertical line, broken
222	Ì	Ì`	I grave, uppercase
223	▀	■	Solid fill character, upper half
224	ó	o'	o acute, uppercase
225	ß	ss	German sharp, lowercase
226	ô	o^	o circumflex, uppercase
227	ò	o`	o grave, uppercase
228	õ	o~	o tilde, lowercase
229	õ	o~	o tilde, uppercase
230	µ	/u	Greek mu, lowercase
231	þ	p—	Icelandic thorn, lowercase
232	Þ	P—	Icelandic thorn, uppercase
233	Ú	U'	U acute, uppercase
234	Û	U^	U circumflex, uppercase
235	Ù	U`	U grave, uppercase
236	ý	y'	y acute, lowercase
237	Ý	Y'	Y acute, uppercase
238	‾	<¦	Overline character
239	´		Acute accent
240	–	—+	Hyphenation symbol
241	±	+—	Plus or minus sign
242	═	—¦ or ═	Double underscore
243	¾	34	Three quarters sign
244	¶	!p or !P	Paragraph symbol
245	§	SO so or s0	Section symbol
246	÷	:—	Division sign
247	¸	,	Cedilla accent
248	°	o	Degree symbol
249	¨	::	Umlaut accent
250	·	·	Center dot
251	¹	^1	One superscript
252	³	^3	Three superscript
253	²	^2	Two superscript
254	■	■	Square bullet
255			Null

Group 1

256	Not Used		
257	☺		Null
258	●		Smiling face
			Smiling face, reversed

Table D-1. Lotus Multibyte Character Set (LMBCS) Codes *(continued)*

Code	Key	Description
259		Heart suit symbol
260		Diamond suit symbol
261		Club suit symbol
262		Spade suit symbol
263		Bullet
264		Bullet, reversed
265		Open circle
266		Open circle, reversed
267		Male symbol
268		Female symbol
269		Musical note
270		Double musical note
271		Sun symbol
272		Forward arrow indicator
273		Back arrow indicator
274		Up-down arrow
275		Double exclamation points
276		Paragraph symbol
277		Section symbol
278		Solid horizontal rectangle
279		Up-down arrow, perpendicular
280		Up arrow
281		Down Arrow
282		Right arrow
283	mg	Left arrow
284		Right angle symbol
285		Left-right symbol
286	ba	Solid triangle
287	ea	Solid triangle inverted
288	" (space)	Umlaut accent, uppercase
289	~ (space)	Tilde accent, uppercase
290		Ring accent, uppercase
291	^ (space)	Circumflex accent, uppercase
292	` (space)	Grave accent, uppercase
293	"^ (space)	Acute accent, uppercase
294		High double quotes, opening
295		High single quote, straight
296		Ellipsis
297		En mark

Table D-1. Lotus Multibyte Character Set (LMBCS) Codes (*continued*)

			Code	Description
298	—		042	Em mark
299			043	Null
300			044	Null
301			045	Null
302	ˇ		046	Left angle parenthesis
303	^		047	Right angle parenthesis
304	:	(space)"	048	Umlaut accent, lowercase
305	˜	(space)~	049	Tilde accent, lowercase
306	°		050	Ring accent, lowercase
307	ˆ	(space)^	051	Circumflex accent, lowercase
308	ˋ	(space)`	052	Grave accent, lowercase
309	ˊ	(space)'	053	Acute accent, lowercase
310	„	"v	054	Low double quotes, closing
311	‚		055	Low single quotes, closing
312	≡		056	High double quotes, closing
313			057	Underscore, heavy
314			058	Null
315			059	Null
316			060	Null
317			061	Null
318			062	Null
319			063	Null
320	Œ	OE	064	OE ligature, uppercase
321	œ	oe	065	oe ligature, lowercase
322	Ÿ	Y"	066	Ÿ umlaut, uppercase
323	-		067	Null
324	-		068	Null
325	-		069	Null
326			070	Left box side, double joins single
327			071	Left box side, single joins double
328			072	Solid fill character, left half
329			073	Solid fill character, right half
330			074	Null
331			075	Null
332			076	Null
333			077	Null
334			078	Null
335			079	Null
336	╨		080	Lower box side, double joins single

Table D-1.   Lotus Multibyte Character Set (LMBCS) Codes *(continued)*

	Code	Char	Code	Description
	337		081	Upper box side, single joins double
	338		082	Upper box side, double joins single
	339		083	Lower single left double box corner
	340		084	Lower double left single box corner
	341		085	Upper double left single box corner
	342		086	Upper single left double box corner
	343		087	Center box intersection, vertical double
	344		088	Center box intersection, horizontal double
	345		089	Right box side, double joins single
	346		090	Right box side, single joins double
	347		091	Upper single right double box corner
	348		092	Upper double right single box corner
	349		093	Lower single right double box corner
	350		094	Lower double right single box corner
	351		095	Lower box side, single joins double
	352	ij	096	ij ligature lowercase
	353	IJ	097	IJ ligature, uppercase
	354	fi	098	fi ligature, lowercase
	355	fl	099	fl ligature, lowercase
	356	n.	100	n comma, lowercase
	357	l.	101	l bullet, lowercase
	358	L.	102	L bullet, uppercase
	359		103	Null
	360		104	Null
	361		105	Null
	362		106	Null
	363		107	Null
	364		108	Null
	365		109	Null
	366		110	Null
	367		111	Null
	368		112	Single dagger symbol
	369		113	Double dagger symbol
	370		114	Null
	371		115	Null
	372		116	Null
	373		117	Null
	374	TM Tm or tm	118	Trademark symbol
	375	lr	119	Liter symbol

Table D-1.   Lotus Multibyte Character Set (LMBCS) Codes (*continued*)

Code	Char	Keystroke	Description
120			Null
121			Null
122			Null
123			Null
124	¤	KR Kr or kr	Krone sign
125	↑	-[	Start of line symbol
126	£	LI Li or li	Lira sign
127	₧	PT Pt or pt	Peseta sign
128	Ç	C,	C cedilla, uppercase
129	ü	u"	u umlaut, lowercase
130	é	e'	e acute, lowercase
131	â	a^	a circumflex, lowercase
132	ä	a"	a umlaut, lowercase
133	à	a`	a grave, lowercase
134	å	a*	a ring, lowercase
135	ç	c,	c cedilla, lowercase
136	ê	e^	e circumflex, lowercase
137	ë	e"	e umlaut, lowercase
138	è	e`	e grave, lowercase
139	ï	i"	i umlaut, lowercase
140	î	i^	i circumflex, lowercase
141	ì	i`	i grave, lowercase
142	Ä	A"	A umlaut, uppercase
143	Å	A*	A ring, uppercase
144	É	E'	E acute, uppercase
145	æ	ae	ae diphthong, lowercase
146	Æ	AE	AE diphthong, uppercase
147	ô	o^	o circumflex, lowercase
148	ö	o"	o umlaut, lowercase
149	ò	o`	o grave, lowercase
150	û	u^	u circumflex, lowercase
151	ù	u`	u grave, lowercase
152	ÿ	y"	y umlaut, lowercase
153	Ö	O"	O umlaut, uppercase
154	Ü	U"	U umlaut, uppercase
155	ø	o/	o slash, lowercase
156	£	L= l= L- or l-	British pound sterling symbol
157	Ø	O/	O slash, uppercase
158	×	xx or XX	Multiplication sign

Table D-1.   Lotus Multibyte Character Set (LMBCS) Codes (*continued*)

415	ƒ	ff	159	Guilder
416	á	a'	160	a acute, lowercase
417	í	i'	161	i acute, lowercase
418	ó	o'	162	o acute, lowercase
419	ú	u'	163	u acute, lowercase
420	ñ	n~	164	n tilde, lowercase
421	Ñ	N~	165	N tilde, uppercase
422	ª	a_ or A_	166	Feminine ordinal indicator
423	º	o_ or o_	167	Masculine ordinal indicator
424	¿	??	168	Question mark inverted
425	®	RO or ro	169	Registered trademark symbol
426	¬	-]	170	End of line symbol/Logical NOT
427	½	12	171	One half
428	¼	14	172	One quarter
429	¡	!!	173	Exclamation point, inverted
430	«	<<	174	Left angle quotes
431	»	>>	175	Right angle quotes
432			176	Solid fill character, light
433			177	Solid fill character, medium
434			178	Solid fill character, heavy
435			179	Center vertical box bar
436	─		180	Right box side
437	Á	A'	181	A acute, uppercase
438	Â	A^	182	A circumflex, uppercase
439	À	A'	183	A grave, uppercase
440	©	CO C0 co or c0	184	Copyright symbol
441			185	Right box side, double
442			186	Center vertical box bar double
443			187	Upper right box corner double
444			188	Lower right box corner double
445	¢	c| c/ c| or c/	189	Cent sign
446	¥	y= y= y- or y-	190	Yen sign
447			191	Upper right box corner
448			192	Lower left box corner
449			193	Lower box side
450			194	Upper box side
451			195	Left box side
452			196	Center horizontal box bar
453			197	Center box intersection

Table D-1.   Lotus Multibyte Character Set (LMBCS) Codes *(continued)*

454	ã	a~	198	a tilde, lowercase
455	Ã	A~	199	A tilde, uppercase
456	╚		200	Lower left box corner, double
457	╔		201	Upper left box corner, double
458	╙		202	Lower box side, double
459	╟		203	Upper box side, double
460	═		204	Left box side, double
461	╧		205	Center horizontal box bar double
462	╪		206	Center box intersection, double
463	¤	XO or xo	207	International currency sign
464	ð	d-	208	Icelandic eth, lowercase
465	Ð	D-	209	Icelandic eth, uppercase
466	Ê	E^	210	E circumflex, uppercase
467	Ë	E"	211	E umlaut, uppercase
468	È	E`	212	E grave, uppercase
469	ı	i (space)	213	i without dot, lowercase
470	Í	I'	214	I acute, uppercase
471	Î	I^	215	I circumflex, uppercase
472	Ï	I"	216	I umlaut, uppercase
473	┐		217	Lower right box corner
474	┌		218	Upper left box corner
475	■		219	Solid fill character
476	■--		220	Solid fill character, lower half
477	┴	/ (space)	221	Vertical line, broken
478	Ì	I`	222	I grave, uppercase
479	■		223	Solid fill character, upper half
480	Ó	O'	224	O acute, uppercase
481	ß	ss	225	German sharp, lowercase
482	Ô	O^	226	O circumflex, uppercase
483	Ò	O`	227	O grave, uppercase
484	õ	o~	228	o tilde, lowercase
485	Õ	O~	229	O tilde, uppercase
486	µ	/u	230	Greek mu, lowercase
487	þ	p-	231	Icelandic thorn, lowercase
488	Þ	P-	232	Icelandic thorn, uppercase
489	Ú	U'	233	U acute, uppercase
490	Û	U^	234	U circumflex, uppercase
491	Ù	U`	235	U grave, uppercase
492	ý	y'	236	y acute, lowercase

Table D-1.   Lotus Multibyte Character Set (LMBCS) Codes (*continued*)

493	Ý	Y'	237	Y acute, uppercase
494	¯|	^_	238	Overline character
495	´	'	239	Acute accent
496		-+	240	Hyphenation symbol
497	±	+-	241	Plus or minus sign
498	≡	-- or ==	242	Double underscore
499	¾	34	243	Three quarters sign
500	¶	!p or !P	244	Paragraph symbol
501	§	SO so or s0	245	Section symbol
502	÷	:-	246	Division sign
503	¸	''	247	Cedilla accent
504	°	^0	248	Degree symbol
505	¨	:	249	Umlaut accent
506	·	.	250	Center dot
507	¹	^1	251	One superscript
508	³	^3	252	Three superscript
509	²	^2	253	Two superscript
510	■		254	Square bullet
511	!		255	Null

Table D-1.   Lotus Multibyte Character Set (LMBCS) Codes *(continued)*

MicroPro®	MicroPro International Corporation
Multiplan®	Microsoft Corporation
Novell®	Novell, Inc.
Novell Netware SFT®	Novell, Inc.
OS/2™	International Business Machines Corporation
PS/2®	International Business Machines Corporation
Softsel®	Softsel Computer Products
Symphony®	Lotus Development Corporation
Tandy®	Tandy Corporation
TI®	Texas Instruments
Token-Ring®	International Business Machines Corporation
TRS-80®	Tandy Corporation
Vector Graphic®	Vector Graphic
VisiCalc®	Lotus Development Corporation
VisiCorp®	VisiCorp, Inc.
VisiFile®	VisiCorp, Inc.
VisiTrend/ VisiPlot®	VisiCorp, Inc.
WordPerfect®	WordPerfect Corporation
WordStar®	MicroPro International Corporation
Xerox®	Xerox Corporation
XT®	International Business Machines Corporation

*Lotus HAL is distinguished from HAL which is a trademark of Qantel for its Hotel and Leisure Software.

Note that this index is separated into four sections: (1) 1-2-3 commands, (2) macro commands, (3) 1-2-3 functions, and (4) general entries.

You're important to us...

We'd like to know what you're interested in, what kinds of books you're looking for, and what you thought about this book in particular.

Please fill out the attached card and mail it in. We'll do our best to keep you informed about Osborne's newest books and special offers.

YES, SEND ME A FREE COLOR CATALOG
of all Osborne/McGraw-Hill computer books.

Name:_____ Title:_____

Company:_____

Address:_____

City:_____ State:_____ Zip:_____

I'M PARTICULARLY INTERESTED IN THE FOLLOWING *(Check all that apply)*

I use this software:
- ❏ Lotus 1-2-3
- ❏ Quattro
- ❏ dBASE
- ❏ WordPerfect
- ❏ Microsoft Word
- ❏ WordStar
- ❏ Others_____

I use this operating system:
- ❏ DOS
- ❏ OS/2
- ❏ UNIX
- ❏ Macintosh
- ❏ Others_____

I rate this book:
- ❏ Excellent ❏ Good ❏ Poor

I program in:
- ❏ C
- ❏ PASCAL
- ❏ BASIC
- ❏ Others_____

I chose this book because...
- ❏ Recognized author's name
- ❏ Osborne/McGraw-Hill's reputation
- ❏ Read book review
- ❏ Read Osborne catalog
- ❏ Saw advertisement in _____
- ❏ Found while browsing in store
- ❏ Found/recommended in library
- ❏ Required textbook
- ❏ Price
- ❏ Other_____

Comments_____
_____

Topics I would like to see covered in future books by Osborne/McGraw-Hill

include:_____
_____

ISBN# 318-2

BUSINESS REPLY MAIL

First Class   Permit NO. 3111   Berkeley, CA

Postage will be paid by addressee

Osborne **McGraw-Hill**

2600 Tenth Street
Berkeley, California 94710–9938